THE
ARMOURED
CAMPAIGN
IN NORMANDY
JUNE—AUGUST 1944

(Courtesy of The History Press)

THE
ARMOURED
CAMPAIGN
IN NORMANDY
JUNE—AUGUST 1944

STEPHEN NAPIER

To the tank crews of all nations that fought in Normandy.

With heartfelt thanks to my wife Nikki for her love and encouragement and to my father, John, for his support and enthusiasm.

Also thanks to Richard Anderson Jnr and William Folkestad in the USA for their assistance.

Cover illustrations courtesy of Battlefield Historian.

First published 2015
This paperback edition published 2017
Reprinted 2024

The History Press
97 St George's Place,
Cheltenham, Gloucestershire, GL50 3QB
www.thehistorypress.co.uk

British Library Cataloguing in Publication Data.
A catalogue record for this book is available from the British Library.

ISBN 978 0 7509 7945 0

Typesetting by Sparks – www.sparkspublishing.com
Printed by TJ Books Limited, Padstow, Cornwall

Contents

THE NORMANDY BATTLEFIELD

●	Town
——	Railway
——	Road
▬▬▬	Caen Canal
▬ ▬ ▬	Département boundary

	Contour 100 metres
	Contour 200 metres
	Contour 300 metres

0   25   50
Kilometres

Bay of the Seine

Cherbourg

Valognes   Quineville
Montebourg
Ste. Mère Eglise   **UTAH**
Barneville

Le Havre

Port en Bessin
OMAHA
Arromanches
Courseulles
St. Laurent
GOLD **JUNO**
SWORD
R. Douve
R. Aure
Carentan   Isigny
Bayeux   Ouistreham   Cabourg
Houlgate
Lessay
R. Taute
Périers
R. Drôme
R. Seulles
Caen
Argences
Lisieux
M A N C H E   St. Lô   Caumont
R. Odon
Coutances
R. Vire
Villers Bocage
Mézidon
R. Touques
C A L V A D O S
R. Dives
Falaise
Condé
Granville
Vire
R. Orne
Flers
Argentan
Avranches
Mortain   **O R N E**
Domfront
R. Sélune
Alençon
R. Mayenne
Fougères
Mayenne

(*Courtesy of The History Press*)

Introduction

The sun did not come up on the morning of 6 June 1944 along the Normandy coastline. Instead the darkness of the stormy night was replaced by an overcast sky above heavy seas still streaked with the white caps of breaking waves. As the light improved, the tense and increasingly awestruck German sentries saw that the once empty horizon was now filled with an armada of ships of every size and shape coming straight for them. The defenders manning the strongpoints of Hitler's Atlantic Wall were tired because of the constant false alerts since 0100 hours; now they could see with their own eyes that the alerts were real. Formations of low-flying aircraft with black and white stripes on their wings suddenly appeared out of the low-lying clouds and made straight for the defenders who immediately took cover. Most of the bombers missed their targets, however, as they were concerned about hitting the ships of the invasion fleet and their bombs detonated harmlessly in the areas behind the beaches.

Steadily the armada came closer, and the individual ships became more distinct. The outlines of grey behemoths became battleships and appeared along with the sleek lines of their smaller consorts such as cruisers and destroyers. In front of them were hundreds of smaller angular landing ships, rocket ships and landing craft, some of which were heading for the shore while others were performing a circular dance as they waited for their turn for the run-in to the beaches. Suddenly the warships were lit up by flashes of gunfire along their lengths, and seconds later the howl of the approaching shells caused the defenders to hug the ground in their shelters and trenches closer. All along the Normandy coastline, giant mushrooms of dirt and debris erupted and the ground shook with the detonations of the shells. The air filled with smoke and dust and the strong smell of cordite. Amongst the terrified Germans, the religious (and some not so religious) began to pray for their salvation. Would the bombardment ever stop?

In the noisy, cramped landing craft of the initial assault wave, Allied soldiers huddled together facing the exit ramp, their helmeted heads bowed. Spray from the rough sea and the occasional desultory German retaliatory shell exploding nearby soaked most men before they had even landed. Those that weren't seasick gripped their weapons more tightly; the religious and the suddenly converted amongst them offered silent prayers …

Amongst the assortment of landing craft moving to the shore were dozens of what looked like small boats but which were actually amphibious tanks, an Allied secret weapon developed especially for this moment in history. As they moved sluggishly through the heavy seas, several disappeared from view altogether.

Since the United States had entered the war in December 1941 and were persuaded by the British and Churchill to follow a 'Germany first' policy, the Americans had wanted to launch a cross-Channel invasion of France (Operation Roundup) from Britain. They considered this the shortest and quickest route to strike directly at Germany itself and honour promises made to the Russians to start a second front. However, once the Americans had committed to the British Mediterranean strategy in North Africa and Italy, Operation Roundup was repeatedly postponed until the British were finally forced to commit to a date of 1 May 1944 at the Teheran Conference in November 1943. Even then, the Italian Anzio landings caused a further postponement of a month.

The secret amphibious tanks were the first armoured units to touch down on French soil in a campaign that was expected to see the Allies victorious and the war ended by Christmas 1944. In this book, attention is devoted to the performance and deficiencies of the DD tanks; there are many fine accounts of the D-Day assault and the 'Funnies' of the 79th Armoured Division already available, but the story of the DD tanks has not been told in full before. The attack on each of the invasion beaches is examined, with particular emphasis on the armoured debacle on Omaha Beach, where the assault almost failed.

Both green and veteran armoured units were fielded by the Allies in Normandy: a division from Canada, three divisions from Britain and two from the United States. The Canadian 4th Armoured Division, the Guards Armoured Division, the 11th Armoured Division and the US 3rd Armored Division were all inexperienced units, although a veteran regiment from North Africa (the 3rd RTR – Royal Tank Regiment) had been incorporated into the 11th Armoured Division. Montgomery had transferred the veteran 7th Armoured Division – the 'Desert Rats' – from Italy for the Normandy campaign. Independent tank brigades or battalions to support the operations of the infantry divisions were also deployed. Opposing the Allies were much-vaunted and experienced German panzer divisions (one untried in battle) against which only the British had fought previously and for whom they had developed a begrudging respect.

There are many accounts of the Normandy campaign already, but this is the first from the perspective of the armoured units and their generals, commanders and tank crews. It compares the intentions of both the Allied and German army and corps commanders in the major battles of the campaign with the outcomes of those battles and how they came about. It was in Normandy that the relationship between Eisenhower and Montgomery became seriously strained, and the background to this irretrievable breakdown is explored.

The daily life of the tank crews is described as well as the organisation for the repair and replacement of tanks and crews after the devastating consequences of being hit by an armour-piercing shell.

Many historians have written only cursorily of tanks in Normandy, while others, in writing about the major operations such as Goodwood, have stated very different tank loss statistics. The main reference used by many historians is the Military Operations Unit (MORU) report No. 23 prepared in October 1946, which gives the daily losses for all the armoured brigades and their reconnaissance regiments for the four days of the battle. According to the MORU report, a total of 493 tanks were damaged, knocked out or destroyed, which has given rise to the accepted figure of around 500 tanks lost. Canadian Lieutenant-Colonel Roman Jarymowycz, for instance, writes that 'the plain before Borguebus was covered with nearly 500 burning British tanks'. Anthony Beevor gives 200 tanks as lost but only writes about the first day, while Max Hastings claims 400 were lost. Others are more circumspect; Eversley Belfield and Major-General Essame give a total of 400 tanks lost but state that many were later recovered and repaired, while Major-General Belchem gives no account of the losses. Ian Dalglish also fails to give a total estimate of tanks lost, despite devoting a whole book to Operation Goodwood. John J.T. Sweet attempts a more rigorous analysis and arrives at the figure of 300 tanks 'stopped' for all causes and 140–150 tanks actually destroyed.

This book establishes for the first time the true number of tanks lost in Operation Goodwood and the other major battles of the campaign up to the closure of the Falaise Gap in August 1944. This is achieved by using official documents, reports, war diaries and regimental histories of the men and units involved, and, where possible, first-hand accounts of those tank men who were in the front line. These have been obtained from research at archives in Britain, the United States and Canada.

The performance of each armoured division in the campaign is examined in relation to the tank training and doctrine of the time, along with the impact of the bocage hedgerows, a terrain for which no Allied tank crews had prepared and which perfectly suited those in a defensive role.

The development of the main German and Allied tanks is examined, as is the considerable performance gap between the German and Allied tanks, which was well known to British leaders (who attempted to prevent any negative reports from reaching the press or the tank regiments).

It took considerable courage for tank crews to go into combat: four or five men crammed into a metal box with little visibility when under fire and expecting to be hit at any second by an anti-tank round that could mean a fiery death...

This is their story.

1

D-Day Tanks

One of the bitter lessons that the British had learnt from the Dieppe raid in 1942 was that armoured support was essential for supporting the assaulting infantry. At Dieppe, half of the Churchill tanks that landed on the beach either lost tracks in the shingle or had difficulty crossing a sea wall to get off the beach and support the troops inland. Of the twenty-nine Churchills landed, only fifteen tanks were able to get onto the promenade before road blocks eventually halted their progress inland and forced them to return to the beach. A total of eighteen tanks were immobilised by gunfire that knocked their tracks off and four more tanks got stuck in the chert shingle on the beach.[1] The Germans could not believe the British would abandon their latest tanks on the beach to be examined at their leisure and presumed the Churchills were obsolete tanks that the British could afford to lose.

It was not an auspicious combat debut for the Churchill tanks but their sacrifice helped identify many of the challenges of an opposed landing. The Operation Overlord planners moved to address some of these problems with the formation of the 79th Armoured Division a year before D-Day under Major-General Percy Hobart to develop and test the specialist armoured vehicles needed to overcome the obstacles expected to be encountered in future landings in France. The 79th Armoured Division also provided training for men to operate this equipment; the US Army had no equivalent organisation.

A shortage of landing craft influenced Allied planning; a proposed landing in the south of France (Operation Anvil/Dragoon) had to be delayed until after the invasion of north-west France (Operation Overlord) as there were not enough craft to make simultaneous landings. Given the shortage, the British were concerned that landing craft would be vulnerable on the run into the beach from shore defences. One devastating hit on a landing craft from a gun could eliminate four or five tanks in one stroke. This was despite the fact that at Dieppe no tank-carrying landing craft were lost on the actual run-in to the beach although many were damaged and several sank *after* off-loading their tanks. The Royal Navy did, however, lose more than thirty landing craft of all types in the operation. One solution was to convert a number of landing craft to fire rockets for close support after the naval bombardment had ceased but this only compounded the shortage of such craft. Another solution was to provide the tanks with flotation equipment so they could swim in under their own power, thus presenting smaller and more dispersed targets. On touchdown on the beach, the tanks would then be immediately available to support the infantry.

Work on a floating tank had already begun using a design originally conceived in 1941 by an American, Nicholas Straussler, and successfully used on Valentine and Tetrarch tanks. As these tanks were outdated and the British were standardising their armoured units around the Sherman M4 as their main cruiser tank, the design had to be altered to suit the Sherman. The realisation of the floating tank concept became one of Major-General Hobart's projects.

To enable the tanks to float, a rubberised canvas screen fitted around the top of the tank hull was erected and held taut by a combination of metal struts and inflatable pillars filled with bottled compressed air. The canvas screen was raised by thirty-six pillars when compressed air was pumped into them via a pneumatic system, and thirteen metal struts fixed between the tank and the screen helped to keep it erect. The screen itself was attached to a boat-shaped metal framework welded to the tank's upper hull. This system could be inflated in 15 minutes and could be quickly deflated when the tank reached a depth of 5ft or less. The tank floated according to Archimedes' principle: with its additional canvas screen, it displaced more water than it weighed. The struts were fitted with a hydraulic quick-release mechanism to collapse the screen and allow the 75mm main gun to come into action when the tank arrived on the beach. If the screen was not properly lowered, the bow machine gun could not be used. Once the screen was deflated and ejected, the tank had the full use of its turret and could operate as a normal tank.[2]

A modified Sherman tank was known as a DD tank, so named for its double or 'duplex drive' systems that by means of a pair of propeller screws at the rear could propel the tank in water at a speed of up to 4½ knots as well as power it on land. The Americans inevitably nicknamed the DD tanks 'Donald Ducks'.

The Sherman II (M4A1), as used by Americans at Omaha and Utah sector beaches, had a freeboard of 3ft in front and 2.5ft at the stern when unloaded. The slightly larger (by 5½in) Sherman V (M4A4), as predominantly used by the British, had a freeboard of 4ft at the bow and 3ft at stern.

To launch from their landing craft, a tank drove on its tracks down the lowered modified ramp into the water and then engaged the Duplex Drive to operate the propellers. This meant a dangerous delay of a few seconds in which large waves could potentially push the tank back into the ramp or the landing craft could run down the tank if a wave caused it to suddenly surge forward. Once launched, the tanks could not get back on the landing craft. When the screen was erected, the driver's vision hatch was blocked, so steering was by means of a periscope and a gyroscope and following the tank commander's instructions. The driver steered the tank by means of a rod linkage that swivelled the propellers at the rear of the tank. The commander, as his view out of the turret was also blocked by the screen, helped steer the tank by using a simple detachable tiller linked to the steering mechanism while standing outside the tank on a plate welded to the back of the turret. The commander was very exposed in this position outside the tank and as soon as the enemy opened fire he was forced to duck back into the turret while the driver continued to steer by means of his gyroscope. However, heavy seas made the gyroscope very unstable and difficult to read so at the most crucial time of the landing, when under fire and nearing the beach, the tank was virtually blind. The limited vision of the DD tanks, particularly under fire or in heavy seas, was recognised as a problem and during Operation Overlord a navigation boat was to be used to guide the DD tanks to a point where they could clearly see their intended landfall. Once launched, the raised canvas screen gave the DD tank in the water the superficial appearance of a smaller infantry assault craft and it was hoped that this would disguise the tank during its approach to the shore.

Prior to being loaded on the landing craft, each tank had to be waterproofed by applying a putty-like compound to all joints, access plates, hatches and bolts before covering the putty itself with Bostik glue. The crews undertook extensive training in the form of launch drills, combined exercises and even practised escaping from a tank that had sunk. Scottish lochs and various lakes around England were used for these training exercises throughout the five months prior to Overlord. At Fritton Park, escape training was conducted with all tank crews wearing modified Davis Escape apparatus (as used in submarines) which provided a limited source of air. The crew took their place in a Sherman at the bottom of a concrete tower and water was rapidly pumped in, flooding the tank to a depth of 10ft. The crews then had to get out of the tank and swim to the surface, an operation particularly hazardous for the tank driver as he was the last of the crew to leave. A piece of equipment added to the DD tanks at the last minute for the Normandy invasion was an inflatable life raft of the type used by the RAF, a last-minute suggestion of Admiral Talbot, commander of the Sword sector Royal Navy forces in the assault.[3]

The performance of the DD Shermans in rough weather was found to be poor during the training exercises. The 13th/18th Royal Hussars lost two tanks in Operation Cupid in March 1944 when the weather turned bad during an exercise after the tanks had already been launched.[4] In Operation Smash, April 1944, the 4th/7th Royal Dragoons lost six tanks when they were launched in a heavy swell and conditions then worsened; six men were drowned.[5]

The DD tanks were demonstrated to General Eisenhower on 27 January 1944 and he was enthusiastic about their potential, directing the US forces to use them in their landings on the basis that any measures that might preserve landing craft were worth taking. The benefits of the deployment of the DD tanks in the first assault wave were thought to far outweigh any potential disadvantages. However, the deployment of DD tanks by both the British and American armies meant that there would not be enough DD conversion kits to go round, so a British expert was flown to the USA with the design drawings and the Firestone tyre company began the manufacture of kits with the intention of sending them to England. As the tanks had to be modified to install the screens, it was far more efficient for US manufacturers to install the kits in America and the first 100 DD-equipped tanks arrived in Liverpool, England, six weeks later.[6]

The planned use of DD tanks was not greeted enthusiastically by all Americans, however. General Gerow, the commander of V Corps and on the COSSAC (Chief of Staff to Supreme Allied Commander) planning staff, was not keen on the DD tanks as he had successfully landed tanks from landing craft directly onto beaches the previous year in the invasion of Sicily and thought the DD tanks impractical.

Ultimately, a shortage of DD kits meant that only two companies or squadrons of each battalion or regiment earmarked for D-Day would be equipped with DD tanks. The third company or squadron would be equipped with tanks with deep wading vents similar to those that had been used successfully in the Sicilian landings. Two trunks, or stacks, were fitted to extend the air intakes and exhausts of the tank which then enabled fully waterproofed tanks to drive off landing craft into water up to 6ft deep.

For the British, the shortage of DD tanks for Overlord was only overcome by taking over the training tanks of the 79th Armoured Division and by the transfer of eighty M4A1 DD tanks from the Americans in March 1944. The Americans' initial order was for 350 DD tanks, and as only ninety-six were required for the operational use of the three tank battalions, with another ninety-six being for training, the Americans had plenty spare. First, however, they had to be shipped to England. As a result of this, many regiments did not receive their DD tanks until late May and there were few opportunities for training. Time at the firing ranges was even more limited as the DD tanks had to be transported by road which required the waterproofing to be redone before the tank could take to the water again. Travel was also restricted as the DD tanks were a secret weapon and any road movements risked them being seen by enemy agents. The Americans turned down the British offer of training instructors from the 79th Armoured Division for the DD tanks and practised at Gosport and Torcross for their D-Day landings under their own instructors.

Each British and Canadian regiment would have two squadrons of nineteen tanks in the assault. As each landing craft Mk III had space for five DD tanks in its hold, there was room for an extra tank to be used. On 17 May the RAC (Royal Armoured Corps) approved the use of forty tanks on D-Day if there were sufficient tanks and crews available. Eighty-five DD tanks were finally allocated to each of the 2nd Canadian and 8th Armoured brigades and forty-two to the 27th Armoured Brigade, but some of these tanks were in the workshop for repair.[7] The 13th/18th Royal Hussars in the 27th Armoured Brigade actually used forty tanks on D-Day, along with the Canadian Fort Garry Horse Regiment.

On 26 April 1944, General Hobart alerted the War Office and the ACIGS to a potential problem with the top rail of the canvas screen on Sherman M4A4 tanks. Owing to faulty manufacture it was very weak and liable to break, especially in rough weather. An investigation was undertaken and rectification work consisting of bolting a length of angle iron to the top rail was immediately carried out on

126 tanks under the supervision of the contractor, Metro Cammell. This fault affected only the kits made in England installed on M4A4 tanks and was apparently not present in US-made kits, although these were made from British plans with the same specification. A British interim report in May stated that a steel tube with a higher tensile strength was now being used in production.[8] The repairs were to be trialled by B wing of the 79th Armoured Division in rough weather before D-Day but these trials had to be cancelled – owing to bad weather! There is no evidence that the Americans were informed of the potential problems before D-Day.

The training branch of the RAC believed the DD tanks could be classed as underwater craft and therefore the tank crews should be entitled to the same Special Duty Pay as submarine crews but this was rejected by the War Office.

Hobart's team developed a whole range of special-purpose vehicles for use in beach operations, the floating tank being only one of them. A Churchill tank fitted with a short-range mortar that fired a large explosive charge, known as a Petard, for destroying bunkers was developed. The Petard-firing tank was then used to build other special-purpose vehicles to cross obstacles, including a tank to carry a small box girder bridge that could be laid across trenches and a tank to carry a bundle of planks (fascine) that could be dropped into ditches and trenches to enable other vehicles to traverse them. Another version (Bobbin) carried a canvas carpet for placing over soft ground to prevent vehicles from getting bogged. As these tanks were issued to army engineers, they were called Armoured Vehicles for Royal Engineers, or AVREs. Once the AVRE tank had completed its task, it was then able to operate as a normal Petard-firing tank. Another useful vehicle developed by Hobart's team was the Flail, also known as a Sherman Crab, which was a Sherman fitted with a rotating drum with attached chains at the front of the tank to beat the ground ahead of the tank and explode any mines in its path.

The Overlord Plan

The Allies had two years in which to plan their return to Europe and in that time extensive information about the German defences was gained by aerial reconnaissance and reports from the French Resistance. General Morgan's original COSSAC plan called for a simultaneous assault by three divisions in the Normandy area (Caen and Bayeux) and for a parachute division to capture Caen. The port of Cherbourg was an early objective, as were the coastal ports of Brittany to the west. The need to secure a firm lodgement and build-up of forces ashore before attacking southwards and eastwards to the River Seine was recognised.[9] Normandy was selected rather than the nearer Pas de Calais as it was considered to be less heavily defended by coastal fortifications and was the most distant from Luftwaffe bases. The advantages of Normandy, which was still within the range of Allied fighter planes based in southern England, outweighed the disadvantages of a longer sea journey for the invasion forces and the lack of a deep-water port.[10] On reviewing the plan early in 1944, General Montgomery ordered it to be expanded to employ five divisions and three airborne divisions in the assault but the fundamentals of the plan were largely unchanged.

The sectors that were originally selected by the Allied planners, after very detailed reconnaissance and assessments that included the taking of actual beach sand samples, were known as (from east to west): Juno, Gold and Omaha. An additional sector, Sword, was added to the Second British Army front on the extreme eastern flank and the Utah sector was added to the First United States Army's (FUSA) proposed front farther to the west. However, a lack of available landing craft (as the Americans were determined to mount Operation Anvil) meant that the additional landings could only be mounted on a single brigade or combat team front, unlike the Juno, Gold and Omaha sectors which would deploy two brigades or combat teams in a two-up assault formation.

SHAEF's orders were for the 21st Army Group to secure a lodgement on the continent from which further offensive operations could be developed. Montgomery intended that armoured thrusts by battle groups be made inland the same day if conditions were favourable. The British Second Army was to seize high ground and other strategic objectives further inland before the German defences could regroup and reinforcements arrive. The 8th Armoured Brigade was given the task of capturing Villers Bocage while the 2nd Canadian Armoured Brigade was to advance as far as Evrecy, south-west of Caen. The 27th Armoured Brigade was to support the 3rd Division in capturing Caen, a vital D-Day objective. These armoured thrusts were explained by Montgomery to Churchill, the King and senior officers of the Allied forces at an invasion briefing given at St Paul's School in London on 15 May and were a key element of Operation Overlord. General Bradley of First United States Army (FUSA) remembered Montgomery making comments about tanks even reaching Falaise on D-Day 'to knock about a bit down there'.[11] Having landed with the two Allied armies of 21st Army Group aligned east to west with the Americans on the right of the line, the armies would then wheel or pivot to realign in a north-east to south-west direction while the deep-water ports of Brittany to the west were captured. The advance on a broad front towards Paris and Germany would then begin.

The German defences forming Hitler's Atlantic Wall to repel the expected Allied invasion were of two types. Strongpoints and bunkers (*Wiederstandnester*) containing heavy guns were constructed on the shore to engage any landings on the beaches, while obstacles were erected offshore to prevent boats or landing craft from actually getting to the beach. A variety of concrete bunkers and emplacements were constructed, their size and shape depending on their location and on the availability of guns and materials. Many bunkers had concrete walls up to 10ft thick and were constructed so that the guns inside could fire along the beach rather than out to sea. This enabled a thick concrete wall to be built seawards to offer the bunker protection from naval gunfire. It also meant that they could only be knocked out by guns or tanks that had landed on the beaches. The Atlantic Wall

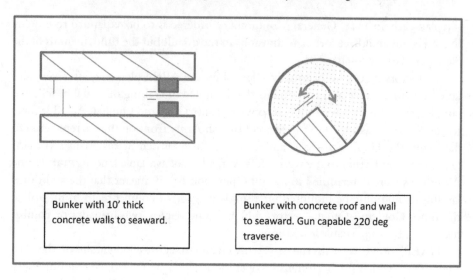

Bunker with 10′ thick concrete walls to seaward.

Bunker with concrete roof and wall to seaward. Gun capable 220 deg traverse.

Diagram of typical beach bunkers from DSOAG King Red Operation Neptune G-2 commanders report (Sword sector). (*Courtesy of The National Archives*)

was designed by the Germans on the principle that armour was not expected in the initial assault and bunkers and strongpoints would only have to deal with infantry, supported by naval gunfire.

The bunkers, pill boxes and emplacements had many different types of guns and anti-tank guns located in them and many were linked by tunnels or slit trenches. The main weapons in the strongpoints were 88mm and 75mm anti-tank guns. A variety of obsolete and captured guns were also used, including 50mm anti-tank guns, French howitzers and the turrets of French tanks. Each strongpoint was surrounded by thick belts of barbed wire and mines. The beaches themselves were also heavily mined in places, as were all the possible exit routes inland.

The second type of defence was formed by placing obstacles on the beach. Offshore, large wooden structures were placed in deep water to block or hinder landing craft from approaching the beach. Known as Element C or Belgian gates, these structures were spaced between 70ft and 140ft apart. The next line of defences consisted of pointed stakes which were simply rows of tree trunks or poles 10ft high and driven into the sand 60ft apart. These were often fitted with a Teller mine or an unexploded shell fitted with a contact fuse mounted on top. Some pointed seawards and others towards the shore so as to cause the landing craft or assault craft to overturn. These stakes were installed in rows closer to the beach and were designed to rip the bottom out of any landing craft, if not blow them up.

The final line of defences in the water were three lengths of 6in angle iron 6½ft long, welded together at their centres to make a form of tripod, with legs sticking up at an angle to leave sharp spikes. They were called Hedgehogs and were placed closest to the beach, up to 15ft apart in rows every 60ft; again, they were designed to damage the bottom of any landing craft.[12]

Sword Sector

The Sword sector was the most easterly of the areas selected for the landings and as such was expected to face the strongest German opposition. German naval attacks on the invasion fleet were expected from E-boats based in Le Havre and the gun battery at Merville was capable of shelling Sword beach, so the most concentrated supporting naval gunfire and aerial bombardment programme of all the proposed Overlord landing areas was devised for Sword.[13]

The beach chosen for the landings in the Sword sector was only 1,600yds long, defined by the River Orne estuary at Ouistreham to the east and rocky shelves offshore to the west near Lion sur Mer, so only a single brigade could be landed at a time. The beach selected was codenamed Queen beach. The coastline in this sector is generally flat with a coastal road, lined with houses along most of its length, linking the two towns. Halfway between the two towns was a major strongpoint, La Brèche, WN20, containing two 88mm anti-tank guns sighted to fire east and west along the beaches, plus numerous other 50mm and 75mm guns. La Brèche was codenamed Cod by the Allies; all coastal fortifications were named after fish, while inland fortifications were named after motor cars. Inland of Queen beach were several major fortifications and strongpoints. Two such gun battery positions were codenamed Daimler and Morris and the headquarters of the 736th Regiment (part of the static 716th Infantry Division) was Hillman. Queen beach itself was just to the west of La Brèche and any landing would face serious opposition from this strongpoint. The coastal town of Lion sur Mer was also heavily fortified with strongpoints, including WN21 (known as Trout), and many houses along the coastal road had been prepared for defence by bricking up windows and constructing machine gun posts in them.

As the Sword sector was closest to Caen, the assault plan was for heavy fire support and the concentration of units on a single beach to facilitate the troops once ashore being able to drive inland to capture Caen on D-Day, in addition to linking up with the 6th Airborne Division holding the bridges over the River Orne at Bénouville.[14] Two assault squadrons of specialist AVREs, instead of the usual one per infantry brigade as on the other British beaches, were detailed to support the single infantry brigade on Sword in order to help the troops get off the beaches quickly and move inland.[15] The 3rd Division was to assault one brigade up on Queen beach, supported by a tank regiment from the 27th Armoured Brigade, the 13th/18th Royal Hussars, with its A and B squadrons equipped with Sherman DD tanks. The Royal Hussars were tasked with then capturing Hermanville, a quarter of a mile inland, and clearing Ouistreham before C Squadron, arriving at H+45 minutes, was to capture the strongpoints codenamed Morris (WN16) and Hillman (WN17).

The Germans had also studied the lessons of the Dieppe raid and considered potential landing sites for the expected Allied invasion. Ports were considered the most likely objectives of any landings and accordingly, the coastal ports of

Normandy, including Cherbourg and Ouistreham, had been heavily fortified to repel any direct landing attempts like Dieppe.

The German 716th Division consisted of two infantry regiments (three battalions each) reinforced by two battalions of *Ostruppen*, formed from men recruited in the countries occupied in the Eastern Front campaign. This single division was expected to defend the Atlantic Wall that protected the Sword, Juno and Gold sectors – 20 miles of Normandy coastline. The 716th Division was a part of the LXXXIV Corps commanded by General Markes, who also had at his disposal the reformed 21st Panzer Division, commanded by Generalmajor Feuchtinger. The 21st Panzer Division had been destroyed in Tunisia in May 1943 at the culmination of the North African campaign and had been reformed with a mix of officers who had managed to escape from Africa and new recruits, many of whom had been rejected by other units. The 21st Panzer Division was not yet rated for service in Russia but had trained extensively in its expected area of operations, digging anti-tank ditches and firing pits for its Mark IV tanks as well as registering potential artillery targets.[16]

The Merville and Le Havre German coastal batteries presented a significant threat to the ships of the landing force as well as the beach itself. During the early hours of 6 June, the paratroopers of the 6th Airborne Division landed and neutralised the former whilst HMS *Warspite* engaged the Le Havre battery in a duel after H-hour, eventually silencing the its guns; however, during the afternoon a single gun began to fire sporadically at the invasion fleet, though its fire would have been more effective if directed at the landing beach.

The 13th/18th Royal Hussars

Following a 24-hour postponement because of bad weather, the Sword invasion convoy S-3 with the LCT Mk IIIs carrying the DD tanks of the 13th/18th Royal Hussars sailed progressively from 0500 hours on 5 June from Spithead. By 0520 hours on D-Day, the LCTs had reached the lowering position for the infantry landing craft 11 miles off shore. A green light shone by the midget submarine X23, which had surfaced after fixing its position and remaining submerged for the previous 24 hours, indicated the course to be taken and the DD tank launching point.[17] Because of the rough seas, the decision was made not to launch at the planned 7,000yds out from the shore but for the eight landing craft to move to within 5,000yds of the beach and this caused a delay. Eventually, the signal to launch was given by raised yellow flags and one by one the DD tanks moved ponderously down the lowered ramps of the landing craft and dropped into the sea. Once their propellers were engaged, they began to slowly move towards the distant shore at a rate of 100yds a minute.

A Squadron

The objectives of A Squadron of the Hussars were to support the specialised AVRE tanks and gapping teams breach the defences on Queen White beach by suppressing and knocking out the fortifications before supporting the 1st South Lancashire infantry battalion in capturing Hermanville. The tanks were to come ashore at H-7½ minutes, before the gapping teams and assault infantry arrived.

Immediately on launching, the DD tanks experienced difficulties. Large waves and a strong lateral current reduced the speed of the tanks to 3 knots and they were forced to steer at an angle of 40 degrees to their intended course just to keep heading for the beach. One DD tank was swamped and sank after its propellers did not engage after launching. A second tank, that of the squadron's second in command, Captain Denny, was sunk by its own landing craft when it failed to get clear of the ramp after launching and a wave caused the LCT's ramp to collide with the tank's screen which collapsed; the tank quickly sank and only Captain Denny survived. The landing craft carrying the AVREs of the gapping teams were following right behind those of the Hussars which were now behind schedule because of the rough conditions and the decision to launch closer to the shore. The result was that the AVRE LCTs were ordered to pass through the columns of swimming DD tanks, unfortunately ramming one tank which subsequently sank in the process. At 1,000yds from the shore, the DD tanks changed formation from four columns of tanks to line abreast in order to arrive at the landing beaches simultaneously. To complicate matters, the AVRE LCTs in front then slowed again as 'short' rockets from the shore bombardment support landing craft fell and exploded all around them and the DD tanks. No tanks were reported hit but one B Squadron troop commander was killed by a piece of shrapnel from the rockets.

The DD tanks then caught up with the AVRE LCTs with the result that the DD tanks and the AVRE vehicles arrived at the beach almost at the same time. Another tank was rammed by an LCT shortly before touching down and, although the tank made it to the shore, it immediately began to ship water and soon had to be abandoned. After dropping their canvas screens to bring their main 75mm guns into action, the tanks began to engage the identified emplacements from their hull-down half-submerged positions at the water's edge. Major Wormald, A Squadron's commander, described the landing on the beach:

> The Naval and Air Bombardment was tremendous and occasional glimpses of the shore were possible, due to the offshore wind which carried the smoke of the bombardment towards us. The tanks were performing well beyond what we thought to be practicable for the apparatus. Four columns each of five tanks (less Cpl Sweetapples) followed the lead of a Landing Craft Personnel (Navigational) the task of which was to lead us to the correct point of 'TOUCH DOWN' on the beach. Our tanks touched down at 07.23. Sixteen tanks got their tracks on the sea bed, moved into water sufficiently shallow to allow them to deflate their screens and to engage the beach defences.
>
> I still remember very clearly the 'brewing-up' of the leading AVRE Churchill tank as it drove down the ramp of an LCT which was beached a few yards to my left front. The turret and the contents thereof spun into the air after a violent explosion, presumably caused by a penetrating direct hit by an anti-tank shell which detonated

the explosive charges which the AVRE was carrying for the purpose of destroying concrete replacements.

I immediately got my gunner to engage a bunker from which I thought that the shot had been fired. His first round hit the target and the gun became silent. We then continued to fire at suspected defensive positions until we could neither see nor hear any firing from the defences.

The Assault Engineers crossed the beach and started to carry out their task of creating 'exits' from the beach. The Assault Companies of the South Lancashires came ashore, crossed the beach with very few, if any, casualties and passed inland.[18]

A total of sixteen A Squadron tanks reached the beach about the same time as the AVREs of the assault squadron but too far away to offer effective support to them as they began clearing their lanes.[19] The rough seas and strong wind caused the tide to come in more rapidly than expected and waves breaking over the rear of some of the tanks on the beach caused their motors to stall. Several tanks were hit and disabled by armour-piercing shells fired from the bunkers and were subsequently swamped by the incoming tide, as were those that lost engine power. Another was blown up when it was jockeying for position amongst obstacles at the water's edge and set off a mine; a total of eleven tanks were eventually swamped and lost.[20]

Anti-tank guns from the La Brèche strongpoint fired along the length of both landing beaches, as did machine guns that took a large toll of the infantry. La Brèche was an initial objective of the men of the 2nd East Yorkshire Battalion but two companies of the 1st South Lancashires having landed in the wrong place, close to the strongpoint, had no option other than to join in the attack. After an intense firefight the La Brèche strongpoint was taken and all serious resistance, apart from an occasional sniper's bullet, had ceased 20 minutes after landing.

Many A Squadron tanks were knocked out and only five eventually left the beach to support the South Lancs in capturing Hermanville inland. Fortunately, in view of the number of tanks lost, not much more opposition was encountered during this part of the operation. The squadron survivors then went west towards Lion sur Mer with the infantry and No. 41 Commando to clear the town and the Trout fortification. Trout was found to be abandoned and Lion sur Mer quickly captured but increasing German resistance centred on the Vaux château in the area meant that Lion sur Mer would be the limit of the westward advance from Sword on D-Day. The 3rd Division was therefore unable to link up with Canadian 3rd Division on the adjacent Juno beach and that evening a gap of 3 miles existed between the Juno and Sword sectors.

B Squadron

B Squadron orders were to support the 2nd East Yorkshire infantry in overcoming the La Brèche Cod strongpoint before advancing inland to capture the fortified Sole and Daimler battery positions. The B Squadron tanks had a more successful swim into their designated beach, Queen Red. However, one DD tank could not be launched when the ramp of its landing craft was damaged by gunfire after the other four tanks had launched, so it was taken back to England. Aboard LCT 467, carrying the five DD tanks of the B Squadron commander, Major Rugge-Price, and the 4th Troop, the first DD tank damaged its screen before launching after a near miss on the LCT. This caused the tanks aboard to lurch into each other and the other tanks were prevented from launching. Major Rugge-Price demanded that the damaged tank be jettisoned but he was overruled by the commander of the landing craft who had received instructions from LCH 185, a headquarters landing craft, to take the landing craft all the way into the shore at H+45 minutes with a subsequent assault wave. Consequently, this landing craft arrived 45 minutes late.[21] This action was initially praised by the S-3 naval commander but the fact that the beach assault was deprived of five tanks at a vital stage was later criticised by Admiral Talbot.

The slow progress of the B Squadron DD tanks meant that they arrived about 5 minutes behind the LCTs carrying the AVREs and the LCAs carrying the assault infantry.[22] The German defences were alert and immediately opened fire on the disembarking 2nd East Yorks infantry which took heavy casualties; their only support for a few minutes was the AVRE tanks. When the fourteen DD tanks arrived and added their firepower, the defences were subdued by H+20 minutes with the assistance of No. 4 Commando. One B Squadron tank was knocked out by shellfire on the beach and two others became bogged in soft sand, all three being subsequently swamped by the incoming tide. A total of five tanks were lost on the beaches and, as one tank had been unable to disembark, only thirteen tanks were able to proceed inland to support the infantry.

Tired of waiting for the assault gapping teams to do their work, a new beach exit was cleared across the sand dunes by Captain Neave (second in command B Squadron), who requisitioned a bulldozer to clear a path through the obstacles and dunes. Five other B Squadron tanks, including the 1st Troop, moved off the beach but turned eastwards by mistake towards Ouistreham and went on to assist the commandos of Lord Lovat's 4th Special Services Brigade in relieving the 6th Airborne paratroops holding the bridges at Bénouville. This was not as per the squadron's immediate orders which were to support the infantry in taking Sole and Daimler but the action was successful, apart from two tanks being lost to anti-tank gunfire south of Bénouville later on in the afternoon. The eight surviving tanks eventually left the beach and helped clear Ouistreham, followed by Sole and Daimler. Two B Squadron tanks appeared at an opportune moment to help knock out two 50mm anti-tank guns at the Casino bunker at Riva Bella that were holding up the liberation of Ouistreham by No. 4 Commando unit. Another two tanks were damaged in these operations. The Daimler fortification near Ouistreham resisted until 1900 hours.

A special so-called 'concrete busting' landing craft was included in the wave of LCTs carrying the AVREs. This was CB 2337, an LCT(A) Mk V landing craft that had been modified to carry two Sherman Vcs (known post-war as Fireflies) on a raised deck in the hold so that the two tanks could fire on the approach to the shore at a specific target. These two tanks were on charge to the I Corps Delivery Squadron but were crewed by the regiment. On landing, the tanks would revert one each to A and B squadrons. CB 2337 was seen to be listing to starboard as it approached the beach after having shipped a lot of water in a difficult Channel crossing. The two tanks did not fire at all on the run-in and landed at H+15 minutes, the tanks moving off to find their squadrons. The tank of Sergeant Ellis located A Squadron and the tank of Lieutenant Knowles, after remaining on the beach for a while, linked up with B Squadron.

C Squadron

The C Squadron wading Sherman tanks landed directly from their landing craft at H+45 minutes opposite the silenced La Brèche position to find the beach crowded with landing craft but relatively calm, apart from intermittent sniper fire. German artillery shells and mortars were still regularly hitting the beach and there were many burning landing craft, swamped vehicles and disabled tanks along the shoreline. The waves were full of debris and the occasional body. On the narrowing beach was a multitude of armoured vehicles waiting to move inland. C Squadron was to support the intermediate reserve battalion of the 8th Brigade, the 1st Suffolks Battalion, firstly to eliminate the Morris bunker and then Hillman. Morris was surrounded by barbed wire and mines but in a two-pronged attack, the three tanks of 4th Troop plus an attached tank approached the strongpoint. Two tanks working with the infantry slowly made their way through the village of Colleville whilst two other tanks worked themselves into position at the rear of the bunker. Before the attack could begin, the defenders abandoned the position without a shot being fired.[23] Forty prisoners were taken under a white flag.[24]

The Hillman position 550yds farther south was still defended and the 1st Suffolks had great difficulty in approaching it owing to the surrounding minefields which were covered by machine guns. The position was the headquarters of the 736th Regiment and had extensive underground bunkers, including two concrete gun emplacements covered with steel domes impervious to all British naval and tank fire. The defenders were able to move between weapon pits and bunkers by means of tunnels and trenches, and the enemy positions had to be eliminated one by one. The defences inflicted nearly 150 casualties on the soldiers of the 1st Norfolks Battalion when they tried to bypass Hillman in the afternoon on their way inland.[25] As the 4th Troop Sherman tanks moved cross-country to engage the bunker from the rear, a hidden anti-tank gun from Hillman destroyed two tanks in quick succession.[26] Two other tanks of C Squadron were knocked out by anti-tank guns from Hillman.[27]

At 1930 hours the tanks of C Squadron were ordered to leave Hillman and form a defensive screen behind a ridge to the south against an expected counterattack by German tanks. The Staffordshire Yeomanry's A Squadron was detailed to cover Hillman in the place of C Squadron.

Meanwhile, the tanks of the rest of the squadron finally broke into the Hillman position and wreaked havoc on the installation, driving over trenches and underground bunkers to make them collapse while tank commanders threw grenades into every weapon pit they could find. The squadron leader's tank fell into what turned out to be the officer's latrine and his tank was damaged, losing a track. Hillman was finally reported captured at 2100 hours but this strongpoint had greatly delayed the 3rd Division's plans and timetable for the day.

The DD tanks of the regiment that had made it to the beach had eliminated three or four 75mm guns, four or five 50mm and numerous 20mm cannon positions.[28] However, the brigadier of the 27th Armoured Brigade, G.E. Prior-Palmer, who had been watching the attack from LCH 185, was reported to have been disappointed with the performance of the regiment.[29]

A Squadron had lost fourteen tanks and had six tanks left at the end of the day when the Sherman Vc from CB 2337 (Sergeant Ellis) rejoined them. B Squadron had lost ten tanks destroyed or damaged. C Squadron had lost six tanks, four being knocked out and two damaged. Therefore the Royal Hussars lost thirty-one tanks out of a total of sixty-three, the regiment's normal complement of sixty-one being bolstered by the two additional DD Shermans in A and B squadrons. This was a 50 per cent casualty rate – but not unexpected as the regiment was in the vanguard. The 266th Field Delivery Squadron servicing the 27th Armoured Brigade was due to land next day with thirty-one tanks, of which seventeen were designated for the regiment. Although the regiment's casualties were initially feared to be high because of a large number of men missing from the drowned or swamped DD tanks, fortunately this was proven wrong. When everybody could be accounted for some days later, the regiment's casualties were relatively light: one officer and fifteen other ranks (ORs) killed and one officer and eighteen ORs wounded.[30]

The Staffordshire Yeomanry

As the tide came in more quickly than anticipated, many beach obstacles could not be cleared; the dry beach area was soon only a narrow strip 15yds wide at high tide. This caused considerable congestion on Queen White beach, to which the seven stranded or swamped tanks of the Hussars added. When the landing craft of the Staffordshire Yeomanry, the second tank regiment of the 27th Armoured Brigade, due at H+195 minutes, landed at 1030 hours slightly ahead of schedule, their tanks disembarked to join the melee at the water's edge. The intention was for the newly arrived 185th Brigade to push on rapidly inland and capture Caen with the infantry of the 2nd King's Shropshire Light Infantry (KSLI) Battalion to be carried on the Staffs Yeomanry tanks towards Caen.

By this time, the fighting had moved inland and there was only sporadic shelling and sniping of the narrow beach which was fortunate as the beach was jammed with vehicles of every description, there being no apparent traffic control or beach organisation. The tanks remained lined up on the beach for more than an hour before they were able to use one of the exits and begin to move to the assembly point to meet up with the waiting infantry. There were traffic jams even on the roads inland from the beach and a different assembly point near Hermanville was chosen to try and avoid the congestion. In the meantime, the commander of 2nd KSLI, having waited for more than an hour until 1230, ordered his men to set off on foot for their objectives.[31]

C Squadron of the Staffs Yeomanry were then sent by 185th Brigade commander to capture and hold Point 61 on the Periers Ridge which was considered vital high ground as it overlooked Queen beach; the tanks achieved this without opposition by 1425 hours and remained there in defensive positions. A Squadron was ordered to assist with the capture of the Hillman strongpoint which was still holding out and had been firing on the units advancing inland towards Caen, causing considerable casualties.

This left only B Squadron and the RHQ (Regimental Headquarters) tanks to continue the advance inland. The armoured thrust inland to Caen as envisaged by Montgomery before D-Day was now being conducted by a few hundred infantrymen on foot, without most of their supporting tanks which had been diverted to secure minor objectives such as Point 61 and Hillman. A well-hidden 88mm anti-tank gun ambushed the advancing tanks of B Squadron and five tanks (including two Shermans from the reserve engineer squadron carrying fascines for the anti-tank ditches located by aerial reconnaissance before the invasion) and the medical officer's half-track were knocked out in quick succession before the gun could be located and destroyed by the remaining tanks.[32] The survivors of B Squadron then took over from C Squadron on Point 61 to guard the right flank of the advance and C Squadron tanks were ordered to take over the advance towards Caen. However, they too struck trouble in the form of a battery of captured Russian 122mm guns in the woods around Periers sur le Dan and were held up.

The 2nd KSLI reached Biéville-Beuville and requested armoured support, so a troop of tanks from C Squadron was sent to help. In turn, C Squadron requested assistance to eliminate the battery of guns holding them up in the woods and a company of infantry was ordered forward.[33] C Squadron, with some recce tanks in front as a screen, then resumed their advance and reached the anti-tank ditch south-west of Biéville-Beuville where two troops of tanks succeeded in crossing.

At this time, about 1600 hours, the recce troop reported enemy tanks moving northwards from Caen. The 2nd KSLI, about to attack Biéville-Beuville, also reported at 1615 hours that tanks were approaching. The Staffs Yeomanry commander immediately requested the release of A Squadron from its support role in the attempts to capture Hillman and the regiment deployed to await the attack. The enemy tanks spotted were the Mark IVs of the 22nd Panzer Regiment of the 21st Panzer Division which, after a frustrating day rushing first east of the River Orne and then back westwards across the only available bridges in Caen while under attack from the air, were about to mount the first serious German counterattack of the day.

The 21st Panzer Division on D-Day was organised into three battle groups, or *kampfgruppen*. The first, Kampfgruppe Oppeln, consisted of the 22nd Panzer Regiment and the 125th Panzergrenadier Regiment with supporting units. The panzer regiment normally had eight companies of Mark IV tanks but was missing

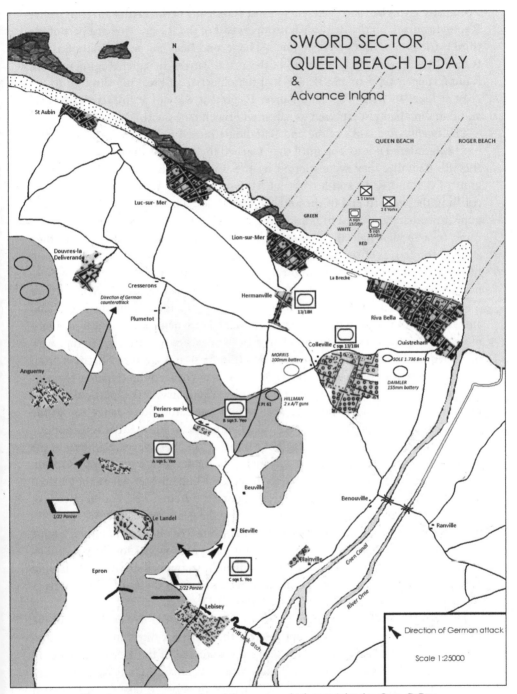

Sword sector, Queen beach and the armoured advance inland to Caen, D-Day

a company as this had had been sent to assist a company of the 125th Panzergrenadier Regiment attack on the British paratroopers east of the River Orne as a part of the third battle group, Kampfgruppe Luck. The second *kampfgruppe* was Kampfgruppe Rauch, which was largely made up of the 192nd Panzergrenadier Regiment; both Kampfgruppen Oppeln and Rauch had the objective of breaking through to the coast at Lion sur Mer. The 22nd Panzer Regiment was not at full strength as the 2nd Battalion had just replaced its captured French tanks with Mark IVs.[34]

The twenty-five tanks of the 2nd Battalion attacked first, travelling fast as they had been ordered not to stop until they reached the coast. As the tanks approached Biéville-Beuville, they were spotted by the waiting tanks, 6-pounder anti-tank guns of the 2nd KSLI and a troop of M10s of the 41st Anti-tank Regiment on reaching the western end of the anti-tank obstacles. The Shermans and anti-tank guns immediately opened fire, knocking out four Mark IVs. The German charge came to a sudden halt and the tanks sought cover behind a ridge while they awaited the arrival of the 1st Battalion. When the formation was complete (about fifty tanks), the attack pushed into the cover of woodland and continued moving northwards towards Le Landel. Two troops of A Squadron of the Staffordshire Yeomanry moved to intercept them when they emerged from the woodland and No. 1 Troop knocked out four more Mark IVs when they reappeared. Once more the Germans resumed their charge to the beaches but diverted farther west of Perier sur le Dan. Three Sherman Vc (Fireflies) and another Sherman from B Squadron that were guarding the right flank then engaged the Germans, knocking out three more tanks.[35] The Staffordshire Yeomanry tanks, particularly the Fireflies, were well sited and were able to aim murderous long-range fire at the German tanks. Kampfgruppe Oppeln, faced with this unexpectedly strong opposition and having lost thirteen tanks, broke off its attack.[36] However, elements of the 192nd Panzergrenadier Regiment, advancing to the left of Kampfgruppe Oppeln at the same time, made it all the way to the coast at Luc sur Mer where they linked up with several German strongpoints at about 1900 hours. The counterattack of the 21st Panzer Division had been deflected into the gap between the British forces in the Sword sector and the Canadian troops in Juno. At about 2100 hours, a huge formation of Allied planes towing gliders and carrying supplies for the paratroopers at Bénouville thundered over the German panzergrenadiers, who, believing they were in danger of being cut off, then retreated from the coast after leaving a company of men to reinforce the radar station at Douvres.[37]

This was the Staffordshire Yeomanry's final action of the day as the rest of the 185th Brigade, after a failed attempt to cross the anti-tank ditch and advance into Lebisey wood, decided not to push on as the outcome of the German attack on their right flank was unknown. The Staffordshire Yeomanry tanks went into harbour for the night at Biéville-Beuville. The British effort to take Caen had been effectively halted by the 21st Panzer Division. It was the closest the British would come to Caen for another four weeks.

Staffordshire Yeomanry casualties were very light in terms of tanks with only five lost that day from the regiment; seven men were killed and three wounded, with seven more missing.

Juno Sector

The sector designated Juno ran from Courseulles to St Aubin sur Mer and was the planned landing place for the Canadian 3rd Infantry Division. The two main landing beaches, codenamed Mike and Nan, were centred on the small seaside town of Courseulles with its harbour built either side of the mouth of the River Seulles. The Courseulles defences included mines, barbed wire, fortified houses and several bunkers. The Canadian division was to assault the beaches with two infantry brigades in a two-up formation with each brigade being supported by an armoured regiment from the 2nd Canadian Armoured Brigade. Their primary objectives were to establish a bridgehead as far inland as the high ground in the area Evrecy–Colomby sur Thaon–Anguerny, seize the airfield at Carpiquet and guard the left flank of the 50th Division landing on Gold. Later, the division was to be prepared to seize the bridges over the River Odon west of Caen.

The landing time for both armoured regiments was H-5 minutes to allow the tanks time to engage and knock out the defensive fortifications and protect the AVREs clearing gaps in the beach defences for the infantry arriving behind them at H-hour. Both regiments had only received their Sherman tanks in May and barely had time to learn to drive them. The Stuart M3 light recce tanks issued to the Fort Garry Horse were driven for the first time on the way to the loading hards for the landing craft. Canadian REME (Royal Electrical and Mechanical Engineers) personnel of the 1st Hussars had worked 24 hours a day 'like Trojans' to prepare newly arrived tanks for the invasion.[38] This late issue of tanks gave the Canadians little time to train with live ammunition, waterproof their tanks and participate in amphibious exercises such as Exercise Fabius III.

H-hour on the Juno sector beaches was the latest of all the Allied beaches in order to allow the tide to cover the many rocky shelves offshore. The landings were originally scheduled for 0735 and 0745 hours for Mike and Nan beaches respectively but were then postponed by a further 10 minutes because of the bad weather which had contributed to a navigational error by some of the landing craft. The LCTs carrying the AVREs destined for Mike beach had entered the wrong swept channel to the beach and the delay of 10 minutes was to allow the LCTs to catch up and assume their proper place in the order of assault. However, the delay and the higher tide than usual meant that the landing craft would be landing amongst the very obstacles the Overlord planners had tried to avoid by landing at low tide when the obstacles would be fully exposed. Two concrete busting LCTs, each carrying two Sherman Vcs manned by soldiers of each regiment, were also part of the initial assault wave (one for each tank regiment) and were tasked with engaging specific bunkers on the way in.

Fort Garry Horse

The DD tanks of the Fort Garry Horse were to be transported by the N LCT squadron of the 11th LCT Flotilla and land with the AVREs as part of the J-2 naval task force. The regiment was to support the 8th Brigade on the left flank landing on Nan beach around Bernières and St Aubin. B and C squadrons were equipped with DD tanks and each squadron took in an extra tank to make twenty tanks. Nan beach had four main defensive strongpoints: WN27 at St Aubin, WN28 and 28A at Bernières and WN29 at Courseulles.

B Squadron

The possibility of the seas being too rough for the DD tanks had been considered by the squadron leaders and LCT flotilla officers prior to and for much of the voyage across the English Channel. Once the launching point 7,000yds offshore

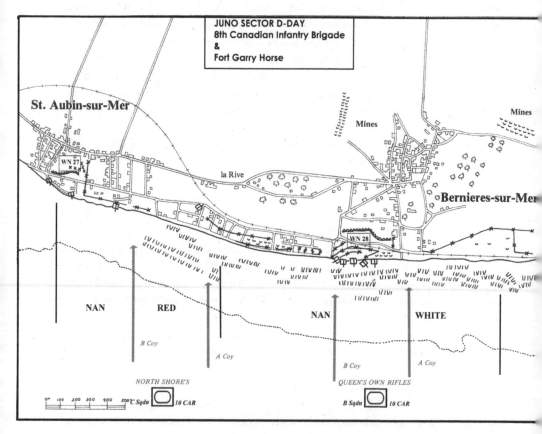

Juno sector, Nan beach. The landings of Fort Garry Horse and the 8th Canadian Infantry Brigade, adapted from *Maple Leaf Route: Caen*. (*By kind permission of T. Copp*)

was reached, the DSOAG (Deputy Senior Office Assault Group) of the DD LCT squadrons asked the senior squadron leader if he wished to launch or move in closer. The decision was taken to move closer but at about 2,000yds from shore, the seas were still considered too rough so the decision was made to take the DD tanks nearly all the way in to the beach. The tanks were finally launched less than 500yds from the shoreline. Paradoxically, this decision to launch the DD tanks closer actually delayed their arrival as the LCTs had to manoeuvre to avoid the other waves of landing craft and the obstacles on the beach.

B Squadron were supporting the Queen's Own Rifles Regiment in their assault on Bernières and the tanks started wading ashore at 0821 hours on Nan White beach. Unfortunately, they were late as the infantry had landed at 0815 hours and were already under heavy fire from WN28 immediately in front of them. The infantry were faced with a series of five pill boxes and fortifications on top of the sea wall which the aerial and naval bombardment had not damaged. The Germans had recovered quickly from the bombardment and all the beach defences were intact. The two leading companies of the Queen's Own infantry suffered heavy losses in making a 100yd dash across the beach to find cover behind the sea wall.

A lance corporal on the beach wrote afterwards:

> Our support craft was knocked out so we had no heavy weapons. The DD tanks had not come ashore. My platoon, approximately 36 strong, went through what we believe was enfilade fire from machine guns. The official battalion KIA figures for 6 June 1944 numbered 63, B Company 34. I don't have the figures for the platoon but I do know that only 9 men moved inland, 3 of whom were walking wounded. Of the ten men in my section, seven were killed and two wounded.[39]

A flak ship moved close inshore and used its guns to pour continuous fire onto the strongpoints, almost running aground in doing so, before the tanks could land and offer effective supporting fire. The tanks moved along the water's edge and engaged the pill boxes and fortified houses that could be identified as holding up the advance. The infantry risked death by staying on the beach, so one by one the pill boxes were attacked and knocked out with the help of the tanks which allowed the infantry to climb the sea wall and cautiously move into Bernières.

However, as the sea wall could not be breached, B Squadron could not get off the beach to support the infantry for over an hour. The gapping teams were not successful until 0920 hours when two exits off the beach were finally opened. The infantry had encountered stiff resistance in Bernières as the previously dazed and stunned Germans recovered and returned to their posts. However, by about 0900 hours, Bernières had been almost secured without the assistance of the tanks which finally arrived in the town at 0930 hours. The Queen's Own Rifles and tanks then prepared to move southwards to capture Anguerny via Bény sur Mer, 7 miles away. B Squadron was then ordered to patrol around Thaon and back to Anguerny; along the way one tank was knocked out and another damaged by artillery. The hill at

Point 70 was reached at about 1500 hours and from there the tanks could see their objective, Carpiquet airfield. The concrete buster LCT(A) CB 2338 came into the beach and the two Sherman Vcs were attached to B Squadron to give it some much needed 17-pounder firepower.[40]

C Squadron

Encountering similar sea conditions to B Squadron, the decision was made to land almost directly on Nan Red beach and the landing craft started to launch their tanks at 0805 hours. After a short swim of 500yds or less, the tanks reached the shore but, because of the heavy seas and manoeuvring to avoid the Element C obstacles, not in the planned order.[41] Tank troops landed in the wrong location, unnoticed by the squadron commander, making co-ordination difficult. C Squadron was supporting the North Shore (New Brunswick) Regiment, timed by the Royal Navy as landing at 0810 hours. Reports vary, but it is likely that C Squadron tanks landed a few minutes after the two companies of infantry in the first wave. Again, the arriving infantry and DD tanks found that the German defences had survived the bombardment and, after an initial lull, quickly came to life. The 50mm anti-tank guns in WN27 on the sea wall in St Aubin began to shoot at the tanks and their landing craft. The first tanks to arrive on the beach were immediately hit, one being quickly knocked out.

Two tanks from LCT 313 were lost after launching, one fell into a shell hole after having deflated its canvas screen and another was swamped after the tank's motors failed.[42] LCT 317 went all the way in to the beach and two tanks disembarked, but the LCT was then hit repeatedly by shell and mortar fire before drifting back out to sea. Three tanks were still aboard, one of which caught fire and drove into the water (flooding the engine) to extinguish the flames. From this half-submerged position the tank began to fire 75mm HE (high explosive) in support of infantry until an AP (armour piercing) round struck the barrel of the 75mm gun, putting it out of action. The crew continued to fire their machine guns until the rising tide forced them to abandon their tank. The crews of the remaining two tanks swam to shore from the damaged landing craft to try and organise a tow for their tanks off the landing craft, but this was not successful and several crew members were killed in the process.

The AVRE tanks and Flails were also late on Nan beach, so the Fort Garry Horse tanks were the only support for the infantry in their fight to capture St Aubin. Three more tanks were drowned reaching the shore and another tank was flooded by the rising tide when its engine stalled while engaging targets on the shore. [43]

Shell and mortar fire made the beaches a dangerous place for the infantry, so they crossed the sea wall and entered the village of St Aubin as quickly as they could. Meanwhile, the late-arriving AVREs had set to work clearing lanes to the sea wall which they then attempted to bridge. Snipers were a particular problem, targeting any tank commander unwisely leaning out of his turret for a better look. Conscious of the fact that the infantry were getting off the beach and needed their support, the tanks of C Squadron attempted to leave the beach before exit lanes had been cleared by the AVRE Flails. Three tanks detonated mines and were immobilised but the rest of the squadron got off the beach to support the infantry. St Aubin was cleared by 1115 hours with the exception of strongpoint WN28 on the western edge of the town. Tanks of the 3rd Troop were sent to assist with the capture of this strongpoint which was protected by mines and a roadblock past which the tanks could not proceed. After a reconnaissance on foot, the tanks broke holes in the perimeter walls and nearby houses to take up firing positions from which they could destroy the two 75mm guns and various other emplacements inside the strongpoint. A tank commanded by Sergeant Walterson finally broke into the strongpoint and ran up and down the trench system until all the occupants had been killed or had surrendered. This troop finally got back to harbour at 2200 hours.[44] Meanwhile, tanks from the 5th Troop circled around Tailleville, destroying various anti-tank guns and forcing German soldiers to flee southwards.

A battalion of the 736th Panzergrenadier Regiment had its command post and ammunition dump in Tailleville at WN23 and this was well defended. C Squadron tanks provided support for the infantry as they slowly worked their way into the position before a Sherman got into the middle of the command post and shot up the trenches with HE at point-blank range.

A Squadron

A Squadron, equipped with deep wading tanks, was to land at H+60 minutes and to proceed inland down the brigade's centre line of advance as far as the high ground and objectives at Colomby sur Thaon. According to the brigade's Overlord plans, the beachhead was supposed to be secured by H+60 minutes before the arrival of A Squadron.[45]

The embarkation of the tanks of A Squadron and RHQ had been a little disorganised owing to the shortage of landing craft. Seventeen tanks were distributed amongst four LCT Mk IVs that landed an hour later on Nan White. Two tanks were due at H+75 minutes, and an LST carrying two RHQ Shermans and a Sherman Vc of the 5th Troop were due to land from H+4 hours.[46] The final A Squadron tank to make nineteen in total was not due until D+8 days.[47]

A Squadron landing craft began beaching unopposed at 0900 hours. An LCT carrying the RHQ and A Squadron HQ tanks struck a mine and whilst manoeuvring to land again detonated a second mine. Fortunately, no casualties occurred and the vessel eventually beached again after freeing its ramp. A Squadron formed up with the reserve infantry battalion from the Régiment de la Chaudière to move towards Bény sur Mer at 1030 hours but the advance through Bernières was held up by a single 88mm anti-tank gun near the town's cemetery. This knocked out three Priests (25-pounder self-propelled artillery) before the infantry organised an attack to eliminate the obstacle.[48] Bernières rapidly became congested with soldiers of the 8th Brigade plus the newly arrived reserve brigade, the 9th Brigade. This brigade was supposed to land at both St Aubin and Bernières but, as fighting was still going on in St Aubin, Nan Red beach had been closed by the Royal Navy and Bernières was the only place that the brigade could land. A Squadron tanks and infantry initially made little progress and apparently waited for artillery to land to support their advance. The A Squadron leader finally arrived after his LCT had beached and assessed the situation. An Orders Group was held and forward progress was resumed with A and B squadrons advancing as planned, incurring some casualties in the process. A Squadron tanks finally reached Anguerny but as there were no infantry with them to hold the town, RHQ and repaired X tank casualties rushed up in support until the Queen's Own Rifles finally arrived to relieve them. The next day the Fort Garry Horse reported eleven tanks being lost (two damaged) with forty-four Shermans and seven Fireflies fit.[49]

Having largely achieved their D-Day objectives, the tanks of the Fort Garry Horse were pulled back as the divisional reserve. The regiment was ordered back to harbour in Bény sur Mer at 2000 hours but the tanks stayed with their infantry well into the night. It was not until 0100 hours the following morning that B Squadron made it back to Bény sur Mer while C Squadron stayed with the North Shores in Tailleville until the following afternoon. The Queen's Own Rifles' history pays tribute to the Fort Garry Horse:

> The tanks ranged far and wide and did valuable work in locating and destroying pockets of the enemy. It was a tank-infantry fight against scattered nests of enemy resistance and never did the cooperation work more smoothly.[50]

The delay at Bernières meant that Carpiquet, one of the D-Day objectives of the Canadian 3rd Division, could not be taken that day and the 9th Brigade and its supporting tank regiment, the Sherbrooke Fusiliers (27th Canadian Armoured Regiment), had to harbour for the night short of their objective. The Fort Garry Horse lost thirteen men killed (one officer and twelve ORs) and twelve men wounded (two officers and ten ORs) on D-Day.

1st Hussars

The DD-equipped A and B squadrons of the 1st Hussars were to land either side of the mouth of the River Seulles at Courseulles at H-5 minutes in support of the 7th Brigade. A Squadron was to support the Royal Winnipeg Rifles Regiment into the western part of Courseulles and B Squadron was to support the Regina Rifles Regiment in clearing eastern Courseulles and then move inland to the bridges over the River Mue at Reviers and further south to Fontaine Henry. The landing craft of K LCT squadron of the 4th LCT Flotilla would transport the DD tanks to their launching positions as part of the J3.111 assault wave composed of DD tanks and AVREs.

The main German strongpoint at Courseulles, WN29, was equipped with an 88m gun and two 75mm guns sighted to fire along the beach from Courseulles to St Aubin.

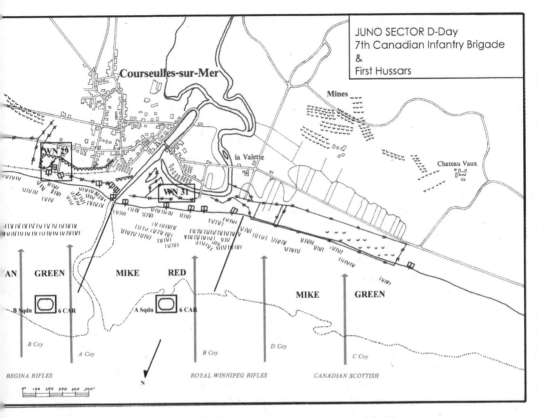

Juno sector, Mike beach. The landings of the 1st Hussars and the 7th Canadian Infantry Brigade,
adapted from *Maple Leaf Route: Caen*. (*By kind permission of T. Copp*)

A Squadron

As arranged at a briefing on 4 June for the tank troop commanders and the DSOAG,
a signal was sent from the control landing craft at 0530 hours querying the advisabil-
ity of launch DD tanks when the LCTs were still 8 miles from the French coast. The
firm reply was that the sea was too rough and to check again when 7,000yds offshore.
At this distance, at 0640 hours, the LCT HQ ship sent a signal that it was too rough
to launch and to proceed directly to the Mike beaches. The tank crews began to
discard excess equipment such as tiller bars, compasses and escape apparatus.

As the LCTs were now ahead of schedule as they had not stopped to launch, the
flotilla turned in a large circle to mark time. However, when the flotilla was lined
up for the beach again at 0725 hours, the bells rang for 'down doors' and the DD
tanks were ordered to launch. The senior squadron leader had decided to launch to
ensure that the tanks arrived as scheduled to support the assaulting infantry. By
this time, German mortars and shells were beginning to range in on the landing
craft. After launching one tank, the chains holding the door ramp of the port
landing craft were shot away and the other tanks could not launch, so the LCT

carried them to the beach, only to hit a mine immediately after the second tank launched. The next tank tried to get off as the LCT began to list to port but it was immediately swamped on launching, blocking the exit of the remaining two tank which were then unable to disembark. Only when the tide went out later in the afternoon could the two tanks get off the beached LCT. Another LCT had its ramp damaged by shell fire and was forced to beach, all tanks getting off successfully, though one was later swamped in the surf.[51]

Therefore only ten DD tanks were launched at about 2,500yds from the beach, nine from the two centre LCTs and one from the port craft. Only seven of these made it to the beach at about 0800 hours, two being swamped or sunk by mortar fire and another swamped by the wash of one of the rocket-firing LCTs moving rapidly inshore to fire a salvo of rockets at the beach.

According to their war diary which also noted that the DD tanks and AVREs were late, the Royal Winnipegs infantry landed at 0749 hours.[52] The Winnipegs were very critical of the effectiveness of the earlier aircraft bombing and naval bombardment which apparently had not put a single defensive position out of action. The Winnipegs were, however, appreciative of the support given by A Squadron, as expressed in a letter written to the Hussars after D-Day which is included in their war diary.

Of the seven DD tanks launched that made it to the beach, three were quickly lost. One tank accidentally deflated its screens too soon when its commander was shot, a second was swamped amongst the underwater obstacles and a third was knocked out by a 75mm anti-tank gun. On the left of Mike beach, No. 3 Troop moved up onto the beach just west of the mouth of the River Seulles where it flows into the sea immediately west of Courseulles. Just inland, the river bent back upon itself, creating a narrow neck of land bordered by water on three sides on which a concrete bunker housing a 75mm anti-tank gun had been constructed. As the tanks forded the river towards the bunker, it opened fire; one Sherman was knocked out and several German machine guns opened fire on the crew as they frantically bailed out. The bunker and machine gun posts were quickly destroyed by the other tanks of the troop. [53]

The four surviving DD tanks of the squadron were joined by the six others landed directly by the LCTs and the ten tanks proceeded to cruise up and down the beach, engaging any targets they could identify. One Sherman blasted the seawall to the east of Courseulles to help the Regina Rifles infantry climb onto the promenade and begin to clear the houses.

Much to the frustration of the infantry, plans previously made to co-ordinate with the tanks were abandoned in the confusion of battle as the tanks milled around, seemingly aimlessly. The squadron's tanks were actually looking for targets to engage but were also reluctant to stop and present themselves as stationary targets to the Germans for any length of time.[54] The first exit from the beach was not completed until 1112 hours owing to the engineers being under constant sniper fire, the congestion on the beach and the high tide.[55]

Only ten A Squadron tanks moved off the beach to make contact with the infantry and these tanks divided up into three groups to support the infantry as they moved inland. The squadron's numbers were reduced even further when one tank broke down near the beach after seawater swamped its engine electrical system and another lost a track. The remaining tanks supported the infantry in clearing La Rivière and at the end of the day the squadron had nine tanks operational.

B Squadron

B Squadron had a similar dialogue with the control landing craft regarding the heavy seas as they approached Nan Green beach. However, no sooner had the decision been made to take the DD tanks all the way in than the commanding officer of the LCT flotilla came alongside the squadron commander when about 5,000yds offshore and asked if the squadron was prepared to launch after all. As the seas appeared slightly calmer, the squadron commander agreed to launch.[56] This caused a certain amount of consternation amongst the tank crews as they too had already discarded some of their DD equipment.

All nineteen DD tanks were launched successfully at about 4,000yds from the beach. One tank developed engine trouble and had to be abandoned before sinking and two more tanks from the same troop were swamped by large waves and sank. German mortar fire began to land amongst the tanks, causing the screen of the squadron commander's tank to collapse after a near miss. The tank quickly sank and the crew managed to make it into the relative safety of the rescue dinghy.

B Squadron lost four tanks drowned on the run-in, and fourteen tanks (plus a tank that arrived much later to the east) reached the beach at 0758 hours, according to a signal from Regina Rifles which sent the code word 'Popcorn' to confirm that the tanks had arrived well ahead of the infantry and AVREs as planned and had begun to engage the beach defences. An account of the amphibious ordeal was given by Sergeant Gariepy:

The night of 5/6 June 44 I was aboard a Landing Craft tank sailing towards France. The night was cold and windy and not many men slept because of the great nervous tension. No one was seasick except two sailors! The coast was sighted early at dawn; H-hour had been changed from 0635 hours to 0735 hours.

Our DD craft were ready for launching but due to a rolling swell in the Channel we were told by Naval officers that we would be beached. That order was never confirmed with embarrassing results. Most of us had thrown our navigation instruments overboard; such as compasses, crew commander's standfast bar and some craft their steering bar.

The order to launch was given at approximately 7000 yards directly in front of our appointed beach. As we became waterborne, commenced terrific rolling and pitching, all five craft were launched but formation was impossible so I decided to make for my designated place on the beach. There was no enemy fire for about 4,000 yards, when we were showered with small arms fire. I then looked around to see who was alongside of me and the only other craft who was parallel was Major Duncan's 30 yards on my starboard side. He seemed to be in difficulties because the dinghy was being prepared. At that point one of my port aft struts broke and the crew had to wedge a fire extinguisher between the hull and the screen. Immediately after two pillars burst through small arms fire, which was increasing in density. I took another look at Major Duncan's DD craft and all I saw was four heads in the water. The other craft were some 200 yards behind me in different positions. I then realized that it was up to me to make for the beach, with God's help we made it. I then followed the crew inside the turret keeping one hatch half open so as to have an occasional look for mines and obstacles at the water's edge. When I judged it safe to deflate we did so and then we immediately opened fire on the pill box which was on our immediate front with 75mm HE. After 5 rounds I advanced another 50 yards and fired 5 more rounds of AP, we were then about 150 yards from target. As there was no other answering fire except small arms I looked back to see if the way was clear for the AVRE. Then I engaged machine gun nests dotting the beach which were playing merry hell along the water line.[57]

Of the DD Shermans that arrived on Nan Green, two tanks were subsequently swamped in the surf. Duels broke out between the tanks on the beaches and the 88mm and 75mm anti-tank guns in the bunkers which the tanks won, not losing a single tank in the firefight. The assault infantry and AVREs arrived 15 minutes later and the AVREs set about making exits off the beach. The tanks began to engage the pill boxes along the promenade in co-ordinated attacks with the infantry. The appearance of the tanks was apparently a complete surprise to the defenders and contributed to their decision to surrender, according to one report in the Hussars war diary.[58] Half an hour later, at about 0900 hours, the first tanks of B Squadron were able to leave the beach and assisted the infantry with the clearing of Courseulles. By 1400 hours, B Squadron only had nine tanks fit; the tank of Lieutenant Seaman had struck a mine assisting the Regina Rifles into Reviers.

Later that afternoon, whilst advancing inland on a reconnaissance patrol of the high ground behind Pierrepoint, five of the squadron's tanks were destroyed in matter of minutes when distracted by a dummy anti-tank gun. By the end of the day, according to the regimental war diary, B Squadron had four tanks fit. Sergeant Gariepy provided a detailed account of the action:

We moved along road past ADEN (codename for Reviers) when high ground reached we deployed – first troop on left, second troop right then HQF covering rear from hull down position on high ground. Small calibre mortar fire was observed in wood behind ADEN. Keeping our formation, we advanced on wood firing HE at the edge. When in valley about 150 yards in front of wood, heavy mortar fire was ranging close to second troop. Second troop leader had no wireless so I called Sun Ray and explained situation and he advised me to withdraw, so I laid down smoke screen to cover our withdrawal. The troop leader realised what was happening and tuned back in two-up formation; troop leader and corporal in front and I in the rear, about ten yard in rear covering with smoke. When top of crest was reached, I saw my troop leader's tank burst into flame. I halted, told my driver to reverse full speed and my gunner to traverse 160 degrees right. When this was almost completed I saw my corporal's tank blown up in turn. I then halted my driver and gave a fire order to bear on the anti-tank gun which was in between the burning tanks approximately 60 yards away. After two rapid round of HE I hit target. I then reported back to Sun Ray who told me to proceed to ADEN. The rest of the squadron followed, the encounter cost us 5 tanks – the anti-tank gun was an 88mm.[59]

Another account of the same action was given by the troop leader, Lieutenant Mcleod, who provided a vivid description of what it was like when a tank was hit:

I was leading the squadron which at that time consisted of the two tanks in SHQ, another troop of three tanks and my troop; we moved to the right or west of the town and swung through the fields towards the high ground south of Reviers. I saw a haystack directly in front at which I fired two rounds of HE. The next thing there was a great jolt in the tank and the turret swung about. The driver reported over the intercom that his periscope had been shot away and the gunner reported that his traverse gears would not work. I immediately gave the order for the driver to swing left and speed up.

A moment late a shell came across the tops of the turret hitting the cupola lids. My face seemed cut and my earphones and tin hat had been knocked off. I then crouched down to give the driver orders to keep going helped by the co-driver who could still see through his periscope. The operator then said the tank was on fire so he pulled the fire extinguisher knobs and used the extinguisher in the turret on the rear hull around the oil canister. The motor quit so I gave the order to bail out. The gunner, operator and myself got out of the turret onto the ground to find the turret was in such a position that the main gun would not allow the driver's or co-driver's hatch to be opened. The screen on the outside was burning by now but I managed to get in the turret and somehow swing it enough for the driver and co-driver to escape through a hole in the basket. The co-driver could not get his hatch off due to Bostik glue. We all laid still in front of the tank in the tall wheat to collect our bearings.[60]

Lieutenant Mcleod was hit in the eye by a piece of shrapnel from the 88mm AP shell that hit the turret hatches and was evacuated back to England.

During the landings, the concrete buster LCT(A) CB 2401 had carried out the destruction of a specific bunker near Courseulles as planned on the run into the beach, each tank using only thirty rounds of ammunition to do so. The ammunition for this task was carried separately in the LCT(A) so that the tanks could land with a full load of ammunition. The two Fireflies (commanded by Lieutenant Irving) joined up with B Squadron but whilst proceeding inland, Lieutenant Irving was wounded when his tank was hit and disabled by a 50mm anti-tank gun.

C Squadron

C Squadron plus the tanks of RHQ, a total of seventeen Shermans V and five Sherman Vc (including RHQ), were scheduled to land at H-hour+45 minutes. The landing craft arrived at 0820 hours on Mike beach to find that, apart from occasional sniping and machine-gun fire, it was secure but a traffic jam was rapidly developing on the beach. By 0900 hours, there were still no exits. The AVREs had been labouring to clear a gap through some flooded ground beyond the sand dunes to a lateral road and one AVRE carrying a fascine had become almost submerged. The fascine was removed by its crew, which then enabled a bridge-layer AVRE to lay its bridge across the top of the sunken tank. Using this perilous exit, six tanks of C Squadron were able to make an exit to the lateral road beyond until the bridge was put out of action by an errant self-propelled artillery vehicle.[61] The tank of the commanding officer, Lieutenant Colonel Colwell, hit a mine while exiting.[62] C Squadron supported the 1st Canadian Scottish infantry in a number of skirmishes and then advanced inland to Banville, another tank being damaged by a mine.

The 1st Hussars was the only regiment on D-Day to reach its objectives. A troop from C Squadron under Lieutenant McCormick penetrated as far inland as Bretteville l'Orgueilleuse and Sequeville Bessin and was in sight of the airfield at Carpiquet. Little opposition was met and the troop tried to contact regimental HQ by radio to inform them of their progress but could not get through. Unsupported, the troop was forced to return to the regiment.

At the end of the day, A Squadron only had nine tanks operational and B Squadron had four so the two squadrons had to be temporarily amalgamated.[63] The regiment reported only twenty-six Shermans and three Fireflies operational next day. Thus the 1st Hussars had thirty-three tanks destroyed or damaged on D-Day, including one of the concrete-busting Fireflies. Most of the casualties were either irreparably ruined by seawater on the beach or damaged in battle and were complete write-offs; the Light Aid Detachment (LAD) when it arrived ashore could only repair several tanks that had run over mines. D-Day casualties in men for the 1st Hussars were heavier than for the Fort Garry Horse because of the greater tank losses – two officers and nineteen men were killed plus a similar number wounded.[64]

Sherbrooke Fusiliers

The Sherbrooke Fusiliers, the reserve regiment with the 9th Infantry Brigade, landed on Nan White beach near Bernières at 1215 hours and after many delays moved to the assembly point designated 'Elder' near Bény sur Mer, arriving at dusk. The Sherbrooke Fusiliers had been using the four tanks per troop model of squadron organisation since training in March 1944 but each squadron was short a tank that was not detailed to arrive until D+8 days. The delays and traffic congestion meant that the regiment had not been able to advance inland and seize its objectives, which included Carpiquet airfield, so preparations were made for a dawn advance next day.

Omaha Sector

The Omaha sector was located between Port en Bessin and the River Vire estuary and linked the Gold and Utah sectors. The proposed landing was on a crescent-shaped shingle beach about 7,000yds long with grass-covered hills behind the beach and cliffs at either end and had been divided into four sectors labelled C to F for planning purposes; these were further subdivided into red (left or port) and green (right or starboard). The beach was on average 100yds wide and rose up to a strip of marshland up to 200yds wide at the base of the steep cliffs, or bluffs. In some places the bluffs were nearly 200ft high and extended from the top of the shingle beach.

In the tidal zone there were three belts of underwater obstacles topped with teller mines. The base of the cliffs and the marshland were also heavily mined. The only exits from the beach for tracked and wheeled vehicles were five narrow natural defiles or draws that cut through the bluffs and led up to the coastal plain. These defiles were heavily mined and strongpoints had been constructed along their length to block the routes away from the beach. There were a total of fourteen strongpoints in the Omaha sector which was the most heavily defended of all the invasion beaches as well as being the most difficult terrain. All but three of these strongpoints could fire along the length of the beaches proposed for the landings. The bunkers had thick concrete walls to protect them from a naval bombardment and could only be attacked by gunfire or tanks on the beaches. They were equipped with a variety of captured French and Russian guns from 37mm to 75mm in size, as well as German 75mm and 88mm anti-tank guns. At the base of the D-1 draw there were a number of villas along a paved promenade that ran parallel to the beach between the D-1 Vierville and D-3 Les Moulins draws. Anti-tank ditches had been dug in front of the E-3 Colleville and D-1 Vierville draws and a sea wall between 4ft and 8ft high, against which shingle had piled up, ran along the western half of the beach, creating yet another obstacle.

The Omaha sector was defended by the newly formed 352nd Division, which had moved into the sector in April to support the 716th Division. The 352nd Division had immediately set about improving the beach defences where there were sufficient materials to do so. The division was formed from the shattered remnants of Eastern Front units, previously wounded men, seventeen- and eighteen-year-old recruits and men from the Eastern occupied countries. Like many of the Allied units, the 352nd Division had never been in action before. Observation posts in the strongpoints were able to direct fire from four batteries of the division artillery positioned inland to support the beach defences. These guns had pre-registered potential targets on the beaches.

741st Tank Battalion

H-hour was the same as Utah, 0630 hours, and was preceded by heavy aerial and naval bombardments. Omaha was farther west than the British sectors and therefore high tides were earlier. So as not to unduly alert the Germans to the imminent invasion, the American naval bombardment would begin at the same time as the British bombardment but because of the earlier high tides, it was only of 40 minutes' duration compared with the 2 hours on British beaches.

The tanks of the 741st Tank Battalion sailed from England as part of Force O-1 in Mk VI LCTs of the 12th US Flotilla; these craft were slightly smaller than the British LCT Mk III and only carried four tanks. The landings were to be on a two-brigade or regimental combat team front, as per Juno and Gold sectors. The 116th Regimental Combat Team (RCT) from the 29th Division was to land on the right and the 16th RCT from the 1st Division land on the left.

The 741st Tank Battalion was to support the 16th RCT on the left flank. The DD tanks of B Company were commanded by Captain Thornton and the company was attached to the 2nd Battalion 16th RCT due to land on Easy Red beach. C Company, commanded by Captain Young, was attached to the 3rd Battalion 16th RCT landing on Fox Green. The DD tanks of both companies were to land when the naval bombardment finished 5 minutes before H-hour.

A Company tanks were to provide support fire to the flanks on the way in from specially modified landing craft and were to land at H-hour across all the beaches being used by the 16th RCT. The landing craft had been modified in the same way as the British LCT(A)s to enable two Sherman M4s side by side to fire over the ramp of the landing craft.

Each LCT(A) carried two M4s and a tank bulldozer for a company total of sixteen M4s and eight tank dozers. The tanks also towed a trailer carrying supplies of ammunition. The extra armour plating and the high centre of gravity created by the elevated tanks on the wooden platform made these LCT(A)s very unstable and they easily rolled and shipped water in rough seas.

As well as supporting the infantry by engaging the German bunkers, the DD tanks also had to support the specialist army and naval engineers clear eight gaps 50yds wide in the beach obstacles and the exits off the beaches. All three companies of the 741st Tank Battalion were to then get off the beach by exit E-3 and support the 3rd Battalion achieve its objectives inland. Tanks from the DD companies were to be used to bring A Company up to strength if required to complete this mission.[65]

B and C Companies

The designated transport loading area for the infantry was 11 miles off shore because of a battery of guns on Pointe du Hoc at the western end of the beach that posed a major threat to the invasion fleet. With H-hour at 0630 hours, the assault landing craft had to be loaded and marshalled in darkness well before that time. Rough seas and strong currents added to the considerable difficulties of the assault units which became scattered on their final approach to the beaches. At least ten landing craft carrying infantry were swamped on the approach and many DUKWs carrying the guns of two field howitzer battalions also sank. The strong offshore current pulled many craft eastwards so they landed on the wrong beaches.[66]

The decision to launch the DD tanks was made after consultation between the two army company commanders by radio and at approximately 5,000yds from shore, the yellow flags for launch were raised. One by one, the ungainly tanks of B and C squadrons trundled to the front of the LCTs and down the ramp into the turbulent sea. One after another, tanks began to succumb to the large waves. Some tanks sank almost immediately while the canvas screens of others collapsed and pumps battled to keep up with the inrushing water. Some tanks, with their crews struggling to hold up the screen, managed to stay afloat for 2 miles before finally going under. The seas became dotted with orange life rafts and surviving crew men.

All sixteen tanks of C Company were lost and all but five tanks of B Squadron sank between 1,000 and 5,000yds from the shore.

Three B Company tanks on LCT 600 were landed directly on the beach at about 0645 hours after the blast from a near miss of an artillery shell caused the leading tank to roll back and damage the screens of the other tanks so they could not be launched. The first tank off then foundered and the LCT stopped to pick up the crew. The fortunate tanks to arrive by LCT were commanded by Sergeants Maddock, Ragan and Williams.

Only two tanks of the twenty-nine that took to the water eventually swam in and they were those commanded by Sergeants Geddes and Sheppard. The 741st Tank Battalion history described the launch:

On the order, the tanks rolled gracefully into the rough sea and many of them sank almost immediately, carrying many men to watery graves. The most fortunate were able to leave their sinking tanks and swim about until rescued. Soon the Channel was a mass of bobbing heads and every available life raft was tossed into the water. Some quick thinking tank commanders anticipated the sinking and in good time were able to inflate the rubber dinghy each tank carried. Not a few men were forced all the way to the bottom of the Channel before getting free and escaping to the surface. For these men their oxygen masks were a Godsend.

Speedy LCIs (Landing Craft, Infantry) did praiseworthy work, zooming about the hundreds of larger vessels picking up men everywhere from the water and taking them to the hospital ships in the rear.[67]

Another survivor, Corporal Hopper, described his near drowning:

The Lieutenant and Merket were trying to hold the canvas out and I was trying to steer it, which was almost an impossible job as the waves were so rough.

When I saw that we didn't have a chance to make it to the beach, I yelled to Snike to come out and Merket yelled to Crouse. We tried unsuccessfully to hold the canvas out when one side caved in so the Lieutenant and Merket inflated one life raft whilst Snike and I tried to inflate the other one but the one we had had been damaged and would not operate. As we were working on it, the tank gave a last shudder and started for the bottom. The Lieutenant and Merket managed to get a hold on one life raft and stayed with it but Snike, Crouse and I went to the bottom with the tank. As I felt it settle on the bottom, I thought I was lost as my cigarettes worked out of my pocket and floated up past my face. I gave up hope as I saw that and started to breathe water; before much longer I opened my eyes again and saw that the water was getting lighter. I finally did reach air and as I looked around I saw Snike about fifty feet from me and trying to swim towards the life raft where the Lieutenant and Merket were. He finally made it. Crouse came to the top a little later, close by me and we tried to make the raft together but couldn't as the water was too rough. Crouse drifted away from me until he was just a speck. One rocket boat passed me on the way to the beach and its commander saluted me which didn't help my feelings any. The LCT I had been on tried to pick me up, but couldn't get close enough so I floated around; every time a wave would raise me up I could see everything that was going on around the beach, then the water would drop me down again till I couldn't see anything. When I saw all the boats pass me by, I really started to get afraid and I started to yell for help. The LCT finally managed to get close enough and threw me a line. I had to wrap it around my arms as my hands were too cold to hold onto it. They pulled me aboard and wrapped me in blankets and I passed out.[68]

The loss of twenty-seven DD tanks meant the initial assault on the left flank of Omaha had very little armoured support for the first quarter of an hour. Easy Red had only five DD tanks on it, one of which was quickly disabled; these tanks were the sole support for 100 infantrymen on Easy Red for the first half-hour. Fox Green had no tanks at all until the arrival of the A Company tanks on both beaches after H-hour.[69]

A Company

Before the landings had begun, LCT(A) 2049, destined for Easy Red, hit a mine and sank at 0200 hours on the cross-Channel voyage so two M4 and a tank dozer were lost to the engineers even before the landings.[70] On Easy Red, three landing craft made it at H-hour or just after and unloaded six A Company tanks and three tank dozers. Of these, one tank sank when it drove into water too deep for its wading equipment, one tank was hit and immobilised by an anti-tank gun on leaving the landing craft opposite the E-3 exit (but continued to engage targets until the rising tide forced the crew to abandon the tank) and another tank was destroyed by gunfire.[71] By H+10 minutes, the tank dozer platoon of four dozers had landed and begun to remove obstacles, clear gaps and unload landing craft, all the while under intense enemy fire. One tank dozer was immediately hit and destroyed by an 88mm gun. Five A Company tanks had been lost on the voyage or soon after beaching and the 16th RCT and engineers now had less than a third of the planned number of tanks to support them. Those that were left went into action between the St Laurent E-1 and Colleville E-3 exits on Easy Red beach.[72]

On Fox Green beach only two landing craft arrived at H-hour, LCT(A) 2037 which was damaged and LCT 210 which was an unarmoured landing craft

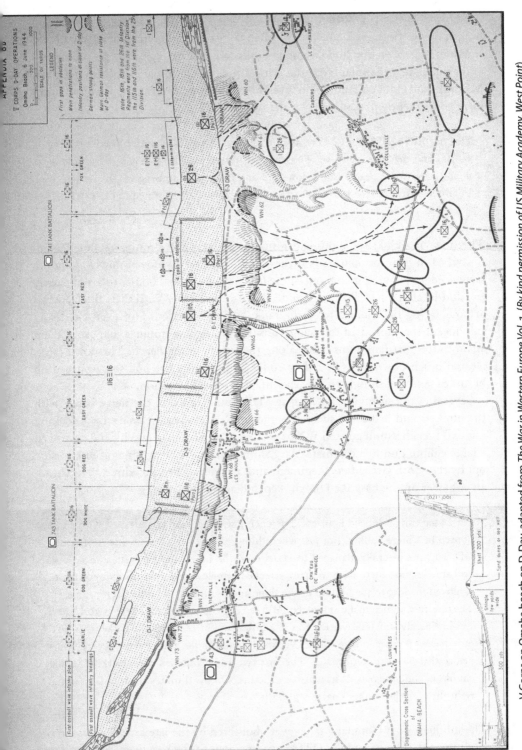

V Corps on Omaha beach on D-Day, adapted from *The War in Western Europe Vol. 1*. (By kind permission of US Military Academy, West Point)

substituted at the last minute in England when the original landing craft had broken down. Both craft quickly unloaded their tanks and retracted off the beach.

Mines, enemy action and swamped tanks reduced the number of A Company tanks supporting the infantry at the critical time of the initial assault from sixteen M4 tanks and eight tank dozers to seven tanks and four dozers. The assault infantry were consequently pinned down at the water's edge:

> During the initial phases of the assault, the beach area was under heavy artillery, mortar and machine gun fire. The assault battalions of the 16th CT were holding about 20 yards of beachhead at low tide and had made no progress inland due to the intense fire. All work carried on by tank dozers was performed under extremely hazardous conditions.[73]

The surviving tanks set about engaging the bunkers and strongpoints of WN60, 61 and 62 in front of them as best they could. The tanks moved slowly along the water's edge, weaving in and out of the beach obstacles and bodies to avoid enemy fire and locate targets. Positioned hull down in the water with their thick frontal armour facing the shore offered the tanks some protection. However, the rising tide meant the tanks had to change position every few minutes, exposing them again to the anti-tank guns firing along the length of the beach. The dozer tanks cleared beach obstacles as best they could whilst under fire and some pushed up berms of sand and shingle to give the infantry some protection.

Several of the surviving B Company DD tanks joined in the fierce battle with the bunkers and had some success. Sergeant Geddes claimed credit for knocking out two French 75mm guns in WN62 and Sergeant Sheppard also hit and destroyed a large calibre gun in a casemate. An 88mm gun in WN61 was reported knocked out by the 726th Grenadiers Regiment at 0720 hours.[74] Private Alfred Whitehead, an engineer on the Easy Red beach, kept a diary:

> For a long time it looked hopeless. The enemy was slaughtering our men with an 88 housed in a huge bunker. But just when things looked darkest, one of our Sherman DD amphibious tanks managed to crawl onto the beach and not get knocked out, probably because there were so many wrecked vehicles the enemy missed spotting it. It moved in close to the bottom of the slope and I ran over and directed it to that 88. The terrain was such that our tank could creep in close enough to where its gun barrel was just barely sticking over the top of a little rise to fire. I told the tanker that he'd only have a few seconds to move over the rise and shoot, then hit the reverse gears before that 88 could return fire. The first two rounds missed their mark, chipping chunks of concrete outside its massive structure. On the third try the round hit home right through the bunker's narrow gun slit.[75]

The numbers of A Company tanks were bolstered by the late arrival of two more landing craft. The damaged LCT(A) 2043 made it to the beach at 0700 hours and a further two A Company tanks waded onto the beach. However, the tank dozer aboard the landing craft would not start and the LCT retracted with it still aboard. The other craft, LCT(A) 2008, arrived at about 0800 hours with its ramp shot away but was able to successfully unload its tanks. At 0820 hours, the battalion commander landed but found he could not contact his tanks as the radio was malfunctioning. Command group officers then directed tanks in person by indicating targets and placing the tanks in more advantageous positions.

The tanks supported the infantry by destroying gun positions and machine gun posts on the cliff tops where possible but communication with the infantry was difficult in the fire and noise of battle. Any tank commander with his head above the turret cupola risked being killed by bullets or shrapnel. The battle on the beach was all too much for one sergeant commanding a tank of HQ company on Fox Green and he abandoned his tank, cowering in a fox hole for most of the day. His tank was ably taken over by a member of the crew who was later asked by a major at a nearby command post why he had not shot the sergeant for not coming out of his fox hole.[76]

At 1100 hours, the 16th RCT decided to make an all-out attack on the E-3 Colleville draw and Captain W. King from 16th Regiment ran along Easy Red beach to give instructions to as many operational A Company tanks as possible. Dodging enemy mortar bursts and machine-gun fire, Captain King made contact with half a dozen tanks, including a DD tank from B Squadron commanded by Sergeant Sheppard. Just as he reached the tank of Staff Sergeant Skiba, an artillery shell landed close by and killed the sergeant. Captain King ordered a corporal to take over the tank which he directed towards the E-3 exit until it lost a track in the shingle and was immobilised. King then approached another tank, also now commanded by a corporal as its sergeant had been hit in the jaw by shrapnel, and directed it along the water's edge towards the E-3 draw. This time Captain King rode in the tank for cover but the tank ran over a mine which had possibly become dislodged from its pole and a track with a bogey of the suspension unit was blown off. All the crew plus Captain King abandoned the tank and ran for the cover of Sergeant Skiba's disabled tank.[77]

Three tanks made it to the E-3 exit and began to move along it, firing at the German bunkers and positions with 75mm HE and machine guns whilst other tanks that had responded to Captain King's orders provided supporting fire from where they were on the beach. The defenders had also been pounded by shellfire from destroyers moving close in to the shore but were still offering strong resistance.

Following behind the lead tank commanded by Sergeant Ball, Sheppard's DD tank was hit by an anti-tank gun on the road ahead and knocked out. The last tank engaged a pill box on the western side of the exit where they thought the fire had come from, but as the exit was too heavily defended both tanks tried to turn around and in doing so one threw a track. The crew abandoned their tank and returned to the beach on foot. The leading tank managed to reverse back to the beach but was later swamped making its way to the E-1 exit.[78]

The E-3 draw was the planned primary exit off the Omaha beaches. Unable to assault the strongpoints and bunkers directly because of the devastating fire coming from them, the infantry were initially pinned down on the beach and the only way off was to climb the bluffs between the German fortifications. As the morning went on, more and more infantry managed this climb and, despite heavy losses, worked their way behind and above the defences (WN62) at the E-3 exit. From there, much to the surprise of the German defenders, they began to knock them out from behind. Meanwhile the remaining tanks continued to engage the strongpoints in the draw from the beach as best they could. The engineer teams suffered high casualties when they landed just after H-hour, some finding themselves alone on the beaches because of the chaotic LCT landings. Only six of the sixteen teams were able to set off their demolition charges to clear small gaps in the rows of obstacles. The assault timetable was in tatters – some landing craft were unable to approach the beach as the obstacles were still intact and many landing craft that had been damaged (or sunk) were unable to return to the troopships offshore for another load.

One by one, the A Company tanks were either knocked out or immobilised, either by mines or by direct hits from anti-tank guns or artillery. A total of five tanks were disabled when they threw tracks in the shingle of the beach.[79] Only one A Company tank survived the day: the tank of Lieutenant Barcelona which lost a track and was immobilised for several hours. The assault on the E-1 St Laurent exit ultimately proved to be more profitable than the attacks on the E-3 Colleville exit. The few A Company tanks that were able to engage the bunkers WN65 and 65 continued to do so, helped by tanks from A and C companies of the 743rd Tank Battalion. The E-1 exit was finally opened to infantry only from 1300 hours.

Once the infantry began to penetrate inland off the beach the amount of direct fire was dramatically reduced, though long-range fire from the 352nd Division artillery batteries inland continued to hit the beach. Between 1200 and 1500 hours, the battalion's tanks were not engaged in combat. By 1530 hours four reserve tanks had arrived on the beach and were quickly directed to the assembly area.[80] These included two HQ tanks and a tank from C Squadron that had been left out of the original landing. One reserve HQ tank got mixed up with the arriving tanks of the 745th Tank Battalion and exited the beach with them, not returning to the unit for another three days. Two armoured recovery vehicles also arrived and began to salvage abandoned tanks, helping repair those that had lost tracks. Late in the afternoon, the battalion's five remaining tanks left the beach by the E-1 exit and went into harbour east of St Laurent sur Mer. Here the operational tanks were allowed no respite and at 2000 hours, one tank was sent to assist the infantry with a mopping-up operation; at 2015 hours, the remaining three tanks under the command of Lieutenant Barcelona were dispatched at the request of the 29th Division to deal with machine gun nests and snipers around St Laurent sur Mer. All four tanks came back at 2300 hours.

At 2315 hours, the 741st Tank Battalion strength was given as three tanks operational, two fit in 24 hours and forty-eight lost.[81] The battalion's entire first wave had been lost except for Lieutenant Barcelona's tank. The reserve tanks provided a nucleus for the battalion to reform around for the coming campaign and it would not see further combat for another two weeks.

The Reasons Behind the Decision to Launch

The likelihood of rough seas on D-Day had been discussed during training and at the briefing before sailing by the LCT commanders and the officers of the tank battalion. The decision to launch the DD tanks had been delegated to the local commanders of the assault force on the basis that the sea conditions might vary from beach to beach and that the sea conditions being experienced by the assault commander's headquarters vessel may not necessarily be the same as those closer to the shore. A procedure was agreed by which the senior LCT naval officer and senior battalion army officer would confer and agree before launching the DD tanks.[82] Unfortunately, this procedure was not followed with the 741st Tank Battalion tanks, as Captain Thornton, the senior battalion officer, made the unilateral decision to launch without consulting with the flotilla officer, Lieutenant J. Barry. A later US Navy report by the 11th Amphibious Force commander, Admiral Hall, was critical of Lieutenant Barry who 'tacitly acquiesced in the decision by his failure to take action to change the order directing the launching'.[83] The report went further and criticised the decision by Thornton as being unsound given the widespread knowledge of the limitations of DD tanks in rough seas. Thornton, for his part, was anxious that the tanks get ashore and support the infantry:

> Captain Thornton succeeded in contacting Captain Young by radio and the two commanders discussed the advisability of launching the DD tanks, the sea being rough, much rougher than the tanks had ever operated in during their preparatory training. Both commanders agreed that the advantage to be gained by launching the tanks justified the risk of launching the tanks in the heavy sea.[84]

Once the tanks were launched, large waves pounded against the flimsy canvas screen and they began to ship water. The top rail of the screens buckled under the force of the waves which also broke some of the struts supporting the screens; this allowed water to pour into the tanks which then sank within seconds, sometimes dragging crew members down with them. The failure of the top rail in the rough conditions is evidenced by the account of Corporal Hopper above and by an operational report of the 79th Armoured Division that stated, 'It was found necessary for the crew to support the top rail with their shoulders on the way in. Much water was shipped and the top rail bent ominously on the impact of the sea.'[85]

These were the same top rails that the British had urgently reinforced in the days before the invasion. Even if the screens did not collapse, water got into some tank motors and they duly stopped, leaving the tank unable to manoeuvre and liable to being swamped. Some tanks did not sink immediately but struggled toward the shore, making for the agreed landmark of the church spire of Colleville. However, the strong cross-current pushed the tanks more and more off course eastwards and they were forced to steer a course which meant that their unstable craft became more and more side-on to the heavy seas which had an even greater effect on the top rail of the canvas screen. After the war, many of the tanks that sank were found on the seabed still lined up in the direction of the church spire at Colleville.[86]

The Sherman Mk II DD tanks used by US forces were supposed to have at least 30in of free board at the stern. Many of the DD tanks were overloaded with extra ammunition and had less freeboard than they had ever operated or trained with before, some as little as 9in. On D-Day the waves were up to 6ft high off Omaha beach, so the DD tanks stood little chance of reaching the shore once launched. The tanks of both company commanders were amongst those that sank. The two tanks that did make the beach did so by steering a course whereby the waves were more behind the tanks so the risk of swamping was reduced. The fact that so many tanks did launch is a testament to the courage and determination of the men of the 741st Tank Battalion.

In view of the number of tanks that sank, the battalion's losses were relatively low: eleven men killed and twenty-six missing. Photographs of men on Omaha beach being rescued from sunken landing craft are actually tank crews in their RAF dinghies. The British report from the 79th Armoured Division concluded:

> It may be that the foundering of some tanks was due to the failure of this rail. It was recommended that, in addition to the top rail being of the proper specifications, an extra strut from the turret front to the centre top rail should be attached in the future.[87]

Clearly, there were problems with the design specification for the strength of the top rail in the sea conditions experienced on D-Day. Many reports of the crews mention the top rail giving way or the crews trying to brace it; one can only imagine their panic as they fought to prevent the rail from collapsing and the tank from sinking. The DD designer, Straussler, would no doubt have argued that the tanks were deployed in conditions that were beyond their capacity, but the top rail was a weakness in the design the British had attempted to address before D-Day. This weakness apparently did not affect DD kits made in the USA. The M4A2 DD tank used by the Americans was 5.5in (14cm) shorter than the version used by the British, therefore any weakness in the top rail would be slightly less critical. The loss of so many American tanks was due to the decision to launch so far out in the rough seas in tanks with an inherent weakness in the top rail. Unfortunately, there is no evidence that the British informed the Americans of the potential problem before D-Day and it is likely that had they done so then more men of the 741st Tank Battalion would have survived.

743rd Tank Battalion

The 743rd Tank Battalion was to support the 116th RCT landing on the right flank of the Omaha sector.[88] B and C companies of the battalion were equipped with DD tanks and the intention was to land 10 minutes before the infantry and engage the beach defences while remaining in the water for protection.[89]

The commander of the LCT flotilla carrying the tanks, Lieutenant Dean Rockwell, was experienced in the use (and limitations) of the DD tanks as he had worked with the tank crews during their training. Well aware that the sea conditions were much too rough to launch the DD tanks, Lieutenant Rockwell followed the previously agreed procedure in the event of poor conditions for launching. In his After Action Report, Rockwell says that at 0505 hours he contacted Captain Elder of the 743rd Tank Battalion as the senior officer present and discussed the decision to launch or not; both agreed to take the DD tanks all the way in.[90] In later years, Rockwell changed his account slightly by saying that 'after launching one or two tanks and having them become swamped by water and go down, I communicated by low power tank radio with Capt Elder ...'[91] Therefore, unless Rockwell was referring to tanks of the 741st Tank Battalion which would have been difficult to see more than a mile away, one or two of the thirty-two tanks were launched, but this is not supported by official reports. All the LCTs except LCT 590, which was badly damaged, were reused later that day.[92]

B Company

The landing craft designated to carry the tanks of B Company to their beach on Dog Green were (Mk VI) LCTs, which landed near the D-1 Vierville draw slightly late at 0630 hours. The Dog Green beach was the westernmost beach for the Omaha landings and was defended by the strongpoints WN70, 71, 72 and 73, equipped with various 75mm and 88mm howitzers and anti-tank guns that could fire along the beach. As the landing craft neared the beach, towering explosions of water and sand from the coastal artillery and mortars showed that the formidable Omaha defences were very much intact.

As the tanks began to disembark from their LCTs, they immediately came under anti-tank fire. The tank of the company commander, Captain Ehmke, drove down the ramp of LCT 591 and stopped to fire its first round at a bunker. The response was immediate: an armour-piercing shell crashed into the tank, filling the interior with black smoke. Fighting the urge to bail out, the men got off two shots; in return, the tank was hit again and penetrated by two more rounds which killed three crew members. Captain Ehmke jumped out of the tank and began to try to attract the attention of other tanks to pick him up but he was killed. Behind Ehmke's tank, the landing craft had started to reverse off the beach before the other three tanks had unloaded; as a result, when they did drive off the ramp the water was too deep and they quickly sank.[93]

All around the tanks the soldiers of the 116th RCT were struggling to find shelter from the machine-gun fire amongst the hedgehogs and poles on the beach:

> Some of the fellows, who were able to exit the boat without getting machine gunned, were being dragged under by the wet combat jackets and heavy equipment. Their life

preservers were of no value. The water was over the head of the average man in my boat. German snipers were also picking them off. The water was being splattered up by bullets, as I ran through it. It was surreal. About 20 feet to my left front were two of our Dual Drive Amphibious medium army tanks, with their rubber sides down. Where are the other fourteen that were supposed be here?

Six 29ers were clinging to the one first to my left and seven were clutching to the one closest to me. The distant tank had a dead soldier hanging from the turret. It had been knocked out. While the tank closest to me was actively firing its 75mm cannon at the enemy.[94]

Another tank was hit and the surviving crew members bailed out to find shelter inside the remaining tanks where possible. One B Company man was taken in by an A Company tank and remained with them for the next two weeks.[95] Eight tanks of B Company and some C Company tanks engaged the bunkers of WN71 and WN72 at the D-1 exit. As radio communications were difficult, during the morning the battalion's commander, Colonel Upham, directed the action on the beaches on foot. The large white numbers visible on the tanks' turrets stood out through the smoke and dust of the battle and enabled Colonel Upham to order individual tanks into position. As the tide came in, the tanks were forced to move to parts of the beach not yet covered by water. Two tanks became snagged on hedgehogs and had to be abandoned as the water level rose inside and flooded them. B Company supported the assault on the Vierville D-1 draw throughout the day and gradually fought their way inland along the elevated gravel causeway of the draw towards Vierville.[96]

Such was the ferocity of the battle between the tanks and the bunkers directly in front of them that they were too busy to engage and knock out the anti-tank guns to the west near the end of the beach at Pointe de la Percee which could fire along the beach. The tanks did, however, make the landings of later assault waves easier as they attracted the enemy fire more than the landing craft.[97]

The destroyer USS *Carmick* came close to shore and helped some tanks that had managed to get on the promenade road and were trying to fight their way westwards towards the Vierville draw D-1. The ship's officers watched where the gunfire from the tanks was landing on the bluff and then used those as aiming points for the guns of the destroyer.[98] Two other destroyers, the USS *McCook* and USS *Doyle*, also shelled the defences of the D-1 and D-3 exits throughout the day, though shore-to-ship liaison was difficult. At noon, for an hour, the battleship USS *Texas* shelled the D-1 exit with its 14in guns and thirty Germans promptly surrendered. At about midday the tide was at its highest and all of the battalion tanks were forced to congregate in the only available dry space on Dog Red beach. Explosives were then used successfully at 1400 hours by engineers to blow up the anti-tank concrete wall; exit D-1 was finally open to infantry but not yet passable for tanks. The After Action Reports of both B and C companies lament the lack of air support during the day.

Using the D-1 exit, B Company finally left the beach about 2130 hours and harboured at Vierville having lost seven tanks during the day, nine being still operational.[99] Three officers and six men were killed, and one officer was wounded.

C Company Action

The landing craft carrying C Company to Dog White beached directly at 0624 hours in equal numbers on Dog White and Easy Green near the E-1 St Laurent draw as some landing craft were carried by wind and tide eastwards. This was defended by WN64 and WN65 with a 75mm howitzer and various 50mm and 37mm guns.[100] C Company tanks ranged over a number of beaches during the day and several A and C Company tanks assisted the remaining 741st Battalion tanks on Easy Red to support the infantry attacking the pill boxes at the bottom of the E-1 St Laurent draw. The C Company tanks were particularly welcome there as there were only four DD tanks supporting fewer than 100 men left of the original assault wave.[101]

The C Company report for 6 June claims that no tanks were lost by enemy action.[102] However, a couple of tanks *were* destroyed. The tank driven by J. Parsons ran over a mine, lost both tracks and was subsequently flooded. Sergeant Preston's tank was hit by a mortar bomb, which killed two crew members, and was disabled while pulling another tank out of a ditch. The life raft of one tank on the beach was set on fire by a mortar shell and the tank was lost in the subsequent fire.[103] Therefore at least two C Company tanks were knocked out. Other C Company tanks on Dog White joined B Company tanks in attacking the D-1 Vierville exit. The rising tide restricted the beach area and the tanks moved to Dog Red beach about midday to avoid being swamped by the rising tide. Movement on the beach was restricted by the high tide, wreckage and the bodies of those killed in action.

C Company finally got off the beach at 2230 hours with thirteen operational tanks, two having been knocked out and one damaged. Casualties to tank crews were light: five men and one officer were wounded.

A Company

A Company landed a few minutes after 0630 hours on Easy Green and Dog Red beaches near the Les Moulins draw. This was defended by WN66, 67 and 68 with various 37mm and 50mm guns, including two 37mm guns mounted in tank turrets on top of the concrete fortifications which were also protected by an anti-tank ditch and concrete wall. A Company was supposed to land across all the 116th RCT beaches to provide fire support and tank dozers for the infantry assault teams. The modified LCT(A)s were equally unseaworthy and A Company had losses before it even landed in Normandy. LCT(A) 2229 sank on the sea passage and two other LCT(A)s would not arrive until the afternoon.

Of the five landing craft (ten tanks and five dozers) that arrived, most beached on Dog Red opposite the D-3 draw. A tank and dozer were lost when Lieutenant Sturbitz, aboard LCT(A) 2307, refused to disembark, claiming that the water was too deep for his wading tank and the bulldozer behind. This was despite the fact that the first tank had driven off successfully. Whilst debating the depth of water, a shell nearly blew the landing craft's ramp off, wounding several crew members. The LCT promptly retracted off the beach with the tanks still aboard but later sank from the damage caused by the direct hit on the bow.[104] Two tanks and a dozer from another landing craft were also immediately lost when they disembarked from LCT into water that was too deep.[105] Therefore on arrival, A Company was further reduced in numbers within minutes to just seven M4s and three dozers.

Staff Sergeant Jenkins dismounted to lead a platoon of tanks and dozers through the beach obstacles after the blade of the leading dozer set off a mine on a pole with unknown consequences for the infantrymen trying to find whatever cover they could nearby.[106] Another tank made it to the seawall and sought a way over onto the promenade, only to find the way blocked by the prone bodies of dead soldiers. One tank had a track knocked off at the water's edge and was subsequently swamped.[107] Of a total of sixteen dozers embarked for the Omaha sector beaches, only six ever reached the beaches and three were disabled by artillery fire.[108]

Captain V. Phillips, the commander of A Company, became the battalion commander at 1300 hours when Colonel Upham, who had been wounded by a sniper earlier in the morning, finally left the beach.

Some A Company tanks supported the remaining 741st Battalion tanks in assaulting the E-1 and E-3 exits while the rest and several C Company tanks engaged the D-3 defences; three tanks attacked WN66 on the western side of D-3 Les Moulins draw and penetrated the outer defences, according to a report in the log of the 352nd Division.[109] A Company tank dozers cut a road on the hills west of the St Laurent E-1 draw in an effort to outflank the D-3 draw defences in WN65 but were beaten back by fierce enemy fire. This road was subsequently used by the remaining 741st Battalion tanks to leave the beach later that evening. The E-1 draw was finally open for infantry to move inland during the afternoon.

During the afternoon the two straggler LCT(A)s 2273 and 2275 arrived, bringing in four tanks and two tank dozers as badly needed reinforcements. After a false rumour in the late afternoon that the D-3 Les Moulins draw was open, the tanks of the 743rd Battalion finally began to leave the congested beach at 2100 hours by the D-1 exit at Vierville. A Company did not harbour until midnight west of Vierville and only eight tanks were left. Eight tanks and six dozers were reported lost on D-Day.[110]

Tank crews on some parts of the narrowing beach or at the entrances to the exits had no choice but to drive over the dead bodies of fellow soldiers. Many parts of the beaches were crowded with wounded and able men seeking cover, and in order to advance, the tanks had no choice other than to run over the bodies. An anonymous tanker commented, 'If there was any sign of life at all, I tried to avoid them. But buttoned up and looking through the 'scope, it was hard to see, you just had to run over them.'[111] Another tanker recorded his horror at finding a soldier's underwear caught in his tracks and fervently hoped the soldier was already dead before the tank ran over him.

Summary

The day at Omaha was won by individual soldiers climbing the bluffs and penetrating inland to attack the bunkers guarding the entrance to the draws from behind or above. Attacking the strongpoints directly was almost suicidal for the infantry without the support of the tanks and as the beach defences were largely intact, the tanks themselves took heavy casualties. The 743rd Tank Battalion tanks were instrumental in destroying key bunkers and providing much-needed fire support for the assault infantry at the D-1 Vierville draw which was open to infantry in the late afternoon. The battalion also played a major role in making up for the lost 741st Battalion tanks on Easy Red to open the E-1 St Laurent draw. It may well have been the heavy and accurate close-range naval gunfire that tipped the balance in the favour of the Americans, but without the tanks of the 743rd Tank Battalion the landings on Omaha might not have succeeded at all.

Once the infantry had left the beaches, the tanks could only continue to engage the bunkers and wait for the exits to be opened. The infantry moved rapidly inland and secured the villages of Colleville, St Laurent and Vierville behind the beaches without the support of the tanks from either tank battalion. The official history of Omaha Beachhead said of the actions of 743rd Tank Battalion on D-Day:

> Their achievement cannot be summed up in statistics; the best testimony in their favour is the casual mention in the records of many units, from all parts of the beach, of emplacements neutralized by the supporting fire of tanks. In an interview shortly after the battle, the commander of the 2d Battalion, 116th Infantry, Major Bingham who saw some of the worst fighting on the beach at Les Moulins, expressed as his opinion that the tanks 'saved the day. They shot the hell out of the Germans, and got the hell shot out of them.'

The 743rd Tank Battalion losses in tanks were seventeen tanks and six tank dozers and there were thirty-eight tanks operational with one repairable in less than 24 hours at the end of D-Day.[112] Nine men (three officers and six enlisted men) were killed and twelve wounded. The 745th Tank Battalion (B Company) due at H+6 hours finally landed at 1630 hours on Fox Green beach after the delays caused by the slow progress of the assault and, after losing three tanks on mines, exited by the newly opened F-1 exit. The 747th Tank Battalion did not arrive until next day.

With the benefit of hindsight, the choice of beaches in the Omaha sector warrants consideration. Putting aside the movement of the 352nd Division to the coast to take over from the stretched 716th Division on this part of the Normandy coastline, the terrain of Omaha made it the potentially the most difficult of all the Allied sectors. The valleys or draws cut into the grass-covered steep hills behind the beach provided the only way off the beach for vehicles and therefore were strongly fortified by the Germans. The Omaha beaches were also not sandy but were of shingle, which had caused so many problems on the Dieppe raid.

So why was Omaha selected, and why was it allocated to the Americans? General Morgan's COSSAC plan, after proposing Normandy as the region for the invasion, identified three sectors suitable for an assault by a division deploying two brigades up with tidal conditions offering the highest future capacity for bringing men, vehicles and supplies ashore. The British had designed and constructed two artificial harbours which would be towed in sections and assembled off the beaches at Omaha and Arromanches. These harbours would provide facilities to unload supplies as there was no suitable deep-water port along the chosen Normandy coastline. The rocky Normandy coastline and the offshore reefs excluded most beaches from being suitable for landing and for bringing in supplies. The beaches that best fitted the criteria were as follows:

- Beach 307 – Lion sur Mer to Courseulles
- Beach 308 – Courseulles to Arromanches
- Beach 313 – Colleville to Vierville

These became Juno, Gold and Omaha sectors. Morgan further proposed that the British forces be supplied from the English ports closest to Normandy. The Americans were then allocated the westernmost beach after the British allocations had been made. Morgan elaborated by describing this selection as the Americans being 'on the right of the line' and the 'British-Canadian forces on the left'.[113] This principle was to be maintained throughout the planning of operations Overlord and Neptune and had a number of important outcomes, not the least of which was that the routes of the assault convoys and follow-up forces would not have to cross over each other. US Army units arriving in England would be billeted in the south-west of England around Plymouth and their invasion convoys could sail from there to the westernmost Normandy beaches without crossing the channels allocated for the British or Canadian vessels. Similarly, transatlantic shipping destined for the American beaches could sail directly to the Omaha sector without crossing British shipping lanes.

Having agreed to the allocation of beaches and the outline of Operation Overlord, it was then up to FUSA to plan and implement the landings in its sectors. For Omaha, FUSA planned to assault the defending strongpoints in the draws frontally and force the exits after they had been targeted by a heavy naval and airforce bombardment. A frontal assault across water from boats is always a risky operation with a high probability of heavy casualties, yet the Americans were prepared to accept these. When the bombardment was not as effective as planned, the task of the assaulting infantry was made much more difficult. No contingency plans seem to have been made to bypass the fortifications and climb the bluffs in the event of the original plan going awry or as part of the actual assault. The 2nd Ranger Battalion successfully scaled the cliffs at Pointe du Hoc in order to blow up the guns of the battery there, only to find when they got to the top that the guns had been moved. A follow-up force, the 5th Ranger Battalion, having received no word of the success or otherwise of the 2nd Battalion, assumed that they had failed and landed on Dog White beach near the D-1 Vierville draw. After a brief pause, the Rangers dashed across the exposed foreshore and climbed the hills; most of the battalion reached the top by 0830 hours. This demonstrated that the strongpoints on Omaha were vulnerable to being out-flanked and such assaults, if planned, would have had a greater chance of earlier success than a direct frontal attack.

Two myths have persisted in the aftermath of the debacle on Omaha beach. The first is that the Americans refused to use the British specialised armour at all and the second is that the Omaha landings nearly failed because British AVREs were not used in the assault.

All of the specialised tanks were demonstrated to Eisenhower and FUSA generals at Tidworth early in 1944 and FUSA rejected them all except the DD tank. One of the reasons given was that the US forces were developing their own M4 versions of the British tanks and that the US Army did not want to add another type of tank, the Churchill, to their inventory. As 115 Churchill flamethrower tanks had already been ordered in February 1944, this was disingenuous of the Americans. As the USA was developing its own mine-clearing tank, the T1E3, the Sherman Flail was also turned down. However, in November 1944 the Sherman Flail was subsequently adopted by all US forces in the ETO and the T1E3 was quickly phased out.[114]

Therefore the first myth is just that, a myth. FUSA was prepared to use whatever vehicles it saw a need for and would employ British designs where necessary if there was no duplication with the US Army's own developments. The refusal to adopt the British Flail tanks was shortsighted, as was the late decision to rely on M4 bulldozers, of which only four were available for each unit on D-Day. It has been argued that the shortage of LCTs prevented the Americans from using the British AVREs which is not true: FUSA simply did not want them.

Regarding the second myth (that US landings at Omaha nearly failed because they did not use the specialised armour), a report of the 79th Armoured Division claims:

> There is no doubt that the troops of the Division were of inestimable value on 'D' Day and thoroughly justified the time and material that had gone into their specialist training and equipment. ... It was the overwhelming mass of armour in the leading waves of the assault, the specialist equipment coming as a complete surprise, that overwhelmed and dismayed the defending troops and contributed a large part to the combination of strategic and tactical surprise which resulted in the comparatively light casualties suffered by our troops on 'D' Day.[115]

While the specialist AVREs had mixed success, the performance of the DD tanks in the weather conditions of D-Day was far from successful and the DD tanks could have been landed directly on the beaches without any significant losses of landing craft and tanks. The DD tanks at Omaha did not contribute their full mass to the assault as many sank before the assault even began.

The initial landings in the Sword, Juno and Gold sectors employed many more armoured vehicles in the initial assault than the US forces did at Omaha and Utah.

Sector	DD tanks	LCT(A)s M4 and tank dozers	Flails	AVREs	Centaurs	Planned TOTAL
Sword	40		26	34	16	116
Juno	78		20	40	32	170
Gold	76		24	40	32	172
Omaha	64	48	0		0	112
Utah	32	24	0		0	56

Although many of the LCT(A)s carrying the Centaurs did not arrive on time, were lost en route or swamped on unloading, it can be seen from the table above that with the Centaurs, Sherman Flails, AVREs and DD tanks, the British planned for much more firepower to be available on their beaches in the first few minutes of landing than the Americans did. Of the LCT(A)s due on Omaha and Utah at H-hour, six did not arrive at H-hour on Omaha (three each carrying the tanks of the 743rd and 741st Tank Battalions) and two did not arrive at all on Utah, so the armour actually available on the American beaches was even less than the totals shown.

Of the Centaurs on the British beaches, only twenty arrived within 15 minutes of H-hour and a further twenty-eight within the next 4 hours, the rest being presumably lost, so the British beach totals were not quite as high as shown in the table.[116] Even so, the numbers indicate that the amount of armour planned to land on the American beaches was only 50–65 per cent of that of the British beaches, so fire support from tanks on Omaha and Utah was always likely to be less effective. This reduction in available fire support was then compounded by the short 40-minute naval bombardment compared to the British area and the inaccurate bombing of the USAAF.

On the British beaches, the Flail and Petard tanks of the AVREs were often the first armoured vehicles to start engaging the German bunkers and they did this with a considerable degree of success, destroying many bunkers despite their own tanks being knocked out. This initial engagement by the AVREs of the beach defences then made the work of the later-arriving DD tanks that much easier, as was seen on Gold, though this was not quite the plan.

The Omaha landings nearly failed because they were not enough gun tanks of any kind on Fox Green and Easy Red beaches to deliver the required suppressing fire onto the bunkers. Once the five DD tanks and the ten wading M4s of the 741st Tank Battalion had arrived at the eastern half of Omaha, the only other armour equipped with large calibre guns due to arrive were the M4 tank dozers, which were already late. The contribution by the 743rd Tank Battalion was significant: not only did the tanks help open the D-1 exit but they also supported attacks on the E-1 exit.

It was the extra firepower of the AVREs that was missed on Omaha beach, not their specialist equipment. As usual, the poor bloody infantry would suffer the consequences.

A final difficulty on the Omaha was the shingle beaches. That the shingle Omaha beaches were chosen appears extraordinary after the problems encountered during the Dieppe raid. Once a tank lost a track in the shingle, it became a stationary target for the defenders and was also at risk of being flooded by the rising tide. Five tanks of A Company of the 741st Battalion and at least one of the 743rd Battalion tanks were immobilised on the beaches after losing a track and these tanks were subsequently lost. In the COSSAC plan, a detailed study (Appendix T) was made of the proposed beaches and there is no mention of shingle being on the Omaha beaches.[117] Apparently neither British nor American planners heeded the warning of the shingle at Dieppe but there was no other alternative beach in the Omaha sector that offered the required unloading capacity and was suitable for the Mulberry Harbour.

Gold Sector

The Gold sector was one of the original three areas selected by the COSSAC plan. The sector ran from the small seaside hamlet of La Rivière in the east almost to the town of Arromanches in the west. The two beaches chosen for the landings were between the fortified villages known as Le Hamel and La Rivière and were codenamed Jig and King with King beach being the easternmost. The 50th (Northumbrian) Division was to land on each beach supported by regiments of the 8th Armoured Brigade. Bayeux was a D-Day objective of the 50th Division, and if conditions were favourable then an armoured column was to penetrate further inland and seize Villers Bocage.

The King Red and King Green beaches west of La Rivière, where many of the houses had been turned into strongpoints, were allocated to the 4th/7th Royal Dragoon Guards. The 1st Nottinghamshire Sherwood Rangers were tasked with landing on Jig beach. Jig and King beaches had gently sloping sand up to a sea wall 4–10ft high behind which there was a strip of sand dunes 3ft high. Extensive belts of anti-tank and anti-personnel mines had been sewn along the sand dunes and in front of the defensive strongpoints. The beach was studded with hedgehogs near the high-water mark and anti-tank obstacles such as posts tipped with mines and Belgian gates were in deeper water.

4th/7th Royal Dragoon Guards

The 4th/7th Royal Dragoon Guards had been converted from a cavalry regiment in the 12 months immediately before the outbreak of war and saw service as part of British Expeditionary Force in France in 1940. In 1944, the Dragoon Guards was the senior regiment of the 8th Armoured Brigade with the mission of supporting the gapping teams before going into reserve in anticipation of any German counterattack.

B and C squadrons were equipped with DD tanks on which they had trained for several months in the lochs of Scotland. The DD tanks were loaded at Stanswood Bay on 2 June and A Squadron and RHQ were loaded a day later; all craft then moored in the bay to await the order to sail for France.

B Squadron was to land on the right flank to support the 6th Green Howards and C Squadron on the left to support the 5th East Yorks, both battalions being part of the 69th Brigade assaulting King beach.

The German defences were manned by two battalions of the 716th Division with their headquarters at Trévières.[118] In WN33 at La Rivière, there was an 88mm gun (plus various other smaller-calibre weapons) that could fire along King beach. In the sand dunes to the west was WN35 at Hable de Heurtot which was built around a series of pill boxes, machine gun posts and mortar pits.

The LCTs carrying the DD tanks finally sailed on the morning of 5 July after the 24-hour postponement. There was much seasickness because of the rough seas and troops had been issued with Hyoscine tablets which, if taken before the onset of nausea, settled the stomach and produced a slight coma-like effect. Hardly anyone had got much sleep the previous two nights with the postponement of the invasion and the anticipation of the next day's landing. As the invasion had been postponed for 24 hours, H-hour was now 0725 hours with the DD squadrons due in 5 minutes earlier; A Squadron was due an hour later at H+60 minutes.

The Royal Dragoons were part of the Gold assault force G-2 destined for King beach and were transported on LCTs of the 12th Flotilla making up the G-4 assault wave.

The naval bombardment started at 0510 hours, engaging all identified German strongpoints and gun batteries. The 6in guns of HMS *Orion* effectively targeted and destroyed the battery of four 120mm guns of WN35A directly in front of the Royal Dragoons planned route of advance through Mont Fleury.[119]

The sea conditions in the Gold sector were no better than those at Sword and Juno. The G-2 naval commander decided at 0726 hours that the sea was still too rough for DD tanks so the landing craft took them in all the way to the beach, the tanks doing a short wade or swim to the shore before dropping their canvas screens and going into action. Naval frogmen, tasked beforehand with clearing lanes through the beach obstacles, could be seen amongst the poles and obstacles off the beach as the tanks swam in.

The decision not to launch meant that the LCTs of the DD tanks were mixed up with the other waves of landing craft and the assault was delayed by nearly 10 minutes as a result.[120]

B Squadron

Once the decision to land directly on the beaches had been made, the landing craft had to turn to starboard away from the beach to allow the subsequent assault waves through and they finally landed after the LCTs carrying the AVREs of the gapping teams, in place of other LCT(A)s which had not arrived at all after an eventful passage across the Channel.[121] These LCT(A)s were carrying Centaur tanks equipped with 95mm howitzers which were supposed to support the infantry on the beach. However, owing to the unseaworthiness of their modified craft, the first two tanks did not arrive until 0900 hours and some never arrived at all.[122]

The regiment's DD tanks landed at H+2 minutes, according to the Royal Navy report.[123] Two landing craft were directed either side of the LCTs carrying the AVREs and the other four LCTs to King Green beach.

There was little opposition for the tanks which provided covering fire as necessary for the AVRE tanks as they cleared lanes in the beach defences. Coloured flares on the beach marked the cleared routes off the beach for the tanks and the infantry which landed approximately 5 minutes after the AVREs and DD tanks.

The AVRE tanks did most of the work in clearing the beaches and supporting the infantry. At Hable de Heurtot, the AVRE Churchills used their Petard mortars to knock out four pill boxes before two tanks got over the sea wall and charged into the position, which was then secured by the closely following soldiers of the 6th Green Howards.

Tanks from a troop in B Squadron came ashore right in front of another bunker on the right of their landing beach which had been misidentified as a machine gun post. Fortunately, the bunker had been built to fire along the beach rather than out to sea and the tanks of 4th Troop stood off in the shallows of the rising tide to fire at the bunker with 75mm HE rounds; a round was reported to have gone through the embrasure, resulting in six Germans coming out with their hands up to surrender. In manoeuvring through the waves towards the bunker, one of the tanks fell into an unseen shell crater and became firmly stuck, resisting all efforts of the crew to get it out. The tank was subsequently swamped by the rising tide and the crew remained on the beach in an unsuccessful attempt to recover the tank in the afternoon.[124]

The Flail tanks began to beat exits off the beaches through the minefields but two gaps were quickly blocked by damaged tanks. A third exit was then successfully created by a single Flail tank commanded by Lieutenant Pear. This tank got onto the lateral road running behind the beach and made for a previously agreed rallying point, a house with a circular driveway. Just past the house which came to be known as 'Lavatory Pan Villa', Pear's tank was halted by a large bomb crater in the road. The bridge-laying tank was brought up and this obstacle was quickly overcome.[125]

The naval bombardment and the specialist tanks of the breaching teams had done their work and the landings of the Dragoon Guards were largely unopposed and without casualties. However, a second B Squadron tank was swamped waiting for an exit off the beach to be cleared.

Using the flailed exit, B Squadron tanks moved off the beach to the rallying point and then inland past the destroyed battery at Mont Fleury.

The advance continued through Villiers le Sec without meeting much opposition but when it reached the river in front of higher ground, the leading tank was knocked out by a Stug III self-propelled gun. The Stug III was in turn knocked out and the tanks crossed the river at St Gabriel before they were engaged by three more Stugs which knocked out one more tank and hit two others without damaging them. After taking up hull-down positions, the B Squadron tanks then destroyed all three Stugs in a brief firefight.[126] The advance continued as far as Brecey before the squadron harboured for the night.

C Squadron

C Squadron was to land near La Rivière on the left in support of the 5th East Yorks Battalion; the main defence on this beach was the WN33 strongpoint with its 88mm casemated gun at the corner of the sea wall sighted to fire along the beach.

Three tanks from C Squadron were drowned coming ashore on the beaches when they fell into shell craters.[127] The advance of 5th East Yorks was held up at La Rivière by heavy fire from fortified houses and the 88mm gun; the infantry were forced to shelter behind the sea wall, unable to advance. Two Churchill AVRE tanks were destroyed by this bunker before a Flail tank of the Westminster Dragoons engaged it.

Lieutenant B. Hoban, a troop leader of the 1st Troop Westminster Dragoons, wrote in his post-war recollections:

> … The familiar juddering thud as the LCT ran aground at La Rivière, the familiar rattle of the chains as the ramp was lowered. From then on things seemed to happen fast. We were soon down into the water, appreciating the fact that our waterproofing seemed to have been efficient. Two AVREs from our LCT charged ahead up the beach until in quick succession they simply exploded. Everything stopped all of a sudden; then got going again in response to the Canadian tones on the wireless of Major Tim Thompstone, RE, our breaching squadron commander, saying 'Get up the bloody beach, all of you'. Luckily Captain Roger Bell on my left, spotted where the fire was coming from, an 88mm in a huge concrete pillbox, and managed to engage, firing through the slot in the pillbox. After his fifth round the gun fell silent.[128]

Once the troublesome casemated 88mm gun was silenced, a Churchill tank led the C Squadron tanks into La Rivière to begin the work of assisting the infantry to clear it.

Meanwhile, other C Squadron tanks were conducting mopping-up operations and advancing inland. There was little opposition apart from snipers, who killed one tank commander and wounded two others.

A Squadron

The landing craft carrying A Squadron started beaching at H+60 minutes. Two tanks from A Squadron were lost when they too fell into deep shell holes while wading ashore, making seven lost on the beaches for the regiment altogether.[129]

Two of these were recovered next day, as the 8th Armoured Brigade war diary reports that the Royal Dragoons had five tanks written off in the actual landings on D-Day.[130]

The Royal Dragoons and the infantry now had a clear exit off the beach and the troops surged inland as waves of reinforcements began to land behind them on the beach.

A Squadron advanced towards the 69th Brigade's objective, St Leger. There was only sporadic resistance from demoralised German conscripts who promptly surrendered when the tanks appeared. Crépon was quickly captured and the tanks pushed on southwards to Creully. On the bridge over the river just north of Creully a German self-propelled gun opened fire, forcing the leading tank to find cover under a hastily laid smoke screen. The armour-piercing shell tore off the Sherman's spare bogey, 8ft of the wireless aerial and gouged out a piece of armour from the glacis near the driver's head. As the squadron's tanks swung right to go around this blocking force, a message was received from the infantry that the enemy tank had retired so the tanks returned to the main road and quickly passed on through Creully. Suddenly four tanks were destroyed in quick succession by another self-propelled gun and the advance came to a halt. Lieutenant Hoban was also accompanying the advance:

> We saw three tanks of the 4th/7th Royal Dragoon Guards hit and starting to burn some 800 yards ahead. We quickly got our tanks behind cover in fire positions. Brian Pear and I were conferring in the open when a 4th/7th subaltern came running up to ask if we had any Fireflies (Sherman tanks with 17-pounder guns) with us; apparently they were fed up of seeing their 75mm AP shot bouncing off the German tank that was causing them so much trouble and damage. Here was early first hand evidence, if we needed it, of how vulnerable our tanks were to German armour.[131]

The assault gun and an anti-tank gun were quickly knocked out by other tanks and an Orders Group was called by the A Squadron commander just south of Creully as the tanks approached the high ground. Unfortunately, the Royal Dragoons were then mistaken for German tanks by a spotter plane for HMS *Orion* and the leading tanks came under heavy naval shellfire at 1940 hours, killing a troop leader and badly wounding another. HMS *Orion* had received an order at 1847 hours to engage an assembly of tanks which it could not initially comply with as its spotter plane was in the process of being relieved.[132] This changeover may have contributed to the friendly-fire episode, as HMS *Orion* was ready to engage the first target reported by the newly arriving spotter plane. At 2012 hours HMS *Orion* was ordered to cease fire and reported 'three tanks destroyed with the remainder scattered'. A total of ten members of the regiment were killed and sixteen wounded with numerous casualties amongst infantry.

Following this setback, the limits of the advance for the day were reached. To add insult to injury, A Squadron were then strafed twice by a USAAF P-47 Thunderbolt that did not see the yellow recognition panels on the tank rear decks before orange smoke grenades could be let off.[133]

The 4/7th Dragoon Guards had advanced inland 6 miles and although they had not reached their D-Day objectives, they had achieved 'a most satisfactory opening to the invasion'.[134] The regiment had lost nineteen tanks from all causes, including at least three knocked out or damaged by shell fire from HMS *Orion* – A Squadron had lost seven, B Squadron nine and C Squadron three.[135] Twelve officers and men were killed and eighteen men wounded.

Nottinghamshire Yeomanry

Jig beach in the western half of the Gold sector was the designated beach for the Nottinghamshire Yeomanry (Sherwood Rangers) Regiment to land in support of two infantry battalions of the 50th Division's 231st Brigade. Jig beach was dominated by the German strongpoint at Le Hamel (WN37), with its casemated 75mm gun and smaller fortifications at Asnelles sur Mer and Les Roquettes (WN40); this made Jig beach more strongly fortified than King beach. As on King beach, many bunkers were built without fields of fire out to sea but were sighted to fire along the beaches. It was planned that the Le Hamel strongpoint be neutralised by the air and sea bombardment beforehand, but unfortunately the naval bombardment was not as effective as on King beach because the German emplacements were well protected and the Eighth Air Force bombers largely missed their targets.[136] Two control craft were also lost during the Channel passage which meant there would be no shoot from self-propelled field artillery from their landing craft on the run-in to the beach.

The tanks were carried by LCTs of the 15th LCT Flotilla as part of the third group of the G-1 assault force destined for Jig beach. As on other beaches, the seas were considered too rough for the landing craft to launch the DD tanks from 7,000yds out so the LCTs were ordered to follow the LCAs in. However, the beach at the waterline was too crowded and LCTs put out to sea again to follow those carrying the SP (self-propelled) artillery in once they had disembarked and their LCTs had withdrawn from the crowded beach.

B Squadron

The DD tanks of B Squadron, which were due at 0730 hours, landed on the Jig Green on the right flank very late at 0758 hours. The landing craft carrying the 1st Hampshire infantry were carried eastward by wind and tide and landed nearly opposite Les Roquettes whilst B Squadron tanks came ashore at the designated point so the infantry were initially unsupported for 25 minutes. The infantry had to destroy the pill boxes and machine gun posts at Les Roquettes, which were actually the objectives of the 1st Dorsetshire Battalion, before moving inland to attack Le Hamel. The forward observation officers for both the naval bombardment ships offshore and the SP field artillery were wounded so no artillery support could be given to the infantry. There was heavy fighting to clear Le Hamel which offered strong resistance. The late arrival of the DD tanks in turn made their LCTs late picking up their next loads from the troopships waiting off shore, further disrupting the timetable for the rest of the day.[137]

There were six gapping teams of flails and AVRE tanks to clear lanes through the minefields and beach exits and these came under accurate fire from the WN37 bunker at Le Hamel. Several Flail tanks were knocked out. Ten Centaur tanks were supposed to land and give fire support yet only five did so, 15 minutes late, and four were quickly knocked out. Only two of the four gapping teams were successful but a route off the beach to the lateral road behind the beach was cleared as soon as 15 minutes after landing.[138]

The intact strongpoint at Le Hamel continued to hamper the landing of the follow-up forces, the 2nd Devonshire Battalion and the 47th Commando, which landed right in front of the strongpoint, losing many men and much equipment as they struggled ashore under fire. The commandos' objective was to seize the coastal town of Port en Bessin and make contact with the Americans to the west at Omaha.

At one stage, the beachmaster on Jig Green beach suspended any further landings directly in front of Le Hamel as all tanks on the beach appeared to have been put out of action.[139] Heavy fire on Jig Green from Le Hamel for most of the morning rendered the gapping teams on Jig Green ineffective. Jig Green was unusable until nearly 1700 hours when Le Hamel was finally taken by the infantry. The only Jig beach exits in use were those on Jig Red where all later landings were made when Jig Green was closed. Strong north-westerly winds meant that high tide was an hour earlier than forecast, so few obstacles could be cleared before they were covered which added to the problems on Jig Green. According to the Gold naval commander:

> If DDs had been able to swim they would have provided much needed support on the right flank to subdue the troublesome small strongpoint at Le Hamel. It is difficult to see how some of them could have avoided becoming obstacles themselves on an already overcrowded beach, in which case their numbers would have been reduced for the later stages of battle in which they are reported to have done so well.[140]

Three DD tanks were drowned on the short run-in to the beach and another four tanks were knocked out on the beach by an anti-tank gun, most likely an 88mm on the high ground overlooking the beach.[141] B Squadron tanks later harboured with those of C Squadron at Buhot.

C Squadron

C Squadron launched 700yds out as it was considered too rough to launch from 7,000yds as planned. The LCTs carrying the AVREs then overtook them and landed first. The 1st Dorsets infantry were carried by the current and landed further east of Les Roquettes than the 1st Hampshires. The C Squadron tanks came ashore on Jig Red behind the infantry, slightly late. After the short swim by both squadrons, two tanks became bogged in clay patches at the water's edge and only thirty-six tanks began the battle to get off the beach.[142]

The gapping teams for 1st Dorsets were more successful as they landed out of sight of the Le Hamel bunker and within an hour three exits were cleared for the infantry which quickly moved inland, supported by the Flail and AVRE tanks in the absence of DD tanks.[143] Le Hamel was bypassed and the infantry moved towards Buhot. Five tanks from C Squadron drowned and two more were knocked out on the beach.[144]

C Squadron was mainly occupied with assisting the infantry in the clearing of the Le Hamel strongpoint. The bunker containing the 75mm gun was finally knocked out when a Petard mortar from an AVRE tank was fired at the rear door. The main problem faced by the squadron was vehicle congestion and getting off the beach, as the tide came in rapidly. C Squadron later rallied and harboured at Buhot. The Sherwood Rangers' casualties were very light: one officer and eight ORs killed.[145]

A Squadron

From 0815 hours, the third battalion of the 231st Brigade, the 2nd Devonshire, began landing on Jig Red with the tanks of A Squadron which arrived at H+90 minutes but it could not get off the beach as planned because of the number of vehicles on the beach. More vehicles of every type were arriving every few minutes and only adding to the congestion. With the closure of Jig Green beach, the follow-up units in the 231st Brigade and the 56th Independent Brigade all had to come ashore on the same beach and the resulting traffic problems disrupted the 50th Division's plans for the remainder of the day.

A Squadron finally got off the beach and moved to the regiment's rallying point at Buhot via Meuvaines in the afternoon. Once clear of the beaches, the regiment met little opposition. The squadron then advanced to capture Ryes with the 2nd Devonshires before retiring to support the infantry of the 2nd Essex Battalion overnight. The regiment lost a total of fourteen tanks on D-Day and, after linking up with the 2nd Essex, harboured just north of Bayeux.

The specialist AVRE tanks had saved the day and the part played by the Sherwood Rangers Yeomanry was small. The B Squadron tanks and infantry on Jig Green had been unable to subdue the strongpoint at Le Hamel and, as a result, the follow-up forces had to use Jig Red, adding to the congestion there and creating large delays in the landing timetable of the 50th Division. Nevertheless, once off the beach, the tanks of the Sherwood Rangers advanced inland as far as Ryes and caused great consternation amongst the German defenders of the 716th Regiment.

Utah Sector

The sector designated Utah was the westernmost of the Allied planned landings and was situated at the base of the Cotentin peninsula. Utah ran from the River Vire estuary westwards to Quinnville and was added by the COSSAC planners early in 1944 to utilise an extra assault division with the objective of capturing the port of Cherbourg. The limited availability of landing craft meant that the 4th US Infantry Division (part of VII Corps) allocated for the assault could only attack on a single regimental combat team front and there would be only one tank battalion in the initial assault on Utah beach to support the designated 8th RCT. This would be the 70th Tank Battalion, a veteran of the North African and Sicilian campaigns that had been re-equipped with DD tanks. H-hour was at 0630 hours, the same as at Omaha and the naval bombardment was again restricted to only 40 minutes.

The beaches chosen for the landings were designated Tare Green and Uncle Red. These beaches were dominated by three major strongpoints: WN5 (four 50mm anti-tank guns, one in a casemate sited to fire along the beach, a French tank turret with 37mm cannon and various mortar and MG posts), WN7 (La Madeleine, headquarters of the 3rd Company of the 919th Grenadier Regiment of the 709th Division) and WN8 (three anti-tank guns and two howitzers). The Strongpoint No. 9 had an 88mm gun that could fire along the beach in front of the other fortifications.[146]

The countryside behind the sand dunes of the beaches was low-lying and had been flooded, leaving four built-up causeways as the only routes inland from the beaches. In the bombing before the assault, WN5 was destroyed and the three other exits had been targeted and bombed very accurately by 277 Marauders of Ninth Airforce which descended below the cloud layer at their assigned bombing altitude to see their targets more clearly.[147]

70th Tank Battalion

A and B companies were allocated the DD tanks and were organised in eight LCTs, each carrying four DD tanks. The battalion's tanks were loaded on 2 June at Dartmouth, England. One C Company M4 stayed in England.

The convoy containing the US 17th LCT flotilla carrying the DD tanks as part of assault wave 1Aa finally sailed for Normandy again on the morning of 5 June after having spent most of the 4 June battling the high winds and rough seas. The Force U convoys had to endure a difficult Channel crossing as it was the longest route of all the invasion convoys and was fully exposed to the strong westerly winds. When the convoy reached the coast in the lee of the Cotentin peninsula, the seas off Utah were found to be not as rough as on the other Allied beaches.

The objectives of the 70th Tank Battalion were to support the infantry in neutralising the strongpoints and securing the beach before proceeding inland to seize the beach access roads to enable the passage of the follow-up forces. The battalion's light tank company (D Company with 16 M5 Honeys) was to land at H+260 minutes and link up with the paratroopers of 101st Airborne Division as quickly as possible.[148]

A and B Companies

The DD tanks of A Company were to land on Tare Green at 0630 hours with B Company bound for Uncle Red beach at the same time. After the difficult sea passage, the LCTs carrying the DDs arrived late in the Transport Area, partially due to an inability to increase speed to make up for lost time en route. Offshore, the assembling assault wave ran into a minefield. At 0521 hours, a primary control landing craft (PCC1261) for Uncle beach hit a mine and the back-up craft for Uncle then fouled its propellers on a marker buoy, so LCC 60 from Tare beach turned back to guide the LCTs that had begun circling with the loss of their guiding craft.[149] At this point, at 0547 hours, LCT 593 detonated a mine off St Marcouf Island and sank immediately with four tanks of A Company. The other LCTs tried to pick up survivors but this put the landing timetable in danger of going seriously astray.[150] Two officers on LCC 60 then made the decision to launch much closer to shore so as to make up for lost time. The commander of LCC 600 gathered together the LCTs with the aid of a bull horn and led them towards the shore, unfortunately not the planned beach but one 1,000yds further east at La Grande Dune. A strong tide and poor visibility due to smoke on the beaches obscuring landmarks also played havoc with the infantry landing craft which landed nearly a kilometre east of their designated point. The infantry assault craft had overtaken the tank LCTs while they were reorganising and were considerably ahead of the tanks.

The DD tanks from the seven remaining LCTs were launched about 1,500yds offshore and twenty-six tanks got to the beach without mishap. One A Company tank was drowned when the blast from the fire of a nearby rocket ship damaged its canvas screen, causing it to collapse and the tank to sink. Another tank developed steering problems and had to be eventually towed to shore.[151]

The southernmost beach for the planned landings was Uncle Red which was astride Exit 3 from the beach. The DD tanks and infantry actually landed with their right flank on Exit 2 on a beach at La Grande Dune previously designated as Victor beach. Rather than amending any orders for the successive waves, it was decided to simply rename Victor beach as Uncle Red and Tare Green; the new Tare Green was now directly opposite the La Madeleine fortification. By landing further east, the assault force had fortuitously largely avoided enemy fire from the WN7 and Strongpoint No. 9 defences. La Madeleine had also been effectively bombed by the air force.

However, the problems prior to launching meant that the DD tanks landed 20 minutes after the infantry.[152] A Company landed on the renamed Tare Green beach in front of La Madeleine while B Company landed slightly further south on Uncle Red, opposite Exit 2. Once ashore, the DD tanks set about engaging any bunkers that were still active and blowing a gap in the sea wall with 75mm gunfire. As the DD tanks were late, the infantry had cleared most of the defensive bunkers and pill boxes that had not been abandoned or destroyed in the naval bombardment without the support of the tanks. The tanks stayed on the beach for half an hour looking for targets while beach obstacles were removed and exits were constructed by the combat engineer battalions.

Once gaps blown in the sea wall, A and B companies moved inland with the infantry. As Exit 3 was covered by 88mm anti-tank guns, A Company could not support the infantry moving along that causeway but went westwards along

Exit 2. Halfway along this causeway, it was discovered that the Germans had blown up the causeway and covered the break with an anti-tank gun and mines. The first tank hit a mine and the second tank was knocked off the causeway by the anti-tank gun which was in turn knocked out by the third tank.[153] A Company then turned north to link up with its infantry just west of Exit 3 and harboured for the night.

B and C companies harboured that night near Les Forges. One B Company tank broke down on a narrow causeway across the flooded fields and had to be pushed off the causeway by a bulldozer.[154] Nine 70th Battalion tanks were lost at sea, five from A Company and four from C Company. Three tanks from A Company and two tanks from B Company were disabled inland by anti-tank guns or mines. The US Naval report of the landing was rather dismissive of the DD tanks, saying that their tardy arrival was not seriously felt.[155]

C Company

C Company was due at H+15 minutes in the third wave of eight LCT(A)s and each LCT(A) carried two C Company wading tanks plus a bulldozer for clearing beach obstacles. Four bulldozers came from the 70th Tank Battalion and four from the 612th Engineer Battalion.[156] C Company was transported in similar landing craft to those modified for use at Omaha. Two LCT(A)s capsized on the voyage from England, LCT(A)s 2301 and 2402, with the loss of all four tanks and two dozers. The remaining twelve wading M4 tanks and six tank dozers started landing on time at H+15 minutes; many C Company tanks arrived ahead of the still-swimming DD tanks. One C Company tank fell in a shell hole on the beach and was swamped.

German 88mm shells and heavy machine-gun fire then began to hit the beach. While the infantry orientated themselves on the unfamiliar beach, the tanks at the water's edge provided covering fire. Once ashore, the company commander, Captain Ahearn, divided his tanks into two forces to look for a gap in the sea wall. One group proceeded south towards Pouppeville and other north towards La Madeleine. The first group found a small bunker that contained a Goliath remote controlled tank which fortunately was not operating as its control cable had been broken in the naval bombardment. Holes were then blown by charges in the sea wall and the battalion bulldozers cleared the debris from the explosions. The engineers went through the gaps but then found themselves in a minefield, so the tanks of C Company drove through to set off the anti-personnel mines. A bunker at Beau Guillot controlling Exit 2 was engaged and neutralised and the tanks pushed on to Exit 1 as well as moving out to the left flank. One of the two tanks of Ahearn's group hit a mine and was immobilised whilst three of the four others on their way to Pouppeville also hit land mines. Two tanks assisted the infantry in engaging a pill box at another beach exit. Pouppeville was already in the hands of the US 101st Airborne troops and the two forces linked up about 1110 hours. The two tanks then went on to assist with the clearing up of hedgerows around an artillery position cleared by the paratroopers. C Company lost two tanks moving inland.[157] Four reserve tanks landed in the afternoon, so the 70th Tank Battalion had forty operational tanks left at the end of D-Day. Only three men were KIA but sixteen were missing, believed lost at sea.[158]

Late in the afternoon a small force of one company of the newly landed 746th Tank Battalion, a platoon of 4th Cavalry reconnaissance tanks and ninety soldiers tried twice to break through to link up with the paratroopers at St Mere Eglise from Exit 2. Both attacks were repelled, one tank being disabled the first time and two tanks knocked out at the second attempt.[159] In total the 70th Tank Battalion lost sixteen tanks, nine of these at sea and seven on land.

By that evening, 15 hours after H-hour, the entire 4th Division was ashore – some 20,000 men and 1,700 vehicles.[160] The main differences between the Omaha and Utah beaches were fewer bunkers and obstacles such as Teller mines on stakes at Utah; this enabled Utah beach to be cleared quickly. The obstacles were not as dense as had appeared in reconnaissance photographs so the original plan of clearing 50yd gaps was abandoned in favour of bulldozers clearing the whole beach, which they accomplished in an hour.[161]

The air force bombing at Utah had been very accurate and effective, unlike on Omaha. The fortuitous landing on the wrong beaches had been opposed by only the small strongpoint WN5 which had been already virtually knocked out by the bombing; the major fortifications at WN8, 9 and 10 played no part in repelling the landings. The Germans had not heavily fortified this beach as they were relying on the inundated lands behind the coastline to deter any invaders.

The circumstances that led to the landings being some 1,000yds further east of where planned had a fortunate outcome and the Utah landings were very successful. Their outcome was never in doubt, unlike on Omaha where the battle hung in the balance for the first 5 hours. Given this, it is surprising that the Operation Overlord planners did not make the original landing beaches those where the troops actually landed.

Effectiveness of the DD tanks

Following D-Day, reports were made by all the units involved in the beach landings of the specialised tanks employed in the assault, including the assault squadrons of AVREs and the tank regiments and battalions as well as the LCT flotilla commanders.

The British and Canadians were generally positive in their reports of the DD tank's performance. The 1st Hussars expressed enthusiasm for the DD tanks, despite their heavy losses:

> A very noticeable event was that very shortly after the tanks deflated back of the underwater obstacles and commenced firing on the beach fortifications, the enemy manning these casements surrendered. It has since been learned from some of these prisoners that the presence of the tanks at this stage of the attack, came as a complete surprise and were the main factor in their decision to surrender instead of fighting.[162]

The commander of the Fort Garry Horse, even though his DD tanks were landed directly on Juno beach, considered that it was 'very important to have these special tanks and to launch them when and where they can best influence the situation'.[163] The performance of the DD tanks in the British tank regiments was also described in the 79th Division's Operational Bulletins and final report:

> DD tanks were launched on most beaches. They were generally successful; out of 130 launched over 80 touched down and fought on the shore. This was achieved in spite of a sea so heavy that a number of purely naval craft foundered, the short steep sea, reported force 4 to 6, and a strong cross current with the wind behind it gave a beam sea of the most difficult kind; conditions were far from ideal for amphibious craft.[164]

The Americans, given what they saw as the poor performance of the DD tanks at Omaha and apparently unwilling to be critical of their own army officers' decisions, were unanimous in their condemnation. In a post-war study, the three commanders of the tank battalions in the first wave ashore were united in their opinion:

> Colonel JC Wellborn, Lt-Col RN Skaggs and Lt-Colonel WD Duncan who commanded the 70th, 741st and 743rd Tank Battalions respectively on D-Day stated that in their opinion, the DD device was not satisfactory for the purpose intended and that medium tanks can be landed more effectively from LCTs directly on to the beach than by swimming in. Losses, in fact, were lower among the units which landed directly on the beach.[165]

This view mirrored that of General Gerow before D-Day. He had protested about having to use DD tanks for the Normandy invasion when tanks had been successfully landed directly ashore from LCTs in the Sicilian landings.

The US Navy conducted its own investigation into the performance of the DD tanks and reached a similar conclusion: the DD tank had limited applications. The commander of the Omaha LCT Flotilla, Lieutenant Rockwell, in his After Action Report concluded that the DD tank was not an effective weapon in amphibious warfare unless ideal sea conditions existed. Admiral J.L. Hall, the US Force O commander, was equally negative in his report, saying, 'Because of the vulnerability of its flotation equipment and the general unseaworthiness of the entire vehicle, the DD tank is not a practicable weapon for use in assault landings of open beaches.'[166] The US reports concluded that amphibious tanks were required for future use but that the DD tanks were found to be wanting in combat and that their development should not be continued.

So how effective were the DD tanks? As part of Operation Overlord, a total of 290 DD tanks were to be launched in the first assault wave on five separate beaches. The heavy seas caused by the high winds and currents made many local commanders change this plan in favour of the landing craft taking the tanks directly into the beaches. Therefore only 180 DD tanks were actually launched, often considerably nearer the shore than planned. A total of forty-seven tanks were lost on the swim to the beach which is 26 per cent of those that were launched; twenty-eight of these were lost on Omaha beach alone. Therefore 133 DD tanks touched down and another 110 tanks were carried directly to the shore, so in the prevailing weather conditions of D–Day, it is clear that the losses of the swimming DD tanks could have been avoided by directing the landing craft all the way to the beach.

Omaha provides an example of the consequences of the non-arrival of the DD tanks – the assaulting infantry and engineers suffered heavy losses from the shore defences and this was the only sector where, for a few hours, the Allied landings were in danger of being thrown back into the sea. Only the tanks of the 743rd Tank Battalion that landed directly on the beach (plus the five surviving DD tanks of the 741st Tank Battalion) provided any form of local fire support for the combat teams of the 1st and 29th Divisions.

However, the performance of the DD tanks also depended on the effectiveness of the aerial bombing and the naval bombardment in suppressing or destroying the beach bunkers before the arrival of the DD tanks. On Sword and Juno, the bombing and bombardment had been adequate but on Gold and Omaha it had been largely ineffective, so the defences were intact. On Gold, the DD tanks that made it ashore had a fierce battle to overcome the beach defences and the Gold landing could not have succeeded without some armoured support on the beach. At Omaha, the aerial bombing had fallen well off target inland and the shortened 40-minute naval bombardment had not been successful in knocking out many bunkers. Only the courage and bravery of the tankers and soldiers ashore with the considerable aid of direct fire from the warships offshore enabled the assault to succeed.

The failure of the normally remarkably well-informed Allied intelligence (owing to its Enigma/Ultra code breaking activities) to detect the relocation of the German 352nd Division from St Lô to the coast also had a critical influence on the events of the day: the soldiers of FUSA were not facing a poorly equipped static division but a combat-ready, standard German infantry division, albeit untried in battle.

A part of the rationale behind the employment of DD tanks was to avoid any losses of landing craft on the approach to the beaches and thereby the loss of four or five tanks at once. D–Day saw this hypothesis tested. Once the decision to not launch the DD tanks had been taken, a total of 110 tanks were carried by twenty-four landing craft through the obstacles and mines directly to the beach. Not a single landing craft was sunk on the run-in to the shore. LCT 590 at Omaha and LCT 313 at Juno were severely damaged, but both were ultimately repaired. Therefore, even on Omaha where the defences were intact, the risk of landing craft being lost was unwarranted; tanks could have been landed directly on the beaches with minimal losses to landing craft and this would have maximised the number of tanks and firepower ashore.

A major objective of the DD tanks was to provide fire support for the assault squadrons clearing the gaps in the defences, gapping teams and the first wave of infantry ashore. To do this, the tanks were required to be ashore before the arrival of the LCTs and LCAs carrying the AVREs of the assault squadrons and infantry to eliminate the bunkers on the beaches. Even if the DD tanks did not arrive at the designated time, it was essential that they get ashore and begin their task before the other units arrived.

Of the DD tanks that were launched on all the beaches, none of the DD tanks arrived at their scheduled times. This was not serious in itself, as on most beaches the AVREs and LCAs carrying the assault infantry were also late, largely because of the heavy seas. However, to be effective, the correct landing order still had to be achieved and only one squadron in the British sector arrived before the AVREs and infantry and that was B Squadron of the 1st Hussars Regiment on Juno.

On Gold beach, the DD tanks of the 4th/7th Royal Dragoon Guards arrived at the same time as the landing craft carrying the AVREs or within a minute or so; several eyewitnesses recall seeing some AVREs being destroyed as they moved up the beaches. The Sherwood Rangers on both Jig Red and Jig Green arrived after the AVREs and infantry; on Jig Green the tanks arrived 28 minutes late and were of little assistance to the infantry which had landed further east. On Sword beach, the DD tanks landed just behind the AVREs whose landing craft had passed through the line of swimming DD tanks.

In the American sectors, only five tanks of the 741st Tank Battalion arrived at Omaha, three of these in LCT 600 at just after H-hour, whilst at Utah the DD tanks of the 70th Tank Battalion arrived 15 minutes after the infantry.[167] In a remarkable image captured on D-Day by the war photographer Robert Capa, who went in with the first wave of infantry on Easy Red beach at Omaha, two DD tanks can be seen with their screens still raised which suggests that they have only just arrived, while to their left wading tanks are already on the beach with infantry huddled behind them seeking cover. As Capa was on Easy Red, the two DD tanks were from the five tanks of the 741st Tank Battalion that did not sink. As the two DD tanks are next to each other, it is more than likely that these are part of the group of three which landed directly on the beach about 0645 hours and went on to perform valiant service engaging the bunkers before being knocked out or disabled.

Those DD tanks in the British sectors that were landed directly by LCT were invariably late, however. This at first appears a little odd – the DD tanks could only make about 3 knots best speed in the conditions on D-Day whilst the Mk III landing craft had a top speed of 9 knots, so in theory the landing craft would have been able to make up any time lost. The problem was that once the decision not to launch had been made, the LCT commander had to make sure all the LCTs in the flotilla received the message and then the flotilla had to insert itself into a different wave of the planned assault without causing any disruption. This meant in most cases that a delay occurred before a suitable landing opportunity could be found and as a result the AVREs and the assault infantry were without armoured support when they most needed it. The Dieppe operation, where the tanks were 10 minutes late, demonstrated the need for the tanks to arrive before or, at the very least, at the same time as the infantry before they began to suffer heavy casualties.

This lesson was forgotten in Overlord and many lives could have been saved by not using DD tanks.

After reviewing a forecast of tank wastage rates before D-Day, 21st Army Group requested that the forecast wastage rate be increased to 25 per cent a month for tanks ashore for the first three months of the campaign.[168]

Regiment	Start no. cruiser tks	D-Day losses all causes	Per Cent	Comment
741 Tk bn	48	47	97.92 per cent	Only one bn tank survived, five reserve tanks landed
743 Tk bn	48	17	35.42 per cent	
13/18 Hussar	63	31	49.21 per cent	Two extra DD tanks
Staffs Yeo *	61	5	8.20 per cent	
1st Hussars	60	29	48.33 per cent	Not inc 2 woCB Vc, one of which was KO. Rcvd thirty-three replacements
FGH	59	11	18.64 per cent	Two extra DD tanks
4/7 RDG	61	19	31.15 per cent	
Sher Yeo *	61	14	22.95 per cent	
70 Tk bn	48	14	29.17 per cent	
*Follow up	**509**	**185**	**36.35 per cent**	

From the above table, a total of 185 medium Sherman or M4 tanks were lost from those that began the assault on 6 June; note that because of the congestion and fighting inland, some craft loads scheduled to land on D-Day were delayed until the next day. The average casualty rate for all the armoured units was 36 per cent, or one tank in three being lost. The wastage rate after one day of fighting was higher than that forecast for the whole month of June, although this is distorted by the much higher losses in the DD regiments. Somewhat pessimistically, 21st Army Group had set aside on paper 190 Shermans to replace all the DD tanks, therefore assuming a 100 per cent wastage rate.[169] As many DD tanks survived D-Day, these gave 21st Army Group a significantly higher number of reserve tanks ashore which would be needed in the ensuing months.

Notes

1 CMHQ Report #107, The Operation at Dieppe 19 August 1942, Further personal stories, 2 November 1943, DHH Ottawa

2 Hunnicutt, R.P., *Sherman: A History of the American Medium Tank* (Novato, CA, Presidio, 1978), p.422

3 ADM 199/1660 Operation Neptune (Naval Aspects of Operation Overlord) – Final report Force S commander, July 1944, TNA

4 Miller, Maj-General C.H., *History of 13th/18th Royal Hussars (QMO) 1922–1947* (London, Chisman, Bradshaw, 1949), p.42

5 Stirling, Major J.D.P., *The First and Last – The Story of the 4th/7th Royal Dragoon Guards 1939–1945*, p.43 (London, Art and Educational, 1949)

6 Hunnicutt, *opcit*, p.424

7 WO 205/748 letter BRAC, 17 May 1944, TNA

8 WO 205/748 Interim report on rectification of bent top rails of DD Sherman M4A4, 6 May 1944, TNA

9 Morgan, General F., Digest of Operation Overlord, COSSAC 43 (32), 27 July 1943, TNA

10 Morgan, *ibid*

11 Bradley, O., *A Soldier's Story*, p.244 (New York, NY, Holt, 1951)

12 RG24 vol 10992 War diary 2nd Canadian Armoured Brigade, May 1944 Appendix 6, Operational Order, Operation Overlord, LAC

13 Operation Neptune (Naval Aspects of Operation Overlord), *opcit*

14 Ellis, Major L.F., *Victory in the West Volume 1: The Battle of Normandy* (London, HMSO, 1962), p.184

15 Anderson, R., *Cracking Hitler's Atlantic Wall*, p.89 (Mechaniccsburg, PA, Stackpole, 2010)

16 Zaloga, S. and Ford, K., *Overlord – the Illustrated History of the D-Day Landings*, p.205 (Oxford, Osprey Publishing, 2009)

17 WO 199/1660 Operation Neptune *opcit* report Operation Gambit, TNA

18 Wormald, Major A., D-Day Recollections, (unpublished, Tyne and Wear Museums)

19 WO 291/246 Opposition on British Beaches Operational Research Report 1944, TNA

20 Wormald, *opcit*

21 ADM 199/1660, Operation Neptune, Force S LCH 185 report, TNA

22 WO 291/246, *opcit*

23 Smith, E.E., Lt, The Assault 6–23 June – The Story of C Squadron (unpublished, Tyne and Wear Museums)

24 WO 171/845 War diary 13th/18th Hussars, June, 1944, TNA

25 Wilmot, C., *The Second World War – the Struggle for Europe*, p.310 (London, Collins, 1952)

26 Smith, *opcit*

27 WO 171/845, *opcit*

28 ADM 199/1660 Operation Neptune, *opcit*, TNA

29 ADM 199/1660 Operation Neptune, *opcit*, TNA

30 Neave, J.A.S., War diary of Julius Neave (unpublished, Tyne and Wear Museums)

31 WO 171/1325 War diary 2nd KSLI, June 1944, TNA

32 WO 171/863 War diary Staffordshire Yeomanry, June 1944, TNA

33 *Ibid*

34 RG319 FMS B-441 Feuchtinger, 21st Panzer Division on 6 June, 1944, NARA

35 WO 171/863, *opcit*

36 Kortenhaus, W., *The Combat History of the 21st Panzer Division* (Solihull, Helion, 2014), p.108

37 *Ibid*, p.110

38 RG 24 vol 10455, Report 2nd Canadian Armed Brigade, Operation Overlord Sequence of events, June 6–11, report 5 July 1944, LAC

39 Lance-Corporal Rolph Jackson quoted in Fowler, W., *D-Day: the First 24 Hours* (Leicester, Silverdale, 2004), p.163

40 RG24 vol 14234 War diary Fort Garry Horse (10 CAR), June 1944, LAC

41 Anon, *Vanguard – The Fort Garry Horse in the Second World War*, p.131

42 *Ibid*

43 RG24 vol 14234 War diary Fort Garry Horse (10 CAR), June 1944, Appendix 1, LAC

44 Vanguard, *opcit*, p.134

45 RG24 vol 10992 War diary 2nd CAB, June 1944, LAC

46 War diary Fort Garry Horse, *opcit*

47 War diary Fort Garry Horse, *opcit*

48 Zuehlke, M., *Juno Beach: Canada's D-Day Victory* (Vancouver, Douglas and McIntyre, 2004)

49 RG24 vol 10992 War diary 2nd CAB radio log, June 1944, Appendix 4, LAC

50 Barnard, Lt-Colonel W.T., *The Queen's Own Rifles Of Canada: 1860–1960*, p.204 (Ontario, Ontario Publishing, 1960)

51 RG24 vol 14213 War diary 1st Hussars (6 CAR), June 1944, Appendix 5, LAC

52 RG24 War diary Royal Winnipeg Regiment, June 1944, LAC

53 Stark, F.M., *History of the 1st Hussars Regiment 1856–1945* (London, Ontario, 1951), p.52

54 Zuehlke, *opcit*

55 CMHQ Report #54 Canadian Participation in the Operations in NW Europe, part 1, June 1944, DHH, Ottawa

56 RG24 vol 14213 War diary 1st Hussars, June 1944, Appendix 6, LAC

57 RG24 vol 14213 War diary 1st Hussars, June 1944, Appendix 8, LAC

58 RG24 vol 14213 War diary 1st Hussars, June 1944, Appendix 5, LAC

59 RG24 vol 14213 War diary 1st Hussars, June 1944 Appendix 8, LAC

60 RG24 vol 14213 War diary 1st Hussars, June 1944 Appendix 7, LAC

61 Ellis, *opcit*, p.182

62 RG24 vol 14213 War diary 1st Hussars, June 1944, LAC

63 RG24, *ibid*

64 Stark, *opcit*, p.62

65 741st Tank Battalion, Field order #1, 21 May 1944, NARA

66 Ellis, *opcit*, p.191

67 'D-Day to VE day – History of 741st Tank Battalion', unpublished history, p.3

68 Hopper, Corporal, quoted in Vitamin Baker, unpublished history, p.26

69 Committee 10, Armour in Operation Neptune, US Army, Fort Leavenworth, KS, Armour School report, 1949, p.83

70 741st Tank Battalion After Action Report, 6 June 1944, NARA

71 741st Tank Battalion Journal, June 1944, NARA

72 Harrison, G., *Cross Channel Attack* (US Army CMH War Dept, 1993), p.315

73 741st Tank Battalion After Action Report, 6 June 1944, NARA

74 RG319 FMS B-388, 352nd Infantry Division, 6 June 1944, NARA

75 Whitehead, A., quoted in Yeide, H., *The Infantry's Armour: The U.S. Army's Separate Tank Battalions in World War II* (Mechanicsburg, Stackpole, 2010), p.140

76 741st Tank Battalion unit journal, 6 June 1944, NARA

77 *Ibid*

78 *Ibid*

79 Anderson, *opcit*, p.200

80 741st Tank Battalion After Action Report, 6 June 1944, NARA

81 741st Tank Battalion unit journal, June 1944, NARA

82 12th LCT Flotilla report, Launching DD tanks on D-Day, 14 July 1944, NARA

83 Action report of DD in the Assault, 11th Amphibious Fleet, letter dated 22 Sept 1944, NARA

84 741st Tank Battalion, After Action Report 6 June 1944, NARA

85 WO 171/583, 79th Armoured Division Operational Bulletin no.1, June 1944, TNA

86 D-Day – the untold story, BBC History website http://www.bbc.co.uk/history/ancient/ archaeology/marine_dday_underwater_01.shtml, accessed 3 December 2011

87 WO 171/583, *opcit*

88 V Corps Operations Plan Neptune, 26 March 1944, NARA

89 Move Out, Verify: The Combat Story of the 743rd Tank Battalion (unpublished history, p.19)

90 *Ibid*

91 Rockwell, D., in Drez, R., *Voices of D-Day – the Story of the Allied Invasion Told by Those who were there* (Eisenhower Centre, 1994), p.233

92 12th LCT Flotilla Report, *opcit*

93 Folkestad, W., *The View from the Turret: the 743rd Tank Battalion during World War II*, White Mane (Shippenburg, 1996), p.5

94 Private Harold Baumgarten, eyewitness, American D-Day.org website http://www.ameri-candday.org/Veterans/Baumgarten_Harold.html, accessed 21 January 2012

95 Folkestad, *opcit*, p.10

96 Folkestad, *opcit*, p.13

97 Armour in Operation Neptune, US Army Fort Leavenworth Armour School report, May 1949, p.81

98 Taylor, C., *Omaha Beachhead*, US Army Forces in Action (War Dept Historical Division, 1984), p.81

99 743rd Tank Battalion, AAR B Company, 6 June 1944, NARA

100 Zaloga, *opcit*

101 Taylor, *opcit*, p.48

102 743rd Tank Battalion AAR C Company, 6 June 1944, NARA

103 743rd Tank Battalion AAR C Company, 6 June 1944, NARA

104 LCT(A)2307 AAR, June 1944, NARA

105 743rd Tank Battalion AAR A Company 6 June 1944, NARA

106 Folkestad, *opcit*, p.8

107 Move Out, Verify, *opcit*, p.27

108 Taylor, C., *Omaha Beachhead*, *opcit*, p.42

109 RG319 FMS B-388, NARA

110 743rd Tank Battalion AAR A Company, 6 June 1944, NARA

111 Move Out, Verify, *opcit*, p.28

112 RG407 Box 1788 Adjutant General 12th Army AFV section reports, June 1944, NARA

113 WO 205/2 COSSAC Operation Overlord; Appreciation and Outline Plan, p.10, TNA

114 General Board, *opcit*, p.6

115 WO 106/4469 79th Armoured Division Final Report 1945, TNA

116 Ellis, *opcit*, p.177

117 *Ibid*, Appendix T

118 Fowler, *opcit*, p.149

119 Ellis, *opcit*, p.176

120 ADM 199/1660, Operation Neptune G-2 Naval Commander's Report, TNA

121 *Ibid*

122 Ellis, *opcit*, p.177

123 ADM 199/1660, Operation Neptune G-1 Naval Commander's Report, TNA

124 Newton, C., *A Trooper's Tale* (self-published, 2000), p.35

125 Zaloga and Ford, *opcit*, p.294

126 Stirling, *opcit*, p.60

127 BAOR, 50th Northumbrian Infantry Division Battlefield Tour, 1947, section VII, p.14

128 Bullock, R., 'D-Day Remembered – Personal Recollections of the Westminster Dragoon Guards' (unpublished, Westminster Dragoons Regimental Association), p.14

129 WO 171/838 War diary 4th/7th RDG, June 1944, TNA

130 WO 171/613 War diary 8th Armed Brigade, June 1944,TNA

131 Bullock, *opcit*, p.15

132 ADM 199/1660, Operation Neptune, Force G Naval Commanders Report Annexure 1 to Appendix C Bombardment Narrative, TNA

133 Fowler, *opcit*, p.155

134 Stirling, *opcit*, p.60

135 *Ibid*

136 Ellis, *opcit*, p.174

137 ADM 199/1660, Operation Neptune, G1 Naval Commander's Report, DSOAG Jig Green report, TNA

138 Anderson, *opcit*, p.169

139 Ambrose, S.E., *D-Day June 6, 1944 The Battle for the Normandy Beaches* (New York, NY, Simon & Schuster, 1994), p.523

140 ADM 199/1660, Operation Neptune, G1 Naval Commander's Report, TNA

141 Lindsay, T.M., *The Sherwood Rangers* (London, Burrup, Mathieson, 1952), p.104

142 ADM 199/1660, Operation Neptune, G1 Naval Commander's Report, TNA

143 Wilmot, *opcit*, p.296

144 WO 171/861 War diary Nottinghamshire Sherwood Yeomanry, June 1944, TNA

145 Hills, S., *By Tank into Normandy* (London, Orion, 2002), p.81

146 Zaloga, *opcit*, p.39

147 Harrison, *opcit*, p.301

148 Jensen, J., *Strike Swiftly: the 70th Tank Battalion* (Novato, CA, Presidio, 1997), p.131

149 Invasion of Normandy: Operation Neptune. Administrative History of US Naval Forces in Europe 1940–1946, vol.V, London, 1946

150 Ambrose, *opcit*, p.276

151 The General Board, US forces ETO Report no. 52 Armoured Special Equipment

152 Armour in Operation Neptune, *opcit*, p.20

153 Armour in Operation Neptune, *opcit*, p.27

154 Jensen, *opcit*, p.140

155 Invasion of Normandy: Operation Neptune. Administrative History of US Naval Forces in Europe 1940–1946, vol.V, London, 1946

156 Ruppenthal, Major R., *Utah Beach to Cherbourg – US Army Forces in Action* (Washington, DC, US Army CMH, 1948), p.47

157 Armour in Operation Neptune, p.31

158 70th Tank Battalion After Action Report June 1944 dated 20 August 1944 NARA

159 Ruppenthal, *opcit*, p.53

160 Ruppenthal, *opcit*, p.55

161 Ruppenthal, *opcit*, p.48

162 RG24 vol 14213 War diary 1st Hussars (6 CAR), June 1944, Appendix 5, LAC

163 RG24 vol 14234 War diary Fort Garry Horse (10 CAR), June 1944, Appendix 6, LAC

164 CAB 106/998, 79th Armoured Division Final Report, July 1945

165 General Board US Forces ETO report no. 52 Specialised Armour, p.21

166 J.L. Hall jnr, Report Force O Commander, 14 July 1944, NARA

167 Harrison, *opcit*, p.304

168 WO 205/112 letter 21st Army Group to Under Secretary of State, 22 May 1944, TNA

169 *Ibid*

2

Fighting the Tank

Montgomery and his Eighth Army in North Africa heavily influenced the standardisation of the British army around the American 75mm gun in 1942. During the first year of the North African campaign, the lack of an effective HE round for the 6-pounder guns in British tanks and anti-tank guns was seen as a great handicap as there was no effective mobile weapons for use against German anti-tank guns such as the famous 88mm Flak gun. This weakness was solved almost overnight with the arrival of the first Sherman M4 tanks from America in September 1942. Not only did the British then have a superior HE gun to the standard 6-pounder weapon with an armour-piercing capability that could penetrate all German tanks so far encountered, but it was also mounted in a tank that was fast and mechanically reliable. The British had already some experience of the same 75mm gun in the American M3 Lee/Grant tanks and the approbation from the Middle East and Montgomery was enough to see it adopted in November 1942 as the future main armament for British tanks.[1] However, the provision of a tank gun with both good armour-penetrating ability and HE performance remained a problem that plagued the War Office throughout the war.

Some within the Ministry of Production (oddly not the RAC) in March 1943 argued that with recent improvements in both the HE and AP ammunition for the 6-pounder, the 75mm gun was now inferior and would be inadequate to defeat heavier German armour in the future:

> It would seem therefore that by adopting the 75mm gun as the standard weapon for the majority of the tanks, we should be gratuitously reproducing in 1943 and 1944 the state of weapon inferiority for which we had to pay so dearly for in 1941 and 1942.[2]

The arguments by the Ministry of Production, which perhaps was perceived as being only interested in rationalising its production, were not powerful enough to persuade those that supported the 75mm main gun such as Montgomery and P.J. Grigg, the Secretary of State for War at the War Office. With promises of a new higher velocity 75mm and 76mm gun, the status quo was allowed to remain and the production of Shermans and new tanks with the 75mm guns continued. Given the subsequent experiences of Allied armour in the invasion of Normandy, the remark by the ministry would prove to be very prescient.

Montgomery and Tank Doctrine

As the newly appointed commander-in-chief of Operation Overlord, Montgomery immediately used his position to influence British tank doctrine by expounding his own particular views on tanks. Since the start of the war, British doctrine had been based on having two types of tanks for different roles: the close support tank for the infantry and a faster, more manoeuvrable cruiser tank for exploitation of the battlefield once gaps had been opened in the enemy lines, or to outflank them altogether. This had seen the creation of the independent Tank Brigades equipped with Churchill tanks to support the infantry whilst the cruiser tanks were allocated to the armoured divisions. Therefore the tank brigades trained extensively with infantry units from the outset and close working relationships were often developed. The armoured divisions with their faster cruiser tanks organised in Armoured Brigades were expected to outflank the enemy or charge through a gap already created in the defences. The 1943 War Office training pamphlet no. 41, 'The Tactical Handling of the Armoured Division and its Components', stated that the role of an armoured division is the complete destruction of the enemy, usually by envelopment or by deep penetration through his defences after a gap has been made in his main position by other formations.[3] In May 1942 the armoured divisions were reorganised and an infantry brigade was substituted for an armoured brigade with more artillery being brought in as well to make a more balanced, independent formation.

Montgomery was opposed to this concept of two types of tank, believing in early 1943 that a single 'capital' tank was needed to fulfil both roles and that the Sherman was best suited for this, being relatively fast and equipped with a 75mm gun that fired both AP and an effective HE round. This meant that the Sherman tanks of the armoured divisions were expected to attack strong enemy defences. By mid-1943 another problem had arisen: British tank production could not produce enough Churchill tanks to equip all of the tank brigades and some had to be equipped with Shermans. This created potential difficulties in that the more lightly armoured Shermans would be more easily knocked out than the Churchill tanks when attacking strong enemy positions thus depriving the infantry of any support.

The tank veteran Brigadier Pyman recognised this problem and wrote a paper in November 1943 advocating separate tactics for the Churchill and Sherman tanks whereby the Shermans would provide support from a distance and 'shoot-in' the advancing infantry. Montgomery was vigorously opposed to this and demanded that all of his tank brigades be capable of carrying out any mission assigned to them. With typical vindictiveness, Montgomery demanded the names of those who had written the paper.[4]

Montgomery, although having led the Eighth Army to victory, was no expert in the use of tanks and at the battle of El Alamein had allowed the retreating forces of Rommel's Afrika Korps to escape when he had the opportunity to cut them off with British armour.[5] So adamant was Montgomery in his views that he even refused to have a Churchill-equipped tank brigade in his army in Italy. In April 1944, Montgomery then tried to have the 6th Guards Tank Brigade disbanded to form replacements for other Guards units but was thwarted by senior Guards officers who approached Churchill directly. In retaliation, Montgomery excluded the brigade from Operation Overlord and put it into reserve. Its subsequent deployment was then contingent on converting 75mm-equipped Churchills back to 6-pounder guns in view of their better armour penetration suddenly seen as essential for Normandy.

Not surprisingly, Montgomery's views held sway and in February 1944 Montgomery's Chief of Staff, Francis de Guingand, an artilleryman, wrote some notes on the employment of tanks in support of infantry for the 21st Army Group wherein the support from a distance was abandoned in favour of tanks being used to:

- Cover the infantry and engineers creating gaps in the enemy defences
- Advance through to the objective without infantry support and hold it until the arrival of the infantry
- Support an infantry attack from positions 200yds behind the leading company

In this latest policy, the tanks in an armour-only attack would once again advance ahead of any infantry. This attempt at a compromise did not differentiate between types of tanks or brigades and assumed the Sherman could withstand enemy fire as much as a Churchill.[6] Perhaps most significantly, this policy maintained the separation of tanks and infantry in battle that was also part of Pyman's policy. For infantry/tank combined operations, 21st Army Group policy was therefore that the infantry should now lead. This was the second change in doctrine within three months and caused much confusion within the armoured units.

Fortunately for many units within 21st Army Group, this doctrine was not rigidly enforced and tank units interpreted these notes in their own way. Units such as the 6th Guards Tank Brigade and 15th Scottish Division that had already started training together continued in the same way when the two formations were finally brought together after Operation Epsom, while the war diaries of the tank regiments of the Guards Armoured Division often describe successful squadron or regiment 'shoots' during the Normandy campaign. How brigades combined with infantry would have important consequences in the Normandy campaign, particularly for the armoured brigades, which, unlike the tank brigades, were not used to working closely with infantry.

The Americans arrived in Normandy with no uncertainty around their doctrine for the employment of tanks. The independent tank battalions had been created to support the infantry divisions and the armoured divisions were designed for exploitation once a gap had been created in the enemy front line, in much the same way as British armoured divisions. 'The most suitable areas for the employment of Armoured force units are on the open flanks or through existing gaps created by penetrations of the enemy's positions.'[7]

A significant difference between American and British doctrine was that the Americans (principally General McNair) believed that the primary role of American tanks was not to fight German tanks which was the function of the tank destroyer battalions with their towed or self-propelled anti-tank guns (M10s). There remained some debate regarding the merits of self-propelled tanks versus towed anti-tank guns but General McNair's views prevailed and the emphasis was on towed tank destroyer battalions, despite the obvious limitations of these weapons being used by an advancing force on the battlefield.

Tank Comparison

The main battle tank in use by the Allies in 1944 was the American Sherman M4 and its variants. The British War Office and the tank industry had failed to develop an adequate cruiser tank in the first few years of the war and following the emergency shipment of 318 Shermans to North Africa after the fall of Tobruk, the British adopted the Sherman tank for its armoured units from September 1942 onwards.[8]

The Sherman was based on the hull of the Lee/Grant M3 tank to which a turret capable of mounting the 75mm M3 gun had been added. Because of a shortage of engines, various different models were developed to utilise the engines produced by different car manufacturers and modifications then had to be made to the hull to accommodate these changes. Other differences were in the manufacturing process: some hulls and turrets were welded and others cast.

The main variant used by the British was the M4A4 which was designated the Sherman V. This was powered by a 'multibank' of five Chrysler car engines which required the hull to be lengthened. The next most common British variant was the M4A2, or Sherman III, which used a diesel engine. The M4A4 was actually rejected by the US Army for overseas service and the US Army generally used the M4A3 with a Ford V8 engine or the M4 and M4A1 with an aircraft Continental R975 engine. Mechanically reliable, the Sherman became popular with British crews and helped turn the tide of war in North Africa. Nevertheless, the Sherman acquired a reputation for catching fire and rapidly exploding when hit which was a feature that did not endear it to crews:

... as we were sitting on top of an underfloor magazine of shells with machine gun ammo each side of you, 100 gallons of high octane petrol behind you, and many gallons of oil in the gear box and final drive in front of you there were much better places to be when it caught fire, and they certainly did very quickly![9]

The tank was nicknamed the Ronson (as in the cigarette lighter advertisement, 'lights every time') by the British and the 'Tommy cooker' by the Germans. Based on combat experience, extra plates of 25mm armour were welded on the sides of the hull (applique armour) at certain places where penetrations were thought to contribute to the tank catching fire or exploding.

Attempts were made to improve the armour-penetrating ability of the M3 gun and a 76mm version, M4A1 (76mm), was available from mid-1944 but, following reluctance from senior officers at FUSA and Patton's Third Army to adopt an unproven tank and incorporate it alongside existing M4s, was not issued to American units in time for Overlord. The 76mm M4 would only be used in separate tank battalions and for the time being would remain at depots in England.[10]

The Sherman was 108in (2.74m) high, only just over 2in (6cm) higher than the Mark IV and lower than both the Panther and the Tiger. The vertical slab sides, which did nothing to deflect any armour-piercing shot, gave the appearance of being overly high, leading to a myth that the Sherman had a high profile that made it an easy target. The Sherman was steered by means of two levers (one for each track) which when pulled, slowed one track or the other (but did not stop them), allowing the Sherman to turn. This gave the Sherman a very large turning circle compared to other tanks. There were no power controls and the driver needed all his strength at times to turn the tank according to the commander's orders.

A powerful electric motor traversed the Sherman's turret at much faster speeds than German tanks were capable of, so in combat this was sometimes an advantage. However, all German tanks were capable of skid turns by stopping one track and very often the driver performed this manoeuvre in combat to help line up the main gun more quickly, at the risk of throwing a track.

Despite adopting the Sherman as its main cruiser tank, British industry continued its efforts to produce a tank of its own and in 1944 this resulted in the A27 Cromwell tank. The Cromwell had a number of variants, like the American M4, based on different engines and armament. The model in use in Normandy, mainly by the 7th Armoured Division, was the Cromwell IV. This was powered by a modified Rolls Royce Merlin engine known as the Meteor and was armed with a 75mm gun based on the British 6-pounder gun modified to fire American 75mm ammunition.

The Cromwell was fast and manoeuvrable and used the same Christie suspension as the Russian T34. The Christie system had been offered to the British before the war but was rejected by the War Office. The Cromwell had a low profile and despite some teething troubles was mechanically reliable. However, it was never popular with crews – a particular weakness was the thinly armoured floor

(10mm) that gave the drivers little protection from land mines compared with the maximum 25mm belly armour of the Sherman. Like the Sherman, the Cromwell was relatively thinly armoured and the 75mm gun had a significantly lower muzzle velocity and hence armour-penetrating ability than German guns. A close support version, the Cromwell VI, mounted a 95mm howitzer and these were issued to regiments on the basis of two per squadron.

Combat experience in other theatres had demonstrated the need to up-gun the Cromwell before it was even issued and early in 1944 a version with a 17-pounder gun called the Challenger was developed with a new turret on a lengthened Cromwell hull. These were introduced into the Cromwell-equipped armoured reconnaissance regiments from August 1944 but the War Office only ordered 200 Challengers as other tanks were being developed.

By 1944, the Allied armoured units had universally adopted the light American tank the M3 (Stuart) and later the M5 (Honey) as their reconnaissance tanks. Only armed with a 37mm gun and a maximum of 51mm of amour, the Stuart was declared obsolete in July 1943 by the US Army but still saw widespread service in north-west Europe in British units along with the M5, which had twin V8 engines fitted. The Stuart and Honey were no match for German tank and anti-tank guns and after significant losses early in the campaign, they were only deployed in restricted roles. Some British regiments even removed the turret altogether to make the tank less visible while on reconnaissance patrols.

As per their early war tank doctrine, the British developed the Churchill tank for infantry support. Again there were a number of different variants, mainly based on armament. The first Churchills were equipped with the 6-pounder gun that had a poor HE shell performance, which was at odds with its purpose of supporting infantry and destroying strong enemy defences. By the time of Overlord

Armour thickness of main tanks in Normandy

	Turret front (mm)	Turret side	Hull front	Hull side	Belly	Speed on road (mph)	Speed cross-country (mph)	Height (m)
Cromwell	76	64	64	44	10	32	18	2.49
Sherman	75	50	50	37	25	21	12	2.74
Churchill	89	76	102	76*	19	15	8	3.25
Mark IV H	50	30	80	35	10	16	13	2.68
Panther	100	45	80	40	30	30	19	3.1
Tiger	100	80	100	80	25	22	13	3

* max

the main version used in Normandy was the Churchill VI, which had been modified to take the 75mm American gun with its better HE shell performance. As the Churchill was heavily armoured, it was naturally slow on the battlefield. The turret ring of the Churchill tank was too small to permit the 17-pounder gun to be installed.

Having developed a potent anti-tank gun in the 17-pounder, enterprising British officers began trying to fit the gun into the Sherman turret even though the Americans said it could not be done. Room was found by turning the gun on its side, cutting out the back of the turret and adding an armoured compartment to the rear of the turret so as to accommodate the recoil of the gun and the wireless set. This higher velocity weapon fired a larger shell and to accommodate these, the tank crew was reduced from five to four by not using a co-driver. As the anti-tank gun was designed to be fired in the open air, when the gun was fired in an enclosed turret there was not quite enough oxygen inside the tank for the propellant charge which burned at a fractionally slower rate. The propellant was still burning when the breech opened to eject the cartridge and a sheet of flame would erupt from the breech, singeing the hair and skin of any of the turret crew in the way. This was investigated by the RAC but found to be 'inconsequential'. A large sheet of flame also came out of the muzzle of the gun when fired and a muzzle brake installed to reduce recoil threw up a lot of dust immediately in front of the tank. The gunner very often could not see whether he had hit the target, so the tank commander had to leave the tank and observe the fall of shot from a few yards away. This was undesirable and not always possible when in action. The dust and flame from the muzzle blast also gave away the position of the tank to the Germans, requiring the tank to either make sure of its first shot or immediately move to a different firing position if possible for subsequent shots. This up-gunned Sherman was known initially as the Vc and then later as the Firefly. The Germans quickly realised the potency of the Firefly and learnt to concentrate all their fire on them first. A further limitation was the gunner's telescopic sights which initially were the standard three power M70 telescopic sights and only accurate to 1,000yds.[11] These were later improved with the installation of Mk 43 telescopes, but some Fireflies continued to arrive in Normandy with the standard sights.[12]

The Firefly standard AP ammunition APC and APCBC could penetrate a Tiger at 1,200yds and the rare discarding SABOT at more than 2,000yds, but the SABOT ammunition introduced in August remained in short supply and was notoriously inaccurate over a range of 500yds. As the HE round was not as effective as the ordinary 75mm HE ammunition, the Firefly was used primarily in an anti-tank role.

On 30 Dec 1944, 2,100 Sherman Vcs were ordered and enough were produced in time for D–Day to equip one tank in every troop of three tanks with the new gun. Thus, only by accident and not official design or policy, did the British get a tank with a gun able to engage German tanks on anything like equal terms.

Armour penetration of main tank guns

Tank	Gun	Range				
		100	500	1000	1500	2000
Cromwell	75mm	93	68	61	54	47
Sherman	M3	90	66	60	55	50
Churchill	75mm	93	68	61	54	47
Vc, Firefly	17-pounder		140	131	112	110
Mark IV H	75mm KwK40 L/48	99		82		
Panther	75mm KwK42 L/70	138	124	111	99	89
Tiger	88mm KwK36 L/56	120	110	100	91	84
Stug III	75mm Stuk40 L/48	99		82		
Jagdpanzer	75mm Pak39 L/48	99		82		
Anti-tank guns						
	6-pounder		87	80	73	67
	6-pounder APDS		131	117	103	90
	75mm Pak40		106	96	80	63
	88mm Pak43			200		167

German data with Pzgr 39 ammunition
Ranges in metres and yards
Data from Chamberlain and Ellis and from original German gun datenblatt where available.[13]

The Americans investigated the possibility of sourcing some Firefly tanks from the British but this did not come about as British production was at full capacity converting enough Shermans to Fireflies for their own use. Montgomery even stipulated that top priority would be given to ensuring that the tank regiments had two Fireflies per troop as soon as possible.[14]

The Germans in Normandy had two main battle tanks: the Mark IV and the Panther. Each panzer division had one Panther tank battalion and one Mark IV battalion, the intention being to ultimately phase out the Mark IVs. The Mark IV tank had been in service since 1937 and was originally conceived as an infantry support tank with a short-barrelled 75mm howitzer as the Mark III tank was the main tank at that time. With the invasion of Russia, the Germans encountered the T-34 and the heavily armoured KV-1, the existence of which came as a great shock and there was an urgent need for the Germans to up-gun and up-armour their tanks. The Mark III was too small to be equipped with any gun larger than 50mm in calibre, so the Mark IV was up-gunned from a howitzer to an anti-tank gun from mid-1942 onwards. The long-barrelled Mark IV came to be known as the Mark IV 'special' in North Africa. By May 1944, most of the Mark IVs in France were the H variant which was equipped with a 75mm KwK L/48 gun and in many cases an additional 5mm of skirt armour on the sides of the hull and turret for extra protection. This extra armour made the Mark IV look larger than it was and many Allied tank crews mistook it for a Tiger tank throughout the campaign.

Following the arrival of the Sherman in North Africa in the second half of 1942 that temporarily gave the Allies parity with German tanks, the next two years saw the Germans introduce a new heavy tank and a new medium tank, the Tiger and Panther respectively.

The Tiger was a heavy tank that had been in development before the war to replace the Mark IV. The development work was given new impetus by the successful production by Krupp of a tank gun based on the famous 88mm Flak gun and the encounters with the T-34 and KV-1 on the Eastern Front. The Tiger made its combat debut in late 1942 at Leningrad and with its heavy armour and enormous firepower quickly earned a deadly reputation. Fortunately, given its weight, complexity and cost, the Germans did not produce many Tigers and they required frequent maintenance to keep them operational. The Germans organised the Tigers in independent battalions of forty-five tanks.

A Tiger tank was knocked out in North Africa by a 6-pounder anti-tank gun and the British mistakenly got the impression that there was not much to fear from the tank. When the tank was shipped to England for trials, RAC reports as to its superior performance set alarm bells ringing in some quarters. However, such was the reputation of the Tiger on the battlefields of Italy and Normandy that senior Allied commanders from Montgomery down were concerned about tank crews developing 'Tiger phobia'.[15]

The Panther tank was developed as a direct response to Russian tanks and was largely modelled on the T-34 with sloped armour, a powerful gun and wide tracks for a good cross-country performance. The tank was developed and put into production within eighteen months of a specification being issued and 250 tanks were deployed at Kursk in 1943, although their deployment was rushed and there was little time for trials. The Panther's combat debut was not successful: many tanks broke down or caught fire whilst others were not well deployed and became bogged. This debut was ironic as the start of the battle had been delayed for the arrival of the Panther tanks, allowing the Russians more time to build their defences. The initial problems were eventually ironed out and the Panther became renowned on the Eastern Front. The Mark III tank battalions in each division were progressively replaced by Panther battalions during the ten months before D-Day. A few Panthers were deployed in Italy but by and large the British and Americans had no experience of fighting them and assumed it was a tank that would be used in small units like the Tiger.[16] The realisation that the Panther tank was a main battle tank did not come until early in 1944 when the British discovered that Panthers would replace all Mark IVs.[17]

The German anti-tank gun ammunition was also largely flashless and smokeless (unlike British ammunition) which helped their tanks and anti-tank guns to remain concealed once they opened fire. In the close countryside of the Normandy campaign, the Germans were largely on the defensive and their advantage of firing the first shot was often retained by the use of such ammunition which allowed a second or third shot before the Allies could react.

Self-propelled Guns

Unlike the Allies, the Germans made great use of self-propelled or assault guns. These typically had a fixed anti-tank gun (capable of up to 15 degrees lateral movement) mounted on an obsolete or standard tank hull. This expedient was less costly than a turret mounted tank and allowed the Germans to keep using the hulls of obsolete tanks such as the Mark II, Mark III and the Czech Pz 38. The 21st Panzer Division had an entire battalion of 75mm anti-tank guns and howitzers mounted on captured French tank hulls. A self-propelled vehicle was about two thirds the cost of a conventional tank and took fewer man-hours to build. The principal assault gun was the Stumegschutz III mounted on a Mark III chassis but when the factory producing them was heavily bombed, the Mark IV chassis had to be utilised. Originally intended as an infantry support tank with a short-barrelled 75mm howitzer, the Stug IIIs were up-gunned to carry a 75mm StuK L/48 gun after the invasion of Russia. In defensive situations in good cover, the Stugs were formidable anti-tank weapons. A replacement for the Stug III, a specially designed anti-tank assault gun, the Jagdpanzer IV, began to be issued to units from March 1944 and saw service with the Lehr, 12th SS and 9th Panzer Divisions in Normandy.[18]

The performance of tanks is measured by three interdependent criteria: firepower, armour and mobility; the heavier the armour and the larger the gun in a tank, the less mobile it will tend to be.

A comparison of the armour thickness and cross-country speeds shows that all the German tanks were as fast if not faster than the Sherman and Churchill but not the Cromwell. The speed of the Mark IV was achieved at the expense of the armour on the front of the turret – only 50mm compared with more than 75mm for the Allied tanks. However, when the penetration powers of the anti-tank guns are compared with the armour thicknesses, there is an immediate contrast between the German and Allied tanks. All the German anti-tank guns could penetrate the frontal armour of the Sherman and Cromwell at over 1,000m distance while the 75mm Allied guns could only penetrate the front of Panthers and Tigers at less than 500yds, if at all. Only the turret front of the Mark IV could be defeated at 1,500yds or less range. The Mark IV had frontal hull armour of 80mm, comparable to that of the Sherman.

Therefore the Allied tanks were at a significant disadvantage at the start of the Normandy campaign as the German tanks could destroy them from long range whilst the Allied tanks needed to get to within 500yds to even have a chance of penetrating the frontal armour of their enemy. The thinly armoured turret and hull sides were the Panther's weak spots, provided the Allied tanks could manoeuvre into defilade. In the bocage countryside that dominated much of the campaign, tank duels took place at close range, so the poorer firepower of the Allies was not such a disadvantage and some German commanders even complained that the long overhanging barrel of the Panther restricted movement amongst the trees and hedgerows. However, the hedgerows and small fields meant that it was difficult for the Allies to quickly outflank a German tank once it had been located and the Germans learned to use their tanks as mobile pill boxes with their thickest frontal armour facing the attackers.

Anti-tank Guns

The main anti-tank guns in use by the British were the 6-pounder and the 17-pounder. The excellent performance of the 17-pounder was in stark contrast to that of the 6-pounder and the British rushed to improve the armour penetration of the 6-pounder by developing a new armour-piercing round, the discarding sabot (APDS), which gave a new lease of life to these guns. The same APDS ammunition could be used in the 6-pounder equipped Churchill tanks, markedly improving their anti-tank performance.

The German 75mm Pak40 anti-tank gun was in widespread use and had a similar performance to the Kwk40 L/48 gun with Panzergranate-39 ammunition but this was considerably improved with the availability of Panzergranate-40. The 88mm dual-purpose Flak guns, as used in North Africa, were a part of the panzer divisions' anti-aircraft battalion and could act in a ground role if required. These anti-tank guns had a high profile, so once they opened fire and their position was revealed then they were easily knocked out by HE. Large numbers of 88mm Flak guns were deployed in Normandy as part of the III Flak Korps of the Luftwaffe, but the use of these guns in an anti-tank role was the subject of much friction between the Heer (army) and the Luftwaffe. Often the Luftwaffe batteries withdrew in the face of impending British attacks but a few batteries played a significant part in some battles. Far more deadly than the Flak guns were the 88mm Pak43 and Pak43/41, versions designed purely as anti-tank guns with a much lower profile. The Pak43 had its own cruciform carriage like the Flak gun, whilst the Pak43/41 was mounted on an FH18 field howitzer chassis.

Infantry Weapons

In 1944 the German infantryman was equipped with a very effective anti-tank weapon: the Panzerfaust. Developed from the 1942 Faustpatrone, the Panzerfaust was a low-cost, single-use recoilless weapon that fired a shaped charge that penetrated 200mm of armour up to a range of 30m. The Panzerfaust was the forerunner of some modern anti-tank weapons and used the same principle as the improvised explosive devices of today. The explosive charge is shaped around the outside of a hollow metal container and when the projectile hits the target the charge detonates and a stream of hot gases are directed by the metal onto a small area of the surface of the armour, which is melted by the heat. The hot gases then penetrate the armour, sending a molten stream of metal and gases into the interior of the tank with devastating consequences. The British army had little or no experience of the Panzerfaust until May 1944 in Italy and the War Office promptly issued a report on the 10 June recommending that protective infantry had to accompany the tanks into battle, which was yet another change in tank and infantry doctrine.[19] The report came a little late for the units already fighting in Normandy and the Panzerfaust would prove to be a formidable weapon in the hedgerows of the bocage.

For anti-tank defence, the British soldier had the PIAT which was a weapon firing a hollow charge rocket up to 115yds that could penetrate the armour of most German tanks. The trigger mechanism used a spring which was difficult to cock while prone. The PIAT had no backblast and tended to be used at close range but it was heavy and cumbersome and not very accurate. The fuses were often faulty and the charge would not go off even if it did hit the target. The PIATs were issued one per platoon so they were not as widespread as the Panzerfaust in the ranks of the infantry in Normandy.

The relative failure of the War Office and the British tank industry to produce a tank that could compete on equal terms or best the German tanks became a political issue; questions were repeatedly asked in the House of Parliament by a small group of politicians, much to the displeasure of Churchill who had established a national coalition government to unite the country politically whilst conducting the war. However, by late 1943 the questions had neither ceased nor been properly answered and eventually a Select Committee on National Expenditure, chaired by John Wardlaw Milne, was set up to report on British tank production. On 11 March 1944, this committee delivered a critical memorandum and Churchill asked the War Office and the Ministry of Supply to draft a short response. MPs like Richard Stokes continued to raise questions in parliament, not just about tanks but also other items of equipment:

16th March 1944

Mr. Stokes asked the Prime Minister whether, in view of the unsatisfactory reports which he has received both as to the inadequacy of British tanks in the field and the waste in production in this country, he will tell the House what action he proposes to take in default of holding an inquiry.

The Prime Minister: I repudiate the allegations of the hon. Member. The next time that the British Armies take the field, in country suitable for the use of armour, they will be found to be equipped in a manner at least equal to the forces of any other country in the world.[20]

30th March 1944

    Mr. McGovern: Will the Prime Minister be prepared to take charge of a Churchill tank and allow the hon. Member for Ipswich (Mr. Stokes) to take charge of a Tiger tank?

    The Prime Minister: I think it might be one way of settling the difference.

In order to try and take some of the heat out of the issue, a secret debate was held in the House of Commons on 24 March 1944. However, the report by the Select Committee was not released by Churchill to MPs prior to the debate as it was allegedly a secret report prepared for Cabinet and not the House. Questions on the performance of British tanks were often answered evasively on the basis of not wanting to give information to the enemy. Stokes continued to ask questions about obsolete tanks and even requested that captured German tanks be brought to Westminster for MPs to see for themselves. By June, a formal reply to the Select Committee report had still not been made and the two 'short' draft responses were so lengthy that summary versions were also in circulation.

To reduce the performance gap between German and Allied tanks, the British developed the 17-pounder anti-tank gun (both in the Firefly and as a mobile anti-tank gun) and improved APDS shot for the 6-pounder guns. The Americans, for their part, although there was a heavier tank in development, had put their faith in a Sherman M4 up-gunned with a 76mm gun.

A second step to close the gap was for some Churchill tank units to remove their 75mm guns and retro-fit them with 6-pounder guns to use the new APDS ammunition developed in 1943. Montgomery wanted it to be official policy for one tank in a troop of four to have a 6-pounder until a way was found for the 17-pounder to be fitted to the Churchill tank.[21] Consequently, three of the independent tank brigades arrived in Normandy with a mix of 75mm and 6-pounder Churchills.

The basic problem was that the Allies were going to Normandy with a main battle tank that was essentially unchanged since its introduction in 1942 while the Germans had introduced the Tiger and the Panther and continued to improve the venerable Mark IV. Montgomery was well aware of the situation, having written in August 1943:

We are badly behind the Germans in this respect and I am anxious as to whether we are thinking far enough ahead. History relates that in the struggle between the gun and armour, the gun always comes out on top.

    To overcome this serious defect it is necessary for our tanks to make the fullest use of ground in order to being effective fire to bear on the enemy tanks. This is a definite handicap when we are the attacker. In pushing forward in a search for good fire positions, tanks often have to expose themselves and casualties happen rapidly.[22]

Churchill was also well aware of the tank gap and the disadvantages faced by the Allied tanks, having written in a minute to the Defence Committee (Supply) in April 1943:

> We shall, I am sure, be exposed to criticism if we are found with a great mass of thin skinned tanks of medium size, none of which can stand up to the German guns of 1943, still less than those of 1944.[23]

General Bradley was also conscious of the tank gap, writing after the war of the North African campaign that US tanks were no match for more heavily armoured and better-gunned German panzers. 'Too often the American tankers complained it cost them a tank or two, with crews, to get the German tanks. Thus we could defeat the enemy's Panzers but only by expending more tanks than we cared to lose.'[24]

Before the British VIII Corps arrived in Normandy, General O'Connor had his staff prepare a report on the numbers and types of German tanks the corps could expect to encounter. By D-Day, the Germans would have an estimated 413 Panthers and 70 Tigers opposing the Second Army which would have landed 187 Vcs in a similar period, increasing to a maximum of 259 by D+15. Further German reinforcements would bring a total of 560 more Panthers and 140 Tigers, making 973 Panthers and 210 Tigers in opposition.[25]

This report seemed to have falsely assumed Mark IVs had all been replaced by Panthers and overestimated the number of Panthers available to the Germans which was a theoretical total of 655 in the panzer divisions eventually deployed in Normandy.[26] Another implicit assumption in the report is the superiority of the Panther and Tiger to the standard Sherman; clearly, senior British commanders were concerned about the threat posed by German tanks and the weaknesses of British armour.

Most tank crews on arrival in Normandy immediately set about fixing or welding track links from destroyed German tanks to the front of their tanks for extra protection. Some commanders, particularly General Patton, frowned upon this because it added extra weight and therefore hindered mobility but the British and Canadians continued the practice throughout the campaign.

The tank gap – the differences in firepower, armour and mobility between German and Allied tanks – meant that in any encounter with German tanks, the Allied main battle tank was likely to come off second best unless it could get within 500yds range or outflank the enemy and hit it in the side. Knowing that the Sherman was at a significant disadvantage to the German tanks, the number of tank casualties in Normandy would also be determined by how the tanks were actually deployed in battle by all the senior officers and commanders at an army, corps and divisional level.

Living in the Tank

The crew of a tank ate, slept and fought in a compartment the same size as a large modern four-wheel drive passenger car. Four or five men living together in such a small space and sharing the experiences and dangers of going into battle in an armoured box containing large quantities of explosive ammunition and fuel meant that crews quickly became tight-knit teams. In action, the fate of the tank often depended on each crewman doing his job and doing it well. The tank commander sat on a folding seat at the right rear of the turret, directly under the large hatch with its two semi-circular flaps; map reading was particularly difficult in the confined space, especially when being jolted around if the tank was travelling cross-country. When the hatch was closed, the commander had to use a periscope which severely curtailed his field of view. Most German tanks possessed a vision cupola with glass blocks all around the outside which permitted a better view of the battlefield in the immediate vicinity of the tank. Therefore most Sherman commanders kept the hatch open during combat, taking frequent quick looks out of the hatch which even some of the experienced German tank commanders did. Having the hatch open made all tank commanders more vulnerable to mortar and artillery fire, as well as snipers, and there was a high casualty rate amongst Allied tank commanders in Normandy. Officers made up 12 per cent of tank casualties, despite being only 8 per cent of the total complement of a regiment.[27]

The tank commander had the best view of the nearby terrain and was usually the first to identify potential targets or threats to the tank. He gave orders over the intercom to the driver who manoeuvred and positioned the tank as quickly as possible. When not driving the tank, the driver was responsible for maintenance. The gunner needed to be well trained and a proficient marksman, especially when engaging moving targets such an enemy tanks. Very often the tank that got off the first shot survived to fight another day and battles were decided by the split-second gunnery and movement of the tanks. The gunner controlled the traverse of the turret by an electric motor and the elevation of the main gun by a handwheel. The loader/operator was required to keep a constant supply of shells up to the main gun in accordance with the commander's instructions for a particular type of shell depending on the target, either High Explosive (HE), armour-piercing (AP) or smoke. When not loading the gun, the loader/operator was responsible for communications over the No. 19 wireless set. This man was the tank's only contact with the outside world, the radio being essential for conveying tactical information and the location of supplies. As the wireless and intercom were not supposed to be operated at the same time, when the tank commander or operator was using the wireless the crew had to perform their duties using their own initiative.

The co-driver operated the bow machine gun to keep any enemy infantry at a safe distance as well as sharing the driving. The co-driver also assisted with maintenance and was usually the odd-job man for the tank as required. In a Sherman, the tank drivers each had a hatch over their heads. The turret itself had a basket or cage containing the turret crew, and the driver and co-driver lower in the hull could only exit the tank via the turret when the turret was positioned in such a way to allow entry to the cage. Behind the co-driver was an escape hatch in the floor of the tank that was kept well-oiled in case of the need to bail out. The tank crews practised this regularly and sometimes for the driver and co-driver this belly hatch was the only means of escape if there was no access to the turret cage and the main gun was positioned above their own hatches, preventing them from being opened. If the belly hatch was opened when the tank was on fire then the increased airflow often made the fire worse, to the detriment of those crew members still trying to get out. In a Firefly, the 17-pounder gun blocked the exit of the loader, and for him to be able to get out, the gun had to be fully depressed. As a result of this interdependence among the crew members, discipline in the tank was usually quite relaxed, even if the tank was commanded by an officer rather than a sergeant or corporal.

As the tank was the crew's home, all the essentials for living, such as bedding, cooking materials, food and water, were carried aboard. Unlike most homes, the tank crew shared their living space with ammunition rounds, machine gun belts and a powerful engine at the rear of the tank that required the storage of large quantities of flammable fuel. The Sherman M4A4 used by the British actually had five Chrysler six cylinder aircraft engines mounted radially on a common shaft. Other versions used a Ford V8 tank engine or twin diesels. No matter the engine, the noise was deafening and required the crew to wear earphones, both to protect their hearing and to be able to talk to each other over an intercom system. When the tank was moving, there would be a constant clanging of pieces of stowed equipment banging into each other in addition to the squealing and rattling of the tracks. In combat, these sounds would be accompanied by a cacophony of explosions, orders and shouts over the intercom, the clang of the gun breech closing, the chattering of machine guns and the ringing of spent cartridges hitting the floor. The crew would also be thrown around quite a bit when crossing uneven terrain at speed, making it difficult at times to operate their equipment.

Contrary to popular opinion, the inside of a tank was not hot, oily or dirty. The interior was painted with white enamel paint which the crew kept as clean as possible so as to maximise the amount of light inside. When the engine was running, it drew in fresh air from outside through the turret, so the tank only became hot when standing in the hot sun.[28] The flow of fresh air often meant the crew were cold, especially in winter, despite the zip-up overalls they were issued with. The smells of fuel, paint and the body odour of the crew, who were often confined for long periods, added to the discomfort of being inside the cramped tank. When the tank was not fighting, the crew would open hatches to get better observation of their surroundings and to ventilate the tank.

When the tank hatches were closed down or 'buttoned up', the crew were forced to rely on vision slits made of reinforced glass or periscopes to see what was happening around them. As the crew's vision was thus impaired, each tank relied on accompanying tanks to identify potential threats and radio warnings to each other. Similarly, when moving through dense terrain such as the Normandy bocage, the tanks relied on the infantry they were supporting to keep enemy soldiers armed with anti-tank weapons away from the tanks. When the weather was dry, the movement of tanks often threw up clouds of dust that when combined with the smoke of battle reduced the vision of the crew still further. Dust was a never-ending problem for the tank crew, the tank needing regular maintenance to ensure that the engines and armament functioned correctly.

The first tank crews to land on D-Day were issued with 24-hour ration packs that consisted of small portions of dehydrated food such as chocolate, porridge and tea. A particular boon on D-Day to crew members that got wet were self-heating cans of soup. When the regiment was out of the front line, food was provided by mobile kitchens which provided hot food of a reasonable quality that was eaten by the squadrons at different sittings. However, the squadrons were often in combat and could not avail themselves of the field kitchens and so used three-day Compo ration packs which contained fourteen identical meals; there were seven different varieties of pack available. These packs contained tinned fruit and stews, rolled bacon, spam, corned beef, cigarettes, biscuits, sugar, sweets and dehydrated soup. There were also eighty-four sheets of toilet paper provided. Each tank crew tried to procure its favourite Compo pack and a constant problem was how to divide the fourteen meals amongst the five-man crew for three days. Not surprisingly, the tank crews sought to supplement their food with fresh produce such as cheese, milk and eggs which fortunately were plentiful in the Normandy countryside, although the British troops were prohibited from buying bread from the local inhabitants because of a shortage of grain. Troops were also forbidden to take local livestock such as cows, pigs and chickens but invariably those found their way into the diets of the tank crews when an 'accident' presented an opportunity. Some tins of food were stowed in the hottest parts of the engine so there was always something hot to eat at night if there was no time to cook.[29] Food was supposed to be cooked on a small primus stove which had to be used outside. Consequently, when a tank was closed up under fire, the crew could not prepare any hot food. Most crews used a stove improvised by pouring petrol into a tin full of earth, which burnt suffi-ciently well to heat a pot of water. Similarly, answering calls of nature when inside the tank could be difficult and was complicated further by the overalls the crew wore. Empty shell cases provided some relief and, when necessary, helmets were used. The alternative of leaving the tank was often impossible as this risked death from shellfire or snipers, although most men preferred to find a convenient hedge. Outbreaks of stomach complaints were common and many soldiers in Normandy were affected by a type of dysentery that was particularly difficult to cope with in a tank. All water had to be carried on the tank and so was always in short supply; it had to be chemically disinfected and was not pleasant to drink. A mugful was available for personal hygiene such as shaving every two or three days. Laundry was also difficult and the tank crews were frequently forced to wear the same clothes for weeks on end. The daily life of German tank crews in Normandy was similar:

> We had plenty to eat. Besides the good combat rations which the company sergeants brought forward at night, we obtained a small butter barrel and a cream pot from a dairy in the combat zone – an excellent nerve relaxer. This was necessary to survive the almost constant fire from the artillery on the ground, from the air, and from the sea. In general, one heard the detonations subliminally if they were not in the immediate area, but one could still not sleep deeply. My excellent crew and I slept in a deeply dug, covered trench under our panzer. Those who had no overhead protection had it bad. The trees and bushes blocked one's vision but not the shell fragments from above, which were set loose by very sensitive fuses that were set off by the thinnest branch … There was a problem with water. There were no nearby streams. Undressing and bathing were excessive luxuries but one took every opportunity to shave. The dry summer weather and the constant strain on the nerves caused a powerful thirst, so we drank large quantities of cider, calvados, wine and cognac without getting drunk. Rations could only be delivered at night. They were often taken with our nerve salve from our 'dairy', the butter and cream. To relax ourselves we smoked cigarettes. Their blue haze could not worsen the already unhealthy air.[30]

Allied tank crews were ordered not to drink the local homemade Calvados spirit, as it was implicated in stomach upsets, but this did not usually stop them. Rum was occasionally issued to the ORs, and the officers at regimental HQ often had a well-stocked mess truck that also supplied spirits as required. The policies for rum rations varied from regiment to regiment, sometimes squadron to squadron. Some regiments issued rum rarely whilst others ensured that each tank had a full water bottle.[31]

A regular supply of mail was very important for morale and mail deliveries were made to the tanks by the rear echelons. Letters written by the men were censored by their officers and most men did not want to relate the horrors of war to their loved ones so as to not unduly alarm them. Only officers were permitted to keep diaries, but this regulation was often broken.

Like all soldiers, tank crews were always short of sleep and took naps whenever they were allowed and the opportunity arose. At night it was customary, and a part of British doctrine, for the tanks to withdraw from the front line into what was called a harbour (also sometimes called a 'laager' or 'leaguer') for to stay in the front line there was the threat of enemy infantry creeping up on them in the darkness. Each squadron's tanks were arranged in a defensive perimeter and the crews then had to dig slit trenches to sleep in; sometimes the tank was driven over the top of the trenches to provide added protection from German artillery or mortar fire, or the occasional nocturnal visit from the Luftwaffe. A tarpaulin fitted on a rail on one side of the tank could be pulled out to make a temporary shelter under which the men could sleep with some protection from the elements. If there was no time, or the men came under fire before any trenches could be dug, the crews slept in their tanks. Before anyone could go to sleep, however, the tanks had to be refuelled and rearmed and any essential maintenance carried out so the tank crews often did not get more than 4 or 5 hours of sleep a day. Each Sherman tank carried more than 100 rounds for the 75mm gun; this load was typically made up of fifty to sixty High Explosive, forty Armour-Piercing and ten smoke rounds, all of which had to be manhandled and stowed in the tank. Petrol or diesel fuel was supplied in 4-gallon jerricans which had to be lifted up individually onto the rear deck and emptied into the fuel tanks. Twenty to thirty boxes of machine gun ammunition also had to be loaded. While the tanks were being resupplied, the troop and squadron leaders would attend an Orders Group with the commanding officer to debrief the day's events and work out the plans for the coming day. The attack's objectives, supporting troops, start times, availability of air and artillery support, and information about the enemy all had to be discussed and understood.[32] The tank crews themselves then had to be briefed on the return of their commanders before anyone could have a meal or attempt to go to sleep. Despite being in the rear areas away from the front line, many harbours were anything but quiet and the constant firing of nearby artillery batteries would often make sleep difficult. Deep, unbroken sleep was rare as the night was regularly disturbed by changes of sentries, mosquitoes and enemy aircraft overhead. The Luftwaffe always made sorties over the Allied beachhead at night and those sleeping would inevitably be woken by the fire of anti-aircraft guns and the occasional falling bomb. As it was midsummer, the nights were short and with most operations beginning at dawn, reveille for the tank crews was often at four or five o'clock in the morning.

When not in action, other maintenance had to be regularly performed on the engine, suspension, wireless and armament. As the workings of the tracks could often mean the difference between life and death, particular attention was paid to them every day. The crew worked with the squadron fitters if necessary to replace rollers, suspension bogies, track pads and sprockets. When the engine was not running, a small petrol-driven generator inside the turret was used to charge the batteries and this often gave a lot of trouble, requiring regular overhauls. The main gun had to be cleaned daily with a long rod to remove any dirt or impurities that had built up in the rifling of the barrel.

Organisation

A British or Canadian tank regiment was organised into three fighting squadrons of nineteen tanks in each with a regimental headquarters of four more tanks. Each squadron was divided into either four troops of four tanks or five troops of three tanks with the balance of tanks forming the squadron headquarters. There had been some debate in the tank regiments about the merits of the squadron commander controlling four or five troops at once and the arrival of Sherman Vc Firefly tanks stimulated this debate. All regiments eventually adopted a four-tank troop model with a Firefly in each troop.

The American tank battalions were organised into three companies of seventeen tanks in each with three platoons each of five tanks and two in company headquarters. There were four tanks in the battalion headquarters. Keeping the squadrons of the regiment or battalion fighting were the support echelons that did not accompany the tanks into battle but met up with the tanks either at a designated place (the rally point) or at the squadron harbour.

The A or F fighting echelon vehicles carried the supplies needed to keep the tanks fighting such as fuel, ammunition and water, and generally were as far forward as the battle permitted. The B echelon contained the kitchen and officers' mess trucks plus various stores and maintenance personnel and remained in a rear area behind the front lines. Each regiment had a small workshop capable of carrying out small or simple repairs to the tanks to keep them operational. These were known as Light Aid Detachments (LAD) and were the first line of workshops with brigade workshops being the second line of workshops for repairs that the LAD could not carry out.

German tank battalions were organised in a similar way to the Allied regiments, with a battalion being made up of four or five companies, each company being of three platoons or zugs of five tanks with another two in the company headquarters.

Replacements

The 2nd Armoured Replacement Group (ARG) was set up in 1944 to organise the movement of replacement personnel and the supply of battle-worthy operational tanks for armoured regiments. This unit was hurriedly created just before D-Day and had a series of tank delivery squadrons attached to it operating at the brigade and corps level. The 2nd ARG was also tasked with organising the training of reinforcements. The reinforcements early in the campaign trained on tanks passed by RAC inspectors for issuing to the regiments, but it was quickly found that the tanks were becoming damaged and a pool of training vehicles had to be set up for the use of a specially created training unit.

The pool of replacements was created by new recruits and drafts of trained men taken on by the 2nd ARG from the regiments which took them off strength. Tank crews that were forced to bail out and men who had recovered from wounds also entered the pool prior to joining another unit. The men were then supposed to be taken on by whichever regiment they were sent to. As the first battle casualties began to flow through the 2nd ARG, regiments naturally tried to procure those men originally from their own regiments and rejected others as 'unsuitable', which was against orders and the practice was frowned upon. An exception to this policy was the Guards Armoured Division which drew on its own pool of replacements.

On arrival at the Army Ordnance Depot (AOD) in Normandy, tanks were serviced by a REME AFV (Armoured Fighting Vehicle) servicing detachment unit before delivery to the 2nd ARG. While in the vehicle parks, tanks were exposed to the elements, required servicing and were often damaged in minor collisions. The vehicle parks were designed to hold only 800 vehicles but often had more than 2,000 vehicles on site because of limited space in the small Allied lodgement area and this increased the regular servicing workload and the amount of physical damage to stored vehicles by other moving vehicles.

The tanks shipped from England required servicing before they could be issued to front-line units. This involved the removal of all waterproofing and degreasing, especially the main gun and the machine guns. Tracks had to be tightened up, clutches adjusted where necessary, a radio installed and all communication equipment checked for operation. In some instances, modifications had to be made such as installing an insulated cover for the battery box in Sherman tanks. Additional equipment that the crew needed to operate the tank was then issued to each tank as a kit and included:

- First aid kits
- Binoculars, watches for the crew
- Fire extinguishers
- Spare telescopes
- Water and fuel jerricans
- Gas masks
- Signal lamps
- Verey pistol and flares

Prior to issue, the tanks were inspected by a REME inspection unit and those found to be unfit for battle were sent back for rectification. The tank then had to be fuelled, water and oil checked, and fully loaded with ammunition by the forward delivery squadrons before delivery to the units. From the end of July, vehicles were no longer waterproofed as the beach and harbour unloading facilities had improved. Thus an armoured fighting vehicle ought to reach its user unit fully operational, fully equipped, fully crewed, fuelled and loaded with ammunition.

The tanks suffered mechanical or electrical breakdowns from time to time that required repairs. If the repairs were beyond the crew, the next step was the squadron fitters which came forward in the fighting support echelon. A recovery vehicle was part of this echelon. If a tank needed to be towed or transported off the battlefield, the regimental Light Aid Detachment provided the next level of repairs. The LAD activities included front-line repairs, changing engines and gearboxes, maintaining electrical equipment and recovering vehicles under all kinds of conditions. A large range of spares was carried and basic welding was performed.

Casualties

When an armour-piercing round struck a tank, there was often a resounding clang and a shower of sparks at the point of impact. If it had sufficient kinetic energy to penetrate the armour, the shot would punch a hole in the tank and enter the interior, causing tremendous damage to any flesh and bone in its path. As the shot entered the tank, the armour on the inside around the penetration would spall and break off, showering the inside of the fighting compartment with red hot pieces of metal. These pieces would then ricochet around the tank, hitting ammunition, fuel tanks, electrical cables and crew members. Even if it did not penetrate, a projectile often still caused spalling on the inside from the impact. German 88mm armour-piercing shot and some 75mm rounds had a small burster charge inside the projectile itself that exploded inside the tank after penetration, causing even more lethal fragments to fly through the tank. Allied armour-piercing shot did not have this burster charge (shot was solid) which may have contributed to the tendency for the Sherman tank to catch fire when hit, though this hypothesis does not seem to have ever been tested. A penetration also generated great heat and a pressure wave, which affected the lungs and other organs of the crew.[33]

The Panzerfaust, firing its hollow shaped charges, was a weapon the Allies had not encountered before and the German infantry used them very effectively in the thick hedgerows of the bocage where it was easy to approach a tank unseen. When a tank was hit by a Panzerfaust, the crew were engulfed by a fireball that caused an enormous rise in the interior temperature with a pressure wave pulse that damaged the crew's body organs and hearing. The mixture of hot explosive gases used up all the oxygen in the tank and breathing became very difficult.

With so many metal fragments and hot gases flying around the inside of a tank full of ammunition and combustible fuel, a fire often started which led to a catastrophic explosion. The ammunition would explode, creating bursts of hot gases and flames that shot out of the turret, forming the characteristic black smoke rings that so often marked the loss of another tank in Normandy. A habit of Allied tank crew early in the Normandy campaign of carrying extra ammunition outside of the normal stowage bins may well have contributed to the tendency of Sherman tanks to burn or explode when hit. When this practice was discontinued and stowage bins surrounded by a water jacket were introduced in later Shermans, the tendency to burn was reduced. The effects on the crew of the various agents from an armour-piercing shell included:

- Blast – whole body, ears and lungs
- Spall fragments – penetrations of the body
- Flame – skin and lungs
- Hot gases – lungs
- Light – eyes[34]

The Sherman tank carried a first aid box on the outside of the tank that contained bandages, dressings for burns and morphine which was administered by crude syringes resembling a small toothpaste tube with a needle in it. Ampoules containing chloroform that had to crushed between the teeth were also included. A medical half-track accompanied the support echelons in battle to facilitate the transport of wounded men to the regimental aid post. The removal of the bodies of men out of knocked-out tanks was a particularly gruesome task that the medical team had to perform.

Any tanks being backloaded to workshops in the rear or even England had to be checked for any remaining limbs or organs after some tanks reached England with body parts inside, to the horror of some female drivers.[35] To remove body matter, the insides of the tanks were cleaned with disinfectant, detergent and water; in extreme cases the interior was sprayed with a creosote-based solution which could then be scraped off when hard.

Not all hits by armour-piercing shells penetrated the hull or turret and knocked the tank out. Minor battle damage, such as a broken track or suspension, was categorised as an X casualty (repairable within 24 hours) and could often be fixed by squadron fitters that accompanied the A echelon provided the tank could retire under its own power. More serious damage often required a tow by another tank or the squadron's armoured recovery vehicle after the fighting had ended or at night. Such tanks were repaired by the regiment's Light Aid Detachment which could perform some heavy work including welding. Serious damage was a tank needing 24 hours or more to repair, which was categorised as a Y casualty. If the LAD could not repair the tank, it was transported to the brigade or second line workshops workshops in the rear areas which were also staffed by REME men. The LAD and brigade workshops only replaced assemblies and any vehicle with more severe damage had to be dealt with by a third line workshop.

After a tank had been repaired it could either go straight back to its unit or to the brigade's Forward Delivery Squadron. The delivery squadron was the channel forwards for new or re-worked tanks and for replacement crews. If a tank was knocked out and could not be repaired by first or second line workshops, it was classed as a Z casualty. At the end of August, the additional category Zw was introduced for tank casualties that had been totally destroyed and burnt out.

Repairable knocked-out tanks were collected at corps back loading points, where they were either repaired by a third line corps workshop set up nearby or shipped back to England for repairs. However, the process of shipping tanks back to England took too long and by the end of August, three Advance Base Workshops had been established in Normandy when there were suitable buildings in Caen.

The close range fighting of the bocage meant that many tank casualties were beyond the repair of field workshops and often beyond recovery. As a rough rule of thumb, REME statistics showed that 50 per cent of knocked-out tank casualties were repairable by divisional resources and another 25 per cent had to be backloaded to third or fourth line workshops for long term repair. The remaining 25 per cent were either destroyed or had brewed up and were unrepairable.[36]

The Germans operated a very similar system to the Allies, categorising the damage by the estimated amount of time to repair. Light damage was categorised as that requiring 16 hours or less to repair and included repairs to tracks, the drive train, steering and electrical work that did not require the removal of the gun or turret and was carried out by a battalion workshop. Medium damage requiring the removal of gun, turret or engine estimated to take from 16–60 hours was done at a division workshop. Any work forecast to take longer than 60 hours was done at an army tank workshop or repair battalion and in the severest cases, shipped back to Germany.[37] As the Allies were slowly advancing, they were in most cases in possession of the battlefield which made it very difficult for the Germans to recover knocked out or damaged tanks. If recovery could be done at all, it was done either under fire or at night; often immobilised tanks were towed from the battlefield by other tanks.

Notes

1 WO 165/133 RAC Half yearly progress report no. 7, January–June 1943, TNA

2 PREM 3/427/1 Tank Policy discussion paper, March 1943, TNA

3 War Office Military training pamphlet, no. 41, The Tactical handling of the Armoured division and its components, July 1943, Bovington Museum

4 Buckley, J., *British Armour in the Normandy Campaign 1944* (Oxford, Cass, 2004), p.80

5 Carver, M., *El Alamein* (Ware, Wordsworth, 2000), p.184

6 de Guingand, F., Notes on the Employment of Tanks in support of Infantry in the Battle, 21st Army Group February 1944, LHCMA de Guingand 4/1/7

7 FM17-10 Armoured Force Field Manual US Army, March 1942, NARA

8 Hunnicutt, R.P., *The Sherman – A History of the Medium Tank* (Novato, CA, Presidio, 1978), p.174

9 Taylor, V., *The Armoured Micks 1941–1945* (Irish Guards HQ, 1997) p.27

10 Zaloga, S., *M4 (76mm) Sherman Medium Tank 1943–65* (Oxford, Osprey, 2003), p.13

11 Zaloga, S., *Sherman Medium Tank 1942–45* (Oxford, Osprey, 1993), p.10

12 WO 32/11035 RAC Liaison letter no. 2, September 1944, p.7, TNA

13 Chamberlain, P., and Doyle, H., *Encyclopaedia of German Tanks* (Arms and Armour Press, London, 1993), p.245

14 WO 205/5d, letter Montgomery M507 to Under Secretary for War, 6 July 1944, TNA

15 WO205/5c, letter de Guingand to Montgomery, 26 June 1944, TNA

16 US Army Intelligence bulletin, January 1944, NARA

17 Jackson, Lt-Col G.S., Operations of Eighth Corps, St Clements. London, 1948, p.25

18 Chamberlain, P., and Doyle, H., *Encyclopaedia of German Tanks* (Arms and Armour Press, London, 1993), p.102

19 Harrison Place, T., *Military training in the British Army 1940–1944* (Oxford, Routledge, 2000), p.156

20 Hansard HC Debate, 16 March 1944, vol.398, cc.393–4

21 WO 165/135, Memorandum Montgomery M506 on British Armour, 6 July 1944, TNA

22 WO 165/135, RAC Progress Report no. 9, Montgomery letter to War Office VCIGS, 28 August 1943, TNA

23 Churchill, W., Minute to Tank Board re Minutes of meeting, 23 April 1943, in *The Hinge of Fate: The Second World War, Vol. 4* (London, Cassell, 1951) p.850

24 Bradley, *opcit*, p.322

25 Jackson, *opcit*, p.25

26 Jentz, T., *Panzertruppen Vol. 2* (Atglen, PA, Schiffer Military History, 1996), p.177

27 WO 205/1165 Wright, Capt. H., and Harkness, Capt. R., A Survey of Casualties amongst Armoured Units in NW Europe, p.62, TNA

28 Baker, A.E. Memoirs in Private papers, 1945, IWM document #569

29 Brownlie, Lt-Col W.S., And Came Safe Home, Private papers, 1944, IWM document #2204

30 Ritgen, H., *The Western Front, 1944: Memoirs of a Panzer Lehr Officer* (Manitoba, JJ Fedorowicz, 1995), pp.62–4

31 Graves, D.E., *The South Albertas – A Canadian Regiment at War* (Toronto, Robin Brass Studio, 1998), p.129

32 IWM, Dewar, D., Memoirs in Private Papers, IWM document #3987

33 Owen-Smith, Lt Colonel M.S., Armoured Fighting Vehicle Casualties – Journal Royal Army Medical Corps vol.123, 1977, pp.65–76

34 *Ibid*, p.71

35 Kennett, *opcit*, p.232

36 Kennett, B., and Tatman, J., *Craftsmen of the Army* (Barnsley, Cooper/REME, 1970), p.234

37 WO 171/439, Intelligence summary no 57, part II, 7th Armoured Division G branch, August 1944, TNA

3

Bridgehead Battles

A myth that has persisted over the years is that D–Day was a success largely because of Adolf Hitler being asleep on the morning of D–Day and his orders not to be disturbed resulted in the German counterattacks being delayed. While it is true that Hitler was asleep, the counterattack was deliberately delayed and was due to the success of the Allied deception operation regarding the location of the landings. A convoluted German chain of command in France and Germany also contributed significantly to the confused and uncoordinated counterattacks on D–Day itself. The Seventh Army in Normandy and the Fifteenth Army in the Pas de Calais were part of Army Group B in northern France which was commanded by Field Marshal Rommel. A second Army group, Army Group G, had been set up in May 1944 to defend the south of France. Field Marshal von Rundstedt, as the commander-in-chief of all forces in France, commanded both army groups and reported directly to the OKW (armed forces High Command) in Germany. The training of the panzer divisions in France was the responsibility of Panzer Gruppe West under von Schweppenburg.

Rommel, since assuming command of Army Group B, had disagreed with both von Rundstedt and von Schweppenburg as to how the panzer divisions should be used when the expected landings came. Rommel wanted the reserves to be located close behind the beaches to be able to quickly counterattack when any such assault was at its most vulnerable in the first few hours after landing, before significant numbers had been built up and defences fully established. Von Rundstedt and von Schweppenburg were of a different view and thought that the panzers should be concentrated for a decisive blow when the British intentions were clear and the front line was out of the range of British naval guns. Rommel objected to this strategy on the basis that any movement of the panzer divisions would be subject to interdiction by Allied aircraft which controlled the skies and any delay in attacking would allow the Allies to strengthen their positions in the beachhead. The personalities of Rommel and von Schweppenburg clashed severely and the different strategies were a major topic of discussion amongst the senior Army Group B officers. Von Schweppenburg seems to have been jealous of Rommel's reputation and direct access to Hitler, once describing Rommel as merely 'an experienced tactician'.[1] General Guderian, the inspector general of panzer troops, supported von Schweppenburg, as did von Rundstedt, so Rommel was the only advocate of the strategy of keeping forces near the coast. Von Schweppenburg was bitter that the dispute was never resolved by Hitler and that Rommel was not directed by Hitler to follow OKW orders. Despite personal appeals to Hitler by Rommel, a single strategy was never decided upon by the OKW and the reserve panzer divisions were divided up between the two proponents of the debate. Army Group B under Rommel in March 1944 was allocated the 2nd, 116th and 21st Panzer Divisions. The four other panzer divisions in France, the 17th SS, 12th SS, 1st SS and Panzer Lehr divisions, were designated as a strategic reserve under OKW control and therefore Army Group B could not call on these units without the express authorisation of OKW and Hitler. This compromise by Hitler pleased no one and resulted in the reserves being controlled by himself and OKW, both many miles away from Normandy. In a final kink in the chain of command, the SS panzer divisions in the reserve were trained by Panzer Gruppe West, controlled by OKW and under the control of SS administration offices.

The potential location of the landings was a difficult problem for OKW – the coastline from Brittany to Normandy to Calais had to be defended without any precise knowledge of where the Allies were going to land. There were not enough panzer divisions to locate one on the coast behind every possible landing site, so a mobile reserve had to be maintained.[2] The suggestion by General Markes of LXXXIV Corps of destroying the port of Cherbourg to deter the Allies from even contemplating a landing in Normandy and thus raising the probability of landings at Calais was not taken seriously by Army Group B.

Hitler was still up in the early hours of 6 June when the first reports of Allied parachute landings began to come into the OKW headquarters from Army Group B. Hitler was entertaining Joseph Goebbels and his wife, and was apparently very relieved that the waiting to do battle with the British and Americans appeared to be over. Even more pleasing to Hitler was that the Allied activity was centred on Normandy which he had predicted only six weeks earlier to von Rundstedt, who was convinced the landings would be in the Pas de Calais.[3] Hitler seemed to have completely lost sight of the fact that Germany was already fighting a war on two fronts and the Allied landings would open a third front that would strain Germany's resources to the utmost. Before retiring at about 0300 hours, Hitler left strict instructions that the panzer divisions in the strategic reserve were not to be deployed without his specific authorisation after a reconnaissance later that morning which would provide a better picture of the overall situation. With that, Hitler retired to bed, taking drugs to enable him to sleep.[4] Hitler was not alone in going to sleep; so did Field Marshal Keital at OKW and Hans Speidel (the Chief of Staff to Rommel at Army Group B), as both believed that the paratroops were merely a diversion. Speidel did, however, finally telephone Rommel on leave in Germany at 1015 hours. Von Rundstedt was sufficiently alarmed by the reports coming in to send initial movement orders to the 12th SS Panzer and the Panzer Lehr Divisions at 0400 hours. At the same time, von Rundstedt requested permission from OKW to deploy these strategic reserves and was told in no uncertain terms, in view of Hitler's edict, to cancel his orders. This von Rundstedt duly did, and it is ironic that in view of the dispute between Rommel and von Schweppenburg over the deployment of the reserve, von Rundstedt's first reaction on 6 June was to call for the mobilisation of the panzer divisions before any Allied troops had even landed.

Hitler's adjutant, General Schmundt, and the OKW Chief of Operations, General Jodl, were reluctant to wake Hitler with any news that might turn out to be false and as he was in a drug-induced sleep it was considered dangerous to wake him. Jodl finally convinced Schmundt to awaken Hitler, who appeared, according to different reports, between 0800 and 1000 hours in the Great Hall of the Berghof. The late rise was inconsequential as Hitler was in no hurry to commit the panzer divisions and was apparently optimistic at the news of the landings. 'As long as they were in Britain we couldn't get at them. Now we have them where we can destroy them,' he reportedly told Keitel.[5]

On reviewing the situation on 6 June, there was still great uncertainty amongst the OKW as to whether the Normandy landings were a feint or the real invasion. Jodl believed the landings were a diversion for the real landings to come in the Pas de Calais and even von Rundstedt was convinced the Normandy landings were a feint. OKW had predicted that the invasion would start with a diversionary raid so as to draw away any strategic reserves in the wrong direction. For the last few months, the Germans had also received many reports and pieces of intelligence to the effect that the Allied landings would come in the Pas de Calais. What the Germans failed to realise was that much of what they were receiving was part of a massive Allied deception operation with the objective of convincing the Germans that the real landings would not be in Normandy.

Under the umbrella of Operation Bodyguard, dozens of pieces of false information and diversionary tactics had been deployed by the Allies in separate operations to keep the Germans guessing as to where the real landings would come. Operation Fortitude (South) had the objective of confirming German thinking about the Pas de Calais; in conjunction with this, there were a host of minor operations to further confuse the Germans, such as Fortitude (North), which proposed a landing in Norway followed by a landing in Calais.

In another Allied ploy, an entire fictitious army, the First United States Army Group, had been created under General Patton in the south-east of England to supposedly invade France across the Straits of Dover at Calais. Dummy tanks and landing craft had been set up in Kent and a high level of bogus wireless traffic was constantly transmitted for the benefit of German listening stations. Any movement of troops to the south coast that was observed by German spies in England was interpreted as being part of the build-up of this army. The fictitious army opposite Calais allowed the Allied troops to assemble unnoticed in the south of England for Operation Overlord. Due to the faulty intelligence of the Abwehr, which reported many more divisions than actually existed, the Germans also had a completely inaccurate estimate of the number of army divisions in England. British Intelligence had also completely compromised every German agent being used by the Abwehr in England, to the extent that these agents were being given false information by the British to send back.

In tandem with the failure of intelligence, the Luftwaffe and Kriegsmarine had completely failed to detect the assembly of the invasion fleet in southern England or its passage to France. Before the invasion, the RAF had successfully chased away any Luftwaffe reconnaissance planes from the south coast whilst allowing them passage over south-east England and Patton's 'army'.

On the morning of 6 June, the RAF and Royal Navy had also carried out a number of diversionary operations to further confuse the Germans. Over Normandy, dummies with firecrackers had been dropped by parachute to simulate a small arms firefight and these had subsequently been found by the Germans. The Royal Navy had made attacks on beaches in the Pas de Calais area; six launches made a diversion near Boulogne and eight more near Le Havre. The parachute drops of the American 82nd and 101st Airborne Divisions during the early morning of 6 June had been so scattered by high winds that, although this made their subsequent operations difficult, the dispersal also contributed to the confusion of the Germans.

In Operations Glimmer and Taxable, RAF planes had dropped metal strips (window) to simulate an invasion fleet sailing for the coast of Calais. In the extensive bombing raids in the weeks before D–Day, the RAF had mounted two bombing raids in the Pas de Calais for each one in Normandy so as not to alert the Germans to any special interest in Normandy.[6] Therefore it is not surprising the Germans were not in a hurry to commit themselves to a counterattack without a clearer picture of the landings.

While it was still dark, confusion naturally reigned. From dawn onwards, reports of a massive invasion fleet and a heavy naval and aerial bombardment began to be received. With daylight, more accurate reports were made by the beleaguered coastal divisions to Seventh Army. These units were under no illusions as to the size and scope of the invasion forces that had landed and were now bombarding them. Reconnaissance units from 21st Panzer Division had patrolled south and west of Caen and found nothing. The 12th SS Panzer Division was ordered to send its own reconnaissance units towards the beaches north-west of Caen. An armoured car reached Magny just inland from Arromanches and observed the landings on Gold beach and the naval activity offshore.

With this report, others from Army Group B and even BBC news broadcasts, by 1000 hours the OKW had started to come around to the view that the landings were real, or at least in considerable force. But such was the volume of contradictory evidence and dissension among the OKW generals that Hitler deferred a decision until the afternoon military conference which was further delayed by an hour by the visit of the Hungarian prime minister. The deciding factor for the Germans may well have been the speech by Churchill to the House of Commons at noon announcing the landings.[7]

At about 1430 hours, Hitler finally gave the order for two panzer divisions from the reserves to be released. Even then, the Germans tried to cover the Pas de Calais by leaving the 1st SS Panzer Division in place to support the Fifteenth Army. However, so much time had already elapsed that the panzer divisions would not be in position to attack before the next day at the earliest.

For the Allies, Operation Bodyguard and its associated operations had been so successful that a determined counterattack against the small beachheads was prevented on D-Day. But Operation Bodyguard was not over, for the deception involving the phantom army in England continued to influence German strategy for the next seven weeks.

The 12th SS Panzer Division had moved up to Lisieux but halted after von Rundstedt's early morning order was countermanded. When the order finally came to advance to the coast, the division was aghast at the order which required it to use an unprepared march route when other routes had already been planned, losing more valuable time. In view of the Allied air superiority over Normandy, Panzer Lehr's commander, General Fritz Bayerlein, requested that the march be delayed until darkness but von Rundstedt refused, much to Bayerlein's disgust.[8]

The only panzer unit that counterattacked on D-Day was the 21st Panzer Division, commanded by General Feuchtinger. A Nazi party faithful, the 21st Panzer Division was Feuchtinger's first divisional command and he had no experience in either tank warfare or combat. For these reasons and the fact that Feuchtinger was in Paris on the night of the invasion, he is often blamed for the poor performance of the panzer division on D-Day. However, this performance owes more to the convoluted German chain of command than to any of Feuchtinger's personal attributes or shortcomings. The weather forecast for the Channel and Dutch coast for the night of the 5/6 June had been such that an invasion was deemed 'improbable', and some of the commanders saw an opportunity to take some leave.[9] Feuchtinger was away on leave on 5 and 6 June, but so were Rommel and the commander of the Seventh Army, General Dollmann. Feuchtinger was contacted early in the morning and returned to his command as quickly as possible, arriving before the British landings had begun.

Parts of the 21st Panzer Division were already in action as the 6th Airborne Division had dropped virtually on top of the billets of the 25th Panzergrenadier Regiment east of the River Orne. At 0615 hours, before any Allied troops had landed, 21st Panzer Division was attached to the Seventh Army by Army Group B and given the mission of destroying the British paratroopers to the east of the River Orne. This was as per standing Panzer Gruppe West instructions.[10] On his return from Paris, Feuchtinger protested and requested that his division advance west of the River Orne towards the coast, but this was overruled by Seventh Army.[11] A company of tanks from the 1st Battalion and the reconnaissance battalion was therefore sent towards Bénouville to support the 25th Panzergrenadier Regiment.

As soon as landings in the British sector were confirmed after 0730 hours, the 21st Panzer Division's anti-tank gun battalion, already deployed on the Periers Ridge, and an artillery battalion were subordinated to the 716th Division by Seventh Army and LXXXIV Corps.[12] Feuchtinger's division was therefore deprived of a valuable part of its assets at a critical time by this detachment. General Richter of the 716th Division immediately moved the 88mm guns of the anti-tank gun battalion westwards in response to reports of British tanks inland, thus opening the door for the 185th Brigade and the tanks of the Staffs Yeomanry to penetrate inland later that afternoon in their advance towards Caen.

As reports of the landings were received by LXXXIV Corps, General Markes also became more and more concerned about the size and strength of the British landings in his sector. At 0925 hours, Markes too became a convert to the Rommel strategy and requested the immediate release of the 12th SS Panzer Division to attack west of the River Orne. This was refused as before, so Markes ordered at 1000 hours the only panzer division available to him at that time, the 21st Panzer Division, to attack west of the River Orne.[13] This meant the division's tanks had to turn around and drive back the way they had come through Caen which was under heavy bombardment. There was a delay in Feuchtinger receiving the order and it was not till about 1300 hours that the panzer regiment's tanks were turned around. Once again, Feuchtinger had a decision regarding his division's deployment made for him. Therefore Feuchtinger cannot be held solely responsible for the performance of his division on D-Day. It is easy with hindsight to say that 21st Panzer Division should have attacked vigorously west of the River Orne as a complete unit, but this would have required Feuchtinger to have the initiative to act against orders and to have a clear picture of the Allied landings. Feuchtinger had neither. Nevertheless, with the delays in the British landings, the attack by the 21st Panzer Division at about 1600 hours was enough to prevent the British capture of Caen and some panzergrenadier units did reach the coast in the gap between the British and the Canadians.

Sherbrooke Fusiliers at Buron

The Sherbrooke Fusiliers arrived on Nan White beach at Bernières at 1215 hours on D-Day with twelve Vc tanks (Fireflies), forty Shermans and ten M5 Stuart light tanks. Another six Shermans on two other LSTs did not land until 7 June when they hurried to catch up with the regiment, minus a Sherman and a Stuart that developed mechanical problems. The regiment had been using a squadron organisation of four tanks per troop since training in March 1944. However, each squadron was short a tank, not detailed for arrival until D+8. After many delays, more due to traffic congestion than enemy action, the regiment arrived at its designated assembly point near Bény sur Mer. From there, the regiment advanced to La Mare at dusk when they were forced to harbour without having reached their D-Day objectives.

At dawn on 7 June, the regiment resumed the advance southwards towards Villons les Buissons with the soldiers of the North Nova Scotia (NNS) Highlanders from the 9th Canadian Infantry Brigade mounted on its tanks. The order of advance was:

- Recce troop
- C Company NNS in their carriers
- A Company NNS on A Squadron tanks – right
- B Company NNS on B Squadron tanks – left
- D Company on C Squadron tanks

A Squadron was on the right flank and B Squadron on the left; C Squadron was in the centre on the axis of advance. A troop of Stuart tanks advanced into Buron about 1000 hours and held it for an hour and a half amidst heavy mortar fire and sporadic infantry attacks while waiting for the vanguard of the regiment to arrive. Initial opposition to the advance came from a single anti-tank gun outside Buron but the infantry quickly dealt with this – dismounting from the tanks, they charged the gun position and destroyed it with hand grenades. A small number of German infantry were similarly eliminated by the accompanying infantry and the tanks. The German defenders were a part of a panzergrenadier battalion from the 21st Panzer Division and stragglers from the 716th Division. Nearing Buron, the two squadrons by-passed the village, with the recce troop protecting the left (east) flank. Buron itself was entered and secured at about 1150 hours.[14] The carriers of C Company of the North Nova Scotia Highlanders went on to Authie without armoured support until a number of machine guns opened fire and stopped the advance; heavy mortar and artillery fire was then directed at the Highlanders.

As it advanced past Villons les Buissons, B Squadron opened fire on some half-tracks and supply vehicles in the orchards to the east. After the infantry had dismounted in Buron, the tanks moved to the right of Galmanche to conduct a squadron shoot on some enemy tanks, half-tracks and troops that appeared to be forming up for an attack. The squadron was then hit by heavy and accurate retaliatory artillery fire and a mortar barrage which forced it to retire to the high ground 500yds further north, leaving behind four knocked-out or damaged tanks. Meanwhile, the infantry carried by A Squadron tanks dismounted south of Buron and began digging-in near Gruchy while the tanks proceeded on to Authie and Franqueville. Two tank troops went forward to support C Squadron, already trying to counteract the machine-gun fire holding up the advance of the infantry. Another troop was sent to help B Squadron who at 1410 hours had reported German tanks coming in on the left flank.

The bulk of the 12th SS Panzer Division which had arrived overnight and the 21st Panzer Division were ordered by the 1st SS Panzer Korps to launch an attack at 1600 hours with the aim of breaking through to the coast at Lion sur Mer. The commanders of the 12th SS Panzer Division and 1st SS Panzer Korps met with

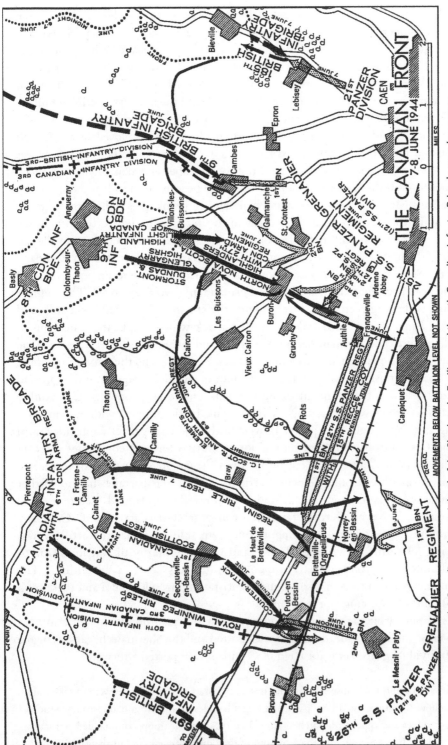

Buron – the Canadian advance inland of the Sherbrooke Fusiliers and the 9th Canadian Infantry Brigade on 7 June 1944, adapted from the *Victory Campaign*.

Feuchtinger at his command post at St Pierre sur Dives at 2000 hours. Kurt Meyer, the commander of the 25th Panzergrenadier Regiment, boasted, 'Little fish! We will throw them back into the sea in the morning!'[15] Only the Mark IV battalion of the 12th SS Panzer Regiment had arrived in time to take part in what would be the division's first action. The battalion had ninety-one Mark IVHs fit on 1 June, but some tanks were left at Elbeuf and did not arrive until the next day. Sturmbannführer Prinz, commander of the battalion, reported to Meyer that approximately fifty tanks had arrived.[16] The tanks and panzergrenadiers were deployed in a v-shaped formation from Franqueville to St Contest for their coming attack and as Meyer watched the Canadian tanks from the tower of the abbey at Ardennes, they advanced further towards the German positions, which had become, by accident, a trap for the Canadians. Meyer ordered the waiting tanks and anti-tank guns to hold their fire.

A Squadron, having pushed on through to Franqueville where they could see their main objective, the airfield at Carpiquet, reported enemy tanks in a valley in front of them. At about 1400 hours, a zug of four Mark IVHs from the 5th Company met the Shermans of A Squadron along the road from Authie to Franqueville, and in the brief firefight that ensued, three German tanks were destroyed. The element of surprise having been lost, Meyer ordered the 5th and 6th Panzer Companies and the 3rd Panzergrenadier Battalion into the attack which caught the Canadians in the left flank. The German tanks opened fire and several Shermans were hit. One troop from A Squadron lost two tanks in quick succession and the remaining Firefly tank took up position in an orchard just south of Authie. C Squadron then moved left to try and outflank the attacking German tanks after dropping off in Authie the soldiers they were carrying. A fierce tank battle erupted with A Squadron being initially caught in a pincer movement by the two panzer companies until B and C squadrons could get into action. The two forward companies of NNS Highlanders in Authie were cut off by the German attack and began to receive so many casualties from a ferocious artillery and mortar barrage that no further advance was possible from Authie and a withdrawal was planned. Before it could commence, however, German tanks and panzergrenadiers arrived.[17] C Company in Authie requested artillery support but were informed that the artillery was moving forward to cover the advance and was temporarily unavailable. Due to communication problems, naval support gunfire was not available either.[18] The Highlanders had a section of 6-pounder anti-tank guns with them and these took a toll on the advancing German tanks.

As C Squadron took over the advance from B Squadron on the left flank, an anti-tank gun screen ahead of them was spotted and the Shermans began to engage the individual guns. Sergeant Reid of C Squadron reported afterwards:

> Mr MacLean quickly dispersed us and instructed us as to the guns we were to take out.
> I believe the gun crew on my particular target had deserted their gun, however, we took
> no chances and quickly dispatched same. The B Squadron troop, commanded as I later
> found out by Lt Steeves and the reminder of the tanks were taking out their guns when

suddenly, out of the blue we got it. I felt a jolt in my tank, looked back and found my blanket box shot through. The next shot unseated my loader/operator, Trooper Galley, and then I saw what was hitting us. There were 18 hornets lined up in hull down positions about 2500 yards away and they had us cold; their third round went through my engine and quickly after that they struck Lt MacLean's and Lt Steeves' almost simultaneously.[19]

All available Shermans from B and C squadrons were ordered forward to meet the German tanks and assist the NNS. After regrouping, B Squadron had ten operational tanks left and at about 1400 hours the squadron moved off towards Authie with a troop of four tanks covering the left flank, only to run into the same hull-down German tanks. Lieutenant Davies of B Squadron reported afterwards:

I found myself all alone with about seven or eight enemy tanks at 1000 yards on my left. I halted, stopped two of them with the 17 pounder, advanced, halted and fired again, scoring another hit, then all Hell seemed to break loose. There were tanks coming up at full speed to my rear (our own), tanks to my left firing at us, A/T blazing away from our left and rear, and tracer and 75mm gun flashes all over the place. I moved forward again, apparently to a hull down position which turned out to be a bottle neck as it was practically a tank trap in an orchard, huge logs barred our way. Tanks were hit and burning all around us by then and it was impossible to keep track of who was who, one was hit directly in front of me, one right beside me, 88mm tracer was cutting down trees all over the place so I decided to withdraw what was left of no. 2 and no. 3 troops. Number 1 troop had meanwhile stood to and covered our flank but had left themselves open by doing so and Lt Steeves' tank went up in flames a couple of hundred yards away.[20]

The advance of the Nos 2, 3 and 4 Troops from C Squadron to the left of Authie was stopped in its tracks. Sergeant Thompson in No. 4 Troop described the situation:

We started for the woods and the next time I looked around, I seen five of our tanks on fire, two from no. 3 troop, one from B Squadron and two recce tanks. While we were trying to take cover a tank came from behind the hedge running wild with no one showing out of it and was making straight for my tank, we pulled hard right and ran up on a stump and near upset the tank and was held there solid. We all got out of the tank where several more tanks were and this tank from B Squadron pulled up and stopped. When they got out I asked them what was wrong, they told me their commander had been badly hurt, they put him out on the ground then went on but none of them would take over as commander. We then all sat around there when one tank started back for Buron and just as he passed the hedge he was hit and the tank caught on fire, I do not know who it was. We then all sat around under the tank as the enemy were shelling us. After it stopped, Sgt Cathcart hauled my tank off the stump and we started back. There were several wounded and they started back, before that some were badly burned, one officer Mr Kraus had a broken leg and his gunner had been killed but did not get out of the tank.[21]

As the casualties amongst the tanks and crew members increased, the surviving troop leaders of the different squadrons gathered together their surviving tanks and made a rapid retreat back past Buron to where D Company of the NNS had prepared hastily dug trenches between Buron and Les Buissons.

The heavy German artillery fire appeared to be coming from the direction of St Contest to the east, so the CO of the Sherbrooke Fusiliers then ordered C Squadron to assist B Squadron on the left flank in order to reduce or eliminate it. As the C Squadron troops were already committed, only the three tanks of squadron HQ were available, reinforced by a tank that had just come up from the beach. The troop moved to near St Contest and engaged the advancing German tanks, knocking out two from the 7th Panzer Company supporting a battalion of panzergrenadiers and causing a third to retreat. The panzergrenadier battalion commander was decapitated by a shell from one of the Shermans before they were forced to withdraw by the remaining Mark IVs.[22] The German commanders watched the Canadian tanks, infantry and carriers streaming back from Authie in full retreat.

Two waves of German infantry supported by tanks then attacked at 1830 hours and Buron was reoccupied. Those Highlanders that were able to moved back to hastily prepared positions just south of Les Buissons where the remnants of the Sherbrooke Fusiliers (twelve tanks) moved back to support them. The defensive position of the Highlanders just north of Buron was overrun by Germans charging with fixed bayonets and only a counterattack by the remaining twelve tanks and heavy artillery fire restored the situation. The panzergrenadiers retreated back to Buron as both sides subjected each other to heavy shelling and mortar fire. The attack by the 12th SS Panzer Division was then called off by the 1st SS Panzer Korps in order to conserve forces for subsequent counterattacks. Buron was recaptured by the Canadians but there were insufficient men left in the NNS Regiment to hold the position overnight, so a withdrawal was made to Villons les Buissons.

The Sherbrooke Fusiliers had requested reinforcements, but Brigadier Wyman of 2nd Canadian Armoured Brigade ordered the regiment to hold its positions while putting the Fort Garry Horse on alert to move if necessary. Wyman finally decided the situation was in hand and no reinforcements were sent; the Highlanders were not assisted during the afternoon by the other two infantry battalions in the 9th Infantry Brigade either.

In what was the first action of both German and Canadian units, the honours were shared as the tank losses for both were similar. The Canadians claimed thirty-three German tanks destroyed plus five probables. In the 12th SS Panzer Division, the 6th Company lost five Mark IVHs but destroyed more than ten Shermans.[23] Only five tanks from the 8th Company arrived to support the 1st Battalion of the 25th Panzergrenadier Regiment in its attack towards Cambes, but one broke down and the other four were damaged or disabled. The 12th SS Panzer Division reported thirteen Mark IVs lost and nearly twenty damaged.[24]

For their part, Sherbrooke casualties were greater than admitted to by the war diary for 7 June, which reported the loss of only fifteen tanks. The post-war regimental history states that twenty-one cruisers tanks were destroyed plus seven others damaged.[25] The war diary does give casualties in a later appendix as a total of twenty-five Shermans, including six Fireflies destroyed or abandoned, with four more lost due to mechanical breakdowns. Two M5 Stuart tanks were also written off. The regiment had thirteen men killed, twenty-seven wounded and twenty-one were missing.

The advance of the 9th Canadian Brigade to Carpiquet had been repulsed with heavy losses. While not a planned ambush, the Germans had the advantage of visibility of the battlefield from the abbey and redeployed their forces accordingly. Despite this, the Canadians were able to inflict enough casualties on the Germans for their attack to the coast to be halted. Most casualties were to the NNS Highlanders: only thirty-five men came back from A and C companies and eighty-four men were killed, thirty wounded and 128 taken prisoner.[26]

The failure of the 21st Panzer Division to join the assault by the half-strength 12th SS Panzer Division, in what was a significant opportunity for the Germans to counterattack, was the main cause of the attack being stopped. Meyer and Feuchtinger blamed each other in post-war accounts and the reasons for the apparent reluctance of Feuchtinger to become involved are not clear.

Given the Canadian advance straight into his positions, Meyer had no option but to give battle. Meyer claims that he briefed Feuchtinger on the situation before requesting support, but whether this was done by radio or dispatch rider is not specified by Meyer.[27] In turn, Feuchtinger claimed that insufficient forces from the 12th SS Panzer Division had assembled in time for the attack. Only one panzergrenadier battalion had established contact as planned with the left wing of the 21st Panzer Division and then only at 1600 hours, more than 2 hours after the fighting began. Feuchtinger also claimed that, when contact was made at Epron, the panzergrenadiers were too exhausted to continue the attack and that there was no 12th SS artillery in position to support the attack.[28] The last is certainly not true, as there was at least one heavy artillery battalion involved in the action which caused many casualties amongst the Highlanders in Authie and Buron.[29] Meyer stated that the attack by his forces was stopped when they ran out of fuel but Feuchtinger refuted this, claiming he had plenty of fuel if Meyer needed it.[30] Meyer later stated that the attack was halted because of the advance to Bretteville of other Canadian units past his left flank.[31]

The reality was that the 21st Panzer Division was tied down in the fighting both sides of the River Orne that day and was unable to disengage and join any counterattack.[32] The elements of the division were dispersed with some units fighting east of the River Orne, some blocking the path to Caen and others attached to the almost destroyed 716th Division. The division's Kampfgruppen Rauch and Oppeln that had counterattacked on D-Day were forced on the defensive by the continued British armoured attacks near Lebisey.[33] The D-Day counterattack had also given Feuchtinger a healthy respect for Allied anti-tank guns, and he later remarked that his Mark IV tanks had been knocked out from 2,000m range and that the Mark IVs could not get even close to the British tanks.[34]

German Counterattacks

The attempted counterattacks by the panzer divisions in the first week of the invasion were hampered for the first time by the problems that would continue to dog their operations throughout the Normandy campaign. These were the Allied dominance of the air, which delayed the arrival of reinforcements, and the lack of mobility of their own infantry divisions, which prevented them from being able to rapidly relieve panzer divisions already committed in the front line so as to free them up for an attack. In addition to these fundamental difficulties, the problem of the convoluted chain of command, which affected the operations of the 21st Panzer Division so much on D-Day, would continue to plague German operations for the next four weeks.

However, the first week of the campaign was the most vital in terms of the need for a successful German counterattack against the Allied beachheads then at their most vulnerable. Seventh Army believed that no matter which strategy was followed, Rommel or von Schweppenburg's, a decisive counterattack had to be made within three to four days of the landings.[35]

Having finally been given their mobilisation orders, Panzer Lehr and the 12th SS Panzer Divisions commenced their approach marches to Caen but were set upon by Allied fighter-bombers and their progress to the front line severely delayed. At 1507 hours on 6 June, all three panzer divisions had been subordinated to the 1st SS Panzer Korps which was commanded by Sepp Dietrich who had risen through the ranks of the SS from being Hitler's bodyguard in the early 1930s. Although having seen action in Poland and Russia, Dietrich was more of a leader of men in battle rather than a tactician and was not regarded as an intellectual by von Rundstedt.[36] In recognition of this weakness, Panzer Gruppe West under von Schweppenburg was given control of the panzer divisions on 7 June to co-ordinate their actions. However, von Schweppenburg did not arrive until the evening of 8 June and until then the counterattacks were Dietrich's responsibility, supported by Rommel. The three panzer divisions were then subject to the control and orders of six higher commands: the 1st SS Panzer Korps, Seventh Army, Panzer Gruppe West, Army Group B (Rommel), von Rundstedt (C-in-C West) and the OKW in Germany; this did not make for clear lines of command and control.

The 12th SS Panzer Division only had one of its panzer battalions and one panzer-grenadier regiment for the attack on 7 June as the division's movement to the front line had been delayed by Allied aircraft and preparations for the counterattack at 1600 hours were interrupted by the Canadian advance to Buron. Whilst the 12th SS Panzer Division was entering the battle, the Panzer Lehr Division was only at Thury Harcourt, having been delayed at a bridge over the River Orne that had been damaged by British aircraft.

Another problem faced by the Germans was the disruption of their communications networks, again by Allied aircraft. Towns at regional hubs in Normandy such as Argentan, Caen, St Lô and Caumont had all been heavily bombed, damaging the telephone connections between units. Wireless communication was often difficult as the radio cars of front-line units were harassed by Allied fighter-bombers and identified headquarters were shelled by naval guns and artillery. Panzer Lehr had difficulty even locating the 1st SS Panzer Korps headquarters on 7 June after the death of a liaison officer carrying codes to the division. When Bayerlein finally met up with Dietrich, plans were issued by the 1st SS Panzer Korps for a renewed attack next day by the 21st and 12th SS Panzer Divisions aimed at the coast at Courseulles via Bretteville. Panzer Lehr was to follow up as soon as it arrived.

Some forward elements of the Panzer Lehr arrived at their assembly area near Bronay at dawn on 8 June to find units of the 12th SS already there so they were forced to withdraw. The northernmost part of the assembly area was also held by the Canadians, further adding to the early morning confusion. This situation was the result of poor staff work by the 1st SS Panzer Korps, a rapidly changing situation on the ground and the failure of communications. It is possible that the two panzergrenadier regiments of the 12th SS were supposed to shift their positions to the right before the attack to close a gap between them and the 21st Panzer Division but did not receive their orders, although no evidence has been found of this.[37]

The newly arrived 26th Panzergrenadier Regiment began its attack in the early hours of 8 June without any armoured support from the Panther tank battalion which had again been delayed by Allied aircraft. Putot was captured briefly from the Canadians, who were overrun, but the situation was restored by the Canadian Scottish Regiment, assisted by artillery and the tanks of the 1st Hussars. Bronay was occupied by the 2nd Battalion of 902nd Panzergrenadiers of Panzer Lehr, who were subjected to naval gunfire:

> Here we encountered the most terrible image of war. The enemy had virtually cut to pieces units of Panzer Lehr Division with heavy weapons. Armoured personnel carriers and equipment had been ripped apart and next to them on the ground, even hanging from trees, were body parts of dead comrades. A terrible silence covered all.[38]

As Panzer Lehr fought for its jumping off positions for the attack and waited for its tank battalions to arrive, Rommel drove to Bayerlein's command post and ordered the attack to stop and for the division to shift its position in preparation for an attack next day on Bayeux. The Seventh Army had ordered the 1st SS Panzer Korps to carry out this attack, much to the incredulity of its Chief of Staff, who complained after the war that the Seventh Army expected an attack to be made by panzer divisions without understanding that they were already engaged holding together the front line in support of the badly mauled infantry divisions.[39]

To emphasise the apparent remoteness of Seventh Army and the communication problems, General Dollman had to go to the command post of 1st SS Panzer Korps on 8 June to inform himself first-hand about the situation as, according to the Seventh Army war diary for 8 June, no counterattacks had apparently taken place.[40]

That evening, the first two companies of the Panther tank battalion of the 12th SS Panzer Division finally arrived on the battlefield and an attack was made on Bretteville L'Orgueilleuse after dark by the tanks and a company of motorcycle infantry mounted on them. The Panthers ran into a 6-pounder anti-tank gun screen and many tanks were knocked out and caught fire. The mounted infantry immediately went to ground and the Panthers rashly carried on the attack directly into Bretteville without their support. The infantry and anti-tank guns of the Regina Rifles were able to knock out five Panther tanks, including several at close range that had penetrated into Bretteville as far as the battalion command post.

Panzer Gruppe West assumed command of the panzer divisions on the evening of 8 June and von Schweppenburg visited the command posts of each division.[41] Either von Schweppenburg was not told of the proposed attack next day by Panzer Lehr or it was permitted to go ahead as its tank battalions were finally due to arrive overnight. Panzer Lehr duly attacked towards Bayeux on 9 June but was still missing its Panther battalion. The plan of attack was to employ the 901st Panzergrenadier Regiment, reinforced by an anti-tank battalion on the right flank and the Mark IV Battalion plus the 1st Battalion of the 902nd Panzergrenadier Regiment on the left flank. The reconnaissance battalion was to secure the left flank from Ellon to Trungy. However, at the last minute, the 901st Panzergrenadier Regiment had to be diverted to defend Tilly and so less than half the division started the counterattack which got as far as Ellon when it was ordered to halt by the 1st SS Panzer Korps. The division was redirected eastwards to go on the defensive against the British 50th Division driving on Tilly and Point 103. On the way back to Tilly, the tanks of the division were forced to travel along a narrow stretch of open ground between two woods and here the division was again hit by fire from naval guns, artillery and anti-tank guns as the British advance had reached the northern outskirts of Tilly. Von Schweppenburg at Panzer Gruppe West was apparently not informed by Rommel either of this decision to switch to the defensive.

12th SS Norrey, 9 June

The Forward Delivery Squadron for the 2nd Canadian Armoured Brigade (C Squadron, Elgin Regiment) landed in Normandy at 0500 hours on 8 June and immediately moved inland to link up with the brigade. The squadron was supposed to have thirty-one Sherman tanks for the three regiments but was forced to cannabalise two tanks before departing England just to ensure that the remaining twenty-nine were operational.[42] On learning of the brigade's D-Day losses, eight tanks under the command of Major C. Tweedale were sent ahead to the 1st Hussars, arriving at C Squadron later that day. Although the reinforcement tanks came from three different regiments, under the reinforcement system of the 2nd ARG the reinforcements were to be taken on strength by whichever regiment needed them. In this instance, seven of the tanks were crewed by men from the Fort Garry Horse and even though these crews were originally part of, and had trained with, the Garrys, on 8 June they became Hussars. On 9 June, the now overstrength C Squadron (six troops instead of five) was ordered to support an attack on Bretteville l'Orgueilleuse and Norrey by the Regina Regiment. After seeing the infantry into Bretteville, the tanks proceeded further south to shoot up Norrey with their machine guns.

That afternoon, the twelve Panthers of the 3rd Company that had not been involved in the previous night's action at Bretteville L'Orgueilleuse were ordered to attack towards Norrey. After using an underpass to cross the railway line south of the village, the company commander ordered the tanks to swing left so as to present the thick frontal armour of the Panthers toward Norrey. The five tanks of the third section hugging the railway embankment were forced to speed past the second section in order to keep a straight line of tanks facing Norrey. The four tanks of the first section had by this point slowed to form a reserve. Unfortunately for the 3rd Company tanks, this turn, though protecting them from the 6-pounders in Norrey, exposed their flanks to the advancing C Squadron Shermans which spotted them first. The Shermans deployed in a line and opened fire at less than 1,000m range. A Firefly commanded by Lieutenant Henry hit the tank nearest the rail-line first. Adolf Morawetz was commanding a Panther tank:

> At that moment after a muffled bang and a swaying as if the track had been ripped off, the vehicle came to a stop.
>
> It was quiet inside the tank. I thought we had driven onto a mine. When I looked to the left to check the situation, I happened to see the turret torn off the panzer driving on the left flank. At the same moment after another minor explosion my vehicle began to burn. The machine gun ammunition caught on fire and there was a crackling like dry wood burning. Since we were to push into Norrey, I had closed the hatch moments before. I tried, without success to open the turret hatch. I could only lift it with the spindle but could not swing it out. Paul Veith, the gunner sitting in front of me had apparently been seriously injured by fragments from the hit. Veith did not move. I tried for a long time with all my strength to swing out the hatch. I was only successful when I tried different height settings on the lift crank. It had probably been damaged by the hit. I jumped out, fell on the rear and was unconscious for a short time. Then I saw flames coming out of the open hatch as if from a blow torch. I got up and tried to jump off the tank. However I could not keep my balance and landed head first on the ground. I do not know how long I lay there. Then I got to my feet and saw to my left along the same line as my tank, other burning panzers.[43]

Veith did not get out of the Panther, and seven others were quickly dispatched in the next 4 minutes. Major Tweedale recorded the incident:

> We were busily 'brassing up' Norrey en Bessin, and an ammo train at the station (cross fire with co-ax etc in a good hull down position), when I noticed a hell of a big tank with a long gun pass our front about 900 yards away and going at a good speed. We

called up and told the right troops about it. When lo and behold, six 'Panthers' came up to the crest in orderly fashion and slowly, about 850-1050 yds range. We let them have it and knocked out the six without them firing a shot at us or traversing their guns in our direction. We thought there were only five but found we had knocked out six on later inspection. The right troops got the lead tank, which no doubt a lot of the Regiment saw on the road between Bretteville and Norrey; our Garry tanks accounted for three. We later found a company of Regina Rifles had been isolated out there and over-run; these men were saved by our action. Also four more Panthers were there but did not come into view and retired with the loss of the one tank commander, picked off by the company commander's batman who could not resist the temptation, even though the whole company had been told to lie low in their weapons slits. So there you have an action where nine Shermans took on eleven Panthers, knocked out seven and routed four without loss from a range as stated above (Lt Henry of the 1st Hussars had a 17 pr). The crew commanders I can remember were Sgt Graham and Sgt Chadioisky. My gunner was Tpr Bennett and loader Tpr Argue; the boys of the other tanks claimed Bennett and Argue got off three rounds before any of the others fired. Bennett's first shot from his tank knocked out a Panther at 850 yards, the second shot missed the tank aimed at and hit another, it exploded and blew off the turret.[44]

Trooper A. Chapman, the gunner in Lieutenant Henry's Firefly, established a bridge-head record of sorts – when the six Panther tanks appeared, he held his fire until all were visible and then fired five times, knocking out five Panthers with five rounds. A sixth Panther became the victim of a tank commanded by Sergeant Boyle.[45] Chapman's record was made possible by distracting HE fire, provided by other tanks at the crucial moment, and the Germans did not detect the presence of the C Squadron tanks until too late, not even managing to traverse their turrets to return the fire.

While there is a discrepancy in the accounts, it is possible that some Panther tanks were hit more than once. In the 3rd Company, fifteen men were killed and nearly all the other crew members were wounded or burnt. The few survivors, including the wounded, bailed out of their destroyed tanks and fled back towards the underpass as an artillery barrage began to pound the area. The attack by the panzergrenadiers preparing to assault Norrey with the Panthers had been stopped cold, as had the other attacks over the previous 24 hours by the 12th SS Panzer Division.

The first Panzer Lehr Panthers did not arrive until 10 June. Kurt Meyer met with von Schweppenburg after the failed attacks on Norrey and Bretteville and explained the impossibility of capturing the fortified villages from the Canadians who were strongly supported from the air and by artillery. According to Meyer, von Schweppenburg looked at him quickly and said, 'My dear Herr Meyer, the war can now only be won by the politicians.'[46]

Having assumed control of the three panzer divisions, Panzer Gruppe West planned for a major counterattack by the 1st SS Panzer Korps during the night of 10/11 June so as to negate the effects of Allied observed artillery and naval gunfire. However, the location of von Schweppenburg's staff headquarters in a château at La Caine was revealed to the British in an Ultra decrypt and the château was attacked by Typhoons and Mitchell bombers, killing most of the Panzer Gruppe West staff and rendering it incapable of functioning.[47] The proposed attack had to be cancelled and the Seventh Army made a transition to defence all along its Normandy front in anticipation of the arrival of more reinforcements in the form of the 2nd SS Panzer Korps from Russia. The control of the panzer divisions was returned to the 1st SS Panzer Korps.

After only a week of fighting, the strengths of the three panzer divisions had been severely reduced and no massed counterattack had been made against the Allied beachheads. The activities of Allied aircraft had not only delayed their arrival at the front line but also caused shortages of fuel and ammunition by preying on the vehicles of the rear echelons. The Germans were forced to commit the panzer divisions in a piecemeal fashion as soon as they arrived to either meet a Canadian or British advance or to mount a limited counterattack towards the landing beaches. Both the 12th SS and the Panzer Lehr divisions were flung into battle hastily and the attacks were then called off, wasting scarce resources such as men, tanks, fuel and ammunition. The result was that the divisions were not committed fully assembled and, despite temporarily halting the Canadian advances, any counterattack was insufficient in strength to break through to the coast. Once committed to the fighting, the panzer divisions, especially the 21st Panzer Division, found it very difficult to disengage as they were blocking British breakthrough attempts and preventing the whole front line from collapsing. German infantry divisions did not have the mobility for rapid deployment and their movement was further hampered by Allied aircraft. The German forces were severely handicapped by the absence of the Luftwaffe due to the Allied air supremacy. The Luftwaffe could not during the day provide cover for the troops on the ground, interfere with the Allied build-up on the beaches, chase observation aircraft away or even provide reconnaissance information on the troops being landed in Normandy.

Hanging over the German High Command was the threat of further landings in the Pas de Calais which prevented the transfer from that area of any infantry divisions and initially the 1st SS Panzer Division. Had the 1st SS Panzer Division been moved to Normandy early on then it could have heavily influenced the outcome of the fighting there.

For the 12th SS Panzer Division, it was a week of mixed fortune. Having beaten off the attack at Buron, the division suffered from being committed piecemeal and straight off the march without adequate reconnaissance. Other assaults, such as the attacks on Bretteville at night and Norrey by unsupported tanks, 'leave the impression of rather hasty and ineffective improvisation. The attacks were pressed with courage and determination but with no particular skill.'[48] The same can be said for the operations of the 2nd Canadian Armoured Brigade, such as at Buron and Le Mesnil Patry where hastily mounted attacks and insufficient reconnaissance resulted in heavy losses. It was the first time in action for both units, however, and both were determined to be successful. After the battle at Le Mesnil Patry on 11 June (see following chapter), General Simonds of the 2nd Canadian Corps told the Hussars that their action had thwarted a counterattack by a panzer division:

While the battle yesterday seemed futile, it actually put a panzer division on skids, thereby saving 7CIB from being cut-off and in the broader picture it helped British 7th Armoured Division to advance on our right flank.[49]

This was not strictly true as the panzer attack had already been cancelled by the Germans in response to the destruction of Panzer Gruppe West. What is certain is that it was the efforts and sacrifices of the men of the Canadian 3rd Division and the 2nd Armoured brigade around Bretteville, Putot and Norrey that consistently blocked the attacks of the 12th SS Panzer Division in its weak attempts to break through to the sea during the first week after D-Day. The conversation between Meyer and von Schweppenburg on 9 June would be prophetic regarding the outcome of the Normandy campaign for the Germans. The tank battles in the first week also demonstrated both the vulnerability of the M4 Sherman to the German high velocity 75mm and 88mm anti-tank guns and the ability of the Sherman Firefly to match the firepower of the Panther tank. The British decision to mount the 17-pounder anti-tank gun in the Sherman was beginning to pay dividends.

The 11th of June marked the end of the opening phase for the Allies with their two armies, the British Second Army and FUSA, well established ashore in Normandy. Not a single threatening counterattack had been made by the feared German panzer divisions. With the closure of the gap between Omaha and Utah on 10 June, the separate bridgeheads of D-Day now formed a continuous lodgement all along the front. The construction of the artificial harbours, at Arromanches in the British sector and St Laurent in the American sector, was well advanced and Allied aircraft could now operate from temporary airstrips in France to give them longer flying time over the battlefield. Churchill was so confident of the outcome of the Normandy campaign that the British Cabinet had already drawn up a draft of the instrument of German surrender.[50] Montgomery signalled the CIGS with his intention to 'pull the Germans onto 2nd Army so that 1st Army can extend and expand'.[51]

Although intended to achieve the original D-Day objectives, the armoured thrusts inland by the Canadians and British in fact served to keep the Germans off-balance and forced the commitment of the panzer divisions. As the attacks continued to be unsuccessful around Caen and Tilly, Montgomery then shifted his attention further west to Villers Bocage in order to capture Caen by the back door.

Notes

1 FMS B-258 von Schweppenburg History of Panzer Gruppe West, NARA, p.8
2 Meyer, H., *The 12th SS – the History of the Hitler Youth Panzer Division Volume 1* (Mechanicsburg, Stackpole, 2009), p.41
3 Shulman, M., *Defeat in the West* (London, Secker and Warburg, 1947), p.96
4 Wilmot, C., *The Second World War – the Struggle for Europe* (London, Collins, 1952), p.269
5 Irving, D., *Hitler's War* (London, Focal Point, 2002), p.682

6 Ellis, Major L.F., *Victory in the West Volume 1: The Battle of Normandy* (London, HMSO, 1962), p.103

7 RG319 FMS B-284, Blumentritt OB West, 6 June–24 July, NARA

8 RG319 FMS B-258, von Schweppenburg, *opcit*

9 CMHQ Report no. 50 Canadian Directorate of History and Heritage, Ottawa, p.8

10 RG319 FMS B-466, von Schweppenburg Panzer Gruppe West June–July 1944, NARA

11 RG319 FMS B 258, von Schweppenburg, *opcit*

12 RG319 FMS B-441, Feuchtinger – 21st Panzer Division on D-Day, NARA

13 *Ibid*, p.21

14 CMHQ Report no. 54, Canadian Directorate of History and Heritage, Ottawa

15 Shulman, M., *opcit*, p.105

16 Meyer, H., *opcit*, p.139

17 CMHQ report, no. 54, *opcit*

18 RG24 vol 15122 War diary North Nova Scotia Highlanders, 7 June 1944, LAC

19 RG24 vol 14287 War diary Sherbrooke Fusiliers, June 1944, Appendix A, C sqdn account, LAC

20 *Ibid*, Appendix A, B sqdn account

21 *Ibid*, Appendix A, C sqdn account

22 Stacey, C.P., *The Victory Campaign, Operations in North West Europe 1944–1945* (Ottawa, DHH, 1960), p.132

23 Meyer, H., *opcit*, p.141

24 Szamveber, N., *Waffen SS Armour in Normandy – the Combat History of the SS Panzer Regiment 12* (Solihull, Helion, 2012), p.41

25 Jackson, H.M., *The Sherbrooke Regiment* (Montreal, Christian Bros, 1958), p.126

26 CMHQ report no. 54, *opcit*

27 Meyer, K., *Grenadiers* (Mechanicsburg, PA, Stackpole, 2005) p.223

28 RG319 FMS B-441, Feuchtinger, *opcit*

29 Meyer, H., *opcit*, p.138

30 Special Interrogation Report Kurt Meyer, *Canadian Military History*, vol.11, no.4, Autumn 2002, pp.59–70

31 Meyer, K., *opcit*, p.226

32 RG319 FMS C-024 Kraemer, 1st SS Panzer Korps in the West, p.20, NARA

33 Ritgen, H., *The Western Front, 1944: Memoirs of a Panzer Lehr Officer* (Manitoba, JJ Fedorowicz, 1995), p.37

34 RG319 FMS B-441, Feuchtinger, *opcit*

35 RG319 FMSB-234, Pemsel, M., The Seventh Army Pre Invasion, NARA

36 Shulman, M., *opcit*, p.104

37 Meyer, H., *opcit*, p.163

38 Meyer, H., *opcit*, p.170

39 RG319 FMS C-024, Kraemer, *opcit*, p.24

40 Ritgen, *opcit*, p.40

41 RG319 FMS B-466, von Schweppenburg, *opcit*, p.24

42 Anon, *Vanguard. The Fort Garry Horse in the Second World War*, p.124

43 Meyer, H. *opcit*, p.190

44 *Ibid*, pp.126–7

45 Stark, F.M., *History of the 1st Hussars Regiment 1856–1945* (London, Ontario, 1951), p.66

46 Meyer, K., *opcit*, p.231

47 Ellis, *opcit*, p.258

48 Stacey, *opcit*, p.137

49 Stark, *opcit*, p.74

50 CAB 66/51/15, Draft Instrument Surrender, 10 June 1944, TNA

51 WO 205-5b, Signal M14 Montgomery to CIGS, 11 June 1944, TNA

4

Operation Perch – Villers Bocage

As the Germans were present in force along the direct route from the coast to Caen and had successfully defeated all attacks in that direction, Montgomery decided on an enveloping operation around the city using the veteran divisions that had served under him in North Africa. The operation was to commence on 10 June and was codenamed Operation Wild Oats. The eastern pincer would be created by the 51st (Highland) Division passing through the small bridgehead over the River Orne and striking south for Cagny. In the west, the 7th Armoured Division of XXX Corps, commanded by Lieutenant-General Bucknall, would make an armoured thrust through Villers Bocage and Noyers before crossing the River Odon and capturing the high ground near Evrecy. The 1st British Airborne Division would then be dropped into the gap between Cagny and Evrecy to complete the encirclement of Caen.[1] However, Air Marshal Leigh-Mallory was not keen on this use of airborne troops as he thought their numbers would be insufficient to hold off the inevitable counterattack by the Germans. Montgomery was not pleased by what he perceived as a lack of support but the plans were amended and the revised operation renamed Operation Perch. Supporting attacks were to be made simultaneously by the 2nd Canadian Armoured Brigade to the high ground around Cheux via Le Mesnil Patry and by the 8th Armoured Brigade to Cristot in order to keep pressure on the Germans and protect the flank of the western pincer.

In the east, the attack by the 51st (H) Division and the supporting 4th Armoured Brigade was delayed for two days as the infantry could not assemble in the bridge-head on time due to the fighting in progress between the 6th Airborne Division holding the bridgehead and the German 346th Division attacking to eliminate it. Once the paratroopers' front line was stabilised by the capture of Bréville on 12 June, the infantry brigades of the 51st (H) Division began their attack on 13 June only to be met and held by Kampfgruppe Luck of the 21st Panzer Division near Cuverville. As the infantry casualty rate rose, any further attempts to expand the bridgehead in the east were discontinued.

The other arm of the pincer began its attack on 10 June with the intention of 7th Armoured Division advancing through the 50th Division to Hottot and Tilly initially before exploiting further southwards. The 131st Brigade of the 7th Armoured Division had only just landed in Normandy and was unavailable, so the 56th Brigade (an independent brigade) was attached; the 56th Brigade and the 1st Rifle Brigade were the only infantry support for the tanks. The 8th Armoured Brigade was also part of the offensive and was tasked with the capture of Lingèvres as well as supporting the 7th Armoured Division. Opposing XXX Corps was the Panzer Lehr Division.

The small fields and high hedges of the bocage were unfamiliar to the men of the 7th Armoured Division who were also using their new Cromwell tanks in battle for the first time. They were about as far away from the deserts of North Africa as they could get. The sunken roads and hedges restricted the tank commander's visibility and any commander with his head out of the cupola was vulnerable to sniper fire.

The initial advance was slowed by pockets of Lehr panzergrenadiers, supported by single tanks or anti-tank guns which used the terrain skilfully to repeatedly ambush the tanks as they advanced without any infantry. A troop of 5th RTR tanks stumbled into a German tank harbour and knocked out a Mark IV. The regiment later lost two Cromwells to a Panther tank in Berniere Bocage.[2]

The 4th County of London Yeomanry (4th CLY) also lost two tanks to friendly fire from the tanks of the 8th Armoured Brigade, but C Squadron did knock out a Mark IV tank, losing three Cromwells and a Stuart recce tank on the first day.[3] The 7th Armoured Division advanced only 6 miles the whole day and lost a total of six tanks.

For the following day, 11 June, units were reorganised to create two mixed forces of tanks and infantry to better cope with the bocage countryside but this first experiment was not that successful. The 4th CLY were attached to the 56th Brigade, with which they had never worked before, and in any case, the tank regiments were not well trained in combined operations. Despite a need for more infantry in the difficult country, the tanks tended to forge on ahead unsupported. The 5th RTR with the 2nd Essex battalion advanced to the woods north of Lingèvres, losing an M5 Honey to a self-propelled gun in Berniers-Bocage. Panther tanks were also present in the area, hidden in the edge of the woodland. One Panther hit a Firefly and two more Cromwell tanks were knocked out by another Panther tank using a sunken road for cover; as the wood was apparently impenetrable to tanks, the regiment withdrew to harbour. A German counterattack that night with two flame-throwing tanks that came in on the infantry in the woods was only just contained by the 2nd Essex battalion with artillery support.[4]

The lost Firefly had been commanded by a Corporal Bridge and the previous evening he had approached his troop commander to say that he had lost his nerve and wanted to be relieved. Bridge, a veteran of North Africa, had been married only a few weeks previously. Unable to immediately do anything as the squadron was due in action again next morning, the troop commander promised to help Bridge, provided he manned the Firefly next day. The armour-piercing shell that had hit the Firefly penetrated the cupola of the turret whilst Bridge was standing up and the shell cut him in two, killing him instantly.[5]

The other mixed group, the 56th Brigade and C Squadron of the 4th CLY Regiment, fought their way into Tilly but could not capture it and withdrew to a position just north of the village. Two Panthers, one disabled, were encountered blocking the road to Tilly and C Squadron knocked out one while infantry with PIATs got the other. As the infantry attacked Tilly, C Squadron moved to out-flank the village from the right flank and were ambushed in close country, losing a Sherman Vc and three Cromwells in quick succession to panzergrenadiers hiding in the hedgerows.[6] The 7th Armoured Division managed to advance just one mile that day, considerably less than the previous day.

12 June

An XXX Corps command conference was held at noon and because of the difficult countryside and consequent slow progress, it was decided that the 7th Armoured Division should try to go around the flank of the Panzer Lehr Division. To the west, the American V Corps was advancing to Caumont and it was hoped that the British

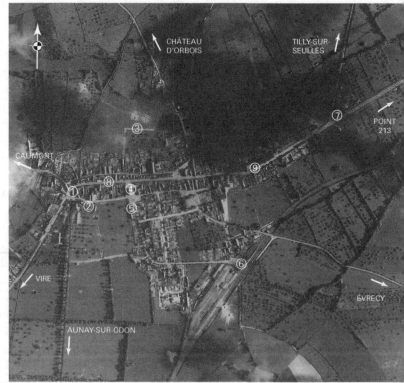

① Place Jeanne d'Arc
② Church
③ Anti-tank ditch (incomplete)
④ Town hall
⑤ Post office
⑥ Railway station
⑦ Calvary
⑧ Rue Pasteur
⑨ Rue Georges Clemenceau (RN 175)

Villers Bocage from the air. This aerial photograph was taken on the morning of 12 June. (*By kind permission of Keele University Photo Archive*)

could exploit the gap created by following in the wake of the American advance and then swinging around eastwards behind the Germans. The advance began at 1600 hours but stopped as soon as it met resistance at Livry from a single anti-tank gun and its attendant infantry. By the evening, the 7th Armoured Division's own infantry brigade, the 131st Brigade, had finally caught up with the division from Bayeux.

Morale of the 7th Armoured Division

By the end of 1943, when Montgomery had been appointed commander-in-chief of the invasion forces, Britain was close to exhausting its manpower resources. Therefore Montgomery requested the return of some veteran units that had performed well in North Africa, notably the 7th Armoured Division and the 50th and 51st (H) Divisions. After a few months in the Italian campaign, the 7th Armoured Division was ordered back to England, leaving their Sherman tanks behind. The division arrived home in England during the first week of January 1944 and after settling in at their spartan accommodation in Norfolk, most men were granted leave on the basis of the number of years of service. Those that had been away for between two to four years got three weeks' leave and those away for more than four years got four weeks. This leave perhaps sowed some seeds of discontent amongst a few of the desert veterans as relationships with wives and loved ones were happily renewed and some men even took the opportunity to get married. Long-suppressed emotional bonds were re-established as the men tried to adjust to life on the Home Front. Britain at that time was full of servicemen from other countries, particularly the USA, but most of these had seen no combat. The prospect of being sent to fight again in Europe was not an attractive one for some men and this generated some ill feeling and unrest during the spring of 1944. These men thought they had done their bit for King and country, and that others should be allowed to go into battle. On their return from leave, the men tried to settle into the routines of training, paperwork and discipline which were all very different to those followed by the division in the field. Some veterans applied for postings to other units:

> Several non-commissioned officers who had splendid records of gallantry and devo-
> tion to duty as tank commanders, applied to transfer to units less likely to be in the
> frontline again. They were undoubtedly influenced by their wives, from whom they
> had been separated for several years and who resented their husbands going into the
> heat of battle again, when so many others had been in Britain all that time and not
> risked their lives in action.[7]

At the request of the commander of the 7th Armoured Division, General Erskine, Montgomery addressed the 22nd Brigade on the 17 February; many men were unhappy and slogans such as 'No leave, no Second Front' had even appeared on the walls of some Nissen huts. Montgomery, in his usual manner, urged the soldiers to break ranks and gather around him while he stood on the bonnet of a jeep to address them. The men were told bluntly by Montgomery, to cheers from some of the men (mainly the officers), that there would be no more leave but they would be getting a second front.[8]

Montgomery's pep talk did not dispel the mood of some men which was further deepened by the poor standard of billeting in the Norfolk cold and damp, and widespread discontentment with the new Cromwell tank. The Cromwell was regarded with deep suspicion as it was British made and must therefore be unreliable compared with the American-made Shermans that the division had used in North Africa and Italy. Having been in action since 1941, the 7th Armoured Division had been forced to use every type of British tank produced in the war so far and the crews were far from impressed with the inferior products of the British tank industry. The Cromwell was small, cramped and had a slab-sided turret compared with the latest German tanks. These objections rather ignored the reality that the Sherman also had larger slab sides and that the Cromwell was faster and had a lower silhouette than the Sherman. Modifications did have to be made to the escape hatches of the Cromwells for them to work properly, however. Whilst being asked to use the new Cromwell, the veterans were also given the new 17-pounder Sherman Vc (or Firefly) which seemed to contradict all that they were being told about the Cromwell. The Firefly was slower and a larger target than the Cromwells and as a troop of tanks could only move at the pace of the slowest tank, the Vc would slow the faster Cromwells down. There was much debate as to how the Sherman Vc should be used and it was finally decided to allot them one per troop of four tanks, the theory being that the Sherman Vc would hang back and knock out the German tanks once they had been located by the tanks in front.

Despite their misgivings, the 7th Armoured Division still had to be prepared for the coming campaign but even the return to paperwork and training was not well received by the men, particularly when conducted by instructors who had not seen any action. Such were the feelings of resentment that the commander of the 5th RTR finally asked all the regiment to sign a loyalty letter, or chit, declaring that the men were prepared to embark for France without further ado. In the resulting furore, a sergeant who refused to sign was arrested. When word of the trouble within the 5th RTR ranks reached the echelons above, the commander was eventually forced to leave on 4 May whilst the offending sergeant was posted to another unit.[9] The 7th Armoured Division history, however, recalls this period of training as being 'agreeable' and notes that it gave more time for leave and recreation than was allowed the home army.[10]

13 June

At 0545 hours, the 7th Armoured Division resumed its advance as part of the western pincer into the rear areas of the Panzer Lehr with the 4th CLY leading.

The town of Villers Bocage was reached at 0800 hours and the inhabitants reported that there were no Germans about. The division had recce troops out in front and on the flanks which reported the presence of German troops nearby but not in any concentration. The commander of the 4th CLY requested a proper reconnaissance be made before a further advance, but Brigadier Hinde, who was anxious to make up for lost time, refused. A Squadron of the Yeomanry then quickly left the town and advanced to the top of Point 213 on the road to Caen which was the division's objective, so the tanks duly halted. A long column of tanks and the carriers of the motorised infantry company 1st/7th Queen's stretched almost back to Villers Bocage.

During the night, 1st SS Panzer Korps had ordered the 101st SS Schwere (heavy) tank battalion equipped with Tiger tanks into position near Villers Bocage as a mobile reserve behind Panzer Lehr. After a 70-mile overnight march during which several Tigers broke down, the 2nd and 3rd Company tanks had arrived in position to the north-east of Villers Bocage and that morning their crews were resting or servicing their tanks.

The commander of the 2nd Company, Obersturmführer Michael Wittmann, was 200yds south of the Caen to Villers Bocage road when his crew saw the leading elements of the 4th CLY drive by and then stop near the crest of the hill. As an Orders Group had been called by the regiment's commander, Lord Cranley, many of the British crew members got out of their vehicles to answer calls of nature and brew cups of tea. Without waiting to contact the rest of his company, Wittmann drove his tank straight from cover towards the middle of the British column. Firstly, he destroyed the two rear tanks of A Squadron, a Cromwell and a Firefly, to prevent the rest of the squadron turning around to engage his tank. Then he turned towards Villers Bocage and proceeded down the length of the column, systematically destroying the 4th CLY recce troop Stuarts and the carriers and half-tracks of the Queen's infantry. By now the other Tiger tanks had heard the noise of battle and quickly moved into action, engaging the now isolated head of the column.

Just outside town were the Cromwell tanks of the Yeomanry RHQ which Wittmann destroyed one by one as they started to back away. One Cromwell, commanded by Captain Pat Dyas, managed to back into a side street, out of the advancing Tiger's path. Shots from the retreating Cromwells had ricocheted harmlessly off the advancing leviathan as it loomed out of the smoke towards them. Sergeant Jack Pumphrey was in the tank of the Major Carr, the 4th CLY's second in command:

> It was deserted and quiet, unnaturally quiet; broken only by the rumble and clatter of steel tracks on the cobblestones of the streets. You listened instinctively for the sharp crack and answering echoes betraying the presence of snipers. There were none of the usual signs of devastation, the houses and shops were intact, but with shutters up and doors closed, and a complete air of desertion. The only sign of life, a mongrel dog

sniffing at garbage in the gutter. It was all wrong, no laughing crowds shouting and waving tricolours – wrong and somehow eerie.

Eeriness shattered into grim reality by that crack-brrrmmmph-bang that can come only from an 88. A Honey tank ahead was transfigured into a mass of roaring red and crimson flame, and the silence dissolved into the pandemonium of tanks at war.

Wireless silence was broken by the Colonel with urgent orders to deploy for battle. We were near the end of town, and a small paddock bounded by thick woods was off the road to our right. Not much space for manoeuvre, but anything to get off that road. Even as Tom reversed 'left hand down' I saw the second Honey, immediately ahead of us share the same fate as its leader. One moment a tank, the next something without shape or form, belching flame and smoke from its turret, the ammunition inside exploding and red and yellow tracers weaving fantastic patterns around it, in-termingled with vivid red and green glows of Very light cartridges. With a glimpse of its commander baling out of the turret and sliding forward to open the hatches above the driver and bow gunner. The swirling black oily smoke obscured him – a long burst of Spandau fire – he didn't reach those hatches.

'Traverse right! RIGHT!' as I brought the turret round. Harry slammed a 75mm armour piercing shell into the breech and the black hull of a Tiger tank appeared across the telescope hairs. No need for Gunnery School orders. Forty yards range and from the way it dominated the telescope, it might have been four. I aimed low, into its engine plate and felt the kick of the 75mm almost in the same second as I saw the tracer flatten against the Tiger's hull and the fly off at a mad tangent. Harry had slammed in another shell before the first case had ceased rattling down into the deflector bag; another, and yet a fourth before we realised that there was no answering sheet of flame from the Tiger's engine. They hadn't pierced, its skin was too thick. Ridiculous … it was uncanny. And slowly, devilishly slowly, its turret traversed round towards us. The black cross bordered with white, on its side came square on, then at an angle more acute until it seemed as if the black circle of the 88's muzzle brake was resting on the front of our tank …

Five years or five seconds could have passed. There was a terrific roaring and crack-ling and my eyes didn't want to open. Everything was red. Flames which wrapped themselves around the guns, the ammunition bins, the periscopes, making them all appear black in silhouette. And there was nothing to breathe, no air, nothing but smoke and fire. I'd got to get out … out of this hell. It was sheer instinct that made me reach to grasp the cupola: instinct that reasoned that if I got leverage and foothold on the commander's seat and then on the turret-ring behind, I should be out. It was more as if I floated than stood up. Blessed movement. I could feel the hinges on the cupola beneath my fingers and the commander's seat giving support to my left foot. And my head was outside. Wonderful light … and air that you could suck in, down to lungs that seemed themselves on fire inside. One more step, a push and I should be out.[11]

Sergeant Pumphrey was badly burnt, and along with the rest of the crew, he was taken prisoner. The tank of the RHQ troop commander, Lieutenant John

Cloudsley-Thompson, backed off the road into a farm and tried to engage the Tiger tank as it passed. The Tiger stopped and returned fire immediately; an 88mm shell penetrated the front of the Cromwell, passed between the wireless operator's and driver's heads, just missed the gunner's shoulder and then went between the lieutenant's legs before striking the engine where it exploded, spraying the inside of the tank with flaming fuel and shrapnel. The five occupants bailed out unhurt and hid in the bushes, under machine-gun fire. The tank of the regiment's sergeant major was also destroyed. Lord Cranley's Cromwell was also destroyed but he had gone ahead to A Squadron for the Orders Group on Point 213 in a scout car.

Wittmann then entered the town which was not usual German practice as tanks are vulnerable to hand-held anti-tank weapons in built-up areas. Wittmann must have believed that German infantry would arrive or that if none were available, then his tanks still had to enter the town to continue the destruction of the British column nonetheless. The next victims of his Tiger were an OP Sherman and Cromwell of the 5th Royal Horse Artillery; the Cromwell too tried to escape by reversing into a side street but was seen by Wittmann, who reversed his Tiger tank slightly to fire at and destroy the tank. The Cromwell, commanded by Captain Pat Dyas, then proceeded to follow Wittmann's tank, hoping to hit the Tiger in its thinner armoured rear. Seeing the Tiger tank stationary ahead, Dyas claims to have hit it with two armour-piercing shells that had no effect.

What happened next has been the subject of much debate over the years. According to Wittmann's own simple account, he advanced to the middle of the town where his tank was immobilised by an anti-tank gun when one of the Tiger's tracks was hit. Wittmann then proceeded to shoot at anything in sight before finally deciding to abandon the tank.

In British accounts, Wittmann either exchanged shots with a Firefly tank on the main street further on in the town and turned around to withdraw the way he had come, meeting the Cromwell of Dyas, which he destroyed before being immobilised by the anti-tank gun, or saw Dyas following him and knocked out the Cromwell by firing his gun over the rear of the Tiger before proceeding to the encounter with the Firefly. Eyewitness accounts differ in the confusion and smoke of the battle and to complicate matters Wittmann was not commanding his own tank that day and the number of his tank has not been confirmed. This has made piecing together the exact sequence of events from eyewitness accounts and photographs after the battle much more difficult. To complicate any reconstruction of events, the Germans recovered some damaged Tiger tanks before 100 RAF Lancasters bombed the town on the night of 14 June and again on 30 June.

Significantly, Wittmann did not try to blow up his tank, believing it would be salvaged. German infantry had indeed begun to infiltrate the town and were providing supporting machine-gun fire and sniper fire along some streets. Wittmann then walked 10 miles to the command post of the Panzer Lehr at Orbois and informed them of the situation at Villers Bocage. Fifteen Mark IV tanks that could be spared from the battle with the 50th Division were dispatched to block the northern exit road from the town. Wittmann returned to the command post of the 1st Company of his own battalion and directed the action of the Tiger tanks in entering Villers Bocage. Meanwhile, on Point 213 the Yeomanry tanks were being stalked and knocked out one by one by the other Tigers of the battalion. The first tanks of the squadron had been knocked out and, as Wittmann had already destroyed the rearmost tanks, the remainder were trapped on the road, apparently unable to escape from the cutting they were in with destroyed vehicles slewed across the road. The last wireless message was received at 1240 hours from Lord Cranley, requesting permission to blow up his scout car before being taken prisoner.[12]

The other Tiger tanks then entered Villers Bocage and a 'confused' battle between the Tigers and the tanks of B Squadron of the 4th CLY and the anti-tank guns of the 1st/7th Queen's infantry took place. Six Tigers and a Mark IVH were knocked out or disabled on the streets of the town, demonstrating the vulnerability of tanks in built-up areas. Panzergrenadiers and reconnaissance elements of the 2nd Panzer Division started to arrive in the afternoon and began to exert further pressure on the British units in Villers Bocage.

Meanwhile, the 5th RTR was at Tracy Bocage, with C Squadron overlooking the battle unfolding beneath them but unable to intervene. Tiger tanks began to appear in the woods in front of them later in the day. One was persuaded to withdraw by a Firefly, but one Cromwell was damaged and another knocked out. Four tank crews abandoned their tanks rather than duel with the Tigers.[13]

Brigadier Hinde decided to withdraw from the town altogether to the high ground at Amaye sur Seulles where the remnants of the 4th CLY and the 5th RTR plus their infantry formed a desert-style defensive box. German artillery then shelled the position heavily while the British were supported by neighbouring US artillery which was used effectively to break up the assemblies of German infantry prior to their attacks. The 1st RTR held another position further north at Briquessard, protecting the division's line of communication to the rear.

14 June

Next day the German troops continued to put pressure on both the 7th Armoured Division positions at Amaye and Briquessard. Again, the British were well supported by American artillery and RAF Typhoons that attacked Villers Bocage and any vehicles moving around Point 213.

However, the ongoing attack by the 50th Division had made no progress southwards towards the positions of the 7th Armoured Division which was now out on a limb. It was decided by XXX Corps to withdraw as soon as possible. No thought seemed to have been given by Bucknall to reinforcing the positions with infantry to retain the ground captured. That night, the troops withdrew, covered by RAF Lancasters that bombed Villers Bocage, and arrived exhausted at 0600 hours on 15 June at La Maulotiere.

Losses 13 June

- 29th Brigade
- 5th RTR one Cromwell (War Diary 4)
- 4th CLY eighteen Cromwells (War Diary 20)
- Three Stuarts (recce troop)
- Four Fireflies
- 1st RB fourteen half tracks
- Eight Bren carriers
- Eight Lloyd carriers
- 5th RHA two tanks

Losses 14 June

- 1st RTR three Cromwells
- 4th CLY one Stuart

A large number of the casualties on 13 June were inflicted by Wittmann's single Tiger tank but the exact numbers may never be known. What is certain is that a few Tiger tanks of 101st SS Schwere battalion assisted by tanks and infantry from the Panzer Lehr Division had stopped Montgomery's western pincer attack cold and the veteran 7th Armoured Division was repelled with a bloody nose.

There were recriminations at every level. The tank crews were shocked by their first battle in Normandy. Their fast Cromwells had been unable to manoeuvre in the bocage and were then found to be completely useless against the Tiger tanks. Tank commanders had been sniped at continuously as they stood in their turrets straining for a better visibility of the countryside around them. None of the division's pre-invasion training had been conducted in terrain resembling the bocage. On the advance to Villers Bocage, some men had inspected a knocked-out Panther tank and were awestruck: 'I took a good look and decided that I would examine no more of them as it was bad for my morale to see that thick sloping front and the length of the barrel of the gun.'[14] The division's senior officers also felt it their duty to report on the events at Villers Bocage. Brigadier Hinde wrote a report for General Erskine and was critical of British strategy:

> The idea of a massed weight of armour punching a hole in blind country in face of anti-tank guns and tanks of superior quality is not practical. As was foreseen about a year ago, we are at a grave disadvantage having to attack Panthers and Tigers with Cromwells and Shermans. This disadvantage largely disappears when the enemy attacks us …
>
> … From experience so far gained it appears that the only way to reduce the disparity between Allied and German tanks is to have more 17-pounder tanks and SABOT for that gun.[15]

To the weight of this report was added a number of reports by XXX Corps officers that eventually reached Montgomery and the War Office. These were not comments made by inexperienced men but by veteran tank officers who had fought in North Africa. Dempsey, commander of the Second Army, in a letter to 21st Army Group on 24 June used the comments of his commanders to call for better armour-piercing ammunition for the Sherman, more improved 17-pounder SABOT ammunition and for more Firefly tanks. Dempsey concluded his letter by saying that 'our armour is fighting under a considerable handicap'.

In response, the RAC's Major-General Richards dismissed the claims of the tank commanders as 'sweeping statements' and 'misleading' while extolling the virtues of the 17-pounder Sherman. This ignored the fact that Fireflies were in short supply, comprising only one tank in a troop of four. Richards referred to a report written in April 1944 and apparently issued to all formations and units in which it was stated that the 75mm Sherman gun was no match for the Tiger or the Panther. Richards concluded that 'nobody should have been surprised when they found out what was said in theory was proved correct in practice' and that faulty tactics were 'probably' to blame.[16]

While the political debate continued in England (which is covered in a later chapter) the British and Canadian tank crews had no alternative but to continue to do battle in the tanks they were issued with.

Le Mesnil Patry

At a Canadian 3rd Division commanding officers' meeting on 10 June, an operation was planned for the 1st Hussars armoured regiment to break through the German lines next day and seize the high ground between Cheux and Granville sur Odon via the village of Le Mesnil Patry in a right hook. In theory, this would isolate the panzergrenadier regiment defending that part of the front line. On reviewing the plan, it was realised that there was little information known about the enemy and the operation was postponed at 2200 hours on 10 June until 12 June to allow a proper reconnaissance to be made.[17] However, on 11 June at 0800 hours, the brigade was informed that the attack had to be made that very day. Although not specified at the time, the reason for this was to support the advance of the 7th Armoured Division to Villers Bocage as the attack of the eastern pincer around Caen by the 51st (H) Division had been held up by fierce fighting and German counterattacks. The brigade issued verbal orders at 1100 hours to the Hussars and the infantry regiment the Hussars would be supporting in the attack, the Queen's Own Rifles of Canada (QOR).The commanding officer of the Hussars, Lieutenant-Colonel White, asked for more time to prepare for the attack but this was refused. A further order was received at about 1100 hours from General Keller of the 3rd Division to attack as soon as possible.[18] The Hussars' own orders could not be issued until noon for an attack that was supposed to start at 1300 hours. Fortunately, the regiment had moved up into an assembly position near Bray the previous evening. The regiment had just received twenty replacement tanks from the Field Delivery Squadron (C Squadron 25th Elgin Regiment) complete with crews. For many men it would be their first battle, although 'unhorsed' men from D-Day were given priority over green crews. The replacement tanks allowed B Squadron to be reformed with a new squadron leader, Captain Harrison, who was the second in command of C Squadron. That night, the regiment's tank muster was fifty-nine Shermans and six Sherman Vcs so the regiment was slightly overstrength.[19] The extra tanks were put in B Squadron, which would have twenty-one tanks instead of the usual nineteen. The war diary of the Hussars summarised the preparations:

> The plan was that 'B' Squadron and one COY of INF were to seize the initial objective, LE MESNIL-PATRY, while 'C' Squadron deployed on high ground on the right flank to support them with covering fire. There was no time for the Div Arty plan and the shortness of time allowed for planning did not give the sub-unit commanders the chance to brief their men of their own individual tasks.[20]

The original start line for the attack was the rail line south of Bretteville from where it was a straight run south-west to Le Mesnil Patry. At the last minute the start line was changed to Norrey and the tanks quickly moved to take up their new positions; however, the sides of the road from Bretteville to Norrey had been mined, so the tanks could not deploy off the road. B and C squadrons were forced to move in single file through the narrow streets of Norrey as German mortar fire began to hit the village. The Shermans, with their wide turning circles, had to jockey backwards and forwards to negotiate some corners; subsequently, the start line was not crossed until 1420 hours, with D Company of the Queen's Own Rifles riding on the back of the tanks.[21] To now advance towards Le Mesnil Patry, B Squadron now had to move in a westerly direction across the front of the positions of the 12th SS Panzer Division.

No sooner had the Hussars cleared Norrey and begun the 1,200yd advance westwards towards Le Mesnil Patry when a heavy mortar barrage was brought down on the tanks of B Squadron whilst machine guns fired at the exposed riflemen mounted on the tanks. The infantry immediately leapt off the tanks and into the wheat fields, only to find them alive with engineers from the Pioneer battalion of the 12th SS Panzer Division which had been lying low. Furious hand-to-hand fighting broke out, with the tanks trying to assist the infantry with their machine guns and destroying any machine gun posts that could be located while the Pioneers engaged the Sherman tanks with Panzerfausts and tried to attach magnetic mines to them. B Squadron was urged on by Brigade HQ to the first objective of Le Mesnil Patry and had to leave the infantry to their own battle. A smoke screen was put down to screen their advance and Le Mesnil Patry (codenamed Strawberry) was reached about 1500 hours by one troop with another troop reaching an orchard just south of the village. At 1615 hours, tanks were reported on the right flank and 8 minutes later both B and C squadrons began to be hit by armour-piercing shells

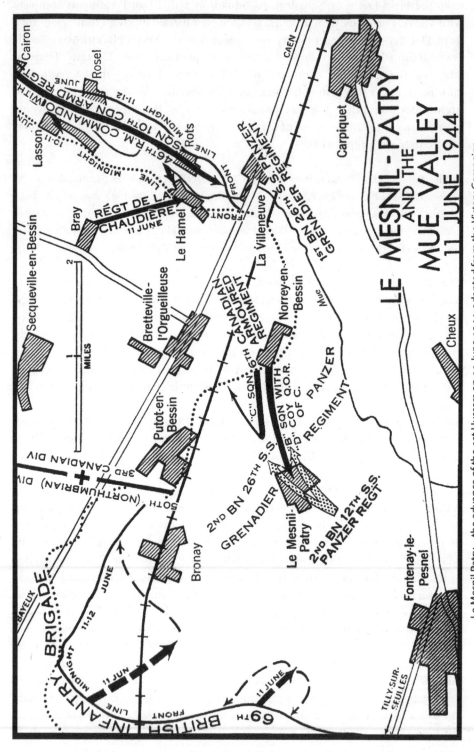

Le Mesnil Patry – the advance of the 1st Hussars on 11 June 1944, adapted from the *Victory Campaign*.

from unseen guns, seemingly shooting from the direction of Cristot.[22] Brigade HQ had earlier received a report that the 8th Armoured Brigade was in Cristot and this information was passed to the Hussars along with the order not to open fire. Lieutenant-Colonel White instructed the two squadrons to fly their recognition flags and Major Marks, the commander of C Squadron, even got out his tank whilst under fire to check that all his tanks were flying the correct flag. The volume of armour-piercing shell only increased, however, and permission was finally given for the two squadrons to return fire.

The line south of Cristot was defended by the panzergrenadiers of the 26th Regiment with their anti-tank guns and three Mark IV tanks of the 8th Company. The Sherman tanks of B Squadron ran straight into the waiting anti-tank guns just as the Mark IVs moved up to the fighting. Untersturmführer Jeran was in an 8th Company tank:

> As we rolled forward, and during an observation stop, I recognised from the agitated gestures of some grenadiers who were pointing in the direction of the enemy with their spade that acute danger was facing us. 'Ready for action.' On this order, the hatches of the three tanks closed as if by themselves. The gun barrels were wound down to firing elevation. Anti-tank shells were loaded on the move. A hedge was still obstructing our view of the enemy on the left. When the hedge suddenly disappeared and our point tank was in the midst of our own infantry, several Shermans were spotted rolling at a dangerous distance towards us through the orchard of a farm. We had driven right in front of their barrels and were showing them our vulnerable flanks. 'Enemy tanks from the left – 9 o'clock – 200 – open fire.' This was all the commander of the point tank could do, he was also the commander of the 8th company. But nothing else was required. The months-long battle drills and battle experience of the crews now proved themselves. The driver jerked the tank to the left, bringing it into a firing position. Even before the fighting compartment ventilation fan, crucial for the survival of the crew, go to full speed, the closest enemy tank had been hit. Within a minute or so, four or five Shermans were burning. Only the last one, which had worked its way to within 100 yard on the far left, brought sweat to the commander's brow. It had only just been spotted and was already swinging its gun towards us. 'Enemy tank – hard left – 10 o'clock – 100.' Barrel was now turning towards barrel, muzzle against muzzle. Through the gun sights they were close enough to touch. For an instant, the gunners may have lined up the cross hairs of their gun sights on each other. Then came a blow, a flash of fire from the breech of the gun, the cartridge dropped into the sack and the enemy tank exploded.[23]

Both B and C squadrons suffered heavy losses and other German tanks were coming in on both flanks. While the 8th Company attacked from the east, the other available Mark IV tanks of the 2nd battalion skirted Le Mesnil Patry to the west and attacked C Squadron before it could go to the aid of B Squadron. C Squadron had managed to advance as far as the command post of the 7th Company of the 26th Panzergrenadier

Regiment which was defended by 50mm and 75mm anti-tank guns. As both squadrons were now in danger of being destroyed, the order was given for the regiment to withdraw to the start line. The surviving C Squadron tanks began to retire, but there was no reply from B Squadron which had either been completely destroyed by then or was unable to disengage. The three Mark IVs pursued the retreating Shermans but were in turn knocked out by anti-tank guns south of Bretteville.

The Hussars' Shermans picked up what infantry they could from the battlefield between the two villages and withdrew back through Norrey which was now being heavily shelled by German infantry and mortars. Lieutenant-Colonel White's tank in the village was destroyed by a direct hit. Rubble from the destroyed church steeple then blocked the streets, so an alternative route through the village had to be found. A tank knocked down a wall to make a new exit, only to fall into the cellar of a house. By 1746 hours, the surviving tanks had formed up near the railway line, along with the Fort Garry Horse Regiment in expectation of a German counterattack, but none came.

Throughout the rest of the afternoon and evening, stragglers made their way back through German lines to the Canadian position but the regiment had suffered heavy casualties that day. Only the surviving tanks of C Squadron and a few crew members of B Squadron who had bailed out when their tanks were hit made it back to the railway line or Norrey.

In what came to be known as the Black Day of the Hussars, there were only two of B Squadron's twenty-one tanks left and these had broken down before entering the battle.[24] Only one B Squadron officer survived and he was taken prisoner; eight officers and forty-seven men were killed, six were posted as missing and a further twenty were wounded.[25] It was an even darker day for the infantry, however: D Company of the Queen's Own Rifles had ninety-eight casualties out of nearly 120 men, fifty-five of whom were killed. The regiment itself lost a total of twenty-five Shermans and three Fireflies, not the thirty-seven tanks claimed by some historians; thirty-seven was the total stated as lost by the whole brigade for that day.[26]

The Hussars claimed that they knocked out fourteen German tanks, including Panthers and a number of anti-tank guns.[27] Trooper Chapman, in his Firefly, claimed three more German tanks. However, no Panther tanks took part in this action, as the attack was met by the Mark IVs of the 2nd battalion of the 12th SS Panzer Regiment which recorded only three Panzer IVs as being lost that day.[28]

Both the war diaries of the 2nd Canadian Armoured Brigade and the 1st Hussars state that the action had resulted in a major German attack being defeated, but this was incorrect. The Germans had already postponed any planned major counterattack until more panzer divisions had arrived, so the losses inflicted on the Hussars were simply from the Germans reacting to their advance. The parallel attack on the right by the British 69th Brigade had been delayed, so the entire Mark IV battalion was able to be concentrated to resist the Canadians. The verdict of the Canadian historian on the operation was succinct, describing the operation as a 'complete and costly failure' in the Canadian official history.[29]

Next day, the 2nd Canadian Armoured Brigade sent a plaintive message to the RAC at the Second British Army HQ requesting that friendly AFV recognition procedures be standardised. An RAC liaison officer also reported that the brigade was being outgunned and that more Sherman Vcs were needed. Communication problems were ascribed to the failure of the radios in DD tanks due to saltwater contamination from the D-Day landings.[30] On the night of 16/17 June, Le Mesnil Patry was finally occupied without any opposition since the Germans had withdrawn in response to progress by the 50th Division on the right.

Cristot

On 11 June, the 50th Division was ordered by XXX Corps to continue its advance and clear St Pierre, Cristot and the nearby woodlands. It was intended that this would reduce the pressure on the 7th Armoured Division's drive southwards as well as protecting its left flank. The 69th Brigade, positioned east of the River Seulles, had been fighting for the strategic hill of Point 103 near St Pierre for the previous two days. On 11 June it was tasked with enlarging the salient it occupied which ran though Audrieu and St Pierre and given the specific objectives of capturing Cristot and Point 102, on which a considerable number of troublesome German mortars were thought to be located.

Prior to this attack the CO of the 4th/7th Royal Dragoon Guards' B Squadron had conducted a reconnaissance in his tank of the approaches to the village of Cristot and Point 102 and had seen a considerable number of infantry but there was no strong reaction. Enemy fire was received from hidden snipers and machine gunners, who seemed to be in every hedge, but the tanks were impervious to this and had no casualties. This reconnaissance may have disrupted a German attack in the process of forming up, but it also alerted the Germans to possible British intentions.[31]

The attack would be in the afternoon by the 6th Green Howards battalion, supported by the tanks of the 4th/7th Royal Dragoons plus two batteries of self-propelled artillery. It would be the first combined tank/infantry operation by the Royal Dragoons and it was organised as per previous training and then current doctrine, with the tanks in the leading wave with the infantry and more tanks in successive waves behind.[32]

At 1500 hours, the 6th Green Howards passed through the 1st Dorsets in the front line and began the advance eastwards, either side of the track from Point 103 to Cristot and Point 102. The guns of the mobile artillery fired on known targets and one hedge immediately ahead of the advance in order to try and eliminate any hidden German positions.[33]

For the attack, the infantry went in two companies up with B Squadron tanks supporting on the right and C Squadron on the left. B Squadron was somewhat understrength with only nine tanks available for the attack. Having crossed the start line, the infantry soon met opposition at about 1700 hours from machine guns and snipers. In the close bocage countryside, with its small fields and long, thick hedges, the tanks of the Dragoons quickly got separated from the infantry who lagged behind. It was impossible to see the enemy positions until they opened fire, and the infantry began to suffer heavy casualties.

Just before the advance along the track reached the Cristot–Les Hauts Vents road, two B Squadron Shermans were knocked out by a hidden anti-tank gun south-west of Cristot. The vanguard crossed this road but heavy machine-gun fire from the top of a sunken lane straight ahead temporarily stopped the advance. The infantry deployed one company either side of the lane with another company to charge straight up it. B Squadron moved into a small orchard on the right to bypass the lane and began to receive anti-tank fire from a dug-in Panther tank and the same anti-tank gun, losing two more tanks. The remaining B Squadron tanks pushed on and traversed a hedge into another small field immediately south of Cristot. Still in view of the Panther tank, the remaining tanks of B Squadron were hit, including the tank of the B Squadron's second in command. Lance Corporal Jackie Weir was the driver:

> The Squadron Leader's tank was hit some thirty yards on our left, and he and his crew bailed out. This left our own commander, Captain Abel, in charge of things and in control of the remaining tanks. He gave the order to leave the orchards and to get into the open country to our left. I drove on to open ground in a wide arc, and began to think luck was with us. Suddenly the tank received a heavy blow as if a huge hammer was using it as an anvil. We stopped almost dead and the driving compartment filled with big sparks and flakes of burning paint and metal, some of which showered over us. When I flicked the catch which allowed the hatch cover to rise, nothing happened. I had always been careful to keep the catch well-oiled, to ensure that the hatch would open. Now, it was obvious the hatch was damaged. This meant that I would have to leave by the hatch of my co-driver – but I saw that he was still in his seat. So I scrambled over the large gear box casing between our seats, and told him to get moving. One member of the crew – our gunner – was already on the ground on our side; the commander and the radio operator were crouched against the Sherman on the other side.
>
> At this time, all hell let loose from the enemy positions, with machine-gun and mortar fire. They were about two hundred yards away. One mortar bomb landed close to the two chaps on the other side of the tank. We were completely exposed, with no cover, and were being sprayed with earth as bullets from a Spandau raked the ground all around us. We were huddled together; I felt Jack, the co-driver, jerk violently as he was hit in the legs by several bullets. We could not stay where we were and decided to shelter under the tank by crawling in from the rear. We managed to drag Jack with us. I got a great shock when I looked through the gap in the bogey wheels and saw that Captain Abel was dead and Bob (the loader/wireless operator) badly wounded. It seemed that they had been hit by mortar fire, but Bob managed to join us underneath the Sherman. All the while, bullets were peppering the side of the tank: I pressed myself into the cool grass and tried to think. Suddenly there was an almighty crash, as another shell from the enemy 88mm found its mark. It actually

lifted the tank off the ground. As we lay there, we could hear the ominous hissing and whacking noises as the tank began to 'brew-up'. We realised that we had a choice: the fuel from our tank, or the fire from the enemy. A sniper began to aim his shots between the bogey wheels systematically going along the length of the tank. I told the lads to move back, and as I moved, a bullet hit the ground where my head had been a moment before. We came out from under the tank, and again, all hell let loose, so we crawled to the side of the tank which seemed to offer most cover. Stray bullets were still ricocheting off the side of the tank though there was nowhere to go. Bob was bleeding badly from his neck and arm and Jack was in great pain from his leg. The rest of the Squadron had now withdrawn under cover of a smoke screen, but the smoke between them and the Germans left us on the enemy side. I noticed that, on our left, was a line of trees and shrubby undergrowth. To reach this cover meant crossing open ground. We discussed it and after realising that there was little chance of survival where we were, decided to make a break for it.[34]

Jackie Weir was taken prisoner along with the other wounded crew members who were apparently shot in cold blood. In another savage episode, a Dragoons troop leader, Lieutenant Moore, who had also been captured, was killed when he was tied to the branch of a tree and left out in the open when British artillery fired at the German positions.

Seven B Squadron tanks had been lost in a matter of minutes. On the northern side of the sunken lane, out of sight of the anti-tank gun and the Panther tank, C Squadron and the infantry reached the outskirts of Cristot but were beaten back by heavy fire from the village. The turret of one C Squadron tank was hit several times by an anti-tank gun in Cristot and the crew abandoned the tank.[35] The attack had now run out of momentum and, as the Germans had obviously reinforced the area since the morning reconnaissance, the attack was called off. A smoke screen was put down and two tanks from C Squadron covered the withdrawal, picking up what wounded infantry they could. The Green Howards lost twenty-eight men killed and the Dragoons thirteen troopers. The folly of separating tanks and infantry was amply demonstrated in this attack against a well-concealed enemy: the Dragoons lost eight tanks and the infantry suffered heavy casualties when their armoured support was knocked out.

Montgomery's Operation Perch to encircle Caen had been a complete failure. The operation demonstrated that hastily or poorly planned attacks against determined resistance in the bocage countryside were doomed to fail. The impetuous advance of the 7th Armoured Division through Villers Bocage without adequate reconnaissance had led to disaster for the western pincer. The Canadians had suffered heavy casualties in a rushed and unreconnoitred attack on Le Mesnil Patry just to support the attack of the 50th Division which was attempting to pin the Panzer Lehr Division whilst the 7th Armoured Division advanced behind it. The attack by the 51st (Highland) Division forming the eastern pincer had been stopped at Bréville with heavy casualties. All three of the Montgomery's veteran divisions had failed to take their Operation Perch objectives. In a letter sent on 14 June, Montgomery had already given his version of events to the CIGS Alan Brooke:

When 2nd Panzer suddenly appeared in the Villers Bocage-Caumont area, it plugged the hole through which I had broken and 'I had to think again' and 'be careful not to get off balance … So long as Rommel uses his strategic reserves to plug holes that is good' but I 'had not got sufficient strength to be offensive on both flanks of Second Army.' He (Montgomery) had therefore decided 'to be defensive in the Caen sector on the front of I Corps but aggressively so' and to use all the offensive power of XXX corps on the right of the enemy. I shall hold strongly and fight offensively in the general area Caumont-Villers Bocage, i.e., at the junction of the two Armies.[36]

For Montgomery to have claimed a 'breakthrough' when the front line had not yet even formed was bizarre, and then to blame the failure of Operation Perch on the arrival of a few advanced elements of the 2nd Panzer Division was simply disingenuous. Caution seemed to have been the order of the day at XXX Corps, although Dempsey and Montgomery do not appear to have been following the developments in Villers Bocage very closely either. For his part, Dempsey was extremely unhappy with the attack conducted by XXX Corps and the 7th Armoured Division and he claimed after the war:

The attack by the 7th Armoured Division should have succeeded. My feeling that Bucknall and Erskine would have to go started with that failure … If he (Erskine) had carried out my orders he would never have been kicked out of Villers Bocage but by this time the 7th Armoured Division was living on its reputation and the whole handling of that battle was a disgrace. Their decision to withdraw was made without consulting me; it was done by the Corps commander and Erskine.[37]

Dempsey did not, however, say what his orders for Erskine were. Within the 7th Armoured Division, the view was taken that the disaster had been caused by the 4th County of London Yeomanry forging ahead without adequate reconnaissance, but this was not correct as Lord Cranley had requested to make a reconnaissance before moving to Point 213 and was told to push on by Brigadier Hinde.[38] Lord Cranley was taken prisoner at Villers Bocage and therefore could not defend this charge at the time.

Other post-war historians see the defence of the box at Amaye as a victory in terms of the numbers of casualties inflicted on the German infantry and think that the position should have been reinforced, not given up.[39] If there were no real morale problems in the 7th Armoured Division before Villers Bocage, there certainly were after Operation Perch.

The Germans, for their part, had succeeded in roping off the Allied lodgement but had failed to mount any serious planned counterattack to the beaches. The Allies had not yet captured their D-Day objective of Caen and the Germans continued to resist every attack in that direction. However, to contain the British attacks, the Germans had been forced to use three of their panzer divisions from the strategic reserve; these divisions had then become entangled in the front line, unable to disengage and regroup for any counterattack. For Montgomery, the immediate goal was to continue the build-up of the Allied forces ashore.

Notes

1 Ellis, Major L.F., *Victory in the West Volume 1: The Battle of Normandy* (London, HMSO, 1962) p.246

2 WO 171/867 War diary 5th RTR, June 1944, TNA

3 WO 171/619 War diary 22nd Armed brigade, June 1994, Appendix Y, TNA

4 WO 171/867 5RTR, *opcit*, TNA

5 Urban, M., *The Tank War* (London, Little Brown, 2013), p.240

6 WO 171 /856 War diary 4th County of London Yeomanry, June 1944, TNA

7 Carver, M., *Out of Step – Memoirs of a field Marshal* (London, Hutchinson, 1989), p.178

8 Delaforce, P., *Battles with Panzers – The Story of 1st RTR* (Stroud, Sutton), p.92

9 Urban, *opcit*, p.227

10 Anon, *History of the 7th Armoured Division, opcit*, p.23

11 Allen, W., and Cawston, R., *Carpiquet Bound: A Pictorial Tribute to 4th County of London Yeomanry (Sharpshooters), 1939 to 1944* (Epsom, Chiavari, 1997) p.68

12 WO 171/619 War diary 22nd Brigade opcit, TNA

13 Urban, *opcit*, p.251

14 Urban, *opcit*, p.242

15 WO 171/619 War diary 22nd Armoured Brigade opcit TNA

16 WO 205/422 21st Army group reports – letter RAC to 21st Army Group 22 June 1944, TNA

17 RG24 vol 10445, 2nd Canadian Armoured Brigade Operation Overlord – Assault on the Beaches of Normandy June 6–11, LAC

18 RG24 vol 10992 War diary 2nd Canadian Armoured Brigade, June 1944, LAC

19 *Ibid*

20 RG24 vol 14213 War diary 1st Hussars 6CAR June 1944, LAC

21 *Ibid*

22 RG24 vol 10992 War diary 2nd Canadian Armoured Brigade Events log, 11 June, TNA

23 Meyer, H., *The 12th SS, Volume 1: the History of the Hitler Youth Panzer Division* (Mechanicsburg, PA, Stackpole, 2009), p.222

24 Stark, F.M., *History of the 1st Hussars Regiment 1856–1945* (Ontario, London, 1951), p.70

25 Stark, *opcit*, p.73

26 RG 24 vol 10992 War diary 2nd Canadian Armoured Brigade, radio log, June 1944, TNA

27 RG 24 vol 14213 War diary 1st Hussars, June 1944, LAC

28 Meyer, *opcit*, p.223

29 Stacey, C.P., *The Victory Campaign Operation in North-West Europe 1944–1945* (Ottawa, DHH, 1960), p.140

30 RG24 vol 10992 War diary 2nd Canadian Armoured Brigade, June 1944, LAC

31 Stirling, Major J.D.P., *The First and Last – The Story of the 4th/7th Royal Dragoon Guards 1939–1945* (London, Art and Educational, 1949), p.65

32 *Ibid*, p.65

33 BAOR Staff Battlefield Tour 50th Infantry Division, 1946

34 4th/7th RDG Association newsletter, September 2011

35 Meyer, *opcit*, p.217

36 Ellis, *opcit*, p.261

37 Dempsey, quoted in D'Este, C., *Decision In Normandy* (London, Collins, 1983), p.196

38 Sgt Bramwell quoted in Neillands, R., *The Desert Rats – the 7th Armoured Division 1940–1945* (London, Weidenfeld and Nicholson, 1991), p.221

39 Carver, *opcit*, p.187

5

Operation Epsom

By mid-June both Hitler and General Montgomery were concerned, though for different reasons, by events following the D-Day landings. The Allies had linked up the beachheads of their five landing sites and had begun slowly to expand their occupied zone south and westwards. In the Cotentin peninsula, Carentan had fallen and the Americans were now pushing towards their goal of the port of Cherbourg. All German counterattacks had failed and the Allies had complete command of the skies during the day which allowed their fighter-bombers to roam the battlefield at will, attacking any build-up of German forces. Observer planes for the artillery and navy operated unhindered. Heavy Allied bombers continued to conduct bombing missions on the German communication centres at the road and rail junctions of the transport networks that serviced Normandy.

But Hitler did not have just France to worry about: Germany was now fighting a war on three fronts which went against all German military training and doctrine. The Allies had captured Rome and were surging northwards towards the next defensive line hurriedly being prepared, the Gustav Line. On the Eastern Front, the forces of Russia continued to sap the human and material resources of the German Army. Hitler believed that the war would be decided in France; if the Allied invasion could be thrown back across the Channel then the capacity and will of Britain and America to mount any further offensives would be severely reduced for some time which could even lead to them suing for peace, allowing Germany to concentrate on the battle in Russia.

Despite Hitler and OKW ordering counterattacks to throw the Allied troops back into the sea on 6, 7 and 9 June, the Allies were unmoved and growing stronger every day as the build-up continued unchecked. The Kriegsmarine, which could not match the strength of the combined US and British fleets after the destruction of most of the U-boats sent to attack the invasion fleet, had resorted to extensive minelaying and even the use of human torpedos. Similarly, the Luftwaffe was reduced to mounting night attacks with medium bombers such as the JU88s which delivered only pinpricks to the Allies. For two years, the Luftwaffe had been building up its fighter strength to defend German towns, cities and industry from the Allied strategic bomber offensive and the development of jet fighter aircraft and rockets had been given priority over a replacement for the obsolete HEIII twin-engine bomber.[1] Therefore the Germans lacked a heavy strategic bomber with which to attack the British beachhead and disrupt the build-up of men and material. During the day, only a handful of ME 109s or FW 190s fighters could make low-level attacks on individual targets with small bombs or 20mm cannon. Overshadowing all of this was the threat of a further landing near Calais by General Patton's phantom army group, which, according to all German intelligence reports, was still poised in England for a further landing. The weekly report of Army Group B on 2 July 1944, using information supplied by the German Abwehr, stated that there were a further sixty-four large formations standing by in Britain, fifty-four of which could be transferred to France.[2] The only bright spot for Hitler was the successful start to the V-1 missile campaign against Britain which he hoped would bring Britain to its knees. Ironically, the Abwehr office also warned that these weapons, which were being launched from the Pas de Calais, might actually encourage a new Allied landing in that area.

On 17 June 1944, Hitler held a command conference at a bunker prepared for him at Soissons in France in 1940 for the invasion of England. Rommel and von Rundstedt attended, along with their chiefs of staff and Generaloberst Jodl from OKW. First Rommel and then von Rundstedt gave pessimistic overviews of the military situation. Von Rundstedt requested and was granted permission from Hitler for the forces resisting the Americans in the Cotentin peninsula to withdraw slowly into Cherbourg which would then be turned into a fortress. Rommel outlined his intentions for a major counterattack by six panzer divisions to split the American and British armies and reach the coast before wheeling either left or right to roll up one or the other Allied armies. Four of the panzer divisions in France (1st and 2nd SS, 2nd and Lehr Panzer divisions) were to be supplemented by the 9th and 10th SS Panzer divisions of the 2nd SS Panzer Korps, recalled from the Eastern Front on 12 June. At last the 1st Panzer Division was to be released from Fifteenth Army in Belgium. Hitler ordered detailed plans to be made, and these were drawn up over the next 48 hours by Rommel and his staff. Rommel prepared two scenarios for what was deemed the final counterattack but cautioned that the plans would fail if the problem of Allied naval gunfire could not be eliminated. On 20 June, the OKW ordered that the offensive begin as soon as possible after two conditions had been met. The first condition was that panzer divisions in the line had to be relieved by newly arriving infantry divisions, the 16th Luftwaffe Field Division and the 276th and 277th divisions. The second condition was more onerous and stipulated that the enemy east of the River Orne was to be destroyed before the main counterattack began.[3] Several attacks by 21st Panzer Division since D-Day to try and achieve this had been unsuccessful. Army Group B began to prepare movement orders for the relevant formations and with the continued bombing of the road and rail networks dramatically slowing the movement of units into Normandy, it was anticipated that the attack could not begin until the first week of July.

Meanwhile, General Montgomery, although relatively comfortable with the progress of Overlord, was concerned by delays to the build-up of forces ashore which limited his future options. In addition to this, the Allies had still not taken their D-Day objective of Caen and the extended beachhead had been effectively roped off by the Germans. The British and American armies were not operating jointly in the same direction as the Americans were moving westwards on Cherbourg while the British were still trying to capture Caen. The attack by the 7th Armoured Division on Villers Bocage in an attempt to penetrate the still coalescing German lines had been a dismal failure and as a consequence, the Germans had succeeded in roping off the bridgehead, albeit with both infantry and panzer divisions as links in the chain. Accordingly, Montgomery issued a directive M502 on 18 June:

> It is clear that we will now have to capture Caen and Cherbourg as the first step in our overall plan. Caen is really the key to Cherbourg. Its capture will set free the forces which are now tied down in securing our left flank. On 21st June, the Second British Army and First US Army will have new reserves available.

Montgomery concluded the directive as follows:

> The enemy divisions are weak and there are no reserves. We are reinforced, have a large number of tanks and can call on a strong air force for support. I hope to see Caen and Cherbourg in our hands on 24 June.[4]

This forecast was to be slightly optimistic. On 19 June, a severe gale developed in the English Channel that lasted for three days and made it impossible to unload any of the men and the equipment from Montgomery's reserves waiting to come ashore. A particular concern was a shortage of ammunition, stocks of which were aboard the ships waiting to unload off the Normandy coastline. During the storm, about 800 small boats and landing craft were driven onto the beaches and large sections of the artificial harbours were damaged; the American installation was so badly affected as to be unusable for the next ten days.[5] With the discovery that LSTs could be beached and unloaded as the tide went out, the disruption to the flow of supplies was not as significant as it could have been.

Montgomery's original plan was to encircle Caen with two simultaneous attacks on 22 June from either side, the main thrust being launched from the small bridgehead east of the River Orne. This was almost a carbon copy of the ill-fated Operation Perch conducted two weeks earlier. The storm caused the starting date to be postponed by four days to allow supplies and men to come ashore. When General O'Connor, the newly arrived commander of VIII Corps, reviewed this plan he pointed out that the bridgehead was too small to mount such an attack and the plan was changed to develop the main thrust in the west, with a more limited attack from the east. Three corps would attack in the west: XXX Corps and I Corps, which had been in action since D-Day, and VIII Corps which was untried in battle and mainly consisted of green troops that had not seen action before. These included the 15th (Scottish) Division and 43rd (Wessex) Divisions plus the 11th Armoured Division with the desert veterans of the 3rd RTR. In total there were more than 60,000 men, 700 artillery pieces and 600 tanks. O'Connor had performed well in North Africa until his capture and VIII Corps was 'fresh from England and eager for battle.' Defending the Cheux region was the battle-weary 12th SS Panzer Division, composed of a few thousand 'teenagers'.[6] The strength of the division was actually 18,000 men and 112 tanks, as 2,550 men had become casualties since D-Day.[7] The bad weather meant that the offensive, codenamed Operation Epsom after the racecourse in England, would now not start until 26 June but a limited attack to the east from the River Orne bridgehead would start on 23 June so as to pin the German forces. These delays gave the Germans a few valuable days free of air attacks to move up reinforcements and supplies and improve their defensive positions. However, OKW's attention was fixed on the Eastern Front where the Russians, after waiting to see the success or otherwise of Operation Overlord, had launched a massive offensive on 23 June, almost on the anniversary of the German invasion in 1941.

23 June

The attack from the Orne bridgehead was carried out by the 152nd Brigade from the 51st (H) Division (part of I Corps) and had the objective of capturing St Honorine further south on the east bank of the River Orne. The brigade was supported by the 13th/18th Royal Hussars from the 27th Armoured Brigade. In a surprise attack before dawn at 0300 hours, without the usual artillery barrage to alert the defenders of Kampfgruppe Luck from the 21st Panzer Division, the infantry were able to occupy St Honorine before light with only minimal resistance. Concentrated mortar fire from Kampfgruppe Luck then forced the infantry back to the northern part of the village, leaving the tanks of the Hussars exposed for an hour.[8] An estimated thirty to forty tanks of the 21st Panzer Division assembled for a counterattack and advanced in a long column, protected by a ridge, before turning north-west towards St Honorine. With an excellent vantage point up a tree to observe the movements of tanks and assault guns, Captain Wardlaw of the Hussars directed the long-range fire of the well-positioned tanks. The German tanks retreated and the accompanying infantry of the 125th Panzergrenadier Regiment were unable to retake the village. The Hussars claimed to have destroyed thirteen tanks for no loss of their own.[9]

25 June

A subsidiary operation, Operation Martlet, was carried out on 25 June to capture the elevated village of Rauray to the west. Only slightly more elevated than the ground around it, Rauray nevertheless had good views and hence fields of fire over the proposed right flank of the British attack. In its first action, XXX Corps was detailed to capture first Fontenay and then the village of Rauray, supported by tanks of the 8th Armoured Brigade and thirteen field and medium regiments of artillery. The 49th (West Riding) Division would lead the assault against the defensive lines of the Panzer Lehr.

At 0400 hours on the 25 June, the artillery barrage began and the infantry of the 49th (West Riding) Division, supported by the tanks, moved off downhill towards the first objective, Fontenay. The dust and fumes of the barrage thickened the early morning mist and co-ordination between the advancing units was often lost. B and C squadrons of the Notts Staff Yeomanry were each supporting a brigade of infantry but quickly lost contact with them. The British advance was initially opposed by the 1st battalion of the 901st Panzergrenadier Regiment from Panzer Lehr, supported by other panzergrenadiers and the Mark IVs of the 8th Company from the 12th SS Panzer Division. Coming out of their bunkers after the artillery barrage had passed, the panzergrenadiers, having had time to prepare their defences, used mortar and machine-gun fire to great effect to stop the forward progress of the attack through the rubble of Fontenay and after a day's confused fighting, they still held the town. One Mark IV tank was knocked out by an anti-tank gun firing from Fontenay.

The advance to Rauray would not be completed for another three days. However, the pressure from XXX Corps was strong enough that day to convince the Germans that this was the main focus of the British attack. Consequently, the Panther tank battalion of the 12th SS was moved westwards to prevent a break-through around Rauray, away from the section of the front line where Operation Epsom was to be launched.

The Panther tanks started arriving in the early afternoon, some reinforcing the panzergrenadiers in Fontenay. The attack by the 8th Armoured Brigade was halted after a fierce tank battle around the Tessel Wood. The 1st SS Panzer Korps ordered a further reinforced counterattack for the next day with the 5th, 6th and 7th Mark IV companies of the 2nd Battalion less the 8th Company, which was already engaged around Fontenay, and the 9th Company, which was defending Carpiquet airfield.

26 June

The final Operation Epsom plan was a bold one. Using VIII Corps, the 15th Division would advance two brigades up, supported by tanks of the two regiments of the 31st Tank Brigade, to break through the German lines. The third brigade of the division would then move through the gap created and seize the bridges over the River Odon. The tanks of the 11th Armoured Division would pass through and advance southwards to Evrecy and the bridges over the River Orne before turning eastwards towards Bretteville to surround Caen. The Germans had not destroyed any of these bridges over the River Odon as they were required for the

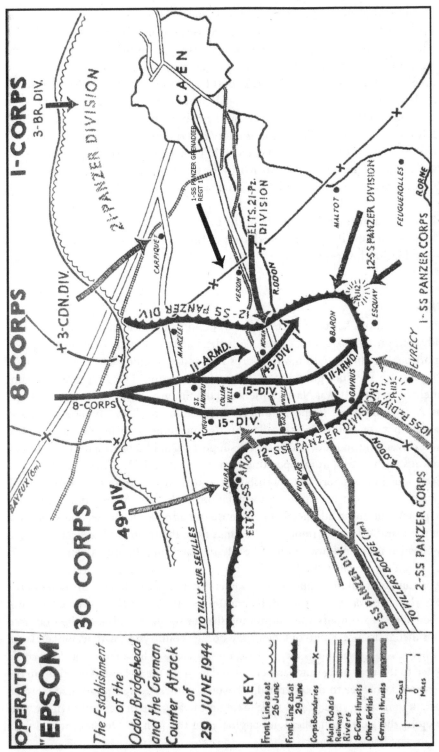

Map of the progress of armour in Operation Epsom, adapted from *Operations of Eighth Corps*.

movement and planned attacks of their own forces. H-hour was at 0730 hours and the infantry of the 15th Division had arrived at the front line only the day before after being unable to disembark from their boats during the three days of gales, without any food other than their own emergency rations. There was little time to plan the next day's attack with the tanks of the 31st Tank Brigade which themselves had only arrived on the 22 June. The brigade would be using its Churchill tanks in the traditional infantry support role as per British doctrine, advancing just behind the advancing lines of soldiers. Montgomery had ordered there be no delay for the start of Operation Epsom, as decrypted Ultra intercepts had reported the arrival in Normandy of the 2nd SS Panzer Korps for the planned German counterattack. The operation would be mounted in two phases:

- Phase 1 – advance to and capture of the bridges over the River Orne
- Phase 2 – occupy the ground north-east of Bretteville sur Laize and be prepared to exploit southwards to Falaise[10]

7th RTR

A and B squadrons left their start lines at 0730 hours following the artillery barrage to advance on Cheux 2 miles away with the infantry of 46th Brigade they were supporting. For the operation, VIII Corps had under its command 532 25-pounder field guns, 112 medium guns and 48 heavy artillery guns. This firepower was supplemented by three Royal Navy cruisers and the monitor HMS *Roberts* with its 15in guns. A programme of support from RAF medium and heavy bombers was also organised but this had to be cancelled on the morning of 26 June because of bad weather over England. Local tactical air support would be provided by the fifteen squadrons of the 83rd Group operating from forward airfields in Normandy.[11]

Each squadron supported a Scottish battalion with two troops of tanks to each company of infantry. In another interpretation of the 21st Army Group infantry/tank policy, one troop advanced alongside the infantry while the second supported from the rear.[12] Within 30 minutes, nine tanks from the regiment had been damaged in a German minefield just south of Le Mesnil Patry and the subsequent confusion caused the tanks to fall behind the advancing infantry. The artillery barrage had done its work and only limited opposition was encountered, particularly as the tanks of the 12th SS had been drawn off towards Rauray by the attack of XXX Corps. Cheux was reached about 1030 hours and on pushing further south, the advance then ran into determined resistance. South of Cheux, the bocage countryside, with its sunken lanes, high hedges and small fields, began to cause problems. The infantry on foot could only see to the next hedge and tank commanders, from their elevated positions in the turret, could only see to the next hedge beyond; numerous well-positioned German anti-tank guns and camouflaged tanks held up the advance of the tanks which were harried by the panzergrenadiers and engineers of the 12th SS Division, armed with

Panzerfausts and magnetic mines. Co-operation with the infantry was difficult as the tank radio sets were not working and the close countryside meant that tanks could only move using the open fields or roads whilst the infantry negotiated the hedges and woods so the two arms were quickly separated.

The regiment finally harboured near Cheux, fortunately not losing any more tanks. There were a considerable number of casualties amongst the tank commanders who were victims of sniper fire; seven officers and twenty-six other men were killed or wounded.[13]

9th RTR

Advancing on the left flank with the 44th Brigade, the tanks of the 9th RTR joined the infantry in following the artillery barrage at H-hour. A and B squadrons each supported a battalion of infantry with tanks following the infantry. The objective of A and B squadrons was to reach the Caen–Fontenay road and St Manvieu, where C Squadron would push on through to Colleville just north of the River Odon. However, before even reaching the start line, two tanks fell into a shell crater 30ft deep from one of the warships providing naval fire support. The advance was initially without major incident, although a tank commander was killed by a German mortar and three tanks were damaged; two tanks ran over mines and a third temporarily immobilised when an anti-tank gun hit a front idler.[14]

St Manvieu was the location of the battalion headquarters of the 1st battalion 26th SS Panzergrenadier Regiment of the 12th SS Panzer Division and it took until 2000 hours to secure the village following fierce hand-to-hand combat and the use of flame-throwing Crocodiles. A German counterattack by panzergrenadiers and a few tanks of a newly arrived company from the 21st Panzer Division was decimated by British artillery.

After the delay caused by the tenacious resistance in St Manvieu, the attack by the 227th Brigade and 9th RTR's C Squadron to push through the gap created by the two other brigades began at 1915 hours without any preliminary artillery bombardment. The 227th Brigade was composed of the 10th battalion Highland Light infantry, 2nd battalion Argyll and Sutherland Highlanders and the 2nd battalion Gordon Highlanders. The actual attack was to be made by the 10th Highlanders and the 2nd Gordons, supported by the 9th RTR, with the 2nd Argylls in reserve. C Squadron advanced cautiously through the rubble-strewn streets of Cheux but when the tanks moved through the wheat fields towards Colleville and went over a ridge, they were hit by anti-tank gunfire and fire from Panthers. Visibility was poor in the rain and gloom, making it difficult to see the German positions. The squadron was then divided into two with half to engage the tanks shooting at them and the other half to support the infantry into Colleville. A tank commander, Sergeant Hall, reported afterwards:

We were to advance through the village of Cheux and up on to the ridge where there would be little opposition. Then we were to move on to the next ridge and try to secure a crossing of the River Odon. It started to rain and as we were approaching the ridge on the right flank, we saw some tanks had been hit and set on fire. I saw green tracer coming towards us, one to the left and one to the right. The third was a direct hit on the turret. We fired back along the ridge at what was either a Tiger or a Panther, and reversed to be able to come up again in a different position. This we did and ended up three-quarters on to him. We came under fire straight away and received several more hits, mostly on the hull. Because we were at an angle to the enemy none of the shots penetrated the armour, but when we tried to reverse prior to coming up on to the ridge again, my driver, Bill Cruickshanks, told me he had lost his hydraulics. As we were still under fire it was only a matter of time before we would lose the crew as well as poor old 'Ilkley.' I gave the order to get out, and we all met up in a large shell-hole nearby. We came under mortar and sniper fire, but due to the very wet cornfield no one was hit, although many mortars landed very close. We all walked back through Cheux and reported to the B echelon vehicles. I have a blank as to what followed. I remember sleeping that night in a tent, and later we were kitted out and given a new tank.[15]

The 9th RTR lost a total of nine tanks on this day, five being totally burnt out, four more being severely damaged and three tanks repairable within 24 hours. Eight tanks were lost from C Squadron alone.

As darkness fell, some infantry of the 2nd Gordons entered Colleville but not in sufficient strength to hold it, so the surviving tanks moved back to Cheux carrying those soldiers they could find in the gathering gloom. The tanks of B and C squadrons finally harboured near St Manvieu that night after their first action.

German Reactions

Believing the previous day's advance on Rauray by XXX Corps to be the point of main effort of the British attack, the 12th SS Panzer Division had been ordered to counterattack. A reinforced battlegroup, Kampfgruppe Wunsche, was assembled to attack towards Juvigny, this time with both of the division's tank battalions supported by artillery and one company of panzergrenadiers. The Mark IV tank companies of the 2nd battalion moved from their positions around Cheux overnight to be in position for the dawn attack on 26 June. No sooner had the kampfgruppe's attack got underway at 0500 hours than it clashed with the tanks of the 8th Armoured Brigade attacking from Tessel Wood. Later, with the opening of the bombardment at 0730 hours around Cheux, the 1st SS Panzer Korps realised that the main attack was taking place there and not Rauray so the 2nd battalion was ordered to return to their previous positions around Cheux. The 5th and 7th companies were able to disengage and move eastwards to Le Haut du Bosq, where they were able to interfere with the British advance that afternoon and were later reinforced by the 8th Company. A panzergrenadier regiment from the 1st SS Panzer Division was also ordered to bolster the defences in the area.

11th Armoured Division

It was clear to General O'Connor of VIII Corps that the attack was going much more slowly than planned and at about noon he decided to order the reconnaissance regiment of the 11th Armoured Division, the 2nd Northants Yeomanry in their Cromwell tanks, to dash forward from Cheux and seize the bridges over the River Odon. At this time, the Northants Yeomanry only had two squadrons of tanks ashore in Normandy and only one was to be used in the attack. A Squadron struggled through the rubble-strewn streets of Cheux and then moved southwards, under sniper fire and the occasional Panzerfaust attack from panzergrenadiers. The Germans had recovered from the artillery bombardment and progress was slow against the camouflaged German positions while bypassing them was even more time consuming. One troop of the squadron got as far as the railway at Grainville where they shot up some 20mm flak guns. The remainder of the squadron reported that they could see the intact bridges but were unable to make any further progress towards them. Two tanks were lost to Panzerfausts and the regiment was ordered to retire at 1630 hours.[16]

Acting on the information received, O'Connor then ordered the tanks of the 29th Brigade forward to assist the action of C Squadron 7th RTR and the 227th Brigade in seizing the bridges. However, it was getting dark, was raining heavily and as the attack of the 227th Brigade had already faltered, the infantry and Churchill tanks of 31st Tank Brigade were retiring to Cheux to rest and replenish fuel and ammunition.

Cheux was now crammed with tanks and infantry through which the tanks of 2nd Fife and Forfar had to pass. C Squadron decided to move round west of the town but the advance south, along narrow, sunken roads was difficult for both squadrons. By this time, after the earlier British advance, many German panzergrenadiers had reoccupied their positions which were difficult to locate in the close countryside and continued to offer determined resistance. No sooner had one position been identified and eliminated, another one sprang to life, taking a toll on nearby infantry and tanks before it too could be destroyed. Armed with Panzerfausts, they hunted the slowly advancing tanks of the 2nd Fife and Forfar while anti-tank guns engaged them when the tanks moved into more open countryside. The tanks and 10th Highland Light Infantry got as far as Le Haut du Bosq but were unable to capture the village. A Squadron lost two tanks and C Squadron seven tanks; other tanks were damaged in the series of ambushes.[17] As it grew darker, it became clear that to push on was dangerous and the regiment was finally recalled. One tank commander said that he had only managed to find his way to the regiment's harbour by the light of the flaming wrecks of tanks scattered about.[18] At the apparent withdrawal of the British forces, the exhausted engineers and panzergrenadiers were elated that their lines had held.

During the afternoon, the tanks of the 23rd Hussars had worked their way south around and through Cheux for B and C squadrons to support the attack on Colleville. Just as the Churchills of the 9th RTR were knocked out as soon as they appeared over a ridge, so were the tanks of the Hussars. These were the regiment's first casualties:

Those who witnessed it will always remember the shock of seeing for the first time one of the regiment's tanks go up in flames. One moment an impregnable monster, with perhaps a crew containing some of one's best friends, forging irresistibly towards the enemy; the next a crack of terrific impact, a sheet of flame – and then, where there had been a tank, nothing but a helpless roaring inferno.[19]

C Squadron lost three tanks and had another one damaged at about 1900 hours before the regiment moved back into harbour.[20] The area was defended by the 5th and 7th companies of Mark IVs that had hurriedly returned from Rauray and the assault gun battalion of the 21st Panzer Division which had moved up from Verson.[21]

Although the Germans had so far contained the British attack, the Seventh Army commander, General Dollman, was sufficiently alarmed by the size of the attack and the possibility of a breakthrough from Cheux that he requested a counterattack by the newly arriving 2nd SS Panzer Korps. Unwilling to commit this formation, which was moving into an assembly area near Caumont for the planned final counterattack to the coast, Rommel ordered a tank battalion from each of 21st and 2nd Panzer Divisions plus a battlegroup from the 2nd SS Panzer Division at St Lô to move up and reinforce the defences. Two more Nebelwerfer brigades would also be transferred to the beleaguered 1st SS Panzer Korps.[22]

27 June

The miserable conditions and the rain of the previous day continued. VIII Corps was ordered to resume the attack at 0445 hours with the 10th Highlanders and the 2nd Argylls of 227th Brigade, again supported by the tanks of the 31st Tank Brigade. The Highlanders were to advance through Le Haut du Bosq and the Argylles had the mission of passing through the dispersed Gordons' position along the route to Colleville and finally capturing the bridges over the River Odon. The tanks of the 29th Armoured Brigade would also support this thrust by the 227th Brigade.

The four remaining Mark IVH tanks of the 8th Company of the 12th SS Panzer Regiment had relocated the previous evening from the fighting at Fontenay and occupied positions located just south of Le Haut du Bosq, well protected by the embankments of a small stream. After a sleepless night in the front line, these tanks stopped the morning attack by the 10th Highlanders with machine guns and later repelled the attack of the supporting 7th RTR Churchills moving towards Grainville. The 7th RTR claimed to have knocked out three German tanks without loss, but the combined attack was called off before noon having barely got beyond its start line.

The tanks of the 2nd Fife and Forfars then advanced towards Mouen and the river crossing north of Gavrus but also ran into the same 8th Company anti-tank screen about 1200 hours, delaying their movement southwards. Three tanks from A Squadron were lost as soon as they crossed the ridge. Other tanks worked their way eastwards to outflank the well-positioned German tanks which by now had twelve British tanks burning in front of them. Hans Siegel, commander of the 8th Company, made the following report:

At approximately 1030 hours, the fourth wave prepares for the attack. This time, it appears there are more tanks. The same drama as before is repeated, but during the frontal tank duels, an antitank shell coming from the right suddenly rips open the floor of the chief's panzer. The lone tank mentioned before had sneaked close, and while our turret is still moving to the 3 o'clock position, a shell hits the front right and, like a flash, the chief's panzer is engulfed in flames. Hatch covers fly open, the gunner bails out to the left, in flames, the loader dives out to the right. The chief wants to get out through the top turret hatch but is caught by the throat microphone wire. He then tries to make it through the loader's hatch to the right but bumps head violently with the radio operator who could not open his own hatch. The barrel, having been turned half right is blocking it. The chief has to move backward. He pushes the radio operator through the hatch, is engulfed in flames for some seconds, in danger of fainting. Still he manages the jump to safety. But he still has the steel boom of the throat microphone at his neck, he cannot pull it over his steel helmet. So he is hanging at the panzer skirt, almost strangling himself while machine gun salvos are slapping against the panzer. With a desperate jerk, he rips loose.[23]

Siegel was badly burned but survived; his gunner did not. The remaining three tanks saw off the attack of the 2nd Fife and Forfars. So well hidden were the German tanks that their positions could only be spotted by their muzzle flashes, and these were Siegel's undoing.

After the 10th Highlanders could make no progress, the commander of the 11th Armoured Division, General Roberts ordered the 2nd Fife and Forfar, late in the day, to advance on Grainville without any infantry support. The advance was fortunately without any opposition until Grainville itself was reached. Churchill tanks of A and B squadrons of the 9th RTR were also in the area and helped fight off a German counterattack and support the infantry attempting to enter Grainville. George Rathke of B Squadron 9th RTR later wrote:

On 27 June B Squadron was given the job of taking Grainville-sur-Odon, a small village completely surrounded by orchards. Number 10 Troop went in and came under anti-tank fire. Sgt 'Cushy' Simmons' tank was hit and Simmons wounded, and the other two tanks were pinned down and unable to move. Number 9 Troop under Teddy Mott was then sent to try an out-flanking movement round the southern side of the village. We moved off, myself as troop sergeant in 'Immune' on the right, Teddy in 'Inspire' in the centre, and Cpl Jakeman in 'Impulse' on the left. We came to a gap in the trees and being on the right I was the first to turn into the opening. I found myself facing the village church some 150 yards away, and in front of the Church a Honey recce tank burning fiercely – I never did find out who it belonged to. I halted and Teddy came alongside on my left and proceeded a few yards further forward and then halted. I had just started to talk to Teddy when there was a big flash and 'Inspire' was hit, flames belching out of the turret. I saw the wireless-op Jimmy Deem throw himself out of the turret and then heard a shell, presumably aimed at my tank, whistle overhead. I had by then told my wireless-op Bert Watson to send out smoke from the 2-inch mortar; I also directed my gunner George Rawe on to the spot where I thought the shots were coming from, and we fired two AP rounds and began to reverse, having concealed ourselves in smoke. Having reversed about 100 yards I halted and looked around for any survivors from 'Inspire'. I spotted Jimmy Deem running toward some other tanks of the squadron amongst the orchards. Suddenly several German machine guns opened up on him and he fell to the ground. We engaged the machine guns with Besa and also fired a couple of HE shells into the hedgerows concealing the German machine guns. All this happened in a matter of minutes – which seemed like hours. I reported the incident to the Squadron Leader, Major Bob Warren, and was instructed to return to the squadron. Having got back and dismounted from Immune I heard a shout, and moving to the edge of the trees I saw Jimmy Deem, limping badly, coming towards us. Several of us ran forward and helped him back, and he was soon on his way to hospital.[24]

Therefore two Churchills were destroyed near Grainville but at the end of the day the village remained in German hands. The 7th RTR, advancing through the hedgerows south of Cheux, made little progress during the day either.

As well as the 8th Company, Mark IV tanks from the 5th Company also defended the Cheux/Le Haut du Bosq area, taking a toll of the slowly advancing Sherman tanks while their own numbers dwindled until only three were left. Three more 2nd Fife and Forfar Shermans were knocked out in the early afternoon. The bocage countryside caused each unit's actions to degenerate into a series of independent, individual engagements and any cohesion with nearby supporting units was rapidly lost. However, as the British forces ground forward, they threatened to surround the three remaining tanks of the 8th Company which were running low on fuel and ammunition and eventually had to pull back.

The 2nd Fife and Forfars spent the day defending against small German counterattacks from the right flank. Having not made much progress to the River Odon, the regiment harboured just east of Le Haut du Bosq. On the left flank, German reinforcements, which included the 101st SS Schwere battalion of Tigers, were slowly arriving from the east. The eighteen operational Tiger tanks distributed themselves in twos and threes across the whole front from Rauray to Verson, where they proved to be formidable rocks in the swirling battle south of Cheux. One of the panzergrenadier regiments from the 1st SS Panzer Division was also on its way to Verson and was due to arrive the next day.

Only one company of seventeen Panthers (not the promised battalion) from the 2nd Panzer Division arrived that day and mounted an attack towards Cheux. The attack, unsupported by infantry and uncoordinated with the defenders, was poorly implemented. After initially causing great consternation in Cheux, the attack was beaten off by infantry using PIATs and the anti-tank guns of the 10th Highland infantry. The Churchills of the 31st Tank Brigade also helped repel the attack but the Scotsmen would later lament the fact that Cheux was crowded with British tanks, all of whom were oblivious to their appeals for help. Six Panthers were lost in this wasted attack.

The infantry of the 2nd Argylls, supported by the tanks of the 23rd Hussars, captured Colleville at about 0930 hours. This cut the main Caen to Villers Bocage road which was the main German artery for the supply and movement of their forces behind the front line. The Hussars pushed on further south towards Mondrainville, losing two Stuart recce tanks (knocked out by a single shot from a German tank) and another tank, which was hit near Mouen. The regiment's tanks entered the village and another two were hit by an unknown tank, possibly a Tiger, and destroyed.

The advance of the 2nd Argylls and the 23rd Hussars had struck a weakly defended part of the German line that was largely only defended by armoured cars of the 12th SS Reconnaissance Battalion and a couple of Tiger tanks. The Hussars were out of touch with the Argylls which was fortunate as there was little need for infantry/tank co-operation and mutual support that afternoon.

The Scottish infantry pushed onto the River Odon and captured the small stone bridge at Tormauville at about 1700 hours. The news of the capture was radioed to the 11th Armoured Division HQ which immediately ordered the 23rd Hussars to cross the river. Two Shermans were knocked out near Tourville while doing so; later a solitary Panther in the east fired at traffic moving towards the bridge. A troop of four tanks from A Squadron was sent out to deal with this tank, but only one tank returned. After some confusion as to whether the stone bridge could support the weight of their tanks, the first Hussar tanks crossed at 1900 hours.[25] By 2200 hours, B and C squadrons of the Hussars and all of the 2nd Argylls plus their 6-pounder anti-tank guns were across the river and had harboured at Tourmauville. The 11th Armoured Division's infantry, the 159th Brigade, moved to the front line to take over from the weary Argylls. As the British advance led by the men of the 15th (Scottish) Division had made only slow progress, another infantry division was committed to the battle. The 43rd (Wessex) Division was ordered to move into the Cheux region to fill the vacuum left by the Scots and firm up the base of the Scottish salient.

The 3rd RTR were ordered to support the 23rd Hussars across the river but only after they had been relieved by a regiment from the 4th Armoured Brigade and so they did not move until the 3rd CLY arrived at 2130 hours. The regiment duly harboured in Colleville for the night. According to the 29th Brigade war diary, a total of nineteen tanks were knocked out and three damaged that day.[26]

General Dollman considered the morning to have been a success defensively. A battlegroup from the 2nd SS Panzer Division, Kampfgruppe Weidinger, had now arrived and was under command of the 1st SS Panzer Korps. Originally scheduled to attack on the 29 June, Kampfguppe Weidinger and one company of Panther tanks would shore up the positions of the Lehr divisions and defend a line from

Mondrainville and Grainville to Rauray and Tessel Wood on the western side of the British salient the next day.

Dollman was further encouraged by the progress of the two divisions of the 2nd SS Panzer Korps assembling as a reserve and the arrival of the first panzergrenadier regiment from the 1st SS Panzer Division. However, other news later in the day was not so uplifting. Hitler had ordered a court martial into the rapid capture of Cherbourg by the Americans and the report later in the evening that the British had secured a bridgehead over the River Odon was particularly unwelcome.

28 June

In response to the British capture of the bridge at Tourmauville, at 0810 hours General Dollman ordered the 2nd SS Panzer Korps to attack immediately from the south-west and eliminate the breach south of Cheux. At the same time, the newly arrived panzergrenadier regiment from the 1st SS Panzer Division would attack from Verson in the east to cut off the British bridgehead which would in turn be invested by the remaining 12th SS troops and tanks to prevent any further enlargement. However, the 2nd SS Panzer Korps reported that it had still not fully assembled and could not attack for at least 24 hours. For Dollman this was the final straw. Already under considerable pressure, having commanded the Seventh Army since D-Day against the Allies who were now threatening to break through and in receipt of Hitler's telegram regarding the Cherbourg inquiry, Dollman wrote a reply to Hitler and then committed suicide at about 1000 hours.[27] It was not until 1300 hours that day that the 2nd SS Panzer Korps stated that it would be ready to attack early on the 29 June.

The Scottish Corridor

The panzergrenadier regiment of the 1st SS Panzer Division, five remaining 4th Company tanks from 21st Panzer Division and some Tigers from 101st SS Schwere Tank Battalion advanced westwards along the line of the railway to Mouen, which was captured by early afternoon, knocking out three Stuart tanks from the 3rd CLY. The 10th Highland infantry plus the 3rd CLY were ordered to clear the area and extend the corridor eastwards. Just after 1900 hours, their attack began and three Shermans were destroyed; the attack was unsuccessful in dislodging the Germans but did prevent them from advancing further westwards. The Shermans of the 3rd CLY took their toll on the German tanks:

Round about 1700 hours the Mk IV tanks of our company found themselves in a tri-angular field bounded by the railway line running between Mouen and Cheux. It was a dangerous position, and when the enemy attacked, we found ourselves engaged in a bitter battle with enemy tanks and anti-tank guns. Tank 413 had a track broken by a shell, but the crew repaired it covered by their 'little brothers' of the SS panzergrenadiers. Then the commander of tank 421, standing up in the turret, had his head blown off by shell; the crew were so horrified that the driver reversed abruptly and broke part of the track mechanism. Both these two crippled tanks retired, moving very slowly. Tank 422 was the next to be damaged; its turret jammed by a hit, it reversed into a sunken road to carry out its repairs. Tank 425 first had it engine put out of action, then its gun; immobile, it lay in the middle of a close quarter fight between the SS panzergrenadiers and the enemy infantry. All its commander could do to help our men was to chuck hand grenades out of the turret. It was hit again and caught fire. Finally, Tank 412 the leader's machine, went up in flames. We had lost two tanks and had three seriously damaged.[28]

In Grainville after the failure of the previous day, a determined effort was made by the infantry of the 9th Cameronians and A Squadron of the 9th RTR to take and hold the village. The first attack was disrupted by German artillery and it was not until just after midday that the tanks and infantry began to enter Grainville. No sooner had they done so than the Germans entered the opposite side of the town and a fierce battle ensued for the next few hours. The Panther tanks of the 2nd Panzer Division, properly co-ordinated this time with Kampfgruppe Weidinger, made the German attack. Churchill and Panther tanks stalked each other through the orchards near the railway line north of Grainville, A Squadron losing another two Churchill tanks.[29] Jim Hutton, a tank driver in No. 1 Troop, described the scene:

Anyway, in the action at Cheux, my troop was engaged in taking on two German armoured vehicles, I believe one was a Panther and other was a Mark IV. We were told that they had been knocked out, that smoke was coming from the Mark IV and we went up to this hedgerow, and as you know the driver on a hedgerow is just looking at the hedge and turret is in a hull down position and just the turret poking over the top. Tony Lyall nipped off in between the tracks and the hedge and he was doing his business. And while this was going on, this German tank gunner climbed back into what we thought was the knocked out Panther and opened up. He fired a shot and it hit the top of the turret next to Trooper Butterfield who was sitting on the top and it splashed him with fragments and I remember his face getting smothered in blood. But it just nicked a little vein on his forehead and, of course, the blood spurted out because it was a red hot fragment that hit him. The next thing we got one smack in the turret which it penetrated the triangle dead centre on the front of the turret and the shot penetrated the 2 inch phosphorus grenades and set them off. Kit Harlow, our gunner, was sprayed with all the phosphorus. He came out screaming his head off and bailed out and Jimmy Bennell took the full force of the shot through his stomach and that killed him instantly. I was knocked unconscious with the impact and when I came around the pannier door was open and my co-driver was gone and I happened to shake myself and get me head together and doing so I got a perforated eardrum and me ear was terrible, terrible pain I got from me left ear. And I got out and we managed to get hold of Kit Harlow and we got together the crew and we made our way around the back of the tanks to where the infantry were. German snipers and the Germans and the British were all firing at us because they didn't know who we were, they thought we were Germans and the others thought we were British and it was all over the place. Anyway we got back to where we thought the British were and they happened to be the 53rd Welsh Division who we were with at Charing. This Welsh chap called out 'Hande hoch, stick yer hands up' and I said to him 'You get stuffed you Welsh git, I'm English' and they said 'Oh alright boyo' and we made our way back. Anyway we got back and we went back to forward recovery and we managed to get a new tank and replenished and we spent the night at the back and came forward again to the regiment.[30]

The village of Grainville was finally secured by 1500 hours. A thrust was made by another battalion of the 46th Brigade, supported by the tanks of B Squadron 9th RTR, to seize the important crossroads at Le Valtru which was achieved by 1100 hours. Late in the day, at 1900 hours, two squadrons of the 7th RTR and the 8th battalion Royal Scots infantry advanced southwards from near Le Haut du Bosq to the railway just west of Grainville. After a brief skirmish, the tanks returned to near their starting positions to harbour. In the meantime, further south, patrols from the 2nd Argylls holding the Tourmauville bridge were able to move along the River Odon and capture the undefended bridges at Gavrus. At this point the British offensive had carved a narrow salient some 5 miles long through the German lines; this salient became known as the Scottish corridor owing to the fact that it had been made and was defended by infantry of the 15th Division. The corridor had several choke points: Cheux itself, the narrow bridge over the River Odon at Tourmauville and the Caen-Villers Bocage railway with its deep cuttings that could only be crossed at the level crossing in Colleville.

The Attack on Hill 112

The 2nd Argylls near Hill 112 had been relieved during the night by the 159th Brigade from the 11th Armoured Division and occupied the village of Gavrus further to the west. The 159th Brigade was at last reunited with its tanks after having been left out of the battle for the previous two days. At 0530 hours, B Squadron of the 23rd Hussars began their advance to Hill 112 and the northern half of it was occupied by noon. The advance was slow and cautious, giving the Germans time to react.

During the night, three Panther companies of 12th SS tanks had been recalled back across the Odon to the area between Esquay and Evrecy with one company left to guard Hill 113 west of Esquay. The 5th and 8th companies of Mark IVs had also been pulled back from south of Cheux. The division had a total of only thirty operational Panther and Mark IV tanks, supported by two or three Tiger tanks around Hill 112.[31]

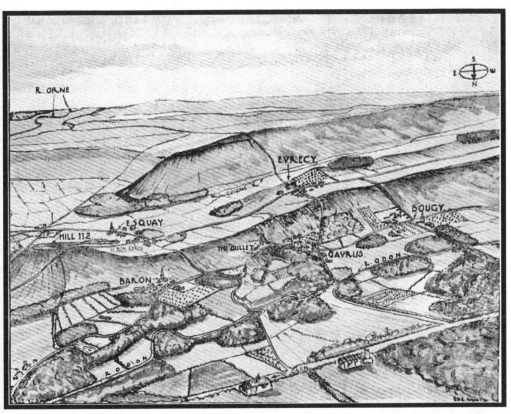

A sketch looking southwards of the River Odon Battlefield, adapted from *History of 34th Armoured Brigade*, BAOR, private, 1945.

The Mark IVs of the 5th Company attacked up the southern slopes of Hill 112 and stopped the advance of the Hussars' B Squadron; C Squadron tanks were directed to move up on their left in support. By midday, A Squadron and HQ had arrived along with eight replacement tanks from the 270th Field Delivery Squadron for B Squadron. However, three of these tanks were immediately knocked out as they moved into position. The Field Delivery Squadron had worked its way through the congested streets of Cheux and across the River Odon to being up twenty-three replacement tanks for the division. The 3rd RTR were watching the eastern side of Hill 112 around Baron where one tank was lost on a mine in Baron and then blocked the road.

By 1030 hours, the 2nd Fife and Forfar were also across the River Odon and were deploying to guard the right flank and attacks from direction of Esquay. The regiment claimed to have knocked out tanks at long range and a whole battery of 88mm anti-tank guns.

The 44th RTR from the 4th Armoured Brigade also came over the River Odon and deployed westwards towards Esquay, so there were by then four tank regiments across the river in the bridgehead. The planners of Operation Epsom had allocated all of the 4th Armoured Brigade to provide flank protection to the south-west for the advance to the River Orne bridges but the other two tank regiments were needed to defend the flanks of the Scottish corridor. On Hill 112, German anti-tank guns and Nebelwerfers engaged the 23rd Hussars tanks and infantry, and the regiment could make no further progress southwards off the hill to the bridges of the River Orne 5 miles away.

At noon, General O'Connor ordered the 11th Armoured Division to hold or improve its positions around Hill 112 but to advance no further. The British had received reports of the arrival of the two divisions of the 2nd SS Panzer Korps near Villers Bocage and aerial reconnaissance photographs had revealed that all the roads to Caen from the south and east were full of German vehicles moving towards the front line. Despite having four tank regiments now over the River Odon, caution set in amongst the British generals.

By the afternoon, the 23rd Hussars were running out of ammunition, so at 1530 hours they were relieved by the 3rd RTR. As there was very little cover, tanks on the crest of the hill were very exposed and vulnerable to long-range fire from Panthers, 88mm anti-tank guns and Tigers deployed around the hill. Attacks by Mark IVs from the southern slopes could not dislodge the British either, for as soon as they advanced they were met with withering fire from the Shermans. Some German tanks occupied prepared defensive positions in a small wood on the southern slope of Hill 112 where they defied all attempts to knock them out with rocket-firing Typhoons, artillery and self-propelled anti-tank guns. For a tank of either side to move from what little cover there was meant that it would almost certainly be knocked out. The German tanks in the wood changed positions regularly to avoid being hit by the British tanks. Artillery from both sides bombarded the hilltop and infantry tried to find what cover they could in a small wood as the landscape was swept by mortar fire and rocket fire. The Germans engaged targets on the hilltop from Esquay, the Château du Fontaine to the north-east and from the south-east.

Firing went on until 2230 hours when it was too dark to shoot any more and the 3rd RTR tanks moved back to harbour at base of the hill just east of Baron.

The death of General Dollman had far-reaching consequences for the Germans. Half an hour after the news, Hitler called a strategic conference for next day which included Rommel and von Rundstedt who were compelled to leave Normandy that afternoon to drive to Germany. While they were en route, Hitler made a number of changes in the command of Seventh Army. The commander of the 2nd SS Panzer Korps, General Paul Hausser, was made the temporary commander of the Seventh Army until the return of von Rundstedt. Hausser and his staff were still planning the next day's attack and changing the corps commander the day before a major attack did nothing but unsettle the corps units. At 1700 hours that afternoon, the four corps, including all the panzer divisions then fighting or about to arrive in Normandy, were again put under control of von Schweppenburg's Panzer Gruppe West which had largely been inactive since its headquarters was destroyed by British planes on 10 June. Panzer Gruppe West was to plan and implement the long-awaited attack to the Normandy beaches as soon as possible and had been given responsibility for the eastern half of the Normandy front with the Seventh Army to manage the operations against the Americans. However, before this could happen, the situation around Cheux and Hill 112 had to be resolved as the 12th SS could not continue to hold the line on its own. Therefore the planned attack by the 2nd SS Panzer Korps to relieve the situation was allowed to continue, even after this was queried by von Schweppenburg. After the war, von Schweppenburg complained bitterly about what he saw as the misuse of the 2nd SS Panzer Korps in terms of the direction of its attack which he thought should have been more northwards into the rear-right flank of the British forces rather than in the north-easterly direction to cut off the River Odon bridgehead.[32]

29 June

The weather, which had started to improve the day before, was fine on 29 June and this allowed the Allied fighter-bombers and observer aircraft to take to the skies once more. The attack by 2nd SS Panzer Korps was planned to start at 0600 hours; the 9th SS Hohenstaufen was to attack north of the River Odon and the bulk of the 10th SS Frundsberg to attack south of the river towards Hill 113 and Gavrus. The 10th SS Frundsberg was a comparatively weak panzer division as it only had one tank battalion in its panzer regiment.

On the British side, the 44th RTR were ordered to occupy Hill 113 and put pressure on Esquay whilst the 3rd RTR were to remain on Hill 112. The 44th RTR did not advance until 0910 hours, C Squadron moving cautiously to just north of Hill 113. First contact was at 1030 hours when two Stuarts were knocked out by guns from the woods just east of Bougy.[33] C Squadron immediately put down covering fire whilst A Squadron moved towards Esquay and shot up any vehicle moving in the vicinity. B Squadron gave support fire to the 3rd RTR which was moving up onto Hill 112 and claimed to have destroyed a Mark IV and some anti-tank guns engaging the 3rd RTR tanks. At about 1230 hours, reports of German armour saw the regiment redeploy to meet the coming attack. C Squadron, on top of Hill 113, clashed with an advancing company of Stug IIIs. These self-propelled guns were not supposed to be used in an attack in the open as their role was normally to provide anti-tank defence from concealed positions because of their thinly armoured sides and low silhouette. However, as this firefight took place in open terrain, the Stugs were able to spot the advancing Shermans and halted to engage them from long range with their powerful 75mm guns. Three Shermans of No. 2 Troop were hit and began to catch fire. The No. 3 Troop with the troop of Sherman Fireflies returned fire and scored hits on the Stugs, but more Shermans were struck by the accurate 75mm fire. The turret of the Firefly commanded by Lieutenant Colbeck-Welch took a direct hit and he ordered the crew to bail out. The lieutenant tried to reverse the tank out of action, but the tank was hit again and knocked out, killing the officer. Finally, B Squadron put down smoke and the remnants of C Squadron withdrew.[34] The 23rd Hussars, having been relieved from the top of Hill 112 by the 3rd RTR and withdrawn to Tourmauville, reinforced the 44th RTR during the afternoon. The 23rd Hussars then covered the positions of the 44th RTR while they subsequently withdrew, losing one tank, which was later recovered.

C Squadron's battle was not over, however. Later the tanks of two other companies of the 10th SS Panzer Division arrived and their Mark IVs joined the Stugs in attacking the 44th RTR which was now supported by M10s of the 75th Anti-tank Regiment. The intention of the 10th SS Panzer Division was to advance to Hill 112 via Esquay and Hill 113 to destroy the British forces south of the River Odon and recapture the bridges. The right wing of the division's advance could be seen from Hill 112 and spotter aircraft above and so concentrated artillery barrages were brought down very quickly on the panzergrenadiers, disorganising the attack. Their progress was hesitant in the face of this heavy artillery fire and the defence of the 2nd Argylls around Gavrus. Some tanks penetrated into Gavrus, which became the contested ground between the two forces, but the bridges over the River Odon at Gavrus remained in British hands. One Mark IVH tank was knocked out by infantry using PIATs in Gavrus.

At about 1640 hours, panzergrenadiers supported by tanks began to attack along the Gavrus–Tourmauville road and penetrated into the woods north and east of Gavrus. A battery of 17-pounder self-propelled anti-tank guns (Achilles) retreated, exposing the positions of the 44th RTR. Three C Squadron tanks were hit from these woods, two tanks bursting into flames. Such was the German pressure that the tanks of B and C squadrons had to withdraw and form a last line of defence in some woods to block any further progress of the Germans towards the vital bridge at Tourmauville. A Squadron were on the extreme left of this line, still in the open ground between Hills 112 and 113, and began to come under fire as the regiment received instructions to retire over the River Odon. Two troops of B Squadron reinforced A Squadron which covered the withdrawal across the river. As late as 2020 hours, an A Squadron tank was knocked out by a direct hit on the turret. Having by now run out of smoke to cover their withdrawal, A Squadron and RHQ finally crossed the river at 2300 hours and harboured back at Cheux. The 44th RTR lost a total of thirteen tanks including two Sherman Vcs (Fireflies) and two Stuarts in this action.[35] The German attack remained stalled at Gavrus and the objectives of Hill 112 and Esquay were not achieved. The 10th SS Panzer Division claimed twenty-eight tanks destroyed for the loss of only two of their own.[36]

North of the River Odon, the attack by the 9th SS Panzer Division, reinforced again with Kampfgruppe Weidinger and tanks from the 2nd Panzer Division, finally got underway at 1400 hours in a concentrated thrust to take Cheux and Mouen and cut off the British bridgehead. The British had an infantry brigade at the crossroads at Le Valtru plus other brigades defending Grainville, Mondrainville and Mouen. Though having served on the Russian Front, the division had not been subjected to an Allied bombardment before and the experience proved to be both shattering and overwhelming. The German assembly areas for the attack were subjected to naval gunfire, fighter-bomber attack and intense artillery fire and the start of the attack had to be delayed. In particular, the assembly area for the tank regiments at Noyers and the woods at Bas de Forges were targeted by devastating naval gunfire and fighter-bomber attacks. Some authors have claimed that these tanks were bombed by 100 Lancasters, but this is not mentioned in the VIII Corps war diary or the official British history.[37] RAF Bomber Command made no raids in this area that day.[38]

The preparations of the 9th SS Panzergrenadiers were so disrupted that they were not ready to attack after their own artillery barrage had begun. About 1400 hours, the panzergrenadier regiments finally began their assaults on Le Valtru and Grainville. The 9th RTR had remained in position around the Le Valtru crossroads and the machine guns of the Churchills tanks inflicted heavy casualties on the German infantry. Four Mark IVs broke into the Scottish infantry positions at Le Valtru but were knocked out by PIAT weapons. Well supported by artillery, the crossroads were held. Five hundred yards further to the north, Grainville was similarly being attacked. During the morning, the 7th RTR plus infantry of the 44th Brigade had pushed south from its harbour near Cheux towards Grainville to the same part of the railway line at Grainville as the previous day. The tank regiment was well positioned to receive the full force of the 9th SS Panzer Division's attack and the Churchill tanks played a major part in blunting the advance but lost twelve of their number doing so.[39] Both infantry battalions held their positions, despite some forward positions being overrun.

Late in the day when the German attack had been turned back, the Cromwell tanks of the 2nd Northants Yeomanry were ordered to make a sweep from Cheux to Grainville. The objectives of this order were to ensure that the Germans had retired and to link up with the infantry again to boost morale. The advance did not get going before dark and as progress cross-country was difficult in the failing light, the tanks proceeded in columns through the gaps in the hedgerows and embankments. One tank of C Squadron was destroyed by an unseen anti-tank gun and then the squadron nearly ran into four Mark IVs. One German tank was knocked out and the other three disappeared into the gloom, so there were no more losses to C Squadron which went on to meet up with the grateful infantry. A Squadron got separated into two groups in the darkness and one group of seven tanks missed their rendezvous and ventured too far west, straight into the German positions. A firefight broke out in the dark, lit only by the flames from burning tanks. For either side to shoot meant that a gun's muzzle flash would reveal its position. However, one by one, the Cromwells were knocked out and after twice having had requests to withdraw refused, all contact was lost with the tanks at about 0100 hours.[40] The burnt-out hulks of the tanks were found next morning.

The 3rd RTR harboured at the northern base of Hill 112 and at 0430 hours reoccupied their former positions on the hilltop and remained there in observation all day. From 1010 hours, Typhoons appeared and attacked the German tanks and gun positions periodically throughout the day. Breakfast on the crest was interrupted by a salvo of Nebelwerfer 'Moaning Minnie' rockets, which killed four men unlucky enough to be caught outside their tanks.

At 1000 hours, General O'Connor again ordered the 11th Armoured Division to remain in its present positions. Allied fighter-bombers claimed to have destroyed nearly 200 German vehicles moving up to the front line and these were clearly the supply echelons for the panzer divisions; a major attack was therefore believed to be imminent. British artillery continued to pound the area around Hill 112 while the Germans had only enough ammunition for their artillery to fire an estimated 10 per cent of the total rounds expended by the British.[41]

The 3rd RTR attempted to improve their positions and eliminate some of the German gun positions from which tanks and anti-tank guns were firing at them. A Squadron was ordered to attack Esquay, but as soon as they moved they were engaged from what seemed like three directions. The tank of a troop corporal was hit and then Major Close, the A Squadron commander, urged the troop further forward. Sergeant Reay's tank was hit and it burst into flames; the sergeant and his gunner jumped out with their clothes alight, only to land on a wire fence. Sergeant Reay rolled around on the ground to extinguish the flames, but he was badly burnt. A half-track from the supporting infantry of the 8th Rifle Brigade picked him up, but on the way to the Regimental Aid Post the half-track was struck and penetrated by an armour-piercing shell that hit both his arms. Shipped back to England swathed in bandages, Reay was taken on 4 July to a specialist burns and plastic surgery unit at a hospital in Basingstoke. There he remained, in great pain and unable to see, for two days. A further operation was needed for an aneurism in his left arm as result of injuries caused by the shell:

> My face had begun to heal up and all the burnt skin had peeled off. I was walking down the corridor one morning, having had all the dressings removed, when I caught sight of my reflection in a glass door. At first I thought there was someone standing behind me. There was this image, not a hair on his head, eyes all distorted, bottom lip hanging down over his chin, upper lip shrunk right up under his nose, or where his nose should have been, both cheeks in a hell of a mess and both ears missing. I made my way back to the ward and laid on my bed and cried my eyes out. For two days I didn't eat or talk to anyone … not even my best friends. I didn't sleep for two days and nights trying to think things out. Then I came to a decision. I would make the best of a bad job. At least I was alive. There were lads in Normandy who would never make it out of their tanks.[42]

As if the burns were not enough, Sergeant Reay's lower left arm had to be amputated and his right hand was crippled. The previous day, on the approach to Hill 112, Reay's tank had broken down. Contravening an unwritten rule that a sergeant stayed with his tank, Major Close had ordered him to take over the troop corporal's tank. Previously in England before embarking for the invasion, Sergeant Reay had declared that he had lost his nerve and wanted to leave the army. The response from the commanding officer, Colonel Silvertop, was that Reay had to 'carry on like the rest of us'.[43]

In the afternoon, a company of men from the 8th Rifle Brigade supported by other tanks of the 3rd RTR did manage to capture the devastated small wood on the southern side of Hill 112 to slightly lessen the amount of accurate German fire being directed at the regiment.

During the day, Montgomery and O'Connor had been receiving a steady flow of Ultra decrypts of German signal traffic which all indicated a build-up of panzer divisions. Information had also been obtained from prisoners and a set of plans and maps for the German counterattack found on a dead SS officer. The bridgehead over the River Odon was badly exposed and the single supply-line through Cheux and Colleville serving it was badly congested with traffic, as well as being under attack from both flanks. The attack by the 9th SS Panzer Division was regarded by the intelligence officers of the 21st Army Group and Montgomery as being merely the opening of a major offensive that would eventually utilise all of the German panzer divisions.

Late in the evening, VIII Corps ordered General Roberts at 2200 hours to pull back the tanks from south of the River Odon. Roberts was apparently disappointed, but this disappointment was not shared by the men of the 3rd RTR in their exposed tanks on top of Hill 112 and few regretted leaving the hill.[44] The 3rd RTR had lost twelve tanks, five from A Squadron. The 29th Brigade in turn received its orders at 2250 hours to move back across the river and one by one the tank regiments moved, in the dark, back across the river in good order.

At Berchtesgaden, Rommel and von Rundstedt's meeting with Hitler began at 1800 hours. The military situation in Normandy was discussed and Hitler directed that the present front lines be held; the major counterattack was to begin as soon as possible. Rommel tried to bring up the subject of a political solution but was rebuked by Hitler and told to focus only on the military situation. Rommel made one more attempt to raise the matter, looking to Goebbels and Himmler for support, but none was forthcoming and Hitler angrily dismissed Rommel from the conference. Orders affirming Hitler's directives were issued by the OKW later that evening.

30 June

The 9th SS Panzer Division tried a night attack during the darkness of 29/30 June in order to lessen the effects of the naval and artillery fire, but by dawn this attack had petered out. The renewed attacks by 9th and 10th SS divisions were hampered again by a lack of co-ordination between the tanks and the panzergrenadiers in the darkness and by devastating British artillery fire.

Early in the morning, Montgomery ordered the end to Operation Epsom as he considered that it had reached its 'maximum offensive usefulness'. General O'Connor redeployed VIII Corps in expectation of a major German offensive and the area around Cheux bristled with infantry, tanks and artillery pieces.[45] The topographically insignificant but tactically vital Hills 113 and 112 were 'recaptured' by the 10th SS after an artillery bombardment, but the British had already withdrawn during the night. Any advance further northwards by the Germans over the River Odon proved to be impossible.

Rommel and von Rundstedt did not arrive back at their command post until late on 30 June. Hitler, by summoning the two officers to Germany for a meeting, had deprived the German forces fighting the battle of their two most senior commanders at the critical point of Operation Epsom.

1 July

The 9th SS Panzer Division renewed the assault into the gap between Rauray and Le Haut du Bosq. Again, the forward British infantry positions were overrun but the attached anti-tank guns and defensive artillery barrages called down on any concentration of German forces won the day. The German counterattack to clear out the breach at Cheux had failed. Shortages of ammunition and a complete lack of aerial reconnaissance or protection all contributed to the German failure as well as the stout, concentrated defences of the British infantry brigades.

The situation report of the 9th SS Panzer Division on 29 June referred to the high intensity of Allied artillery being like the drumfire of the First World War that caused all attacks to be nipped in the bud. The division's tank losses were six Panthers, sixteen Mark IVs and ten Stugs but forty-nine British tanks were claimed knocked out by the Stugs of the 7th and 8th companies and thirteen tanks destroyed by the 1st Panther Battalion and the 5th and 6th Mark IV companies.[46]

On the morning of 1 July, having returned to Normandy, von Rundstedt received a report from von Schweppenburg as to the progress of the offensive; the report stated that the planned major counterattack could no longer take place as the panzer divisions had been weakened too much and it advocated a withdrawal out of range of naval gunfire with an evacuation of the Caen salient to establish a new front line. It was proposed that this be done with the newly arriving infantry divisions in order to enable the panzer divisions to be moved into reserve to prepare for the major offensive. Von Rundstedt once again requested freedom of action in a letter to OKW and forwarded a copy of the report from von Schweppenburg plus endorsements from Hausser and Rommel, all of whom were apparently in agreement with one another. Von Schweppenburg and Rommel did argue over the use of the newly arriving infantry divisions which Rommel reportedly refused to throw into the front line, saying that 'the infantry cannot do this anymore and is not prepared to do it'.[47] Rommel's refusal to pull out the 12th SS and 21st Panzer divisions from the front line and use them as a mobile reserve in the 1st SS Panzer Korps was apparently because this would have meant abandoning Caen which was against Hitler's direct orders. Given that Rommel's single concern since D-Day was a massed panzer counterattack to the Allied beaches and the only way of assembling enough panzer units to do this was by pulling them out of the front line, this was an odd statement for Rommel to make, if indeed he did say it and it has not been taken out of context. Von Schweppenburg, perhaps in a further attempt to discredit Rommel, also hinted that Rommel may have been acting with political motives in view of the later plot to kill Hitler. There was no love lost between Rommel and von Schweppenburg, and Rommel cannot answer this charge which was made during post-war interrogations.

The request and report from von Rundstedt must have come as a shock to Hitler, who had personally issued specific directives to his two senior commanders fighting the Allied invasion less than 48 hours previously at Berchtesgaden. At 1740 hours, the reply from OKW was received and it again ordered that the present positions were to be held. By then von Rundstedt was quite pessimistic about the military situation in Normandy and told General Keital as much in a telephone conversation that evening:

'What shall we do?' asked Keital.

'What shall we do? Make peace, you idiots,' said von Rundstedt. 'What else can you do?[48]

The next day, von Rundstedt was given a letter of dismissal along with the Oak Leaves to his Knight's Cross medal. Field Marshal von Kluge was appointed the supreme commander OB West and arrived on 3 July to take up his new command, much to the dismay of Rommel who was hoping to be given that promotion. Von Schweppenburg was also dismissed the same day and was replaced as the commander of Panzer Gruppe West by General Eberbach.

Panzer Gruppe West was subordinated to Army Group B, not Seventh Army on 28 June, and it was therefore under Rommel's direct control, but Rommel apparently refused to move the panzer divisions. Von Schweppenburg later maintained that a co-ordinated attack could have begun on 29 June as the 2nd and 2nd SS Panzer divisions were idle.[49] However, in the absence of both Rommel and von Rundstedt, who were in Germany that day, General Hausser, not having any contrary instructions, believed the relieving counterattack by the 2nd SS Panzer Korps was more appropriate and necessary in the circumstances. Hitler himself had stipulated that the situation around the River Orne had to be cleared up before the major counterattack to the coast. The Seventh Army daily summary on 29 June stated that 'the arrival of the divisions of 2nd SS PZK, barely in time, made possible the prevention of the enlargement of the breakthrough on all sides. Further, the breakthrough was compressed against an enemy who was superior on the ground and in the air.'[50]

Thus the 9th and 10th SS Panzer divisions were thrown into the Normandy maelstrom as soon as they arrived and carried out a failed counterattack which severely weakened their combat effectiveness for future operations in the campaign.

Tank Casualties

In their first battles, the British armoured units suffered significant casualties. Using information from the war diaries of the units involved and the daily 21st Army Group summaries, the total tanks lost can be determined.

	Sherman	Sherman Vc	Churchill	Stuart	Cromwell
31st T Bde			35		
2nd NY					14
29th A Bde	49	8		21	
44RTR	10	2		3	
3CLY	5			3	
	64	**10**	**35**	**27**	**14**

In the attempted breakthrough, exactly 150 tanks had been knocked out or required repairs needing more than 24 hours. Given the planned build-up of armour ashore, these losses were acceptable to the British. More armoured units, such as the Guards Armoured Division, the 6th Guards Tank Brigade and the 34th Tank Brigade had either not yet left England or were only just arriving in Normandy.

The Germans, on the other hand, lost an equivalent number of tanks that could not be replaced and therefore they could ill afford to lose.

	PzIVH	Panther	Stug III	Tiger
21st Pzd	24			
2nd Pzd		13		
12th SS Pzd	26	11		
9th SS Pzd	16	6	10	
10th SS Pzd	14		7	
101st SS Schw bn				8
	60	**30**	**17**	**8**

A total of more than 120 German tanks had been destroyed or damaged in Operation Epsom, almost the equivalent of an entire new panzer regiment. The operational strengths of each German panzer regiment involved in Operation Epsom had been significantly reduced in preventing the British breakthrough and the commitment of the two divisions from the 2nd SS Panzer Korps had achieved nothing. With the exception of the tank casualties in the 12th SS Panzer Division, most of the damaged tanks were not recovered and were ultimately lost as the British were in control of the battlefield. Such were the losses to the reconstituted Panzer Gruppe West that, as per von Schweppenburg's report of 30 June, the planned major offensive to the coast could no longer be carried out unless the front line was shortened by abandoning Caen and allowing the panzer divisions to rest and refit.

For the Germans, the orders given by Hitler and Seventh Army on 28 and 29 June were crucial to the whole Normandy campaign. Hitler's calling of a meeting in Germany following Dollman's death meant that the two senior commanders, Rommel and von Rundstedt, were absent; once again, Rommel was uninvolved in the Normandy campaign at a critical time. There is no doubt that the attack of the 2nd SS Panzer Korps should have been stopped or, failing that, redirected in conjunction with attacks by the 2nd and 2nd SS Panzer divisions. The preparations for the attack were rushed and further hindered by Hitler's decision to promote the corps commander to command the entire Seventh Army. Believing he was continually being let down by Wehrmacht generals, Hitler chose to appoint an SS general to be the first SS commander of an army and in so doing he contributed to the command problems instead of resolving them. The two newly arrived panzer divisions were then frittered away in a failed counterattack straight into the part of the British front line where four infantry brigades with all their supporting anti-tank units and the best part of two tank brigades were expecting an attack. The opportunity to mount the strongest possible mass panzer attack was irretrievably lost. The weekly Army Group B report claimed that the attack was needed to restore the German lines in the sector held by the 12th SS Panzer Division; in reality, the British discontinued the attack because of their expectation of a new offensive by the combined panzer divisions and not just the attack by the 2nd SS Panzer Korps.

The British and German casualties from Operation Epsom were very high. For the British, 470 men were killed, 2,185 wounded and 706 were missing: a total of nearly 3,500 men.[51] The majority of these casualties were suffered by the 15th (Scottish) Division, with 2,331 casualties (288 men killed, 1,638 wounded and 794 missing) from 27 June to 2 July. Beginning the battle with nearly 15,000 officers and men, the Scots had lost 15 per cent of their men, more if the numbers of men in the rear echelons are taken into account. The 11th Armoured Division had 257 men killed.[52]

The German panzer divisions also suffered similar losses of about 3,500 men. There were 1,145 casualties in the 9th SS Panzer Division and 636 men lost from Kampfgruppe Weidinger.[53] The 12th SS Panzer Division had 1,240 men killed or wounded.[54]

Aftermath

Montgomery always knew German armour would arrive in Normandy and that he had to attack first. In Epsom, the British gained 5 miles of territory but failed to break through the German lines and certainly created no significant threat to Caen.

Montgomery's response the day Operation Epsom was cancelled was his M505 directive of 30 June to Bradley and Dempsey which indicated a significant change of plan. The British army was to prepare for the expected German counterattack, make plans for taking Caen and continue to hold as many German forces around Caen as possible whilst FUSA would mount a new offensive to clear the Cotentin peninsula and occupy Brittany. FUSA would pivot to form a line from Caumont to Vire to Avranches before sweeping south and eastwards. Eisenhower was unhappy at the change of strategy as he expected the Allied breakout to be from around Caen. Before Operation Epsom, Montgomery had written to Eisenhower on 25 June and informed him that the coming operation would be would be a 'blitz attack' which would 'continue until one of us cracks and it will not be us'.[55] On 18 June, Montgomery had asked Bradley to take Cherbourg and Dempsey to take Caen; the Americans had done as ordered, but the British had not achieved their objective, which was now apparently being changed. Montgomery had quickly moved the goalposts and revised the British objective after judging the difficulties too great for immediate execution.[56] The hallmark of a good commander is being flexible and being able to change a plan in response to changing conditions. However, when changes are made, the next important step is to ensure all stakeholders are advised and that they understand the reasons for the change. This clearly did not happen. Instead of a 'blitz', Operation Epsom resulted in the British carrying out a First World War-type set piece attack on a narrow 4-mile front complete with infantry advancing in rows through fields of wheat, supported by a huge weight of artillery. An advance of 5 miles was achieved, hardly the breakthrough operation intended to encircle Caen.

The VIII Corps planners must take some of the blame for the slow progress of the operation. It took the vanguard of the VIII Corps two days to advance the 5 miles from their start lines to the River Odon, despite having a greater number of tanks and overwhelming artillery and air support. The 11th Armoured Division had 154 Shermans at the start of the operation and the 31st Tank Brigade had 120 Churchills, not including the Stuart Recce tanks of each regiment and the 40 Cromwells of the 2nd Northants Yeomanry. In comparison, the 12th SS Panzer Division had just 126 tanks operational on the 26 June.

The bocage countryside certainly favoured the defenders. However, VIII Corps seems to have planned the operation with little regard for the countryside and the local road network. From Cheux, only one road led south to each of Grainville and Colleville and these were initially well defended by the Germans. Cheux itself was on the centre line of the attack and became a bottleneck for British units trying to get into battle and for the supply echelons bringing up the rear. This bottleneck in turn became a target for the German Nebelwerfer brigades and artillery which added to the traffic problems around Cheux. The Scottish Corridor itself only used one bridge across the River Odon at Tourmauville to supply the bridgehead over the river and any traffic moving south from Cheux had to use the railway crossing at Colleville as the railway line could not be crossed at any other location because of embankments and cuttings. VIII Corps made no provisions for advancing quickly in the bocage to the river and relied on the tremendous weight of artillery and the determination of the Scottish infantry to get forward.

Yet it was the British who cancelled the attack and gave the initiative back to the Germans. Montgomery did this because of the threat of a further armoured attack and an intelligence appreciation that the 2nd SS Panzer Korps attack was simply a probe, the prelude to a much larger offensive. This was perfectly correct:

the 2nd SS Panzer Korps attack was to cut off the bridgehead over the River Odon before the planned and long-awaited panzer offensive to the coast. Montgomery chose to exercise extreme caution based on the information he had at the time. It may be that once the panzergrenadiers of the 1st and 2nd SS Panzer Divisions were identified in the battle, it was presumed that their tank regiments were not far away and another much larger attack was imminent.

However, the same British intelligence appreciation that failed to realise that the panzer regiments had not arrived with the panzergrenadiers also overestimated the strength of the Germans. In particular, the extent of the casualties in men and tanks of the 12th SS were not appreciated; neither was the fact that their lines were near breaking point. The infantry of the 15th and 43rd Divisions, well equipped with anti-tank guns (711 in VIII Corps alone by 23 June) and devastatingly powerful artillery fire, had effectively contained the attack by the 2nd SS Panzer Korps. The 1st SS Panzer Division was still en route and would not be fully assembled before 5 July.[57]

From early on 28 June, the complete 11th Armoured Division and another tank regiment were over the River Odon and formed a powerful strike force of more than 200 tanks which unfortunately was not ordered to press forward with any great vigour. Despite overwhelming air and artillery superiority, the 29th Brigade tanks were reduced to effectively becoming target practice for the thirty remaining tanks of the 12th SS Panzer Division. Dempsey and O'Connor always knew there were German panzer divisions on the way to the front; the only question was the date of their arrival. The 28 June was the golden opportunity to push on the few miles to the bridges over the River Orne, and it was lost; the 29th Brigade tanks spent the day either in reserve, in 'observation' or being sniped at by 88mm tank guns.[58] General Roberts was rightly disappointed at the cancellation of the operation, and this was reflected in the division's history:

> … the general feeling that in spite of tank losses, a further sweep southwards from Hill 112 coupled with the continued repulse of enemy attacks on the flanks, was well within its powers …[59]

Thus the mere threat of further German attacks was enough for the British to call off the offensive, despite the fact that the armoured spearhead of the 11th Armoured Division was poised to break through the stretched and depleted lines of the 12th SS. Caution had won the day and the British were unable to crack the Germans; it would be another four weeks of fighting before Hill 112 was finally in Allied hands. Operation Epsom had come nowhere near to achieving its objectives; it had not even achieved those stipulated in phase one and so can be regarded as a failure. The offensive did, however, force the premature commitment of the panzer divisions slated for the planned counterattack which led to the attack being halted. For the Germans it was a pyrrhic victory. The 2nd SS Panzer Korps and the 12th SS Panzer Division lost so many men and tanks that any future opportunity for a decisive counterattack to the coast had been lost.

Infantry/Tank Co-ordination

The 11th Armoured Division had not performed well in its combat debut during the first two days of Operation Epsom. The 2nd Fife and Forfars had been held up to the south-west of Cheux without any supporting infantry when ambushed and the 23rd Hussars had made only a slow rate of advance to the River Odon, also without any supporting infantry. Indeed, the 11th Armoured Division tanks had been ordered to support the infantry of the Scottish Division on 27 June but had been virtually out of touch with the infantry they were supposed to be support-ing.[60] Roberts commented afterwards, 'The cooperation between the Scotsmen and the 11th Armoured was not very close; they rather went their separate ways.'

VIII Corps had thrown in the division's understrength reconnaissance regiment, the 2nd Northants Yeomanry, to try and achieve what the 29th Brigade could not, namely the capture of the bridges over the River Odon. General Roberts said, 'It was thought that being tanks, they would have a greater chance of breaking out. I never thought much of their luck if they had to make a fight of it.'[61] In view of the German resistance, it is fortunate that no more than two tanks were lost to the Panzerfaust-wielding engineers of the 12th SS Panzer Division.

The division's organic motorised infantry, the 159th Brigade, was not used in the first two days of the battle and then was hurriedly moved overnight into the bridgehead over the River Odon, only to be left there until 5 July, under fire but undefeated when the division's tanks retired back across the river on the night of 29 June. The tanks and infantry clearly did not co-operate or support each other and this problem was not confined to the 11th Armoured Division. The tanks of the 31st Tank Brigade had not trained with the 15th Division infantry before and their attempts to work with each other were not very successful. On 26 June the tanks of the 7th RTR ran into a minefield, forcing the infantry to continue the attack without them. Radio sets in the tanks did not work, making visual signals and direct speech the only methods of communicating with the infantry. Given the noisiness of the tanks, which required their crews to wear headphones, and the limited visibility through the narrow vision ports of the tanks, even these forms of communication were not reliable. In the heavy rain on the afternoon of 26 June, the Churchill tanks had trouble seeing and communicating with each other, let alone infantrymen outside the tanks. The result on a number of occasions was Scotsmen being killed or wounded by machine-gun fire from the tanks.

The bocage countryside also contributed to the problems of infantry/tank co-operation. The terrain certainly favoured the German defenders who had time to prepare their bunkers, determine arcs of fire and site well-concealed anti-tank guns. The small fields and orchards lined with earthen embankments and tall hedgerows reduced the visibility of the attackers. The sunken roads of the terrain also made vis-ibility of the flanks difficult for the advancing tanks and afforded opportunities for determined panzergrenadiers to ambush any vehicles on the road. A well-camouflaged and sited anti-tank gun could dominate a road and once the leading tank was knocked out, it often blocked the road so the other tanks had to move cross-country where they fell victim to other tanks or anti-tank guns. The infantry could move through the hedgerows and woods more easily than the tanks which had to find gaps and open ground to make progress but these too were often covered by anti-tank guns.

When the Germans had to attack, the roles were reversed and it was the British soldiers who had the advantage of concealed anti-tank guns and found the German tanks just as potentially vulnerable to their PIATs as the British tanks were to the Panzerfäuste.

Infantry were needed by tanks to locate the hidden anti-tank guns whilst the infantry needed the tanks to neutralise machine gun posts. The tanks needed the infantry to keep away German snipers and infantry armed with the short range Panzerfaust whilst the infantry needed the tanks as mobile gun platforms. The British armoured divisions were beginning to learn a painful lesson. As the 7th Armoured Division at Villers Bocage had found out to its cost, armoured columns could not go tramping about the bocage countryside as if they were on manoeuvres in the desert. In such Normandy terrain, the tanks could not dominate the battlefield which was often reduced to the size of the field the tank found itself in. The front line in Operation Epsom became 'a mass of small engagements and disconnected fighting on both sides whereby the operations of one part of the force had little or no effect on the local situation of the other'.[62] In the past, many tank battles had been fought with only a few infantry. In much of the Normandy campaign, it was the infantry that would come to dominate the battles and there was an urgent need to address this in the organisation and training of the armoured divisions. The outcome of future battles would depend on how well the Allied commanders understood and resolved this problem.

Notes

1 RG319 FMS Ethint 49 Jodl and Keital, NARA
2 Army Group B weekly report, 27 June – 2 July 1944, in Wood, J.A., (ed) *The Army of the West* (Mechanicsburg, Stackpole), p.79
3 Meyer, H., *The 12th SS: The History of the Hitler Youth Panzer Division Volume 1* (Stackpole, Mechanicsburg, 2009), p.318
4 WO 229/72/30, HQ 21st Army group Directive M502, 18 June 1944, TNA
5 Ellis, Major L.F., *Victory in the West Volume 1: The Battle of Normandy* (HMSO, 1962), p.272
6 McKee, A., *Caen – Anvil of Victory* (London, Souvenir Press, 1984), p.145
7 Meyer, *opcit*, p.329
8 WO 171/845 War diary 13th/18th Royal Hussars, 23 June 1944, TNA
9 *Ibid*
10 Jackson, Lt Col G.S., *Operations of Eighth Corps* (St Clements, London, 1948), p.28
11 Jackson, *opcit*, pp.30–1
12 Dalglish, I., *Over the Battlefield – Operation Epsom* (Barnsley, Pen and Sword, 2007), p.55
13 WO 171/868 War diary 7th RTR, June 1944, TNA
14 Beale, P., *Tank Tracks* (Stroud, Sutton, 1997), p.46
15 Beale, *opcit*, pp.49–50

16 WO 171/860 War diary 2nd Northants Yeomanry, 26 June 1944, TNA

17 WO 171/853 War diary 2nd Fife and Forfar, 26 June 1944, TNA

18 Sellars, R.G.B., *The History of the Fife and Forfars*, 1960, p.160

19 Blacker, C.H., *The Story of the 23rd Hussars 1940–1946*, p.46

20 Blacker, *ibid*, p.46

21 Meyer, *opcit*, p.372

22 Wilmot, C., *The Struggle for Europe* (London, Collins, 1952), p.378

23 Meyer, *opcit*, p.396

24 Beale, *opcit*

25 WO 171/848 War diary 23rd Hussars, 27 June 1944, TNA

26 WO 171/627 War diary 29th Brigade, June 1944, TNA

27 Irving, D., *The Trail of the Fox* (London, Futura, 1977), p.561

28 Kortenhaus, W., quoted in Mckee, *opcit*, p.170

29 Beale, *opcit*

30 Beale, *opcit*

31 Meyer, *opcit*, p.422

32 RG319 FMS B-258 Geyr, Von Schweppenburg

33 WO 171/873 War diary 44th RTR, June 1944, Appendix 2, TNA

34 *Ibid*

35 *Ibid*

36 Tieke, W., *In the Firestorm of the Last Years of the War – the 2nd SS Panzer Korps* (Manitoba, Fedorowicz, 1999), p.92

37 Tieke, *ibid*, p.89

38 RAF Air Historical Branch letter to the author, October 2013

39 WO 171/868 War diary 7th RTR, June 1944, TNA

40 Neville, Capt R.F., and Scott, Lt Col G., *The 1st and 2nd Northamptonshire Yeomanry 1946*, (Uckfield, Naval and Military, 1946 reprint), p.117

41 Jackson, *opcit*, p.47

42 Sgt Reay, quoted in Moore, W., *Panzerbait with the Third Royal Tank Regiment 1939–1945* (London, Leo Cooper, 1991)

43 Close, Major, W., *View from the Turret* (Tewkesbury, Dell and Bredon, 1998), p.107

44 Close, *opcit*, p.119

45 Jackson, *opcit*, p.53

46 Tieke, *opcit*, p.98

47 RG319 FMS B-466, Geyr, von Schweppenburg, NARA

48 Churchill, W.S., *Triumph and Tragedy* (London, Cassell,1953), p.23

49 RG319 FMS B-466, *opcit*, Geyr

50 War diary AOK7, 29 June, quoted in Meyer, H., *opcit*, p.432

51 Jackson, *opcit*

52 Clark, L., *Operation Epsom* (Stroud, Sutton Publishing, 2004), p.109

53 Tieke, *opcit*, p.98

54 Meyer, *opcit*, p.437

55 CAB 44/248, signal M30 Montgomery to Eisenhower, 25 June 1944, TNA

56 *Ibid*, p.15

57 Lehmann, R., and Tiemann, R., *The Leibstandarte, Vol. IV* (Manitoba, JJ Fedorowicz, 1993), p.129

58 WO 171/866 War diary 3rd RTR, June 1944, TNA

59 Palamountain, E.W.I., *Taurus Pursuant: The History of the 11th Armoured Division* (BAOR, private, 1945), p.20

60 Jackson, *opcit*, p.39

61 How, J.J., *Hill 112 – The Cornerstone of the Normandy Campaign* (London, Kimber, 1984), p.46

62 Jackson, *opcit*, p.39

6

Battle of the Hedgerows

The US 2nd Armored Division had fought in North Africa and Sicily and was the only unit of the USA Armored Force in Normandy to have seen action apart from the 70th Tank Battalion. The first elements of the division came ashore in France on Omaha beach on 9 June 1944 after one LST carrying men and vehicles of the division hit a mine in the English Channel and sank.[1] Seven men were killed or went missing and sixty-six were wounded; seventeen medium M4 tanks and fourteen M5 light tanks were lost and another medium tank of D Company was drowned when it drove off its LST into deep water.[2] After removing the waterproofing materials, the men and vehicles of Combat Command A (CCA) were the first to arrive at their assembly point near Mosles which was in the V Corps sector to the west of Carentan. They were assembled by midnight. The area around Carentan had been defended by the paratroopers of the US 101st Airborne Division since D-Day and supplies and ammunition were running low. The American beachhead was at its narrowest at Carentan and was therefore the most vulnerable part of the American front line; the capture of Carentan was vital in order for the Omaha and Utah beachheads to be joined.

By 12 June, the 2nd Armored Division's Combat Command B (CCB) had also landed and was assembling around Littry and Lemolay while CCA had received orders to take up positions south of Carentan for an attack next day. The task for CCA was to hold the bridge over the River Vire at Isigny and link up with the units of the 101st Airborne in the area, offering support where required. During the previous night, the Germans, also running low on ammunition, had withdrawn from Carentan to a new defensive line to the south and US paratroopers were able to occupy the town that morning. That night, the First United States Army (FUSA) commander, General Bradley, had also received Ultra intelligence and aerial reconnaissance reports of a German build-up for a counterattack and he consequently ordered General Gerow to move a battalion of tanks into the area to support the paratroopers.[3]

After moving out at 0322 hours, the 2nd battalion of the 66th Armored Regiment with a battalion of armoured infantry from the 41st Infantry Regiment arrived without incident at the River Vire west of Isigny; the armoured infantry immediately sent out patrols to the south to locate friendly units and make contact with any enemy in the area. Plans were being made to clear the Germans from the western edge of Carentan and south of the Carentan–Isigny road when orders were received to help defend Carentan. Earlier at about 0630 hours, the panzergrenadiers of the 17th SS Panzer Division and elements of the 6th Parachute Division supported by a few assault guns had counterattacked the two parachute regiments just south of Carentan and pushed them back to within 500yds of the town. The 2nd Battalion tanks and armoured infantry moved to the eastern end of Carentan and then launched their own counterattack at 1430 hours down the Carentan–La Campagne road with the objective of seizing the road junction at La Campagne before capturing Méautis.[4] D Company M4 tanks and the battalion of armoured infantry led off, meeting only light resistance from small-arms fire for the first 500yds while the parachute regiments also attacked from either side of Carentan. Heavy German artillery, mortar and anti-tank gunfire was then received and the advance slowed:

> D Company attacked at 1400 hours along the route running between Carentan and La Campagne … It was a rainy and dismal afternoon. The terrain was evenly divided into small squares by ditches and hedges. The Germans were well entrenched. D Company charged the hedgerows and ditches, traversing each hedgerow with machine guns and firing into the occasional tree top for snipers. The total results were scores of dead, three 75mm anti-tank guns, one Mark IV tank and no prisoners. D Company reached a line running north–south through the village of Douville where it was relieved by F Company 66th Armoured Regiment. The company had expended 75000 rounds of .30 calibre ammunition, 225 rounds of 75mm HE explosive, 750 rounds of 0.45 calibre and 25 hand grenades. Our losses were 1 M4 tank, one officer wounded and one enlisted man injured. This hard hitting initial assault against an entrenched and determined SS panzergrenadier regiment cracked their line and broke their will to resist further in this sector.[5]

The Germans believed they were attacking a few lightly armed paratroopers and the appearance of the tanks came as a great shock to them. Having left their defensive positions to attack, the Germans were caught in the open by the tanks and field artillery of the CCA task force. Despite their determination and the support of the assault guns, each German attack was thrown back with heavy casualties, totalling 500 men killed and more than 1,000 wounded. CCA suffered very light casualties in contrast, only eight men killed, including two officers.

The 2nd Battalion tanks advanced to a point east of Cantepie and as it was getting dark, the battalion decided to harbour after the forward positions were secured by the infantry. The battalion had knocked out four 75mm self-propelled Stug III assault guns, destroyed two anti-tank guns and killed an estimated 400 Germans. Three of the Stug IIIs were knocked out by one M4 Sherman tank with three single armour-piercing shells.

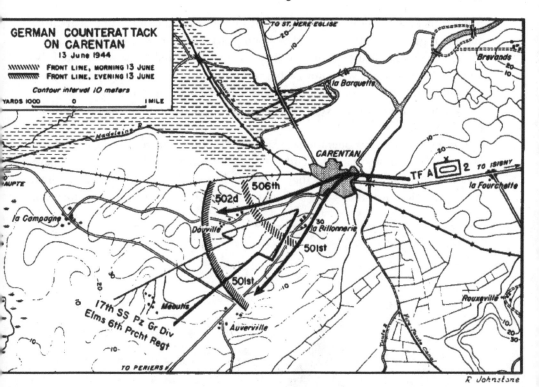

CCA of US 2nd Armored Division and the German counterattack at Carentan, adapted from G. Harrison, *Cross-Channel Attack (USCMH)*.

During the day, the 1st Battalion had also launched an attack from Carentan towards Auverville which was secured at 2100 hours. The 66th Armored Regiment's total tank casualties in this operation were three M4 Shermans and a Stuart tank lost.[6]

It had been the first action of the men of CCA and the tanks of the 66th Armored Regiment fighting in the hedgerows and even though they had only managed to advance 2 miles, it was successful. The men of CCA were able to adapt very quickly to the difficult bocage countryside, with its sunken lanes, small fields bordered by embankments and high hedges. Tanks found they could not manoeuvre through the hedges and were largely restricted to moving through existing gaps in the hedges or along the roads, both of which were usually covered by German anti-tank guns. German snipers and rifle fire from positions that had been dug into the hedgerows had taken a toll on the infantry accompanying the 2nd Battalion tanks.

The American forces had not trained to fight in the bocage and at first it was a bewildering experience for most of them. German infantry, often supported by an assault gun, would open fire from defensive positions in the hedgerows at short range with devastating effect. The Americans learnt to spray the hedgerows in front of them with automatic weapons fire and to make use of the liberal artillery and naval gunfire support available, although fixing their own position and that of the enemy on a map was often difficult as each field and hedgerow looked the same. The hedgerows were impassable to the tanks and any tank trying to push through them either got stuck, exposing its thin belly armour, or overturned. Only a bulldozer or explosive charges could create a gap in the hedge for vehicles to pass through.

The First US Army operational plans for Neptune had readily identified the bocage as being not suitable for tanks and yet the American planners seem to have given little thought as to how they would fight in this terrain once ashore. The report itself describes the bocage as being of 'rough, hilly terrain', with no mention

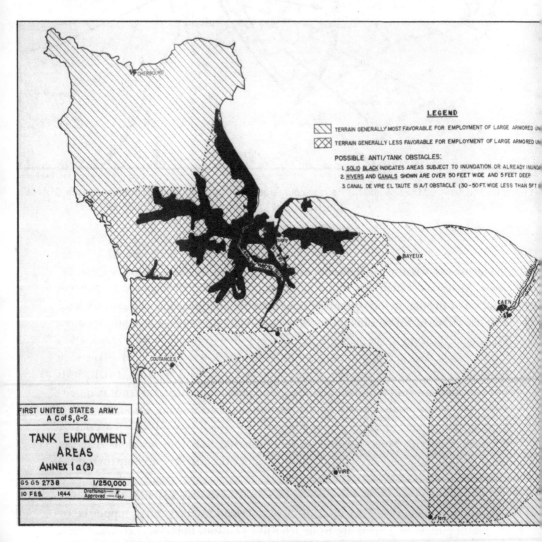

Map of terrain for the employment of tanks from FUSA Operation Neptune operational plans.

of small fields and high hedgerows.[7] Perhaps more concerned with getting ashore, no training in similar terrain had been conducted by the invasion units stationed in England. The American forces, largely located in Devon and Cornwall which in places resemble the bocage, did not take the opportunity to train and, in any case, off-road movements and training were strictly controlled by the British. It is also possible that the Americans did not comprehend how the bocage physically looked, as this was the first time nearly all the men of the First United States Army had been in France. The only likely source of information would have been those senior British officers of COSSAC that had travelled to France in 1940 or before and these were apparently not consulted, nor did they offer any advice.

On 14 June, the 2nd Battalion continued its attack towards La Campagne and reached the objective of the road junction there without any opposition by 0800 hours. The remainder of the morning was spent in a reorganisation of the regiment which gave each battalion a company of light tanks and two companies of medium tanks. This was a more balanced structure, as previously the 1st battalion had three light tank companies and the 2nd and 3rd battalions contained only medium tanks. In the afternoon, the reorganised tanks of the 66th Armored Regiment drove the Germans out of Méautis. A reconnaissance in force was made next day (15 June) by two CCA armoured task forces but, after meeting stiff resistance, the units returned to their start lines and the 2nd Armored Division, FUSA's most experienced tank unit then went into reserve, attached to VII Corps, for the next four weeks until Operation Cobra.

3rd Armored Division

FUSA's build-up was disrupted by the storm in the Channel of 19–21 June. New arrivals after the storm subsided included the infantry divisions of VIII Corps and the 3rd Armoured Division. The first units of this armoured unit arrived in Normandy on 24 June 1944 and two days later its CCA proceeded to St Clair to support the 29th Division in its defensive role. The division was activated in April 1941 and had yet to see combat. The CCA was then ordered by XIX Corps on 29 June to eliminate a German salient 2,000yds deep around Villiers Fossard, from where the Germans could observe and shell Carentan and Isigny from the high ground in the salient. Bad weather prevented any American aerial reconnaissance from 26 June to 3 July and little was known about the German defences. Previous attacks by the 29th Division to eliminate the salient had been unsuccessful as they had broken down in the face of machine-gun fire from the corners of every field entered and accurate mortar fire that had been registered on all likely avenues of attack.

The 3rd Armored Division was committed in its first battle to attack into the difficult bocage hedgerows against largely hidden defensive positions held for several weeks by the same enemy forces. The German defenders initially were only three companies of the 353rd Fusilier battalion from the 353rd Infantry Division, supported by mortars and some artillery.

Three task forces were formed for the attack which was to start at 0900 hours on 29 June. Task Forces X and Y each had a battalion of tanks and armoured infantry, whilst Task Force Z was held in reserve. The task forces were further broken down into teams of one company of tanks and one company of infantry supported by a platoon of tank destroyers with two or three bulldozers to break through the hedges.

CCA's objective was the high ground south and south-east of Villiers Fossard, and it was expected to achieve this in one day before being relieved by infantry from the 29th Division.[8] Villiers Fossard itself is only 5 miles from the regional centre and road hub of St Lô. The weather on the morning of the attack was overcast and the low cloud and fine rain caused the planned air support to be cancelled. The artillery bombardment began as planned 20 minutes beforehand and at 0900 hours the advance began, only for Task Force Y to immediately run into a storm of small-arms fire and mortar fire as the German troops had unexpectedly moved forward of their own lines to escape the artillery bombardment.

Task Force X advanced with little resistance until it reached the high ground near La Forge where it was ordered to stop as Task Force Y had not been able to advance at the same rate. Despite using a procedure developed in training a few days previously, Task Force Y was only able to make small advances. Heavy and accurate German machine-gun and mortar fire forced the infantry to go to ground which isolated the tanks from the accompanying infantry. This enabled German soldiers to engage the tanks at close range with Panzerfäuste, resulting in nine tanks being knocked out. German anti-tank guns also knocked out tanks as they drove into the fields using natural gaps before the tank commanders learnt to use the bulldozers to create new gaps. Several bulldozers broke down and engineers had to place explosives manually to blow gaps in the hedges. The armoured infantry tended to take cover at every opportunity and officers struggled to ensure that the infantry even fired their weapons to provide covering fire which then resulted in a lot of unaimed fire and wasted ammunition. There was a lack of aggression from the infantry in advancing, particularly when attacking immediately after an artillery barrage on the objective. This created a delay that allowed the Germans time to recover and reoccupy their positions, inflicting more casualties on the attacking infantry.[9] The tanks themselves did not aggressively push forward, although this was difficult in the hedgerows without close infantry support and seven tanks were abandoned in the field by their crews.

The first day of fighting for the 3rd Armored Division achieved an advance of just over 1 mile for the reported loss of thirty-one tanks, 400 men injured and twenty-five men killed. The 32nd Armored Regiment had tank losses as follows:

- Mines – one light tank M5
- Panzerfäuste – nine medium tanks M4

- Mortar fire – one medium tank M4
- Anti-tank gunfire – two medium tanks M4
- Abandoned on battlefield – seven medium tanks M4

Another four medium tanks and one light tank broke down and, of the above casualties, one light tank M5 and eight medium tanks M4 were unrepairable.[10]

The attack was an improper use of a tank regiment to straighten out the front line; the division was given a limited objective only 1 mile away and was expected to achieve this by making a frontal attack in difficult terrain. The XIX Corps commander, General Corlett, tried to use the armoured division in a role normally performed by the independent tank battalions that usually supported the infantry divisions as per the then current US doctrine. The 3rd Armoured Division had trained for exploitation roles in the attack and not to support infantry. Villiers Fossard was not an attack of exploitation but was simply a frontal attack to reduce a salient. However, the fighting did serve to give CCA its first combat experience and allowed General Corlett to tidy up the battlefield, albeit with forces not normally part of his corps.

After its somewhat inauspicious combat debut at Villiers Fossard, CCA had time to review its performance whilst the rest of the division assembled. The destroyed tanks were replaced and some M4 Shermans were fitted with two large steel forks to help batter a path through the hedgerows. The division remained attached to XIX Corps for the next offensive, which was not long in coming.

St Lô

The principal objective of the First US Army in June was the capture of Cherbourg by VII Corps. While this battle was in progress, V and XIX Corps held the line to the south with only limited operations and advances southwards to keep pace with the operations of the British Second Army to the east while trying to prevent German units from being transferred from the east to aid the defence of Cherbourg. Strong German counterattacks were anticipated to attempt to eliminate the American beachheads but none eventuated which was fortunate for the First US Army.[11] The German Seventh Army, for its part, was relieved that the Americans did not attack southwards in any force as this freed up its forces to fight the British around Caen and defend Cherbourg until the Americans finally sealed off the Cotentin peninsula on 19 June.

With the capture of Cherbourg and its demolished harbour on the 26 June and the continued build-up of men and supplies in the beachhead, FUSA planned a major offensive to begin on 3 July across its entire front when sufficient forces had arrived in France. This was to be a breakout operation, designed to achieve one of the strategic objectives of the Operation Overlord plan which was to seize the ports in Brittany or, if this was not possible, construct a new port at Quiberon Bay. A deep-water port was regarded as essential for the build-up of supplies and reinforcements for the Allied armies. Therefore the breakout had to be made by FUSA westwards while the British Second Army continued to hold as many German forces at Caen as possible. This was Montgomery's stated strategy both before and after the failure of the British Operation Epsom. Caen had still not been taken and with the failure of the two planned armoured thrusts inland on D-Day and Operation Epsom, the British lodgement area or base was smaller than anticipated and was now crammed with soldiers, tanks and guns with little room for the construction of extra planned airfields.

To achieve the port objective, FUSA needed to capture more of the Cotentin peninsula at least as far south as Avranches in order to provide more room to deploy Patton's Third US Army before it attacked westwards towards Brittany.

American history over the years has downplayed the importance originally attached to Bradley's offensive, preferring to focus on the later breakout achieved in Operation Cobra. This has been done by separating Bradley's July operations into two phases: firstly the advance to St Lô and then the breakout. In fact, they were two separate operations with the same objectives after the first breakout attempt failed. General Bradley recalled:

> By July 10 we faced a real danger of First World War type stalemate in Normandy. Montgomery had taken the northern outskirts of Caen but the city was not by any means in his control. The airfield sites still lay beyond his grasp. My own breakout had failed. Despite enormous casualties and loss of equipment, the Germans were slavishly following Hitler's orders to hold every yard of ground.[12]

Bradley's FUSA breakout operation on a broad front required his three corps to attack one after the other. VIII Corps began its attack on 3 July and VII Corps on 4 July; XIX Corps did not begin their operations until 7 July. Opposing XIX Corps initially were units of the 17th SS Panzer and the 275th Division as a part of Kampfgruppe Heintz. A panzer regiment from the newly arriving 2nd SS Panzer Division was also attached to the 17th SS Panzer Division for armoured support as, despite being called a panzer division, the 17th SS actually had no tanks apart from three companies of assault guns. The division had eighteen Stug IIIs assault guns left of the original forty-two, having been fighting since D-Day.

After the 30th Division had made reasonable advances during the day, having crossed both the River Vire and the Vire–Taute canal as well as capturing St Jean de Daye, General Bradley ordered the 3rd Armored Division to be pushed through the 30th Division and to make a drive to the high ground south-west of St Lô.

CCB, organised in three task forces, began to move at 1930 hours on 7 July and the leading elements crossed the River Vire at Aire. Task Force X received small-arms fire only 600yds south of the crossing and discovered that the 30th Division had not advanced much further south than that point. All three task forces decided to harbour in the vicinity of the east–west road between St Fromond and Le Dézert.

The Germans recognised the threat from the American advance and scrambled to bring in reinforcements to block the advance. Units from the 2nd SS Panzer

Division, including the 6th Panzer Company of the 2nd Panzer Regiment plus a battalion of panzergrenadiers and engineers, were committed to the area as Kampfgruppe Wisliceny to which the troops of Kampfgruppe Heintz were subordinated.[13] In its battle against FUSA, Seventh Army insisted on deploying the 2nd SS Panzer Division units piecemeal to support other units and the division was never committed in Normandy as a complete unit, much to the chagrin of its commanders.[14]

The next day, 8 July, was notable for the tremendous confusion in the XIX Corps advance. The original XIX Corps plan had been for CCB to proceed through the three regiments of the 30th Division by using the east–west road to St Jean de Daye and then turn due south along the road to Pont Herbert while the infantry were ordered to keep the roads clear for the tanks. However, in view of the limited ground that the 30th Division appeared to hold south of the River Vire and that the Germans were likely to be covering the one good road in the area, rather than use the road to move due west to St Jean de Daye, General Leroy Watson ordered CCB to advance cross-country in a south-westerly direction. This unfortunately meant that the CCB would be trying to advance across the direction of the infantry attack.

At 0645 hours, CCB Task Force X (2nd Battalion of the 33rd Armored Regiment) began its advance and almost immediately ran into five Mark IV tanks from the 2nd SS Panzer Division. D Company of the 2nd battalion were leading and went into action:

> During their first fifteen minutes of combat, a tank crew commanded by Sgt. Dean Balderson knocked out three German Mark IVs. Balderson pulled out of a small orchard at dawn, and his gunner, Cpl. 'Swede' Anderson, immediately spotted the enemy. Four Kraut tanks were in position on the road ahead, their guns pointed in the opposite direction and evidently waiting for another company of the 3rd to advance.
>
> Anderson's first round, an HE, caught the nearest Mark-IV flush on the turret, and things began to happen. The enemy tank blew up in a sudden gust of flame and black smoke! Immediately afterwards, the remaining Jerry vehicles were alert and moving. Excited, Anderson called for an armor piercing shell, but his loader, Pfc. Bill Wilson, threw in a second HE. This shell duplicated the first, and a second Mark-IV blew up. Wilson found an AP round for the third shot, and Anderson sent this projectile crashing through for number three. Three enemy battlewagons in less than fifteen minutes of combat! Sgt. Balderson and his crew decided that war was a soft snap. Another week of fighting convinced them that it was just the opposite.[15]

After this brisk early morning action, during which the 2nd Battalion lost one tank for the destruction of the five Mark IVs, the difficulties began. The men and tanks of CCB set about advancing methodically through one field after another, only to encounter men from the 2nd Battalion of the 19th Infantry Regiment trying to enter the same field from a different hedgerow. Wild, confused firing took place, with tanks firing at friendly infantry in the hedgerows and vice versa. To add to the confusion, the 3rd Battalion of the 33rd Armored Regiment was then ordered to cross into the small bridgehead over the River Vire using the same bridge at Aire the rear echelons of CCB were using. A single tank battalion with a 60yd spacing between vehicles occupies 12 miles of road and there were now three reinforced tank battalions for the 3rd Armored Division plus the rear echelon vehicles of the 30th Division all trying to use the same bridge.[16]

The result was terrific traffic congestion around St Fromond. A conference was held between the respective commanders and a route agreed for the tanks to advance along, a large part of which was still cross-country. Other infantry advancing later south of St Jean de Daye complained that CCB tanks were cutting across their front and they could not advance until the tanks moved off. In exasperation that night, General Corlett attached CCB to the 30th Division to ensure maximum cooperation between the tanks and infantry. Corlett himself was unwell and incapacitated for much of the time, so his aide, Major-General Walker, directed a lot of the battlefield movements. To bolster the right flank of the attack, XIX Corps now directed CCA of the 3rd Armored Division, with the attached 113th Cavalry squadron, to enter the battle from St Fromond and cross the battlefield westwards to Goucherie to secure the right flank while the 30th Division and CCB advanced. This order predictably created yet more traffic congestion on the St Fromond-Le Dézert road. CCB Task Force X finally halted to harbour at Le Bernadrie after an advance of only 2,000yds for the day and Task Force Y moved up to take over the advance early next morning.[17]

During the day, the tanks, engineers and panzergrenadiers of Kampfgruppe Wisliceny arrived at Belle Lande and the engineers immediately established a defensive position astride the main road from St Jean de Daye to Pont Hébert. However, it was difficult to locate the individual units of Kampfgruppe Heintz, making coordination impossible. Seventh Army also planned to reinforce the area with a battalion of paratroops from the 3rd Parachute Regiment from reserves and Mobile Brigade 30, a bicycle brigade then attached to the 352nd Division. Rommel, at Army Group B headquarters, ordered the commitment of the Panzer Lehr against XIX Corps after it had made a withdrawal from the British sector at Tilly.

During the early morning of 9 July, reports of German armour on the move created major concern at XIX Corps about a possible German counterattack. When the American attack resumed that morning, progress was slow as CCB was still muddled up with the 119th Infantry Regiment. Task Force Y, now leading the advance, only managed to advance 600yds during the morning and after criticism from the commander of the 30th Division, the CCB commander, General Bohn, ordered the tanks to get on the road and use it to advance more quickly. In response, a company of tanks from the 1st Battalion carrying infantry, commanded by Lieutenant-Colonel King, dashed down the road towards Les Hauts Vents.

At about 1500 hours, the expected German counterattack was launched either side of the 2nd Battalion of the 120th Infantry Regiment which was being supported by the 743rd Tank Battalion. Two platoons of 743rd Battalion B Company tanks were caught in a devastating ambush when they pursued two German Mark IV tanks acting as decoys down a minor road towards a forked road junction. Several other Mark IVs, with sirens wailing, moved rapidly towards the American tanks on the parallel road from the junction and engaged them from the flank, knocking out the first and last tanks so the M4s could not withdraw.[18] In a matter of minutes, nine M4 tanks and a bulldozer tank were destroyed. Another three disabled tanks had to be abandoned by their crews when the supporting infantry withdrew (having seen their armoured support destroyed) which meant that nearly all of the B Company tanks were lost in a single day.[19] All the XIX Corps divisional and Corps artillery was concentrated on the highway and the attack of the advancing German forces ground to a halt before withdrawing, leaving five wrecked Mark IV tanks behind.

The 117th Infantry Regiment had become increasingly nervous with the reports of German tanks approaching. The 1st battalion, east of the highway, began to report fire from enemy tanks to the south at 1537 hours; then fire from friendly tank destroyers; then trouble with friendly artillery fire falling short. Then, at 1620 hours, the 1st Battalion reported ten tanks coming towards them; in the next half hour some elements of the battalion began to pull back along the road in a movement that threatened to expose the positions of anti-tank guns and the attached tank destroyers.[20] Almost at the same time, CCB's Task Force Z (3rd Battalion of the 33rd Armored Regiment) moving westwards had reached the Pont Hébert road at 1630 hours but mistakenly turned north instead of south. The tanks of I Company approached the positions of the 117th Regiment, which, after checking with their HQ that there were supposed to be no friendly tanks in the area, opened fire with its anti-tank guns. The leading I Company tanks returned fire, but two tanks were knocked out before both parties realised their mistake. One tank commander was killed. When it finally moved off in the right direction, Task Force Z, using only minor roads, made good progress southwards. With considerable artillery support pounding the enemy positions ahead of the advance, the German defensive line was breached by the two task forces. Task Force Z, advancing parallel with Task Force Y, reached Belle Lande and the high ground of Les Hauts Vents, followed by the tanks of the 1st battalion in Task Force Y shortly afterwards. CCB then requested permission to continue the advance, but as the tanks were now well out in front of the 30th Division and further German armoured counterattacks were expected, permission was refused and the task forces were ordered to harbour in defensive positions north of the objectives. Seven tanks from I Company failed to receive the orders to return to harbour and were left on the high ground overnight in front of the American positions. To add to their feelings of isolation and discomfort, these tanks were later strafed by P-47 aircraft. The news that the CCB tanks were on their objectives was unfortunately received with scepticism by both the XIX Corps and 30th Division headquarters.[21]

CCB had made good ground that day and, having made little contact with any Germans, successfully reached its objectives, only to be told by XIX Corps to withdraw and harbour. That evening, as a consequence of the confusion of the previous 36 hours which was certainly not all of his making, General Bohn was relieved of command of CCB and replaced by Colonel D. Roysden.

Next day, 10 July, at 0600 hours, the attack on Les Hauts Vents was resumed and was directed in person by Colonel Roysden who ordered Task Force Y with the 1st Battalion to take the hill. The 1st Battalion only had two light tanks and six M4s operational at that time after two days of combat and was unable to take the hill. The nearer Task Force Y got to the objective, the heavier was the German fire. The Germans had reorganised their lines of defence during the night and had tanks and anti-tank guns covering the main axis of advance along a sunken road. When the M4 tanks were knocked out, their hulks blocked the roads before they could be towed away and this slowed the attack as the other tanks were unable to manoeuvre around the obstruction. Finally, the German fire became so intense that the task force was forced to halt altogether. Task Force Z then attempted join the attack but was hit by anti-tank fire from Belle Lande which was supposed to be in the hands of the 119th Infantry Regiment. Belle Lande, reported unoccupied the night before by the tanks of Task Force Z before being ordered to withdraw, was now defended in strength by enemy forces which had deployed four tanks in the hamlet. At 2000 hours, two platoons of tanks from the 1st Battalion's E Company were ordered forward to clear Belle Lande. The Germans opened fire and knocked out one of the accompanying tank destroyers of Task Force X which was covering the Pont Hébert road from a ridge. The E Company tanks returned fire, hitting one enemy vehicle and advanced to the edge of the hamlet where troops of the 119th Infantry Regiment reported three dug-in tanks. A reconnaissance was attempted but, in the growing darkness, had to be abandoned. The infantry regiment resorted to subjecting the German positions to an intense artillery barrage.

On 10 July CCA was attached to the 9th Division, having been instructed to attack towards Les Perry and Les Lands. These orders were changed in view of intelligence reports about a German counterattack and instead of attacking, the CCA made defensive preparations. The tanks of E Company were sent to the important road junction directly south of St Jean de Daye while St Jean de Daye itself was reinforced by tank destroyers. These defensive moves were continued on the morning of 11 July with F Company being moved to just north of Le Dézert.

The Counterattack of Panzer Lehr

On the night of 9/10 July, the Panzer Lehr Division began to arrive in the sector, its approach march having been delayed by air attacks along its route. The 902nd Panzergrenadier Regiment assumed responsibility for the line from Belle Lande to the River Vire. Panzer Lehr's commanding officer, General Bayerlein, had been given the mission of destroying the American advance south of the Vire–Taute canal with a counterattack that was to begin on 11 July. However, Panzer Lehr had been ordered to leave one tank battalion and an artillery battery behind at Tilly to support the newly arrived 276th Division which had taken the division's place in the line. Therefore Panzer Lehr could not attack as a complete division and the units assembled for the attack were already under strength as a result of four weeks of fighting around Caen.

The available forces for the attack were assembled into three battle groups:

- 1st and 2nd battalions of the 902nd Panzergrenadier Regiment and a battalion of twenty tanks to attack north from Pont Hébert
- 1st Battalion of the 901st Panzergrenadiers and two companies of assault guns guns (twenty Stug IIIs) to attack through Le Dézert
- 2nd Battalion of the 901st Panzergrenadiers with eleven Panther tanks from the Bois du Hommet, driving east and north-east[22]

The initial objectives of the three attacks were, respectively, Cavigny, St Jean de Daye and Le Mesnil Véneron and the three battle groups intended to link up around St Jean de Daye from where a further advance to the coast would be coordinated. This would be the strongest counterattack mounted by the Germans since the invasion.

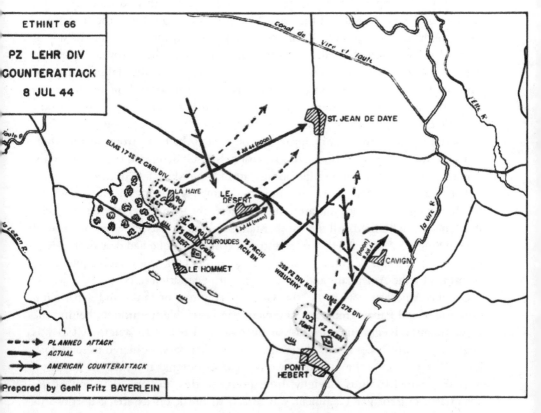

Plan of the attack of Panzer Lehr on 11 July, drawn by General Bayerlein. Note that Bayerlein was apparently mistaken with the date.

The Panzer Lehr attack began at 0600 hours on 11 July, with the strongest part of the attack falling on the right flank of XIX Corps which had been reinforced by CCA of the 3rd Armored Division and the 9th Division only the day before. The attack struck between the 39th and 47th Infantry Regiments which were pushed back by the fury and intensity of the assault before the attack was met north of Le Dézert in the afternoon by the tanks of CCA (F Company of the 32nd Armored Regiment) and the M10s of the 899th Tank Destroyer Battalion.

Advancing towards La Caplainerie (north of Le Dézert), the battle group of the 2nd battalion 901st Panzergrenadiers, supported by eleven Panther tanks, was stopped by two M10 tank destroyers. The CCA tanks were located in orchards on either side of the road, waiting to take part in a 47th Infantry Regiment mission while the two M10s were holding positions on the road about 200yds from the American tanks. When the Panther tanks appeared, F Company opened fire but inexplicably used HE rounds which at a range of 400yds had no effect on the Panthers. The leading Panther broke through to duel with an M10 at a range of 120yds. The Panther was damaged by the first shot from the M10, but it returned fire, hitting the M10 and wounding or killing three members of the crew. The other M10 then opened fire, finishing the Panther off with two shots. Another Panther tank was spotted and the same M10 fired ten rounds into the suspension system of the second Panther, which sideslipped helplessly into a bank on the side of the road and was immobilised, caught in a tangle of matted hedgerow and churned mud. The Panther crews bailed out and were later captured after taking refuge in a nearby farmhouse.[23] A second column of tanks was destroyed on another tree-lined road north of Le Dézert when the first and last tanks were knocked out, trapping the remainder which were then shot up one by one. The long, overhanging barrel of the Panther tanks apparently prevented the tanks from turning their turrets to fire back at the Americans. Bayerlein himself described the Panther tank as not being suitable for use in the bocage, unlike the Mark IV tanks.[24]

The destruction of the German armour continued and P-47s joined in from the air, diving on the assault guns around Le Dézert. By 1600 hours, the Panzer Lehr attack had been blunted. All the Panther tanks used in this attack were lost, as well as nine Stug IIIs.[25] The 899th Tank Destroyer battalion alone had destroyed eleven Panthers and a Mark IV tank. These wrecked Panther tanks would subsequently be examined by the Americans and used in armour penetration tests.

On the American left flank, the German columns of tanks and a battalion from the 902nd Panzergrenadier Regiment had been able to infiltrate behind the 119th Infantry Regiment lines east of highway and reached Cavigny. CCB was preparing to attack Les Hauts Vents once more when it was ordered to send Task Force Y to the aid of the infantry; two companies of tanks from the 1st Battalion were dispatched towards Cavigny. In response to this, the 2nd Battalion of the 902nd Panzergrenadier Regiment was forced to break off its attack northwards and help defend Cavigny. Task Force Y lost another six tanks to German self-propelled guns apparently firing from across the river at St Gilles, but the Germans were unable to penetrate the American lines in any great strength and their attack faltered. Later that afternoon the Germans withdrew from Cavigny.

A second German column advanced in the early morning into the positions of the 3rd Battalion of the 120th Infantry Regiment at Le Rocher. Unchallenged by sentries, tanks and armoured cars supported by panzergrenadiers on foot reached the battalion command post before the Americans realised what was happening and opened fire.[26] In the ensuing firefight in the dark, the Germans lost a further five Mark IVs tanks and four armoured cars and the attack was beaten off.[27]

Combined with artillery and air support, these actions were enough to defeat the advance by the two battle groups of the 902nd Panzergrenadier Regiment. The Panzer Lehr Division was forced to go on the defensive for the rest of the campaign.

CCB resumed the attack on Les Hauts Vents with the attack still being led in person by Colonel Roysden. As Panzer Lehr had attacked north-eastwards during the day, CCB had also advanced in the opposite direction in an effort to capture Les Hauts Vents again. When CCB pushed forward, the battle groups of the Panzer Lehr Division had swept past it on either side.

Les Hauts Vents and the strategic Hill 91 were finally recaptured by the combined efforts of Task Forces Z and X at 1736 hours and defensive positions were set up. The 2nd battalion (Task Force X) lost three tanks but knocked out a Mark IV just north of Pont Hébert.[28] CCB held Les Hauts Vents from 12 to 16 July waiting for the arrival of the remainder of the 30th Division. The 33rd Armored Regiment had thirty-one tanks destroyed or damaged, mainly by Panzerfäuste and all of these were M4s except for one M5 light tank.

In defeating the attack of the Panzer Lehr kampfgruppe around Le Dézert, CCA (32nd Armored Regiment) had tank casualties of three M4 medium tanks knocked out (one to Panzerfäuste) and two damaged but repaired plus two tanks unfit, with mechanical problems.[29] During the whole action, the 32nd Armored Regiment lost a total of twelve tanks destroyed, including two M5 light tanks, while twenty-seven tanks were repaired.[30] Twenty-four new tanks were issued by Ordnance to the division in this period. The 3rd Armored Division maintenance battalion repaired other tanks with routine mechanical problems, making a total of fifty-two tanks lost or damaged during the course of this battle. On 16 July, Colonel Boudinot, commander of the 32nd Armoured Regiment, assumed command of CCB to replace Brigadier Bohn.

The 2nd SS Panzer Division during this battle up to 23 July lost thirteen Mark IVs and thirty-one Panthers destroyed or damaged plus fourteen Stug IIIs destroyed or damaged. In the same period, Panzer Lehr lost twenty-one Mark IV and sixteen Panther tanks, with an estimated ten Stug IIIs also lost.[31]

The similar tank losses of the Americans and Germans demonstrated the difficulties of advancing in the hedgerows that gave the tactical advantage to the defenders. The initial American advances were strongly resisted by fewer German troops, but the counterattack by the Panzer Lehr Division was no more successful, many of its tanks being knocked out by well-sited American anti-tank guns, tank destroyers and M4 tanks at close range in ambush positions. The better firepower and armour-penetrating abilities of the German Mark IV and Panther tanks compared with the M4 Sherman were to some extent negated by the close ranges (less than 400yds) that most tank combat took place where the Sherman 75mm gun could penetrate the side and rear armour of the German tanks. This was provided the M4s could outflank the German tanks which was very difficult to do quickly in the hedgerow country even once the positions of German tanks were known. Therefore the German tanks on the axis of most American attacks were able to keep their thick frontal armour facing towards the Americans which the M4 could not penetrate and thus were very difficult to knock out. When the German tanks attacked, they lost the benefit of the cover provided by the hedgerows and American anti-tank guns on the flanks of the German advance were able to knock out the tanks by hitting them on their less well-armoured sides.

The XIX Corps infantry divisions continued their slow advance, and St Lô was finally reached on 18 July, representing an advance of less than a mile a day.

Overcoming the Hedgerows

The bocage countryside was unlike anything the US Army had operated in before and proved to be a formidable obstacle to the separate infantry, tank and artillery units. Not only were the hedgerows themselves obstacles but the German soldiers effectively utilised them to form a series of strong defensive positions by burrowing into the earthen banks at the base of the hedge to make shelters and firing slits. These shelters were then covered with tree branches and soil so as to make them virtually impenetrable to American artillery fire. Machine guns, some of them operating remotely, were fired on fixed arcs from positions in the hedgerows to cover the open field and flanking hedgerows. Observers for artillery and mortar batteries climbed trees in the hedgerows behind those being attacked to call down fire on the attackers. Where available, well-camouflaged tanks were positioned about 20yds apart as close as possible to the hedgerows and used as armoured fortifications with a squad of panzergrenadiers nearby for protection.[32] Provided the Americans could not outflank such positions, they were almost indestructible and were only vulnerable to a direct hit by a large calibre artillery shell. Anti-tank guns were set up to cover the only gaps in the hedgerows that allowed vehicles to enter the fields and thus eliminate any attempts to outflank a position.

Throughout June and the first half of July, most American infantry and armoured officers gained first-hand experience of the bocage and studied the problem of fighting in the hedgerows. The challenge was to combine the mobility and firepower of the separate arms so as to create a combined team that could rapidly fight its way through the hedges of successive fields. An example of the scale of the problem is described in this report from the history of the 17th SS Panzer Division:

At a range of 400–500 metres, an American tank cut a hole in the wall and hedgerow with its cutting spade. The tank commander went into a well-concealed firing position with his tank. An American tank drove through the gap, exhibiting no apparent concern, and out into the meadow. Three more of the same followed. As the fifth one showed itself in the gap, the right moment had come for the tank commander. The first round from his 75mm gun tore the turret off the American. The American tank stayed there, burning, and blocked the gap. The other four then fired in every direction, except at our panzer. Before they had figured out where their enemy was, the tank commander had knocked them all out.[33]

An obvious part of the solution was the need for infantry and tanks to work closely together in order to offer each other mutual support and harness the firepower of the tank's machine guns and main armament. The infantry had to protect the tanks so that the tanks could engage and neutralise enemy fire directed at them. The tanks provided a mobile platform for both machine guns to suppress enemy defences (thus allowing their own infantry to manoeuvre) and for the 75mm cannons to fire high explosive shells at enemy positions and anti-tank guns as a form of mobile artillery.

For the tanks and infantry to work together more effectively, problems of communication had to be overcome. In the din of battle and the noise of the operating tanks themselves, it was difficult for the infantry to communicate with the tanks which in any case were often closed up. One infantry officer fired his pistol at the turret of a tank in order to get its attention and, when the tank commander opened his hatch, he was promptly shot by a sniper in a nearby tree.[34] Hand signals were not very efficient and so telephone handsets were provided on the rear deck of tanks for the infantry to talk to the crew inside via the tank's intercom system. Radio communications were also improved with more radio sets being issued to the infantry. A practice that worked well was for an infantry officer to ride in the command tank of the supporting armoured unit while in radio contact with his own infantry so that tanks could quickly be directed to where they were required.[35]

The Allied air superiority allowed the artillery units of the infantry division to make liberal use of spotter planes above the battlefield which quickly allowed heavy and accurate artillery fire to be provided when required. Again, extra radios and communication links (especially VHF radios) between the ground and the air facilitated this process.

Improved tank/infantry cooperation was, however, only part of the problem. A means of physically forcing access to the fields through the hedgerows where the Germans were not expecting an attack was needed to outflank German positions.

The most successful way to force a gap in the hedgerows was with bulldozers, but as these were not plentiful or heavily armoured and were prone to breaking down, other methods were experimented with. One of these was to use explosives buried in the base of the hedgerow; this method, although often successful in creating a gap when the correct amount of explosive was used, still signalled the Germans as to the direction of the coming attack. The transport and placement of the explosives could also be a hazardous process for those men involved if under German mortar or artillery fire. As it was time consuming to bury sufficient charges, two steel prongs were welded to the front of an M4 tank to make holes in the earthen bank into which the explosive charges could be quickly inserted. It was then found by accident that an M4 tank with these prongs could force a gap completely through the hedge without the front of the tank rising up and exposing the thinly armoured underside of the tank to enemy fire. Various types of hedge cutters were devised by different units and fixed to the front of M4 tanks to enable a tank to ram a hedge-row and smash its way through a small section to make a gap to allow the entry of

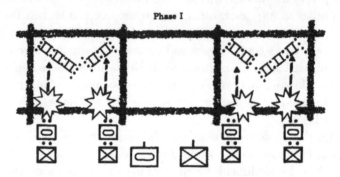

Phase I—Dozer tanks or engineer teams gap hedgerows as indirect fire falls on German positions. Tank and infantry teams attack along outer edges of fields, then sweep across the objective.

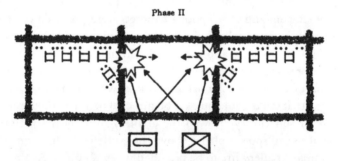

Phase II—Parent companies move forward and provide suppressive fire as friendly forces gap hedgerows of center field. Tank and infantry teams assault German position from the flanks.

The 3rd Armored Division plan of attack in the hedgerows, adapted from Captain M. Doubler, *Busting the Bocage. (By kind permission of Combat Studies Institute, US Army)*

a waiting platoon of tanks into the field. The most famous and effective device was that devised by Sergeant Culin of the 102nd Cavalry Reconnaissance Squadron in the 2nd Armored Division. Hundreds of Culin's device and other designs utilising similar metal forks and blades were hastily manufactured and welded to M4 tanks in time for Operation Cobra.

With this two-part solution of combined tank and infantry teams able to communicate with each other and tanks that could physically break through the hedgerows, each division found its own tactical solution to the problem and a common system was not ever adopted by FUSA. For example, the 3rd Armored Division adopted the tactics of attacking three adjacent fields at a time by forcing gaps in the two outer fields and then entering the fields with teams of tanks and infantry which worked their way along the perimeter of the fields. The centre field would then be attacked and breached simultaneously from three different directions.

These tactics were trialled at Villiers Fossard by CCA of the 3rd Armored Division and were not entirely successful as the tanks and armoured infantry managed to get separated and bulldozers broke down. However, this was perhaps more due to the combat inexperience of the men of CCA which trained intensively to perfect the tactics over the following weeks.

The 2nd Armored Division came up with a system of tank-mounted infantry attacking in two waves behind a first wave of only tanks. The infantry of the second wave dismounted to deal with targets located by the first wave and to protect the tanks while the third wave dealt with any enemy positions missed by the first two waves.[36]

The solutions devised by each armoured and infantry unit, although different, were all potentially successful and FUSA was now ready to try and get out of the bocage country once and for all into the open countryside south of St Lô.

Notes

1 Trahan, E.A., ed, *A History of the Second Armored Division 1940–1946* (Atlanta, GA, Love, 1947)

2 Houston, D., *Hell on Wheels – the 2nd Armored Division* (Novato, CA, Presidio, 1995), p.199

3 Harrison, D., *Cross Channel Attack* (Washington, DC, US Army CMH, 1951), p.365

4 RG407 After Action Report 66th Armoured Regiment, June 1944, NARA

5 AAR D Company 66th Armoured Regiment, August 1944, quoted in Bando, M., *101st Airborne – The Screaming Eagles at Normandy* (Minneapolis, MN, Zenith, 2011), p.101

6 RG407 AAR 66th Armored Regiment, August 1944, NARA

7 FUSA Operation Neptune Plan, 1944, NARA, p.125

8 Bryan, Major J., The Operations of Task Force Y, CCA at Villiers Fossard, MCOE Fort Benning paper, 1948–49

9 Bryan, *ibid*

10 32nd Armored Regiment S-2 report 30 June 1944, University of Illinois

11 FUSA Report of Operations 20 October 1943 to 1 August 1944, NARA, p.73

12 Bradley, O., *A General's Life* (New York, NY, Simon and Schuster, 1983) p.272

13 Weidinger, O., *Das Reich 1943–1945* (Manitoba, JJ Fedorowicz, 2012), p.153

14 *Ibid*, p.131

15 Dugan, H., *Spearhead in the West – The Third Armoured Division* (Paducah, KY, Turner, 1991)

16 Dugan, H., 'First Combat' (essay dated 17 July 1986, University of Illinois), p.3

17 2nd Battalion 33rd Armored Regiment log and journal, July 1944, University of Illinois

18 Taylor, C., St Lô 7 July–19 July 1944, US Army CMH, Washington, DC, 1946, p.29

19 Daugherty, L., *Battle of Hedgerows* (St Paul, MBI Publishing, 2001), p.151

20 Taylor, *opcit*, p.31

21 Dugan, H., *The 3rd Armoured Division Saga in World War II* (University of Illinois, 1986)

22 Rg319 EHINT 66 Bayerlein, Lt. Gen F., interview Panzer Lehr division Jan–28 July 1944, NARA

23 Taylor, *opcit*, p.39

24 RG319 EHINT 66, *opcit*

25 Rg319 EHINT 66, *opcit*

26 RG407 AAR, 3rd Battalion 120th Infantry Regiment, 11 July 1944, NARA

27 RG407 AAR, 30th Infantry Division July 1944, NARA

28 2nd Battalion 33rd Armored Regiment Log and Journal, July 1944, University of Illinois

29 32nd Armored Regiment journal and log July 1944, University of Illinois

30 RG407 3rd Armored Division G-4 journal July 1944, NARA

31 Zetterling, N., *Normandy 1944 – German Military Organisation, Combat Power and Effectiveness* (Manitoba, JJ Fedorowicz, 2000), p.390

32 RG 319 EHINT 66, *opcit*

33 Weidinger, *opcit*, p.158

34 Creamer, Major F. W., The Operations of XIX US Army Corps in Normandy, MCOE Fort Benning, 1946, p.27

35 Doubler, Capt. M., Busting the Bocage – American Combined Arms Operations in France 6 June to 31 July 1944, Combat Studies Institute, Fort Leavenworth, 1988, p.37

36 *Ibid*, pp.54–5

7

Operation Goodwood

Operation Goodwood is one of the most studied battles in modern history as it was the first Allied mass employment of tanks (three armoured divisions) in the Second World War. However, for all this research, the outcome continues to be debated along with the number of British tanks lost. The official British history is circumspect on the outcome, stating that although the position on the east of the River Orne had been improved, all the intended objectives were not met and in some respects execution fell short of intention.[1] Belfield and Essame state that the Germans had resisted 'any breakthrough' and lament the lack of co-operation between infantry and armour.[2] The British Cabinet history reflects Montgomery's final plan to dominate the area of Bourguébus-Vimont and Bretteville whilst writing down German armour and states that these objectives were largely attained.[3]

Interestingly, the Cabinet history is non-judgmental and gives the different opinions of Montgomery, Dempsey and O'Connor on the outcome. In his biography General Bradley suggests that the whole operation and subsequent commotion was part of a deliberate attempt to deceive the Germans about the place and date of the American breakout. Yet, as Belfield and Essame point out, this was the most powerful attack yet by the British in the Normandy battle which does not support an objective of merely attempting to deceive the Germans. The debate over Operation Goodwood continued long after the war as both Eisenhower and Montgomery used their biographies and articles to explain their positions and intentions, thereby perpetuating the controversy. Both were aided by various members of their command staff, such as General Bradley for Eisenhower and General Belchem for Montgomery, publishing works that supported their leaders' positions.

The background to the development of the plans for Operation Goodwood is worth examining in detail as the evolution of the plans directly influenced the outcome of the battle. The planning process itself also directly contributed to the furore that erupted after the battle which marked the beginning of the long-standing feud between Montgomery and Eisenhower.

Following the capture of Cherbourg, Montgomery's orders of 30 June were for Bradley to continue offensive action on the right flank by advancing south and then pivoting to face east to provide a protective line behind which the Third Army was to move south and west into Brittany.[4] Whilst Bradley's army was doing this, the Second British Army would continue to try and hold as many German forces as possible on the left flank around Caen.[5]

After a period of time for replenishment and replacements to arrive, FUSA had resumed major offensive action on 3 July. However, in the bocage countryside and the many low-lying flooded areas, the Americans made very slow progress, the daily advances often being measured in hundreds of yards or the number of fields or hedgerows gained in the face of tenacious German resistance. With the British left flank not making progress either, Churchill, Eisenhower and General Marshall (the US Army Chief of Staff) were concerned that a stalemate was developing in Normandy. Eisenhower wrote to Montgomery on 7 July lamenting that a 'major full dress attack' be mounted 'with everything we could bring to bear' had not yet been made and even offered the use of an American armoured division. In response to this growing criticism, Montgomery met with Dempsey and Bradley on 10 July and asked them both to come up with plans for major operations. Montgomery's instruction to Dempsey on 10 July was as follows:

Second Army will retain the ability to operate with a strong Armoured force east of the River Orne in the general area between Caen and Falaise,

For this purpose, a corps of three Armoured Divisions will be held in reserve, ready to be employed when ordered by me.

The opportunity for the employment of this corps may be sudden and fleeting. Therefore the study of the problems arising will begin at once.[6]

At the same time, Bradley was ordered to maintain the FUSA offensive southwards and westwards as per the previous directive and to link up with the British at Beny Bocage. On 11 July, Bradley began to conceive of a breakthrough operation from the high ground of St Lô at the southern edge of the bocage into the open countryside in what would ultimately be codenamed Operation Cobra.

Dempsey, in particular, was mindful of recent discussions with General Adam, the Adjutant General from the War Office, who had recently visited Normandy. Adam had reported that, given the high casualties so far in the campaign, if casualties continued at the same rate then there were only enough British infantry replacements until the end of July. It had also come to Dempsey's attention that there was a build-up of tanks in the beachhead. By mid-July, the British had approximately 2,250 medium tanks and 400 light tanks in three armoured divisions and five independent armoured or tank brigades within the bridgehead.[7] Dempsey's solution was to utilise these tanks in a major operation, thereby reducing the possibility of further casualties and having to cannibalise one or more infantry divisions to form replacements for other divisions. In arriving at this solution, Dempsey was clearly not aware of the emerging replacement crisis in trained personnel for the armoured units.[8]

Both Dempsey and Bradley were impressed by the power and success of strategic bombing during operations to capture northern Caen (Operation Charnwood) so they included it in their plans. Bradley would later claim he had already been working on the idea of using strategic air power following its limited use in capturing Cherbourg.[9] Dempsey enthusiastically laid out a plan for a concentrated armoured attack that would break through the German lines and then use the good tank country south of Caen to thrust deep into the German rear echelons, as far as Falaise. This would also have the secondary benefit of helping the Americans with their operation on the western flank if the Germans could be encouraged to retain their armoured divisions deployed around Caen – the so-called hinge, or pivotal point in the Normandy front line.

After initially rejecting Dempsey's plan, the usually cautious Montgomery accepted it next day and told Dempsey to develop the details. Thus both Dempsey and Bradley came up with remarkably similar plans for the breakout of their respective armies. Both would harness the power of strategic bombers and both would be heavily dependent on armour. Bradley's operation was scheduled for 18 or 19 July whilst Dempsey's plan, codenamed Operation Goodwood, was scheduled for the same dates. However, Bradley and Dempsey would use armour in different ways. Bradley would use infantry conventionally to make a breach in German lines and exploit it with two armoured divisions to penetrate deep behind the German lines before pivoting westwards to cut off all the enemy units in the front line around St Lô. Dempsey, on the other hand, in yet another departure from established doctrine, would use the tanks to make the breach itself in the German lines after the German defences in depth had been heavily bombed.

Dempsey presented his plan to Montgomery on 11 July and it was reluctantly approved. Both realised that the success of the operation depended on airpower, so on 12 July, Montgomery wrote to Eisenhower and Air Chief Marshal Tedder asking for their all-out support and promising fireworks. If Montgomery could have the 'whole weight of air power', he said, his 'whole eastern flank' would 'burst into flames'. The results would be 'decisive'.[10]

Faced with another request for heavy bomber support after what they saw as poor returns for the strategic air force assisting the ground forces during Operation Charnwood, despite northern Caen having been captured, Tedder and General Spaatz of the US air force were initially not very receptive. Having prepared the ground with his letter to Eisenhower, Montgomery, aware of the reluctance at 21st Army Group, then bypassed Tedder and Spaatz and sent Brigadier Richardson to England on the 16 July to pose the question directly to Air Chief Marshal Arthur Harris who quickly affirmed RAF support for the operation.

Dempsey's first operational order to the VIII Corps commander, General O'Connor, was made on 13 July. The instruction was for VIII Corps to cross the River Orne and 'establish an armoured division in each of the following areas, Bretteville sur Laize – Vimont – Argences – Falaise'. A copy of this order went to SHAEF headquarters and Eisenhower. The inclusion of Falaise as an objective at this stage, 20 miles behind the front line, clearly suggested a breakout was the objective.

Montgomery also sent a letter on 14 July with marked-up maps to the British CIGS, Brooke, explaining the plan of attack and stating that the objectives were to destroy all possible enemy troops in the general area of Caen, Mézidon, Falaise and Evrecy. Once a breach had been opened by the Guards and 11th Armoured Divisions, the 7th Armoured Division was to surge forward as far as Falaise, pushing a screen of armoured cars in front. Montgomery even suggested that victory in the east could help FUSA achieve its objectives.[11] The inclusion twice by Montgomery of Falaise as an objective confirmed the intention to breakout. Eisenhower and the staff at SHAEF began to get excited by Montgomery's proposed operation and gave their enthusiastic support. Eisenhower's reply to Montgomery on 14 July indicates his understanding of the intentions of both operations in that Goodwood would be a breakout attempt:

> I am confident that it will reap a rich harvest from all of the sowing you have been doing over the past weeks. With our whole front acting aggressively against the enemy so that he is pinned to the ground, O'Connor's plunge into his vitals will be decisive …
>
> I am viewing the prospects with the most tremendous optimism and enthusiasm. I would not be at all surprised to see you gaining a victory that will make some of the 'old classics' look like a skirmish between patrols …
>
> [Bradley] would keep his troops fighting like the very devil twenty four hours a day if necessary to provide the opportunity your Armoured Corps will need, and to make the victory complete.[12]

Clearly Eisenhower had either misunderstood the two operations entirely or expected the breakout to come from the British whilst the US troops kept the Germans busy. If Montgomery said anything to Eisenhower apart from the information contained in the Operational Orders of the 13 July that caused him to have this impression will never be known, but Montgomery was sufficiently alarmed by Eisenhower's enthusiasm to take two steps to downplay the importance of the operation. Firstly, he wrote some notes to Dempsey on 15 July, modifying the operation's objectives to liberating the rest of Caen and establishing a strong bridgehead south of the River Orne, only being prepared to exploit further if casualties were light and the opportunity presented itself. Montgomery emphasised that the advance southwards could only continue if the Canadians had secured Caen, as he had concerns about a German armoured counterattack from the west into the flanks of any attack southwards. Secondly, Montgomery despatched to London his own emissary, in the form of Lieutenant-Colonel Dawnay, to brief Brooke personally on the operation and downplay any notions of a breakout. At the same time Montgomery offered the tantalising possibility to Brooke of '700 tanks loosed on the Caen–Falaise road – anything may happen'.[13]

Therefore, in the space of 24 hours, Montgomery had undergone a major change of heart in terms of the objectives for the operation but still offered the hope of something else happening with '700 tanks loose'. It was almost as if Montgomery had a sudden attack of nerves and sought to downplay the operation in case it did not succeed. One historian has suggested that Montgomery's caution was due to both the fear of failure and the fear of success.[14] If the attack was unsuccessful then the British forces holding the Germans around Caen would be weakened; if the attack was successful then the Allies would have to plan and execute a series of exploitative battles in a fluid and unpredictable environment. This was a long way from Mongomery's preferred comfortable strategy of building up superior forces, staging a set piece battle and then 'crumbling' the enemy, as demonstrated at El Alamein.

It is also possible that Montgomery was alarmed by Eisenhower's reply of 14 July, as the reply provided further evidence to support his belief (shared by Brooke) that Eisenhower did not understand the strategy in Normandy. If this was a simple misunderstanding then the normal procedure would have been to arrange a meeting or send a letter to clear up any confusion, but Montgomery did not do this.

Not only did Eisenhower not receive the benefit of any later briefing, he did not receive a copy of Montgomery's notes of 15 July with the revised objectives either. The stage was set for massive recriminations if the operation was unsuccessful, as Eisenhower clearly had different expectations of Operation Goodwood.

On 16 July Dempsey issued his revised instructions to VIII Corps which incorporated the revisions into the Operational Orders issued that day to the corps units. The objectives had been changed to merely dominating the areas around Bourguébus, Vimont and Bretteville and only being prepared to exploit southwards if the conditions were 'favourable'. Note that even Bretteville is still 10 miles south of Caen. To reinforce the changes, Dempsey then issued notes of his own on 17 July confirming the objectives as Vimont, Hubert Folie and Verierre on the Bourguébus ridge. A copy of these notes were also apparently sent to SHAEF headquarters but were never received.

Bradley was forced to postpone Operation Cobra when it took FUSA, after struggling for two weeks through the bocage, until 18 July to capture St Lô. St Lô was to be the jumping-off point for Operation Cobra and time was needed to prepare for the attack. The decision was made by Montgomery to press on with Operation Goodwood, however. The onset of bad weather from 20 July effectively grounded the required heavy bombers and caused a further delay for FUSA until 24 July.

In planning the operation, Dempsey and his staff had a number of problems to contend with. Dempsey planned an armoured attack on a very narrow front, thereby relegating the tanks to the role of a battering ram, rather than one of exploiting their mobility. The Allies had three armoured divisions to use in the operation: the 11th Armoured Division; the veteran 7th Armoured Division; and the recently arrived Guards Armoured Division which had yet to be blooded in battle.

The bridgehead east of the Orne held since D-Day was very small, being hemmed in by the German-held area of southern Caen and positions to the east around

Bavent and Troarn. Attempts to expand it in June had been effectively resisted by the 21st Panzer Division. The planning challenges facing Dempsey included:

- A shallow bridgehead on the east bank of River Orne
- How to conceal preparations from the Germans
- Sufficient crossing points over the River Orne
- Minefields
- German defences and the battlefield terrain
- The German panzer divisions in reserve

The bridgehead held east of the River Orne did not have enough area to accommodate the infantry, armoured divisions and artillery earmarked for the attack and was in any case under German observation. Therefore it was proposed that the bulk of the armour and infantry divisions would be concentrated west of the river the night before and only cross the river after the attack had begun.

This created the second problem in that there were not enough bridges over the River Orne to take all the vehicles moving into battle. New bridges could not be constructed prior to the attack in daylight without alerting the Germans, so it was decided to begin construction of new bridges capable of carrying armour only on the night before the attack. I Corps was tasked with building three more bridges north and south of the existing three pairs of bridges across the Caen canal and the River Orne, whilst in the Canadian sector two more crossings would be built, including a raft ferry suitable for tanks.

The next problem facing Dempsey was the huge numbers of Allied mines that had been hastily laid as defences against a possible German counterattack; these had to be lifted and cleared to create safe channels for the armoured regiments to advance through. Again, this work could not be done in daylight without alerting the Germans and so work did not begin until two nights before the attack.

The Allies believed that the planned aerial bombardment would shatter the German front lines and then allow their tanks to 'crack about' behind German lines. The aerial support would be on a scale never seen before and would consist of:

- 1,056 RAF bombers using HE to attack the flanks, i.e., Colombelles in southern Caen, Cagny and the villages of Toufvreville, Sannerville and Bannville on the eastern flank to reduce the risk of a counterattack
- 483 medium bombers from USAAF to attack the area immediately in front of British positions along the intended centreline of advance with fragmentation bombs so as to not crater the ground excessively

A further 539 heavy US day bombers were to attack the areas around the villages of Four, Soliers, Bras and Frénouville to neutralise identified gun positions beyond the range of Allied artillery. Operation Goodwood would be cancelled for any reason, including bad weather, if air support was not available.[15] Tactical fighter-bomber support was to come from the RAF 83 Group, which was to attack outlying villages and provide direct air support as requested, as well as intercepting any German reserve units observed moving up to the battle.

Artillery would be provided by the guns of three corps and would target known German gun positions and anti-aircraft batteries as well as providing a rolling barrage along the centre line of advance behind which the tanks would follow. Due to the limited space in the bridgehead, the artillery too had to be concentrated west of the River Orne with the tanks. Once the armoured divisions had advanced beyond a certain point, they would then be out of support range and dependent on their own mobile artillery. Three Royal Navy ships, including the monitor HMS *Roberts*, with its two 15in guns, were detailed for counter battery fire.

General Roberts of the 11th Armoured Division queried the planned use of supporting infantry with the VIII Corps commander, General O'Connor, when battalions from his own brigade were detailed for the early capture of Cuverville and Démouville, only 2 miles from the start line. Once these infantry were detached, the tanks would then be on their own apart from a motorised company with each regiment. Roberts objected to this plan in writing but was bluntly told by O'Connor that if he did not like the plan then one of the other divisions could lead; Roberts backed down despite the plan being completely against current doctrine.

Once over the River Orne bridges, the terrain was largely of open fields and long gentle slopes up to the Bourguébus Ridge. To the tank commanders, who had been struggling in the closeness of the bocage terrain, this was an opportunity to 'give their horses their heads' once the planned intense aerial bombardment and artillery barrages had neutralised the German defensive positions. To further reduce the numbers of defenders, Montgomery also ordered diversionary attacks west of the River Orne (Operations Pomegranate and Greenline) to draw off the panzer division reserves and make the Germans think Caen would be encircled from the west rather than the small bridgehead to the east.

German Defences

Field Marshal Rommel had always expected an attack from Caen as this was the easiest route from Normandy in terms of favourable terrain and distance to the River Seine and Paris beyond. This was obvious from maps of Normandy and from German war games that had been conducted in the area since 1940.

From observation posts in the industrial area of south Caen (Colombelle), the relative heights of the Bourguébus Ridge and the high ground to the east which almost overlooked the invasion beaches, the Germans were able to observe British preparations. Any movement of tracked vehicles brought up clouds of dust, so much so that the attempts at deception were fruitless. German reconnaissance aircraft dropped flares nightly and were able to see the vast quantities of tanks and artillery being amassed around the wrecked gliders of the 6th Airborne Division that had captured the vital Ranville bridge over the River Orne on D-Day. Dietrich mocked his captors after the war by claiming that he could hear the British tanks moving up by putting his ear to the ground in Red Indian fashion.

In the front line, at the expected place of attack, was the 16th Luftwaffe Field Division and elements of the 21st Panzer Division. The 21st Panzer Division, having been in continuous combat since D-Day, was sorely in need of a rest and refit. The bulk of the division had been placed in reserve behind the Luftwaffe division, which had also been badly mauled in the fighting for Caen and was in reality nothing more than a screen for the German positions. However, Feuchtinger had not been idle and had prepared many defensive positions and firing pits for his tanks and assault guns. These defences were inspected regularly by Rommel and General Eberbach, the new commander of Panzer Gruppe West. The countryside south of the River Orne along the intended line of attack was a chess board of small, open wheat fields studded with small stonewalled villages every mile or so. By occupying and defending these villages, the Germans were able to create carefully planned arcs of fire and killing zones for their high velocity anti-tank weapons. The open Normandy countryside, which the British so coveted for their airfields and which was good tank country, was even more perfect for defence with its long, uninterrupted views and lines of fire. The British would also have to negotiate two raised railway lines that crossed the battlefield and would generally be attacking uphill, allowing the Germans to have a good view of the battle as it unfolded below them.

The Germans had several panzer divisions available for defence. The complete 1st SS Panzer Korps had recently been moved into the area. The 1st SS Liebstandarte Adolf Hitler was in reserve south of the Bourguébus Ridge around Bully and Bretteville sur Laize whilst the 12th SS Panzer Division was also resting in reserve around Potigny and Garcelles. The 1st SS Panzer Korps also had a heavy tank battalion (101st Schwere SS) attached of approximately twenty-five Tigers, with sixteen tanks operational on 16 July.[16] The 21st Panzer Division had only fifty Mark IVHs operational plus a battalion of fifty self-propelled guns converted by its commander, Major Becker, from captured French tanks. Thirty powerful 75mm Pak 40 anti-tank guns had been mounted on the chassis of Hotchkiss tanks and another twenty converted to fit 105mm howitzers. Firing pits, offering good camouflage and a low profile, had been prepared for each vehicle to move into and out of as the tactical situation required. Major Becker had organised these hybrid assault guns into five batteries, each of six anti-tank vehicles and four self-propelled artillery guns and deployed them in the various fortified villages along the anticipated British line of advance. The 503rd Heavy Tank Battalion, equipped with Tiger tanks, had taken the place of the second tank battalion of the 21st Panzer Division. Twelve of these Tiger tanks were the new Tiger IIs or King Tigers, at the time the heaviest and most powerful tank of the war.

German operational tanks and SP guns 17 July (per Zetterling)

	PzIVH	Panther	Stug III	Tiger I	Tiger II	SP A/t Guns
1st SS LAH	59	46	35			
21st Panzer	50					30
503rd tank bn				27	12	
101st SS tank bn				16		
Total	**109**	**46**	**35**	**43**	**12**	**30**

The 16th Luftwaffe Division had two Stug IIIs and the 346th Division had eight Stug IIIs as part of their mobile anti-tank sections. On the eve of the battle, the Germans could therefore muster fifty-five Tigers, forty-six Panthers, 109 Mark IVHs and seventy-five assault guns for a total of 285 armoured vehicles in the front line. In reserve, the 12th SS Panzer Division had twenty-one Panzer IVHs and eighteen Panthers operational on 16 July, giving the Germans a total of 324 tanks and self-propelled guns, including the reserves. It was accurately estimated by the British that the German armour in the front line numbered 250 tanks.[17]

The Germans also had a large number of anti-tank guns and dual-purpose 88mm Flak guns in the area. Three batteries of six 88mm anti-tank guns of the 21st Panzer Division were located on the Bourguébus Ridge as were up to seventy-eight dual-purpose 88mm flak guns of the III Flak Korps which had been deployed in a crescent from Bourguébus to Cagny to provide air defence for Caen.

The two panzergrenadier regiments of the 21st Panzer Division also had an anti-tank capability. The heavy support company of each battalion (there were two battalions to a regiment) had three 75mm Pak 40 anti-tank guns and two of these had been mounted on Somua half-tracks (another of Major Becker's hybrid vehicles) making a total of twelve 75mm anti-tank guns. These were dispersed in the villages defended by the panzergrenadiers, such as Le Mesnil Frémentel, Grentheville and Le Prieure. Each regiment HQ also had a battery of three 50mm anti-tank guns.

Therefore the Germans possessed a powerful anti-tank defence force. Rommel and Eberbach had created four formidable defensive belts plus had strong reserves in the tanks of the 1st SS Panzer Korps. The German positions were the strongest yet built in Normandy, but the British trusted that the fragmentation bombs of the USAAF along the proposed corridor of advance and the artillery barrage directly on the villages beforehand would neutralise these positions.[18]

On the evening of 17 July 1944, the VIII Corps had more than 750 tanks operational for the coming day's battle and a further 460 tanks to support the infantry divisions conducting the flank attacks. This total excludes the Stuart tanks which were virtually no longer fit for use on the battlefield and the self-propelled M10s of divisional anti-tank regiments.

British Tank Strengths 17 July 1944 (all figures from WO205/636)

	Sherman	Sherman VC	Stuarts	Cromwell	Cromwell CS
11 AD (29th Bde)	153	36	25		
2 NY			11	55	6
7th AD (22nd Bde)		35	34	141	17
8th Hussars				55	6
GAD (5th Bde)	162	36			
2WG				55	6
2CAB	153	23			
27th Armed Bde	60	33			
144 RAC	49	12			
Total	577	175	70	306	35

The 2nd Canadian Armoured Brigade would support the 3rd Division in clearing the industrial area around Colombelle (Operation Atlantic) to complete the capture of Caen. The 27th Armoured Brigade and a regiment from the 33rd Tank Brigade, the 144th RAC, were to support the 51st (H) Division and 3rd Division of I Corps in securing the eastern flank. If the tank forces of the divisions assigned to hold the flanks are excluded, the sabre strength of the three armoured divisions of VIII Corps assigned to make the breakthrough was more than 763 tanks which gave a numerical superiority of 3:1.

Dempsey and the Allied planners believed they had overcome all the potential flaws in the plan. Even when an Ultra intercept just 36 hours before the intended attack indicated that the Germans were expecting a massive operation, the Allies still believed they had the element of tactical surprise on their side and the operation would proceed.

So the stage was set for another Rommel versus Montgomery set-piece battle. The Germans, for their part, were ready and waiting. The only setback to their defensive preparations was the loss of Rommel on the eve of the battle. His staff car was strafed by two Spitfires as it returned from a last-minute inspection of the defences and a visit to Dietrich at the 1st SS Panzer Korps headquarters. Rommel received severe head injuries and was evacuated from Normandy, never to return. Ironically, Rommel had apparently been canvassing Dietrich's support in the event of a coup against Hitler in order to bring about a negotiated settlement to the war.[19]

At 0200 hours on 18 July, the attack was confirmed for daybreak that day. Once again the Allied attack had been named after an English racecourse, Goodwood, and the coming battle or race 'meeting' would give the opportunity for the modern-day cavalry regiments to conduct their favourite manoeuvre: the charge.

The Battle

Montgomery cabled Churchill on 17 July saying that because of his diversionary tactics he was very optimistic about the success of Goodwood: 'Conditions for big attack tomorrow very favourable as main enemy weight has moved to west of the Orne as was intended to oppose my attacks in the Evrecy area ...'[20]

Dempsey had moved his HQ to co-locate with that of VIII Corps on 17 July so he could take over the subsequent exploitation if the attack was successful and 'favourable opportunities' presented themselves. The tank regiments had two sleepless nights assembling for the attack:

> The night moves proved to be horrendous, moving nose to tail along dusty wind-ing tracks, tank commanders peering with bleary eyes out of their turrets trying to maintain station on the tank in front. This first move on the night of the 16th/17th July was accomplished without undue incident and we arrived in an area west of the Orne about 1.00am in the morning. Our orders were to lie up for the day, camouflage our tanks and get as much rest as possible. However the guns and instruments in the tanks had to be cleaned of the appalling dust which covered everything after the night march. We were able to cook meals on our small tank stoves although no fires were allowed and all movement was kept to a minimum in the leaguer area ...[21]

The Guards Division occupied a forming up place before the attack about 5 miles west of the River Orne bridges and only arrived in position at about midnight on 17 July so did not get much opportunity to rest or sleep either.

Just before daylight the British vanguard, the 3rd Royal Tank Regiment (3rd RTR) of the 11th Armoured Division, moved through the newly cleared minefield chan-nels to its starting position. At dawn, 0545 hours, the RAF aerial bombardment using 942 aircraft made up of 667 Lancasters, 260 Halifaxes and fifteen Mosquitos began in clear conditions.

The soldiers of both sides heard and then saw the approach of the massed forma-tion of bombers. The Allied soldiers settled back to watch the show, secure in the knowledge that there was a 6,000yd exclusion zone between them and the bomb-ing zones. The Germans presumed that yet another city in Germany was going to be targeted until coloured flares falling to the ground and the opening of bomb bay doors indicated that this time they were the targets and that they only had a few seconds to find cover. Most of the targets were satisfactorily marked by the RAF's radio direction finding system, Oboe, and at the only target where Oboe failed, the Master Bomber and other Pathfinder crews looked for and found it themselves.

Following behind the British bombers were more than 1,000 American bombers of the Eighth and Ninth US Airforces which attacked their targets with frag-mentation bombs. Some aircraft were unable to see their targets because of the smoke and dust raised by the previous waves of bombers and did not drop their loads. By 0830 hours, a total of 6,800 tons of bombs had been dropped of which

Bomber Command dropped more than 5,000 tons. The 8th USAAF after action report states:

> 644 B-24s are dispatched, in conjunction with Ninth Air Force and RAF Bomber Command, to bomb enemy equipment and troop concentrations in support of the assault by the British Second Army in the Caen area; 249 hit Solier, 146 hit Frénouville, 139 hit Troarn, 23 hit Hubert la Folie and 12 hit the Mezidon marshalling yard; 1 B-24 is lost, 2 are damaged beyond repair and 182 are damaged. 90 RAF Spitfires fly uneventful support for the B-24s.

The aircraft bombed from only a medium height, 5,000–9,000ft, but the combination of the bombing, artillery and naval gunfire quickly subdued many of the defending flak batteries and only six aircraft (five Halifaxes and one Lancaster) were shot down. Allied air superiority over the battlefield by day was complete and no German fighters appeared to hinder the bombing mission. The bombs fell on the German positions, not randomly but in a huge wall of explosions, thunderous detonations and fountains of earth that advanced towards them. As they were engulfed in the inferno, men simply disappeared, torn apart in the maelstrom of high explosives. Heavy Tiger tanks were overturned by the blasts and men cowered in their foxholes or under tanks wondering if they would be next:

> As far as my company were concerned, two Tigers were completely neutralised, two others were so badly damaged that they could not be employed. All the tanks were completely covered with earth and the gun sights had been thrown completely out of alignment by the shock effect. Fifteen men of the company were dead, two further had committed suicide during the bombardments; another had to be sent to a mental hospital for observation. The psychological shock of these terrible exchanges remained with us for a long time.[22]

The casualties amongst the infantry were far worse. The 16th Luftwaffe Field Division virtually ceased to exist, shallow infantry foxholes offering no protection to its infantry against the 500-pounder bombs of the RAF. General Eberbach reported the bombing as follows:

> The hail of enemy artillery shells and bombs had simply swept away not only the remaining half of the 16 LW Feld Div, but also the elements of 21 Pz Div which had been assigned to the second position in the rear. The local reserves had been annihilated or shattered, the guns smashed before they had even fired a shot.
>
> In addition, the telephone communication lines had been cut. The radio stations of the intermediate command staff, in so far as they had not been damaged, had been put out of commission by dust and concussion. The observation posts, in so far as they were not situated in the sector under attack, saw for hours nothing but a screen of smoke, dirt and flames. Thus the batteries which were left intact did not know where

to fire. And if they fired all the same, then enemy fighter bombers immediately dived onto them and silenced them with machine gun fire and bombs.[23]

Such was the chaos and the destruction in the German positions that when the British tank regiments moved into their crowded final assembly positions east of the River Orne before the attack, not a single German artillery shell landed on this tempting target; the aerial bombardment had effectively neutralised the German artillery positions and those of any forward observers in the front line.

At H-hour, 0745 hours, the artillery barrage began, a second creeping curtain of death that marched towards the German lines before enveloping them in another inferno of smoke, dust and explosions. Unfortunately for the waiting British tankers, some rounds fell short and landed amongst the 3rd RTR tanks, killing several officers and men. By the time the subsequent confusion was sorted out, the barrage had moved on and the leading tanks of the 3rd RTR were already behind the barrage and having difficulty in keeping up. The other two regiments followed in column with the 2nd Fife and Forfar leading the 23rd Hussars, each accompanied by their motorised infantry companies and artillery observers.

Once through the channels in the minefields, the 3rd RTR shook out into attack formation two-up, i.e. two squadrons abreast. Each squadron advanced in a square formation with a troop at each corner and squadron HQ in the centre; the tank troops themselves advanced in a V-formation with the Sherman Firefly tucked in behind the three tanks in front; the individual tanks were about 30yds apart.[24] The tanks went as fast as they could but visibility was poor due to the clouds of dust and fumes from the bombardment and tank drivers had difficulty in avoiding shell craters, even though only fragmentation bombs had been used. A speed of only about 5 miles an hour was possible and tanks reached their first objective, the Caen–Troarn single-track railway line, at approximately 0830 hours.

The German opposition to this point was very light. Dazed soldiers who appeared out of the gloom in front of the tanks with their hands up were waved to the rear by commanders as the tanks could not stop to pick them up. The effects of the bombing were felt for about 2 hours by the Germans underneath it and for the first 5 miles of the charge. Captain Lemon of the recce troop of 3rd RTR:

I rather enjoyed the first few minutes as I think most of us did. There was very little opposition and one had a wonderful feeling of superiority as many Germans, shaken by the preliminary bombing and shelling, gave themselves up, As time passed though, they became more aggressive, having overcome the effects of the shells and bombs … I and the tanks around me had some excellent MG shooting at targets that kept appearing in the hedgerows and the villages of Cuverville and Démouville … There were a couple of embankments to cross which proved to be awkward obstacles, but an AVRE with a 'dustbin' did an excellent job of blowing gaps, making the crossing easier. The objective was Falaise and it seemed at the rate we were going we would reach there comfortably …[25]

Lines of defensive anti-tank guns had been smashed by the bombardment and any emplacements showing signs of life were quickly shot up by the tanks. The single-track railway was not thought to be an obstacle by the intelligence officers of VIII Corps, but this proved to be a mistake. Built on a raised embankment up to 6ft high, the railway line was just navigable to the tanks but not to the wheeled vehicles following behind which had to find alternative crossing points such as the level crossing at Lirose. This caused much confusion and a further delay until engineers blew several gaps in the embankment. Two tanks of the 3rd RTR lost their tracks crossing the railway lines.[26]

Once across the railway, the available frontage widened and the 2nd Fife and Forfar came up on the left of the 3rd RTR who were to go to the right of the farm Le Mesnil Frémentel and the 2nd Fife and Forfar to the left of it. A dense hedge, reminiscent of those of the bocage, then barred the way of the 3rd RTR. It could only be crossed by a tank where the earth banks were lowest and the foliage sparsest. A gap was forced by one tank and enlarged by successive tanks passing through, making it passable for the wheeled vehicles following behind.

The artillery barrage stopped at 0905 hours and from then on the tank regiments were dependent on their own mobile field artillery provided by eight self-propelled Sextons with 25-pounders attached to each regiment.

A second hedge just north of Le Mesnil Frémentel was reached at about 0900 hours and searching for a gap caused a further delay. Once through this hedge, the tanks of the 3rd RTR were in plain sight of the defended farmhouse and anti-tank gunfire began to strike the advancing tanks. The position was defended by panzergrenadiers of the 125th Regiment and Becker's 4th Batterie. Concerned by the fire coming from Le Mesnil Frémentel, Major Close of the 3rd RTR radi-oed that he wanted to stop and shell the buildings but was told to keep going by the 29th Brigade HQ:

> This wasn't the usual way to deal with defended villages and I felt most uncomfort-able. We were crossing what was virtually a plain at this time and armour-piercing shot was coming from Cagny and Le Prieure. As the shot hurtled over the corn, you could see it rippling, leaving a wake like a torpedo. The paths were so clear that we were able to take evasive action.[27]

Major Close ordered his tanks to fire into Le Mesnil Frémentel while on the move. Attempting to bypass the position exposed the thinner armoured, more vulnerable sides of the Shermans to Major Becker's 4th Batterie of assault guns within the farm. The 3rd RTR experienced its first casualties, three Shermans being lost in quick succession. An infantry attack by the HQ company of 8th Rifle Brigade and half of its E (support) Company was organised by 29th Brigade HQ but it did not begin until 1030 hours, taking an hour to clear the farm house and surrounding area.

The 2nd Fife and Forfar, going east of Le Mesnil Frémentel, took its first serious casualties when it reached the second railway line embankment, the Caen–Vimont railway. The leading two waves crossed the embankment successfully but C Squadron, in the third wave, was devastated by fire believed to have come from the direction of Cagny to their rear whilst waiting to cross. Trooper John Brown in a Sherman Vc of the 2nd Fife and Forfar recorded:

> It was not long after the earlier euphoria that we realised what was in store for us – thirteen tanks, one of our squadrons knocked out, some burning and what remained of their crews either walking or crawling back from the front. Our tanks reached the Caen–Vimont railway [the second main obstacle] close beside a level crossing in the Cagny area. From our position we knocked out two, probably three German tanks, but it was difficult to recognise this in the carnage.[28]

Thirteen tanks were lost in quick succession at about 0930 hours. Was this Becker's 4th Batterie still in Le Mesnil Frémentel or 88mm fire from Cagny? The 2nd Fife and Forfar history is convinced that it was fire from Cagny. A veteran of the 3rd RTR believed it was the combination of the self-propelled assault guns in Le Mesnil Frémentel and the anti-tank guns in Cagny that did the damage to 2nd Fife and Forfar; smoke and dust from the artillery barrage plus that churned up by the advancing tanks made it difficult to locate the source of the enemy fire.[29]

The Charge Continues

As the leading tanks of the 3rd RTR approached Grentheville, having crossed the Caen–Vimont railway, armour-piercing fire increased from the direction of the village and its orchards. Major Close reported seeing anti-tank guns amongst the trees being turned by their crews to engage his squadron. Five Shermans were hit, their crews baling out. Another of Becker's assault gun batteries, the 3rd Batterie, occupied Grentheville. Again Major Close had to push on, leaving the enemy position to others to deal with. Ordered to get his squadron to the west of the Chemin de Fer Minier railway line that ran north-south over the Caen–Paris railways and roads, Close led his squadron into the relatively peaceful countryside west of the embankment using a culvert under the railway. The tank commanders could now see the industrial suburbs of Caen (Cormelles) and the villages of Hubert Folie and Bras higher up the ridge to the south. Sheltered by the railway embankment from the fire from Grentheville, the 3rd RTR believed they were through the German lines. The rest of the regiment came under the embankment either at the same point or further south and the remaining tanks formed up in line abreast for the advance up the slope. It was then about 1100 hours. An artillery barrage from the accompanying Sextons was put down on Hubert Folie and a Bren gun carrier quickly drove up to the village under cover of the barrage to determine if it was held by the Germans. Drawing no fire, the carrier careered the length of the village before hastily returning to report that Hubert Folie appeared to be unoccupied.

The regiment advanced up the gentle slope through wheat fields towards Hubert Folie and got to within 500yds of it when they were caught in a crossfire of armour-piercing shells. The Germans had either been too surprised by the appearance of the scouting Bren carrier to open fire or had been deliberately laying low. Fire came from Hubert Folie and Bras, as well as from the direction of Bourguébus back across the railway line. Tanks began brewing up and blackened figures threw themselves out of hurriedly opened hatches of tanks that had been hit and from which flames and smoke began to rise. Captain Lemon was now less confident:

> We did not hit the crust of the enemy, the 21st and 12th SS Panzer Divisions – it was just as the leading tanks were level with Hubert-Folie when the fun began. I saw Sherman after Sherman go up in flames and it got to such a pitch that I thought that in another few minutes there would be nothing left of the Regiment![30]

The 3rd RTR had run into the anti-tank gun screen of the 88mm flak guns of III Flak Korps and the anti-tank guns of the 192nd Panzergrenadier Regiment defending Hubert Folie. A battery of 88mm anti-tank guns from 21st Panzer Division may also have been present. The three squadrons lost nearly half their tanks in minutes in the crossfire:

> Bras is at the top of the slope beside a small wood. We started copping it there and I fired back, hitting a couple of SP guns and a tank before the Sherman on my left brewed up. The crew bailed out and came over to my tank carrying the gunner, a Scots lad called Hume who used to play for the battalion football team. I thought 'My God, Hummer, you will never keep goal again.' Both legs were hanging on by sinews. They got him on the back of the tank and I handed them morphine as I had other things to do. Hummer must have been gripping something when the shot entered the tank as one hand was taken off and the other burned black. I decided to get him back and called up the MO. When I had reversed to the bottom of the hill, Mac came up in a half track and took Hummer away but I heard that he died in hospital. By the time I got back up the hill we were getting it really badly and my tank was hit two or three times but not penetrated.[31]

The advance faltered in the face of the fierce German fire and Shermans began to move backwards as fast as they could go, zigzagging from side to side. The troop commanders urged their tanks to find cover of which there was precious little apart from small hedges. By 1130 hours, the 3rd RTR reported that it was in a very exposed position around Bras and Soliers. The regiment remained in this position for nearly 4 hours, waiting for support from other regiments and artillery to arrive.

The 2nd Fife and Forfar, once it had disentangled itself from Cagny, crossed the Caen–Vimont railway line and made for the villages of Soliers and Four but came under fire from Frénouville and Le Poirier and found it difficult to disengage. By 1115 hours, the regiment had apparently reached the limit of its advance as tanks were reported to be 400yds just east of Bourguébus. But this was an error. In reality, the tanks got no further south than south-east of Soliers. The flanking fire from the direction of Frénouville became heavier and more accurate, pinning down the left squadron. The 29th Brigade HQ told the 2nd Fife and Forfar not to worry about Frénouville as the Guards Division were going to deal with it.[32] Four unidentified tanks were spotted moving southwards from Frénouville at 1152 hours by the 2nd Fife and Forfar which were possibly Becker's 5th Batterie moving back from Le Prieure to its next position.[33] German infantry and anti-tank guns were seen in the villages of Four and Soliers while tanks were observed arriving in Bourguébus from noon onwards. B Squadron of the 2nd Fife and Forfar reached the outskirts of Soliers and Four and came under heavy fire from the defenders. The accompanying motorised infantry occupied Four, but this was to be their only success: the Fife and Forfar found it impossible to capture any other villages or make any further progress in the face of the arriving German reserves. The regiment had moved into the German killing zone created between Soliers, La Hogue and Bourguébus, all of which looked down on the advancing tanks from higher ground. John Thorpe, 2nd Fife and Forfar Yeomanry:

I see palls of smoke and tanks brewing up with flames belching forth from their turrets. I see men climbing out on fire like torches, rolling on the ground to try and douse the flames but we are in ripe corn and the straw takes fire.[34]

The 2nd Fife and Forfar tanks began to be picked off one by one and the regiment lost more than twenty tanks in this area; at 1245 hours the regiment reported only twenty tanks left.

The German reserves, in the form of the 1st SS Panzer Division, did not reach the field and attack until about noon so any tank casualties before this were due to the anti-tank guns and tanks of the 21st Panzer Division and Flak guns of the III Flak Korps.

Guards Morning

The Guards Armoured Division planned to attack two-up with the 2nd Battalion Grenadier Guards on the right to attack Cagny and the 1st Battalion Coldstream Guards on the left to attack Vimont, intending to pass to the east of Cagny. The objective of the division was to pass east of Cagny and press on to Vimont which had been described as the 'tailor's shop of the 21st Panzers'.[35] The 2nd Battalion Irish Guards was in reserve. The 11th Armoured Division crossed the River Orne more quickly than anticipated and at 0800 hours a frantic message was sent to 5th Brigade HQ by despatch rider to get the division moving, but the river was not crossed until 0930 hours. Both the Guards and 7th Armoured divisions were moving simultaneously after a VIII Corps staff officer, dismayed that the Guards were

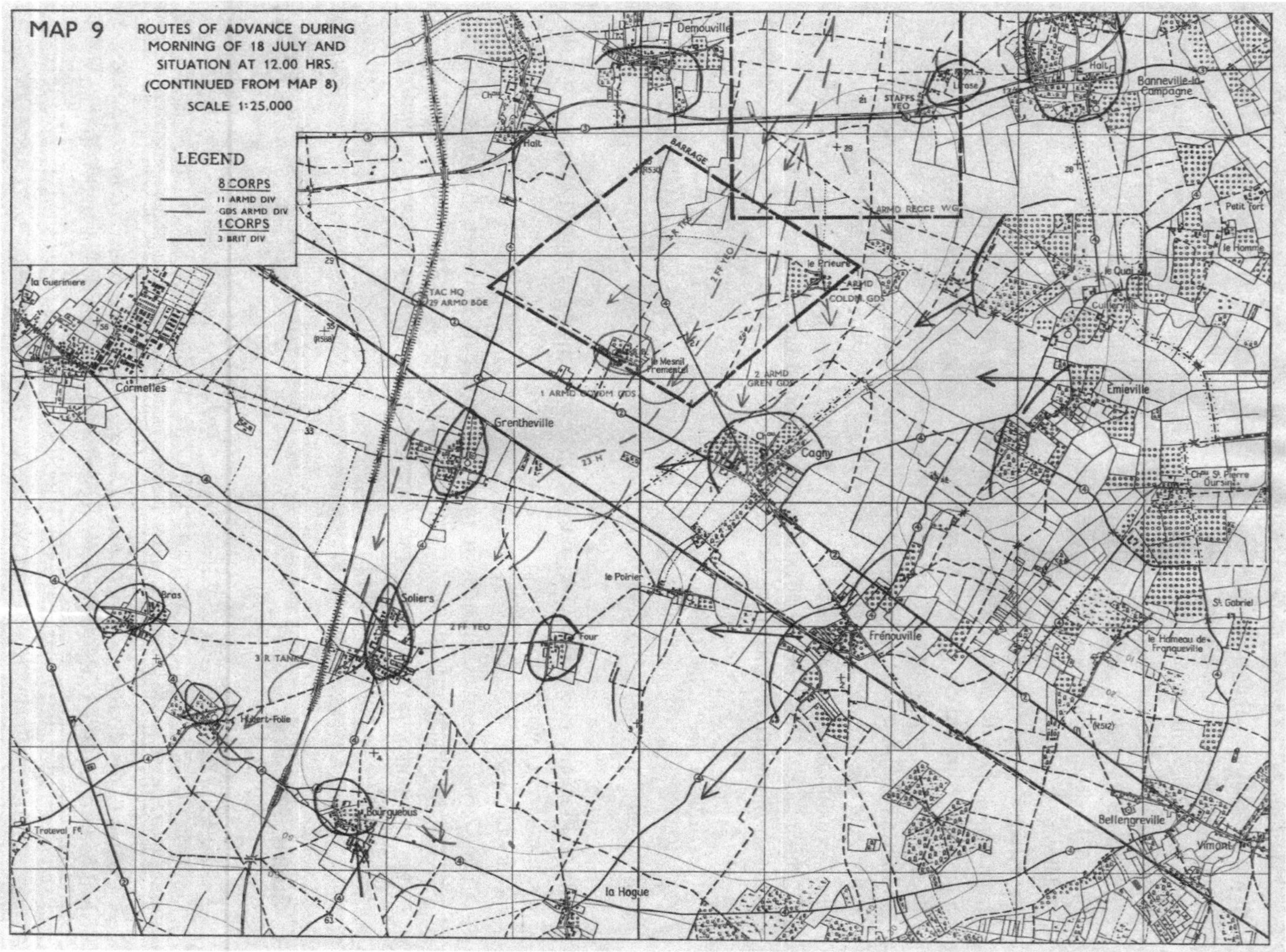

MAP 9 ROUTES OF ADVANCE DURING MORNING OF 18 JULY AND SITUATION AT 12.00 HRS. (CONTINUED FROM MAP 8)

SCALE 1:25,000

LEGEND

8 CORPS
— 11 ARMD DIV
— GDS ARMD DIV

1 CORPS
— 3 BRIT DIV

The limit of the advance of British armour in Operation Goodwood not following the 11th Armoured Division, ordered the 7th Armoured Division to move, despite the fact they were supposed to be following the Guards Division across the narrow start line.[36] The 7th Armoured Division in turn could not cross until the 2nd Canadian Armoured Brigade had used the bridges first, and an armoured traffic jam developed. At 0945 hours the leading Guards regiments were halted near Démouville but were ordered to press on at 1000 hours. At 1045 hours, the 1st Coldstream Guards was 1,000yds west of Emieville. At the same time, the 2nd Irish Guards was reported to be still 7,000yds west of the bridges over the River Orne which gives an indication of the traffic congestion building up around the bridges.

The 1st Coldstream Guards was in its first action of the war and were looking forward to it. From briefings given by General Adair and others, the Guards expected that this was the big offensive that would take them all the way to Paris. The opposition was expected to be 'feeble' after the bombing and there were only a few German tanks to oppose 700 British tanks in wonderful tank country of flat, open cornfields south of Caen.[37] After being ordered to move to cross the start line at 0800 hours, the regiment did not arrive in the vicinity of Le Prieure until 1100 hours because of delays caused by the fighting of the 11th Armoured Division and the 2nd Grenadier Guards ahead of them. Brigade HQ had also moved up to Le Prieure when the leader of the brigade protective troop of tanks saw movement inside the buildings so he opened fire, only for nearly 100 Germans to come out and surrender.[38]

The 2nd Grenadier Guards had a tougher baptism of fire. The initial advance southwards with No. 2 Squadron leading was uncontested until it arrived north of Cagny at 1115 hours; here the squadron began to lose tanks to the 88mm guns in Cagny, losing eight in quick succession. The CO then tried to put No. 1 Squadron around to the east of Cagny whilst No. 3 Squadron moved to protect the eastern flank.

As tanks of the Guards Division finally approached Emieville at about 1100 hours, the thin line of the 2nd Battalion 125th Panzergrenadier Regiment stretching from Emieville to Cagny was reinforced by the first anti-tank guns of the arriving Panzerjaeger Abteilung 1039 with its powerful 88mm Pak 43/41 and a few tanks.[39]

Tiger Attack

Following the cessation of the bombing and artillery barrage on their positions at Manneville, the crews of the 3rd Company of the 503rd Heavy Tank Battalion struggled to make their Tigers operational, a task not helped by the destruction of many of the workshop vehicles. Four tanks were beyond repair or had been turned upside down but, at about 1000 hours, six hastily repaired tanks moved out of Manneville southwards under the command of von Rosen to form a blocking force between Cagny and Manneville. Two tanks quickly broke down but the remaining four tanks took up defensive positions hull down below a small rise south of

Le Prieure. At about 1100 hours, a troop of four Shermans from the 2nd Grenadier Guards appeared from Le Prieure, probing eastwards. In a short, sharp engagement two Shermans were destroyed, forcing the remainder of the troop to retreat the way it had come. When many of the armour-piercing rounds fired at the Shermans missed their targets, the Tiger crews realised to their horror that their gunsights had been knocked out of alignment by the blasts from the bombing. The Tigers moved south towards Cagny to find a better defensive position when suddenly two of them were knocked out by armour-piercing rounds fired from the direction of Cagny, piercing the normally inpenetrable frontal armour of their tanks. This was unprecedented and caused the nervous Germans to fear further casualties, so the move was broken off as 'they could not pinpoint the source of fire and did not want to suffer any further total losses'.[40] With that, the remaining Tigers of von Rosen's 3rd Company limped from the battlefield and took no further part in the action, preferring to concentrate on salvaging what tanks they could from Manneville. By 1600 hours there was only one Tiger tank operational.

Whilst von Rosen's 3rd Company was sorting itself out, the 1st Company under Oberleutenant Oemler, equipped with King Tigers, was also doing the same and by 1100 hours eight tanks were ready for action. Proceeding north from the vicinity of Manneville, the Tigers then turned westwards and began to approach the British columns of tanks, wheeled vehicles and carriers pouring southwards along the corridor from the bridgehead over the River Orne. The Tigers approached the neck of the corridor at its narrowest point which was barely 1 mile across from Lirose to Démouville. As it traversed a wheat field, Oemler's tank fell into a large bomb crater and was immobilised while two other King Tigers were engaged from their flank by a Sherman Vc of the 1st Coldstream Guards which knocked them out. Displaying similar over-caution to von Rosen, Oemler blew up his own tank and the remaining five tanks called off their weak attack. For the rest of the day, the 1st Company along with the 2nd Company defended the area between Emieville and Frénouville before the entire 503rd Battalion was withdrawn when darkness came.[41] Another King Tiger would be lost in unusual circumstances in a confrontation with the 2nd Battalion Irish Guards. As a counterattacking force, the Tigers of the 503rd Battalion were very ineffective in this battle and certainly did not live up to the reputation of their comrades on the Eastern Front who regularly carried out 'fire brigade' actions to restore the front lines. The salvaged Tigers, King Tigers and Panzer IVHs formed ad hoc defensive positions for the rest of afternoon in support of the remnants of 1st Battalion 125th Panzergrenadier Regiment in a line from Cagny to Emieville.

The Cagny Anti-tank Guns

One of the most celebrated stories of the Normandy campaign is that of the German commander of the 125th Panzergrenadier Regiment of the 21st Panzer

Division, Major Hans von Luck, who arrived back from leave in Paris just after the British artillery barrage had ceased. Von Luck commanded a kampfgruppe made up of his 125th Panzergrenadier Regiment and other forces, including the 4th Company of Mark IVHs, which lay directly in the proposed British line of advance. According to von Luck, in an effort to find out what was happening he was driven, still in his dress uniform, in a Mark IV tank to Cagny where he saw the tanks of the 11th Armoured Division streaming past the village to the west. On his way back to the command post von Luck noticed a battery of four Luftwaffe 88mm flak guns, their barrels pointing skywards, in the centre of Cagny. Von Luck then asked the Luftwaffe captain if he knew that there were British tanks already bypassing Cagny and ordered him to move his guns to an orchard north of the village to engage them. The following conversation then apparently took place:

'Major, my concern is fighting enemy planes, fighting tanks is your job. I'm Luftwaffe.' He was about to turn away. At that I went up to him, drew my pistol (which we had to carry for trips to Paris), levelled it at him and said, 'Either you're a dead man or you can earn yourself a medal.'[42]

The captain realised that von Luck was serious and decided to comply with the order, quickly moving his guns into the orchard overlooking the lines of advancing British tanks. Von Luck arrived at his command post just as the barrage ended, so the time was about 0905 hours. The leading elements of the 3rd RTR and 2nd Fife and Forfar reached the Caen–Vimont railway at 0930 hours and were across it 15 minutes later and this is when disaster struck C Squadron of the 2nd Fife and Forfar as they were milling about waiting to cross the railway.

Some doubt has been expressed post-war as to the existence of the battery of 88mm flak guns in Cagny. Doubt has crept in as a result of von Luck's larger-than-life character and a tendency to enjoy telling the story of his part in the battle on post-war lecture tours. Other historians have not been able to find any photographic evidence of flak gun emplacements and so claim they did not exist.[43]

An 88mm Flak 36 gun deployed in anti-aircraft position takes a six-man crew 3.5 minutes to convert it to the travelling position on two bogies and only 2.5 minutes to ready it for a ground fire role whilst still on its bogies in the travelling position.[44] Therefore the 88mm flak battery would need only about 15 minutes to relocate a short distance. It is most likely that it was these 88mms that caused so many losses to the 2nd Fife and Forfar about 0930 hours. The only other possible unit is Becker's 4th Batterie in Le Mesnil Frémentel. However, if this company did not move before 0930 hours, it would have been cut off when the leading tanks of 29th Brigade crossed the railway. The 4th Batterie was able to relocate successfully to just south of Four where it was in action for the rest of the day and so must have moved well before 0930 hours.

As part of the III Flak Korps, German heavy anti-aircraft guns were located in the outlying villages of Caen as protection against the high-flying medium and heavy Allied bombers that had been bombing Caen. Photographic evidence of the Luftwaffe batteries in the area exists.[45] Given the general hostility of the German army towards the Luftwaffe because of its continued absence from the Normandy battlefield, it is unlikely that the German army would credit the Luftwaffe for anything unnecessarily. The timeline from von Luck's confrontation with the Luftwaffe battery commander just after 0900 hours fits with the subsequent losses of the 2nd Fife and Forfar C Squadron at 0930 hours as it took this time to relocate the 88mm guns to new positions to enfilade the advancing British tanks. The loss of the two Tigers moving southwards after engaging the Shermans from the 2nd Grenadier Guards by clean penetrations of the Tiger's frontal armour suggests the actions of an inexperienced Luftwaffe crew faced with large, unidentified tanks coming straight for them.

With the later German decision to abandon Cagny, the 88mm flak guns were destroyed on von Luck's orders so only wreckage could be found after the battle. The Guards Division King's Infantry occupied Cagny late in the afternoon and found three 88mm anti-tank guns.[46] An alternative explanation has been put forward that the self-propelled guns of Becker's 5th Batterie may have stopped to defend Cagny during their withdrawal from Le Prieure to Frénouville.[47] At 500m the 75mm Pak 40 was capable of penetrating 120mm of armour, so at 650m it could have just penetrated the Tigers' frontal armour of 100mm. However, these penetrations would not have been as clean as those from 88mm armour-piercing shells. Von Luck correctly attributed credit where it was due and his only sin is the assumption of a mantle previously worn by Rommel who stopped the British tank attack at Arras in 1940 by ordering the 88mm flak guns to engage the ground targets of the British tank force. Usually located well behind the front lines, 88mm anti-aircraft crews did not expect to become embroiled in fighting as per III Flak Korps policy and their direct involvement occasionally took some persuasion.

An officer of the 2nd Fife and Forfar wrote in his memoirs of his surprise at seeing a German officer in dress uniform surveying the battlefield from Cagny and accordingly fired a couple of 75mm HE shells at him, which missed.[48]

11th Armoured Division Afternoon

At 1210 hours, the infantry attacks by the 159th Brigade on Cuverville and Démouville were still in progress, supported by tanks of the 2nd Northants Yeomanry which, despite being the reconnaissance regiment of the 11th Armoured Division, had been detailed to support the attack on Cuverville in front of the British bridgehead. Roberts thought that if support was lent to his infantry then their task would be completed more quickly and they would then be able to assist the tank regiments. After a bad start losing four tanks on British mines, Cuverville was captured and in the next action at Démouville, the 2nd Northants Yeomanry destroyed two 105mm SP guns that were part of Becker's 1st Batterie. The 23rd Hussars were also involved in this battle around Démouville until ordered to advance to Grentheville at 1205 hours. By then the 23rd Hussars had got more than a mile behind the leading regiments and were unable to offer any immediate support to the regiments in front.

The Panther battalion of the 1st SS Panzer Division began to arrive in the early afternoon and made repeated raids on the 2nd Fife and Forfar tanks, the first serious attack taking place at about 1300 hours. The counterattack was made straight off the march by the tanks as they arrived in Bourguébus, Soliers and Frénouville from their position in reserve. Tactical air strikes were called in by the British on the tanks moving up towards Bourguébus, but despite causing some damage they could not slow the stream of arriving German armour.

The Panthers charged straight down the hill towards the British tanks and a confused tank melee developed in which the long-range superiority of the over-committed Panther tanks was largely negated as tank fought tank at close range. The commander of the 1st SS, Theodore Wisch, tried to recall the Panthers in a message at 1250 hours as evidenced by a message intercepted by the Canadians. The reply was also intercepted, to the effect that the Panthers were too heavily engaged to withdraw.[49] The 1st SS Panzer Division had not learnt from the close range tank battles of Kursk a year earlier.

When the 1st SS Panthers finally managed to withdraw, ten were left behind as smoking wrecks. From then on, the Panthers made more judicious raids on the largely immobile Shermans below them while other Panthers worked themselves into good positions to fire on the British tanks from long range. The Tiger tanks from the 101st Schwere SS Battalion arrived later in the afternoon and added to the enormous firepower of the Germans, bringing destruction to the helpless Shermans in the cauldron below them. In the 2nd Fife and Forfars, Captain Hutchinson of A Squadron took up a flank guard position facing south-east from just north-east of Four and in this role destroyed two Panthers.

A VIII Corps command conference was held at 1300 hours between O'Connor and the commanders of 11th and 7th Armoured divisions and at 1350 hours it was decided to continue the attack towards Bourguébus with the two divisions. Roberts was at pains to point out the need to eliminate the village strongpoints using artillery and infantry as the tanks could not capture and hold them on their own and in the meantime were receiving many tank casualties from the anti-tank guns there. The 23rd Hussars were to move to the left of the 3rd RTR to attack towards Soliers and Bourguébus, east of the Chemin de fer Minier railway. The 3rd RTR was effectively isolated from the rest of the division as they were positioned west of the embankment of the Chemin de Fer Minier towards Caen.

Since 1255 hours, the 23rd Hussars had cautiously moved up to support the 2nd Fife and Forfar and, after crossing the Caen–Vimont railway, they could see the battlefield ahead littered with burning tanks. B Squadron advanced straight into the ring of flaming tanks and immediately its own tanks began to be knocked out by a largely unseen enemy. Reaching Soliers, a firestorm of shot then descended on B Squadron, forcing them to move back to a hedge, which afforded precious little cover:

> Every five minutes there was a crack of armour-piercing shot passing through the air, the shattering crash as it penetrated a Sherman, the shower of sparks, the sheet of flame and then black figures silhouetted against an orange glow as they jumped to the ground, sometimes pausing to drag a wounded comrade after them. The slow crackling as the tank began to burn, black smoke pouring out of the turret, and later, at intervals, the vivid crimson flashes and violent rending as the ammunition blew up.[50]

Since they were advancing along the same centre line as the 2nd Fife and Forfars, it is not surprising that the 23rd Hussars ran into the same trouble. Smoke and dust made visibility poor (one reason why the 1st SS Panthers may have opted for the raids on the Shermans in the valley below that resulted in the close quarter duels) and the well-camouflaged German positions were extremely difficult to spot. The 23rd Hussars radioed Brigade HQ at 1425 hours that there appeared to be so few 2nd Fife and Forfar tanks left that if they began the attack as ordered then a gap would be left in the front line.[51]

C Squadron moved up out of sight of the rest of the regiment behind a ridge toward Four. A sudden volley of armour-piercing shot decimated the squadron:

> … almost in one minute, all of the tanks of three troops and Squadron Headquarters were hit, blazing and exploding. Everywhere wounded and burning figures ran or struggled for cover, while a remorseless rain of armour-piercing shot riddled the al- most helpless Shermans. Major Shebbeare's tank was one of the first to be hit. He was never seen again. Dazed survivors ran to and fro helping the many wounded, beating out flaming clothing with their hands until the intense heat and violent explosions drove them back to the cover of the railway line.[52]

The 23rd Hussars had run into Panther tanks that had reinforced Four and the 4th Batterie of Becker's assault guns that had relocated from Le Mesnil Frémentel.

Finally, at about 1500 hours, the surviving tanks of the 2nd Fife and Forfar were withdrawn through the 23rd Hussars, back across the Caen–Paris railway to a position east of Grentheville behind Hutchinson's troop which had by then lost two tanks. On assessing their losses, thirty-seven tanks were found to be missing. The regiment claimed the destruction of two Panthers, two Mark IVs, five self-propelled guns and three 88mm anti-tank guns. At dusk, six Tiger tanks attacked in the last action of the day. Grentheville itself had still not been cleared and having been a source of trouble for the armoured regiments for most of the afternoon, it was not secured until 1800 hours by the motorised infantry accompanying the 23rd Hussars.

By 1500 hours, the 23rd Hussars had lost the equivalent of a squadron of tanks and were continuing to lose more. Faced by this overwhelming onslaught and unable to advance, the 23rd Hussars retired back as best they could over the Caen–Paris railway line at about 1800 hours.

Meanwhile, the 3rd RTR was coming under increasing pressure from the German tanks and at 1400 hours had to withdraw from the slope leading up to Hubert Folie to a position next to the Chemin de Fer Minier railway embankment near Soliers.[53] This move at least sheltered them from fire from east of the railway but not from Hubert Folie and Bras. The regiment stayed in this exposed position until 1700 hours when it pulled back further to a position 500yds northwest of Soliers. Mixed groups of Panthers and Tigers mounted attacks during the rest of the afternoon and evening as they tried to outflank the 3rd RTR.[54] One attack from Soliers was led by a captured Sherman, but this did not fool an alert gunner in an M10 self-propelled anti-tank gun who knocked it out along with two Panthers.

At 1515 hours, in a last throw of the dice, Roberts ordered the 2nd Northants Yeomanry to the aid of the pinned-down 3rd RTR. Throwing the Cromwells of the reconnaissance regiment into the fray after the decimation of the Sherman-equipped sabre regiments was a desperate move by Roberts to get the attack moving again. At 1640 hours, the 2nd Northants Yeomanry arrived in the area but initially one squadron could not find a way across the Caen–Vimont railway. Another squadron found a culvert under the railway west of Grentheville and started moving towards Bras, only to be halted by fierce fire 1,000yds from it. C Squadron also incurred many casualties around Soliers. The Northants Yeomanry were then hit by a counterattack by the Stug IIIs of the 1st SS assault battalion making a pincer attack around the village of Bras about 1800 hours. A total of sixteen Cromwells were knocked out in quick succession.

At 2230 hours, the remaining tanks of the 3rd RTR withdrew further north to a harbour in the lee of the Minier railway embankment; only twenty tanks of the regiment survived the day, thirty-six having been knocked out and five more damaged.[55] The 23rd Hussars lost twenty-three tanks and the 2nd Fife and Forfar forty tanks, but this was subsequently revised to thirty-three tanks with four breaking down.[56]

However, the onset of darkness gave no respite to the 2nd Fife and Forfar. After midnight, parachute flares dropped by German bombers over the River Orne Bridgehead revealed the masses of wheeled vehicles and soldiers drawn up in support of the attack. The subsequent bombs could not fail to hit any targets and unfortunately several fell close to where the 'unhorsed' Fife and Forfar crews were recovering after their ordeals of the day; six officers and men were killed and forty-three wounded. The next day the 2nd Fife and Forfar could only muster twenty-five serviceable tanks, with twelve in A Squadron and eleven in C Squadron. By

1900 hours, all armoured regiments (except the 3rd RTR) had been forced to retire back over the Caen–Vimont railway in the face of the ever-increasing numbers of German tanks.

Thus ended the charge of the 11th Armoured Division. Initially halted by the fierce defensive fire of the 21st Panzer Division's assault guns and the anti-tank guns of the surviving 125th and 192nd Panzergrenadier Regiments, the arrival of the SS Panthers and Stug IIIs unhorsed so many riders that the race had to be abandoned.

Guards Afternoon

At 1527 hours, three Tiger tanks and two Mark IVHs were reported moving north-west out of Cagny towards the British corridor.[57] This was possibly a late warning of the attack earlier by the 1st Company of the 503rd Tank Battalion but certainly indicates that some German tanks had recovered from the bombardment.

Due to a misunderstanding between the commanders of the 11th Armoured and Guards Armoured divisions that Cagny was heavily defended, the British delayed attacking it until more infantry had arrived. In fact, it would have been possible to have cleared it much earlier in the day with the motorised infantry of the 1st Grenadier Guards Battalion. As the 32nd Guards Brigade of infantry prepared to attack Cagny at about 1600 hours, von Luck ordered the 88mm flak guns in Cagny that had caused so much havoc to be blown up and the village abandoned.

The 2nd Grenadier Guards were ordered to occupy Cagny and this was duly achieved in an hour at about 1800 hours with the tanks accompanying the King's Company of infantry from the 1st Battalion of Grenadier Guards. Tank losses for the regiment for the day were fifteen Shermans and one Stuart destroyed or disabled and six other tanks damaged but repairable within 24 hours.[58] The squadron leader of No. 2 Squadron, Arthur Grant, was killed, and the regiment commanding officer lamented his death:

> [Grant] is the greatest (loss). He was quite excellent. His squadron was the first into battle and he was exercising a most wonderful control of it. I always felt he knew far more about this Armoured business than any of us here.[59]

The 2nd Irish Guards

The 2nd Battalion Irish Guards, the reserve regiment, following behind the Grenadier and Coldstream Guards, did not cross the start line until noon and suffered its first casualty at 1300 hours when a Sherman was hit and brewed up as they advanced.[60]

At about 1500 hours, other tanks were engaged from the direction of Emieville by the newly arrived Panthers which were well hidden in the orchards around

Le Prieure. A low ridge runs southwards from Emieville and the ground between Cagny and Emieville is open to this ridge which is crossed by a few hedges and roads.

The 5th Brigade HQ ordered the 2nd Irish Guards at 1600 hours to push onto Vimont, so No. 2 Squadron charged up this ridge east of Cagny with the objective of entering Frénouville to the south before moving on to Vimont. Lieutenant John Gorman, after bogging his tank in a small stream north of Cagny, took over another tank in his troop of three and moved uphill, following a line of pylons before turning north-east along a lane. This lane led back towards Emieville, so Gorman was actually going in the wrong direction, away from Frénouville. In a field in hull down positions just below the crest of a hill, a King Tiger tank, a Tiger I and a Mark IV were stationary and engaging targets as they moved southwards down the corridor of the advance towards Cagny. This was a mixed group of surviving tanks from the 503rd Heavy Tank Battalion and the 21st Panzer Division. The King Tiger, number 122, had taken part in the abortive attack by the 1st Company of the 503rd Battalion earlier that day. Both sides were as surprised as each other at the sudden appearance of Gorman's tank and as the King Tiger began to traverse its gun towards the Sherman, the Sherman's 75mm gun jammed. Thinking quickly, Gorman ordered his driver to increase speed and ram the King Tiger before it could bring its gun to bear. The Tiger, in an effort to bring its gun to bear more quickly, began reversing and tried to turn towards Gorman's charging tank. With a crash of metal, the Sherman struck the Tiger in the left rear flank. Both crews quickly abandoned their tanks and took cover. The other German tanks had turned to counter this new threat and when the remaining tank of Gorman's troop appeared over the hill, their concentrated close-range fire immediately destroyed it.[61]

Undaunted by this experience, Gorman returned to Cagny on foot and found a Firefly that had just been hit. The German AP round had penetrated the tank and killed the commander but otherwise left the tank relatively undamaged. After removing the body from the tank, Gorman took command and returned up the hill towards the Germans. This time he avoided the lane and, using the hedges of the field in which the German tanks were positioned for cover, moved into a firing position by nosing the Firefly into the hedge from where he could see the Germans. He first aimed at the King Tiger and after a few rounds caused it and his previous Sherman to catch fire. Return fire from the other tanks began to come uncomfortably close, so Gorman backed out of the hedge and moved 100ft to a new firing position and then destroyed a Tiger I with several rounds. Other tanks from his squadron then arrived and a firefight developed, forcing the German tanks back into Emieville.

For the rest of the day the 2nd Irish Guards battled tanks, self-propelled guns and 88mm Pak 43 anti-tank guns of the 1st SS along the line Frénouville to Emieville, losing at least eight tanks knocked out and two damaged in exchange for the King Tiger no. 122, a Tiger I, two Panthers, two Stugs and two anti-tank guns.[62] The 2nd Irish Guards finally harboured just north of Cagny that night.

At 1200 hours, the 1st Coldstream Guards, unable to make any further progress south-east towards Vimont, were instructed to try to get around Cagny from the west. This new order required the 1st Coldstream Guards to advance along the same route as that of the slowly arriving 7th Armoured Division. As the leading squadrons of Guards tanks neared the Caen–Vimont railway line, they could see the wrecked and burning tanks of 2nd Fife and Forfars on the rising ground in the distance. The commanding officer of the 1st Coldstream Guards decided that his regiment would not become a part of the unfolding disaster.[63] After skirting Cagny westwards, the regiment proceeded slowly and cautiously towards Frénouville, moving between Cagny and the Caen–Vimont railway and made no attempt to cross the railway line. Meanwhile, the 2nd Fife and Forfars were receiving heavy flanking fire from the direction of Frénouville and Le Poirier, and their brigade HQ was expecting the Guards tanks to eliminate this problem by advancing on Frénouville. But the Coldstreamers, not having any accompanying infantry to winkle out any of the hidden anti-tank guns engaging them from Le Poirier and Frénouville, halted. No. 2 Squadron moved back to a wood and a wall running north–south from Cagny to the railway and spread out along the wall where they remained in the same exposed position for the next 4 hours. Panther tanks stalked the Shermans, taking occasional pot shots and forcing them to change positions by moving a few yards. As the Sherman tanks moved cautiously about, they tried to avoid falling into the large bomb craters. The regiment's technical adjutant arrived with three ARVs in the evening but mistakenly drove into an orchard already oc-cupied by three Panthers. In a rapid exchange of fire, one ARV tank was knocked out before they made a hasty escape. Later, two tanks did fall into bomb craters on their way to the harbour.[64]

An attempt by the 1st Coldstream Guards to capture Le Poirier just across the Caen–Vimont railway using its Grenadier Guards motorised infantry also failed and the unit harboured south of Cagny. The regiment had no tank losses in battle for the day (one Panther was claimed hit) and the only other casualties were seven guardsmen wounded in the harbour that night during a German air raid. Next day, the regiment took up defensive positions north of Cagny.

That afternoon twenty-seven tanks were claimed as destroyed by three 88mm anti-tank guns of the newly arrived 1039 Abteilung blocking the advance of the Guards towards Vimont, which would not taken by the British for another six weeks.[65]

The 2nd Grenadier Guards and 1st Coldstream Guards saw no further action in Operation Goodwood. An attack by the division towards Vimont was planned for the next day but then cancelled so the regiments remained in position for a day or so before moving back to rest around the bridgehead over the River Orne. The 2nd Irish Guards had a Firefly damaged the next day in an exchange of shots with Germans near Emieville. Frénouville and Le Poirier were occupied by infantry but the battle was over for the Guards Armoured Division.

Casualties in the Guards Division were relatively light. The 2nd Grenadier Guards had twelve men killed and twenty-nine men wounded or missing, and the Irish Guards had six men killed and nine wounded or missing, whilst the Coldstream had no battle casualties.

7th Armoured Division

Led by the 5th RTR, the 7th Armoured Division began to move from its starting position at its designated time and reached the River Orne bridges 1 hour later at about 0900 hours. From then on, its progress was very slow as the 5th RTR had to wait for Canadians to get across London bridge first while the 2nd Irish Guards, bringing up the rear of the Guards Armoured Division, crossed York bridge. By 1130 hours, the 5th RTR was only just south of Cuverville, having only advanced 3 miles and the 1st RTR was still only crossing the river. The operations of the 159th Brigade with the 2nd Northants Yeomanry tanks clearing Démouville also delayed the 5th RTR and at about 1300 hours, the regiment lost its first tanks (a Vc and a Stuart) in the vicinity of Démouville to the recovering Germans.[66]

At 1340 hours, despite continued exhortations from VIII Corps to keep moving forward, more traffic congestion was reported by the 5th RTR which had caught up with the tails of the 29th and 5th Armoured brigades. The later movement of the 1st Coldstream Guards westwards around Cagny also hampered the advance of the 5th RTR. The 5th RTR was then ordered to push on to La Hogue but by 1600 hours was only approaching Grentheville from the north. Two hours later, the 5th RTR was east of Grentheville after crossing the railway but the 1st RTR was only at Démouville and the 4th County of London Yeomanry tanks were still crossing the River Orne bridges.

The 5th RTR was then directed to send a squadron towards Four where Panthers were reported; C Squadron advanced cautiously towards the village but immediately came under accurate German fire at 1900 hours from two Panthers and two Mark IVHs. Two of these were destroyed, as were two Cromwells.[67] Artillery was then used to force the Germans back into Four whilst the 5th RTR then claimed that they could not manoeuvre around Four because of 29th Brigade tanks in the area.[68] A Squadron of the 5th RTR was then ordered to attack Soliers but was held up by twelve German tanks; by 2200 hours the squadron had not gone much further southwards from Grentheville and eventually harboured there for the night. The rest of the regiment harboured at Le Mesnil Frémentel whilst 22nd Brigade HQ did the same just south of Démouville. The 5th RTR lost a total of six Cromwell tanks that day. The progress of 7th Armoured Division had been painfully slow due to the traffic congestion and a great deal of caution as it proceeded slowly southwards through the smoking, wrecked Shermans of the 11th and Guards Armoured divisions.

19–20 July

The Germans launched minor probes and reconnaissance patrols during the morning which delayed British preparations for resuming the attack. At 0700 hours, the panzergrenadiers in Four succeeded in reoccupying Le Poirier. The 2nd Northants Yeomanry performed a reconnaissance at first light towards the orchards south of Cormelles but came under fire from tanks and anti-tank guns on the ridge.

After a restless night, the 3rd RTR moved out early in the morning and slowly advanced up the ridge towards Bras and Hubert Folie again. Another firestorm from German artillery and anti-tank guns descended on them and several tanks were quickly knocked out.[69] It was clear the Germans were still present in force and where possible had improved their defences overnight. Realising that a more co-ordinated attack was required, the 3rd RTR were forced to retire back behind the Caen–Paris railway to reorganise. Other reconnaissance patrols reported German infantry reinforcing Four.[70]

As if shell-shocked from the previous day's operation, the British could only manage a slow start next morning. General O' Connor scheduled a command conference for 1200 hours for the divisional commanders where they presented their operational plans for what was left of the day. This time the plans had been formulated by the commanders themselves rather than having been imposed on them by Dempsey and O'Connor. The 159th Brigade had finally been reunited with the rest of the 11th Armoured Division overnight and was available to work with the regiments. Tanks, infantry, motorised infantry and artillery would be used in several scaled-down limited attacks to try and capture the villages that had been the previous day's objectives. Given the failure on the first day to break through, Dempsey had apparently lost interest in the battle.[71]

The Germans were not idle during this unexpected reprieve, regrouping and reorganising their defences as the remainder of their reserves came up into line; the 12th SS Panzer Division was positioned both sides of Caen–Vimont road. New defence lines were created further to the rear and the infantry of the 1st SS Panzergrenadier Regiments relieved the 192nd Panzergrenadier Regiment of the 21st Panzer Division.

The 2nd Northants Yeomanry were ordered to attack at 1600 hours and take Bras with a company of the 8th Rifle Brigade and, when that was done, the 3rd RTR were to assault Hubert Folie with fire support to be provided by the 2nd Northants Yeomanry. General Roberts specifically warned the 2nd Northants Yeomanry not to go too far west towards Ifs as strong German anti-tank forces had been located there the previous day.

Despite the warning, the 2nd Northants Yeomanry strayed westwards and a barrage of well-aimed fire from Ifs stopped the attack cold; within 20 minutes it was obvious the attack could not succeed. Five tanks were lost very quickly and the attack came to a halt. The Germans had seen the build-up of British armour and had decided to withdraw from Bras for the attack, leaving only two Stug III assault guns to defend the village. In the interim, the Stug companies were gathered as a mobile reserve behind Hubert Folie.[72]

The commanding officer of the 3rd RTR, Colonel Silvertop, suggested that his regiment could attack Bras (despite only having three squadrons of ten tanks in each left) as the 3rd RTR could not complete its own mission for the day of taking Hubert Folie without the support of the 2nd Northants Yeomanry. This offer was accepted and following an artillery barrage, motorised infantry from the 8th Rifle Brigade charged through the cornfields towards Bras whilst 3rd RTR tanks shot them in before rampaging through the village, destroying anti-tank guns wherever they found them. Within an hour, Bras was taken, there being only light resistance from a few remaining panzergrenadiers and the two Stug IIIs. The tanks remained in observation and finally withdrew to harbor at 2300 hours in the A echelon area.

As the 3rd RTR had now occupied Bras, the 2nd Northants Yeomanry was ordered to attack Hubert Folie. As they moved into position, a report was received that Cromwell tanks from 22nd Armoured brigade had already occupied the village. A delay ensued while this was clarified during which the Germans opened fire and six tanks were quickly knocked out by Tiger tanks. By about 1830 hours, the regiment was reduced to a single squadron and could not continue the attack. The 2nd Northants Yeomanry casualties for the day were another seventeen Cromwells that included two 95mm close support tanks.

The 2nd Fife and Forfar were again allowed no rest and were ordered to attack Hubert Folie, following the failure of the 2nd Northants Yeomanry attack. After a heavy artillery barrage at 2000 hours, the attack succeeded without further tank losses and Hubert Folie was handed over to a motorised company of the 8th Rifle Brigade. The 2nd Fife and Forfar then retired back across Caen–Vimont Railway. Their fellow regiment, the 23rd Hussars remained in reserve all day.

7th Armoured Division

Such was the traffic congestion in the River Orne bridgehead that the tail of the 7th Armoured Division did not complete the crossing of the Orne bridges until 0430 hours on 19 July. The plan the second day was for the 7th Armoured Division to play an active part in the battle and help achieve the original objectives, as clearly there was going to be no opportunity to exploit or break through to Falaise. The 22nd Brigade was instructed to clear Soliers, Four and Bourguébus. A German reconnaissance in force from Four towards the 5th RTR positions just after 0700 hours was beaten off.

The 5th RTR attacked Soliers and was able to clear it by 1130 hours as it was defended by only a few panzergrenadiers but fierce fighting took place around Four before midday. Accordingly, plans were later changed for the 5th RTR to break off from Four and attack Bourguébus at 1700 hours whilst the 1st RTR was to resume the attack on Four.[73] B Squadron of the 1st RTR attacked Four at 1400 hours and after heavy fighting until 2200 hours, the village was cleared with assistance from a company from the 1st Rifle Brigade.

In the afternoon attack on Bourguébus, the 5th RTR found that, unlike Soliers, it was defended by three Tigers and two Panthers. A brief firefight at close range in the village saw two Tigers and one Panther destroyed for the loss of two Cromwells and a Firefly from B Squadron. The regiment subsequently retired to Soliers where they spent a nervous night in unsecured positions as German infantry continued to infiltrate Soliers and Four in the darkness.

By now, Bourguébus was almost surrounded on three sides, yet still could not be captured and continued to be defended by German tanks. At last light, the situation was very confused; German tanks were infiltrating between the villages into firing positions on higher ground and conducting long-range fire whilst panzergrena-diers tried to creep back into the villages. However, by midnight on 19 July, most of Operation Goodwood's revised first-day objectives had been taken with the exception of Bourguébus, Frénouville and Vimont. The last word on the day's fighting can be left to the chief tactical planner of Operation Goodwood, General O'Connor of VIII Corps:

Summary of Ops 19th July

Although only a short advance had been made, the ground gained was of great tactical importance and had considerably improved the position of the Corps compared with the situation at the start of the day. The positions won had entailed hard fighting and even during the morning while the 'sorting out' was in progress, there was a steady toll of casualties in personnel and tanks, but the total day's casualties were much less than on the previous day, particularly in II ARMOURED DIVISION.[74]

On 20 July, B Squadron of the 5th RTR moved back at first light into Bourguébus. Here they encountered a solitary Tiger barring their advance, which was duly outflanked and destroyed. The regiment was then relieved and moved back to Démouville.

The reserve regiment of the 7th Armoured Division came into action for first time on this day. The 4th County of London Yeomanry advanced to the Caen–Falaise road between Bras and Hubert Folie, the Germans having moved back to new defensive positions. B Squadron advanced to the Beauvoir Farm south-west of Bras, while C Squadron shot in the Canadian infantry in their attack on Troteval Farm before retiring.

A thunderstorm produced heavy rain later that day at about 1600 hours, halting all further fighting and bringing time for both sides to rest and reorganise. The heavy rain made vehicle movement very difficult and all air support was grounded. Having not broken through the German lines on the first day, despite their best efforts, Operation Goodwood was brought to a close by the British. For their part, the German lines had once again buckled under the British onslaught but had just held. However, many irreplaceable men, tanks and self-propelled guns had been lost and the chains containing the British beachhead were stretched to breaking point.

Conclusion

At 1600 hours on 18 July, Montgomery made the following report to the CIGS Alan Brooke:

> Operations this morning a complete success. The effect of the air bombing was decisive and the spectacle terrific. VIII Corps advanced at 0730 hours. Present situation as follows:
>
> 11th Armed div reached Tilly 0760 (Tilly la Campagne)-Bras 0663. 7th Armed divn passed area Démouville 1067 and moving on La Hogue 0960. Guards Armd divn passed Cagny and now in Vimont. 3rd infantry Division moving on Troarn. Have ordered the armed car regiments of each div, supported by armed recce regt, to reconnoitre towards and secure crossings over Dives between Mezidon and Falaise.[75]

For a commander who had gone to great lengths to ensure his instructions for Operation Goodwood were implemented, this report was extraordinarily inaccurate. The 11th Armoured Division had got nowhere near Tilly and had made no further progress south since noon that day, having spent the afternoon largely trying to find cover from the German anti-tank fire and avoid further casualties. The Guards Armoured Division were not near Vimont and had not even captured Cagny at the time of this communiqué. The 7th Armoured Division was still 4 miles away from La Hogue and only the 5th RTR had crossed the Caen–Paris railway. A solid defensive line had been created by the 1st SS Panzer Division and it would have been impossible, if not suicidal, for the lightly armed reconnaissance forces to venture further south than the Caen–Paris railway. Just how Montgomery came to this appreciation of the day's fighting is almost beyond belief; how could the most senior British officer be so ignorant of the real situation on the battlefield? Did O'Connor and Dempsey fail to reveal the true situation to Montgomery? The divisional commanders of the 11th and Guards Armoured divisions had not been backward in reporting their difficulties to O'Connor. Were O'Connor and Dempsey holding on to a faint hope of a breakthrough?

It was almost as if Montgomery had already prepared this report before the day's battle and it was sent out accidentally. However, just to underline that the report was intentional, a similar statement was released soon afterwards for the BBC evening news and the story of Montgomery's apparent 'breakthrough' was telegraphed around the world.

For a few brief hours, to the watching world, Montgomery of Alamein had again achieved a miracle victory and the stalemate in Normandy had been broken. However, just as quickly as Montgomery was feted, when it became apparent that the attack had failed to break through, a storm of protest led by the Americans and the British air chiefs descended on Montgomery. Eisenhower sent a strong letter to Montgomery on 21 July expressing his disappointment with the outcome of the battle. 'I thought that at last we had him and were going to roll him up. That did not come about.'[76]

The reaction of the CIGS to the results of Operation Goodwood is not recorded in his normally meticulous diaries. Indeed, Brooke that day was more concerned about rehabilitating Montgomery in the eyes of Winston Churchill who believed that Montgomery had banned him from visiting Normandy.[77] Brooke retrieved the situation by flying to see Montgomery on 20 July and dictated an apologetic letter for him to send to Churchill. Suitably mollified, Churchill finally visited Montgomery (and Eisenhower) on 22–23 July; no recriminations were targeted at Montgomery who smoothed the way with a gift of a bottle of vintage brandy to Churchill. In discussions with Eisenhower, Churchill was apparently content with the situation.

In private, Eisenhower was far more explicit, raging after Churchill's visit that 'Monty had sold Winston a bill of goods.'[78] Montgomery was suffering the fallout from his ambitious promises to Eisenhower and SHAEF and for failing to keep Eisenhower fully informed. Montgomery's relationship with Eisenhower was irretrievably damaged and their differences would remain until the end of the war and beyond.

Tank Losses

The actual tank losses during the battle are difficult to determine from the records that have survived the battle. The main reference used by many historians is the Military Operations Unit (MORU) report No. 23 prepared in October 1946, which gives the daily losses for all the armoured brigades and their reconnaissance regiments for the four days of the battle. According to the MORU report, a total of 493 tanks were damaged, knocked out or destroyed and this has given rise to the accepted figure of 500 tanks lost.

MORU Operational Study Operation Goodwood no. 23

	17th	18th			19th			20th		
	P	P	Q	R	P	Q	R	P	Q	R
27 AB	220	201	6	18	194	4	4	195	-	-
29AB 11AD	214	91	13	115	96	12	16	132	5	9
2NYeo	72	46	1	15	35	4	16	46	-	1
22AB 7AD	216	198	10	8	191	11	4	199	12	3
8H	72	67	3	2	62	8	2	70	-	-
5GB	235	153	1	62	198	15	18	166	5	27
2WG	68	63	1	4	68	1	3	66	2	4

18th 224 in total r cas
19th 63 in total r cas
20th 44 in total r cas

From the MORU study data for the three armoured divisions, the total 'R' casualties are 331 tanks with another 104 damaged.

The MORU report indicates that the Guards Armoured Division reported sixty-five tanks lost on 18 July and then continued to report losses of twenty-five and twenty-seven tanks for the next two days, even when the tank regiments were not in combat. As the armoured regiments disengaged and there was more time for a better assessment of casualties and damage, the more accurate figures were reported. However, the MORU report does not recognise this and merely totals the unit's reported daily tank states so that in some instances tank losses have been counted twice.

Post-war historians and authors have also made errors that have subsequently become held as truths over the years. An VIII Corps report claims that the 2nd Northants Yeomanry lost thirty-seven tanks on the second day of the battle, as does Daglish.[79] However, the second day's figure is the two-day total losses for the regiment as confirmed in the regiment history and 11th Armoured Division reports.[80]

The actual losses of the Guards Armoured Division have been hard to determine from war diaries and many official divisional histories have also not provided much detail, even when written by serving officers. Most authors have not distinguished between tanks merely knocked out and tanks written off which has added to the confusion.

Servicing the Guards Armoured Division, the 268th Field Delivery Squadron supplied twenty-four Shermans, five Cromwells and three M5 Stuarts between 19 and 25 July 1944 so it can be assumed these were direct replacements for those tanks written off. The Guards Armoured Division REME commander's report details the tanks lost in Operation Goodwood as follows:

- Zw – (destroyed and burnt) – sixteen
- Z – damaged, major repairs required in 3rd echelon workshops – nineteen
- Y – repairable longer than 24 hours – thirty-one

Therefore the Guards Armoured Division lost thirty-five tanks as Z casualties and thirty-one tanks were damaged for a total of sixty-six knocked out.[81] A further twelve 'X' (repairable within 24 hours) casualties were repaired by regimental LADs.

In the heavy rain after the battle, it took the REME some time to examine all the knocked-out vehicles and much information was lost as two regimental adjutants had become casualties themselves. Using regiment war diaries and official reports, a more accurate summary can be put together.

As can be seen in the table below, the total number of tanks destroyed or disabled for more than 24 hours was 213 with an estimated further sixty-two X casualties for a total of 275, which is a lot lower than the MORU report and other previous estimates.

	Sherman	Sherman X cas	Cromwell	M5 + others	Total cas
11th Armoured Div*					
Repaired by LADs		40			
Not yet recovered	15		14	9	
Process of recovery	13		6		
Written off	26		2	2	
In 2nd line workshops	5		4	4	
In 3rd line workshops	18			3	
Inc 2nd NY recce **Tot**	**77**	40	26	18	**161**
Guards Armoured div **					
Written off Zw	15			1	
Third line Z	19				
Second line Y	30	12		1	
inc 2nd WG recce **Tot**	**64**			2	**78**
7th Armoured div			8	2	
27th Armoured Bde	12				
2nd Canadian Armd Bde	3	10		1	
Tot	**15**		8	3	**26**
Total Goodwood	**156**	**62**	**34**	**23**	**275**

Sources:
* WO 171/248 DDME HQ 2nd Army, July 1944, Appendix, Operation Goodwood
** WO 171/386 Guards Division CREME report Goodwood, September 1944

The British Cabinet history, after quoting the MORU report, then gives a revised figure of 156 tanks lost, which is the number of tanks in the Zw category and thus totally written off.[82] The bulk of these losses were in the 29th Brigade of the 11th Armoured Division, which had reported 118 tanks knocked out with eighty-five of these being in the Z category. This was the equivalent of two entire armoured regiments being lost. The DDME Operation Goodwood report for the 11th Armoured Division gave the total tanks knocked out or damaged as 161 with forty of these being X casualties repaired by regiment LADs, so the division had 121 tanks knocked out, which corresponds with the 29th Brigade report.

German losses have been researched by historians such as Niklas Zetterling and Wolfgang Schnieder. The major difficulty with German tank casualties is the Panzertruppen policy of not writing off any recovered tanks in long-term repair as being lost to enemy action. German losses between 17 and 21 July were as follows:[83]

- 21st Panzer Division … twenty-eight Panzer IVs (twenty-two recovered by the British from the bombed area around Manneville)
- 1st SS Panzer Division … twenty-six Panthers and sixteen Stug IIIs damaged or lost around Bourguébus and Soliers

- 503rd Schwere Tank Battalion … seven Tiger Is and three Tiger IIs[84]
- 101st SS Schwere Tank Battalion … three Tiger Is

The total of German armoured vehicles lost or damaged in Operation Goodwood was therefore eighty-three tanks and self-propelled guns, almost the strength of an entire panzer division at that time in Normandy. Montgomery had certainly achieved one of his objectives, of writing down German armour. With few replacements reaching the panzer divisions, this loss brought the situation in Normandy to a critical state for the Germans.

Casualties

One of the significant planning factors of Operation Goodwood was the high infantry casualty rate sustained to that point in the Normandy campaign and the looming shortage of infantry replacements, coupled with a surplus of tanks building up in the beachhead ordnance parks. Post-war, Dempsey claimed that the loss of 500 tanks was not unreasonable and he was prepared to lose many more.[85] In reality, 275 tanks were lost or damaged and infantry casualties (killed, wounded or missing) were as follows:

- I Corps 1,656
- VIII Corps 1,818
- XII Corps 449
- 2nd Canadian Corps 1,614

Therefore the total of men killed, wounded or missing during the period of Operation Goodwood, 18–22 July, was 5,537, including the limited flank and diversionary actions taking place elsewhere.[86] As the total cumulative losses of the 21st Army Group from D-Day to 22 July were 45,795, Operation Goodwood was responsible for a further 12 per cent of British Second Army casualties, hardly the preservation of infantry said to be so dear to Montgomery and Dempsey. Clearly, Operation Goodwood failed in its objective of casualty minimisation. However, Dempsey did not acknowledge this in his post-war interview with Wilmot:

> Our tank losses were severe but our casualties in men were very light. If I had tried to achieve the same result with a conventional infantry attack, I hate to think what the casualties would have been.[87]

Note that the MORU report into Operation Goodwood gives total casualties of 4,011 killed, wounded or missing, which is still 8.76 per cent of the total Normandy casualties to 22 July. RAC casualties in the armoured divisions (excluding infantry) were as follows:

	Killed		Wounded	
	Officers	Other ranks	Officers	Other ranks
11th AD	13	84	28	176
Guards AD	4	23	5	53
7th AD	3	9	7	39
Total	**20**	**116**	**40**	**268**

As RAC fatalities only totalled 136, this is another indication that fewer tanks were lost than officially reported. As the number of tanks knocked out was 213, the casualty numbers are still fewer than the expected average as per the study by Coox and Naiswald, which found every time a tank was knocked out, an average of one man was killed and another wounded.[88] This can partially be explained by the fact that Sherman crews, after six weeks of fighting, had more experience at bailing out from tanks hit by enemy armour-piercing rounds; some crew members had already bailed out of two or three tanks by the time of Operation Goodwood. The numbers of men wounded are more in line with the expected average if 275 tanks were lost or damaged, bearing in mind that on the night of 18 July, the 2nd Fife and Forfar lost three officers and four ORs killed plus forty-three men wounded in the German air attack.

Failure of the Plan

The build-up of Allied armour before the attack was plainly seen by the Germans from observation posts in chimneys at Colombelles and from the high ground to the east of Caen which undoubtedly led to Dietrich's post-war comment about Red Indians.

The additional bridges required for Operation Goodwood were not all completed until 0200 hours on the second day of the attack, although one bridge was completed by 1745 hours on the first day. However, this was too late: the crossings had acted as choke points and hindered the armoured advance from the start.

By dawn on 18 July, seventeen channels had been cleared through British minefields, so mines did not restrict vehicle movement as much as the bridges had done. Despite the fears of the planners, very few German mines were encountered along the centre line of the advance with the exception of the southern suburbs of Caen where several Canadian tanks were damaged. In fact, shipments of German mines to the Normandy front had been delayed in Paris by the Allied bombing of the railway system.

The axis of the VIII Corps advance was far too narrow: the initial frontage that was allowed for the advance of three armoured divisions was that normally used for a single armoured brigade. This narrow frontage for the attack prevented the armoured regiments from spreading out as well as not allowing any other supporting arms to move up with them. This made the armoured regiments dependent on their own motorised infantry brigades to capture villages and flush out anti-tank guns. As there was only one motorised battalion per brigade, this allowed only one motorised company for each regiment. O'Connor had ordered Roberts to use the 159th Brigade to clear the villages of Cuverville and Démouville so these men were unavailable to Roberts for the rest of the day. Therefore on 18 July the lack of availability of infantry hampered the British as there were not enough motorised infantry to accompany the tanks into battle and seize the fortified villages on the route of the advance.

The narrow frontage of advance further played into the hands of the German defenders as accurate anti-tank gunfire could be directed from the orchards and villages of Cagny, Emieville and Cuillerville on the left flank across the corridor of advance. The advance southwards exposed the thinner side of armour of the Shermans to this enfilade fire which slowed the advancing tanks as they took casualties. The 7th Armoured Division took from 1045 hours to 1900 hours for the 5th RTR, the leading regiment, to take up a position on the left of the 11th Armoured Division. It should be noted that the general advance resembled not so much a cavalry charge but a gentle trot: the leading regiments of the 11th Armoured Division took more than 2 hours to get across the main Caen–Vimont railway which was more than double the time allowed by VIII Corps planners.[89]

Once out of range of the heavy corps artillery AGRA (Army Group Royal Artillery) regiments to the west of the River Orne that could not be moved up to follow the advance, the armoured divisions were dependent on their own self-propelled field artillery just as they moved forward into terrain largely untouched by the morning's bombing south of the Caen–Paris railway. The British tanks had to undertake the final exposed 4,000yds of their advance with no support from heavy artillery or the air when it was most needed. The vehicle carrying the Forward Air Controller for the 11th Armoured Division was knocked out early in battle (although his place was taken by a junior officer) so tactical air support was perhaps not as effective as it could have been. The heavy aerial bombing by the first and second waves was effective on the flanks and along the path of the armoured divisions; the third wave with its 100-pounder and 20-pounder fragmentation bombs on the designated areas of Hubert Folie and Bourguébus was not so successful, the target areas being obscured by smoke and dust and the fall of bombs widely scattered.[90] Some planes did not bomb at all because of the poor visibility. It was in these areas that the German anti-tank guns and Flak guns halted the VIII Corps attack.

Much heavy artillery was still west of the River Orne on 19–20 July and so could not support any further operations. On 20 July, the heavy rain grounded the tactical ground support aircraft altogether, so Operation Goodwood was finally called off, though in reality the outcome had been decided on the first day.

O'Connor met specifically with Adair and Erskine to emphasise the importance of the 7th and Guards Armoured Divisions taking up positions alongside the 11th Armoured Division as soon as possible so as not to leave the 11th Armoured

Division isolated. But this is exactly what did happen as the Guards and the 7th Armoured divisions displayed a reluctance to get forward and into battle. The Guards' initial enthusiasm for their first action was tempered by the casualties suffered by the 2nd Grenadier Guards and then blunted by the sight of the burning 2nd Fife and Forfar tanks the other side of the railway. Blaming a lack of infantry to tackle the hidden anti-tank guns, the Guards made little progress towards their objective of Vimont and did not venture across the railway line to put pressure on the Germans in Frénouville who were taking their toll of the 2nd Fife and Forfar and 23rd Hussar tanks around Four and Soliers. The 1st Coldstream Guards, despite being in the vanguard of the division's advance, did not lose a single tank to enemy fire. The Guards Armoured Division on its formation, like all Guards units, had to be commanded by a Guards officer. As this was the first Guards unit to be equipped with tanks, there were no Guards officers who had served in tanks before, so the division was extremely lacking in tank battle experience. General Adair later commented:

> Goodwood was a badly designed battle from the Corps point of view. Our advance rather resembled a cavalry charge with its momentum lost once 11th and Guards division became deeply involved at Cagny. Our tanks were picked off by well-sighted German anti-tank guns.[91]

The historian Liddell Hart, after talking post war with General Hobart (then in the 11th Armoured Division), concluded that 7th Armoured Division, commanded by General Erskine, had also showed 'pervading caution' during the advance, 'resulting from the division's disillusioning experience in the early stages of the invasion'.[92]

After meeting with officers from the Guards Division and 23rd Hussars, at 1145 hours Brigadier Hinde sent an extraordinarily imprecise signal to 7th Armoured Division headquarters saying that the situation was obscure and that the enemy was somewhere in front between the 11th Armoured Division and the Guards Division.[93] Later in the afternoon Brigadier Hinde met with General Roberts at his tactical HQ north of Le Mesnil Frémentel, and Roberts was disappointed by what Hinde had to say: 'There are too many bloody tanks here already; I'm not going to bring my tanks down yet.'[94] Before the surprised Roberts could reply that the tanks in view had actually been knocked out, Hinde took off for somewhere else.

At O'Connor's afternoon meeting, Roberts explained the situation to General Erskine and the need for the support of the 7th Armoured Division to neutralise the defended villages; O'Connor ordered Erskine to provide this support and attack towards La Hogue. But the 7th Armoured Division regiments were still strung out all along the corridor of advance after the delay in crossing the bridges over the River Orne. Erskine believed the whole operation was a gross abuse of armour and seemed determined to keep his tanks out of it as long as possible, a belief that was reinforced by Hinde's reports.[95] When O'Connor demanded that the 7th Armoured Division advance, Erskine then maintained that there was no room between the two divisions ahead. The 5th RTR did not cross the Caen–Paris railway until about 1800 hours and was too late to influence the battle. It is clear that both Erskine and Hinde were not keen on participating in Operation Goodwood which they both regarded as being poorly planned and were determined to avoid another catastrophe befalling the division similar to that of Villers Bocage.

This reluctance to get forward combined with the poor planning that caused such massive traffic jams at the start allowed the Germans to repeatedly attack the exposed left flank of the 11th Armoured Division from where the 7th Armoured Division was supposed to be positioned. The narrow frontage of the British attack allowed the arriving German reserves to be quickly marshalled to parry the lone spearhead of the 11th Armoured Division.

The morning advance of the 11th Armoured Division was halted primarily by the improvised assault guns and anti-tank guns of the 21st Panzer Division that survived the terrific aerial bombardment. The much-vaunted Tiger tanks played little or no part in stopping the attack and the two sorties made by the 503rd Heavy Battalion, although damaged in the aerial bombardment, can only be described as half-hearted. At one point a company of King Tigers, the largest and most power-ful tanks then in existence, threatened to cut the British axis of advance but they were deterred by a few determined Shermans of the Coldstream Guards.

Montgomery had said in January 1944 that he would not use an armoured corps again, yet at Goodwood employed three armoured divisions at the same time in VIII Corps.

A Victory or a Defeat?

In order to determine whether Operation Goodwood resulted in a victory or a defeat for the Allies, its stated objectives must be compared with actual outcomes. It is clear from the early briefings that Montgomery was planning a breakthrough and communicated so to SHAEF and the CIGS Brooke. However, this was subse-quently revised and downplayed by Montgomery and lesser territorial objectives of enlarging the bridgehead over the River Orne were set. However, most regimental commanders believed that they were participating in a battle for a breakthrough; Dempsey, as confirmed by the movement of his HQ before the battle to that of VIII Corps plus his post-war interview with Liddell Hart, certainly believed this. Thus, if a battle for territory only took place, the Allies were successful in achieving an enlarged bridgehead with the added bonus of the destruction of eighty-three irreplaceable German tanks. Despite losing 213 tanks, which could be replaced from the reserves, then Operation Goodwood was successful.

If, on the other hand, the objective of the battle was a breakthrough to Falaise then as the German lines held and inflicted 275 tank casualties on the Allies, the outcome was unsuccessful and can be regarded as a German victory. However, the

German victory was another pyrrhic one, as the loss of precious tanks contributed to the gradual whittling away of the effectiveness of the panzer forces in Normandy.

In his notes after Operation Goodwood, O'Connor himself stated that the second objective of Goodwood was a 'breakthrough the Caen–Falaise plain with a view to an armoured thrust in the direction of Falaise'.[96] In a post-war interview with Liddell Hart, Dempsey said:

> It was always possible the enemy's resistance might breakdown and it was therefore necessary to foresee such a situation arising and be mentally prepared for it.

Given the documents and correspondence that have come to light in the last seventy years, it is quite clear that Goodwood was intended as a breakthrough by Dempsey, who thought that 'an enthralling battle to seize all the bridges was possible'.[97]

Montgomery and his supporters continued to play down the failed operation after the war, even claiming it was part of a deception campaign to keep the German forces near Caen while the Americans tried to break out. The diversionary operations, the heaviest yet air force bombings, the use of three armoured divisions and even Montgomery's signal to Brooke all indicate this was a break-out attempt. Liddell Hart makes the point that Operation Goodwood fell short even of its limited initial objectives. The attack failed to capture and hold the high ground to the south of Caen which had an adverse effect on subsequent attacks to the south in support of Operation Cobra, particularly Operation Spring where the Canadians were repulsed with heavy losses. Montgomery also failed to destroy much of the German armour: the attack was held by the 1st SS Panzer Division with the remnants of the 21st Panzer Division and the 12th SS Panzer Division in reserve was not called upon at all on 18 July. And as for the breakout, any hope of breaking through and exploiting southwards 'to Falaise, or beyond, that faded away on the first day'.[98]

In total, the Allies had extended their control over an extra 7 miles to the east of Caen and destroyed eighty-three German tanks, for their own loss of 275 tanks and over 5,500 casualties, although many of the tanks were repairable. More than 34 per cent of the tank strength of the 11th Armoured Division was lost.

Probably the biggest post-Goodwood claim of success was that the attack reinforced the German view that the British and Canadian forces on the Allied eastern flank were the most dangerous threat. This resulted in the Germans committing their remaining reserves to the front around Caen so that the FUSA forces in the west only faced one and a half panzer divisions compared with the six and a half facing the British and Canadian armies around Caen. The newly arrived 116th Panzer Division from the Fifteenth Army in Pas de Calais was committed to Caen and the 2nd Panzer Division which was to be withdrawn into reserve at St Lô at Caumont was diverted to the area south of Caen.[99] Once Operation Cobra began a week later and finally breached the thin German defensive 'crust' in the west, few German mechanised units were available to block the American advance or counterattack.

Notes

1 Ellis, Major L.F., *Victory in the West Volume 1: The Battle of Normandy* (London, HMSO, 1962), p.351

2 Belfield, E., and Essame, H., *The Battle for Normandy* (London, Parnell, 1965), p.144

3 CAB 44/249 The Liberation Campaign, Book 2, Chapter V, Operation Goodwood, p.146, TNA

4 Blumenson, M., *Break Out and Pursuit* (Washington, DC, US Army CMH, 1961) p.37

5 WO 229/72/28, 21st Army Group directive M505, 30 June 1944, TNA

6 WO 229/72/27, 21st Army Group directive M510 10 July 1944, TNA

7 D'Este, C., *Decision in Normandy* (London, Penguin, 2000), p.354

8 WO205/631 2nd Armoured Replacement group, July 1944, TNA

9 Bradley, O., *A Soldier's Story* (New York, NY, Holt, 1951), p.330

10 Pogue, F.C., *The Supreme Command* (Washington, DC, US Army CMH, 1989), p.188

11 WO 205/5E, Montgomery to Brooke, M511, 14 July 1944, TNA

12 Eisenhower, Gen I., letter to Montgomery S-55476, 13 Jul 44, Eisenhower Centre, Abilene

13 Horne, A., *The Lonely Leader, Monty 1944–1945* (London, Macmillan, 1994), p.207

14 Blumenson, M., *The Battle of the Generals* (New York, NY, Morrow, 1993), p.118

15 BAOR Battlefield Study Tour, Operation Goodwood Spectator edition, BAOR, Aug 1947, p.27

16 Zetterling, N., *Normandy 1944 – German Military Organisation, Combat Power and Effectiveness* (Manitoba, JJ Fedorowicz, 2000), p.178

17 BAOR Study, *opcit*, p.7

18 D'Este, *opcit*, p.368

19 Irving, D., *The Trail of the Fox* (London, Futura, 1977), p.592

20 CAB 22/248, Cable Montgomery to Churchill, 17 July 1944, TNA

21 Close, Maj W., *A View from the Turret* (Tewkesbury, Dell and Bredon, 1998), p.115

22 Von Rosen interview, quoted in Dalglish, I., *Goodwood* (Mechanicsburg, PA, Stackpole, 2009), p.64

23 CMHQ Report No.58 Eberbach, Gen H., The Campaign in NW Europe, DHH, Ottawa, p.79

24 Dalglish, I., *Goodwood* (Mechanicsburg, PA, Stackpole, 2009), *opcit*, p.71

25 Lemon, Capt. R.F., quoted in Liddell Hart, Capt. B.H., *The Tanks – The History of the Royal Tank regiment, Vol 2, 1939–1945* (London, Cassell, 1959), p.366

26 Moore, W., *Panzerbait with the Third Royal Tank Regiment 1939–1945* (London, Leo Cooper, 1991), p.142

27 Close, W., quoted in *Panzerbait*, *opcit*, p.145

28 Delaforce, P., *The Black Bull From Normandy to the Baltic with the 11th Armoured Division* (Stroud, Sutton, 1994), p.55

29 Moore, *opcit*, p.145

30 Lemon, quoted in Liddell Hart, *opcit*, p.386

31 Kite, B., quoted in *Panzerbait*, *opcit*, p.147

32 WO171/627 War diary of 29th Armoured Brigade, 18 July 1944, TNA

33 WO171/627 War diary of 29th Armoured brigade, 18 July 1944, TNA

34 Thorpe, J. quoted in Dalglish, *opcit*, p.118

35 Boscawen, R., *Armoured Guardsmen* (Barnsley, Pen and Sword, 2010), p.26

36 Fitzgerald, D., *History of the Irish Guards in World War II* (Aldershot, Gale & Polden, 1949), p.376

37 Boscawen, *opcit*, p.26

38 Boscawen, *opcit*, p.32

39 Schneider, W., *Tigers in Normandy* (Mechanicsburg, PA, Stackpole Books, 2011), p.148

40 Von Rosen interview, Camberley college 1979, quoted in Dalglish, *opcit*, p.104

41 Dalglish, *opcit*, p.165

42 Von Luck, H., *Panzer Commander* (Westport, CT, Praeger, 1993), p.193

43 Dalglish, *opcit*, p.262

44 TM E9-369A, German 88mm Anti-aircraft gun manual, US War Dept, June 1943, NARA

45 Dalglish, *opcit*, p.159

46 Hill, Colonel E.R., and Parsons, Capt L.M.H, *The Story of the Guards Armoured Division* (London, Geoffrey Bles, 1956), p.40

47 Dalglish, *opcit*, p.260

48 IWM Brownlie, Lt-Col W.S., And Came Safe Home, Private papers, 1944, IWM document #2204

49 BAOR Study Tour, *opcit*, p.41

50 Blacker, C., *The Story of The Twenty Third Hussars 1940–1946* (BAOR), p.75

51 WO 171/627 War diary of 29th Brigade, July 1944, TNA

52 Blacker, *opcit*, p.76

53 WO 171/866 War diary 3rd RTR, 18 July 1944, TNA

54 WO 171/627 War diary 29th Armoured Brigade, 18 July 1944, TNA

55 WO171/627, War diary 29th Armoured brigade, 18 July 1944, TNA

56 WO 171/456 War diary G section 11th Armoured Division, July 1944, TNA

57 WO171/627, *ibid*

58 War diary 2nd bn Grenadier Guards narrative July 1944, Guards Museum, London

59 *Ibid*

60 WO 171/1256 War diary of 2nd Irish Guards, 18 July 1944, TNA

61 Fitzgerald, *opcit*, pp.173–83

62 WO 171/1256 War diary 2nd Irish Guards, 18 July 1944, TNA

63 Boscawen, *opcit*, p.33

64 Boscawen, *opcit*, p.39

65 Scheider, W., *opcit*, p.149

66 BAOR Study Tour, *opcit*, p.44

67 WO 171/867 War diary 5th RTR, July 1944, TNA

68 WO171/867, 5th RTR, *opcit*

69 Moore, *opcit*, p.155

70 WO 171/620 War diary of 22nd Armoured Brigade, 19 July 1944, TNA

71 Dempsey, M., Letter and notes to Liddell Hart, 28 March 1952, LHCMA, LH1/230/22

72 Lehmann, R. and Tiemann, R., *The Liebstandarte, vol IV* (Manitoba, JJ Fedorowicz, 1993), p.158

73 WO 171/620 WD 22nd Armoured Brigade, 19 July 1944, TNA

74 CAB 106/959 Operation Goodwood, TNA

75 Montgomery, B., quoted in Ellis, *opcit*, pp.344–5

76 Eisenhower, letter to Montgomery 21 July 1944 in Eisenhower Papers III, quoted in D'Este, *opcit*, p.395

77 Danchev, A. and Todman, D., (eds) *War Diaries 1939–1945 Field Marshal Lord Alanbrooke, 20 July 1944* (London, Weidenfeld and Nicholson, 2002)

78 Diary of Capt Harry Butcher, 25 July 1944, Eisenhower Presidential Papers, quoted in d'Este, *opcit*, p.398

79 Jackson, Lt-Col G.S., *Operations of Eighth Corps* (London, St Clements, 1948), p.106

80 Neville, Capt R.F. and Scott, Lt Col G., *1st and 2nd Nothamptonshire Yeomanry 1939–1946* (Brunswick, 1946), p.122

81 WO 171/386 War diary CREME Guards Armoured Division, September 1944, TNA

82 CAB 44/249, *opcit*, Appendix B, TNA

83 Zetterling, *opcit*

84 Schieder, *opcit*, p.157

85 CAB 106/1061, Liddell Hart Dempsey notes, TNA

86 WO 171/139 War diary 21st Army Group A branch, July 1944, TNA

87 Wilmot interview with General Dempsey, quoted in d'Este, *opcit*, p.387

88 Coox, A. and Naisawald, L., ORO T117 – A Survey Allied tank casualties in World War II, US Army Operations Research Office, March 1951

89 Liddell Hart, Capt. B.H., *The Tanks – The History of the Royal Tank Regiment, vol.2, 1939–1945* (London, Cassell, 1959), p.369

90 CAB 44 /249, Operation Goodwood map G, TNA

91 Lindsey, O., *A Guards General: The Memoirs of Major General Sir Allan Adair* (Michigan, Hamilton, 1986), p.147

92 Liddell Hart, *opcit*, p.386

93 Dalglish, *opcit*, p.185

94 Dalglish, *opcit*, p.185

95 Wilmot, C., *The Struggle for Europe* (London, Collins, 1952), p.399

96 CAB 106/959, Operation Goodwood O'Connor notes, TNA

97 CAB 106/1061, Liddell Hart – Dempsey notes, TNA

98 Liddell Hart, *opcit*, p.369

99 Wilmott, *opcit*, p.404

8

Operation Cobra

With the failure of Operation Epsom and FUSA's renewed offensive to gain much territory in early July, there were fears of a stalemate developing in Normandy. Churchill, at a meeting on 6 July with the CIGS Alan Brooke, had launched into a tirade about Montgomery and his slow progress; Brooke was forced to defend Montgomery.[1] Churchill had also apparently met previously with Eisenhower to voice his concerns and iterated that Eisenhower had only to ask for the dismissal of any British officer and it would be approved.[2] Eisenhower, in his letter to Montgomery on 7 July 1944, had expressed his concern:

> It appears to me that we must use all possible energy in a determined effort to prevent a stalemate or of facing the necessity of fighting a major defensive battle with the slight depth we now have in the bridgehead.[3]

When Montgomery met with Bradley and Dempsey on 10 July and asked both to come up with plans for major operations, Bradley was a little despondent because of FUSA's failure to break through the German lines. In response, Montgomery was very conciliatory, if a little condescending, towards Bradley: 'Never mind. Take all the time you need, Brad.' And then later he said, 'If I were you, I think I should concentrate my forces a little more.'[4]

Bradley had been trying since 3 July to advance the FUSA on a broad front through the difficult bocage countryside and Montgomery attempted to get Bradley to consider a change of tactics. Montgomery later reported on this meeting to Brooke:

> First Army is cracking ahead and I have been carefully into its various thrust lines with Bradley. There is no doubt that the enemy is very severely stretched on my western flank and he has very few reserves there with which to hold us; if we maintain the pressure he will crack eventually.[5]

Montgomery's orders to Bradley and Dempsey on 10 July (M510) required Dempsey to plan for a major operation with three armoured divisions but contained no reference to a similar operation for FUSA. They stated that FUSA's right wing should continue to exert strong pressure southwards to Avranches while the whole army was to eventually wheel southwards and eastwards, using its left flank as a pivot. In the meantime, FUSA was to continue its efforts to seize Brittany, followed by a wide sweep eastwards towards Alençon. For FUSA, the M510 directive was similar to that of 30 June (M505).

Following Montgomery's suggestion to concentrate his forces, on 11 July Bradley devised a plan for another major offensive designed to achieve the much sought-after breakthrough. This plan was developed in detail by the FUSA General Staff and approved by Bradley on 13 July with a start date of 19 July. Operation Cobra was to be a heavy daylight air bombardment of a small section of the German front line 5 miles west of St Lô followed by an attack by three infantry divisions to breach the front line. The British had used heavy bombers for the first time on 7 July in support of a ground operation in the successful attack to capture Caen so the availability of air power was very much in the minds of Dempsey and Bradley. Two armoured divisions would then charge through the breach and drive to the west coast at Coutances, thereby cutting off the left wing of the entire German Seventh Army in the Cotentin peninsula. The breakthrough would then provide the opportunity for the deployment of Patton's Third Army to continue the advance into Brittany. The main FUSA forces in the operation would be those of VII Corps while the other three corps would exert pressure all along their fronts at the same time in support. On 13 July Montgomery affirmed his intentions in a telegram to Eisenhower:

> Am going to launch two very big attacks next week. Second Army begin at dawn on 16 July and work up to the big operation on 18 July when VIII Corps with three armoured divisions will be launched to the country east of the Orne. Note change of date from 17 to 18 July. First Army launch a heavy attack with six divisions about 5 miles west of St Lô on 19 July. The whole weight of airpower will be required for Second Army on 18 July and First Army on 19 July.[6]

There is no mention here of Montgomery's avowed strategy of the British Second Army holding the German forces around Caen while the Americans break out in the west and clearly both armies were attempting to make a break through the German lines and a subsequent breakout at the same time. Montgomery confirmed this with his message to Brooke on 14 July in which he stated his intention to have a real 'showdown' on the eastern flank and loose a corps of three armoured divisions into the open country on the Caen–Falaise road.[7]

The jumping-off point for Operation Cobra was to be the Perier–St Lô road which was not then even held by the Americans who were still attacking through the hedgerows from the River Vire towards this road and St Lô. Once this line was attained, a pause of 48 hours would be required to resupply and reposition the artillery and divisions for the attack.

St Lô was not captured until 18 July and any further major offensive action by FUSA was called off on 19 July so as to be able to prepare for Operation Cobra. Since 3 July, FUSA with twelve divisions had advanced only 7 miles west of the River Vire and half that distance east of the river. Casualties numbered more than 40,000 men, most of them infantrymen, although one tank battalion after a week of action was unavailable for any action whatsoever due to the loss of so many tank crews.[8] Continuous bad weather in England then kept the aircraft required for the operation's initial bombardment grounded and conditions were not forecast to clear until 24 July, forcing the start date to be postponed to that date.

The employment of armour in the hedgerow battles had been a major problem for the Americans fighting in Normandy but with the development of combined arms teams, better communications and various techniques of making gaps in the dense hedgerows, the Americans had overcome this. The hedgerow cutter design of Sergeant Culin of the 102nd Reconnaissance Battalion in the 2nd Armored Division was demonstrated to Eisenhower on 14 July and put into mass production. After a huge effort which involved tank transporters moving steel from German beach defences to workshops inland, three out of every five tanks at the start of Cobra had hedgerow cutters welded to them. Such tanks became known as Rhinos.[9]

After modifications by General Collins at VII Corps, the final Operation Cobra plan called for three infantry divisions – the 9th, 4th and 30th Divisions – to make the initial penetration immediately after the air bombardment and create a 'defended corridor' for the exploitation forces, which were to race westward towards the sea. The motorised 1st Division, with CCB of the 3rd Armored Division attached, was to thrust directly toward Coutances as the main force to cut off the German units in the Cotentin peninsula to the north. The 2nd Armored Division, with the 22nd Infantry Regiment attached, was to establish blocking positions from Tessy-sur-Vire to the Sienne River near Cérences to prevent any German counterattack from the east interfering with the operation. The rest of the 3rd Armored Division was to remain in reserve pending the operations of the other armoured units.

Before the start of the offensive, the 2nd and 3rd Armored Divisions each received fifty-two of the first M4s with the 76mm gun that had better armour-piercing capabilities than the current 75mm gun.[10] These 76mm M4s had been warehoused in England prior to D-Day as none of the generals had been keen to utilise them but, given recent experiences against the German tanks in Normandy, the 76mm M4 was suddenly seen as a solution to the poor armour-piercing performance of the M2 gun equipped M4 tanks. The 76mm gun could penetrate 93mm of homogenous armour at 500yds and 88mm at 100yds compared with the 75mm M2 performance of 60mm and 55mm at the same ranges.[11] As well as the aerial bombardment, for added firepower VII Corps was allocated a large part of FUSA's artillery – nine of its twenty-one heavy battalions, five of its nineteen mediums and all seven of its non-divisional light batteries.

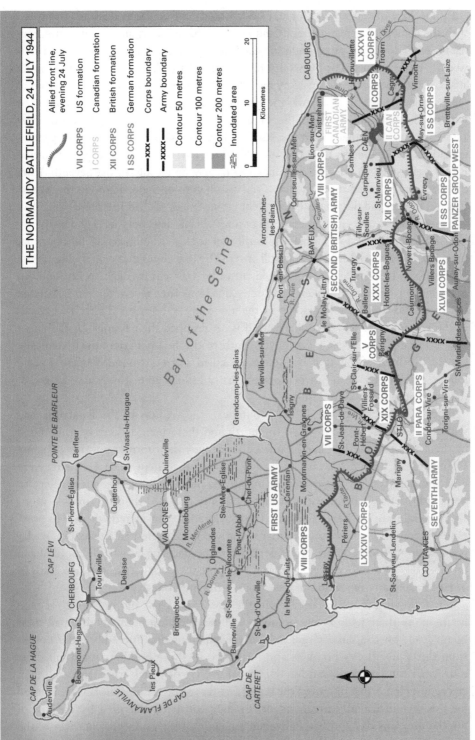

The Normandy Battlefield, 24 July 1944. (*Courtesy of The History Press*)

By the start of Operation Cobra, FUSA would have fourteen divisions compared with the depleted German divisions and kampfgruppen which amounted to no more than nine divisions on paper, eight of which had been in combat for more than four weeks.[12] It was estimated by FUSA that the men of VII and VIII Corps assembled for the attack outnumbered the Germans by more than five to one. Immediately in the path of the intended American attack was the Panzer Lehr Division that had been reinforced with two battlegroups, one from the remnants of the 275th Division and the other the 14th Parachute Regiment from the 5th Parachute Division. A battlegroup of panzer-grenadiers and engineers from the 2nd SS Panzer Division that had been supporting Panzer Lehr since 19 July was withdrawn to Gavray on 24 July. In the Seventh Army, the Germans only had about 150 tanks and assault guns operational, 100 in the 2nd SS Panzer Division and fifty in the Panzer Lehr.[13] The Americans had assembled more than 600 medium M4 tanks for the attack plus scores of tank destroyers and light tanks.

H-hour for Operation Cobra was finally set for 1300 hours on 24 July but that morning, the skies over St Lô were still covered by low cloud that would obscure the targets from the bombers. A postponement order was sent by radio to England but many aircraft had already taken off. Some squadrons later received a recall message but many did not, including some of the 1,600 heavy bombers. Thirty-five planes of the second wave and 300 of the third wave dropped their bombs on the target area, a rectangle 2,500yds by 7,000yds south of the St Lô–Periers road. Tragically, twenty-five men of the 30th Division were killed and 131 wounded when a plane leading a flight of sixteen others dropped part of its load prematurely and the rest of the flight promptly followed suit.

Before the arrival of the USAAF bombers, the soldiers in the front line had withdrawn for safety 1,200yds to the north and these men, having been bombed by their own planes, then had to attack to reoccupy their former positions as some Germans had moved forward to escape the bombardment. The Germans were now thoroughly alert to the impending attack and began to use their artillery to bombard the forward American troops who only regained their original positions after several hours of heavy fighting. General Bradley considered whether to postpone Operation Cobra as the Germans clearly now expected an attack, but, under pressure from Montgomery and Eisenhower, the decision was made to go ahead the next day. A number of changes were supposedly made to the air force plans in order to avoid any repetition of the errors of the previous day.

The following morning, on 25 July, the skies were clear and beginning at 1100 hours, more than 1,500 heavy bombers and 380 medium bombers dropped their bomb loads on the same target area as the previous day. Incredibly, the bombs from thirty-five heavy bombers and forty-two medium bombers again fell short into American positions, causing 601 casualties, 111 of which were fatal.[14] Human error, dust clouds that obscured the target and wrong target indicators were blamed for this second friendly fire incident. Bradley had been horrified by the loss of life the previous day and had convened a meeting between representatives of the army and air force at which the air force was asked to approach the target parallel with the front line so as to avoid flying over any American troops. The air force had objected on the basis that this would not achieve the desired concentration of bombs in the target area and the meeting had concluded with the army under the misapprehension that its request would be met. After the short bombing, the American infantry and artillery units struggled to deal with their casualties and reorganise for the attack; one battalion had lost its entire headquarters staff, artillery observation posts were destroyed and telephone lines were cut. However, the effects on the Americans were slight compared with the devastation wrought on the German defenders. Having survived the previous day's bombing, the Germans were confident that they could do so again and did not realise that the first bombing had been in error and that many planes had been recalled. This time, their positions were turned into a lunar landscape of overlapping bomb craters and more than 1,000 men were killed, tanks overturned and anti-tank positions obliterated. Three battalion command posts were demolished and all control by Panzer Lehr was lost. As the American infantry, supported by tanks, began to move forward, the shattered defenders could only offer feeble resistance.

The initial objectives of the three infantry divisions, each supported by a tank battalions, were the towns of Marigny and St Gilles 3 miles away; when captured, these towns would form the corridor for the waiting two armoured divisions to charge through. The initial American advance was slow and cautious, hindered by mines and cratered roads and as time went by, the Germans began to recover from the effects of the bombing. To their surprise, the Americans began to encounter an increasing level of resistance and it soon became clear that the bombing had not been as effective as hoped. German artillery, although short of ammunition, was still very active and had not been knocked out by the bombs as the locations of the batteries were not known by the Americans. Some battalions made good progress through areas that had been saturated by bombs, but resistance was stronger in the areas that had not been hit heavily.

The 743rd Tank Battalion had been tasked with supporting the 30th Division on the left flank to St Gilles via the high ground at Hebecrevon and during the bombing by the medium bombers, an M4 tank and an M5 light tank were damaged and had to be evacuated. When the planes had departed and H-hour was approaching, some tank crew members could not be found. The battalion's tanks had formed up in two columns with the light tanks leading as little opposition was expected. At H-hour, the tanks slowly began to pick their way through the unnatural fog of dust and explosives residue that cloaked the barren landscape. Mines on the road required several halts while they were cleared and engineers attempting to do this came under small-arms fire, causing some delays. In one column, two platoons of light tanks of D Company led an M4 company with a company of infantry and progress was difficult along the mined roads; the column was soon forced to stop at a road junction before a small stream to make a reconnaissance. The best route cross-country was determined by the force commander, Captain Miller, and orders were issued but, when Miller reached the stream in his tank, he saw that no other tanks were following. Going back on foot to the road junction, Miller berated the other tank crews: 'Now listen, by Christ, if I can go up there on foot you can take your tanks, you have protection!'[15]

Just then several German tanks opened fire from an orchard on the crest of a small hill on the other side of the stream, knocking out one Sherman and damaging another when it fell into a roadside ditch while taking evasive action. This effectively stopped the advance and with no way around and unable to find a road leading to Hebecrevon, the tanks withdrew, leaving the infantry of the 119th Regiment to go on alone.

The other column of A Company tanks and a platoon of light tanks encountered a roadblock on the road to St Gilles of three Panthers supported by a few panzer-grenadiers. The infantry tried to work in closer under HE fire from the medium tanks to use their bazookas while the light tanks began a flanking manoeuvre. One of the M5 tanks saw a Panther:

> Sergeant Caroll Hibness, one of the tank commanders, fired two quick rounds at one of the German tanks. The Mark V slowly began to turn its turret gun around at the light tank and before it could fire on Hibness' tank, the latter got off another shot. All three ricocheted off the Mark V and the 37mm shell was not effective. Colonel Duncan remembers hearing Sergeant Hibness' doleful voice come over the radio: 'Good God, I fired three rounds and they all bounced off.'[16]

The Panther's first shot was a direct hit and Sergeant Hibness and his crew bailed out before their tank was hit three more times and began to burn.[17] The infantry of the 30th Division then tried to outflank the roadblock, only to come under fire from German artillery and infantry in other positions which forced them to go to ground. Two Shermans trying a flanking manoeuvre were also lost to the Panthers which were finally dislodged by a combined tank/infantry assault that knocked out one Panther and compelled the others to withdraw. A Company of the 743rd Tank Battalion also knocked out two Panthers in this action.[18] As the VII Corps attack had not achieved its initial objectives, in the late afternoon the battle group was instructed to keep going and capture Hebecrevon which did not happen until midnight with the support of the C Company tanks of the 743rd Battalion working in almost total darkness.

The other infantry divisions also made little progress. In the centre, the 4th Division, supported by the 70th Tank Battalion, attacked the positions of the 14th Parachute Regiment opposite. The division was tasked with advancing to high ground south of the St Gilles–Marigny road. The infantry battalions were beset by problems caused by the short bombings, difficult terrain and having to pass through friendly positions. The depleted German parachute regiment put up a determined resistance in many instances from positions in woods and orchards and was supported by accurate artillery and mortar fire. The 70th Tank Battalion had lost a tank in the bombing and the supporting tanks were unable to keep up with the infantry because of the hedgerows, streams, felled trees and cratered roads; infantry/tank cooperation was further hindered by a lack of radios and there were at least four instances of where tank/infantry cooperation failed.[19] In one unfortunate incident, a tank using its hedgecutter burst through a hedgerow only to bury an American soldier in a ditch on the other side. The tank crew helped dig out the soldier by using the tank to pull another tree out; the soldier survived, only to be killed by an artillery shell a few minutes later.[20]

The 9th Division had been tasked with reaching both La Chapelle en Juger and Marigny with the 746th Tank Battalion attached for armoured support. The division had many casualties in the bombing and its attack plans were thrown into chaos. By nightfall, the division was just west of La Chapelle en Juger but still more than 2 miles from Marigny.

At about 1800 hours, the 4th Division was given the new objective of La Chapelle en Juger to the west after it became clear that 9th Division would not be able to capture it that day. However, the 4th Division's commander, General Barton, ordered a halt as his division had been attacking for nearly 12 hours and needed some daylight to form firm defensive positions. Chapelle en Juger was an important objective that had to be cleared for the armoured advance but the infantry division halted less than a mile from the village.

That evening, in the face of the continuing German resistance, it was the opinion of most American division commanders that their combined forces had not forced a break in the German lines and that the Germans, having had ample warning of the attack, had assembled reserves and were about to counterattack. At the end of the first day of Operation Cobra, Marigny, St Gilles and Chapelle en Juger had not been captured and VII Corps had only advanced just over one mile. Infantry/tank cooperation had been extremely difficult as the tanks had been unable to keep up with the infantry in the deeply cratered terrain and the results of any training were not realised.

General Collins, although acknowledging these concerns, believed that the German resistance was local and uncoordinated and the German lines were virtually destroyed. Knowing that he would have the full support of IX Tactical Air force, Collins decided to take a gamble and that the two armoured divisions should attack next day. Given the relative failure of the infantry to make a deep penetration, this was the only course of action open to Collins and the armoured divisions would first have to take the objectives originally assigned to the infantry. A partial gap had been created in the German lines but a corridor for the armoured advance would not exist until Marigny was taken.

The German reaction to the day's events was somewhat muted, perhaps due to a lack of information from the disruption of communications by the American bombing and a failure to appreciate the size of the attacking force. Von Kluge had his hands full dealing with the Canadian Operation Spring around Caen, as intended by Montgomery while General Hausser of the Seventh Army did not seem unduly alarmed, despite his front having been penetrated in several places. Battlegroups from the 275th and 353rd divisions were attached to von Choltitz's LXXXIV Corps for a counterattack to seal off the front once more. The 941st Infantry Regiment, after many delays caused by the persistent Allied fighter-bombers, counterattacked eastwards in the late afternoon.[21] However, this was right across the path of the three advancing infantry divisions and was doomed to failure. The 985th Regiment from the 275th Division was ordered forward to support Panzer Lehr but was pinned down by Allied aircraft north of Marigny where it could only form defensive positions. The 983rd Regiment was ordered to move overnight to La Chapelle en Juger to stop the American advance there.[22] Hausser also decided to reinforce Marigny with what reserves he had from the 2nd SS Panzer Division which were only a tank company and a company of infantry.[23]

Had von Choltitz and Hausser known Panzer Lehr and its reinforcements had been virtually destroyed and Hebecrevon captured with the road to St Gilles open, their reaction may well have been stronger, although they possessed few reserves.

CCB 3rd Armored Division

The 1st Division, with the attached CCB of the 3rd Armored Division, had the mission of attacking along the Coutances to Periers road via Marigny and seizing the high ground around Coutances so as to block the retreat of German units from the Cotentin peninsula to the north. CCB, commanded by Colonel Boudinot, was divided into three teams along with the motorised 18th Combat Team of the 1st Division for the advance to Marigny. As Marigny had not been captured on the first day of Operation Cobra, the 1st Division would have to fight its way to Marigny before advancing through the corridor to Coutances and the coast. The 18th Infantry Regiment would attack either side of the Tribehou–Marigny road to finally force a gap in the German lines but the infantry would only advance on foot as no great penetration of the enemy lines had been made. CCB moved up to the start line during the night of 25 July and began the advance next morning at 0704 hours, led by the reconnaissance company of the 33rd Armored Regiment reinforced with a platoon of tanks and a tank dozer to repair the roads.[24] Pushing down the road to Marigny, the vanguard had to deal with the cratered road and frequent roadblocks set up by a few German tanks or self-propelled guns which could only be cleared with the help of artillery and attendant P-47 fighter-bombers. The reconnaissance company ran into a roadblock near Montreuil of two Stug IVs and two 75mm anti-tank guns which they outflanked and destroyed, taking twelve prisoners.[25] At about 1030 hours, the CCB bulldozer was knocked out by artillery fire and the tanks found themselves unable to advance at a faster rate than the infantry. By 1330 hours, Team 1 was just north of Marigny but was meeting increased opposition from some Mark IV tanks of the 2nd SS Panzer Division, a few anti-tank guns and infantry from 353rd Division. While a tank firefight was going on, the team attempted to outflank the town from the right but found movement cross-country across sunken roads and through hedges slow and difficult. The manoeuvre was unsuccessful and CCB harboured one mile to the west of Marigny at 1812 hours, finding itself out in front of the infantry. Team 1 had knocked out three Mark IV tanks and three 75mm anti-tank guns during the day around Marigny.[26] Believing that the advance of his 18th Infantry Regiment was lagging and that Marigny had been secured by CCB, the infantry commander ordered the regiment to keep advancing to the high ground east of Marigny where they arrived at about midnight. Despite facing only pockets of resistance and Allied planes having completely neutralised the counterattack of the kampfgruppe from the 275th Division during the day, the anticipated American armoured charge had been reduced to less than a gentle stroll and Marigny remained in German hands. FUSA HQ had received reports that M4s were in the town, but these reports proved to be false and a clear corridor still did not exist through the German lines.

Next day, CCB resumed its attack towards Coutances, leaving Marigny to be secured by the 18th Infantry Regiment. A company of infantry entered the town at 0640 hours only to meet fierce small-arms fire and was forced to withdraw, leaving two platoons cut off. The capture of Marigny would take the 18th Infantry Regiment most of the day. The road to Coutances ran south-west, parallel with a ridge to the north formed from three hills along its length which dominated the road and the approaches to the town. The axis of CCB's advance was the main road to Coutances itself in order to make up for lost time. The initial objective of CCB that day was Camprond which after being secured was to be handed over to the 18th Infantry Regiment following behind. CCB was also ordered to capture the three hills along the ridge that overlooked the road. The tanks of the 4th Cavalry Mechanised Reconnaissance Squadron moved along the northern flank while infantry of the 16th Combat Team protected the southern flank. Later the 16th Infantry Regiment, moving on the side roads, was given the objective of blocking the roads north of Coutances.

Two CCB teams drove side by side rapidly down the highway towards Coutances, preceded by the reconnaissance company which was bolstered by a platoon of supporting tanks and two squads of armoured engineers. All day the American advance ran into isolated groups of German infantry, sometimes supported by tanks; such a typical action was reported by Ernst Barkmann of the 2nd SS Panzer Division whose lone Panther tank apparently ambushed the advance of CCB, causing it to come to a sudden halt:

> At dawn on 27 July, Panther 424 was able to follow the company into its new combat sector. They reached Le Lorey near the main road Coutances-St.Lo. On the curving road, at the exit of town, Panzergrenadiers and supply soldiers came running to the Panzer. 'US tanks are advancing on Coutances,' they yelled at them. But that was where they were going! From the distance Barkmann could hear the noise of the battle and aircraft engines, then fire from sub-machine guns and rifles. The Spiess and Schirrmeister, both wounded, approached his Panther. They reported American tanks driving on the road to Coutances, together with a long column of vehicles. 'Ready for Action!' Barkmann ordered. Panther 424 rolled ahead slowly until the crossroads were in view. It was ideal firing position, 100 m to the crossroads, covered at the side by an earth mound with bushes.

'Tanks coming from the left, we will fire on the two point tanks.' Gunner Poggendorf had the first tank in the crosshairs, the first shell ripped the turret off the enemy tank. Then the second tank at the point was in the cross hairs, it too was set on fire. With this, the crossroads were blocked for the following tanks. They turned back, even those vehicles which had already passed the crossroads retreated.

'Open Fire!' The Panzer gun fired shell after shell into the personnel carriers, jeeps and ammunition trucks. Within minutes, the crossroads resembled a burning auto graveyard. Suddenly, Barkmann spotted two Sherman tanks driving off the main road and approaching from half left. A duel Panzer against tank began. The first Sherman burned brightly after the second shot. Barkmann took two hits from the second Sherman before it, too, caught on fire after a hit to the rear. Fighter-bombers then appeared over the Panther, the first bombs tumbled earthward but did not hit. But with each dive they came closer, a violent explosion made the Panther tremble and shake. Fragments ripped apart a portion of the tracks and explosive rounds hit the turret and hull. A number of Shermans closed in and opened fire. Barkmann managed to knock out two more before his Panzer sustained heavy damage from hits. A shell ripped apart the welded dovetailing of the Panther hull, another shell blew the track from the teeth of the driving sprocket, and the ventilation system in the interior failed. There were more hits to the rear as the crew tried to move the Panzer back into cover with the track blown off and a damaged driving sprocket. This maneuver required the highest concentration, but it was successful. Another Sherman, which had pushed ahead the furthest, was also knocked out, before the Panther limped back to a farm house in the village of Neufbourg where the most critical damage was repaired. Barkmann's battle at main road to Coutances had stopped the advance of the US troops in the rear of German units long enough to allow many units, which had already appeared lost, to save themselves from threatened encirclement. As the last one to break off contact with enemy, Barkmann's Panther, with two others in tow, reached Coutances on 28 July.[27]

From this German account of the battle, which does not give the time of the engagement, it is difficult to determine which units of CCB were involved in this action. Team 1 was following the reconnaissance company and neither the CCB nor the 33rd Armored Regiment reports for 27 July mention the claimed loss of seven tanks. The report of the 33rd Armored Regiment does, however, state somewhat laconically that Team 1 reached La Chapelle and encountered armoured resistance in the form of three Panther tanks, which were 'thrust aside'.[28] The 3rd Armored Division G-4 report for 27 July for CCB reports three M4 tanks damaged, only one of which required a replacement.

After the skirmish at La Chapelle, Team 1 turned northwards and seized the hill at Camprond at 1540 hours without much difficulty and waited for the 18th Infantry to arrive to relieve the tanks as ordered before they could push on. Caught up at Marigny, the relieving force struck more resistance later in the day moving to La Chapelle which required air support to be overcome. CCB was not relieved until 2250 hours when it was far too late to continue the advance. A whole afternoon was therefore lost while the tanks were waiting for their relief. In the interim, Team 1 moved 500yds further west and harboured on Hill 158, the second objective. Team 2 also had more difficulty keeping abreast of Team 1 as it was not using the main road but was travelling cross-country parallel with the road.[29] Once again, CCB had not advanced very far and the territory captured by day's end more resembled that gained by a walk rather than an armoured dash.

Advancing south of the Coutances road, the 16th Infantry Regiment had also encountered German troops that blocked their movement around Marigny and did not reach a point south of Camprond until midnight. Although there was no organised German defence, as with CCB, isolated pockets of infantry supported by a few tanks continued to put up determined resistance before either withdrawing or being destroyed by the advancing Americans.

By the end of the day, CCB and the 1st Division were still only halfway to Coutances and the grand plan of slashing across the rear of the German forces and trapping them was in danger of failing.

The left wing of the Seventh Army had begun a withdrawal in response to the slow but steady FUSA advances and units of the 2nd SS Panzer Division plus a battalion of engineers from 17th SS Panzer Division tried to construct an ad hoc defence line from Coutances via Cambernon to Savigny. German forces north of CCB were able to infiltrate back across the American lines of advance to the relative safety of the south in the night. Von Kluge, still not apparently aware that Panzer Lehr was destroyed, ordered a counterattack by Panzer Lehr and a tank battalion of the 2nd SS Panzer Division, the latter with only fourteen tanks operational. During the night, a German horse-drawn artillery column blundered into the harbour of Team 1 and was destroyed in a brief engagement.

CCB was ordered at 0810 hours on 28 July to seize Monthuchon and after being relieved by the 26th Infantry Regiment, was to attack towards the high ground north of Coutances. However, Bradley had become concerned at the slow progress of VII Corps and therefore ordered VIII Corps, advancing further west along the coast, to put pressure on the extreme left flank of the Seventh Army and to take the VII Corps objectives of Coutances and Monthuchon that day.

VIII Corps was able to make good progress and quickly captured Monthuchon before the leading elements of CCB which did not move out of their harbour until 1130 hours. When CCB later occupied Cambernon without difficulty and was ready to drive on Coutances, CCB was ordered to halt by Collins as VIII Corps troops were by then near Coutances. The tanks of Team 1 were forced to stop at Cambernon within sight of their objective of Coutances, only 2 miles away below them.

Meanwhile, the 16th Infantry Regiment was still attacking in the direction of Monthuchon and ran into determined resistance, four M4 and two M5 tanks from the 745th Tank Battalion being destroyed. CCB was ordered at 1730 hours to reverse its course altogether and to go to the aid of the 16th Regiment. This manoeuvre caught the German defenders from behind and caused their defences to crumble. The 26th Infantry Regiment later arrived and performed mopping-up operations.

The 1st Division and CCB had largely failed in their mission, having advanced slowly and taking only 565 prisoners. Coutances had not been captured as planned and large numbers of Germans that had not been trapped in the Cotentin peninsula north of the St Lô–Coutances highway were continuing to withdraw southwards. During the night of 28/29 July, Team 1 continued to have contact with German forces infiltrating through their positions. Next morning, orders were received to assemble the entire division at Cerisy-la-Salle but Colonel Boudinot requested a few hours of rest for his men and the division did not move until the afternoon.

CCA 3rd Armored Division

The bulk of the 3rd Armored Division had been kept in reserve depending on the success of the other units in the offensive and General Collins on 26 July was sufficiently confident of the progress made by VII Corps to commit the division to the battle. On 27 July it commenced a thrust between CCB and the 2nd Armoured Division to secure the roads south of Coutances via Cerisy-la-Salle. Again it was anticipated by Collins that the initial advance would be through areas already secured and would therefore be rapid but the division had to fight south-west from Marigny onwards. The division was split into three task forces and struck trouble around Marigny about 1245 hours in the form of a German strongpoint, which either had not been cleared or had been set up by soldiers infiltrating back. Four medium M4 tanks were lost before the head of the armoured column, nearly 10 miles long, could disengage and bypass the resistance. There were similar problems at Quibou: the leading tank of C Company was hit by an anti-tank gun and blocked the road. As the tanks moved off the road, a second was hit and began burning. A single anti-tank gun supported by a few infantry on an embankment along the only good road meant the division had to destroy the roadblock before they could advance further. Further delays ensued while the attack was organised and by nightfall the division had still not reached Cerisy-la-Salle. The German resistance continued to coalesce and the commander of the 3rd Armored Division, General Watson, was concerned about his armoured task forces receiving flanking fire from the developing German line as they moved southwards. Watson decided to turn his forces westwards at the start of the next day rather than turning much later at Cerisy-la-Salle as planned.

The next day, 28 July, was to provide no outstanding success for the 3rd Armored Division either. The advances by the three task forces were slowed either by late starts as supplies had difficulty getting through the traffic congestion in the rear of the columns, or the difficult terrain which was crossed by a poor road network. Pockets of German resistance were also a constant threat that further delayed the advance while they were cleared. The Germans had been expecting the Americans to advance southwards from St Lô rather than the initial movement south-west towards Coutances and had reinforced the south with what reserves were available. A US task force with the objective of advancing to Coutances via Carantilly only got 5 miles to the west of Carantilly before it ran into opposition. The other two task forces charged with capturing Montpinchon and Cerisy-la-Salle were prevented from doing so by elements of the 17th SS Panzer Division tenaciously defending the high ground. In the evening, two M4 tanks and an armoured car were destroyed west of Cerisy-la-Salle.[30] The Germans then withdrew overnight which allowed the high ground to be occupied the next day without casualties and the task forces to continue exerting pressure on the German forces retreating southwards. Panzer Lehr was forced to abandon its repair depot at Cerisy-la-Salle with the loss of thirty damaged tanks.[31]

On 30 July the 3rd Armored Division, now reunited, was to attack as a whole to seize bridges over the River Sienne at Gavray. The 83rd Reconnaissance Battalion led the attack with CCA following and found that the bridge at Gavray had been destroyed. Opposition increased south of the river and while a small bridgehead was held by the infantry, a bridge was constructed during the night of 30 July. However, at midnight CCA was attached to the 1st Division and given a new mission of advancing to Brecy and the River See the next day. Despite heavy fighting round Villedieu les Poêles, both columns reached their objectives by the evening of 31 July and many prisoners were taken. The area was congested with American troops trying to advance and German stragglers trying to escape.[32]

CCB on the left flank with its own reconnaissance company and mixed team of armoured infantry, engineers and F Company tanks from the 33rd Armored Regiment leading, reached the River Sienne south of Hambye at La Sayerie where a bridge had to be constructed by the engineers. The team then made the crossing under heavy shell fire. Meanwhile, the reconnaissance company column was cut in two places amid increasing German resistance and another team was forced to come to its aid. CCB eventually harboured for the night with all around defences set up at the bridgehead and around Hambye.[33]

CCB was preparing next day to continue the attack to Villedieu les Poêles when it was placed under the command of the 4th Division along with the 83rd Reconnaissance Battalion. With the slow American advance, most German units had by then been able to fall back in front of the American attack and none were completely encircled as envisioned in the plans for Operation Cobra. CCA had lost eight M4s and one tank dozer so far in the operation.[34]

CCA 2nd Armored Division

As the 3rd Armored Division had done, the 2nd Armored Division reorganised its armoured columns for the attack as the objective of St Gilles originally assigned to the infantry now had to be taken by the division. The light reconnaissance tanks originally expected to lead were replaced by heavier assault teams based on medium tanks and armoured infantry. The task of the 2nd Armored Division was essentially a protective one to the east in order to prevent German reinforcements moving westwards and striking the American advance in the flank. Having to secure St Gilles first, CCA tanks began their advance in two columns at 0945 hours on 26 July to secure the high ground at Le Mesnil Herman but immediately lost an M4 tank as they crossed the Periers–St Lô road. Undeterred, the two armoured columns pressed on as fast as the bomb-cratered roads permitted, meeting only sporadic resistance and light artillery and anti-tank fire. The advance received significant assistance from the fighter-bombers on call constantly overhead and from observation planes which reported the presence of enemy troops in front of the advance before directing artillery fire at the same. However, the combat commands of CCA 2nd Armored Division and the 3rd Armored Division were forced to use the same road to Marigny in a continuous armoured column which contributed to the already considerable traffic congestion in the area.

Just outside St Gilles, a strong roadblock of four Mark IV tanks along with anti-tank guns was quickly overcome by M4 tanks with air support and by mid-afternoon CCA entered St Gilles. The advance continued relatively unhindered down the road towards Canisy. This road marked the boundary between Panzer Lehr and the 352nd Division (as well as being a corps boundary) and as the road was the responsibility of Panzer Lehr, which was no longer operational, the advance was largely unopposed. After smashing another roadblock outside Canisy, the columns passed through the village at 1510 hours and then diverged, one half proceeding in the evening to St Samson de Bonfosse and the other to Le Mesnil Herman. That day, CCA only lost three M4 tanks, a half-track, a truck and a jeep.[35]

St Samson de Bonfosse was entered about midnight and Le Mesnil Herman (8 miles from the line of departure) was secured next morning at 0800 hours after a brief halt to refuel and rearm. Three tanks were lost to German infantry wielding Panzerfäuste on entering Le Mesnil Herman.

Next day, two reconnaissances in force were made, one in the direction of Villebaudon by the 3rd Battalion and the other towards Tessy-sur-Vire by the 1st Battalion. All forces harboured at the end of the day back near Le Mesnil Herman. On 28 July CCA was reorganised into three columns and the 2nd Battalion attacked towards Beaucoudray (with the objective of Percy) as part of the middle column. The 2nd Battalion lost one tank in a minefield near Moyen and in the town itself, a tank battle developed between the battalion's M4s and ten Panthers with four assault guns. The battalion knocked out two of the Panthers and two assault guns for the loss of three medium tanks but was unable to capture the town. A wide flanking movement to take the town from behind was unsuccessful and another tank was destroyed by a Panther. The left-hand (eastern) column of the 1st Battalion met strong opposition from tanks and 88mm flak guns when advancing to Le Mesnil Opac and destroyed four anti-tank guns and five Mark IVs for the loss of only one M4 tank. As the task force was under heavy mortar and artillery fire, it was unable to make any headway and withdrew.

The right-hand column (3rd Battalion) reached Villebaudon on 28 July and advanced towards Percy where there was heavy fighting for the next two days and the column was periodically cut off. CCA was battling with the remnants of Panzer Lehr and the 2nd Panzer Division, which had arrived that morning after having been sent by von Kluge to Tessy-sur-Vire in response to Operation Cobra. The 2nd Panzer Division blocked the Villebaudon to Tessy road at Hill 133 near Le Mesnil Opac and succeeded in capturing the La Denisiere crossroads further west, cutting the 1st battalion column.[36] Also defending in the area were other battlegroups from the 2nd and 17th SS Panzer divisions. The 116th Panzer Division would also join the 2nd Panzer Division next day to support the Seventh Army around Tessy and Vire.

At 1530 hours on 29 July, on the same day the reconnaissance battalion of the 116th Panzer Division arrived in the area, the CCA 3rd Battalion finally reached Percy. The bulk of the division was due in two more days. The 1st Battalion column could only manage an advance of 1 mile that day from Le Mesnil Opac before harbouring back at le Mesnil Herman. CCA was now confronted by the vestiges of four panzer divisions which continued to put up strong resistance. The unique 'heavy' structure of the 2nd and 3rd Armored divisions, with two tank regiments in each division, paid dividends here as CCA contained an entire regiment of tanks which enabled it to sustain losses and maintain the offensive against the considerably weakened German divisions. The 2nd Panzer Division largely had only its Panther battalion as it was forced to leave two companies of the Mark IV battalion to reinforce the 326th Division around Caumont until 27 July and had no more than twenty Panther tanks operational.[37]

The 2nd Battalion of the 66th Armored Regiment continued the advance towards Tessy on 30 July from Villebaudon and, against determined resistance, only managed to capture the crossroads south of the town by the evening before withdrawing to a harbour area, leaving the town in the hands of the infantry. After heavy fighting, Percy was finally captured on the evening of 30 July by the 3rd Battalion.

The next day the 1st Battalion was ordered to secure the left flank and high ground around Dumont. The advance reached a ravine where there were German tanks on the far side and a spirited firefight across the ravine ensued in which four German tanks were claimed as destroyed. The battalion was unable to force a crossing amidst the heavy artillery and tank fire being received.

On 1 August, the 3rd Battalion task force attacked towards Tessy 5 miles away. In the misty conditions, a German transport column was encountered on the road which was shot up and destroyed. Resistance increased around Tessy and two M4s were lost on the outskirts of the town when they ran onto mines covered by anti-tank guns; on bailing out, the tank crews were captured. In other skirmishes, two German Panthers cut the battalion convoy and before being driven off, four tanks were lost while the rest of the column kept moving eastwards under cover of a smoke barrage. Two more M4s were knocked out by Panthers west of La Poemeliere. The attack resumed at 1430 hours with H and G companies either side of the road to Tessy-sur-Vire and four more tanks from G Company were knocked out. By the time the high ground north-west of Tessy-sur-Vire was reached at about 1800 hours, the battalion had lost fifteen M4 tanks and a light tank. Tessy-sur-Vire was finally captured and cleared that evening.

CCB 2nd Armored Division

CCB was committed only at 1100 hours on 27 July in its originally planned role of setting up blocking positions between Lengronne and Notre Dame de Cenilly by following CCA to Canisy and then turning south-west. The start had been delayed by traffic congestion and the slow progress of CCA in clearing resistance around Canisy. Three hours later, the leading elements had reached Canisy when their mission was changed by VII Corps to make a thrust to the coast at Brehal, 10 miles south of Coutances, in a last-ditch attempt to cut off the German forces still in the Cotentin peninsula.[38] CCB was organised into two columns but as there was only one road, the two columns were intermingled until after reaching Canisy where the two columns were able to deploy. Led by the 82nd Reconnaissance Battalion, the leading troops of the right column came up against a sizeable German force defending between Quibou and Laisney. While the recce tanks, self-propelled artillery and fighter-bombers engaged the German positions, the vanguard found a way around and moved through Dangy at 1900 hours and then later reached Pont Brocard. Limited resistance from anti-tank guns, armoured cars and infantry was overcome and the town was secure at midnight. By 0200 hours on 28 July, the right column and the reconnaissance battalion were in Notre Dame de Cenilly.

After clearing Canisy, the left column used the secondary roads to reach its objective of the high ground east of Dangy by 2000 hours on 27 July but then found further progress difficult in the terrain; the column was forced to move westwards back to the main road at Pont Brocard. That night the mission of CCB was then changed back by General Collins to its original mission of establishing blocking positions between Lengronne and Notre Dame de Cenilly.

At 0900 hours on 28 July, Company H of the 67th Armored Regiment, less a platoon of tanks but with a company of armoured infantry and a company of engineers, moved to occupy Cambernon on the planned route of the right column. After overcoming a force of six German tanks at the crossroads north of St Denis le Gast, the battle group reached Cambernon at 1600 hours and this effectively cut the highway south from Coutances to Gavry.[39] Later that day, a Kubelwagon drove into the roadblock and all occupants were killed; amongst them was the commander of the 2nd SS Panzer Division.

Before the main body of the right column could get going that day, a small German battle group of Panthers from 2nd SS Panzer Division and a few units of 275th Division tried to breakthrough from the direction of Cerisy-la-Salle towards Notre Dame and Pont Brocard where the 183rd Field Artillery Battalion was positioned. The attack was broken up by the intervention of the reserve Combat Command, including tanks of the 3rd Battalion of the 67th Armored Regiment.[40]

During the day, platoons from the 82nd Reconnaissance Battalion continued to roam far and wide as far as Cerences and Lengronne where they found the bridges over the River Sienne still intact, while another platoon reached the crossroads north of St Denis le Gast. Before nightfall, the reconnaissance platoons reassembled in the vicinity of the La Panetiere crossroads.[41]

An early Sherman DD training tank – note the wooden gun barrel. The three rails that support the screen can be seen, as well as some of the supporting struts at the front. The tank commander's perch can be seen on the rear of the turret. *(IWM MH 3660)*

D-Day Omaha sector, Easy Red beach. Two wading tanks of the 741st Tank Battalion with infantry sheltering behind them have arrived before two DD tanks, which are in the process of lowering their screens. Note small exhaust stack on DD tanks. *(Magnum Photos)*

D-Day Sherman tank of 1st Hussars, Juno sector. *(Battlefield Historian)*

D-Day, Omaha beach, afternoon – a wading M4 or Sherman knocked out. *(US Navy)*

A Sherwood Rangers tank unloading from an LCT on Jig beach on D-Day. Note shell crater in the foreground. *(Battlefield Historian)*

D-Day, German bunker WN 18 La Breche on Sword beach – note how the extended thick wall facing the sea protects the bunker from naval fire. The bunker has been hit repeatedly by shots from tanks. *(Battlefield Historian)*

Some 741st Tank Battalion crew members in a life raft reach Omaha sector beach on D-Day. This famous image was captured by US Army Signals Corps photographer Private Louis Weintraub. *(Battlefield Historian)*

Panthers on their way to Normandy. Moving the trains in daylight was almost impossible because of Allied air superiority. *(Battlefield Historian)*

Lingèvres, 14 June 1944: one of Panzer Lehr's Panthers knocked out by Sergeant Harris of the 4th/7th Royal Dragoon Guards. *(Battlefield Historian)*

Bretteville l'Orgueilleuse – one of the 12th SS Panthers knocked out on the night of 8 June 1944. *(Battlefield Historian)*

The PIAT (Projector Infantry Anti-Tank) was as feeble as it looked. But in the bocage, where the operator was able to get close to the target, it could be effective. *(IWM B8913)*

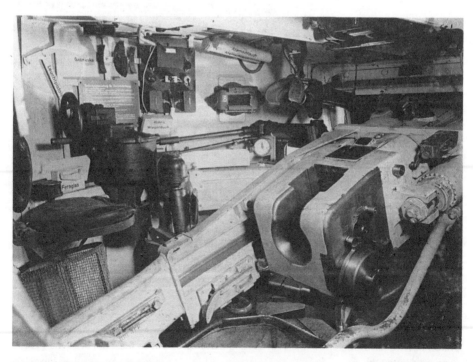

Interior of a Tiger I turret. *(USNA)*

Two Tiger I tanks of 101st SS Schwere Tank Battalion on the move. *(Battlefield Historian)*

The Sherman Firefly's 17-pounder provided the only effective anti-tank gun for the British armour and there were none available to the Americans. *(IWM B51300)*

Stuart V light tank of 7th Armoured Division, photograph dated 15 June 1944. A 'Desert Rat' symbol can just be made out on the glacis. *(IWM B5608)*

One of SS-Obersturmführer Michael Wittmann's many victims on 13 June 1944. The Cromwell jammed a track while trying to turn to escape and the tank was taken out by Wittmann with a single shot. *(USNA)*

Close to the *mairie* in the centre of Villers Bocage, and illustrating the folly of tanks entering built-up areas, two German tanks have been knocked out – a Tiger (right) and a Panzer IV of Panzer Lehr Division. *(USNA)*

Operation Epsom: a Churchill tank of 7th RTR and infantry on 28 June 1944. *(Battlefield Historian)*

Operation Epsom: Churchill tanks of 9th RTR move through the ruins of Norrey en Bessin. *(Battlefield Historian)*

Fontenay: a knocked-out Sherman and Panther in Operation Epsom, 27 June 1944. Note the penetrations of armour-piercing shells in the front hull of the Sherman. *(IWM B6043)*

A Sherman Vc or Firefly keeping watch in the Normandy hedgerows – note the length of the 17-pounder gun barrel and the section added to the rear of the turret to accommodate it. *(Battlefield Historian)*

Knocked out during Operation Charnwood, this dug-in Mark IV tank is 'camouflaged' by the remains of a shed near Lébisey. *(Battlefield Historian)*

Operation Bluecoat: a surviving DD tank, possibly of the Sherwood Rangers, moving up near Ondefontaine on 4 August 1944. *(IWM B8588)*

Second bombing, Operation Totalize, 8 June 1944. The fighting vehicles are lined up to advance southwards and the ambulances are ready to go back north to the rear area where 'friendly' bombs are falling. *(Battlefield Historian)*

A tank dozer crosses the bridge at St Fromond accompanied by US infantry during the push to St Lô, around 7 July 1944. US engineers had repaired the bridge and built other foot and vehicle bridges nearby. *(USNA)*

A Sherman is towed to Le Dézert around 11 July 1944 for repair. Unlike the Panzer Lehr tanks, damaged US armour could be recovered, repaired and sent back into battle. *(USNA)*

Operation Totalize: the morning after – one of the hazards of tanks advancing at night. *(Battlefield Historian)*

The Falaise Gap: a knocked-out Mark IV with two crew members who did not survive the action –
a fate feared by all tank crews. *(IWM B9657)*

One of the very few Tiger Is to escape destruction in Normandy. Tiger '213' – a late model – got as far as the River Seine but found all the bridges bombed. Shortly after this picture was taken, the crew destroyed the tank. (*From* The Tiger Tank Story, *Mark Healy*)

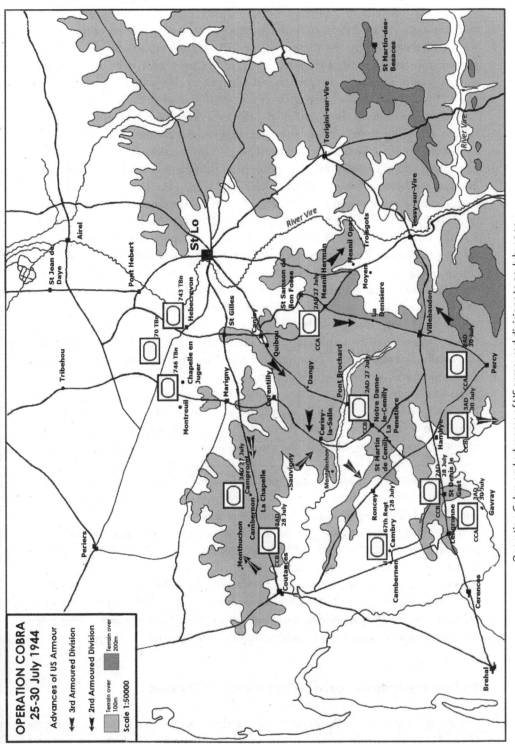

Operation Cobra and advances of US armoured divisions to 30 July 1944.

The CCB left column continued to move slowly down the same road being used by the heavily engaged right column ahead of it. Small detachments of the column were sent ahead during the night to seize and establish roadblocks on the crossroads 2 miles north-west of Hambye, north of St Denis le Gast and at Lengronne. Only sporadic resistance to these moves was put up by isolated elements of the 353rd Division and these objectives were successfully reached during the night.

With the creation of these roadblocks, the left wing of the Seventh Army was at last cut off, although by a single over-extended combat command. The situation at Hausser's HQ was chaotic. Communications, and hence control, had been lost with many units and the rapidly advancing American columns had caused total confusion in the rear echelons of the divisions in LXXXIV Corps. Hausser himself had almost been captured as American forces reached Gavray whilst Bayerlein's command post near Dangy had to be evacuated the previous day when American tanks appeared outside; Bayerlein, at least, had been finally able to report the destruction of his division to Hausser. The commander of the 17th SS Panzer Division who was now commanding what was left of both the 2nd and 17th SS Panzer divisions, having not heard from Hausser, assumed the Americans had cut the Cotentin peninsula and accordingly made preparations to breakout southwards towards Brehal. Hausser, meanwhile, managed to get in touch with von Choltitz, the LXXXIV Corps commander, and ordered him to break out to the south-east so as to link up with troops supposedly assembling for a counterattack near Vire. Von Choltitz protested, as this would mean the western end of the German line would lose contact with the coast and allow American forces to surge around the German left flank unopposed, but Hausser insisted on his orders being carried out. Von Kluge was furious when he found out about this order and immediately countermanded it but Hausser was unable to contact von Choltitz. By the time a messenger conveyed the order to von Choltitz, he had lost touch with many units and it was too late as the German forces trapped were already making preparations for their own breakout attempts. The planned attack to the south-east, as ordered by Hausser, would take them straight into the 2nd Armoured Division's CCB blocking positions.

Aware that the Germans would attack in an effort to breakthrough their positions, CCB recalled some of its more distant units from Cerences, creating a 10-mile gap between Lengronne and the coast that would have considerably helped any breakout attempts made by the Germans due south. Still north of the CCB positions were the 2nd SS Panzer Division, parts of the 17th SS Panzer Division, the 6th Parachute Division and the 243rd and 91st divisions. This force was concentrated around the Roncey and Montpinchon area.

29 July: the Roncey Pocket – 2nd Armored Division

During the night, the advance elements of the 4th Division began to arrive in Notre Dame de Cenilly to relieve the CCB right column. Both the 1st and 2nd battalions of the 67th Armored Regiment were heavily engaged to the west of St Martin de Cenilly while a company of armoured infantry blocked the road further to the south-west. A company of men from the 4th Division and four tank destroyers formed a roadblock in the early hours of the morning at the La Panetiere crossroads between St Martin de Cenilly and Notre Dame de Cenilly.

Just before dawn, at 0400 hours on 29 July, a column of thirty German vehicles coming from the direction of Roncey, including fifteen tanks, tried to break through the roadblock; they overran the company of infantry and reached the positions of the 78th Armored Field Artillery Battalion. The self-propelled 105mm field guns were forced to fire over open sights at the attackers. With the aid of an additional four guns from the 702nd Tank Destroyer Battalion and artillery fire, the attack was held off for 30 minutes until reinforcements from the armoured infantry arrived to defeat the attack altogether. Seven Mark IV tanks were destroyed and 125 Germans killed.[42]

As the right column was heavily engaged with this early morning breakout attempt, the left column of CCB moved off to reinforce the previously established blocking positions but progress was slow as the area between St Martin de Cenilly and Hambye was being used by Germans retreating southwards. Enough of the 4th Division had arrived at Notre Dame de Cenilly by 1200 hours to relieve the forces of the right column and these then advanced rapidly to Lengronne and St Denis le Gast. The 2nd Armored Division Combat Command Reserve later occupied St Denis le Gast.

Planes from the IX Tactical Air Command spotted and attacked a concentration of German vehicles in the area around Roncey. Two large columns of vehicles on separate roads that converged at Roncey had created a massive traffic jam: vehicles were stationary and bumper-to-bumper. It was a fighter-bomber's paradise, and the Thunderbolts and Mustangs set about their task with a savage enthusiasm. For 6 hours squadrons rotated over Roncey and attacked whatever vehicles were still intact while CCB tanks and artillery directed a barrage of HE fire into the village. More than 100 armoured vehicles and 250 soft vehicles were found wrecked, damaged or abandoned in the Roncey pocket a few weeks later. That night the surviving soldiers would attempt a final breakthrough of the CCB line and formed independent groups supported by a few tanks to press against the CCB cordon, desperate to find a way through back to their own lines.

30 July

At 0300 hours, elements of the 2nd and 17th SS Panzer Divisions (600 men and ninety armoured vehicles, including twenty tanks) attacked the 2nd Armored Division Combat Command Reserve around St Denis. The headquarters of both the 41st Infantry Regiment and the 3rd Battalion of the 67th Armored Regiment were overrun; a Panther tank put its gun muzzle through the hedge and shot up the tank battalion command post in the field where it was harboured. A German column, headed by an 88mm self-propelled gun, entered St Denis le Gast itself, the infantry using Panzerfäuste and throwing grenades. An M5 light tank, commanded by Sergeant Douglas Tanner of A Company of the 67th Armored Regiment, engaged the German column head-on in order to allow his fellow soldiers time to fall back and get out of the way of the Germans. Tanner's tank exchanged shots with the self-propelled gun and was hit twice, bursting into flames. The driver of the M5 pulled Tanner out of the turret and laid him on the side of the road, but Tanner was mortally wounded. For his bravery, Tanner was awarded the Silver Star and the Croix de Guerre with bronze star.[43] Such was the force of the German assault that the American line was broken and St Denis had to be temporarily yielded to the Germans.

In the midst of the confusion and intense enemy fire in the darkness, the remaining roadblocks were strengthened and all available headquarters personnel joined the fight.[44] The German soldiers were more intent on breaking through the American outposts than stopping to engage in any firefight which meant any contact was brief but savage.

The capture of St Denis allowed the surviving Germans to continue their flight southwards for a short period before a CCB counterattack retook the village at about dawn. The men of the division reserve killed 130 Germans and wounded another 124 which were taken prisoner along with 400 others. At least twenty-five vehicles were destroyed, of which seven were tanks. American losses were almost 100 men and twelve vehicles.[45]

Eleven vehicles of the German force that got through at St Denis took a wrong turn in the darkness and headed westwards until they reached the harbour of the 78th Field Artillery Battalion, 2 miles west of St Denis, at about 0215 hours. This was the same artillery battalion that was involved at the La Panetiere crossroads previously. The sentries mistook them for American vehicles and allowed the group to proceed past an M10 parked at the side of the road into the encampment. Here the mistake was realised when an American officer challenged the occupants of the vehicles in German. A firefight immediately broke out at very short range and when the leading and rearmost German vehicles were destroyed, the German survivors were forced to flee on foot. The column, including two Stug III assault guns and a 105mm self-propelled artillery gun, was completely destroyed.

Further north on the Coutances to Gavray road near Cambry, which had been held since the afternoon of 28 July by a small isolated force of the reinforced H Company of the 2nd Battalion of the 67th Armored Regiment, other units from 2nd Battalion finally arrived in Cambernon at 1800 hours on 29 July and linked up with H Company. Other tanks were ordered to take up defensive positions along the road from Cambernon to Grimesnil. At about 0100 hours, more than 2,500 German soldiers of a mixed group of units, which included elements of the 2nd SS Panzer Division, attacked the recently arrived Americans who were still digging-in. German soldiers who tried to infiltrate past the defences in the darkness were followed by a column of armoured vehicles, led by a Mark IV tank and a Hummel self-propelled gun. Several M4 tanks at Cambry were knocked out, and the German tanks threatened to overrun the entire position until an M4 tank destroyed the leading vehicle that blocked the road at Grimesnil, allowing the 2nd Battalion to regroup. A furious firefight developed in the darkness. The crew of the Hummel self-propelled gun were killed by rifle fire and their vehicle blocked the road with its engine still running. The history of the 2nd Armored Division describes the events:

> ... an infantry sergeant who under intense small arms fire, made his way to a friendly tank, mounted its back deck and guided it to a position where it could destroy the enemy's lead tank. The sergeant beat off enemy infantry by firing his sub machine gun and by using hand grenades as he guided the tank forward. The destruction of the enemy's lead vehicle blocked the road and stopped his advance. Vicious hand to hand fighting broke out on all sides and each friendly vehicle became an island of defence around which our troops rallied and fought off the more than five to one numerical superiority of the enemy ...
>
> Throughout the entire engagement fighting was at extremely close quarters. Bazookas, hand grenades and bayonets were used extensively by both sides and tankers fought hand to hand with German troops that attempted to mount their tanks. Officers went from tank to tank and group to group, giving orders to each in an attempt to maintain a semblance of organisation in the face of almost complete darkness and battle confusion, which made it nearly impossible to identify friend or foe.[46]

The Americans were pushed back and only after immediate artillery support was called for, virtually on top of their own positions without waiting for targets to be registered, did the German advance falter. The infantry of the 41st Armored were then able to restore the situation after a 6-hour battle with the help of tanks and close mortar and artillery support. Three hundred German infantrymen who attempted to outflank the American positions to the east through a swamp were caught by a platoon of tanks and more than 250 of them were killed. German casualties were 450 men killed, 1,000 taken prisoner and about 100 vehicles of all types destroyed. American losses were about fifty men killed and sixty wounded.

The 2nd Battalion lost seven tanks and nine half-tracks in this action.[47] However, CCB reported only one tank and one half-track destroyed for the entire operation.[48]

A Panther tank commander in the 2nd SS Panzer Division, Fritz Langake, described the chaos amongst the German units cut off by the American advance as he tried to break out during 29–30 July:

> I got to the bunker, snapped to attention and reported to the regimental commander and asked for orders. He didn't have any for me, and I left the shelter. For the next two or three hours I was quite busy. I ran back 200–300 meters down the road looking for vehicles from our task force and others. Most of the men who had abandoned their

vehicles were back now. I found two operable Panthers and one Panzerkampfwagen IV. With them I was able to move enough obstacles so that our halftrack and wheeled vehicles could pass. We formed quite a column. I told those with me that, come darkness, we would break out. I reported this fact to the regimental commander and checked in another two or three times. He finally told me not to make any noise and wait. He would, under cover of darkness, sneak stealthily through the American blockade with his infantry and all the stragglers, without shooting …

… Shortly after my last encounter, some seasoned parachute non-coms came and said to me: 'You poor bastard. You're the only one around here who doesn't know what's cooking. Those guys don't plan anything. They are going to surrender.' I felt ashamed for my stupidity. I went over to the bunker and told them I would start with my column at 2200 hours that evening and the hell with them. Then two officers came to my tank. One, a major, was the commander of an assault gun battalion, and the other was his adjutant. They had camouflaged their two vehicles in a sunken lane close by. They asked me whether they could join our column. By that time I had given up wondering why an officer of his rank would ask a platoon leader, who wasn't even an officer, if he could join instead of taking over command. I then drove with my tank back to the road and broke two passages through the hedgerow on the left side in order to pass the big gun and other destroyed vehicles in front of us. In the attempt to move the destroyed vehicles to the side of the road, one of my Panthers had broken a sprocket wheel and had to be abandoned.

I set up a march formation. First my tank with grenadiers on the left side and about 50 to 60 paratroopers on the right side as a safeguard against close combat fighters with bazookas. Then the two assault guns, the wheeled vehicles of our task force, various stragglers, self-propelled infantry guns and mobile flak followed. The rear was brought up by the Panzer IV and my second Panther. The frequency of our radio communication was set, and at 2200 hours we started. Of course, no scouts had moved at all before this …

… On the right side a farm was in flames. In the wavering light I thought I saw a Sherman in the field to the left. We fired twice and hit it, but it didn't burn. Then I drove full speed across the Hambye-Roncey Road, where I expected stiff American resistance and, if I remember correctly, we rolled over an anti-tank gun. I shot into the lane that led into the main road from the other side and stopped. Passing the intersection, I saw two Shermans to my right side standing at right angles, sticking their heads into the hedgerow. Now I realized these were the machine guns that had fired at our paratroopers when we started and had wounded a number of them. We had to be quick to use the surprise effect, so I ordered the assault guns to rush to the crossing, turn right and knock out the two tanks that showed them their sides. They hesitated and started deliberating. I was enraged. I turned my turret and told them to start immediately or I would knock them out. They did, turned right and had no problems destroying the American tanks. I proceeded down the lane. To my right side there was a wider field with a hedgerow bordering it. Along this hedge a number of armoured vehicles were parked, pointed toward the main road. I was lucky. We hit the last one, probably an ammunition carrier, and it was like fireworks at a summer festivity. The flare ammunition with the different colours was a fantastic sight. The whole area was illuminated, and I could easily pick out another four to six of these armoured halftracks. I don't remember the exact number. With all this, a great many soldiers of the infantry units behind the north-south road were encouraged to jump up and follow us. They did this in an unmilitary manner, with shouts and yells, firing in the air and the like. At first I was appalled, but then I realized it was quite useful. The Americans seemed to be completely surprised and even dumbfounded. They left a number of cars, which were taken over by Germans, and there was practically no further resistance. I drove on and maybe 150 meters in front of me an American tank raced from the right toward the road. We wanted to stop it, and that thing happened that all tank crews are most afraid of – you pull the trigger or push the button, and the gun doesn't fire. Figuring that was the end for us, I turned my head and got an even bigger shock. From the south, four American tanks rushed onto the road that joined ours, which came from La Valtolaine. They turned back and disappeared at full speed. I again looked forward. That first tank had such momentum when it hit the road that it couldn't stop in time and got stuck with its nose in the ditch next to the road. Only with great trouble could it get out, turn around and get away. We were sitting there in our Panther, not only undamaged but even unmolested and almost couldn't believe it.

The column we had started with comprised about 300 men. By now it was around double that number. As we moved farther, our progress was made easier by a number of captured [Allied] vehicles. Some stragglers joined us, while others separated and chose different ways. We were a motley, mixed bunch. I figured that combat action would occur in this intersection area, which appeared to be more than a mere road-block. I ordered the other Panther to take the lead, and I brought up the rear. Radio communication still worked, and we began our erratic wandering. We first reached Lengronne, continued to Cerences, crossed the Sienne River and drove on to Gavray.

When we reached the town, it was under fire. Here our column became mixed with a number of other vehicles. Outside the town we continued without loss and turned toward St. Denis-le-Gast, but before reaching it, we left the road and drove to the bridge at La Baleine. As we approached, our movement nearly stopped. I climbed out of my Panther to find out the reason. Artillery fire, which continued sporadically, or bombing had damaged this bridge, the sides of which were partly destroyed. The drivers were very reluctant to go on it. I then took over, organized the approach to the bridge and directed each vehicle across. When our tank crossed, as the last vehicle, only half the width of the tracks found footing in some places. On the south side of the river, tactical signs of quite a number of units were installed, and the column could dissolve. Most of them now knew where to go. My self-appointed mission was finished. It was full daylight by now, and the first planes appeared. We drove into a lane that led up a hill, and at the first farm with an orchard we stopped. I told the crew we would now have a good nap after three nights of nearly no sleep at all. We crawled under our tank and were lost to the world around us. It was high noon when we were awake again, and we were alone.[49]

Daylight revealed the results of the desperate battles during the night. Hundreds of wrecked vehicles, dead horses and corpses littered the countryside. The 2nd Armored Division alone had killed an estimated 1,500 Germans and taken 4,000 prisoners for the loss of nearly 100 men killed and 300 men wounded.[50]

Operation Cobra was over, and the German Seventh Army was in pieces with its left wing up in the air and the US 4th Armored Division moving south past it towards Avranches. The advance continued next day and the bridge over the River Selune at Pontabault was captured intact, opening the door to Brittany for Patton's Third Army.

Aftermath

In the first few days of Operation Cobra, 6,000 German prisoners were captured by FUSA and by the end of the month this total had risen to 20,000 prisoners.[51] However, many men of eight German infantry divisions and the 2nd and 17th SS Panzer Divisions had either managed to evade the 2nd Armored Division cordon before it was set up or fight their way through the American lines. These divisions that had been in combat since D-Day had virtually disintegrated into small groups of men who had lost or discarded much of their equipment and could only be formed into small kampfgruppes for attachment to other units in the future.

Von Kluge, preoccupied with the Operation Spring offensive around Caen, was furious when he discovered the full extent of the American gains during Operation Cobra. He was not slow in putting the blame on Hausser for his order for the retirement of the left wing of Seventh Army to the south-east away from the coast. Von Kluge was also critical of the defensive arrangements made by Hausser in the relative calm of the few days before Operation Cobra was launched when the Panzer Lehr had been left in the front line and not withdrawn to form a mobile reserve. Acutely aware that Hausser had been appointed by Hitler himself only the previous month, von Kluge took no action against Hausser but dismissed the Chief of Staff of the Seventh Army, Max Pemsel. The commander of LXXXIV Corps, von Choltitz, was also relieved and von Kluge took personal control of Seventh Army on 30 July.[52] Von Kluge had made no effort to check the dispositions of Seventh Army prior to Operation Cobra and therefore must bear some of the responsibility for the collapse of the army.

For the Allies, and FUSA in particular, Operation Cobra was an outstanding success after a hesitant start and the first breakthrough and breakout achieved by the Allied forces in Normandy. The route between the shattered left wing of the Seventh Army and the western Cotentin coast was now open for the Americans to advance through and invest the Brittany ports which had been a key Overlord objective. On 1 August, General Patton's Third Army was officially activated and came under the new 12th Army Group along with FUSA.

American casualties in Operation Cobra were nevertheless quite heavy. Until Operation Cobra, FUSA combat units had suffered 11,597 men KIA and 42,092 wounded.[53] To 1 August, FUSA had lost 15,676 men KIA with 65,871 wounded, and therefore the casualties from Operation Cobra were 4,072 men killed and 23,779 men wounded.[54] VII Corps alone had suffered 17,627 casualties.[55]

A large number of tanks were also lost or damaged in the offensive. The 3rd Armored Division had forty tanks replaced in July.[56] However, most of the tanks lost in July were during the action of CCB at Les Hauts Vents in the first offensive of the breakout attempt. The division's losses in Operation Cobra were very light: CCA had ten tanks knocked out or damaged whilst CCB losses were five M4 tanks and one M5 tank damaged, of which one M4 and one M5 required replacement.[57]

Another 3rd Armored Division casualty was the commanding officer, General Watson, who was relieved of command on 30 July by General Collins. Collins believed that Watson 'failed to demonstrate the leadership and control required for the command of an armoured division'.[58] The 3rd Armored Division's performance had been unspectacular earlier in July with the coordination problems during the fighting to reach St Lô, and then CCB had not reached its objective of Coutances in Operation Cobra while CCA had also struck determined opposition at Montpinchon that had delayed its advance. According to some reports in the divisional headquarters, very early one morning Watson had called Collins, who was asleep, to discuss the coming day's attack. Collins was unimpressed and before Watson made the call he was a temporary general commanding a division and when he had finished he was a permanent colonel without a command.[59] However, during Operation Cobra, CCB was under the command of the 1st Division and so cannot be held entirely responsible for its slow progress; for example, on 27 July CCB reached its objective but then had to wait for the relief force, which had been held up at Marigny, to arrive. General Collins changed the orders several times of the 2nd and 3rd Armored divisions and while flexibility is a hallmark of leadership, too many changes can lead to disorder and confusion and are an indication of a lack of control of the situation.

The rapid commitment of the armoured divisions and the frequent changes of orders certainly helped the Americans maintain an attacking 'tempo' that enabled them to retain the initiative. The Germans, with their communications already badly disrupted by the bombing and little information coming from the front lines, were kept off balance and uncertain as to the forces opposing them and their intentions.

Collins was certainly responsible for the chaos and traffic congestion around Marigny when both the armoured divisions were ordered to advance through the narrow gap between Marigny and St Gilles even though Marigny had not even been captured. Despite an overwhelming superiority in numbers of infantry, artillery and complete dominance of the air, the attack by the three infantry divisions had made very little progress by the end of the first day. The independent tank battalions operating with the infantry divisions had been unable to keep up with the advance of the infantry on foot and this resulted in few opportunities for the new combined tank/infantry tactics to be practised. The only successful tank/

infantry operation on the first day was the capture of Hebecrevon at midnight by the tanks of the 743rd Tank Battalion and the 119th Infantry Regiment from the 30th Division; in the words of the 30th Division's historian, 'infantry tank cooperation was excellent'.[60]

The advance of the 2nd Armored Division's CCA is also a possible exception. CCA had trained extensively with the 22nd Infantry Regiment from the 4th Division during the week before the start of Operation Cobra, practising combined arms small unit tactics.[61] When committed on 26 July, CCA advanced 7 miles to Canisy and St Martin de Bon Fosse, although the combat command used roads whenever possible and the chosen route was along the poorly defended boundary between the LXXXIV and 2nd Parachute Corps, so it is not clear how often hedgerow tactics were required or employed. Even though the Germans were outnumbered by more than three-to-one, enough Germans survived the bombing and artillery bombardment to prevent the American infantry from making a breakthrough on the first day of Operation Cobra. One historian suggests that, despite the American superiority in numbers, the objectives of the infantry divisions, particularly Marigny, were too far away and the divisions were too weak to realistically attain them.[62]

The 2nd Armored Division was more heavily engaged in tank-to-tank combat when CCA pushed towards Tessy-sur-Vire where it fought with tanks of the 2nd and 116th Panzer Divisions. The division had forty-five M4s and two M5s replaced during July and as the division was in reserve until Operation Cobra, this total was lost during the breakout.[63] The 3rd Battalion of the 66th Armored Regiment (CCA) alone had thirty-five tanks damaged or destroyed during Operation Cobra for the destruction of only four German tanks.[64] The 2nd Battalion of the 66th Armored Regiment also had fourteen tanks knocked out or damaged and received a Presidential Unit Citation for its efforts.

There were six independent tank battalions attached to the infantry divisions of the three corps of the FUSA engaged in Operation Cobra and a total of forty-nine tanks were lost by these battalions.[65] Therefore at least 109 American medium tanks were knocked out in Operation Cobra, the majority of which were destroyed and had to be replaced.

German armour losses during Operation Cobra are difficult to estimate. The 2nd SS Panzer Division on 23 July had seventy-eight tanks and twenty-five assault guns operational but by the time of Operation Luttich on 7 August only had twenty-five tanks and perhaps fifteen assault guns operational.[66] Therefore an estimated fifty-three tanks and ten assault guns were lost in Operation Cobra by this SS division.

Panzer Lehr was occupying the front line directly under the aerial bombardment and there were 347 panzergrenadiers killed in July with another 1,480 missing following the bombings of 24 and 25 July. Reports vary as to the number of tanks lost. Certainly some Panther tanks were lost in the bombing, either buried or overturned, as photographs exist of these tanks. One report states that forty tanks in the front line were destroyed by the American bombs but another says that the Mark IV battalion was withdrawn to form a mobile reserve and very few Panther tanks were actually knocked out.[67] The division records show the same number of Mark IVs operational (fifteen) on 1 August as on 23 July while the number of operational Panthers has decreased from sixteen to twelve in the same period, so it would appear that only four Panther tanks were lost during Operation Cobra. One war correspondent counted nineteen tanks knocked out or abandoned along 2 miles of the road to St Gilles but did not identify the type or unit.[68] With the capture of the division's repair facility at Cerisy-la-Salle, the entire tank strength of the division was reduced to only thirty-three tanks and assault guns by 1 August, less than two full-strength companies. Panzer Lehr would never fight again as a division and the survivors could only form a battle group which was attached to other units over the next few weeks.

Therefore the Germans lost an estimated seventy tanks and assault guns in Operation Cobra, the bulk of these being from the 2nd SS Panzer Division. The eight infantry divisions in LXXXIV Corps also had companies of self-propelled anti-tank guns (Marders) and Stug III assault guns as part of their organic anti-tank units and those that were still operational attempted to break out through the American lines with their infantry. Most of these armoured vehicles were destroyed in the Roncey pocket and in the clashes with CCB of the 2nd Armored Division during 29–30 July.

Operation Cobra utilised the strengths of FUSA and developed into an outstanding success. The initial attack of three infantry divisions well supported by an abundance of artillery and heavy air support concentrated on a narrow front did not go well and it was left to the 1st Division and the combat commands of the 2nd and 3rd Armored divisions to force their way through the German lines the next day. After some initial difficulties around Marigny for the 1st Division, the two armoured divisions were then able to move through the gap and make rapid advances against the defeated and disorganised Germans in a textbook armoured attack. Unfortunately the failure of the 3rd Armored Division to form a secure cordon quickly enough allowed many Germans and their equipment to evade the trap being set before the 2nd Armored Division finally established a line further south on 29 July. With the apparent early success of the operation, Montgomery issued a directive (M515) on 27 July that claimed credit for the success of his plan:

> ... the main blow of the whole Allied plan has now been struck on the western flank; that blow is the foundation of all our operations, and it has been well and truly struck.[69]

A day later, in a cable to Brooke, Montgomery was even more confident in the outcome: 'It begins to look as if policy we have been working on for so many weeks is now going to pay a dividend.'[70] In another telegram the same day, this time to Brooke, Montgomery stressed the importance of the pending Operation Bluecoat in which 'all caution would be thrown to the winds' in another British breakout attempt.

Notes

1 Danchev, A. and Todman, D., eds, *War Diaries Field Marshal Lord Alanbrooke* (London, Weidenfeld and Nicolson), p.566

2 D'Este, C., *Decision in Normandy* (London, Penguin, 2000), p.303

3 CAB 44/248, letter Eisenhower to Montgomery, 7 July 1944, TNA.

4 Letter Dempsey to Liddell Hart re Operation Goodwood, 28 March 1952, LHCMA LH1/230/22

5 CAB 44/248, letter Montgomery to Brooke, 10 July 1944

6 CAB 44/248, signal Montgomery to Eisenhower, 13 July 1944

7 CAB 44/248, signal Montgomery to Brooke, 14 July 1944

8 Blumenson, M., *Breakout and Pursuit* (Washington, US Army CMH, 1961), p.177

9 Blumenson, *ibid*, p.207

10 Zaloga, S., *Armored Thunderbolt – The US Army Sherman in World War II* (Mechanicsburg, PA, Stackpole, 2008) p.166

11 Hunnicutt, R.P., *A History of the American Medium Tank* (Novato, CA, Presidio, 1978), pp.562–4

12 Wilmot, C., *The Struggle for Europe* (London, Collins, 1952), p.432

13 Zetterling, N., *Normandy 1944 – German Military Organisation, Combat Power and Effectiveness* (Manitoba, JJ Fedorowicz, 2000), p.325 and p.390

14 Blumenson, *opcit*, p.236

15 Miller, Capt E., Interview by Capt Hechler for Operation Cobra, 6 September 1944, NARA

16 Korrison, Lt D., Interview by Capt Hechler for Operation Cobra, 6 September 1944, NARA

17 Anon, *Move Out Verify – Combat History of the 743rd Tank Battalion* (Frankfurt, 1945), p.65

18 RG407 AAR, 743rd Tank Battalion, July 1944, NARA

19 Carafano, J.J., *After D-Day – Operation Cobra and the Breakout* (Mechanicsburg, PA, Stackpole, 2008), p.163

20 Hall, C., *History of the 70th Tank Battalion* (Louisville, KY, Southern, 1950), p.75

21 RG319 FMS A-984 353rd Infantry Division 14 July–15 September 1944, NARA

22 RG319 FMS A-973, 275th Infantry Division Combat Operations in Northern France, NARA

23 Blumenson, *opcit*, p.248

24 AAR 33rd Armored Regiment, July 1944, 3rd Armored Division Archives, University of Illinois, Urbana

25 RG 407 603 AAR CCB 3rd Armored Division, July 1944, NARA

26 RG407 603 AAR 3AD CCB, July 1944, NARA

27 Fey, W., *Armour Battles of the Waffen SS* (Mechanicsburg, PA, Stackpole, 2003), pp.117–9

28 AAR 33rd Armored Regiment July 1944, 3rd Armored Division Archives, University of Illinois, Urbana

29 RG407 AAR CCB, *opcit*

30 32nd Armored Regiment journal and log July 1944, 3rd Armored Division Archives, University of Illinois, Urbana

31 Zetterling, *opcit*, p.388

32 RG407 603 AAR CCA 3rd Armored Division, July 1944

33 RG407 603 AAR CCB 3rd Armored Division, July 1944

34 Journal 32nd Armored Regiment July 1944, 3rd Armored Division Archives, University of Illinois, Urbana

35 RG407 Operations Report 66th Armored Regiment, July 1944, NARA

36 RG319 FMS B-763 Pemsel, M., The Seventh Army June and July 1944, NARA

37 Zetterling, *opcit*, p.315

38 Blumenson, *opcit*, p.272

39 Johnson, Lt-Col B.P., The Operations of the Second Armoured Division in the Saint Lo Breakthrough, 26–30 July 1944, MCOE Monograph 1946–47

40 Blumenson, *opcit*, p.275

41 RG407 AAR 82nd Reconnaissance Battalion July 1944, NARA

42 Committee 3, Pilsbury, G., et al, Employment of the 2nd Armored Division in Operation Cobra, MCOE paper, 1950, p.56

43 Bando, M., *Breakout in Normandy – The 2nd Armoured Division in the Land of the Dead* (France, Editions Heimdal, 2013), pp.106–7

44 Johnson, *ibid*, p.9

45 Blumenson, *opcit*, p.279

46 Trahan, E.A., ed, *Second Armoured Division 1940–1946* (Nashville, Battery Press, 2002)

47 *Ibid*

48 RG407 AAR 67th Armoured Regiment Operation Cobra 1944, NARA

49 Winter, G.J. (Sr), *World War II* magazine, November 2003

50 Exton, Colonel H.M., The 2nd Armored Division in Operation Cobra, Military Review, August 1947

51 FUSA Report of Operations August 1943 – July 1944, p.116, NARA

52 Ellis, L.F., *Victory in the West Volume 1: The Battle of Normandy* (London, HMSO, 1962), p.385

53 US Army Office of Adjutant General, Army Battle Casualties and Nonbattle Deaths in World War II, Final Report: 7 December 1941–31 December 1946, 1953

54 FUSA report, *opcit*, Table 4, Cumulative casualties

55 History of VII Corps, p.40

56 FUSA, *opcit*, Operations report, Appendix 2, annex 9, p.203

57 RG407, 3rd Armored Division, G-4 operations report, July 1944, NARA

58 Collins, J.L., Letter to Eisenhower, 1 August 1944. J. Lawton Collins Papers, Box 3, 201 Personal Letter File, 1944, Dwight D. Eisenhower Presidential Library.

59 Haynes, D., The 3rd Armored Division Saga in World War II, 1988, 3rd Armored Division Archives, University of Illinois, Urbana

60 Hewitt, R.L., *Workhorse of the Western Front – The Story of the 30th Infantry Division* (Washington, DC, Infantry Journal Press, 1946), p.38

61 RG407, AAR 66th Armored Regiment, July 1944, NARA

62 Carafano, *opcit*, p.184

63 FUSA operations report, Appendix 2 annex 9, p.203

64 Zien, Col. H., Operations of the 3rd Battalion 66th Armored Regiment in the St Lô breakthrough, MCOE paper, 1946–47

65 FUSA Operations report, Annex 9, Armoured section report, p.199

66 Zetterling, *opcit*, p.325

67 Zetterling, *opcit*, p.387

68 Wilmot, *opcit*, p.434

69 WO 229/72/24, 21st Army group directive Montgomery M515, 27 July 1944, TNA

70 CAB 44/248, signal Montgomery to Brooke, 28 July 1944, TNA

9

Operation Bluecoat

Operation Cobra had been in progress for two days by 27 July. The German forces in the St Lô area were in disarray and the FUSA had broken through the German lines but had not yet achieved a strategic breakout or cut off the Seventh Army.[1] Despite the valiant efforts of the Canadian forces during Operation Spring on 25–26 July as part of Montgomery's stated master strategy to hold the German panzer divisions around Caen, the 2nd Panzer Division slipped away on 26 and 27 July bound for the St Lô area. The division made a forced march during daylight from the River Orne to the River Vire, taking considerable casualties en route from the persistent attention of the Allied fighter-bombers. The 116th Panzer Division was also ordered to St Lô on the 28 July by Army Group B and this arrived on 29 July. This was a considerable blow to Montgomery's stated strategy of pulling all the German armour onto the Second Army's front. The Germans were so strong around Caen that the British could not mount another attack in that area for another week after the losses of Operations Goodwood and Spring.[2] In Operation Spring, hastily organised to support Operation Cobra, two Canadian infantry divisions had attacked the Verriers Ridge south of Caen and had been bloodily repulsed by the combined efforts of three panzer divisions. Therefore Montgomery needed to mount another operation as quickly as possible in a less well-defended area to prevent the migration of more panzer divisions from one front to the other. The key topographical feature in the chosen area was Mont Pinçon near Caumont which dominated the surrounding countryside and would provide the Germans with an ideal anchor for their right flank opposite the Americans whilst their left flank retired to absorb the momentum of Operation Cobra. Accordingly, in his directive M515 of 27 July, Montgomery wrote that the main blow of the whole Allied strategy had been delivered by the FUSA as planned and that there was a need for a further British operation with six divisions west of Noyers on a relatively undefended part of the chains that the Germans had put around the Allied beachhead.[3] However, Montgomery was jolted into action more quickly than he had anticipated by a letter on 28 July from the CIGS Brooke, who noted in his diary:

Now, as a result of all this talking and the actual situation on your front, I feel personally quite certain that Dempsey must attack <u>at the earliest possible moment</u> on a large
scale. We must not allow German forces to move from his front to Bradley's front or
we shall give more cause than ever for criticism.[4]

Clearly, all was not well in the Allied camp. Montgomery's failure in Operation
Goodwood had damaged his own credibility further and caused increased tension within SHAEF; matters were not helped at all by the movement of the two
panzer divisions from Caen to the American front.[5] On reading the M515 directive,
Eisenhower added his own message, complete with veiled criticisms of previous
operations, requesting no further delays:

I feel very strongly that a three division attack now on the Second Army's right flank
will be worth more than a six division attack in five days time. Follow up units if
needed can reach the scene while the initial breakthrough progresses as now, as never
before, opportunity is staring us in the face. Let us go all out the line you have laid
down in your M515 and let us not, repeat not, waste an hour in getting the whole
affair started. Never was time more vital to us and we should not, repeat not, wait on
weather or perfections in details of preparation.[6]

From the above message it is clear that Eisenhower was once again expecting
a breakthrough operation from the British. That same morning, Montgomery conveyed his intentions to Dempsey with a date for Operation Bluecoat revised from
2 August to 30 July. The sector chosen for the new offensive, around Caumont, was
believed to contain no panzer divisions. After declaring to the CIGS on 14 June that
the British Second Army would continue to exert pressure in this sector and then
putting all efforts into the opposite end of the front line at Caen, Montgomery was
now turning his attention back to the Second Army right flank around Caumont.
The revised starting date immediately threw the British planners into turmoil as,
following the first planning meeting at 1645 hours in Creully, it gave them less
than 36 hours to plan the operation and move the required forces from positions
around Caen to their assembly points. This required a march of 25 miles for the
11th Armoured Division and 45 miles for the Guards Armoured Division which
had to move from the bridgehead east of the River Orne.

As previously, Montgomery sent that day a hugely optimistic signal to Brooke,
declaring that 'it will be on the largest scale and have everything thrown in' and
that he had instructed Dempsey 'to throw all caution overboard and take any
risks he likes, and to accept any casualties, and to step on the gas for Vire'.[7] Once
again, Montgomery offered a goal to his superiors that was way beyond what his
real intentions were and, in any case, Vire was an objective of the US XIX Corps
advancing from St Lô as part of Operation Cobra. The easternmost FUSA Corps,
V Corps, was actually going to be pinched out as a result of the south-easterly
advance of XIX Corps and ultimately had to stop just north of the town.[8]

Montgomery's directive M515 of 27 July was vague regarding Vire and stated that a strong British force should be held ready for a rapid exploitation towards Vire, the capture of which would facilitate the movements of FUSA.[9] The operational orders of VIII Corps for Operation Bluecoat say nothing about Vire. The primary intention of Operation Bluecoat, as stated in the VIII Corps orders, was for XXX Corps to assist FUSA in its breakout attempt by capturing and denying the use of the high ground at Mont Pinçon to the Germans to use as an anchor or hinge for their Seventh Army.[10] The VIII Corps objective furthest south given was that of Petit Aunay which was just north of the River Souleuvre and nowhere near Vire.

An attack by six British divisions was planned into the worst bocage countryside in Normandy. To the usual small fields, high hedgerows and sunken lanes of the bocage were added heavily wooded areas and many steep hills, ridges and valleys. So bad was the terrain that the German 326th Division, defending part of that sector, had no tank support apart from two companies of Mark IV tanks left behind by the 2nd Panzer Division and its own anti-tank company, comprising fourteen Marders and ten Stug III self-propelled guns, as the Germans thought the country to be unsuitable for tanks.

In order for FUSA to concentrate its forces for Operation Cobra, Second Army had extended its responsibilities on 23 July to include part of the line previously held by the 5th US Infantry Division so the 15th (Scottish) Division was moved into the line next to the Americans.[11] This allowed the inexperienced US 5th Division to attack on a small, single regiment front which they had been doing since 26 July but had only managed to advance 3 miles in the difficult countryside before Operation Bluecoat.

The short space of time available to mount Operation Bluecoat meant that when the first operational orders were issued by VIII Corps on 29 July to the two divisions leading the attack, the 11th Armoured and the 15th Divisions, the times for the start of the attack could not be given as the details of the air support had not yet been determined. Once again, as in the previous breakout attacks of Operations Goodwood and Cobra, extensive air support had been organised to assist with the breakthrough of the German lines. When finally confirmed, the air support plan was for 700 RAF heavy bombers to bomb targets in front of XXX Corps between 0855 and 0955 hours and 900 USAAF bombers to support VIII Corps at the same time. Cloudy weather on the first day of Operation Bluecoat then interfered with the air support programme. Only 480 RAF bombers were able to locate their targets and all fighter-bomber squadrons were grounded. The USAAF successfully carried out its mission in support of XXX Corps.[12] Learning from Operation Goodwood, a further bombing raid had been organised for the afternoon to assist with the advance through the German defences that were organised in depth as was their usual practice. If Operation Bluecoat was not ever intended as a breakout operation, the need for this second air raid is not clear. A second air raid had been requested by VIII Corps planners for Operation Goodwood and had been refused. The war diaries of the 4th Grenadier Guards and the 3rd Scots Guards Armoured regiments state that Operation Bluecoat was intended both as a breakthrough and breakout battle. Nevertheless, Montgomery was again hedging his bets with his orders for VIII Corps which were only to be prepared to exploit southwards whilst at the same time conveying to the CIGS and Eisenhower what they wanted to hear.

Operation Bluecoat involved four corps of the Second British Army, principally the British VIII and XXX Corps which were to be supported by simultaneous attacks by units of XII Corps and the 2nd Canadian Corps further east. The main advance was to be made by XXX Corps whose final orders were to capture the area of high ground at Point 361 west of Jurques using the 50th and 43rd Divisions, supported by the 8th Armoured Brigade with the 7th Armoured Division in reserve. When this was completed, the 7th Armoured Division was to be prepared to pass through and either capture Le Bény Bocage, Vire or dominate the Mont Pinçon feature.

VIII Corps was to advance on a two-division front with the 15th (Scottish) Division on the left and 11th Armoured Division on the right; its mission was to protect the right flank of XXX Corps, capture the high ground east of St Martin des Besaces (Point 309) and advance as far as Petit Aunay. The main effort was to come from the 15th (Scottish) Division as the 11th Armoured Division, after being mauled during Goodwood, was only involved as there was no other infantry division available.[13] The Guards Armoured Division was in reserve.

Following the difficulties of fighting in the bocage experienced over the previous eight weeks by the Allies, the British armoured formations reorganised to try and find the best structure for infantry tank cooperation. In VIII Corps, the 15th Division was reunited with the 6th Guards Tank Brigade with which it had trained before the invasion. Two troops of three Churchill tanks with a seventh Churchill with 95mm howitzer from the 4th Grenadier Guards were allocated to each company of the 227th brigade.[14]

The Guards Armoured Division in VIII Corps also reorganised at the specific instruction of General O' Connor. An infantry battalion and an armoured battalion were grouped together. The two Grenadier Guards battalions were at last reunited but the Coldstream and Irish Guards units remained separated so that the 1st Armoured Coldstream worked with the 3rd Irish Guards and 2nd Irish Guards worked with the infantry of the 5th Coldstream. This reorganisation was done in great haste, within 90 minutes, on the basis of which battalions were camped next to each other in adjacent fields and was far from ideal.[15] The motorised battalion of the Grenadier Guards was thus lost to the other armoured regiments, further restricting their mobility and flexibility.[16]

The 11th Armoured Division reorganised into two battle groups. The division's 159th Brigade would work with the 2nd Fife and Forfar Regiment whilst the rest of the 29th Brigade would be supported by an extra infantry battalion brought into VIII Corps, the 3rd Monmouth. Although not of equal size, General Roberts hoped that the two battle groups would give a more flexible and integrated organisation that would produce results in the bocage. Both battle groups were supported by divisional and corps artillery plus AVREs from the 79th Armoured Division.

Opposing the forces of the two British corps was a single German division, the 326th Division, which had been transferred to Caumont from the Fifteenth Army in the Pas de Calais after Operation Goodwood, relieving the 2nd Panzer Division on 23 July. Having been in possession of this area for nearly seven weeks, the Germans had laid many minefields, built road blocks and carefully sited their anti-tank guns and machine guns to take advantage of the terrain and cover likely bottlenecks in any enemy advance. The relative weakness of the Germans in this sector was known to Eisenhower who referred to it in his cable to Montgomery on 28 July: 'On that ten mile front the enemy now has only four regiments and the occasional dug-in tank.'[17]

The usefulness of the outstandingly successful Operation Fortitude was almost at an end as the Germans no longer believed in a second landing around Calais and had begun to transfer troops from the Fifteenth Army. Units on their way to Normandy since Operation Goodwood included seven infantry divisions and the 9th Panzer Division from the south of France.

30 July

XXX Corps

The 43rd (Wessex) Division advanced with the tanks of the 27th Armoured Brigade in support but made very little progress as 'the enemy had laid mines thickly and booby traps were plentiful'.[18] A stream running east–west through Briquessard with high banks that had been mined, proved impassable and the only crossing points were strongly defended by anti-tank and machine guns. By mid-afternoon, the advance had not even reached Cahagnes so any further attacks that day were postponed.

15th Scottish/6th Guards Tank Brigade

H-hour for Phase 1 having finally been confirmed for 0655 hours, the 227th Brigade attacked two-up with the 9th Cameronians supported by two squadrons of the 4th Grenadier Guards with the objective of Sept Vents and the 2nd Gordons to clear the Lutaine Wood with the No. 3 Squadron. The brigade was given 2 hours to reach the start line for phase two, which would commence at 0955 hours immediately after the bombing. There was no preparatory artillery barrage until H-hour when smoke was put down on the distant ridge to hamper German observation and hopefully any defensive artillery fire. Despite the smoke, the Germans reacted swiftly to the advance with well-aimed mortar and artillery barrages. Movement south on the roads was obstructed by anti-tank mines while the thick hedgerows restricted visibility and made navigation difficult. One company of the 9th Cameronians got lost in the difficult bocage countryside. Five Grenadier Guards tanks went up on mines on the same road and their advance had to be halted whilst Flail tanks were used to clear them. By the time the Grenadier

Guards got to Sept Vents at 0915 hours, another two tanks had been lost to mines. Sept Vents was strongly defended by the Germans and was not captured until 1300 hours. One squadron of Grenadier Guards used the 20mm cannon of its anti-aircraft tanks in an infantry support role during the capture of the village.

The advance to Lutaine Wood with No. 3 Squadron was more successful and the objective was reached by 0900 hours, the wood being cleared by noon. A single Churchill tank managed to penetrate the wood and charged through the German defences, creating mayhem before retiring to its own lines. Two tank commanders, including the squadron leader, were killed by snipers – one being shot while a group of Germans were surrendering to him; the group was immediately 'liquidated'.[19]

While the mopping-up operations were in progress, the bombers passed overhead towards their targets. The two remaining battalions, the 2nd Argyll and Sutherland Highlanders and the 10th Highland Light Infantry, having formed up with their supporting tanks, crept forward towards the start lines where they could see and hear the fighting in progress ahead of them. The phase two start line was 1,500yds south of Sept Vents and as there was still fighting in Lutaine Wood, considerable confusion developed as the infantry and tanks destined for phase two became embroiled in the fighting of the mopping-up of phase one. No plan had been made for any units to clear the area of the start line between the two points.[20]

As the phase one objectives had not been attained by 0955 hours, which was X-hour for the start of phase two, it was decided by VIII Corps that the other two armoured regiments and their infantry should pass through and push on ahead as the timetable was in danger of falling behind with the second bomber raid due at 1555 hours. The 2nd Argylls with the tanks of the 3rd Scots Guards were to take Hill 226 near Les Loges at the same time as the 10th Highlanders, supported by the Coldstream Guards, were to advance to Hill 309. However, the infantry and their tanks quickly got separated on the way to the start lines and as a result, the tanks crossed the start line well ahead of the infantry. The 4th Coldstream Guards lost two tanks on mines just before they reached the start line which they crossed at 1030 hours; the 3rd Scots Guards eventually crossed their start line at 1105 hours after also losing two tanks on mines.

An artillery barrage accompanied the start of phase two after the bombing and was timed to give an advance rate of 100yds in 4 minutes for a total of 2,500yds. However, due to the difficult country the tanks were unable to keep up with this barrage. The objective of the Coldstream Guards in phase two was the high ground south of Hervieux. This was reached at about 1130 hours and it was secured as far as possible by the tanks within 30 minutes. The infantry did not arrive until 1400 hours. The tanks of the Coldstream Guards were then supposed to carry another battalion of infantry, the Glasgow Highlanders on to Point 309 but the infantry had not arrived at rendezvous.

The 3rd Scots Guards crossed their start line without the 2nd Argylls infantry, which had become embroiled in the fighting around Lutaine Wood and Le Bourg, so the tanks went on alone. The advance was without much opposition and the

tanks shot up every hedgerow and farmhouse along the way. After halting for an
hour to wait in vain for the infantry to catch up, the two leading squadrons then
moved off to the objective. By 1530 hours, the infantry had at last arrived and the

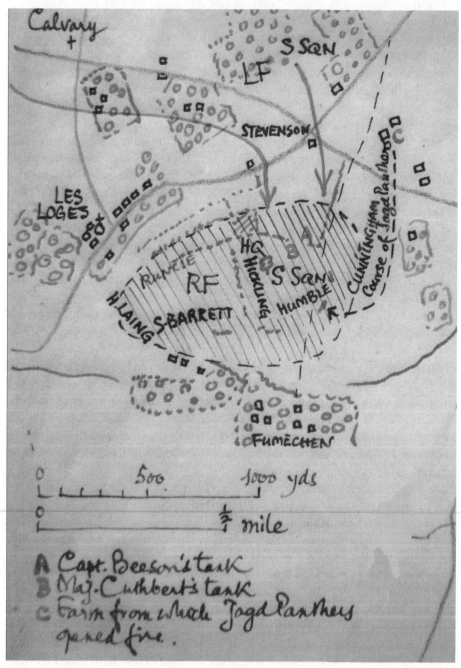

Sketch map of plan of action of 3rd Scots Guards on Hill 226, 30 July 1944, during Operation Bluecoat.

village of Les Loges was secured while Hill 226 was also occupied. The Scots Guards were ready to push on with phase three but permission was refused as while the 15th (Scottish) Division had created a deep penetration into the German lines, the XXX Corps advance on the left had been slower than anticipated and the division's left flank was now exposed. The Scots Guards were told to hold the position at all costs and wait for the anti-tank gun company of the Argyles to come up to support them.

After repeated German artillery barrages on the exposed top of Hill 226, the infantry retired back to the comparative shelter of the village of Les Loges leaving the Scots Guards tanks hull down below the crest of the hill. At 1800 hours, a very heavy barrage of 150mm and 120mm artillery hit their positions and one tank was knocked out. Ten minutes later, the easternmost troop of three tanks of S Squadron was knocked out by fire from two Jagdpanthers located in a wood some 500yds to the left rear of the squadron.

The two Jagdpanthers then moved out of the woods, covered by a third, and advanced straight through S Squadron, shooting at any tanks in their path. A large hedge separated and screened S Squadron from the left flank squadron to the west which did not see the German tanks. The regiment's second in command chose that moment to return from checking on the positions of the left flank squadron and his Churchill tank met the enemy head-on. The Churchill was penetrated through its thick frontal armour and the tank's ammunition exploded, blowing the turret cleanly off.

Armour-piercing shells from the Churchills struck the advancing Jagdpanthers but simply bounced off their thick, sloped armour. The two German self-propelled guns then veered away and disappeared over the hill in a northerly direction.[21]

The action was observed by S Squadron's commander, Captain Whitelaw:

The mortaring and shelling suddenly intensified. Then I saw the left hand tank of my left forward troop go up in flames closely followed by the other two. Immediately I started to return to the hill. As I was driving up the field I saw all three tanks of my left flank troop go up in flames, and as I approached the top of the hill, I saw a tank moving from right to left in front of me. Suddenly it appeared to me (wearing a headset) as if the turret of this tank had been quietly lifted off and put down on the ground some yards away. It was only when I saw the flames that I realised that this tank had in fact exploded. All six tanks in my two left hand troops together with the battalion second in command's tank had been knocked out ... in a little over a minute.[22]

Eleven Churchill tanks were destroyed in this brief action. A track of one of the Jagdpanthers was damaged by a shot from a Churchill and after travelling about a mile to the east, the crew abandoned their vehicle after setting fire to it, apparently unable to make any repairs.

The German self-propelled guns had the village of Les Loges at their mercy and could have cut the line of the British advance to Hill 309 but did not press the attack. If the British infantry that withdrew had been in their previous positions, the Jagdpanthers would not have been able to stalk the British tanks unnoticed before opening fire.

The second bombing raid, which was the prelude to phase three, started as scheduled at 1555 hours. The Coldstream Guards were ordered to advance to Hill 309 at 1630 hours without any infantry as the designated infantry, the Glasgow Highlanders, had not arrived and would now be carried by the tanks of the Grenadier Guards behind them. The advance got underway 15 minutes late. No. 3 Squadron encountered an anti-tank gun in La Morichesse and decided to by-pass the village, but the RHQ rear link tank did not follow the detour and went straight ahead into the village where it was immediately knocked out. Two other tanks in La Ferrière au Doyen were also hit and immobilised by an anti-tank gun which was then silenced by an artillery barrage called down on its location. The two squadrons of Coldstream Guards tanks got to Hill 309 at 1900 hours and the infantry finally arrived at 2230 hours; the regiment harboured there for the night.

The Grenadier Guards received new orders that afternoon to proceed onto Hill 309 with all squadrons, picking up the late Glasgow Highlanders en route north of Hervieux along the main road from Caumont to St Martin de Besaces. A further tank was damaged on a mine around Sept Vents and the advance was held up by another 88mm anti-tank gun covering the road south of Hervieux at La Morichesse. The infantry dismounted and proceeded to infiltrate into the village, supported by the tanks of No. 2 Squadron which had one tank knocked out but in turn destroyed the anti-tank gun. As it was now late evening, the regiment decided to harbour a mile further north and found themselves in a traffic jam with other vehicles coming down the road. The order to harbour was countermanded but as it was too difficult to turn around, the regiment was diverted onto a track where it eventually harboured at La Ferrière.[23]

11th Armoured Division

At 0700 hours, the 11th Armoured Division's advance began in the two groups previously described. The 29th Brigade was the easternmost group (left) and the 159th Brigade was on the right; the divisional orders were to protect the right flank of XXX Corps.

The 23rd Hussars and Monmouth infantry were in the vanguard of the 29th Brigade group and their route benefited from the earlier actions of the adjacent 15th Division in clearing a path. Passing to the west of Sept Vents, one tank was knocked out by an artillery barrage and two tanks were lost in minefield. The advance had to be halted whilst the Flails were brought forward to clear a passage. The small fields and narrow lanes made it very difficult for the tanks to keep up with the infantry although the tanks were under the command of the infantry battalion. The advance was slow but met only isolated pockets of resistance and mines, which had to be cleared before forward progress could be resumed. At La Morichesse, the reserve group of the 3rd RTR and the 8th Rifle Brigade passed through and took over the advance from the Hussars. After a firefight in the darkness, St Jean des Essartiers was captured and the tanks then harboured.

The right-hand column of the 2nd Fife and Forfar tanks and Hereford infantry struck more opposition and minefields. B Squadron lost seven tanks as soon as it had crossed the start line and the Herefords spent most of the day clearing the village of Cussy, less than 1,000yds from start line. Guessing that the German lines had been pierced and conscious of the tight timetable, the regiment was then ordered by VIII Corps to advance as rapidly as possible. Lieutenant Steel Brownlie of A Squadron relished the chance to advance at speed:

> We were told to move and move fast. We called it 'baffing'. No more creeping through hedges and grinding about in first gear, but doing what we had been trained to do, move. A Squadron went first, and I was leading troop. It was a case of motoring flat out, 35mph on the straight, for the faster you went the harder you were to hit. There were Germans all over the place, running and scampering. We fired wildly at them, overtook them and left them far behind. There were targets at every turn of the road. It was exhilarating.[24]

The other two tanks of Brownlie's troop were knocked out and Brownlie's own tank was damaged by a direct hit that jammed the turret. The squadron eventually reached the high ground north-west of St Ouen des Besaces, which was where the group harboured for the night.[25]

The German Army Group B command was already preoccupied with dealing with the threatened American breakout at Avranches when it received news of the attack near Caumont. General Eberbach at Panzer Gruppe West did not want to move any more armoured units away from Caen, so von Kluge decided to first send a kampfgruppe of the 21st Panzer Division to the aid of the 326th Division. Later in the evening, the remainder of the division was added when it was realised that the British had advanced as far as the 326th Division's rear artillery positions at St Jean and La Ferrière. After having been in action since D-Day, the 21st Panzer Division had been pulled out of the line on 27 July to rest and refit prior to the planned major armoured counterattack. Three batteries of 88mm guns were also sent from the III Flak Korps.[26] The easternmost division of the Seventh Army, the 3rd Parachute Division, which was the sole unit of the 2nd Parachute Corps, became increasingly nervous about what appeared to be the collapse of its neighbouring division and began to pull back from its own positions towards Vire.

31 July

XXX Corps

The 43rd Wessex Division made slightly better progress and captured Cahagnes, advancing to a stream south of the village. The 50th Division, after managing an advance of only a few hundred yards, finally captured Orbois. Clearly no break-through was going to occur on the XXX Corps front.

11th Armoured Division

The tired infantry of the KSLI and A Squadron of the 2nd Fife and Forfar were roused early in the morning and advanced in the darkness to the main road just west of St Martin des Besaces. This force was subsequently ordered to capture the town which was defended by a single Mark IV tank that knocked out a Sherman as it crossed the road. The rest of the troop returned fire along the road and the track of the Mark IV was damaged, requiring it to be towed from St Martin by another tank before the arrival of the British. St Martin was secured by midday but not before a second tank was lost in this operation.[27] The town was then handed over to the infantry of the 15th (Scottish) Division so that the 11th Armoured Division could continue its advance.

2nd Household Cavalry

C Squadron of the Household Cavalry Regiment was attached to the 159th Brigade group and at dawn had moved southwards in their armoured cars to probe the German lines. Two armoured cars crossed the road west of St Martin des Besaces before the operation had begun to clear it and proceeded south into the Forêt l'Evêque. There they carefully followed a German armoured car southward and reached the village of La Ferrière on the other side of the forest. The two scout cars drove on south and east along various tracks until they came to a small stone bridge over the River Soulevre. The single sentry was ruthlessly dealt with and while the two cars were hidden in nearby bushes, the information on the capture of the bridge was wirelessed to the Household Cavalry HQ which quickly passed it on to the 11th Armoured Division HQ. The 2nd Northants Yeomanry were ordered to reinforce the position at the bridge as soon as possible. C Squadron got two troops of Cromwells over the road and the railway west of St Martin but the remainder of the squadron was held up by enemy fire. After moving somewhat more cautiously than the armoured cars, the tanks arrived at the bridge at 1405 hours.

Elated at the news of the seizure of the bridge, at 1400 hours VIII Corps issued new orders to the 11th Armoured Division as there was now an alternative route for the assault on Le Bény Bocage from the west, south of the River Soulevre, rather than the previously planned frontal assault from the north across the river. The 23rd Hussars were ordered to reinforce the bridge carrying the 3rd Monmouth infantry on their tanks, taking the supposedly faster main road around the Forêt l'Evêque to the bridge. The rest of the brigade groups were to advance south from St Martin as soon as possible.

The orders for the rest of the day were carried out with only one difficulty: the circuitous route of the 23rd Hussars and the reminder of the 2nd Northants Yeomanry tanks around the Forêt l'Evêque was held up by an American column moving along the same road southwards at Petite Aunay, despite VIII Corps having earlier requested the US V Corps to keep the road clear. B Squadron of the Hussars took about 3 hours to reach the bridge, which they did at 1800 hours, whilst the rest of the regiment arrived at 2100 hours. B and C squadrons made a brief recce across the bridge to the wooded hillside opposite but, after losing one tank on the mined road, decided to return to harbour around the bridge as darkness set in. A brief firefight resulted in the capture of a soldier from the reconnaissance battalion of the 21st Panzer Division.

Meanwhile, the 3rd RTR had also arrived and cleared La Ferrière of infiltrating German paratroops of the 3rd Parachute Division. During the night, the American troops that had been met on the road at Petite Aunay dug in between the bridge and La Ferrière to underscore the apparent breakdown of communications between the British and Americans.

From a later intercept of a German radio message, it was learnt that the River Soulevre bridge and the track through the Forêt l'Evêque were not only the boundary line between the II Parachute and the LXXIV Corps but the same line was also the boundary between the Seventh Army and Panzer Gruppe West.[28] As such, each of the adjacent German units thought the other was guarding the bridge and as a consequence the bridge was left relatively undefended. The men of the Household Cavalry were given no time to rest and were instructed to patrol towards Vire. As the 11th Armoured Division was making more rapid progress, the major roles in Operation Bluecoat were then reversed by General Dempsey. The objective of Le Bény Bocage was taken from XXX Corps and allocated to VIII Corps while the 15th (Scottish) Division would now protect the left flank of the 11th Armoured Division; XXX Corps, in turn, would protect the flank of the Scottish Division.

General Dempsey also ordered VIII Corps to bring the Guards Armoured Division into the battle because of the lack of progress and the division advanced at 1630 hours from Caumont. By dusk, the Guards had advanced to contact with the Germans south-east of St Martin des Besaces on the hill at Point 238. The tanks of No. 2 Squadron 2nd Irish Guards, along with the 5th Coldstream infantry, tried to capture the hill late in the evening in a hastily planned and unreconnoitred attack that was unsuccessful, losing the tank of the squadron's second in command which was found next morning burnt out. Other advance elements of the 21st Panzer Division had arrived on the hill in the afternoon and the rest of the division deployed overnight, including forty-one Mark IV tanks and the surviving King Tiger tanks of the 503rd Schwere Battalion.

By late afternoon, the advanced elements of the 21st Panzer Division had begun to arrive in the area around the Bois du Homme. General Feuchtinger had arrived the previous evening and had met with the LXXIV Korps commander who was adamant that a counterattack be made as soon as possible. Feuchtinger was pessimistic that his weakened division could hold a front line that ran from the Bois du Homme to Le Bény Bocage and preferred to use his men to block the British advance rather than frittering them away in a pointless attack.

A limited counterattack was made by the LXXIV Korps reserve of the 326 Fusilerbattalion, the reconnaissance battalion of 21st Panzer and a few Jagdpanthers towards Cahagnes, but this was stopped by artillery and air attack. Feuchtinger was later reprimanded for not committing all of the 21st Panzer Division to this attack and was threatened with a court martial if he did not attack with all his forces on the next day.

1 August

All the other elements of the 21st Panzer Division arrived overnight and were deployed in blocking positions from Le Bény Bocage to the Bois du Homme and, apart from the remnants of the 326th Division, were the only German force defending against the British operation.

The main counterattack of the 21st Panzer Division that day was directed at Hill 309, east of the Bois du Homme, which was still being held by the 6th Guards Tank brigade. After heavy artillery and mortar fire, small groups of infantry, accompanied by tanks, began to try and infiltrate the British forward lines. The Coldstream Churchills changed position frequently and were able to repel the German attack with the loss of only two tanks. The Coldstream regimental history wrote of the attack:

> At a quarter to seven the enemy infantry was seen advancing from La Ferrière with Tiger tanks in support. Tanks and small arms fire soon disposed of the infantry but against the Tiger tanks they were powerless. The battalion had just been equipped with the latest SABOT ammunition and it bounced off the enemy tanks like ping-pong balls. It was only the medium artillery that kept the Tigers at bay – that and the inability of the Tigers to move over ground which Churchills would have crossed with ease. All day the attack continued and there was little intermission in the heavy shell fire that came down on the hillside. The prolonged noise and tension and heat wore down nerves and judgement and crews would direct their fire upon Tigers which proved to be only bushes and huts; but Major Hambro on whose flank the bulk of the attack had fallen, remained calm, and his control of the squadron and the supporting artillery fire was complete. At last, at four o'clock in the evening, the Germans began to withdraw across the open ground between La Ferrière and the Bois du Homme.[29]

The Bois du Homme was used by the German panzergrenadiers as a forming-up point for their attack and the woods were repeatedly shelled by British artillery which disrupted every attack, causing heavy losses. The 21st Panzer Division, already weakened, was not strong enough to continue the attack and could barely hold the line in the face of the British numerical and firepower superiority. Feuchtinger's pessimism proved to be correct and further reinforcements were required to stop the British attack.

11th Armoured Division

The 3rd RTR took Le Bény Bocage that morning with little resistance and afterwards pushed eastwards towards Catheolles to seize another important bridge over the River Souleuvre and a road junction. One Sherman tank was knocked out and another one became bogged. A road block was set up and many unsuspecting German vehicles trying to get through Catheolles were shot up. This position was effectively behind the 21st Panzer Division which had its headquarters at St Pierre Tarentaine, only half a mile away. Once the news of the British road block was received, the headquarters staff began a rapid withdrawal from the area, resulting in the cancellation of any further attacks on Hill 309.

This advance caused further consternation in the German command as clearly the British were poised to make a breakthrough. Many British armoured formations previously identified as being around Caen had now moved to the Caumont sector and so it was reasoned by von Kluge that German tank units could be moved from Caen as well. At 1605 hours, both the 9th and 10th SS Panzer divisions were ordered to disengage from around Caen and proceed to the Caumont sector to shore up the crumbling defences of the 21st Panzer Division and the 326th Division. A Tiger tank battalion, the 102nd SS Schwere Battalion, was also dispatched to the area.

Vire was a vital road junction and supply hub for the Seventh Army to its depots in Paris and further east. The 10th SS Panzer Division would be used to block the advance of XXX Corps whilst the 9th SS Panzer Division was given the mission of plugging the gap in the German lines, restoring contact between the two armies and breaking the armoured spearheads of the 11th Armoured Division. On 1 August, the 9th SS Panzer Division had operational thirty-one Panthers, seventeen Mark IVs and twenty-eight Stug III assault guns to carry out these tasks.[30]

That day, the two 29th Brigade regiments continued the advance: the 23rd Hussars occupied Le Bény Bocage while the 2nd Fife and Forfars crossed the River Souleuvre to Carville, east of Le Bény Bocage, without opposition.

Guards Division

The 32nd Brigade of Guards and the Shermans of No. 1 Squadron of 2nd Irish Guards resumed the attack on Point 238 south of St Martin de Besaces next morning. A sudden mortar barrage caused the infantry to go to ground and as the tanks came up in support, they were hit by fire from several well-placed and camouflaged Mark IVs in hull down positions in a sunken lane. Two tanks were knocked out and the attack was recalled in order to regroup. The German tanks also withdrew to new positions from where they stopped a second attack, causing four more Shermans to be lost, although this time a Mark IV was spotted and destroyed by one of the Shermans before it was itself knocked out. The conditions were summarised in the 2nd Irish Guards war diary:

One of the main difficulties we had to overcome now and later was the close country, thick hedges and sunken lanes which prevented deployment and limited vision to 100 yds or less, with the result that 2 or 3 well hidden guns or tanks could shoot up a whole troop before being spotted.[31]

For the regiments of the Guards Armoured Division, this was their first time fighting in the bocage and their experiences mirrored that of all other units. A flanking attack was made by No. 2 Squadron around the eastern slopes of the hill only for the Germans to promptly withdraw. That morning A Squadron lost a total of seven tanks before the hill was taken.[32] The German tank knocked out was found to be from the 2nd Panzer Division and the two companies left behind to support the 326th Division when it moved towards St Lô.

The village of St Denis Maisoncelles was occupied about 1300 hours by the Irish Guards and later in the afternoon a patrol of Stuart recce tanks and infantry approached the bridge over the River Soulevre at Le Tourneur, only for the leading tanks to be knocked out by a Panther tank defending the bridge. No further progress was made that day until the bridge was taken by two companies of infantry in an attack later that night. The capture of the bridge at Le Tourneur was important as it provided VIII Corps with a second crossing over the River Soulevre. However, the 1st Coldstream and 2nd Grenadier Guards saw little action that day as most of it was spent in traffic jams on the dusty road from Caumont. As the Guards Armoured Division had still not crossed the River Soulevre, the left flank of the 11th Armoured Division that had advanced further was now exposed.

In the west, FUSA had captured Avranches and thus sealed off the entire Cotentin peninsula. American armoured divisions were now rapidly passing through the town and fanning out west and southwards into the interior of Brittany largely unopposed. During the day, other patrols of 2nd Household Cavalry reached Vire and reported that it was undefended.

XXX Corps

The 7th Armoured Division was introduced into the battle to advance from Caumont to Cahagnes, Breuil and Aunay. Led by the 1st RTR, the division made little progress against small but determined resistance, encountering frequent road blocks and mines. Progress was also impeded by traffic jams around Caumont caused by the tail of the 50th Division. The 43rd Division, however, made better progress and took the hill at Point 361 south of the Bois du Homme.

2 August

XXX Corps

The 1st RTR led the advance for the day and met increasing resistance from mines and small groups of infantry with Panzerfäuste. Units of the 10th SS Panzer

Division that had been committed against XXX Corps around Aunay sur Odon had started to arrive and had taken up defensive positions. C Squadron reached the high ground north-west of Sauques at a cost of six tanks lost to mines, Panzerfäuste and anti-tank guns.[33] A trooper in 1st RTR wrote in his diary:

> … Bloody awful bad show. Tank went over mine, blew bottom in, these Cromwells no use on mines … Had to stop in the wood until midnight when the SPs (of Norfolk Yeomanry) took over – glad to because Tigers were milling about somewhere in front.[34]

The 7th Armoured Division had only advanced 7 miles in two days. The reasons for this slow advance were queried by the XXX Corps commander, Lieutenant-General Bucknall, and General Erskine's response at 1520 hours was as follows:

> Mist not cleared until 1200 hours. Heavy traffic on centre line. 43rd Division had not captured Robin (the crossroads south east of Cahagnes) and finally 1/5th Queen's were shelled from Point 238 and had to debus earlier than planned.[35]

The 8th Armoured Brigade had also been slowly advancing in support of the 50th and 43rd divisions since 30 July. Having captured Cahagnes the day before, the Sherwood Rangers advanced towards Jurques and La Bigne:

> We started at dawn with my tank about fourth from the front. The infantry of the 7th Hampshire were with us, walking alongside the tank and covering the flank. Then we arrive at a T-junction which was mined along with the fields around it. The column halted to allow the sappers to come up and clear the mines when suddenly a Tiger tank emerged from cover and moved to the high ground overlooking the road. It opened fire at about 2000 yards and hit a tank further back in the column. With both ends of the column now blocked, we were bottled up and the Tiger was out of our range.
>
> I shouted, 'Gunner, traverse right! Steady on Tiger. Smoke 1750 yards. Fire when ready.' Our shot landed just in front of the Tiger and the smoke soon obscured it from view. We fired again, this time just to the left of the tank, aiming to keep plenty of smoke between us and it. Other tank commanders did the same whilst the air officer accompanying us called up four Typhoon fighter bombers off the cab rank to fire their rockets at the Tiger. We fired some red smoke to identify the target and then the planes came in, very low and with a tremendous roar. The second plane scored a direct hit and when the smoke cleared, we could see the Tiger lying on its side minus its turret and with no sign of any survivors. It was an awesome display of firepower and demonstrated only too clearly how important control of the skies was to our ultimate success.[36]

The tanks of the Sherwood Rangers carrying their infantry got into the village of Jurques later that morning.

VIII Corps

The Guards Armoured Division was ordered by VIII Corps to resume its advance, this time towards Vassy. The division would advance in two columns, codenamed HOT and COLD, and share the road to Catheolles before taking different routes to Vassy. The left-hand column of the Grenadier Guards (HOT) was instructed to advance via Catheolles to Montchamp but was held up by German tanks and anti-tank guns on the high spurs south at Arclais and Drouet occupied by the 9th SS Kampgruppe Meyer. In the subsequent fighting the Grenadier Guards lost a total of ten Shermans plus three damaged and three Stuarts knocked out in the course of the next few days of Bluecoat.[37]

Meanwhile, the 2nd Welsh Guards reconnaissance regiment with its Cromwells had probed almost to Montcharivel (modern spelling is Montchauvet) on the narrow winding road between the two spurs of high ground when the leading tank was hit and destroyed, blocking the road. Stug IIIs of the 7th Company of the 9th SS Panzer Division and stragglers from the 326th Division had moved into Montcharivel and St Charles de Percy in the early morning. As the route northwards was blocked, the regiment moved southwards and No. 3 Squadron lost five tanks at St Charles de Percy before moving east towards Montchamp, losing another tank.

With orders to advance to Vassy via St Charles de Percy and Estry, the right-hand column (COLD) of the 2nd Irish Guards was to follow the left-hand column at 0715 hours but could not move off until noon because of the traffic on the road ahead of it. The force was then caught in another traffic jam, caused by the rear elements of the left column that had stopped because of the fighting ahead in Catheolles. Eventually the tanks of the Irish Guards forced their way through the vehicles lining the road after the Coldstream infantry abandoned their lorries and mounted the tanks. As the tanks arrived at St Charles de Percy to cut the main road from Vire to Villers Bocage, the main gun of the second tank accidentally fired while negotiating the crossroads, hitting the rear of the leading tank and killing three crew members. The advance continued but was soon held up by two Jagdpanthers in Courteil that proved particularly troublesome. The advance was held up for 5 hours while preparations were made for an attack until the brigadier of the 5th Brigade arrived to see what was causing the hold-up. The regiment was ordered to immediately bypass Courteil and push on to the high ground near Estry and the commanding officer was relieved of command and ordered to rest.[38] In rushing to carry out these orders in the growing darkness, the column got separated: No. 2 and 3 squadrons harboured at La Marvindiere and No. 1 Squadron harboured with RHQ some miles back at Sieurnoux.

11th Armoured Division

The 11th Armoured Division received new orders to redirect their advance to the east of Vire rather than continue southwards as per the previous day as it had now been confirmed by Montgomery that Vire was an American objective.[39] Unknown to them, advance elements of the 9th SS Panzer Division were arriving and about to counterattack. A pincer movement was planned by the Germans with the two pincers converging on Le Bény Bocage. Kampfgruppe Meyer, making up of the bulk of the division, was to attack Le Bény Bocage from the east and Kampfgruppe Weiss, composed of the 102nd SS Schwere Tank Battalion and the 9th SS Reconnaissance Battalion, was to attack from the west via Vire. In the meantime, soldiers from the 3rd Parachute Division would occupy Vire and prepare it for defence against both the American XIX Corps in the western outskirts or the advancing British. The battle groups of the 11th Armoured Division made slow progress along the narrow roads of the difficult terrain and units became strung out in long columns and often became separated. There were sporadic clashes involving German units that were moving south-west across the lines of the British advance.

The 23rd Hussars were ordered to advance from Le Bény Bocage to Le Desert, Presles and Chenedolle. On the Estry ridge above Presles, the leading tank of B Squadron knocked out two armoured cars from the 9th SS Reconnaissance Battalion and fought off some Panzerfäuste-wielding infantry. Descending down into the valley and the village of Presles, two more German self-propelled guns were knocked out from the same reconnaissance regiment. The Hussars RHQ stopped in the middle of Presles only to see a Panther tank moving down the road towards them from the direction of Estry. The Panther was engaged by a Firefly whilst a troop of tanks worked their way around to fire at the Panther from the flank and it was duly knocked out. Other Panther tanks were spotted and A Squadron was pushed out to cover the regiment's left flank. Leaving a narrow track, the squadron began to deploy into a field. The regimental history recorded what happened next:

> At the other end of the field, playing the usual 'lying in wait' game which was the delight of the German tank man, lay hidden a number of Panthers. At close range, and with well distributed fire, they all opened up at once, with devastating effect. All but four of A Squadron's tanks were hit and blazing within a matter of minutes, and the remaining four fought their way back to cover, destroying three Panthers as they did so.[40]

Five Sherman tanks were quickly knocked out in this ambush.[41] Although the history and war diary mention Panther tanks, it is likely that the 23rd Hussars had run into Kampfgruppe Weiss moving to Vire. The 1st Company of Tigers engaged the Hussars while the 2nd Company hurried on to Vire. The Hussars' B Squadron was unable to get across the difficult countryside to assist and pushed on into Chenedolle to immediately have a tank knocked out by a Tiger tank that blocked the main street. Infantry from the Rifle Brigade stalked the Tiger only to see the shots from their PIATs have no effect other than causing the Tiger to reverse out of trouble. As strong German armour was coming in on their left flank, the regiment decided to withdraw with the infantry to a defensive box on the high ground between Chenedolle and Presles on the ridge just south of Le Bas Perrier.

The 2nd Fife and Forfar reached the village of Burcy and pushed on to the Vire–Vassy road where they set up a road block with two squadrons of tanks, beating off attacks by Panther tanks and infantry coming from the direction of Vassy. At nightfall, the two squadrons were withdrawn to a harbour near a farm called La Pavée except for a road block of one troop of tanks and fifteen men from the 3rd Monmouthshire Regiment:

> … I arranged an all-round defence of our little pocket. No smoking and anyone found asleep would be shot. The infantry dug in with their hands, shovels too noisy. Barbed wire and Hawkins grenade were stretched across the road. Tank guns were pointed at possible approaches and the plan was to fire everything full blast if there was an attack. We sat, pricking our hands with pins to keep awake, and listening to German tracked vehicles moving somewhere to the south; and wishing we were somewhere else.[42]

With the 29th Brigade group, the 3rd RTR occupied the hamlet of Le Grand Bonfait after encountering a small group of German tanks and infantry threatening the rear echelons of the division around Point 138. The infantry of the Shropshire regiment managed to knock out one Panther tank with a PIAT, but in the fading light C Squadron lost three tanks brewed up.[43] The 2nd Northants Yeomanry on the right flank were ordered to Etouvy on the extreme right and tanks from C Squadron reached the outskirts of Vire unopposed at 2000 hours but were instructed not to enter the town as it was in the American sector.

At 2230 hours the 11th Armoured Division HQ ordered the leading regiments to hold their present positions as the division was now considerably exposed, there being no support on the left.[44] The 9th SS Panzer Division was where the Guards Armoured Division was supposed to be. Although well positioned for a further exploitation south to Vire, once again the British commanders decided to halt the advance in order to wait for the Guards to make progress to Estry and to await the inevitable German counterattack. Although the defenders in that type of terrain often had the advantage, this decision displayed the identical caution shown in Operation Epsom when the mere threat of an attack was sufficient to halt the attack just as it was poised to achieve a major success. The 29th Brigade reported thirty tanks damaged or destroyed, including six Fireflies, that evening.

The German counterattack had not been successful. The eastern pincer of Kampfgruppe Meyer had clashed continuously with the strung-out units of the 11th Armoured Division and had been unable to penetrate to Le Bény Bocage. The 2nd Company of the 102nd SS Schwere Battalion of Tiger tanks had reached Vire in the evening after taking a detour around the road block of the 2nd Fife and Forfars on the Vire–Vassy road while the 1st Company of Tigers stayed in the vicinity of Chenedolle and Estry. The close countryside made an impression on the battalion as recorded by a tank commander, Unterscharfuehrer Streng:

> The bocage was a cruel area. Every road, every little field and meadow was surrounded by thick hedges two or three metres in height. It was full of frightening opportunities for tanks and anti-tank guns to hide in ambush. The fighting was confused and difficult; each crew member had to react in a flash to any threat or danger. Tank clashes at short range, sometimes only a few metres, were not unusual.[45]

That evening, von Kluge anxiously studied his strategic maps. The news that Vire had not been captured was an enormous relief in view of the new orders that had arrived from Hitler after midnight confirming Operation Luttich (the Mortain counterattack) as Vire was a vital road junction on the route east to west

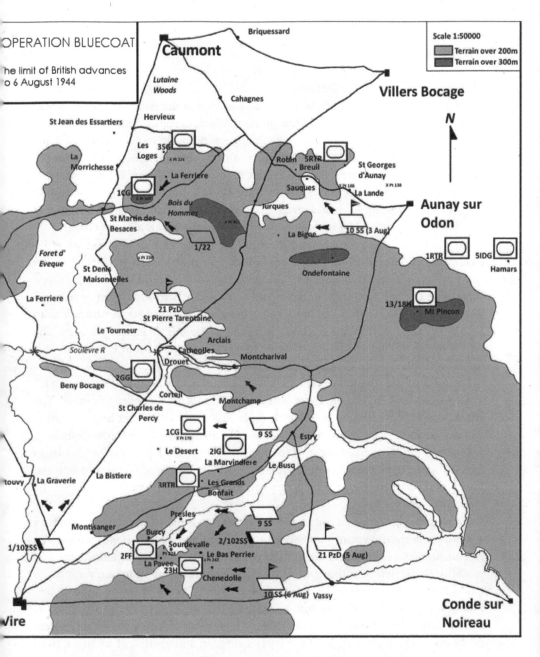

The limits of the advances of British armour in Operation Bluecoat, 6 August 1944.

required by the assembling German armour. General Eberbach ordered the 12th SS Panzer Division to supply a small battle group, Kampfgruppe Olboeter, to secure the Vire–Vassy road and keep it open. This kampfgruppe, consisting of thirteen Panther tanks of the 2nd Company plus a company of panzergrenadiers with six self-propelled artillery guns, got underway that night.

3 August

VIII Corps – 11th Armoured Division

Having been ordered to halt in their present positions at the end of the previous day, the two battle groups of the 11th Armoured Division occupied four defensive positions. The 23rd Hussars and the 8th Rifle Brigade of the 29th Brigade group occupied the ridge north of Le Bas Perrier with the rest of the brigade group back across the valley on the ridge at Point 218 above Presles. A Squadron of the 3rd RTR was further east at Les Grands Bonfait. The 159th Infantry Brigade box was further west around Forgues while the 2nd Fife and Forfars group with the 3rd Monmouths were around Burcy, La Pavée and Point 224, only 1,200yds west of the position of the Hussars.

The Germans at least recognised the strategic importance of Vire and were determined to hold it at all costs. A more limited pincer attack was planned with the two pincers to meet this time at La Bistiere on the road north of Vire. Kampfgruppe Weiss with the 2nd Company of the 102nd Schwere SS Battalion (seven operational Tiger tanks) plus the 9th SS reconnaissance battalion would attack northwards from Vire at the same time as the engineer battalion of the 9th SS Panzer Division. The 1st Company of Tigers and Kampfgruppe Meyer would attack from Estry westwards to link up with the 2nd Company at La Bistiere.

For most of the day, the 2nd Fife and Forfar box near Burcy, La Pavée and Hill 224 was attacked by the engineer battalion of the 9th SS Panzer Division. The attack was unsupported by artillery or tanks and eventually, after heavy fighting and considerable defensive artillery fire, the Germans were forced to withdraw.

On the Vire–Vassy road an early morning German attack led by the Panther tanks from Kampfgruppe Olboeter destroyed the road block and forced the 2nd Fife and Forfar tanks back to Burcy where they anxiously prepared for the advance of the Germans from Presles.

Kampfgruppe Meyer of the 9th SS Panzer Division continued its attack in a south-westerly direction, parallel with the Estry and Perrier ridges, to cut the British lines of communication to their forward boxes, construct a new line and reaching La Bistiere. Panther and Tiger tanks accompanied by infantry advanced along the valley between the ridges and attacked Presles at about 1000 hours. Presles was captured in the afternoon, isolating the battle group of the 23rd Hussars and the Rifle Brigade on the Perrier ridge. The Hussar tanks and the infantry were deployed on the reverse slope of the Perrier ridge in anticipation of an attack from Chenedolle and as their tanks were visible to the German tanks in the valley below, they found themselves under long-range fire as the regiment history portrayed:

A series of resounding cracks followed by sudden puffs of dust rising round our tanks announced that we were under fire from their guns. B Squadron and RHQ were on the most exposed side of the hill and had to bear the brunt. RHQ had a hedge which partially concealed them but B Squadron were unavoidably in full view. They fired back but the range was too great for the seventy fives of the Sherman to have any effect. Gradually these ominous puffs of dust began to creep nearer to our tanks as the Germans found the range. The crack and whistle of enemy armour-piercing shot grew in intensity, mingling with the roar of our seventeen pounders as they retaliated. Inevitably there was soon a crash and spurt of flame. A cloud of black smoke rose from a B Squadron tank which had been hit.[46]

Losses continued to mount and to add to their difficulties, German mortar and artillery fire began to sweep the exposed position. The nine Firefly tanks left forced the German tanks to keep their distance and change their firing positions regularly. The 9th SS Panzer Division claimed that eleven Shermans were knocked out that day, although the actual total was four.[47]

A small group of German tanks were spotted near the hedges close to the British position at Les Grands Bonfait. A Squadron of the 3rd RTR had harboured as instructed by the second in command in a tight defensive desert-style harbour with the tanks closely grouped together in an orchard. At 0930 hours there was a sudden savage German mortar barrage that caught most of the tank crews out of their tanks. Seven German tanks, supported by infantry, were observed around their position. Sergeant Buck Kite saw two Panzer IVs working their way down a hedge 200yds away, coming towards his tank. He jumped into his tank instead of underneath it like the other tank crews and began to engage the Germans:

> I managed to halt the two tanks I'd first seen – they got out of it but whether they were hit or whether they had reversed out of the field into the road I don't know. In any case, by this time three more had appeared and were having a go … We fired so many shots at these three Jerries that I ran out of armour-piercing and started to use HE which wasn't a great deal of use against armour but was better than nothing.[48]

Sergeant Kite then noticed that the troop Firefly was nearby and was not in action, so he ran with his gunner to the Firefly and stood on the rear deck behind the turret to direct the 17-pounder's fire. The Firefly was then hit several times, forcing Sergeant Kite back to his own tank where he fired off the remaining HE shells. A human chain was then formed to transfer, under fire, more armour-piercing shells to Kite's tank until another Panther appeared:

> We were concentrating on one Panther when I realised another was swinging his gun straight at us. I said to my gunner, 'Right a bit, Herbie … on' but before he could fire, I saw the flash of the Jerry's gun. The corn bent as the shell passed over it and I thought, 'This is it. Goodbye.'[49]

The shell struck the Sherman's turret and exploded, knocking Kite unconscious. Luckily, it was a high explosive shell as the Panther tank had apparently run out of armour-piercing shot as well. Kite survived and was awarded a bar to his Military Medal. During this attack, heavy defensive artillery fire had been brought down around the German tanks and eventually the attack petered out; the Germans withdrew, leaving A Squadron to count the cost of the action. Three Shermans and a Firefly had been lost in this battle.[50]

2nd Northants Yeomanry

At 1200 hours, A Squadron was covering the Vire–Vassy road north-east of Vire. C Squadron was in reserve around Etouvy and B Squadron was covering the road north of Vire. At about 1500 hours, the Tiger tanks advanced out of Vire and immediately knocked out three Cromwell tanks of B Squadron. The 75mm armour-piercing shells of the Cromwells simply bounced off the frontal armour of the Tigers. B Squadron was ordered to form a road block but this was attacked from the front and outflanked by Tigers; six more Cromwells were quickly knocked out. A Squadron tried to call in corrections to an artillery shoot but priority was given to the calls from an artillery observer plane which was in communication with a squadron of Typhoons on call that day. Unfortunately, this plane was then shot down by the Germans and the Typhoons could not be given a target so the delayed artillery barrage missed the advancing Tiger tanks. One Tiger tank emerging from behind a building to get on to the main road was hit in the side by one of the RHQ Cromwells at La Bistiere and was knocked out. A couple of Tiger tanks, possibly from the 1st Company, came in from the east so RHQ and A Squadron were pulled back as they were in danger of being cut off. The small, hedged fields meant that even when the Cromwells tanks had a flank shot at a Tiger, the velocity of the 75mm armour-piercing shells was sometimes reduced by the hedges and little damage was done. The Tigers engaged C Squadron which had moved up in support of the other squadrons and tanks began to trade shots with each other. A troop of M10 tank destroyers was located a mile to the north but did not come to the aid of the Northants Yeomanry. However, the dense hedgerows restricted the visibility and movement of the heavy Tigers and in response to counterattacks by British tanks and infantry armed with PIATs, the 2nd Company Tigers eventually withdrew, leaving two tanks at the vital road junction and their accompanying infantry to dig in. The 1st Company, having fought its way through to La Bistiere, stayed near La Graverie where they had linked up with the 3rd Parachute Division. SS Rottenführer Trautmann was the gunner in the company commander's tank:

> The commander of the reconnaissance battalion had told us that friendly patrols were out in front. We had scarcely reached the fork in the road when we were able to identify a tank and several men in the hedge along the road about 500 yards from us. It could not be determined with certainty whether it was the enemy. Suddenly, however a small armoured car moved up behind the tank and then took off to the

north. Because it could only be seen for a few seconds, it could not be knocked out. A fire command was immediately issued – engage at will!

While the first few rounds hit the tank, there was a howling above us in the air. The infantry jumped under cover. Our location was within enemy artillery range.

Schroif issued orders – continue to advance!

Although the tank in front of us had been hit several times, it did not fly into the air. Closely behind it and along the side roads were four Cromwells, all of which were knocked out. We then stopped for a short period until the infantry had closed up.

The terrain in front of us sloped downwards, only to climb up again further on. The last three Tigers provided cover; the main body rolled down the hill and then up the other side. The remaining tanks then followed with infantry aboard.

Our attack objective, a small village could be seen about 600–700 yards ahead. The infantry proceeded to the left and right through the fields, the Tigers then moved out. Soon they had reached the first buildings.

Then it got crazy! Close to the road, hidden from view by the buildings and high hedges were enemy tanks. Shermans! But the two lead tanks, Loritz and Streng worked in an exemplary fashion together and knocked out one tank after another. Those of us in the remaining tanks had our hands full as well. We were getting a lot of fire, especially from the high ground to the left which was filled with row after row of hedges. It looked like we were dealing with tanks, nothing but tanks! We notified each other by radio whenever we were hit, so the others could get out of the enemy's line of fire. We were struck many times by armour-piercing shells, especially in the running gear. Schroif gave orders again and again to fire into this or that hedge. We slowly found our targets. In one place a shot of flames rose to the sky, then at another place. The enemy fire became weaker. The road started to climb uphill. When we were next to the last building, the middle of the column was heavily engaged again while the lead elements continued to advance. The armour-piercing shells landed between and among us like dazzling bolts of lightning. There was another hit to the running gear. The company commander had all tanks fire off to the left! Once again massed fire … groups of bushes off to the left. Two tanks flew into the air again! It was an engagement at point blank range, 50–100 yards.

Schroif continued to receive hits from the building he was in front of, until several high explosive rounds put an end to this defensive effort. The advance then continued. The road climbed; the attack objective was reached. It was then imperative to find a good defensive position in the terrain. The lead elements had reached the hill top when new fire from the left flank was received. We were hit, the radio stopped working. Had something bad happened? What was the matter with the radio operator? The driver? By physically grabbing hold of the gunner and shouting at him, he was told to fire in the direction of where the enemy fire was coming from. The first round had hardly been fired when the Tigers to the rear joined in. They knew what was happening and immediately supported us with heavy fire. The lead platoon continued to move briskly down the slope and climb the hill on the far side. Now, at the most important moment, the radio had stopped working. What was to be done?

Schroif signalled Harlander to come up to him; Harlander had to pass on orders to the rest of the company:

Stop immediately ... objectives reached! Jupiter 1: take position on the line oriented north with me! Jupiter 2: Screen to the right and left at the road intersection 100 yards behind us.

The Tigers rolled into their assigned positions. Rosowski was in the process of turning when he received six direct hits from about 30 yards away. The seventh round was from Rosowkski's tank, it was fired into the hedge from where he had taken the hits. A long tongue of flame shot skyward and a loud bang signalled the effectiveness of this shot – the enemy tank flew into the air![51]

The 2nd Company of Tigers claimed seventeen tanks for the previous day; the Northants Yeomanry tank state that evening recorded five Cromwell tanks knocked out and four damaged along with two Cromwell CS tanks.

That night, A Squadron lost a further eight tanks to marauding German paratroops armed with Panzerfäuste. Next morning, in the face of a renewed German infantry attack, the battered regiment withdrew to Le Brien with two more tanks being lost to Panzerfäuste on the way. At 1900 hours, a troop of anti-tank guns was put under the regiment's command and the surviving tanks were ordered to form a roadblock. In the previous hard-fought 24-hour period, eighteen Cromwell tanks of the Northants Yeomanry were completely destroyed.

XXX Corps

The movement of the 10th SS Panzer Division from its position around Hill 112 near Evrecy had been delayed by the slow relief of their units and Allied air attacks along the route of their march. Although the advance elements of the division had set off on the afternoon of 1 August, the main body of the Division did not arrive around Aunay and Ondefontaine until 3 August. In the advance elements were the reconnaissance battalion, the second tank battalion and the 21st Panzergrenadier Regiment which mounted an attack (supported by a battalion of Jagdpanthers) towards Hill 188 near St Georges d'Aunay and the advancing 7th Armoured Division.

That morning, the 5th RTR had been ordered to seize Point 138 which was on a low ridge that overlooked Aunay in order to shell German vehicles moving on the road below. Advancing through the morning mist to the railway bridge in La Lande, A Squadron spotted and knocked out a Mark IV waiting to ambush the leading troop the other side of the bridge. Point 138 was occupied by 1100 hours and the tanks began shelling traffic on the road below. Their position was, in turn, overlooked by another ridge further to the south occupied by the Germans and artillery fire began to land amongst the Cromwells. Twelve German tanks from the 10th SS Panzer Division started to infiltrate through La Lande, accompanied by panzergrenadiers, while another company of panzergrenadiers approached from the north supported by the Jagdpanthers. The infantry of the 1st Rifle Brigade became involved in a firefight with the panzergrenadiers and B Squadron was sent forward to reinforce A Squadron. A Squadron continued to duel with the advancing Mark IVs, and three Cromwells and a brand new Challenger tank, which did not have time to align its gun sights, were knocked out in exchange for two Mark IVs. As the day progressed, German pressure began to mount and a sudden attack after an artillery bombardment caused the Rifle Brigade infantry to withdraw, leaving the tanks surrounded in the orchards around La Lande. As darkness fell, one troop from B Squadron broke out under cover of a smoke screen, one tank being destroyed in the process. Panzergrenadiers, armed with Panzerfäuste, then began to stalk the isolated Cromwell tanks in the darkness; showers of sparks marked the position of Sherman tanks periodically being hit by the Panzerfaust projectiles. The decision was taken to attempt a mass breakout and the tanks lined up one behind the other before charging westwards through the German positions, taking casualties as they did so but eventually reaching the safety of the British lines. A Firefly was abandoned by its crew who opted to try and get back to safety on foot in the darkness rather than in their tank. Of the twelve tanks left that made the breakout, nine reached safety.[52] According to the regiment's war diary, only seven Cromwells were lost that day but an eyewitness account puts the total much higher, with A and B squadrons losing eighteen tanks between them.[53] The men of the 21st Panzergrenadier Regiment alone claimed fourteen tanks destroyed by Panzerfäuste.[54] Owing to the heavy losses, A and B squadrons were amalgamated next day for future operations. Over the course of the next week, the 263rd Field Delivery Squadron sent eleven Cromwells, two Sherman Vcs and a Challenger, making fourteen replacement tanks in all for the 5th RTR.[55]

Guards Armoured Division

The squadrons of the Irish Guards reunited at dawn at La Marvindiere and moved out to resume the advance to Estry and Vassy via the village of Le Busq. The division was ordered to bypass Estry if necessary but VIII Corps was completely unaware that the 9th SS Panzer Division had arrived overnight and was now occupying positions in Estry. With No. 3 Squadron leading and covered by the other two squadrons, a farm north of Le Busq was reached at about 1000 hours:

> No. 3 Sqn with an infantry Coy, which by now was very tired, crossed the little stream at 732378, and worked its way up the far slope through high hedges and orchards. As they came to the crest by a sunken lane, enemy tanks opened fire at close range and knocked out a tank in Lt. Liddle's troop. Reconnaissance on foot by Capt. P. Stobart and careful observation discovered 7 or 8 Tigers and Panthers just on the reverse slope, escorted by about one company of infantry. Our own infantry dug in by the sunken lane, and the rest of the day was spent playing hide and seek in and out of orchards and hedges. The advantage, of course, lay with the Germans as, no matter what is said in Parliament, their guns penetrate our armour, and the 75mm does not penetrate theirs.[56]

The Irish Guards/Coldstream group made no further progress and remained on the defensive all day opposite the Germans on the Estry ridge. Groups of tanks and infantry of 9th SS Panzer Division continually infiltrated past their positions from the north-east throughout the day. A battery of self-propelled field artillery (Sextons) to the rear was attacked and only rescued by the timely intervention of some M10 tank destroyers of Q battery of the 21st Anti-tank Regiment. A convoy of support echelon vehicles driving to Siernoux for supplies was forced to turn around and return to La Marvindiere where the whole regiment eventually harboured to spend another night isolated.

The Guards Armoured Division was only making slow progress against the constant infiltration and attacks by groups of 9th SS troops and tanks from the north-east and it was finally forced to halt altogether. XXX Corps received new orders at 1900 hours to seize the plateau of Mont Pinçon and the town of Aunay. The 3rd Division was attached to VIII Corps as reinforcements and infantry of the 185th Brigade were sent to provide much-needed support to the battle groups of the 11th Armoured Division.

That evening, General Erskine of the 7th Armoured Division and the XXX Corps commander, General Bucknall, were summoned to a meeting with General Dempsey whose patience had finally run out. Erskine was replaced by General Verney from the 6th Guards Tank Brigade and Bucknall by General Horrocks.

The attacks of the 9th SS Panzer Division were not successful largely because the division had not been concentrated, attempting to reach La Bistiere, Point 176 and Montchamp simultaneously. Despite having made the breakthrough and threatening to rampage about in the German rear areas, the decision by Dempsey to stop the British advance meant that the initiative was regained by the Germans and it was they who were marauding behind the leading British units.

By nightfall, the 9th SS Panzer Division was effectively holding a line from Burcy to Montchamp and only had twenty-eight Panthers, seven Mark IVs and nine Stug IIIs operational – less than a British armoured regiment – but had stopped the advance of two British armoured divisions.

4 August

The Germans continued to occupy Chenedolle which had become a critical point in the new German front line being fashioned that was intended to run through La Bistiere–Le Dézert–Estry–Montchamp. By creating this line the Germans would keep possession of the Vire–Vassy road but first had to deal with the two British boxes already behind their proposed front line.

Infantry from the 3rd Division, the 2nd Warwicks, recaptured Presles in an attack at midnight and during the morning began to relieve the 8th Rifle Brigade in the hamlet of Le Bas Perrier. A strong German attack was mounted just as the handover commenced and although panzergrenadiers occupied Le Bas Perrier they were unable to make any further progress across the open ground up the ridge. Very heavy artillery fire was called down on the Germans from all available VIII Corps artillery with devastating effect. Heavy bombardments from both sides continued to sweep the Perrier ridge and surrounding areas and although the 9th SS Panzer Division made several more probes, no further large-scale attacks were mounted; the positions at the end of the day remained largely unchanged.

The 2nd Fife and Forfars with the Monmouths spent an unpleasant day also under a continuous German bombardment. The battle group had been isolated at Burcy and La Pavée for 48 hours and all the men were tired and hungry. With the recapture of Presles, the supply lines were restored to the 23rd Hussars group at Le Bas Perrier; supplies and reinforcements could be brought up and the wounded evacuated. On the XXX Corps front there was heavy fighting throughout the day around Hill 188 and La Bigne but little progress was made.

The other Guards units tried to move out of their positions towards Montchamp assisted by infantry from the 15th (Scottish) Division, which cleared the spurs of high ground at Arclais and Drouet. Shermans of the 1st Coldstream Guards occupied the northern outskirts of Montchamp before they were immediately counterattacked by infantry of the 9th SS and six Panthers. Tanks stalked each other through the village until heavy losses compelled the Coldstream Guards to withdraw.[57] The Irish Guards group moved out towards Le Busq but again made no further progress and in the afternoon they came under attack from Germans trying to reach Montchamp to form the new front line. The regiments of the Guards Division would remain largely static for the next two days with the Grenadier Guards holding Catheolles and the Coldstream Guards clearing Point 176.

Groups of German infantry and tanks that remained behind the lines of the 11th Armoured Division were now themselves in danger of being cut off as their attack failed. A German group of four Stug IIIs and some captured vehicles of the Guards Armoured Division was ambushed by 17-pounder anti-tank guns attached to 3rd Battalion Irish Guards at Maisoncelle.[58]

North of Vire, constant British pressure from artillery and the arriving infantry of the 3rd Division compelled Kampfgruppe Weiss and 9th SS Panzer Reconnaissance Battalion to withdraw at 2230 hours from their positions at La Bistiere back to Vire.

That night, the 10th SS Panzer Division broke contact with XXX Corps to move to Vassy in preparation for the Mortain offensive as ordered by Hitler. Although it would not arrive in time for the main attack on 7 August, the 2nd SS Panzer Korps had been designated as the follow-up force. While Operation Bluecoat prevented the immediate transfer of the 2nd SS Panzer Korps, its inclusion in the counterattack was a result of the movement of British armoured divisions away from Caen that allowed the Korps to move as well. The 21st Panzer Division, the 276th Infantry Division and what was left of the 326th Division were to withdraw to a new front line from Thury Harcourt to Presles via Estry and Roucamps.

5 and 6 August

The Perrier ridge was the key to the battlefield and if the British were thrown off it then they would have to retreat back to the River Soulevre. The German intention to mount Operation Luttich also meant that the British positions had to be eliminated as quickly as possible in order that the timetable for the attack not be disrupted. Von Kluge decided to not wait for the 10th SS Panzer Division to get into position to mount a joint attack but for the 9th SS Panzer Division to continue its efforts alone. As reinforcements, the 2nd Company of the 102nd Schwere SS Battalion Tigers returned to Chenedolle to join the 1st Company which was already there with the 9th SS Reconnaissance Battalion now reinforced by the Army Pioneer Battalion 600 from Korps reserve. The defence of Vire had been taken over by the newly arrived 363rd Division and the paratroops of the 3rd Parachute Division moved to positions south of Burcy to link up with the 2nd SS Panzer Korps.

During the day, tanks and panzergrenadiers periodically attacked the positions of the Hussars three times but were unable to break into the British positions. A similar attack was mounted on the 2nd Fife and Forfar positions at La Pavée. The heaviest attack came at about 1730 hours after a relatively quiet day; Tiger tanks, which had got into position on the high ground that overlooked La Pavée to the west of Chenedolle, supported the attack with long-range fire. Some infantry and 2nd Fife and Forfar tanks reoccupied Burcy and this time they were able to hold it, allowing the supply lines to be reopened.

As suddenly as it started, the German attack stopped; the 9th SS Panzer Division was exhausted and could no longer continue the assault; its sister division would have to take over the mission next day.

That night, the 1st Norfolks infantry battalion left La Bistiere after relieving the 2nd Northants Yeomanry and moved to reinforce the Fife/Monmouth position at La Pavée. As the situation seemed quieter at Le Bas Perrier, the 23rd Hussars took the opportunity to withdraw A and B squadrons back across the valley at midnight, leaving one troop as additional support for C Squadron.

Next morning a heavy mist lay over Burcy and Presles which covered the arrival of the 1st Norfolks to relieve the Monmouths at La Pavée. However, the Monmouths were unable to withdraw as German mortar fire destroyed the motor transport of the Norfolks about to be used by them. The Monmouths decided to stay and fight on with the Norfolks which was fortunate as just as the Norfolks had taken over the slit tranches of the Monmouths at 1500 hours the attack by the 10th SS Panzer Division began, preceded as always by a heavy mortar and artillery bombardment. Tanks, panzergrenadiers and SP guns attacked the Pavée position from three directions and the 2nd Fife and Forfar tanks were in the thick of it:

> There was much shelling which rose to a climax till suddenly, in the afternoon, Don Bulley's and Cpl Newman's tanks burst into flames and we heard the whine of AP shot. Tanks, SP guns and infantry came towards us from Dump wood and

C Squadron on our left reported being attacked by Tigers. Our infantry were rolling back in confusion. Obviously a big attack was coming in. Pinkie Hutchinson got as Mark IV, and I got an SP while we killed many of the advancing infantry. The squadron, already depleted, lost four more tanks. Cpl Ives came crawling back through the corn with three or four wounded. They sheltered under my tank and were lucky to be unhurt when a shell hit the near-side track and bulged the armour. A shell landed on the back of Cpl Croney's tank which disappeared in a huge cloud of feathers – he had liberated a few civilian mattresses. We were not, however, pushed off our positions, the attack on us had failed and my No.4 troop was still intact.[59]

Two Tigers and a Mark IV tank supporting the attack were forced to withdraw by a troop from C Squadron after two tanks from another troop had been knocked out. Other Tigers continued to fire from long range from the high ground near Chenedolle.

A determined German attack was also made on the positions of the Hussars. Tiger tanks sniped at the C Squadron tanks during the morning and then at 1600 hours a major assault was launched, preceded by the usual fierce bombardment. Other Tigers worked their way up into overlooking positions to fire as infantry began to infiltrate and get within Panzerfaust range. Sherman tanks and artillery used HE air bursts into the tops of trees with devastating effect on the advancing German infantry. An infantry patrol in Le Bas Perrier village was hard pressed and a troop of three tanks was sent to help them:

By the time we had reached the village there were only two of us (what happened to the other tank I never knew). The leading Sherman, commanded by Sgt. Smith, probed further into the village while we in our tank, commanded by Sgt. Jackson, came to a halt on the outskirts. As we stood there, we looked through the periscope and I saw a Panther tank half hidden in the trees. A long-barrelled gun was pointing in our direction and our 17-pounder was aimed at them. It was an uncanny situation, facing each other with no sound disturbing the scene. The ominous silence was suddenly broken by the sound of a rifle shot fired by a German sniper hidden in a tree. I heard the bullet ping against the rim of the turret hatch and ricochet harmlessly in another direction.

The order came from the hill above, 'Return to the Squadron!' Our driver tried to start the engine, but it failed. He tried several times but without any result. Just then, Sgt. Smith returned in his tank to find us in a hopeless predicament. With no thought of the danger he and his crew, together with Sgt. Jackson, jumped out of their vehicles and quickly fastened a hawser to ours and slowly began to tow us back to the hill. We had only gone a few yards before what we had assumed was the abandoned German tank suddenly came to life. A shell landed just a few feet from our tracks. After what seemed an age we reached the top of the hill to rejoin the squadron, amazed and very relieved to have made it back unscathed.[60]

Given no time to reconnoitre or plan the attack, the 10th SS Panzer Division had thrown its forces in waves straight at the front of the two boxes instead of employing their usual tactics of infiltration or attacking the flanks. The objective at La Pavée of Point 224 was reported as captured by the panzergrenadiers but then reported lost. As daylight faded, the German attacks diminished and after having been compelled to pull back into a tight harbour, the La Pavée position remained unbroken. The Hussars also managed to hold, despite having been considerably weakened by the withdrawal of the two tank squadrons overnight. British artillery fire played a significant part in breaking up the attacks by the panzergrenadiers.

At about midnight, the 10th SS Panzer Division broke off its attacks in order to regroup before travelling to Mortain. By end of the day, the 10th SS Panzer Division only had five Mark IV tanks and five Stug IIIs operational and was in no condition to take part in the Mortain counterattack.

7 August

On 7 August, C Squadron of the 23rd Hussars was relieved at midday by the tanks of the 3rd RTR and withdrew to La Barbiere to join the rest of the regiment. Attacks on the 2nd Fife and Forfar position continued. Tank losses made it necessary to amalgamate A and C squadrons and the composite squadron knocked out two Mark IVs that came too close. Two Tigers which had succeeded in occupying a hilltop east of Le Haut opened fire at long range, knocking out five tanks that were exposed. The Tigers were engaged by a troop of tanks and one was knocked out, although this was later towed away by other Tigers. It was not until the next day, 8 August, that the tanks of the Scots Grey regiment arrived to take over from the 2nd Fife and Forfars. Meanwhile, five American divisions finally completed the capture of Vire with 3,000 casualties.[61]

On the XXX Corps front, the disengagement of the 10th SS Panzer Division and the shortening of the German front line permitted some territorial gains against little resistance, including the capture of some long-contested positions. The 50th Division finally captured Villers Bocage on 4 August, and the 7th Armoured Division entered Aunay on 5 August. The mission of capturing the Mont Pinçon feature was then taken away from the 7th Armoured Division and given to the 43rd Wessex Division with the 8th Armoured Brigade in support. The 129th Infantry brigade plus the tanks of the 13th/18th Hussars would lead the assault on the imposing steep-sided plateau. After unsuccessful attacks on 4 and 5 August, on 6 August the Hussars broke through the German perimeter and found a perilous narrow track on the side of the plateau to the summit. One tank slipped sideways and overturned in a quarry and another had a track blown off by an anti-tank gun but under the cover of a smoke screen, one tank reached the top and the six others quickly joined it.[62] Once the infantry arrived and began digging-in, a fog descended on the whole plateau and prevented any German counterattack or anti-tank guns from shooting at the regiment's tanks climbing the track to the summit.[63]

After eight days of fighting, the stated main objective of Operation Bluecoat, the capture of Mont Pinçon, had been achieved although fighting continued around Estry (Operation Grouse) for another week.

Aftermath

After a slow start, the British attack in Operation Bluecoat made a break clean through the German lines and caused the redeployment of three German armoured divisions from the Caen area. As Montgomery's strategy was to keep the German armour occupied around Caen whilst the American army broke out in the west, the movement of these panzer divisions westwards was an unfavourable outcome. As the panzer divisions were subsequently no longer required around Caen, they were then allocated to the Mortain counterattack.

However, by bringing these formations into a battle in a different sector, the ensuing fighting served to weaken these already depleted formations further although this was not a stated objective of Operation Bluecoat. The 10th SS Panzer Division reported on 7 August that it had only five tanks and five self-propelled guns operational (from a total of thirty-five available at the beginning of August). The 9th SS Panzer Division was similarly reduced to a total of twenty-three fit armoured vehicles. These losses would have important consequences for future German plans.

Having made the breakthrough and advanced rapidly, the British did not exploit the situation. Instead, they stopped to await the German counterattack and handed the initiative back to the Germans. The opportunity to achieve a breakout as decisive as Operation Cobra with the capture of Vire was lost. If the objective of Operation Bluecoat was the capture of Mont Pinçon to the east, why was the point of main effort switched to VIII Corps on the second day of battle? VIII Corps could not have been expected to swing due east and advance across the front of XXX Corps units. Having displayed flexibility in the operation by giving VIII Corps the task of continuing to advance south and capturing Le Bény Bocage, this flexibility was then disregarded in favour of defence as soon as the first units of the 2nd SS Panzer Korps arrived and the great strategic prize of Vire went unclaimed.

Vire was reported by the patrols of the Household Cavalry on 1 August as being largely undefended and could have been easily occupied by the 2nd Northants Yeomanry and supporting infantry on either that day or the next. The confusion as to which army had the responsibility for Vire originated from Montgomery as there was certainly no confusion amongst the Americans in XIX Corps; General Bradley had directed FUSA in his orders of 29 July to capture an area that included Vire.[64] If there was any confusion at all, it was up to Montgomery to clarify the army boundaries and objectives and he did not do this until the British units had arrived at the town. Why Montgomery chose to leave the town as an American objective is not clear. Perhaps Montgomery did not want to irritate the Americans further by capturing the strategic town ahead of them. Or perhaps the rapid advances of Bluecoat on 31 July were too much for the normally cautious Montgomery. But there was much to gain from the capture of Vire, not least for Montgomery to practise his avowed policy of casualty conservation and save the Americans from having to attack the town later. If Montgomery's aim were to prevent the movement of German reinforcements to the west then the capture of Vire would have certainly done this and would have completely disrupted the preparations for Mortain. The 1st SS Panzer Division was able to travel on 6 August through Vire from Caen on the Vire–Vassy road in time for the counterattack.

With the arrival of the 2nd SS Panzer Korps in response to Operation Bluecoat, the British opted for caution and stopped their advance on defendable hilltop positions within range of the supporting corps artillery. Although the advanced British positions were cut off for periods of time and lacking in vital supplies, they were able to repel repeated German attacks with the help of the considerable artillery and air support available. Again, British intelligence seems to have overestimated the strength of the attacking German divisions which had no more than 150 tanks between them, the equivalent of just three British armoured regiments. At the start of Operation Bluecoat, the British had three entire armoured divisions and two armoured brigades, totalling more than 700 tanks. Caution may have been appropriate for VIII Corps with the information they had available at the time but the failure to seize Vire was a golden opportunity that was wasted. Montgomery had achieved a major breakthrough but once again the British failed to exploit their own success. As Major J. How commented, 'The failure to seize the town of Vire was a tactical error of great consequence. Its seizure would have been a knock-out blow for the German Seventh Army.'[65] Montgomery had so nearly achieved the boasts of his pre-battle messages but at the last minute had become fearful of his own success.

Casualties

After the initial breakthrough was made by VIII Corps, Operation Bluecoat essentially became a meeting engagement between opposing armoured divisions with the advantage going to the force that used its reconnaissance to warn of the approach of enemy vehicles and then used the countryside to quickly deploy into a defensive role. When the British were advancing, their armoured spearheads were vulnerable to the sort of action that nearly destroyed A Squadron of the 23rd Hussars on 2 August. When the Germans had to attack the British defenders, they too had heavy casualties such as the 21st Panzer Division suffered in its hasty attacks to retake Hill 309 and the 9th SS Panzer Division suffered attacking the positions of the Guards and the 11th Armoured Divisions.

British tank losses in Operation Bluecoat

	Sherman	Vc	Cromwell	CS Cromwell	Stuart	Churchill	Challenger	
XX Corps								
th AD		2	16	2			1	
ch A Bde	12	8			6			
III Corps*								
estroyed	42	1	9			9		
vacuated to LADs	22	3						
vacuated to CBPs	5	3	2			3		
waiting repair	62	11	9			8		**Total**
	143	**28**	**36**	**2**	**6**	**20**	**1**	**236**

* VIII Corps figures from DDME 2nd Army report, 16 August 1944 WO 171/248

The cost of Operation Bluecoat was very high in terms of tanks. Between VIII Corps and XXX Corps, 236 tanks became Y or Z casualties that required repair in second or third line workshops. This excludes all X casualties repaired by regimental LADs. By 11 August, 104 of these tanks had been repaired but fifty-eight were complete write-offs with another eight Churchills waiting to be assessed in the field.

German tank losses in Operation Bluecoat

	Panzer IV	Panther	Tiger	King Tiger	Stug III
21st Panzer	23				
9th SS	8	24			21
10th SS	15				10
102nd SS bn			5		
503rd bn				4	
KG Olboeter		6			
	46	**30**	**5**	**4**	**31**

The Germans lost far fewer tanks than the British but they still lost more than 100 tanks and assault guns, due in part to the hastily prepared attacks they were ordered to make on British positions and the effects of Allied air and artillery superiority. The two panzer divisions of the 2nd SS Panzer Korps were reduced to just over thirty operational tanks between them which precluded them from taking any effective part in the Mortain counterattack. Montgomery's stated intention of launching an attack where the panzer divisions were less concentrated only caused them to be moved from Caen to meet this attack which had the fortunate outcome of severely reducing their combat strengths.

Operation Bluecoat saw the dismissal of the XXX Corps commander Bucknall and the commander of the 7th Armoured Division, Erskine. But these were not the last of the changes within the 7th Armoured Division, now commanded by General Verney. On 7 August, Brigadier Hinde was removed from command and there followed a series of meetings and conferences with the officers and men to discuss morale and tank problems.

On 10 August, General Verney visited the 22nd Brigade and next day General Horrocks of XXX Corps addressed the officers and NCOs of all regiments. Later in the day, Brigadier Fisher and Major-General Briggs from RAC also arrived at 22nd Brigade to discuss personnel and issues with Cromwell tanks.

Two days later, on 13 August, there was a further conference for 22nd Brigade HQ and 7th Armoured Division HQ with Major-General Richards from the RAC at 21st Army Group regarding personnel problems. Finally, 100 officers and men were posted out of the 7th Armoured Division.[66] Forty of these men were from the 5th RTR.[67] The 1st RTR also received a new commander on 17 August.

In response to these changes, the absentee rate at the 7th Armoured Division increased dramatically. Twenty-four men were convicted of desertion, drunkenness or insubordination in August compared with four the previous months.[68] However, General Verney was unable to turn the division around and retained the post for only four months until November. His impression of the division was not a favourable one:

> There is no doubt that familiarity with war does not make one more courageous. One becomes cunning, and from cunning to cowardice is but one short step. The infantryman who does not want 'to have a go' can find opportunities for lying low at the critical moment, the tank man can easily find a fault in his engine or wireless and thus miss taking part in the battle. This is a disease that spreads rapidly. The commander who finds his men getting 'canny' soon losses his confidence and becomes nervy himself. If he happens to also have done a lot of fighting and especially if he has been 'brewed up' in his tank once or twice himself, he gets slow and deliberate; and is quite unable to take advantage of a situation that requires dash and enterprise. This is a most important point in an armoured division which exists to exploit a favourable situation quickly.
>
> The 7th Armoured and 51st Highland were extremely swollen headed. They were a law unto themselves, they thought they need only obey orders that suited them … both these divisions did badly from the moment they landed in Normandy.[69]

The 7th Armoured Division's initial recklessness in Normandy had given way to excessive caution and a poor performance. This caution resulted from the division's reaction to both German tank superiority and the effectiveness of their anti-tank guns as reported by General Erskine after Villers Bocage.[70]

Any criticism of 7th Armoured Division needs to be put into context, however. The division had seen service in three theatres since 1941 and was fighting in very unfamiliar and difficult countryside for which no Allied units had trained:

> Montgomery had asked too much of the 7th Armoured and that the amount of time it had spent in action was blatantly unfair when compared, for example, to the Guards Armoured Division.[71]

The lesson of the need for good infantry/tank co-operation had to be learnt by the 7th Armoured Division as it had to be by every other armoured formation in Normandy.

The Desert Rats continued to view the Cromwell tanks with great suspicion although they performed well in the pursuit after Normandy. The division was heartened temporarily in August by the appearance of a few Challenger tanks (modified Cromwells fitted with a 17-pounder gun) although a few weeks later the Challengers had to be handed over to the reconnaissance regiment which had no Fireflies. A promise by the RAC to supply the division with the first new Comet tanks was not kept, with the tanks going to the 11th Armoured Division.

Notes

1 Jackson, Lt-Col G.S., *Operations of Eighth Corps* (London, St Clements, 1948), p.118

2 Wilmot, C., *The Struggle for Europe* (London, Collins, 1952), p.436

3 Montgomery, B., *Normandy to the Baltic, vol.II* (London, Hutchinson, 1947), p.347

4 Bryant, A., *Triumph in the West* (London, Collins, 1959), p.245

5 Hastings, M., *Overlord: D-Day and the Battle for Normandy 1944* (London, Michael Joseph, 1984), p.242

6 CAB 44/248, Eisenhower cable to Montgomery, 28 July 1944, TNA

7 CAB 44/248, Montgomery cable to Brooke, 28 July 1944, TNA

8 Blumenson, M., *Break Out and Pursuit* (Washington, DC, US Army CMH, 1961), p.450

9 WO 229/72/24, Montgomery directive M515, 27 July 1944, TNA

10 BAOR, Operation Bluecoat Battlefield study tour, Appendix 6, BAOR, 1946

11 Dalglish, I., *Over the Battlefield – Operation Bluecoat* (Barnsley, Pen and Sword, 2009), p.14

12 Jackson, *opcit*, p.127

13 How, Maj J.J., *Normandy – The British Breakout* (London, Kimber, 1981), p.40

14 Dalglish, *opcit*, p.31

15 Fitzgerald, D.E., *History of the Irish Guards in World War II* (Aldershot, Gale & Polden, 1949), p.396

16 Verney, Maj-Gen G.L., *The Guards Armoured Division – A Short History* (London, Hutchinson, 1955), p.53

17 CAB 44/248 Eisenhower cable to Montgomery, 28 July 1944, TNA

18 Anon, Club Route History of XXX Corps, 1946, p.34

19 War diary narrative 4th Grenadier Guards, August 1944, Guards Museum, London

20 Dalglish, *opcit*, p.43

21 WO 171/1258 War diary 3rd Scots Guards, July 1944, Appendix K1, TNA

22 Whitelaw, W., quoted in Dalglish, *opcit*, p.73

23 BAOR, *opcit*, p.19

24 IWM Brownlie, W.S., And Came Safe Home, Private papers, 1944, IWM document #2204

25 WO 171/853 War diary 2nd Fife and Forfar, June 1944, TNA

26 How, *opcit*, p.34

27 WO 171/853 War diary 2nd Fife and Forfar, August 1944, TNA

28 Palamountain, E.W.I., *Taurus Pursuant – A History of the 11th Armoured Division* (BAOR, 1945), p.32

29 Howard, M., and Sparrow, J., *The Coldstream Guards 1920–1946* (London, Oxford University, 1951), p.304

30 Tieke, W., *In the Firestorm of the Last Years of the War – the 2nd SS Panzer Korps* (Manitoba, JJ Fedorowicz, 1999), p.149

31 WO 171/1256 War diary 2nd Irish Guards, August 1944, TNA

32 WO171/1256 War diary 2nd Irish Guards, August 1944, TNA

33 Verney, *opcit*, p.214

34 Delaforce, P., *Churchill's Desert Rats* (Stroud, Sutton, 2003), p.73

35 *Ibid*, p.72

36 Hills, S., *By Tank into Normandy* (London, Cassell, 2002), p.121

37 War diary narrative 2nd Grenadier Guards, August 1944, Guards Museum, London

38 WO 171/1256 War diary 2nd Irish Guards, August 1944, TNA

39 How, *opcit*, p.220

40 Blacker, C., *The Story of the 23rd Hussars* (BAOR, 1946) p.93

41 WO 171/627 War diary 29th Armoured brigade, August 1944, TNA

42 Brownlie, *opcit*, p.27

43 How, *opcit*, p.107

44 WO 171/627 War diary 29th Brigade, August 1944, TNA

45 Streng, SS Unterscharführer quoted in How, *opcit*, p.86

46 Blacker, *opcit*, p.98

47 How, *opcit*, p.127

48 Moore, W., *Panzerbait with the Third Royal Tank Regiment 1939–1945* (London, Leo Cooper, 1991), p.163

49 *Ibid*, p.164

50 Close, Maj W., *A View from the Turret* (Tewkesbury, Dell and Bredon, 1998), p.133

51 Trauttman, quoted in Schnieder, W., *Tigers in Normandy* (Mechanicsburg, PA, Stackpole Books, 2011), pp.194–6

52 WO 171/867 War diary 5th RTR, August 1944, TNA

53 Urban, M., *The Tank War – The Men, the Machines and the Long Road to Victory* (London, Little Brown, 2013), p.288

54 Tieke, *opcit*, p.148

55 WO 171/892 War diary 263rd Field Delivery Squadron, August 1944, TNA

56 WO 171/1256 War diary 2nd Irish Guards, August 1944, TNA

57 Howard and Sparrow, *opcit*, p.276

58 Howard and Sparrow, *opcit*, p.276

59 Brownlie, *opcit*, p.29

60 Slarks, E., On the Perrier Ridge, August 1944, BBC History website http://www.bbc.co.uk/history/ww2peopleswar/stories/36/a6115736.shtml, accessed 2 December 2012

61 How, *opcit*, p.208

62 *Ibid*, p.453

63 Miller, Maj-Gen C., *History of 13th/18th Hussars QMO 1922–1947* (London, Chisman, 1949), p.122

64 Ellis, p.403

65 How, Major J.J., *Normandy – The British Breakout* (London, Kimber, 1981), p.92

66 Verney, *opcit*, p.215

67 Urban, *opcit*, p.291

68 Buckley, J., *opcit*, p.206

69 Verney, Maj-Gen G. quoted in d'Este, *opcit*, p.273

70 WO205/422 Combat reports GOC 7th Armoured Division – Impression of fighting in Normandy, 17 June 1944, TNA

71 Urban, *opcit*, p.295

10

Operation Luttich – Mortain Counterattack

There were two basic problems within the OKW, the first being Adolf Hitler himself. After the failed attempt on his life on 20 July in which he suffered concussion and damaged eardrums, Hitler had drawn the wrong conclusions from his seemingly miraculous survival. Like all politicians who are in power for long periods, Hitler genuinely believed that he, and only he, knew what was best for Germany and could lead her to ultimate victory. The failure of the bomb plot convinced Hitler that it was his destiny to continue to lead Germany and therefore he would continue to involve himself in the day-to-day decisions of the OKW, with disastrous results. Hitler believed that most of the titled generals of the Heer had let him down and wanted to end the war by negotiation with the Allies as soon as possible to cover their own shortcomings, and that his SS divisions were the only reliable, effective fighting force – hence the promotion of SS General Hausser to command the Seventh Army in Normandy. This change was made at a critical time during Operation Epsom just before the major German counterattack to restore the front line and it subsequently disrupted German preparations. When faced with an American breakout from the Cotentin peninsula along the coast at Avranches following Operation Cobra and Americans advancing into Brittany, Hitler knew decisive action was called for. The OKW Normandy situation map revealed that the width of the corridor through which the American divisions were flowing was very narrow and hence vulnerable. If the Germans could assemble a powerful force and drive through to Avranches, the German front line would be restored and the American spearheads cut off, to be dealt with at the Seventh Army's leisure. Hitler then placed on the map the unit pins for the panzer divisions. In theory, an unstoppable army of five or maybe six panzer divisions could quickly be assembled and drive to the coast. What Hitler failed to take into account was the poor condition of the panzer divisions after weeks of fighting. At that moment, Hitler became one of the despised generals from his own experiences in the First World War: a château general, divorced from reality, who simply manoeuvred pins on a map.

The second problem within OKW was that no one was prepared to stand up to Hitler and at least argue alternative viewpoints. The German army in Normandy was under a cloud of suspicion, having failed to mount a major counterattack to defeat the invasion and several senior officers implicated in the bomb plot.

On 31 July, von Kluge arrived at Seventh Army HQ to discuss plans to restore the German front line by reconnecting with the coast on the left flank of the army. That day, American forces had captured the bridge at Pontaubault intact and could now breakout from the Cotentin peninsula. All the panzer divisions in Panzer Gruppe West from the eastern sector would be made available in a new formation called the Fifth Panzer Army. The attack would be mounted as soon as possible when all the panzer divisions had been assembled which was subject to their successful disengagement from the front line and their replacement by new infantry divisions as they arrived in Normandy. Hausser also wanted to evacuate the occupation forces from the Channel Islands and Brittany but this was denied by OKW which hoped the Americans would expend time and resources in capturing the fortresses of Brittany.[1]

The decision was taken that the Fifth Panzer Army would attack along the isthmus between the Rivers See and Selune with the assembly area for the attack to be around Mortain and Sourdevalle. The planned area for the attack had a natural anti-tank obstacle in the form of the River See to protect the northern flank of the proposed drive whilst to the south the ridge parallel to the River Selune afforded good observation of the intended line of attack and positions on which to deploy heavy artillery for support. While offering some benefits, the area chosen for the attack had the small fields, dense hedgerows and hills of the 'Suisse Normande', similar to that encountered by the British in Operation Bluecoat.

By 1 August, however, both flanks of the Seventh Army were threatened. The Americans had captured Avranches and Pontaubault in the west and the 326th Division in the east had all been but destroyed by the British in Operation Bluecoat. The Seventh Army was experiencing considerable pressure all along the length of its front line. With the loss of Villedieu to the Americans, the front line could be shortened by a withdrawal to the Forêt St Sever that allowed the 116th Panzer Division to be partially disengaged for the coming attack but some elements were still caught up in defensive fighting. The 84th Division was on the way to replace the 116th Panzer Division but had not yet arrived. For a while, the British breakthrough in Operation Bluecoat looked very ominous for the Germans: not only were units such as the 2nd SS Panzer Korps destined for the planned attack still engaged but Vire, through which the panzer divisions designated for the attack would have to pass, was also threatened. Fortunately for the Germans, despite Vire being relatively undefended on 2 August, the British attack had halted in response to the counterattack by the 9th SS and 10th SS Panzer divisions. This allowed elements from the 3rd Parachute Division, supported by two batteries of 88mm Flak guns in a line from Vaudry to La Papillionaire to create an anti-tank screen, to occupy Vire. It was against this background that Hitler, on 2 August, ordered Operation Luttich to proceed.² While Hitler regarded the planned attack as a masterstroke, von Kluge was unenthusiastic: to assemble the required panzer divisions meant weakening further the forces around Caen and the intentions of Patton's Third Army to the south were still not clear. At best, von Kluge believed that the attack would restore the front line at Avranches and force the Allies back on the defensive.³

The 2nd Panzer and 2nd SS Panzer divisions were withdrawn from the front line, their place being taken by the arriving 363rd Division. The 116th Panzer Division continued to be hard pressed and had to abandon Brecy while struggling to defend St Pois.

The 275th Division was also being strongly attacked at this time by the Americans and was forced to give ground in the face of heavy artillery bombardments and aerial support. Two assault guns sent to reinforce it were knocked out by Allied fighter-bombers. Juvigny and St Barthélemy north of Mortain were lost and the reconnaissance battalions of the 2nd Panzer and Lehr divisions were committed to supporting the 275th Division around Mortain. The armoured columns of Patton's Third US Army were on the move and an anti-tank gun screen with the self-propelled guns of the 341st Assault gun Brigade could not prevent the capture of Rennes.

The 9th Panzer Division, also part of the coming attack, was coming up from the south of France and had reached Alençon. From 4–6 August, the Seventh Army had more cause for optimism. The situation at Vire had been stabilised by the actions of the 2nd SS Panzer Korps and Kampfgruppe Olboeter from the 12th SS Panzer Division, but the Korps could not immediately leave the Vire sector and was a vital part of German plans. The American advance south from Pontaubault was then not as rapid as feared and was expected to swing westwards towards Brittany as per the invasion plans captured on D-Day.⁴ As Vire was still in German hands, the 1st SS Panzer Division had been able to begin its move from Caen to the assembly area around Tinchebray, being due there on 6 August.

Rather than waiting for the arrival of the 2nd SS Panzer Korps which was not anticipated for another three or four days at the earliest, and given that the strategic situation by then was impossible to predict with the assembling forces increasingly at risk of being detected and bombed from the air, von Kluge decided to attack on 6 August with the immediately available forces. Given the enormous air superiority of the Allies, all-out support was requested from and promised by the Luftwaffe. The German panzer divisions, incorporated into the XLVII Panzer Korps led by General von Funck, would attack as follows:

- 116th Panzer Division on the right flank north of La See River (thirty Mark IVs and thirty-two Panthers operational on 30 July*)
- 2nd Panzer Division (reinforced) in the sector La See and St Barthélemy (sixty tanks and fifteen Jagdpanzer IVs)
- 2nd SS Panzer Division either side of Mortain (twenty to twenty-five tanks)
- 9th Panzer Division and 708th Division to follow when they arrived.

- 1st SS Panzer Division (fifty-seven Mark IVs and forty-six Panthers operational on 5 August)

★ All operational figures from Zetterling

The main point of effort, or *schwerepunkt*, was to be with the 2nd Panzer Division which was to be reinforced by one panzer battalion from each of the 1st SS and the 116th Panzer divisions with the objective of taking Avranches via Juvigny, 21 miles away. The additional thirty Panthers from the 116th and thirty from the 1st SS Panzer divisions gave the 2nd Panzer Division a strike force of 135 tanks in the main thrust. Colonel von Kluge, von Kluge's son, reported that the attack would be made with 145 tanks. Owing to its late assembly, the entire 1st SS Panzer Division was to take over from St Barthélemy onwards for the drive to Avranches. Each panzer division would attack in two columns, with the 116th Panzer Division to advance north of the River See and protect the right flank of the 2nd Panzer Division from the advancing Americans.

The Americans continued to make attacks all along the front line in the first week of August which particularly caused problems for the 116th Panzer Division as the 84th Division had not yet fully arrived; each time units of the division tried to disengage they were required to mount a counterattack to seal off the front line again. Mortain was captured on 3 August by the US 1st Division. On 5 August Patton's Third Army swung eastwards to threaten Mayenne which was a great concern to the Seventh Army and required the formation of a blocking force composed of the 708th Division, an engineer battalion from the 5th Parachute Division and the reconnaissance battalion of the 9th Panzer Division. A small kampfgruppe from Panzer Lehr was also ordered to join this force. Laval was lost on 6 August and again the Germans were surprised at the speed of the advance of the Americans.

Still on the march, the 9th Panzer Division was not available for the attack and the 116th Panzer Division was still heavily engaged against the US 9th Division which was attacking towards Sourdeval. The battalion of tanks from the 1st SS Panzer Division also had still not arrived by the designated start time of 2200 hours, so the start was postponed until midnight, losing two valuable hours of darkness for the attack. A kampfgruppe from the 17th SS Panzer Division also joined the 2nd SS Panzer Division for the attack for which a maximum of 180 tanks had now been assembled.[5]

Reinforcements would be provided by the 9th and 10th SS Panzer divisions and the new Panther battalion of the 9th Panzer Division. On 6 August, Hitler suddenly got involved in the planning of the operation and committed the 11th Panzer Division which was moving up from the south of France.[6] Hitler also wanted the attack to be led by General Eberbach and for von Kluge to wait for all the panzer divisions to be assembled; von Kluge insisted that the attack go ahead at once in view of the rapidly changing tactical situation. From an attack to restore the front line as planned by von Kluge, Hitler saw this attack as determining the outcome of the battle in France. Only two US divisions had been identified (30th Division and part of the 3rd Armored Division) in the area and an early morning fog was forecast to provide additional cover. The Luftwaffe had promised 300 fighters to protect the advancing armoured columns.[7]

American Preparations

Ultra intelligence, which had the decoded intercepts of both Hitler's orders of 2 August and von Kluge's reply next day, provided Montgomery and Bradley with a complete picture of German intentions.[8] Therefore every disposition made by Bradley from 4 August onwards was made with the impending counterattack in mind. Bradley's dilemma was whether to maintain the advance south by the Third Army and risk it getting cut off if the German attack was successful or switch to the defensive and forego the possibility of encircling the Seventh Army. Another issue was that Bradley did not want to reveal the source of his intelligence about a German attack and did not even warn his senior commanders. A compromise was reached whereby Bradley decided to halt some units, ostensibly to rest and refit, while on 5 August, after a day's rest after capturing Mortain on 3 August, the 1st Division with CCA of the 3rd Armored Division was directed to advance south towards Mayenne.

After two days' rest, the 30th Division took over responsibility for Mortain on the evening of 6 August and the 1st Division withdrew, leaving the 30th Division to occupy its positions. The 30th Division had been attached to three different corps in the three days prior which is evidence of the uncertainty in the FUSA command and its eventual deployment was directly in the path of the intended German attack.

Meanwhile, CCB of the 3rd Armored Division, which had been attached to the 4th Division advancing to Villedieu and St Pois, was ordered to rest on 6 August at Reffuveille after reaching Le Mesnil Adelée across the River See.

The commander of the 3rd Armored Division, Leroy Watson, had been relieved and demoted on 30 July by General Collins and was not replaced until 7 August by Maurice Rose from CCA of the 2nd Armored Division. As a result, the 3rd Armored Division HQ had been inoperative since the end of July and remained that way throughout the Avranches counterattack.

While CCA of the 2nd Armored Division was attached to a battalion of the 30th Division fighting around Vire, the remainder of the 2nd Armored Division, including the 67th Armored Regiment, was attacking south-east on 6 August from St Sever Calvados towards Champ du Boult as a part of XIX Corps. Having succeeded in this task, the division was relieved at 1800 hours by the 28th Division and put into reserve around St Sever but was then placed on alert to move the next day.

It was expected that by the evening of 6 August the 1st Division and CCA 3rd Armored were to have captured Barenton during their advance to Mayenne.

Barenton was briefly held, but the infantry were ejected from all but the southern outskirts of the village by a German counterattack and it was planned to resume the attack next morning. Because of the gap that would develop between the US forces in Mortain and those approaching Mayenne, General Collins of VII Corps requested that XIX Corps transfer the 2nd Armored Division to him to support the 1st Division drive south-east from Barenton. This was approved by Bradley and the 2nd Armoured Division received its orders late on 6 August for a move next day.[9]

The 1st Division and CCA of the 3rd Armored Division then continued their rapid advance south and reached the Varenne River, 25 miles further south-east at Ambrieres, on their way to link up with the Third US Army at Mayenne. At midnight, all VII Corps units received a warning from VII Corps HQ that a German attack was possible within the next 12 hours as German units had apparently been spotted from the air.[10] The Allies also had complete decrypts of Luftwaffe signals regarding the proposed operation and this allowed the British and US Air Forces ample time to make plans for the next day.

7 August

The German attack by the panzer divisions started at midnight as planned but without the additional 1st SS tank battalion for the left flank attack of the 2nd Panzer Division which had been reportedly delayed until dawn by an aircraft crashing on its column and blocking the road. In order to try to achieve surprise, the attack began without any preparatory artillery bombardment.

The 116th Panzer Division was already fighting before the attack began and, lacking the element of surprise, was unable to advance along the northern bank of the River See towards Le Mesnil Gilbert with its depleted forces towards the objectives of Hill 211 and La Mardelle, north of Cherence. The XLVII Panzer Korps commander leading the attack, von Funck, contacted Hausser on the evening of 6 August to say that the 116th Panzer Division had not released its Panther battalion for the attack (which was untrue) and that its commander should be relieved because of his defeatist attitude. Having detached the tanks as ordered, the 116th Panzer Division had no more than twenty-five tanks operational and lacked the numbers and firepower to advance.[11]

The right flank attack of 2nd Panzer Division, reinforced with the Panther battalion from the 116th Panzer Division (Kampfgruppe Schake), advanced quickly to Le Mesnil Tove after passing through Belle Fontaine. The 39th Infantry Regiment from the US 9th Division was in Cherence, attacking north-eastwards towards Gathemo and heard tanks moving towards Le Mesnil Tove before calling down artillery fire on them. The regiment's roadblock at Grand Dove was quickly demolished by the German advance which cut off the three infantry regiments to the north from their divisional HQ, anti-tank gun company and artillery.[12]

The left attack of the 2nd Panzer Division and the attached 1st SS Tank Battalion did not start in earnest until 0500 hours owing to the late arrival of the Panther battalion. Two Panthers with some panzergrenadiers had moved off at the originally designated starting time and approached St Barthélemy from the north-east which was defended by the 117th Infantry Regiment. After some initial skirmishes with sentries and patrols, at about 0200 hours the Panthers attacked a roadblock consisting of a 57mm anti-tank gun and a platoon of infantry, knocking out one anti-tank gun but alerting the Americans to the attack in progress. These tanks then waited for the rest of the division and the 1st SS unit to catch up. This delay allowed other anti-tank guns, including four 90mm guns, to be quickly deployed in and around St Barthélemy. When the Germans resumed their advance in force at about 0500 hours, their artillery shelled St Barthélemy heavily. One American anti-tank gun knocked out the leading Panther which blocked the road for an hour. Dense fog had by this time reduced visibility to only 20yds, concealing the movements of attackers and defenders from each other. A second Panther was destroyed by the same anti-tank gun and the attack again halted to wait for more infantry to come up. Meanwhile, other German tanks began to attack St Barthélemy from different directions and infiltrate past the anti-tank guns positions. American soldiers were able to stalk Panther tanks in the fog and knock out several with bazooka rockets. Now behind schedule, the Panthers and Mark IVs advanced straight into St Barthélemy, losing another tank to a 90mm anti-tank gun on the outskirts. However, one by one the anti-tank guns were put out of action by the Panthers and panzergrenadiers which then rounded up the crews and any soldiers they could find. Instead of then heading straight for Juvigny, the 2nd Panzer Division column halted for 90 minutes to reorganise and allow the advance to be taken over by the Panthers of the 1st SS Battalion as arranged. At about noon, the tanks started forward again, only to be fired at by a single anti-tank gun which promptly knocked out the leading tank and damaged a second before being destroyed by other Panthers. By this time, the morning fog had burnt off to a bright sunny day and the planes of all nationalities took to the skies. Forewarned of the Luftwaffe plans, British and American fighters intercepted the German planes near their bases or en route to the Mortain area so that not a single Luftwaffe plane reached the operational area.[13] The only planes in the skies over Mortain were Allied and the fine weather permitted them to go to work on the German columns. Werner Josupelt, a panzergrenadier, wrote later:

> Our Panzers stood on an asphalt road. We were not moving forward. We infantrymen sat on the Panzers. Luckily there was thick fog. I thought 'They must think we're still in Russia, where you can get away with big assemblies of Panzers like this.' But today, German planes were supposed to be keeping the air space above the attack sector clear.
>   We finally got off the Panzers which rolled into the fields and camouflaged themselves. The fog lifted. There weren't any German planes, there were only Allied

planes. We all cursed Hermann's Luftwaffe. If he wasn't going to fly today, when was he going to fly?

The fighter bombers circled our tanks several times. Then one broke out of the circle, sought its target and fired. As the first rejoined the formation of 20 planes, a second pulled out and attacked. And so they continued until they had all attacked. Then they left the terrible scene. A new swarm appeared in their place and fired all their rockets. They had it well organised!

Black clouds of smoke from burning oil climbed into the sky everywhere we looked. They marked the dead Panzers. There were dozens of clouds of smoke from our area alone. Finally the Typhoons couldn't find any more Panzers so they dived down on us and chased us mercilessly. Their rockets fell with a terrible howl. One hit right next to a comrade of mine but he did not get hurt. These rockets burst into just a few big pieces of shrapnel, and a man had a chance of not being struck.[14]

Later that month the British Operational Research unit examined the Mortain battlefield:

Conditions on the afternoon of the 7th August were ideal from a pilot's point of view as no opposition was encountered from enemy aircraft and nor, till late in the day was there any appreciable flak reaction. Under cover of mist and low cloud, the Germans seem to have neglected all normal precautions and, when the weather cleared, they were sighted in large numbers head to tail in narrow road and lanes. The pilots reported that they were able to go in very close to attack, rockets being fired at 1000 yards range and cannon and machine guns from even closer.[15]

It was only 3 miles from St Barthélemy to Juvigny, but the attack by the 1st SS Panthers was stopped halfway by the aerial storm unleashed by the rocket-firing Typhoons of the 2nd Tactical Airforce, which arrived from noon onwards.[16]

That day, Typhoons from ten squadrons of the RAF 2nd Tactical Air Force flew 294 sorties and US planes made a further 200 raids.[17] Over the three days from 7–10 August, pilots claimed 153 enemy tanks destroyed, forty-three probables and fifty-six damaged: a total of 252 tanks. As this was more than the number of German tanks involved, clearly some of these claims were incorrect. After the battle, the wrecks on the ground in the area were examined and out of thirty-three Panther tanks and ten Mark IVs found knocked out, only six Panthers and three Mark IVs were found to have been destroyed by rockets and 500-pounder bombs. A total of 125 German vehicles (tanks, armoured cars, half-tracks, car, lorries) were found on the battlefield, of which only thirty-three were confirmed as being hit by aircraft.[18] Although the Germans may have taken many damaged vehicles with them when they withdrew, it appears that the effects of the aerial support were more psychological than physical and the mere appearance of the planes over the battlefield was enough to halt the advance and force the vehicles off the road into whatever cover they could find. One of the determinants of the success of the

German operation was support from the Luftwaffe and, thanks to Ultra, this support did not appear. The advance was taken over by the Mark IV battalion of the 2nd Panzer Division until the two leading tanks were knocked out by a bazooka team and blocked the road to Juvigny, effectively ending the German advance for the rest of the daylight hours.

At Mortain, the 2nd SS Das Reich Division attacked both sides of the town and captured it after a short fight. However, men of the 2nd battalion of the 120th Regiment held their position on Hill 317 to the east of Mortain. This hill overlooked the surrounding countryside through which the German forces were advancing and the battalion were able to call heavy and accurate artillery fire down on the roads choked with Das Reich vehicles. Simultaneously, Das Reich assault guns broke through the screen of 4th Cavalry squadron attached to the 1st Division further south near Barenton.

The tanks of the 3rd Armored Division's CCB were undergoing maintenance and rest on the afternoon of 6 August. When its commander General Boudinot got word of a possible German attack at 0115 hours on 7 August, many of the tanks were missing tracks, guns and engines and work to reassemble them could not begin until it was light. Therefore CCB could not move before noon.[19] At 0744 hours CCB was attached to the 30th Division and at 1015 hours received orders to retake Le Mesnil Adelée and Le Mesnil Tove.

At 1030 hours, the reconnaissance company of the 33rd Armored Regiment moved out to reconnoitre the roads towards Mortain. Task Force 1, including 1st Battalion 33rd Armored Regiment, was ordered to stop the German attack and clear the area around Le Mesnil Adelée and Le Mesnil Tove. Task Force 3 was dispatched to seize the road junction at St Barthélemy.[20]

The tanks of the 1st Battalion reached halfway between Le Mesnil Adelée and Le Mesnil Tove when they were stopped by artillery fire from the north and west. Three or four tanks were knocked out and Le Mesnil Adelée was reported to be swarming with German troops. Two platoons from F Company attacked Le Mesnil Adelée from the south and one platoon from the north after an artillery bombardment. The attack from two directions surprised the Germans and several Panthers were destroyed by the M4s coming from the north. The two southern platoons attacked in a frontal assault but lost six M4s damaged or destroyed.[21] The armoured spearhead of Kampfgruppe Schake had stopped, believing that it was getting too far ahead in the advance and was not being supported by other units. Now the kampfgruppe was being fired at by the combined artillery of three American divisions and had enemy forces on three sides.[22] Once the morning fog cleared, the conditions were perfect for artillery observation and the Americans used their artillery to deadly effect. Under considerable pressure from the American tanks, artillery and armoured infantry, the kampfgruppe withdrew from Le Mesnil Adelée from about 1800 hours, leaving behind six Panthers and two assault guns that were knocked out.[23]

In the south, the Americans counterattacked towards Barenton and the weakened German 275th Division was unable to prevent the village from being captured. The reconnaissance battalion of the 9th Panzer Division was ordered to attack the flank of the advancing Americans but could not disengage from the American tank forces attacking Domfront.

The 2nd Armored Division (less CCA which was fighting around Vire) had begun its move to link up with the 1st Division just after midnight and the 82nd Reconnaissance Battalion that was leading came under machine-gun fire and mortar fire as it approached Cherence. Contact was made with infantry from the 9th Division and it was clear that a major German attack was in progress. The 3rd Battalion of the 67th Armored Regiment reached Le Mesnil Gilbert at 0945 hours, and the tanks and divisional artillery engaged any targets they could see across the river in the fog at Le Mesnil Adelée for the rest of the morning. The commander of CCB offered support to the beleaguered 30th Division but was ordered by General Huebner to keep moving to link up with the 1st Division for the advance to Mayenne. The division was then transferred to VII Corps at 1100 hours and was ordered to move to Barenton with the mission of attacking back to the north towards Ger. The reports of heavy fighting coming in all morning had confirmed Bradley's prior knowledge of the German attack and these orders meant a movement of 50 miles around the German advance to place a strong armoured force on the southern flank of the Germans. When infantry of the 4th Division arrived, the 2nd Armored Division commenced its move westwards, again being led by the 82nd Reconnaissance Battalion which felt its way around the German spearheads. The division crossed the River See and moved through St Hilaire to Barenton where it made contact with Task Force X of the 3rd Armored Division and the 3rd Battalion of the 120th Regiment attached to it. Also a part of the 2nd Armored Division at that time was the 702nd Tank Battalion less Company A which was with CCA. The hilly countryside around Barenton was not suited to armour and the control of the high ground was essential for future operations as the road to Ger lay between two steep hills.

The 35th Division in the south, a part of the Third US Army, was ordered to attack from St Hilaire towards Barenton and was also attached to the 2nd Armored Division. Thus in a short space of time, five infantry and nearly two armoured divisions plus their attached independent tank battalions were in a position to block the German advance and attack its southern flank.

To the north, the 1st SS Panzer Division could make no progress in the teeth of the heavy artillery fire and fighter-bomber attacks, so its vehicles had pulled off the roads into the fields and camouflaged themselves as best they could. The 2nd SS Panzer Division could not take Hill 317 east of Mortain and was under attack around Romagny.

At 1600 hours on 7 August, the commander of the 116th Panzer Division, von Schwerin, was relieved, having not made much progress in supporting the attack of the 2nd Panzer Division. Von Schwerin had believed the attack could never

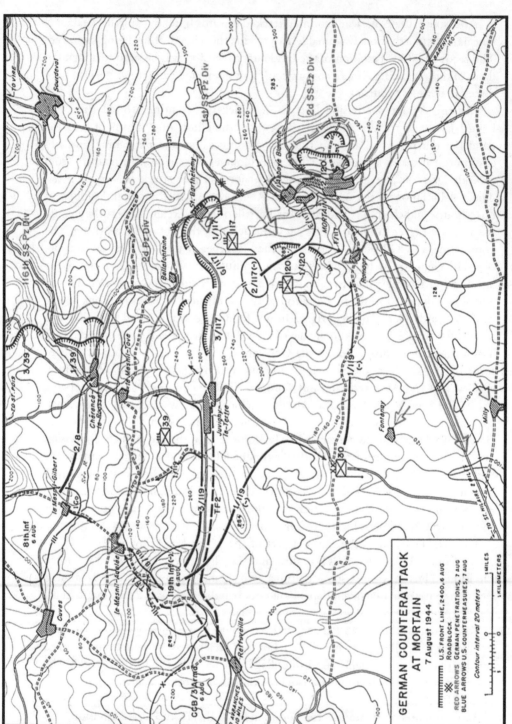

GERMAN COUNTERATTACK
AT MORTAIN
7 August 1944

||||||||| U.S. FRONT LINE, 2400, 6 AUG
⊗ ROADBLOCK
RED ARROWS GERMAN PENETRATIONS, 7 AUG
BLUE ARROWS U.S. COUNTERMEASURES, 7 AUG

Contour interval 20 meters

Operation Luttich: limits of German advance, adapted from *Breakout and Pursuit*. (By kind permission of M. Blumenson, USCMH.)

succeed and that he had insufficient forces to both go on the attack and prevent the front being held by the newly arrived and inexperienced 84th Division from collapsing.[24] The division was expected to attack westwards while being under attack from the north; the division's artillery had to fire in two directions that day.

After the relief of von Schwerin, the 116th Panzer Division finally attacked during the night and reached the railway crossing within 500m of Cherence but was forced back by an American counterattack. The failure of the 116th Panzer Division to advance in parallel with the 2nd Panzer Division exposed the spearheads of the 2nd Panzer Division to strong counterattacks from the 4th Division and CCB of the 3rd Armored Division.

Hitler, meanwhile, was becoming increasingly concerned about the progress of the attack, given its strategic importance, and ordered that afternoon:

> I command the attack be prosecuted relentlessly and daringly to the sea. Regardless of the risk, the 2nd SS Panzer and either the 12th SS or 21st Panzer Divisions must be withdrawn from the Fifth Panzer Army line and committed in the Avranches sector to bring about the collapse of the Normandy front by a thrust into the deep flank and rear of the enemy facing Seventh Army. Greatest daring, determination and imagination must give wings to all echelons of command. Each and every man must believe in victory. Cleaning up the rear areas and in Brittany can wait until later.[25]

By 1930 hours, Hausser was already discussing options with von Kluge for withdrawing; both men believed that the attack had failed. However, despite the advances of the Americans in the south and the attack of 2nd Panzer Division being halted, OKW ordered von Kluge to continue the attack. The 9th Panzer Division was to attack towards St Hilaire with available forces and it was decided to commit the 10th and 2nd SS Panzer divisions next day under a new Korps command, LVIII Panzer Korps.[26]

The German attack, often through narrow sunken lanes, had to contend with restricted room to manoeuvre, fog and American resistance on the ground and in the air, all of which had served to limit their progress on the first day. A spearhead from the 2nd SS Panzer Division attacking on the southern route towards St Hilaire made the most progress, reaching Milly, 4 miles from St Hilaire.

8 August

Pressure from the US units forced the 2nd Panzer Division to pull back its most advanced units that had not already done so from Le Mesnil Adelée on the night of 7 August. The arrival of US 2nd Armored Division at Barenton now threatened the rear of the German attack.

During the day, the US 3rd Armored Division continued its blocking action of the German attack and was able to make up some ground. Task Force 1 of CCB advanced to the north-west of Le Mesnil Tove to make contact with the 8th Infantry

Regiment. The half-track of the forward observer was knocked out and, without artillery support, the advance bogged down when a force of seventeen Panther tanks east of Le Mesnil Tove was encountered. Thirty minutes later, a squadron of P-47s arrived and broke up the German tank formation. That night, the task force harboured on the high ground north-west of Le Mesnil Tove after linking up with the intended infantry at 1912 hours and Le Mesnil Tove had been recaptured. The CCB knocked out three Panthers, two Stug IIIs and a Mark IV.[27]

The 1st SS Panzer Division again made no progress towards Juvigny because of heavy artillery, fighter-bomber attacks and the strong American resistance. D Company of the 2nd Battalion of the 33rd Armored Regiment managed to construct a roadblock between Le Mesnil Tove and Grand Dove late that evening to further contain any German advance.[28] The 2nd Panzer Division was pushed back to a line from east of Le Mesnil Tove to Hill 220 near St Barthélemy.

South of Mortain, the 2nd Armored Division began to put pressure on the Germans by attacking towards Ger. The 2nd and 3rd battalions of the 67th Armored Regiment supported the 41st Armored Infantry Regiment in attacks along the road to Ger with the intention of cutting the road from Ger to Mortain that carried all the supplies for the panzer divisions. Tanks from I Company destroyed two 88mm and two 37mm anti-tank guns in the village of Bousentier. One tank was lost by the regiment on a patrol southwards to St Jean du Corail.

In the south, the relentless advance of Patton's Third US Army continued, and at 1530 hours Le Mans fell, forcing the Seventh Army HQ to relocate. At 2115 hours, von Kluge ordered the attack to halt altogether and preparations to begin for its continuation in the next few days.[29] The Canadian Operation Totalize had started around Caen and von Kluge was now contending with threatened Allied breakthroughs at Caen and Vire as well as the progress of Third US Army to the south.

9 August

CCB of 3rd Armored Division continued its cautious move to recapture ground from the 2nd Panzer Division. Task Force 1 was heavily shelled all afternoon and finally withdrew back to Le Mesnil Adelée, having not made any progress.

The commander of Task Force 2, Colonel Cornog, was killed near Le Mesnil Tove by a German artillery shell that came through the door of a shack in which an orders group was being held. The positions of the 2nd Battalion were under constant mortar and artillery fire and every vehicle movement brought up clouds of dust that attracted so much mortar fire that the infantry of 119th Regiment requested that the tanks stay back.

Task Force 3 carried out a much bolder operation, however. Having been unable to reach the road junction at St Barthélemy as ordered on 7 August due to the presence of German armour, the task force had gone into reserve for the 30th Division.[30] At noon on 9 August, Task Force 3 set off to complete its original mission by making an attack from south of St Barthélemy with infantry of the 2nd Battalion of the 119th Regiment riding on its tanks. The armoured column arrived at Hill 285 to the west of Mortain and then conducted a reconnaissance, meeting troops at the Abbaye Blanche roadblock north of Mortain that had been holding out against Germans since the early hours of 7 August. As the tanks moved through Abbaye Blanche, German artillery fire forced the infantry to dismount and take cover and the tanks went on alone. A battalion of the Der Führer Panzergrenadier Regiment had reinforced German positions with assault guns and anti-tank guns, and nine M4s were lost in 30 minutes. The 2nd Battalion infantry finally came up, but before they could attack their preparations were disrupted by another heavy artillery barrage and the attack did not go ahead. Charles Corbin of the 391st Field artillery was attached to Task Force 3:

By 7 August, we were with Combat Command B again and the 30th Infantry Division to halt a counterattack near Le Mesnil Tove and Mortain. After reaching our objective on 9 August we were ordered to join Task Force 3, whose mission was to take the high ground north of Mortain, to control the crossroads to Mortain. We hit heavy resistance about 300 yards from our objective and the command made plans to go up a hedgerow lane, out left into a field and go through the next hedgerow.

Lieutenant Patterson told our driver, John Manual, to follow the first tank when it made a hole with its blade. We tried to do this twice as the tanks were hit by anti-tank fire. Lieutenant Cooper of I Company pulled up beside us in his tank and while waiting for another hole to be made, he jokingly said 'Wouldn't it be nice to get a million dollar wound and get the hell out of here?' His tank passed us by and was also hit trying to break out of the hedgerow. I could feel the heat of the next shell as we backed up. I saw two tankers get out of the tank and pull Lieutenant Cooper out and carry him past us. He didn't seem to be seriously wounded. I waved to him.

The other tanks had coiled in the field and the German 88 that had been waiting for us cut loose, also mortar, artillery and machine guns pounded our tanks and infantry. The tank next to us went up in flames and a tanker was having trouble getting out. Another tanker jumped on the tank and tried to help but was hit by a bullet. Then a shell beheaded the tanker. At this point we bailed out of the halftrack. I was between two infantrymen and a shell landed behind us and seriously wounded the two of them, although I thought they were both dead. The rest of the 30th Infantry retreated. All or most of our tanks had been hit and what men could get out retreated back to the next hedgerow. A piece of shrapnel hit our driver in the arm and I helped him back.

All of our men were accounted for except Lieutenant Patterson, who was kneeling over the two infantrymen near our halftrack. I waved for him to come back but he waved for me to come to him. He had administered first aid to them and was giving them some morphine shots. We loaded and strapped one man on the left fender and I held the other man on the right fender as he drove the halftrack to safety. We came out on the losing end and with many dead and wounded and 15 of our 17 tanks knocked out. A corporal left was the highest ranking man. It was one hell of a battle witnessed by this 19 year old kid.[31]

Task Force 3 was forced to go into a defensive harbour 100yds from its objective of the road junction.

Overnight, the 10th SS Panzer Division arrived with orders to both relieve the 275th Division and continue the advance towards Avranches, screening the simultaneous attack by the 2nd SS Panzer Division. After the losses in Operation Bluecoat, the division then only had twelve tanks and assault guns operational. South of Mortain, 3rd Battalion tanks from the 67th Armored Regiment continued pushing along the high ground to the west of the road from Ger to Le Breuit. The terrain around Hill 250 was too rugged for tanks, so infantry from the armoured regiment conducted an attack which captured the hill. German vehicles then visible from the hilltop were shot up on a side road. In the afternoon, eight tanks from the 10th SS Panzer Division advanced down the road from Ger and five of them were left burning by 3rd Battalion tanks and the 702nd Tank Destroyer Battalion.

The advance by the 2nd Armored Division was cautious and achieved only 5 miles in three days. The terrain was not suitable for tanks and Ultra intelligence had revealed details of further German plans for resuming the attack, so the division was wary of advancing too quickly. The German Seventh Army tried to regroup for the renewed attack by shortening the front line where possible and the 2nd and 116th Panzer divisions were pulled out of the front line into reserve.

Hitler repeated his orders of 7 August and demanded that General Eberbach be put in command of the renewed assault. Hausser wrote a situation report that outlined the options for resuming the attack provided specific conditions were met regarding reinforcements, air support, supplies and Alençon being secured. If these conditions could not be met, Hausser requested that the attack should be cancelled. Under pressure from the Canadians south of Caen, Hitler ordered anti-tank forces to be transferred from the Calais sector to bolster the line south of Caen and prohibited all unnecessary attacks and unauthorised local withdrawals, even if they overcame any advantages an Allied penetration might have achieved. Hitler also insisted that he alone would determine the timing of the next attack for Operation Luttich.[32] Von Gersdorff recorded the wording of Hitler's order:

A unique opportunity is offered OB West by means of a forceful thrust on Avranches to decisively turn the tide of the entire situation in the west and to gain the initiative. Therefore the attack is to be launched with all available forces after a thorough preparation, taking advantage of the enemy situation which is in our favour ... After reaching Avranches, the main body of the force is to be turned off towards the north east regardless of the enemy forces which have broken through towards the south and the entire Allied invasion is to be rolled up by a simultaneous attack by Seventh and Fifth Panzer army.[33]

Hitler was now completely out of touch with the reality of the situation in Normandy. Von Gersdorff wrote:

The designated objective was pure Utopia and was neither in keeping with the actual strength proportion, nor with the situation on the ground, in the air and in supply. It especially failed to consider the situation on the southern flank. This represented the apex of conduct by a Command ignorant of front-line conditions, taking upon itself the right to judge the situation from East Prussia.[34]

Hausser and Eberbach made plans for the attack, but both men knew that with Hitler's express stipulation that the attack was not to be started until sufficient forces were available, further advances by the Allies would dictate the military situation and make the orders for the attack irrelevant. Von Kluge himself continued the passive resistance to the Hitler's orders and wrote on 10 August, 'Owing to the favourable weather conditions for the enemy and to the time required in bringing up troops, it is not expected that the attack on Avranches can be launched before August 20.'[35]

End Game

Next day, 10 August, the 2nd Armored Division continued in its attempts to cut the Mortain to Ger road. At the same time, the 10th SS Panzer Division attacked towards Barenton but was compelled instead to block the advance of 2nd Armored Division and could make no progress. CCB of the 3rd Armored Division remained around Le Mesnil Tove whilst the fight for the road junction at St Barthélemy, where Task Force 3 was still heavily engaged, continued.

The Third US Army started its advance northwards towards Alençon on 10 August and the next day von Kluge was finally able to dismiss any thoughts of a second German attack by convincing Hitler that the panzer divisions were needed to attack the American forces advancing from the south. A German withdrawal from the battlefield began: the 1st SS and 2nd Panzer divisions were pulled back to a line from Le Bruins to Hill 270 where they went on the defensive to await the arrival of the 9th Panzer Division, two more Nebelwerfer brigades and the Panther battalion of the 9th Panzer Division. During the night of 11 August the Germans abandoned Mortain and at noon the next day the American infantry on Hill 317 at Mortain were relieved. The road junction at St Barthélemy was duly occupied by American infantry early on the 12 August, leaving the CCB task force to count its losses which included fourteen Sherman tanks, two Stuart tanks and three armoured cars.[36]

CCA from the US 2nd Armored Division moved south past Sourdeval and Ger and linked up with its CCB on 14 August in an intended envelopment operation that trapped a few elements of the Seventh Army but by this time most of the panzer divisions had withdrawn eastwards to avoid encirclement. Nevertheless, German losses were once again significant.

Losses

The 2nd ORS (Operational Research Section) No. 4 report examination of battlefield from St Barthélemy to Juvigny found thirty-three Panthers, ten Mark IVs and three self-propelled guns – a total of forty-six tanks – all brewed up. However, the Germans had time to recover salvageable or damaged tanks and actual losses were considerably higher. The 30th Division and its attached units (CCB 3rd Armored Division, the 743rd Tank Battalion and 823rd Tank Destroyer Battalion) had destroyed sixty-nine tanks during the battle, many being hit by infantry bazooka teams or artillery.[37] The 2nd Armored Division, advancing from Barenton, destroyed only five German tanks of the few operational left in the 10th SS Panzer Division.

The Germans lost 120 tanks and assault guns, well over two-thirds of the assembled armoured force. The panzer divisions had now been worn down to the point where they had little offensive capability and would never again pose a threat in Normandy.

The 33rd Armored Regiment processed forty-one replacement vehicles and more than sixty work orders during the short five-day action.[38] Twenty-six CCB M4 and four M5 tanks were destroyed. The 2nd Armored Division had twenty-seven M4s and five M5s knocked out in the period 1–15 August.[39] American losses totalled sixty-six M4 tanks.

Aftermath

Hitler believed that von Kluge had shown poor judgement in the conduct of the attack on 7 August in not waiting until his forces were fully assembled or for favourable weather that would have grounded the Allied fighter-bombers which had both delayed the assembly and wrought havoc during the attack. In many ways these criticisms were unjustified. American advances had changed the strategic situation daily and whilst von Kluge could do nothing about the weather, both von Kluge and von Gersdorff believed that if the attack was going to be made then it had to be made as soon as possible in view of Allied advances further south. But the attack was certainly not well co-ordinated, with some units of the 2nd Panzer Division attacking before the designated start time and the attached units of the 1st SS Panzer Division not arriving until 0500 hours when it was already getting light. The 116th Panzer Division did not attack at all until the evening of 7 August after von Schwerin had been relieved of his command. These mistakes meant that the German armoured punch was not as strong as it might have been and the local Americans units were alerted to the impending attack, although Ultra intelligence had already given a warning. Instead of the planned six armoured columns, the failure of the 116th Panzer Division and the left column of the 2nd Panzer Division to start the attack meant that only three armoured thrusts began at midnight. The commander of the attack, von Funck, did not conduct a proper reconnaissance before the attack which would have revealed not only the US units along the intended axis of the attack but also any gaps between them that could have been exploited.[40] The decision to make the main point of effort towards Avranches in the north via Juvigny rather towards southwards towards St Hilaire was crucial as it meant that the 2nd Panzer Division would be advancing close to the existing front line with the US 4th and 9th divisions nearby.[41] As the 116th Panzer Division had not advanced to protect the flank of the 2nd Panzer Division, it was quickly engaged by three infantry divisions and CCB of the 3rd Armored Division plus their attached tank battalions. The southern route via St Hilaire, the most direct and less defended route, had been originally allocated to the 2nd SS Panzer Korps, which was caught up in Operation Bluecoat and unable to take part. With the unavailability of the 2nd SS Panzer Korps, no thought seems to have been given to changing the direction of the schwerepunkt.

During the actual attack, the attack of the 2nd Panzer Division lacked aggression and coordination. The advance around St Barthélemy was hesitant and lacked determination to either breakthrough or bypass the American resistance. Belle Fontaine, on the road to Juvigny, was taken early on by the left or southern column, but the Germans did not attempt to bypass St Barthélemy or use the fog to infiltrate past anti-tank guns positions. The right column of Kampfgruppe Schake stopped at Le Mesnil Adelée in the belief that it was not being supported and missed an opportunity to capture Juvigny from the undefended north.

Both the 2nd and 1st SS Panzer divisions were understandably reluctant to keep attacking when the fog cleared and the Allied fighter-bombers appeared overhead, with the Luftwaffe conspicuous by its absence. Although their attacks were daunting to units on the ground under fire, the Typhoons destroyed far fewer armoured vehicles than both combatants believed. However, they did cause the leading tanks to seek cover off-road rather than continuing the attack. If von Kluge and the commander of the 116th Panzer Division were not optimistic about the operation then their troops can hardly have been motivated either and it may be that the failure of the Luftwaffe to appear and the stronger-than-expected American resistance offered an excuse for the vanguard to halt.

A thorough reconnaissance of the battlefield before the attack combined with better intelligence on the American units would have also revealed the sizeable armoured forces that were actually confronting the Germans, who believed they were attacking only part of the 3rd Armored Division and an infantry division. The 3rd Armored Division was a 'heavy' division with two armoured regiments, so even though it had been split into two combat commands, each command was almost the equivalent of a standard armoured division. However, each US infantry division also had attached to it an independent tank battalion of sixty M4 tanks, and as there were five infantry divisions involved in the battle, this was an extra 300 American tanks. The 743rd Tank Battalion attached to the 30th Division saw a lot of action during this battle with its companies and platoons of tanks supporting individual battalions of infantry as required. Other tank battalions involved included the 70th, 737th and 746th Tank battalions, and there were also a number of Tank Destroyer battalions present, both towed and mobile, including the 702nd, 629th, 899th and 823rd battalions.

From the 743rd Tank Battalion, B Company was sent on 6 August to Barenton with a battalion of the 120th Regiment while the other companies helped defend the area around Le Mesnil Tove and Le Mesnil Adelée with CCB of the 3rd Armored and the 119th Regiment. Eight M4s were destroyed in this action.

The 823rd Tank Destroyer Battalion, with its towed 90mm guns, was deployed in the St Barthélemy and Abbaye Blanche roadblocks and was instrumental in disrupting the German tanks on 7 August, knocking out seventeen tanks and assault guns plus many more soft vehicles for the loss of twelve guns.

The 746th Tank Battalion was attached to the 9th Division pushing towards Cherence and Mortain in the sector St Pois to Gathemo and created many of the difficulties for the 116th Panzer Division around Cherence on 6 August and in the vicinity of Grand Dove.

The 899th Tank Battalion was attached to the 9th Division directly in the path of the German advance. Supporting the infantry of the 39th Regiment, A Company also fought at Cherence and knocked out five German tanks on 7 August, which stopped any further German advances northwards.

While the German attack had many shortcomings, a significant factor in its defeat was the bravery of the US army forces in resisting the attack which, because of the terrain, did not develop into the massed armour attack planned. Instead it broke down into a number of small tank-infantry engagements which were all won decisively by the Americans.

The appearance of the 2nd Armored Division on the battlefield was an important tactical move, though it saw little combat. This division, with the 35th Division, not only blocked any possible German advance by the easier southern route to St Hilaire but also put pressure on the lines of communication through Ger of the attacking panzer divisions so, when it became evident that the attack had not succeeded, it was stopped by von Kluge. The Allies had learnt that considerable artillery and air support was needed if advances through the difficult countryside were to be successful and the Germans had neither. Bradley's strategy unfolded exactly as he planned and the German attack was blunted within hours on 7 August without imperilling the Third Army which Eisenhower was even prepared to see temporarily cut-off:

Bradley and I, aware that the German counterattack was under preparation carefully surveyed the situation. We had sufficient strength in the immediate area so that if we chose merely to stand on the defensive against the German attack, he could not possibly gain an inch. However, to make absolutely certain of our defence at MORTAIN, we would have to determine the number of divisions we could have in the enemy rear and to sacrifice our opportunity to achieve the complete destruction for which we had hoped. Moreover, by this time the weather had taken a definite turn for the better, and we had in our possession an air transport service that could deliver if called upon, up to 2000 tons of supply per day in fields designated by any of our forces that might be temporarily cut off.[42]

Notes

1 RG319 FMS B-725 Hausser, Avranches Counterattack, NARA
2 Blumenson, M., *Breakout and Pursuit* (Washington, DC, US Army CMH, 1961), p.457
3 *Ibid*, p.457
4 RG319 FMS B-725, *opcit*
5 RG319 FMS B-725, *opcit*, p.38
6 Blumenson, *opcit*, p.459
7 *Ibid*, p.461
8 Cave Brown, A., *A Bodyguard of Lies*, p.784
9 Houston, D., *Hell on Wheels – the 2nd Armored Division* (Novato, CA, Presidio, 1995), p.243
10 D'Este, C., *Decision in Normandy* (London, Penguin, 2000), p.421
11 RG319 ETHINT 17, von Schwerin, 116th Panzer Division in Normandy, p.16, NARA
12 Blumenson, *opcit*, p.469
13 RG319 FMS, B-725, *opcit*, p.42
14 Lehmann, R. and Tiemann, R., *The Leibstandarte, Vol. IV* (Manitoba, JJ Fedorowicz, 1993), p.185
15 WO 291/1331 ORS Report no. 4 Air Attacks on Enemy Tanks and Motor Transport in the Mortain Area, August 1944, TNA
16 RG319 FMS B-725, *opcit*, p.42
17 WO 291/1331, *opcit*
18 WO 291/1331, *opcit*
19 Reardon, M., *Victory at Mortain* (Lawrence, KS, University of Kansas Press, 2002), p.122
20 AAR 33rd Armored Regiment, August 1944, 3rd Armored Division Archives, University of Illinois, Urbana
21 Reardon, *opcit*, p.140
22 Reardon, *opcit*, p.143
23 Reardon, *opcit*, p.140
24 RG319 EHINT 17 Von Schwerin – 116th Panzer Division in Normandy, NARA
25 Blumenson, *opcit*, p.464
26 RG319 FMS B-455 LVIII Panzer Korps, p.5, NARA
27 AAR 33rd Armored Regiment, *opcit*
28 Log book 2nd bn 33rd Armored Regiment, August 1944, 3rd Armored Division Archives, University of Illinois, Urbana
29 RG319 FMS B-725, *opcit*, p.50
30 Reardon, *opcit*, p.162
31 Corbin, C., Letter to Dugan Haynes, 3rd Armored Division Archives, University of Illinois, Urbana
32 Blumenson, *opcit*, pp.482–3
33 FRG319 FMS B-725, *opcit*, p.55
34 RG319 FMS B-725, *ibid*
35 Ellis, L.F., *Victory in the West Volume 1: The Battle of Normandy* (London, HMSO, 1962), p.426
36 RG407 603-CCB Journal and file US 3rd Armored Division CCB, August 1944, NARA
37 RG407 30th Division G-2 Periodic report 12 August 1944, NARA
38 RG407 603-0 Call Me Spearhead, NARA
39 Barnum, Major J., et al – Committee 6 The Armoured Division in a Double Envelopment – The 2nd Armored Division in the Mortain Counterattack, Appendix V, MCOE paper, Fort Knox, Kentucky, 1948
40 Reardon, *opcit*, p.143
41 Blumenson, *opcit*, p.474
42 Eisenhower, D., *Crusade in Europe* (New York, NY, Doubleday, 1948), p.275

11

Operation Totalize

The 2nd Canadian Corps, which had been fighting in Normandy since D-Day, regrouped after the heavy casualties of Operation Spring; in the front line the 4th Canadian Armoured Division took the places of the Guards and 7th Armoured divisions which had moved to Caumont. The newly activated Canadian First Army was ordered by Montgomery at the end of July to try and pin down as many German units as possible to assist Operation Bluecoat whilst also preparing plans for a future offensive. The deployment of the Canadian First Army had been delayed because of congestion in the limited British beachhead. Despite the efforts of the Canadians, the 2nd SS Panzer Korps and the 21st Panzer Division moved westwards away from Caen to Caumont in response to Operation Bluecoat. As the German forces in the Caen sector were now significantly weakened, Montgomery wanted to mount a new attack there as soon as possible.

The most experienced British troops were already involved in Operation Bluecoat and any new operation in the Caen area would have to be undertaken by the Canadian First Army with the attached 1st Polish Armoured Division. Montgomery's directive issued on 4 August instructed the Canadians to launch an attack to breakthrough in the direction of Falaise in order to cut off or hinder the withdrawal of German forces around Caen, with this operation to start no later than 8 August, ideally sooner.[1] Much to the irritation of the commander of the Canadian First Army, General Crerar, Montgomery sent his own staff officers from 21st Army Group to assist with the planning.[2] Crerar, in turn, then left most of the planning to General Simonds of the 2nd Canadian Corps. Simonds had already been working on plans for such an operation since the end of July but, at 2300 hours on 4 August, Simonds was asked if the operation could be brought forward 24 hours in view of the developments in other parts of Normandy and the transfer of the 2nd SS Panzer Korps away from Caen. Simonds agreed, knowing that this would inevitably reduce the time for final plans, the drawing up of orders and preparations for the attack. D-Day for Operation Totalize was now 7 August 1944 with H-hour at 2330 hours.

In a British intelligence summary dated 6 August the Germans are generally described as falling back in disarray and in a later directive Montgomery (M517) stated that the Allied units must pursue the Germans with vigour so as to not allow them to establish new defensive positions.[3]

On the night of 6/7 August, XII Corps crossed the River Orne near Thury Harcourt with the tanks of the 34th Tank Brigade in support of the 59th Division in a diversionary operation. During the initial fighting, the Germans found the plans of the British attack in a knocked out armoured car and decided that the attack by XII Corps was the main effort. Therefore Kampfgruppe Krause from the 12th SS Panzer Division was dispatched to Grimbosq to support the 271st Division along with the 2nd Battalion of the panzer regiment, which moved into the vicinity of Thury Harcourt at Acqueville. Kampfgruppe Krause was composed of the following:

- 3rd Company Panthers – ten tanks
- 2nd Company Panthers – three tanks
- 8th Company Panzer IVs – five tanks
- 2nd Company from 101st SS Schwere Tank Battalion of ten Tiger tanks
- 1st and 3rd battalions of 26th Panzergrenadier Regiment (commanded by Krause)

The kampfgruppe was quickly in action, as recorded by the war diary of the 2nd Canadian Armoured Brigade which reported on 7 August of attacks on the 59th Division defending the bridgehead at 1900 hours by a German infantry battalion and twenty tanks.[4]

For the main attack planned by Simonds, Operation Totalize, the Canadian First Army was composed of the Canadian 2nd and 3rd divisions, the 4th Canadian Armoured Division, two armoured brigades (2nd Canadian and the 33rd Armoured Brigades), the 1st Polish Armoured Division and the British 51st (H) Division.

Simonds' plan, after the by now standard heavy bomber raid as a prelude to any Allied breakthrough operation, was for a series of armoured columns to break through the German line at night. As a second line of German defences had been identified, a second bombing operation would signal the start of the subsequent exploitation phase by the 1st Polish and 4th Canadian Armoured divisions towards Falaise. Simonds was acutely aware of the problems facing the operation. The countryside south of Caen was very open with long uninterrupted fields of fire that suited the high-velocity anti-tank guns of the Germans who were occupying positions they had been in for many weeks. As an ex-artillery officer, Simonds had no experience of handling an armoured division but the availability of heavy bomber support reinforced his pre-war belief that the use of aircraft avoided the need to secretly concentrate the artillery before an attack.[5] Simonds was also conscious of the German tactics of mounting immediate counterattacks and had written a 2nd Canadian Corps memorandum advising that such attacks were to be expected and provisions needed to be made to meet them.[6]

Simonds also believed he was facing considerable German armour, including the four panzer divisions of the 1st and 2nd SS Panzer Korps plus what was left of the 21st Panzer Division. The 4th Canadian and 1st Polish Armoured divisions had not been in battle before and the men of the 2nd and 3rd Divisions were somewhat demoralised after the many casualties suffered in Operation Spring. Simonds carefully considered all aspects of these problems and came up with a series of potential solutions which would work with varying degrees of success.

To limit the formidable firepower of German guns (of which the burnt-out Sherman tanks littering the slopes of the Verriers and Bourgébus ridges provided gruesome examples), Simonds' final plan proposed an armoured attack at night despite no Allied tank units having had training or experience of such operations. British doctrine of the time was for the armoured regiments to retire to a safe harbour at night behind the front lines where the tanks could be protected by the infantry; therefore this was an entirely untried tactic. Tanks also did not fight at night as a certain amount of light was needed to illuminate the optics of the gun sights (the so-called 'periscope light') and therefore the tanks would be unable to return enemy fire accurately. Lastly, to overcome the navigational problems of driving cross-country at night, Simonds hoped that innovative methods of maintaining direction such as searchlights, coloured artillery marker shells, radio direction signal beams and Bofors AA guns firing coloured tracer on fixed lines would adequately mark the direction of travel in the dark.

To break into the German lines, the armour would be organised into six columns, each led by troops of Flail tanks to detonate any mines in the path of the columns. Armoured troop carriers were fabricated by removing the guns from Priest 105mm self-propelled guns and welding armour over the gap in the front. Each 'defrocked' Priest (later dubbed a Kangaroo) could carry a section of men and these vehicles would enable the infantry to accompany the tanks into battle to deal with any anti-tank guns encountered. Armoured personnel carriers had been discussed fruitlessly by the British since the First World War, so this was their first use by the Allies. In contrast, the Germans had been using armoured half-tracks (SdKfz 250/250) for their panzergrenadiers since the outbreak of war.

The operation would be preceded by massive heavy bomber support but this time, learning from Operation Goodwood (as did Operation Bluecoat), a later second bomber raid was planned to eliminate the artillery and anti-tank gun screens of the second line of defences. A considerable pause before the commencement of phase two after the second bombing would allow some artillery to move up to support phase two as the phase one advance would move beyond their range which also had been a major shortcoming of Operation Goodwood. The second aerial bombardment would compensate for the reduced amount of artillery being available for the start of phase two.

Finally, in an effort to boost morale, at an officer's meeting conducted at Simonds' HQ in Cairon on 30 July, Simonds tried to motivate his officers by relating the exploits of a recent British Victoria Cross winner of the Westminster Regiment in its first action in Italy. The officers were told to discuss this and its implications with the men of their commands.[7] Simonds had not been impressed with the Canadian forces (particularly the infantry) in Operation Spring, and he was determined to keep close control of the coming operation.[8]

While planning was going on, Montgomery ordered limited actions by the Canadians in support of Operation Bluecoat which proved to be unsuccessful and costly in terms of men and tanks. These probes and limited attacks by the Canadians effectively signalled the Germans that they intended attacking again in the same direction from Caen towards Falaise which was as Montgomery intended as per his M516 directive to encourage the Germans to keep their forces around Caen.

German Defenders

From 3 August, while the Canadians were planning Operation Totalize and making their small-scale attacks, the German forces around Caen changed in response to Operation Bluecoat, the arrival of infantry divisions as reinforcements and the planned counterattack at Mortain, Operation Luttich. The 21st, 9th SS and 10th SS Panzer divisions were sent to Caumont. On the night of 3/4 August, the 12th SS Panzer Division went into reserve, its sector of the front line being taken over by the 272nd Division.

Finally, the 1st SS Panzer Division was pulled out of the front line into reserve from 5 August as the 89th Division arrived from Norway to take over. The 89th Division, with a single anti-tank gun company, was to occupy a sector previously held by two panzer divisions.[9] The 89th Division was at full strength but had been formed from under 18s, over 40s and East Europeans and was untried in battle.[10] A company of thirteen Sturmpanzers from the 217th Battalion was placed under its command for extra artillery support. As a part of the change in dispositions and the impending Operation Luttich, Panzer Gruppe West, under General Eberbach, was redesignated the Fifth Panzer Army on 5 August.

Both divisions of the 1st SS Panzer Korps, i.e. the 1st SS and 12th SS, were earmarked for Operation Luttich and orders were in the process of being raised for their redeployment with Seventh Army.

The Germans actually hoped that during the first week of August the Allies would mount another Goodwood-type cavalry charge that would allow the combined strengths of the 1st SS and 12th SS Panzer divisions to wreak heavy losses from prepared defensive positions. The tank regiments from both divisions were amalgamated into one Kampfgruppe, commanded by Wunsche, to provide a powerful counterattack in the event of such an attack. Kurt Meyer had been stationed in this part of France in 1942 when the 1st SS Panzer Division was refitting, so the Germans knew the terrain very well.

The planned movement of panzer divisions westwards for Operation Luttich was strongly resisted, especially by Dietrich who, somewhat surprisingly, was very outspoken towards Adolf Hitler.[11] Dietrich was only too conscious that his front was close to collapse and would have great difficulty resisting another attack if the 1st SS Panzer Korps was transferred elsewhere.

Final Plans

Simonds wanted a week of training for the operation but got only one night on 5/6 August for the armoured columns to form up and practise manoeuvering. Further preparations on 6 August were interrupted by church services for all units which were well attended.

A German ambulance and a deserter from 89th Division were captured on the night of 5/6 August and Simonds learnt that the 1st SS Panzer Division had been withdrawn. However, British Intelligence could not answer the question as to its new location.

The plan for Operation Totalize was for two divisions to break into the German lines and create the gaps for the armoured divisions to subsequently exploit. The 2nd Division would attack west of the Route Nationale 158 Caen–Falaise road, with the armour of the 2nd Canadian Armoured Brigade arranged in four columns. The attached 51st (H) Division would attack east of the road with the 33rd Armoured Brigade tanks in two columns.

Each column was four tanks wide and more than fifty vehicles long, the width of the column being determined by the size of the lane which could be cleared by four Flail tanks operating side by side. There was less than 6ft between the vehicles in each row and 20ft separating each row. The actual composition of each column varied from unit to unit, but generally the columns were led by a navigator in a Stuart tank followed by two troops of Sherman tanks which in turn were in front of the Flail tanks. The remainder of the armoured regiment then came behind the Flails, followed by the 'defrocked' Priest troop-carrying vehicles, AVREs and the anti-tank guns of the infantry battalions.

Having only had one night to practice driving in such a column, it was a difficult task for tank drivers to keep formation behind the tank in front whilst the column twisted and turned to avoid any obstacles on the intended route. The movement of so many tracked vehicles threw up huge clouds of dust, which reduced visibility to a few feet on occasions, and in order to maintain the integrity of the columns, a concession was made to allow the tanks to switch on one red tail-light for the vehicle behind to follow.

The columns formed an armoured snake, a sort of twentieth-century throw-back to the ancient Roman testudos. Just like in Operation Goodwood, the tanks themselves would be blasting the gap in the German lines. Instead of the armoured cavalry charge of Operation Goodwood, Simonds had devised an armoured steam-roller. The armoured columns were instructed to bypass all centres of resistance and not stop until they reached their phase one objectives.

Once the objectives of phase one were achieved – when a line from May sur Orne to Fontenay to La Hogue had been secured – the two armoured divisions were to be launched side by side with the direction of their attacks parallel to the Route Nationale 158 towards Falaise. In his appreciation dated 1 August, Simonds believed he was immediately facing two SS panzer divisions with a third, the 12th SS, in reserve. The initial plan was for an operation in three phases:

- Phase one – two infantry divisions, each supported by an armoured brigade, to break into German lines and capture the high ground at Point 122
- Phase two – one armoured division and another different infantry division to break into and open gaps in the second line of defences. The high ground west of Quesnay Wood was to be captured by the armoured division
- Phase three – a second armoured division was to advance to Falaise

Simonds' appreciation recognised two German defensive lines: a forward line that ran from May sur Orne to Tilly to La Hogue and a rear second line that ran from Hautmesnil to St Sylvain; both were to be targeted by the heavy bombers. Simonds fully expected the initial night advance to provoke the usual German counterattack once daylight came on 8 August, and the Canadian units were warned to prepare defensive positions accordingly.

As 7 August approached, intelligence reports of the movements away from Caen by the German panzer divisions must have encouraged Simonds and his planners greatly. At 1000 hours on 6 August, at a final briefing conference, a change was made to the plan on the basis of intelligence that not only had the 2nd SS Panzer Korps moved to Flers but the 1st SS Panzer Division had been relieved by the 89th Division and had moved back to the rear, either around Potigny or as far afield as Vassy.[12] Phase one was expected to be easier, but the phase two attack was still likely to meet strong resistance from the 12th SS Panzer Division which was believed to be in reserve somewhere around Bretteville sur Laize and would provide the main opposition as it had done for the last six weeks.[13] Given this apparent reduction in the numbers of defenders, Simonds changed his plans and decided to launch the two armoured divisions simultaneously, side by side down the road to Falaise thus reducing the operation to two phases.[14]

On the evening of 6 August, Ultra decrypts disclosed that the 1st SS Panzer Division was part of the forces assembling for the Luttich counterattack and, as the Allies also knew that the 12th SS Panzer Division (or at least parts of it) was in action at Grimbosq on the River Orne and around Vire, there appeared to be considerably fewer panzer formations opposing them, if any at all. This was good news for the Canadian First Army, but Simonds certainly did not believe that the Germans would leave the road to Falaise virtually denuded of German tanks after having defended Caen so vigorously since D-Day. However, this was precisely what von Kluge had been instructed to do with the 12th SS Panzer Division allocated to Operation Luttich and about to begin its move westwards to Vire.

The Battle

The formation of the armoured columns on 7 August stirred up a lot of dust and it was feared this would warn the Germans of the impending attack. However, no artillery fire was received, perhaps due to ammunition shortages or the inexperience of the 89th Division.

Without any preparatory artillery bombardment, Operation Totalize commenced at 2300 hours with a bombardment from 1,020 heavy RAF bombers on the flanks of the proposed line of advance to disrupt any enemy units with the potential to mount a counterattack. This created so much smoke and dust that only two-thirds of the planes were able to see their targets and drop their bomb loads. At 2330 hours, the armoured columns began to advance towards their start lines, and an artillery barrage at 2345 hours preceded the advance proper.

The effect of the bombs, smoke from fires and the artillery barrage was a dense smog in which many units lost their way. German artillery began returning fire and a ground mist developed in the early morning which did not help matters. Visibility was often only a few feet and drivers strained to follow the vehicle in front whilst trying to avoid crashing into the back of it during the frequent stops to check the direction or find a way around obstacles. The columns moved at little more than walking pace. Compasses began to spin wildly in response to the bombardment whilst the smog obscured the green tracer overhead from the Bofors guns and the searchlights. Some tank commanders were able to receive the radio direction signal but others had to rely on their maps and aerial photos and try to identify a landmark in the dark to pinpoint their position. There was a tendency for the radio signal to be lost every time the columns changed direction to avoid a bomb crater or find a way through a hedge or across a sunken lane. At the first major obstacles the orderly columns began to break up into little groups, all desperately trying to navigate in the darkness and smog.

Navigators of the 1st Northants Yeomanry in the 33rd Armoured Brigade columns arrived at their end point at about 0230 hours, just north of St Aignan de Cramesnil, much to the surprise of many of them. Only two tanks and three Priests were destroyed on the way after a running fight with some self-propelled guns and anti-tank guns. In the column led by the 144th Regiment RAC, three Stuart tanks of the navigators fell into bomb craters and, as a result, the column broke up into small groups. On reaching the railway line, two tanks were lost to Panzerfäuste but the regiment regrouped and found an alternative crossing before proceeding on to the objective of St Aignan. Just as they arrived, at 0400 hours, a tank was hit by an anti-tank gun and knocked out.[15] The commanding officer of the 144th Regiment RAC, Colonel Jolly, described the night-time advance:

> The air bombardment was going on while we were moving up … So far there was no
> enemy reaction, and at H-hour, half past eleven – we crossed the road which was our
> start line and speeded up to 5 mph. This would, we estimated, bring us close to the

barrage when it opened fifteen minutes later about a mile ahead, just north of Tilly. All went well until the barrage started, when the columns was immediately enveloped in a dense cloud of dust in which it was impossible to see more than a few feet even to see the taillight of the tank in front. Lt Osborne, leading the column, had not so far heard a sound, either dots or dashes from the beam wireless but his compass had been working fairly well. When the barrage started, the needle immediately swung wildly in all directions and the compass became useless. He could see nothing in the dense' dust cloud and, before long, his light tank disappeared into a bomb crater about ten feet deep. The two reserve navigators following behind tried to avoid this crater and went into another ...

The columns soon disintegrated into utter chaos. The confusion was indescribable. Everyone had been told to keep closed up and follow the tank in front, but it was soon apparent it was the blind leading the blind. Great shapes of tanks loomed out of the fog and asked who you were. Flails seemed to be everywhere and their enormous gibs barging about in the dark seemed to add to the confusion. It was not until one chanced upon the road or the railway that one had any idea of one's position. Even so, this was no check of the distance travelled and it was possible to go over the main road without noticing it. In fact some of the Canadians became mixed up in our column and one Canadian tank spent the rest of the night with us ... There was very little sign of the enemy at this stage.[16]

The 4th Brigade infantry in their Priests were to be escorted into battle by two regiments from the 2nd Canadian Armoured Brigade, the Fort Garry Horse and the Sherbrooke Fusiliers plus the 8th Canadian Reconnaissance Regiment. These forces formed three columns on their right axis of the advance and one column on the left axis to act as a flank guard; each column was divided into separate gapping, assault and fortress forces with the assault forces ordered to capture the objectives before dawn and the fortress forces to deploy in expectation of a counterattack.

The gapping force at the head of the columns on the right axis consisted of a navigator, two troops of Shermans from the Sherbrooke Fusiliers and other AVRE, and Flail tanks to remove mines and mark the route. Two troops from C Squadron of the Fort Garry Horse led the left axis column gapping force and the remainder of the squadron formed the fortress force.

The assault force in each column on the right axis was made of one squadron of the Sherbrook Fusiliers less the two troops in the gapping force. The fortress force in each column of the right axis was formed from the remaining two squadrons of Fort Garry Horse tanks distributed across each column and was designed to meet any German counterattack once daylight came.[17]

The left axis column was temporarily halted by fire at a railway bridge 1,000yds short of its objective, a small hill west of Cramesnil, but was unable to determine if this fire was from friend or foe. After exchanging shots in the darkness, the incoming fire died down and the column was able to move on.

The left-most column of the right axis stopped 2 hours before daylight to find itself only 300yds away from the correct objective, the same hill at Cramesnil. It was very difficult in the darkness for the navigators to determine if they were on high ground or not. In the centre column of the right axis most vehicles arrived at the designated area of the quarry near Gaumesnil but the leading tanks kept going westwards and had to be brought back by urgent radio messages. The infantry in the right-hand column of the right axis debussed too early in Rocquancourt whilst the tanks went on a further 3,500yds to the correct unloading point. Once daylight came the infantry were able to move up to join the tanks at Caillouet.[18]

Despite the navigational difficulties caused by the darkness, smoke and dust, the columns all eventually arrived on their objectives by 0600 hours and the fortress forces were deployed to meet any German counterattack.[19] The radio direction equipment had not worked well and the smog was often so thick that even the moon was periodically obscured. The most useful navigational aids were the tracer shells from the Bofors guns and tank commanders found that if they halted and waited for the smog to clear then the green tracers indicating the correct direction would eventually become visible again.

No tanks were lost in the gapping forces of any columns but those Germans that were not terrified by the armoured advance and were able to get over the shock of the bombardments engaged the assault and fortress forces at close range with anti-tank guns and Panzerfäuste. A total of nine tanks were destroyed and three damaged in the advance of 3 miles through the German lines. Any Canadian fears of mines that had so hindered the British advance in Operation Bluecoat were unwarranted as no mines were encountered by the advancing columns, but one minefield was missed by 6ft and another by 12ft.[20]

Meanwhile, the tanks of the remaining regiment of the 1st Hussars were supporting the 5th Brigade in a more conventional attack to the west. A and B squadrons and the infantry were a follow-up force behind the armoured columns with orders to clear any pockets of resistance and push on to secure Bretteville sur Laize. A Squadron supported the Calgary Highlanders into Verrieres at 0400 hours, followed by Rocquancourt and then on to Bretteville sur Laize. Two tanks were put out of action by German artillery. B Squadron was also directed to Rocquancourt and Bretteville, losing one tank to shellfire, but the tanks had a fine time shooting up anti-tank guns and Nebelwerfers. A 2nd Canadian Armoured Brigade report concluded:

This novel use of tanks and infantry in armoured carriers at night was entirely successful. The force accomplished everything it set out to do with the absolute minimum of casualties. During the actual advance to the objective, more than five miles through strong enemy defences, there were no vehicle casualties in the gapping force that led the advance.

The main difficulties encountered were those of keeping direction and organisation in the dark and the most useful aid in this was found to be the Bofors guns.

The searchlight and moon were of limited value in illumination. The searchlights, being off to one flank, and not remaining stationary, were of limited value in keeping direction. One of the major factors in the success of this operation was the extremely good marking of the routes carried out by the AVRE personnel who worked out in the open throughout the whole operation despite enemy HE and AP fire.

An operation of this type can be of the fullest success but could equally well have been a complete and utter failure through loss of direction or enemy counter action. Such a force has little offensive power in the dark and this method of employing tanks should only be used with the greatest circumspection.[21]

German Reaction

When the heavy bombing started at 2300 hours on 7 August, the 1st SS Panzer Korps, having been ordered 2 hours previously to move the 12th SS Panzer Division to Mortain, requested that the division stay attached to the Korps in view of the attack developing. Somewhat ambiguously, this request was approved by the OKW on the basis that the division take all measures for a speedy transfer to the Seventh Army to carry out its role in the forthcoming Operation Luttich.[22] Meyer recalled Kampfgruppe Krause from Grimbosq and also Kampgruppe Olboeter which had been sent to keep open the vital Vire–Vassy road from the British advancing in Operation Bluecoat.

The 2nd Battalion of tanks was also recalled from around Thury Harcourt. From the 5th and 7th Company only seventeen Mark IVs were immediately available, and these were subordinated to Kampfgruppe Waldmuller.[23] As the 12th SS Panzer Division was the only armoured unit in the whole sector, some tanks were later sent to provide anti-tank support for the front-line infantry divisions. A zug of Mark IVs (five tanks) was left with the 89th Division and two zugs were detached with the 271st Division.[24]

It was planned to use the new Panther battalion but this only had a dozen operational tanks after the long road march and the shortage of fuel. Von Kluge then requested that the 9th SS Panzer Division send a tank battalion; when this was reported to be still caught up in the fighting around Estry, the 2nd SS Panzer Korps dispatched instead the operational Tigers of the 102nd SS Schwere Tank Battalion.

Canadian Halt

The Canadian advance was to remain halted for the next 6 hours until the daylight air raids had finished. The first wave of the 8th USAAF planes was due at 1226 hours to bomb the northern targets and the second wave due from 1335–1355 hours for the southernmost targets.

An early morning ground mist also persisted but this allowed the tanks to deploy from their columns without enemy interference. The mist would have caused some difficulties for any further advance until it burned off, though none was planned. The 4th Canadian and Polish Armoured divisions were to move up to their start lines in this period, ready to attack once the phase two bombing finished.

Pockets of German resistance that had been bypassed during the night began to mount localised counterattacks with small groups of infantry accompanied by one or two tanks or self-propelled guns. In particular, the villages of Caillouet, Tilly and Gaumesnil remained in German hands. These actions prevented any supplies or ambulances getting through to the Canadian positions. Caillouet was not captured until midday after the mist cleared and operations continued throughout the day to mop up these pockets of resistance and clear the lines of communication.

Blue on Blue

For the phase two bombing, the Flying Fortresses were instructed to bomb in a direction parallel to the front to avoid a repeat of the friendly-fire bombings of Operation Cobra. This required them to approach the target from the direction of Vire which exposed the planes to a lengthy period of anti-aircraft fire. The first wave bombed without problems although a lot of smoke and dust was created. Inexplicably, a formation of twelve planes veered off the flight path and headed for Caen where they dropped their bombs on the suburb of Cormelles and the road to Falaise. Many vehicles and guns were hit as well as supply units. Troops were caught in the open as they were on the move and had no time to dig slit trenches. Casualties from this incident caused great disruption amongst the troops moving up, especially the supporting artillery for phase two. Cormelles was some 6 miles from the intended line of targets. The units bombed were aghast and shocked; unanswered questions ranged from wondering how the Germans had managed to capture some Flying Fortresses to asking why the Americans were bombing them. The war diary of 2nd Canadian Armoured Brigade commented, 'At approximately 1300B hours, main Brigade HQ at Cormelles along with various gun areas in the immediate vicinity were bombed by American precision bombing. Casualties were heavy in both men and equipment.'[25]

Remarkably, a second formation of twelve planes followed the lead of the previous group and dropped their bombs in the same vicinity. A total of sixty-five men were killed and 250 wounded, including the commander of the 3rd Division. The USAAF would later claim that the lead plane was hit by anti-aircraft fire and was forced to abort its mission before jettisoning its bomb load over Caen.[26]

For the Germans, the halt by the Canadian advance was little short of a miracle and allowed them time to gather together all available forces, deploying them to meet the Canadian attack. Meyer likened the halt to a cavalry charge where the riders had stopped to feed their horses. Reinforcements, in the form of the

85th Division, were due to arrive from 10 August but the 12th SS Panzer Division would have to meet the brunt of the attack in the meantime. The only troops immediately available were subordinated to Kampfgruppe Waldmuller of the 25th Panzergrenadier Regiment along with the seventeen Mark IVs from the 2nd Battalion, the corps and division escort companies plus a company of ten self-propelled anti-tank guns (Jagdpanzer IVs). To this kampfgruppe was added the 3rd Company of Tiger tanks from the 101st SS Schwere Tank Battalion, now commanded by Michael Wittmann. Therefore Kampfgruppe Waldmuller contained the following tanks:

- Seventeen Mark IVs – five from 5th Company and twelve from the 7th Company
- Ten Jagdpanzers IV
- Ten Tigers

Two Tiger tanks of the 3rd Company collided on the route march to Cintheaux and became unavailable for the attack, leaving only eight Tigers. At the last minute two Mark IVs and five Panthers from the repair workshop were added to this formation.[27]

The Germans saw the hundreds of massed Canadian and British tanks that had broken through but had halted in front of them and realised that they could not defeat them with the forty-two tanks of the kampfgruppe. Their only hope was to disrupt the timetable of the advance so as to give them time to establish new defensive positions and reform the front line. The mission of Kampfgruppe Waldmuller was to form a blocking position on the low ridge south of St Aignan de Cramesnil to St Sylvain. The terrain was quite open and the Germans hoped that the long-range superiority of the Tiger tanks would keep the Allied tanks at bay.

Death of Wittmann

The German counterattack was scheduled to begin at 1230 hours and coincided with the arrival of the first wave of Flying Fortresses. Led by the eight Tigers, the German tanks drove quickly towards St Aignan de Cramesnil from Cintheaux astride the Caen to Falaise road. The Mark IVs and Jagdpanzers were echeloned to the right rear, accompanied by the panzergrenadiers of the 25th Regiment. Unseen by the Germans, two armoured regiments had advanced from their earlier positions at Point 122 towards Cintheaux. On one side of the Caen-Falaise road, A Squadron of the Sherbrooke Fusiliers had occupied the Gaumesnil château grounds and taken up firing positions behind a wall overlooking the open ground to the east. Meanwhile, in the east, A Squadron of the 1st Northants Yeomanry had worked their way through an orchard and the woodland south of St Aignan which was occupied by the rest of the regiment and the 144th Regiment RAC. The A Squadron tanks were lined up behind a hedge and had an excellent view of the open ground to the west. When the Tiger tanks appeared in front of their positions, they were caught in a crossfire of armour-piercing shells from the two squadrons. A Northants Firefly hit several of the Tigers, which were peppered by 75mm fire from the other Shermans, knocking off tracks and immobilising them. Several of the Tigers briefly returned fire at the Firefly, forcing it to move before it was knocked out. Five Tigers were destroyed without loss in a few minutes; the tank commanded by Wittmann caught fire and eventually exploded. The German attack can only be described as rash and impetuous, similar to that performed at Villers Bocage but with a very different outcome. Three of the Tigers were knocked out by the Firefly tank (the gunner was Joe Ekins), and it is likely that the Sherbrooke Fusilier tanks accounted for the other two Tigers nearer the Caen-Falaise road. Ken Tout of the 1st Northants Yeomanry was in A Squadron that day and watched the German tanks advance:

'Oboe Able to 3 Charlie. Near enough. Fire! Over.'

'Charlie, OK. Gunner, fire!' In his excitement, Charlie has forgotten to switch back to intercom back but his gunner can hear the A set clearly. 'Gunner, on! Fire!... Got him, you golden boy! Got him! Charlie got him. Over.'

'Able to Charlie. Get the middle one. I'm hitting the first in line to keep his head down. And use your intercom. Off.'

I see a thick sprouting of smoke over the trees beyond my range.

'Oboe Able to 3 Sunray. Charlie's Sunray hit. Get over there and keep Charlie shooting. 3 over.'

'3. On my way. Off'

I traverse gently back and forward but can see no more of the road. The growing cloud of smoke shows where one of the Tigers is blazing. SLAM-CRASH of an 88mm! Almost simultaneous crashes. Flat trajectory. Tremendous muzzle velocity. An anti-aircraft gun used point blank against tanks. Firing and impact explosions coming almost together. No smoke in A Squadron's positions. SLAM-CRASH! Another Tiger fires unseen. A Squadron's 3rd troop leader will be dodging through the orchard trees. Lifting the commander from the turret. Giving orders. Bearing on the middle Tiger. One Tiger blazing and the other two swinging around to look for shelter and still not sure where the pesky Shermans are. We see it clearly in our mind's eye.

BLAM CRASH – slightly different sound, equally imperious, of the seventeen pounder.

'Oboe Able to Oboe. Second Tiger brewing. Am keeping third busy while Charlie bring to bear. Over.'

'Oboe. Bloody good show. Off.'

Black gush of smoke over the trees hiding road. Another Tiger burning. SLAM–CRASH of an 88mm almost together as the BLAM–CRASH of the seventeen pounder. One ... two ... three crashes nearby. An answering roar of sound. New spouts of flame beyond the distant trees. I shout, 'They've got him! They've hit Tiger three!'[28]

Both General Kitching and General Maczek, the Polish commander of the Polish Armoured Division, had expressed concerns to Simonds the day before the operation about the changes to the proposed plan which now required both divisions to advance on a front of less than 1,000yds. Doubts were also expressed about the need for the second bombing raid but Simonds turned down all requests for modifications.

The Polish armoured regiments crossed the start line as planned at 1355 hours and were quickly in action against Kampfruppe Waldmuller at about 1425 hours. The Division HQ and infantry brigade were delayed coming through Caen but they were not required for the first part of General Maczek's plan.

The Canadian Grenadier Guards Regiment was delayed by traffic congestion around Rocquancourt but began a slow advance at about 1200 hours.[29] The Canadians could not cross the bomb line, which ran north of Gaumesnil and Robertmesnil, until the bombing finished, H-hour for phase two being 1355 hours. The phase two forces waited around the low hill at Point 122 just east of Cramesnil. Both the armoured divisions were reported to have crossed the start line at 1355 hours, so the congestion and friendly fire bombing did not delay the start of the attack as claimed by many historians.[30]

What did delay the attack once it started was the omission of a plan to take Gaumesnil, a phase two objective not far from the start line. In a considerable oversight, the village had not been assigned as the objective of any unit. The Royal Regiment of Canada was instructed only at 1300 hours that afternoon to clear the area. Despite A Squadron of the Sherbrooke Fusiliers having been all around the château during its earlier engagement with the Tiger tanks, the squadron had moved back to west of highway to support an attack on Caillouet, so it was not known whether the village itself was occupied.[31] An attack was hastily planned and mounted just as the Germans put down a fierce artillery barrage on the assembling Canadian forces. Gaumesnil was finally captured about 1530 hours with little opposition and this at last freed up the tanks to advance.

With No. 1 Squadron leading, the Grenadier Guards reached a point just north of Gaumesnil at about 1400 hours. Four tanks, including three from No. 1 Squadron, had been lost on mines during the early morning move to the start line. The Shermans moved cautiously past the burning Tigers, perhaps wary of any others that might still be near, and with reason, as one tank was indeed knocked out by a retreating Tiger. By 1600 hours, Brigadier Booth was getting increasingly frustrated at the slow progress and ordered the regiment to push on at all costs. The squadron tried to skirt Cintheaux to the east but was stopped by considerable anti-tank gunfire from the woods near where the 1st Northants Yeomanry was located. No. 3 Squadron then passed through to take up the advance, but again, two tanks were hit and knocked out. The Grenadier Guards tanks had entered a killing ground which had already seen the demise of Wittmann; with a tank battle in progress to the east, their advance in their first action was naturally hesitant.[32] Booth's frustration is reflected in the 4th Canadian Armoured brigade signal log:

1426: 22CAR reached Laughton (road Bretteville sur Laize to St Aignan)

1515: Reported German tanks burning at Gaumesnil

1617: You are reporting no opposition so push on. If there is opposition I should know about it. (Sunray) I must push on. Bypass any opposition the momentum must be carried on.

1700: Advance must continue immediately. 22nd to phase one in 1 hour's time

1702: Fetch sunray – what is the hold-up … phase two in three hours time. I want phase I in 1 hour – no opposition in front yet the going is very slow. I'm not waiting any longer I want you to move fast.

1719: 22CAR reached Laughton 1650

1740: Get on with it, too slow. Get to phase one by 1800 hours. I am going to pass you.[33]

The No. 4 Troop of No. 3 Squadron, commanded by Lieutenant Phelan, was then ordered to proceed to the west of the highway between Gaumesnil and the railway line towards Cintheaux, and considerably less opposition was encountered on this route.[34] In a short space of time, his tank knocked out four 20mm and three 88mm anti-tank guns plus three self-propelled guns in the orchards and hedges to the west of Cintheaux, with only two Shermans damaged.[35]

This would be the furthest the Grenadier Guards regiment advanced that day. Permission to harbour was requested and was, surprisingly, given by Halpenny, and at 2000 hours the regiment harboured back at Gaumesnil. The regiment had lost seventeen tanks damaged or destroyed since midnight on 7 August.[36]

C Squadron of the reconnaissance regiment, the South Albertas, reached Hautmesnil after supporting the Argyll and Sutherland Highlanders into Cintheaux at about 1600 hours, the town being cleared by 1830 hours. One Cromwell tank was lost to an anti-tank gun.[37]

The first day of battle for the 4th Canadian Armoured Division, led by the Grenadier Guards, had ground to a halt 1,000yds south of Cintheaux which was an advance of just over 3 miles. According to the signals log, the 4th CAB HQ still believed at 2200 hours the Grenadier Guards had reached the phase one objective of Bretteville le Rabet when in fact the regiment was still at Cintheaux.

Kampfgruppe Waldmuller

The destruction of the five Tiger tanks was not the end of the day's action for the 1st Northants Yeomanry. At about 1300, hours twenty tanks were observed

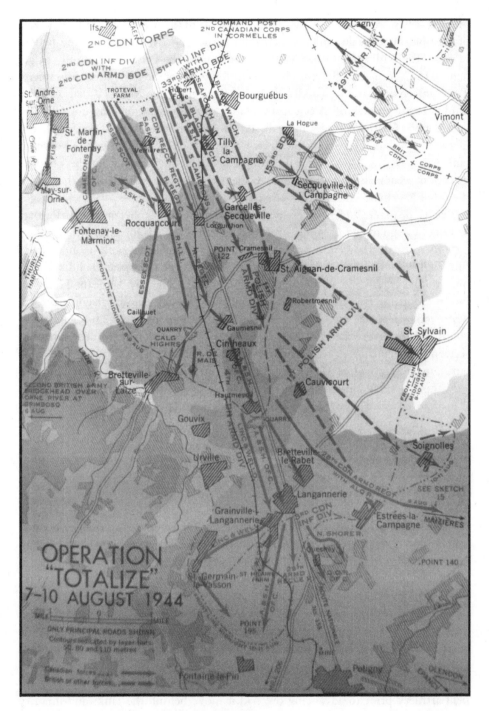

Operation Totalize: the limits of Canadian and Polish advances, 10 August 1944, adapted from the *Victory Campaign*.

moving westwards towards Gaumesnil. These were the Mark IVs and Jagdpanzers of Kampfgruppe Waldmuller which then turned northwards, using the hedges to cover their advance. Other Mark IV tanks used the Petit Ravine gully to get behind the Yeomanry Shermans before climbing out of the gully to surprise them. Tank stalked tank in the woodland around the gully. One Mark IV that was well hidden began to pick off A Squadron's tanks one by one, knocking out six tanks before it was finally spotted. On the basis that the enemy tank could not fire at both of them simultaneously, the squadron leader, Major Skelton, organised another tank to attack the Mark IV at the same time as his own but from the opposite direction. Major Skelton won the duel: the Mark IV was brewed up at the cost of the other Sherman which was destroyed.[38]

The Jagdpanzers advanced at speed, skirting around Robertmesnil before attacking St Aignan and C Squadron from the east. Other Jagdpanzers stood off on a ridge 1,000yds away and knocked out another C Squadron tank. Concentrated fire from the squadron made the two withdraw, but others appeared and knocked out another Sherman. Three Jagdpanzers were engaged by Sergeant Hume of No. 1 Troop and he managed to knock out two of them. Another Jagdpanzer was destroyed by Captain Fox, even though in a hull down position.[39] The deadly hunt continued for several hours until the evening. The 1st Northants Yeomanry lost sixteen tanks, including five Fireflies, in this battle but claimed twenty German tanks, including the five Tigers, four Panthers, six Mark IVs and five Jagdpanzers.[40]

Kampfgruppe Waldmuller, despite its heavy losses, succeeded in delaying the Canadian advance which gave the Germans time to reorganise their defences and for the Panther tanks of Kampfgruppe Wunsche to return overnight from Grimbosq in time to take part in the battle.

1st Polish Armoured Division

Beset by traffic jams and delayed by the American bombing of Cormelles as other units sorted themselves out, the 1st Polish Division slowly moved up to its position on the start line and the leading elements were able to cross the line on schedule at 1335 hours. The division was organised on the same basis as a British division but, owing to a shortage of men, the tank squadrons had only sixteen tanks in them, four platoons of three tanks and four in the squadron HQ. Maczek's plan was for the 10th Cavalry Brigade (the armoured brigade) to advance to Hill 140 and the areas around Estrées la Campagne while the 3rd Infantry Brigade would capture Cauvicourt in the first phase; the 10th Cavalry Brigade was then to advance to Falaise in the second phase. Unlike Kitching, Maczek chose to not deploy his field artillery prior to advancing but had it move behind the tanks and infantry to come into action as required.[41] Therefore the Polish attack began without any preparatory artillery bombardment.

The 2nd Tank and the 24th Uhlan regiments advanced to the east of St Aignan with their flank screened by the reconnaissance regiment, the 10th Mounted Rifles (PSK). By this time the division escort company of the 12th SS Panzer Division and the corps escort company of the 1st SS Panzer Korps that made up the rest of Kampfgruppe Waldmuller had occupied the wooded areas around Robertmesnil and St Sylvain to block any advance in that direction. The two companies were supported by the three other Tiger tanks and the company of Jagdpanzers that had engaged the 1st Northants Yeomanry. The division escort company had at least two 75mm anti-tank guns and the corps escort company had two 75mm howitzers.

The Polish tanks advanced across the open fields and straight towards the waiting Germans, who opened fire. The 2nd Tank Regiment lost twenty-six tanks within minutes, many of the Shermans bursting into flames immediately. The 24th Uhlans saw what was happening to the 2nd Tank Regiment and stopped their advance in a small valley out of sight of the Germans while a hasty reconnaissance was organised. The Polish artillery then came into action at 1450 hours but the attack had been literally stopped in its tracks. Heavy German artillery fire was brought down on the tanks and, in the ensuing chaos, the 24th Uhlans lost fourteen tanks before making it back to the relative safety of the woods around St Aignan and the Canadian lines.[42] The 10th Mounted Rifles also lost three tanks dueling with Jagdpanzers around St Sylvain as they attempted to outflank the 2nd Tank Regiment. The battle was again recorded by Ken Tout:

The tanks were theoretically in open order but only a touch of the gun traverse apart one from another. The gunners in two German Mark IVs must have been utterly flabbergasted to see the sight, but lost no time in firing shot after shot. While Tony Faulkner watched speechless, from Sherman after Sherman there blossomed the unmistakable flowering of flash, smoke, and dust, marking the impact of armour-piercing shot. Then the puff of flame and smoke out of the turret or engine. The scramble of men, some immune, others on fire, out of the blazing vehicle. The devastating roar of turrets being blown off and ammunition sending fireworks high into the air.

Many of the Polish tanks tried to fire their guns but without any clear sighting of opponents. More tanks brewed. Others began to circle and dash for shelter. Machine-gun fire plucked at survivors. Someone remarked that it was like watching a field full of haystacks set on fire by an arsonist …

The defenders had demonstrated that by that time of day, there was no daylight route around east of Robertmesnil on 8 August.[43]

Two Jagdpanzers entered St Aignan and engaged targets in the open to the north until 2200 hours, unsupported by infantry. The Jagdpanzer company claimed a total of twenty-eight tanks knocked out that day, mostly Polish, for the loss of five Jagdpanzers; the three remaining Tiger tanks claimed a further seven tanks.[44] That evening the Polish regiments counted their losses. Next morning they reported the total loss of twenty-five Shermans and six Cromwells.[45] The Poles were critical of their Sherman tanks while Maczek blamed the losses on the Allied artillery and airforce not having neutralised the enemy sufficiently and having to mop up enemy left by the 51st (H) Division, which for its part reported the Polish lack of progress to Simonds.[46] The operations of the AGRA supporting the Canadian First Army were certainly disrupted by the friendly bombing but, in view of this, Maczek should have made sure he had his own artillery available for support before advancing. Simonds was not impressed by the performance of the Polish Division.

9 August

The two armoured divisions had not advanced far that afternoon and, to Simonds' anger, they harboured for the night rather than pushing on. Parts of the Canadian lines of communication were still congested, making it difficult to get troops and supplies forward. However, the capture of Hautmesnil and Bretteville sur Laize by the Canadians made the position of Kampfgruppe Waldmuller difficult and it was ordered to break contact and withdraw that night to the area around Hill 140, north-west of Assy. The kampfgruppe, with its attached Mark IVs, Jagdpanzers and the three surviving Tigers of Wittmann's company, had been pushed to the east towards Soignelles by the Polish advance. Kampfgruppe Krause arrived overnight and assembled with the bulk of the division's remaining armour in Kampfgruppe Wunsche in the Quesnay Wood as a reserve.

Nine Panther tanks had been lost, mainly to heavy artillery fire in the fighting around Grimbosq (in which the 107th RTR also lost twenty-eight tanks), and the kampfgruppe arrived in the Quesnay Wood with four tanks which with the sole survivor from Waldmuller's attack the previous day gave the division five Panther tanks. The ten Tiger tanks of the 2nd Company 101st SS Schwere battalion that had returned from Grimbosq were also in the same location.

The first tanks of the Panther tank Battalion promised by von Kluge on 8 August began to take up positions in the Ouilly Woods near Potigny, but no sooner had they arrived than they were ordered to leave by von Kluge during the afternoon of 9 August to reinforce the attack at Mortain. The elation at having a heavy tank force to meet the expected assault and then losing it was like a 'cold shower' to the German defenders.[47]

By noon on 9 August, thirteen Tigers of the 1st Company of the 102nd Schwere SS Battalion had also arrived from Estry and positioned themselves in Quesnay Wood.[48] The tanks of the 2nd Company were deployed in the sector of the 271st Division to provide much needed support there. The 8th Company of five tanks that was a part of Kampfgruppe Krause involved in fighting on 8 August against Grimbosq bridgehead also assembled in Quesnay Wood before being deployed around Hill 195 on 9 August.[49] The Germans thus managed to collect together another small but powerful force in the Quesnay Wood of twenty-five Tiger tanks (including two 3rd Company tanks), five Panthers and five Mark IVs.

The line of hills around Potigny and to Mazières following the Laison River was the only defendable terrain and the decision was made to make this the new front line, pending the arrival of the 85th Division as reinforcements.[50]

At 1830 hours on 8 August, Simonds had ordered Kitching to continue the advance to Point 195 through the night but the Grenadier Guards were already moving back to harbour. Kitching, in turn, convened his own orders group at 2000 hours with his two brigade commanders and Booth was ordered to advance to Point 195 and Bretteville le Rabet, the latter being a still outstanding objective. The Grenadier Guards would advance at 0315 hours to take Bretteville le Rabet and the British Columbia Regiment with the Algonquin infantry regiment less one company would advance just east of the Caen–Falaise road and parallel to it, past Bretteville before crossing the road to Point 195. By the time Booth's orders group had finished it was 0100 hours, with the start time scheduled for 0200 hours.[51] The final objective of Hill 195 was beyond the range of British artillery but three forward observers accompanied the battle group to provide support once the field artillery had moved up. The British Columbian Regiment was expected to hold the hill until reinforcements arrived.

The initial advance did not begin until 0400 hours, according to the war diary of the British Columbia Regiment, with C Squadron leading and A Squadron bringing up the rear. The tanks went as fast as the darkness and terrain permitted. Arriving just north of Bretteville le Rabet, the leading tanks were fired upon by anti-tank guns and the regiment briefly halted to consider whether to wait until the nearby Grenadier Guards had cleared the village. The commander of the regiment, Colonel Worthington, gave the order to 'Move on anyway, while we still have surprise.' Fire from the Germans intensified as they realised that enemy tanks were passing through their positions. The regiment pushed on, shooting up haystacks and any obvious locations where German soldiers could be hiding on the way.

Dawn brought an end to the uncertainty of navigating at night but had other consequences. The Canadians saw some high ground in front of them and, assuming it was their objective, headed for it whilst the anti-tank gunners of the German defenders could clearly see the Sherman tanks for the first time.

The battle group shot up several half-tracks and lorries spotted in the woods along the route of the advance which had penetrated deep behind the German front-line positions. Arriving at a rectangular field bounded by hedges, the battle group arranged itself in a tight defensive position to await the arrival of reinforcements. Unfortunately, the hill that the regiment occupied was Hill 111 east of Potigny and not Point 195 west of Potigny.

En route, B Squadron had become disorganised in the darkness near Cauvicourt when the first resistance was encountered around Bretteville. After re-forming, the squadron pushed well to the east to avoid any fire from Bretteville and, when it neared Estrées la Campagne at dawn, a further Orders Group was held. At this juncture, the squadron commander, Major Carson, believed that the squadron had got off course and directed the tanks to move in a south-westerly direction to Hill 195. Colonel Worthington then ordered the squadron by radio to 'advance to the high ground in front', which they duly did, except for No. 2 Troop, which proceeded as arranged as far as Point 151. There they were engaged by two anti-tank guns which the tanks knocked out before heading back to Estrées la Campagne where they came across several tanks of A Squadron, similarly uncertain of their way. A Tiger tank then appeared and, in the ensuing firefight, three A Squadron and the B Squadron tanks were knocked out.

The British Columbia position on the hilltop had thirty-one Shermans (sixteen tanks in C Squadron, eleven in B Squadron and four in RHQ) and a Stuart recce tank plus nearly two companies of the Algonquin infantry, and its presence was soon revealed to the Germans as it became light. The Canadians were occupying the proposed location of Kampfgruppe Waldmuller after its withdrawal, and as the kampfgruppe was now only able to withdraw to the east, it was in danger of being cut off. The five available Panthers moved to the east and started to engage the Shermans on the hill whilst the two Tigers from the 3rd Company and three from the 2nd Company that had arrived from Grimbosq attacked from the west. Later, the thirteen Tigers from the 1st Company 102nd Schwere SS Battalion were committed to the battle when they arrived. Other tanks such as Jagdpanzers and Panzer IVs may well have joined the fray periodically.

Two Shermans from A Squadron were the last to arrive in the position but these were the only A Squadron tanks to make it, as the remainder were destroyed en route by the thoroughly alarmed and quick-reacting Germans. The vehicles carrying D Company of the Algonquin infantry were also badly shot up and the remnants of the company made their way back to the north of Bretteville le Rabet to find the rest of their regiment.

On the hilltop, Tiger and Panther tanks began to snipe at the Sherman tanks from long range. A pair of Typhoons appeared at about 0800 hours and, after mistakenly attacking the Canadian positions, they spotted the yellow smoke that identified their targets as friendly. The planes then gave valuable support by attacking any observed build-up or concentration of German tanks and infantry. Other Typhoons appeared overhead regularly during the day and their sorties provided a considerable boost to the morale of the isolated men.[52] Armour-piercing fire came in from a wood 1,000yds to the north at about 0800 hours and then from a small wood on higher ground to the south. One troop went to the north to try to deal with the source but the tanks were all knocked out. Four tanks of B Squadron then drove forward to clear the other wood to the south but were promptly brewed up as well by a Tiger tank. The Sherman tanks did not use flashless, smokeless ammunition like the Germans, so when a tank fired it gave away its position. The Germans were able to pick off the Shermans at long range while the Shermans were unable to return any effective armour-piercing fire due to the poor performance of their

75mm main guns. Only the Fireflies and the Typhoon sorties made the German tanks keep their distance.

One by one the remaining Shermans were knocked out as intense German artillery and mortar fire swept the exposed Canadian position. Polish tanks advancing in the afternoon from St Sylvain mistook the Sherman tanks for Germans and opened fire before the Canadians could let off their yellow recognition smoke.

The Germans turned their attention to the Polish tanks for a while which give the Canadians some respite, but this attention was too close for comfort and the Poles withdrew after getting within 300yds of the hilltop. At 1500 hours Worthington ordered the remaining tanks that were operational to make a run for it back to Canadian lines. Eight tanks made it; the remainder left behind began to run out of all types of ammunition. German infantry tried to storm the position repeatedly but were repelled by machine-gun fire from the tanks. By 1900 hours there were no operational tanks left and the remaining tank crewmen (fourteen) and sixty soldiers of the Algonquin companies decided to make a run for it; most eventually managed to make it back to the Polish lines.

The British Columbia Regiment lost 101 ORs killed, wounded or missing, and six officers killed, five wounded and two taken prisoner. A total of forty-four Sherman tanks and two Stuarts were destroyed. The two companies of the Algonquin Regiment, which began the day with 220 men, had only three officers and seventy-nine men fit for duty next day.[53]

There is no doubt that Worthington's regiment committed a grave navigation error. It is difficult to understand exactly what happened, as Worthington proceeded to compound his original mistake. It is possible that Worthington Force, after becoming disoriented in the darkness and confusion whilst under fire, followed an old straight track called the Chemin Haussé, believing it was the Caen–Falaise road.[54] Yet the Caen road is a sealed asphalt road, and if the Chemin Haussé could be mistaken for a smooth road at night it certainly could not be mistaken at daybreak. Worthington was also supposed to move south-westerly from where his intended route crossed the Route Nationale but the route taken was virtually a straight line south-east to Hill 111. Worthington cannot be held solely to blame, as others had a hand in the planning of this operation. It was at Simonds' insistence, and in turn Kitching's, that the division's advance should continue overnight to make up for lost time. The British Columbia Regiment had very little time to prepare or plan for its first action. Worthington went to brigade HQ at 2130 hours for the briefing, which did not finish until 0100 hours, leaving Worthington just an hour to issue orders to his regiment. The Canadians had not trained or practised an advance at night, yet Brigadier Booth ordered the regiment in its very first action to conduct a night advance of some 10 miles behind German lines while likely to be under fire for most of the way.

Enemy small arms and machine-gun fire cannot injure a tank crew but does force them to 'button up' for protection by closing the hatches, so the crew must then use their vision slits and periscopes which give limited vision at the best of the times. It was a tall order for the regiment and, although the Canadians' luck held for Simonds' first night attack, their luck ran out for Worthington Force.

Worthington seems to have overruled his junior officers on a number of occasions, perhaps refusing to admit he had made a mistake or convinced that his navigation was correct. When Major Carson of B Squadron queried the line of advance, he was told to recall his troops that had started out for Hill 195 and order them to join the rest of the regiment on Hill 111.

At 0748 hours the 4th Brigade HQ requested by radio the regiment's position and it was given by Worthington at 0755 hours as Point 195.[55] When Captain Lewis took some half-tracks carrying wounded back to the Canadian lines mid-morning he also carried a message from Worthington, again saying they were on point 195.[56] Radio contact was unfortunately lost with Brigade from about 1000 hours onwards, but Worthington and other officers were still able to contact other Canadian units. At 1100 hours Worthington requested more ammunition from his supply echelon. The accompanying Forward Observation Officers (FOO) with the field artillery regiments also had a good idea where they really were and were in contact with their own regiments which were moving up to lend support. At about noon, one battery fired three rounds of smoke, which was observed 1,800yds to the north, so at least one field regiment knew the Worthington's location. The FOO with the 19th Field Regiment was also apparently in contact with his regiment for most of the day, until 1830 hours, and yet the FOO with the British medium artillery regiment on the hilltop claimed that he could not find a working wireless set.[57] The war diary of the Algonquin Regiment refers to a discussion mid-morning between Worthington and the senior officer of the Algonquins present where the fact that the battle group was in the wrong position was recognised, but the officers hoped that the information given by Lewis would enable a relief force to be organised and therefore they would hold on for as long as possible. In view of the earlier message given by Worthington for Lewis to take back to the Canadian lines, Worthington still seemed to be in state of denial. Meanwhile, the 4th Brigade HQ was now searching for their lost regiment. A light plane was sent up and a patrol sent out from the 12th Manitoba Dragoons to observe Point 195 but both reported no signs of the battle group.

The heavy tank losses of 1st Polish Armoured Division on 8 August meant that it would not take part in any overnight operations while it regrouped and sorted itself out. Their advance on 9 August did not start until 1100 hours and one of the objectives of the 1st Tank Regiment was the capture of Hill 140. The Poles encountered the British Columbia Regiment about 1500 hours and the Canadian liaison officer with the division reported the presence of Canadian tanks; this should have alerted the 4th Brigade that the British Columbia Regiment was on the wrong side of the Caen–Falaise road. Similarly, the Typhoons did not report the regiment's location although the planes repeatedly returned during the day.

When Worthington decided to let the remaining tanks and vehicles make a run for it at about 1500 hours, this was in effect a death sentence for the tank crews and Algonquins left behind. Perhaps unwilling to surrender to the SS in view of rumours of atrocities, or perhaps realising he had committed a grave error, Worthington was determined to fight to the death. No help was on the way as no one knew their correct location. No purpose was served by continuing to fight on in a battle that the Canadian official historian described as 'a tragic mixture of gallantry and ineptitude'.[58] However, the ineptitude was not just Worthington's; Booth and Kitching were also responsible for the events of that day.

The other operation planned for 9 August was for the capture of Bretteville le Rabet by the battle group of Grenadier Guards and this operation was far more successful. Two squadrons advanced at 0330 hours from Gaumesnil, No. 2 Squadron carrying a company of Lake Superior infantry and, after engaging in considerable speculative shooting en route, the forming-up point for the attack was reached at about 0600 hours. One anti-tank gun was destroyed in the dark when its muzzle flash gave away its position. No. 1 Squadron, with the infantry, then supported the attack on Bretteville le Rabet. A troop leader's tank was knocked out by a Panzerschreck as soon as it entered the town but the infantry and tanks worked well together and methodically moved through the streets, clearing enemy positions. By 1500 hours the town was secure. One tank ran out of petrol after having been operating since 0100 hours the previous day and had to be towed back to harbour.[59]

While the tanks of the South Albertas and the men of the Lincoln and Welland Regiment cleared Langannerie and Grainville-Langannerie further south on the Caen–Falaise road, Brigadier Booth had the dual problem of a missing regiment and the apparently untaken objective of Point 195. Despite the Governor General Foot Guards having been in reserve all the previous day, it was not until 1000 hours that Booth instructed the Foot Guards to urgently begin moving up to Gaumesnil. Half an hour later the CO was given his instructions to push onto Point 195 as quickly as possible. Somewhat ominously, a report of forty-five German tanks just east of Potigny was received at 0938 hours. Once again, the time for planning was very short: the H-hour for the attack was 1330 hours. A battle group of the Foot Guards and A Company of the Algonquins, with a troop of anti-tank guns, was put together and did not advance until all the units had arrived at 1430 hours. Driving east of Bretteville le Rabet, the group progressed without incident to Langannerie, where trouble struck. On reaching a hedge 500yds north of Quesnay Wood, tanks from No. 1 Squadron began to be quickly knocked out by a largely unseen enemy. Three tanks were destroyed and the track of the squadron leader's tank was knocked off. German artillery and mortar fire began to land on the exposed open ground and the Algonquin infantry were forced to take cover in the orchards of Grainville-Langannerie. The regiment had come into range of the tanks of Kampfgruppe Wunsche which had occupied Quesnay Wood that morning. From the edge of the woods the Germans had an excellent view down the gentle slope to Langannerie and Estrées la Campagne 1,500yds away. No. 1 Squadron then tried to move around to the west of the woods but came under more fire, losing another two tanks. The infantry were then requested to clear the woods but apparently the Foot Guards tanks were unwilling to provide support; as contact had been lost with the supporting artillery, the infantry commander decided against an attack. The other two squadrons moved to the hedge in support of No. 1 Squadron; a total of fourteen tanks were lost between them before the regiment harboured near the Algonquins. A Firefly managed to knock out one Tiger tank and its gunner was presented with a bottle of whisky by the CO for bagging the regiment's first tank in battle. No. 1 Squadron had also lost twelve tanks, making a total of twenty-six tank casualties in one day.[60] The advance to Hill 195 had been stopped dead.

If the British Columbia Regiment had not made its navigation mistake, its intended route would have taken it close to the Quesnay Wood about dawn and they would have more than likely been exposed to the same fire from Kampfgruppe Wunsche as was the Foot Guards. Even if some tanks of the regiment had survived and made it onto Hill 195, it may never have been relieved in view of the assembled German firepower.

Poles versus 12th SS Divisionbeigleit Company

At 0900 hours, Maczek gave his orders for the coming day's operations. The 3rd Infantry Brigade would clear the Woods around Robertmesnil that had given so much trouble the previous day and then advance on St Sylvain. The armoured drive towards Hill 140 would be continued at 1100 hours by the 1st Tank Regiment and the 24th Uhlans. This time the regiments advanced more cautiously and were able to make slow progress past Estrées la Campagne and Cauvicourt. The five remaining Jagdpanzers of the previous day occupied the high ground and engaged the advancing Polish tanks whenever they could. The 24th Uhlans advanced west of Estrées la Campagne and also came under fire from the German positions in Quesnay Wood, losing fourteen tanks. The 1st Tank Regiment to the east had approached Hill 140, which was a specific regimental objective, before being forced to retire by fierce German resistance that was determined to eliminate Worthington Force on Hill 111. The 1st Polish Armoured Division's operational report for the day makes no reference to the Canadian tanks occupying the division's objective. The 10th Mounted Rifle reconnaissance regiment operated in front of the infantry and tanks around St Sylvain and Cauvicourt. Nos. 1 and 3 squadrons attacked the positions of the 12th SS Panzer Division escort company in the woodland on Point 84 east of Renemesnil and virtually destroyed it, losing only one tank to a Panzerfaust.

Other attempts to advance further south were defeated by concentrated anti-tank fire from the Germans. The elimination of the British Columbia position and the halting of the Polish attacks allowed the remnants of Kampfgruppe Waldmuller to retire to the new German lines around Conde sur Ifs. While this was in progress, a Polish attack on Soignelles was broken up by two Jagdpanzers which destroyed all the tanks except for two. The 1st Company Jagdpanzers claimed to have knocked out twenty-two tanks that day. However, the Poles were able to occupy Soignelles later without a fight when the Germans withdrew.

In the early evening, the Polish advanced past Hills 111 and 140, as far as Rouvres where they clashed with the newly arrived elements of the 85th Division before being forced to withdraw after losing twenty-two tanks.[61] A staggering nineteen tanks were claimed as destroyed by the same two Jagdpanzers that did so much damage the previous day. Not surprisingly, their commanders, Rudolph Roy and Georg Hurdelbrink, and gunners received a medal for their actions. Fritz Eckstein, the Jagdpanzer gunner in Rudolph Roy's vehicle, claimed to have destroyed eight tanks on 8 August and thirteen the next day; Eckstein was subsequently awarded the Iron Cross (First Class).[62]

10 August

Overnight the last element of the 12th SS Panzer Division, Kampfgruppe Olboeter, returned from Vire and was ordered to defend the high ground at Hill 195 west of Potigny. After the road trip and losses in combat, of the original thirteen Panthers there were only four tanks operational, three needing short-term repairs.[63]

Hill 195 had been reported clear by the Manitoba Dragoons searching for the missing regiment the previous day. The Dragoons had not seen any Sherman tanks on the objective or Germans either and Booth now sought to take advantage of this. A company of the Algonquin infantry with a squadron each of armoured cars and tanks were to advance after dark to capture the St Hilaire farm just north of Point 195, also unoccupied. The armoured vehicles did not arrive at the forming-up point and so the infantry advanced unsupported to the farm, fortunately without incident. Two more infantry battalions then followed up and secured Point 195 before dawn, again without a shot being fired. As it grew lighter, the German realised what had happened and mounted a heavy bombardment of the exposed hilltop with artillery and mortars. The Grenadier Guards Regiment was initially ordered to just move up to Point 195 to support the infantry, but these orders were then changed to drive on further south for Point 206 to the south-west of Potigny. Assembling at the railway embankment north of St Hilaire at 0300 hours, the regiment had halted until dawn. The CO's tank lost a track during this march and was immobilised. With the coming of daylight, this tank had just been repaired when it was knocked out by what was believed to be a Tiger tank lurking in an orchard nearby. No. 1 Squadron advanced towards the farm at 0815 hours and a Sherman and a Firefly were immediately knocked out by two German tanks that had moved up to near the farm and by fire from Quesnay Wood. No. 3 Squadron also lost two tanks to anti-tank fire from the west. The rate of advance was too slow for Brigadier Booth who again urged the regiment in a series of messages to 'get cracking' and 'get on' or the regiment would be taken out of the attack. Booth was evidently under pressure from Kitching to reach the objective as soon as possible. To add to the Grenadier Guards' problems, at 1007 hours twenty-four German self-propelled 88mmm guns were reported on the southern slopes of Point 195. Rather than being vehicles, these guns were more than likely the 88mm Flak guns of the 12th SS Panzer Division forming the last line of defence.

In response to the British advance, the 1st Jagdpanzer Company moved from Mazières to Fontaine le Pin to the west of Point 195 while the operational Tigers in the Quesnay Wood also engaged the Grenadier Guards from long range.

By 1130 hours, the regiment was in a cornfield just short of the crest of Point 195 in hull down positions, both No. 1 and No. 3 squadrons having lost two tanks on the climb to the hilltop. The exposed position was receiving armour-piercing fire from three directions, particularly Quesnay Wood, as well as mortar fire, and there was little cover. Any advance by the tanks over the crest of the hill was met by a hail of armour-piercing shot, so the tanks remained stationary whilst an Orders Group was held. Simonds had apparently threatened to 'pull-out' the regiment if it did not get moving.[64] A plan to advance to Point 206 was devised but it was decided that considerable artillery support was required if this was to be success-ful. At 1155 hours another volley of armour-piercing shells then came in from the left flank from German Jagdpanzers and six Stug III assault guns that had worked closer to the Grenadier Guards' tanks by using the hedges for cover. Three German remote-controlled robot tanks were directed at the stationary tanks without any success, as the vehicles were easy targets for the Shermans. By this time, eight tanks had been hit and were burning. The CO reported that a further advance was now impossible and then at 1228 hours that the regiment would be unable to hold its present position without assistance. The Foot Guards were ordered forward as sup-port whilst the Grenadier Guards were ordered to hold the position at all costs, being down to just fifteen tanks. The situation was becoming desperate for the Canadians on Point 195 and, along with additional air support, the twelve remaining tanks of the British Columbia Regiment were ordered forward. The main attack by the Germans was halted by intense artillery fire but the two Jagdpanzers of Hurdelbrink and Roy worked their way around the right flank to engage the Canadian tanks in the rear. Between them another thirteen Shermans were destroyed. The Grenadier Guards requested to be relieved at 1837 hours, but this was not possible. The two tank regiments and the infantry spent an uncomfortable night in their forward positions, virtually surrounded by Germans.

During the afternoon, an attempt to clear Quesnay Wood by two battalions of infantry failed with heavy casualties. The infantry were told that the woods were lightly defended and that the Germans were pulling back, not that the woods were occupied by a formidable force of tanks and anti-tank guns.

The three operational Jagdpanzers of the 2nd Company arrived at Assy from 1500 hours and occupied positions north of Ouilly.

11 August

At 0745 hours Simonds decided to call off Operation Totalize. Having been ordered to capture Falaise by Montgomery, Simonds was already planning his next operation. Operation Totalize petered out after achieving an advance of only 9 miles but in comparison to previous British and Canadian operations this was a considerable distance.

At 1400 hours the Grenadier Guards began to withdraw one troop at a time from their exposed positions on Point 195. An earlier intense German artillery barrage had knocked out four tanks, and as the tanks moved back towards the St Hilaire farm they came under accurate armour-piercing fire from the Jagdpanzers and lost six more tanks.

Losses and Aftermath

In halting Operation Totalize, the 12th SS Panzer Division, from 7–10 August, lost twenty-two Mark IVs, twenty-six Panthers and six Jagdpdpanzers, a total of fifty-four tanks. Fifteen of these Panthers were lost elsewhere, nine at Grimbosq and six at Vire. A total of six Tiger tanks were also destroyed, making sixty tanks written off in the entire battle.[65] For its part, the Canadian First Army lost more than 180 tanks in Operation Totalize.

Both the war diary and the regimental history for the Grenadier Guards state that a total of twenty-one tanks were lost and not recovered for Totalize and not a single German tank was knocked out.[66] This was later revised by the regiment, and only twenty replacements were requested.[67] The Foot Guards lost at least twenty-six tanks damaged or knocked out but did knock out one German tank for which the gunner was appropriately rewarded.[68]

Total Sherman losses, including Fireflies, were reported as being eighty-one for the 4th Canadian Armoured brigade and fifty-six for the 1st Polish Division.[69] A total of sixty-six tanks were lost by the Polish 10th Brigade in its first engagement.[70]

There is a cliché that no battle plan survives first contact with the enemy and Operation Totalize is an example of this. The attack started successfully as a set-piece battle, but then having made the gaps for subsequent exploitation, Simonds took the conservative approach and the advance was halted in preparation for phase two. However, the achievement of phase two objectives by the armoured divisions was then entirely dependent on the USAAF bombing being effective. Unfortunately, not only was it ineffective but it caused Allied casualties and confusion in the rear echelons as well. Moreover, the Germans were given precious hours to regroup, bring up reserves and organise a limited counterattack which stopped the Canadian advance cold. While some parts of Simonds' planning were innovative and daring, key aspects of the German defences were overlooked.

In the British intelligence summary of 1 August, the presence of positions being dug north of Potigny was mentioned.[71] These were used by the 88mm flak guns of the 12th SS Panzer Division and Luftwaffe III Flak Korps to form a third defensive screen, just as they did in Operation Goodwood. However, the importance of the part played by the III Flak Korps is often overstated as there was a constant conflict between Luftwaffe and Heer as to how and where these guns should be employed, as happened during Operation Goodwood. Meyer refers derisively to III Flak Korps as not helping at all in the German defence during Operation Totalize.[72] Lieutenant Phelan of the Grenadier Guards, in his bold attack on 8 August, destroyed several 88mm Flak guns that were pointing skywards. Even if the Luftwaffe guns were not being used in an anti-tank role during Operation Totalize, there were still the twenty-four 88mm Flak guns of the 12th SS Division itself which were a formidable anti-tank force in and around Potigny.

Simonds failed to plan any action on the third defensive line north of Potigny, despite knowing of it. This area was supposed to be bombed in phase two, with fragmentation bombs to target artillery, anti-tank guns and personnel – air targets 10, 11 and 12. The Intelligence summary of 5 August described this area as largely being unoccupied but with some defences such as 'prepared infantry defences and some bays suitable for the reception of artillery or tanks'. At a final conference to confirm the plans for the air support, Air chief Marshal Tedder said that the targets 10–12 were too large and spread out to be able to achieve the concentration of bombs required to do any damage (i.e., the air force did not want to bomb open fields) and Leigh Mallory suggested these target areas could be handled by roving fighter-bombers of 2nd TAF and US 9th AF.[73] Simonds did not alter his plans: he must have believed that with the aerial and artillery support at his disposal the two armoured divisions would smash through the German lines and on to Falaise.

Having waited hours for the second bombing raid, the results were extremely poor. The phase two air targets were along a bombing line from Bretteville sur Laize to St Sylvain and Hautmesnil. Bretteville le Rabet and Quesnay Wood further south were not included. Unfortunately, the phase two bombing was largely ineffectual, failing to destroy the second line of German defences, hitting friendly troops and contributing further to the traffic chaos in the rear of the Allied front line. Some artillery batteries were delayed moving into position by at least 1 hour, and German resistance continued all afternoon; Bretteville sur Laize did not fall until the evening.

When the advance of Grenadier Guards finally got underway at about 1600 hours after the planning lapse of failing to plan for the capture of Gaumesnil, the Germans by then had had ten precious hours to call back their kampfgruppen, plan a counterattack and resurrect new defences along the Route Nationale. When the advance began it was cautious and was hardly an armoured spearhead, being made by one regiment with one squadron in front. Knowing that there were Tiger tanks about, the Grenadier Guards may well have had Tiger phobia. The few tanks and anti-tank guns of Kampfgrupper Waldmuller were able to successfully impede the advance of two armoured divisions. The Grenadier Guards, from their positions north of St Aignan before the second bombardment, managed an advance of only 2 miles the whole afternoon. The Polish, in contrast, displayed no caution but attacked with their tanks concentrated in a traditional cavalry charge and learnt the same lesson as all other Allied armoured formations about the superior firepower of German tanks and the weaknesses of their own armour.

If the planning by Simonds and his staff was flawed, the planning by the 4th Canadian Armoured Brigade was lamentable in Operation Totalize. Brigadier Booth did not hold his first meeting until 1100 hours on 7 August, the day before the attack. Booth had already been to a meeting regarding Operation Totalize with Simonds and other brigade commanders on 3 August. General Kitching had also again briefed his two brigade commanders at 1800 hours on 6 August. A second conference was held by Booth at 1800 hours on 7 August to finalise details and, in the Grenadier Guards, Lieutenant-Colonel Halpenny did not issue his final orders until 2200 hours for a start 2.5 hours later. This compressed time did not allow much time for officers to familarise themselves with maps or for anyone to get much rest. A period of more than 16 hours had been allowed to elapse before Booth briefed his officers on 7 August regarding their first action.

The first day of battle for both armoured divisions was one of heavy tank losses for the Polish and very little progress by the Canadians. Kitching and, in turn, Booth sent increasingly frustrated messages to the Grenadier Guards. In the late afternoon Kitching went forward to see Booth, only to find him completely drunk in his command tank. Inexplicably, Booth remained in command after only a tongue-lashing from Kitching.[74] The process of giving out orders that evening for the coming day by Booth was predictably chaotic and not helped by Kitching meeting very late with his brigade commanders at 2000 hours. Worthington went to Booth's Orders Group at 2130 hours whilst the infantry and tank commanders assembled their forces, having been given some warning of the plans. Booth's meeting did not finish until 0100 hours for an advance supposed to start at 0200 hours that morning. It was not until 2 hours later that the Worthington battle group finally moved out. The regiment had little time to prepare or rest, let alone familiarise themselves with maps, and the outcome was predictably the almost complete destruction of the regiment.

The morning of 9 August brought Booth another headache with the growing suspicion that something had happened to Worthington Force or that they might, at the very least, need reinforcement. At 1029 hours the Foot Guards, as the reserve regiment, were summoned to 4th Armoured Brigade HQ and given orders to advance to Point 195 to assist Worthington Force. Given that the Worthington's orders were to hold Point 195 behind German lines until reinforcements arrived, it is almost unbelievable that no unit was standing by to relieve Worthington. The Foot Guards were going into its first action at 1330 hours with little more than 2.5 hours' notice but still found time for 'a hasty lunch.'[75] The attack got underway an hour late at 1430 hours and was duly stopped at Quesnay Wood with the loss of twenty-six tanks.

No attempt seems to have been made to take into account the heavy opposition being encountered. The German tanks facing the Canadians could have only come from the 12th SS Panzer Division, and yet again the 4th Armoured Division was advancing with just one regiment up front to Point 195. The SS Division was reported as being depleted before Operation Totalize and yet had successfully repelled all attacks so far after inflicting heavy tank losses; Simonds and Kitching can have only believed that the 12th SS Panzer Division was close to collapse and they could break through with only one regiment. The existence of the gun line of 88mm anti-tank guns was again ignored or left to the air forces to deal with. The Grenadier Guards and the Foot Guards in their Sherman tanks advanced straight onto an exposed hill surrounded by some of the most powerful anti-tank guns and tanks that the Germans possessed.

Simonds does not seem to have grasped what had happened after the initial success of phase one and, by neglecting the third line of German defences, he repeated Dempsey's mistake in Operation Goodwood. The exploitation attacks by individual regiments of the 4th Armoured Division were easily seen off by a handful of tanks, self-propelled guns and anti-tank guns with considerable tank losses. The British Cabinet documents recorded the following:

Day 1 result

The 2nd Canadian Corps had advanced more than seven kilometres down the Falaise road onto the main line of enemy defence, nevertheless the momentum of the attack had been lost.

Later:

It is worth considering whether there was not too much armour, on a limited front, and whether the objectives for the armour were not far too limited. Armoured Divisions should think big! [emphasis in original.][76]

Once again the British, having made a breakthrough, failed to exploit the gaps they had expended so much energy and lives in creating. Once more the German lines were able to reform and stop the British attack but only at the cost of more irreplaceable men and equipment. The Germans continued to be amazed that they were again able to repeat this feat previously performed during Operations Goodwood and Bluecoat in Operation Totalize.

Notes

1 WO 229/72/23 Montgomery M516, 4 August 1944, TNA
2 Hastings, M., *Overlord: D-Day and the Battle for Normandy 1944* (London, Michael Joseph, 1984), p.299
3 CAB 44/248 Liberation Campaign North West Europe – The Breakout and the Advance to the Seine, TNA
4 RG24 vol 10992 War diary 2nd Canadian Armoured Brigade August, 1944, LAC
5 Perrun, J., Best-Laid Plans: Guy Simonds and Operation Totalize, 7–10 August 1944, *The Journal of Military History*, vol. 67, No. 1, 2003, pp.137–73
6 *Ibid*, p.143
7 Copp, T., Reassessing Operation Totalize, *Legion Magazine*, Part 27, 1 September 1999
8 Caravaggio, A., A Re-Evaluation of Generalship: Lt-General Guy Simonds and Major-General George Kitching in Normandy 1944, *Canadian Military History*, vol.11, no.4, 2002, p.4
9 RG319 FMS B-425 89th Infantry Division – Part 1 Invasion to 15 August, NARA
10 BAOR, BAOR Study Tour Operation Totalize, BAOR June 1947, p.7
11 Mitcham, S., *Retreat to the Reich – The German Defeat in France 1944* (Mechanicsburg, Stackpole, 2007), p.113
12 BAOR, *opcit*, p.11
13 RG24 vol 10649, First Canadian Army HQ, Enemy appreciation, 7 August 1944, LAC
14 Reid, B., *No Holding Back – Operation Totalize, August 1944* (Mechanicsburg, PA, Stackpole, 2009), p.100
15 WO 171/878 War diary 144th Regiment RAC August 1944, TNA
16 Jolly, Col. A., quoted in Liddell Hart, Capt B.H., *The Tanks – The History of the Royal Tank regiment, Vol 2, 1939–1945* (London, Cassell, 1959), p.385
17 RG24 vol 10992 War diary 2nd CAB report Operation Totalize, August 1944, LAC
18 *Ibid*
19 *Ibid*
20 Reid, *opcit*, p.181
21 RG24 vol 10992 War diary 2nd CAB report Operation Totalize, August 1944, LAC
22 Reid, *opcit*, p.212
23 Szamveber, N., *Waffen SS in Normandy – The Combat History of the SS Panzer Regiment 12* (Solihull, Helion, 2012), p.125
24 Meyer, H., *The 12th SS – The History of the Hitler Youth Panzer Division Volume 2*, Stackpole, Mechnicsburg, PA, 2005, p.42
25 RG24 vol 10992 War diary 2nd CAB, 8 August 1944, LAC
26 CMHQ report #65 Canadian participation in Operations in NW Europe vol III August 1944, DHH, Ottawa, p.29
27 Szamveber, *opcit*, p.126
28 Tout, K., *Tank – 40 Hours of Battle August 1944* (London, Robert Hale, 1985), p.112
29 CMHQ report #65, *opcit*, p.28
30 Stacey, Col. C.P., The *Victory Campaign* (Ottawa, Dept of National Defence, 1960), p.224
31 Zuehlke, M. *Breakout from Juno* (Vancouver, Douglas and McIntyre, 2011), p.292
32 Reid, *opcit*, p.272
33 RG24 vol 14052 War diary 4th CAB, Signals Log, 8 August 1944, LAC
34 Duguid, A.F., *History Canadian Grenadier Guards 1760–1964* (Montreal, Gazette,1965), p.263
35 RG24 vol 14260 War diary 2nd Canadian Grenadier Guards, August 1944, LAC
36 Duguid, *opcit*, p.264
37 RG24 vol 14295 War diary South Alberta Regiment, August 1944, LAC

38 Neville, R.F. and Scott, G.S., *History of the 1st and 2nd Northamptonshire Yeomanry* (Uckfield, Naval and Military, 1946 reprint), pp.36–7

39 *Ibid*, p.38

40 WO 171/859 War diary 1 NY August 1944, TNA

41 Reid, *opcit*, p.285

42 McGilvray, E., *The Black Devils March. A Doomed Odyssey – the 1st Polish Armoured Division 1939–1945* (Solihull, Helion, 2005), p.22

43 Tout, K.A., *A Fine Night for Tanks – The Road to Falaise* (Stroud, Sutton, 1998), p.112

44 Szamveber, *opcit*, p.168

45 RG24 vol 10798 2nd Cdn Corps HQ log, 9 August 1944, LAC

46 RG24 vol 10942 report 1st Polish Armoured Division in Operation Totalize, LAC

47 RG319 FMS C-024 Kraemer, 1st SS Panzer Corps in Normandy, NARA

48 Meyer, *opcit*, p.41

49 Szamveber, *opcit*, p.131

50 Meyer, K., *Grenadiers* (Mechanicsburg, PA, Stackpole, 2005), p.285

51 Reid, *opcit*, p.304

52 RG24 vol 15000 War diary Algonquin Regiment, August 1944, LAC

53 CMHQ report #169 Canadian participation in the operations in NW Europe, August 1944, p.95

54 Bechthold, M., Lost in Normandy – The Odyssey of Worthington Force, August 9 1944, *Canadian Military History*, vol.19, no.2, Spring 2010, p.21

55 RG24 vol 14052 War diary 4th CAB, radio log, 8–11 August 1944, LAC

56 Reid, *opcit*, p.316

57 Bechthold, *opcit*, p.21

58 Stacey, *opcit*, p.228

59 RG24 vol 14260 War diary Canadian Grenadier Guards, August 1944, LAC

60 Duguid, *opcit*, p.104

61 Meyer, *opcit*, p.40

62 Szamveber, *opcit*, p.259

63 Szamveber, *opcit*, p.127

64 Reid, *opcit*, p.342

65 Schneider, W., *Tigers in Normandy* (Mechanicsburg, PA, Stackpole Books, 2011), p.372

66 Duguid, *opcit*, p.268

67 RG24 vol 14260 War diary CGG, August 1944, Appendix 17, LAC

68 Jessup, Major A.R., *Regimental History of Governor General Foot Guards* (Ottawa, Mortimer, 1948), p.104

69 WO 179/2622 War diary BRAC First Canadian Army, August 1944, TNA

70 Maczek, Gen Report of Operations 1st Polish Armoured Division, *Canadian Military History*, vol.15, no.2, Spring 2006, pp.51–70

71 RG24 vol 13645 First Canadian Army Intelligence Summary no. 33 on 1 August 1944, LAC

72 Meyer, K., *opcit*, p.289

73 AIR 37/763 Operation Totalize air support notes, 5 August 1944, PRO

74 Reid, *opcit*, p.301

75 RG24 vol 14255 War diary Governor General Foot Guards August 1944, LAC

76 CAB 44/248, Operation Totalize, August 1944, TNA

12

Operation Tractable

For Montgomery there were at last signs that the stalemate in Normandy was about to be broken. Patton's Third Army was advancing largely unopposed towards the major German supply hub for the Seventh Army at Alençon and the doomed counterattack by the German panzer divisions had been defeated at Mortain, leaving them concentrated on the extreme left flank of the Seventh Army. It was General Bradley who first recognised the possible encirclement of the Germans in Normandy and raised it with Montgomery, who agreed to pursue what would become known as the short hook.[1] In a signal to Brooke on 8 August, Montgomery mentioned for the first time the possibility of encirclement and stated that he was trying 'to get to Falaise and Alençon as the first step in closing the ring behind the enemy'.[2] Only 24 hours earlier, Montgomery had impressed on Crerar of the Canadian First Army that whilst Falaise was the objective of Operation Totalize, the army (especially the Polish Division) was to advance no further eastwards than the River Dives until the situation at Mortain had been resolved. On 8 August Bradley directed Patton to develop the southern pincer by an advance to Alençon and Argentan to meet the advancing Canadians.

Three days later, the situation had become clearer as Patton swung northwards towards Alençon and the German offensive did not resume in any great strength, despite the orders of Hitler to continue the attack after regrouping.[3] Montgomery in his directive of 11 August referred to the developing encirclement and ordered that as a prelude to closing the gap behind the main enemy forces it was 'vital' that the Canadian First Army 'quickly' capture Falaise and Argentan to choke off the German supply lines that ran through the area.[4] Having committed the experienced British armoured divisions to a breakout attempt in Operation Bluecoat, the changing strategic situation offered the opportunity to encircle the German Seventh Army but Montgomery only had the inexperienced Canadian First Army to spearhead the attack to Argentan. In his regular evening signal to Brooke the same day Montgomery outlined the day's progress:

On the Second Army front, there has been very heavy fighting on the fronts of all three Corps and each one has made definite advances. On the front of the Canadian Army, no (repeat no) progress has been made today.[5]

General Crerar and Simonds were only too aware that there had been little progress, as Operation Totalize had come to a halt in front of the hastily regrouped tanks and anti-tank guns of the 12th SS Panzer Division. General Crerar issued orders on 13 August to attack and seize the road net north, east and south of Falaise but not the town itself, as this would be taken by the British XII Corps. Once this was done, the army was to drive south-east to Trun to form the northern pincer while the Americans advancing from the south would form the other pincer to encircle the Germans. Simonds immediately set about planning the next operation to achieve the breakthrough that had been so sought after by the Second British Army since D-Day. Again, he would have the 2nd Canadian Corps and the British I Corps at his disposal.

As the Caen–Falaise road was strongly defended by the Germans in the villages and high ground along its length, Simonds wanted to make more use of the open ground to the east of the Route Nationale. The plan was to attack with the 4th Canadian Armoured Division on the right flank and the 3rd Division on the left. The attack would again be led by the armoured divisions, including the 2nd Canadian Armoured Brigade under command of the 3rd Division. The 1st Polish Armoured Division had been relegated to the role of corps reserve as Simonds was so displeased by their performance that he had considered having the division disbanded.[6] Simonds looked at what had worked in Operation Totalize, chiefly the advance of the armoured columns at night that had broken into the German lines and applied similar thinking to what became known as Operation Tractable (originally Operation Tallulah). This time the operation would start in daylight to avoid the navigational problems of the night advance and the advance would be conducted behind a huge smoke screen to reduce the effectiveness of the waiting German anti-tank guns. To offset the strong likelihood that anti-tank gunfire would quickly cause the columns to break up, the armour would be grouped in solid phalanxes. The tanks would therefore charge on in a dense mass, regardless of the unfortunate victims lost on the outside of the formations to anti-tank guns, relying on sheer weight of numbers to smash through the German lines along the River Laison and reach their objectives. This plan was a throwback to the heavy cavalry charges of the Napoleonic era or the advances of the Roman legions in ranks. Once again, heavy bomber support would be provided in two waves to protect the flanks from counterattack and bomb the defensive positions around Quesnay Wood on which Operation Totalize had foundered.

German Defenders

Following Operation Totalize, the exhausted Germans constructed new anti-tank gun screens and deployed their armour where it could be most effective in the terrain. This task was aided once again by the capture of a complete set of plans for Operation Tractable on 13 August when an armoured car on reconnaissance was knocked out after losing its way and driving into the German lines. Armed with these plans, the Germans scouted for good defensive positions along the route of the intended Canadian advance to Falaise.[7]

The newly arrived 85th Division was holding the right flank of the 1st SS Panzer Corps around Jort whilst the 12th SS Panzer Division was in reserve behind the remnants of the 89th Division on the Caen–Falaise road with the 271st Division further west. As the German armour had withdrawn from around Thury Harcourt during Operation Totalize, this had allowed the Canadian 2nd Division to advance into the vacated areas supported by the Sherbrooke Fusiliers Regiment. This force managed to establish a bridgehead over the River Laize at Clair Tizon on 13 August. Overnight, the Germans moved Kampfgruppe Krause (this time composed of the 3rd Battalion 26th Panzergrenadier Regiment and the division escort company) to eliminate this bridgehead which they were able to achieve next morning.

The 12th SS Panzer Division had suffered heavy losses in the defensive fighting of the last eight weeks. On 11 August, it had only seven Panthers, seventeen Mark IVs and five Jagdpanzers operational, a little more than a British squadron.[8] Three days later the number of operational Panthers had increased to fifteen.[9] The panzergrenadier regiments and the divisional artillery had been reduced to half strength. The two battalions of Tiger tanks remained in the area, deployed in twos or threes. The 101st SS Battalion had eleven Tigers operational on 11 August and the 102nd Battalion had thirteen tanks operational on 13 August.

'Advance Now'

The armoured regiments used the few days after Operation Totalize to receive replacement tanks and crews and repair minor damage. The Field Delivery Squadron delivered in two days thirty-seven Shermans and two Vc tanks to the British Columbia Regiment, two M5s to the South Albertas and nine Shermans and a Stuart to the Grenadier Guards. These replacements completely depleted the delivery squadron and were still not enough to bring the regiments up to full strength again. The 4th Canadian Armoured Division workshop also managed to repair twelve tanks and these would be the only replacements available during the coming operation.[10]

The total strength of 4th Canadian Armoured Division on 13 August was 259 A vehicles.[11] This gave the division a strength of about 75 per cent. The estimated tank states of the regiments were as follows:

- GGFG – thirty-seven Shermans and nine Vcs
- CGG – forty-one Shermans and seven Vcs
- BCR – forty-five Shermans and six Vcs

On 13 August, Crerar and Simonds addressed the commanding officers of the tank regiments in the division and stressed the need for 'pushing the armour to the limits of its endurance' and that 'any thought of the armour requiring infantry protection for harbouring at night or not being able to move at night was to be dismissed immediately'.[12] Simonds was a little more forthright in his own address and accused them all of being rotten and 'yellow and henceforth you will command from your tanks'.[13] This instruction illustrated how little Simonds knew of the tactical handling of armour as it was impossible to command a tank in battle while co-ordinating the actions of three squadrons and supporting arms. General Crerar did not want a repeat of the slow, hesitant advances of Operation Totalize, while Simonds was angry that his original plan had not succeeded and clearly held the armoured regiments responsible for the outcome of Totalize.

Meanwhile, two American infantry divisions had pushed northwards as part of the southern pincer and were just south of Argentan on 13 August but had halted so as not to cross the inter-army boundary between the US and British forces which was Argentan itself. Bradley had reached Argentan as ordered by Montgomery but was unwilling to advance further north to close the gap.

Bradley accepted responsibility for this after the war and stated that his reasons for ordering the halt were two-fold: firstly, he did not want two Allied armies to advance head on into each other, and secondly, he did not want the necks of the Americans occupying the gap being broken by the German forces 'sluicing back'.[14] The first reason is specious, as with radios, liaison officers and agreed recognition procedures there would have been little confusion and the second not much more logical, as there was no general German withdrawal underway at this time, nor did it begin in earnest until 16 August.

Another explanation for the halt, although contradictory, is that incorrect American intelligence reports may have convinced Bradley that the bulk of the German forces had already fled the encirclement.[15] An 18-mile gap still remained between the American and Canadian forces.[16] General Patton, with his customary diplomacy, asked Bradley for permission to keep advancing and push the British back into the sea for another Dunkirk. When Bradley politely refused, Patton kept his army moving by directing two XV Corps' divisions eastwards towards the River Seine as a part of a longer envelopment.

On the morning of 14 August, the armoured regiments of the two Canadian armoured brigades began to form up in the area from Cauvicourt to St Sylvain into Simonds' desired formations. These movements were in full view of the German defenders and were conducted as if they were on a parade ground. Each armoured brigade with two regiments up occupied a box about 800yds long by 120yds wide. Troops of Flail tanks and AVREs carrying fascines were attached to each regiment.

Behind the armoured phalanxes came the infantry carriers, anti-tank guns, field artillery, recovery vehicles and medical half-tracks of the infantry division.

The 4th Canadian Armoured Division was to advance across the River Laison at Rouvres and Mazières and move on to Versainville and the high ridge north-east of Falaise at Point 159.

The 2nd Canadian Armoured Brigade was to advance to the river at Montboint and then the high ground at Point 170 west of Olendon and then the ridge south-west of Olendon at Point 175 (Orme des Gresles) and up to Point 184. The Sherbrooke Fusiliers Regiment continued to be attached to the 2nd Canadian Division which was attacking directly down the Caen–Falaise road towards Soulangy.

It was another sunny day and the wheat fields of the terrain at the start lines had been untouched by the war so far. The tanks gleamed and sparkled in the summer sun and the armoured regiments were each drawn up in four rows of six tanks like a Napoleonic cavalry unit. At 1142 hours, the command was given for the advance as forty-five medium Mitchell and twenty-eight Boston bombers began to bomb targets on the defensive line to the north of the River Laison and in the valley itself around Montboint, Assy and Mazières. The armoured phalanxes started forward in unison, steadily picking up speed to 12 miles an hour. A barrage of smoke shells began to fall in front of the advancing tanks to make a smoke screen behind which they advanced, the barrage lifting 500yds every minute:

> ADVANCE NOW. Then all hell broke loose. The fog of war descended and the confused din of the battle broke with a rumbling roar. The whole earth trembled with the rattle of a thousand speeding vehicles and the shock of gun recoil and discharge. The acrid air throbbed with the hum of engines and the explosion of all manner of screaming missiles. An incomprehensible range of reverberating vibrations struck upon the senses until only the sights of the gun and the red disc of the sun could be seen through the quivering misty veil. For the first two minutes the original formation was maintained, but before the first half mile, a concertina movement developed on account of minor bottlenecks caused by bomb craters, a sunken road, and other irregularities of the terrain. Then all were running blindly forward with pedals to the floor, in mixed groups of Grenadier, Foot Guard and Churchills.[17]

The formation began to break up only a mile from the start line as visibility was lost and tanks began to be knocked out by German mines, 2nd Company Jagdpanzers and anti-tank guns firing at very close range. The leading tanks used their main guns and machine guns to destroy those infantry outposts they could see to shoot at. The smoke screen was not uniform and in some places quickly dispersed, exposing the tanks to the waiting anti-tank guns north of the river as they passed through the German lines. Other tank drivers could see nothing apart from the pale outline of the sun through the clouds of dust and smoke and they steered towards this, causing many of the formations to veer eastwards. The tanks encountered batteries of anti-tank guns and 105mm artillery which were all rapidly destroyed. Two Tiger tanks were knocked out by Fireflies of A Squadron of the 1st Hussars. The armament of Sergeant Gariepy's tank of the Hussars' B Squadron was put out of action, but during the afternoon he collected 342 prisoners and led them to the rear.

When the leading tanks reached the River Laison, they received a shock as the river was found to be impassable. Simonds and his planners had used aerial photographs and a reconnaissance by the 6th Canadian Field Company engineers the previous day to deduce that the river was not an obstacle to tanks.[18] Although only 10ft wide and a few feet deep, the muddy river bottom and steep banks meant that any tank trying to cross got bogged. The charge of the tanks was reduced to an armoured mass milling around at the river's edge and the hedges along its banks, looking for a crossing. Many tanks became bogged in waterside meadows. One bridge was found to be damaged but it was not known that there was a suitable ford nearby.

Prior to Operation Tractable, the limited numbers of operational German tanks were deployed in small groups along the front line. The eight Tiger tanks of the 2nd Company of the 101st SS Battalion were supporting 89th Division positions along the northern ridge of River Laison between Assy and Potigny as a part of Kampfgruppe Prinz with the majority of the Mark IVs.[19] Also in the area were five Jagdpanzer from the 2nd Company in the orchards from Ouilly le Tesson to Rouvres.[20] Three Tigers from the 2nd Company of the 102nd Schwere SS Battalion were supporting the fifteen operational Panthers in the sector of 271st Division around Clair Tizon and Tournebus.[21] Kampfgruppe Olboeter, with two Mark IVs, was supporting the 89th Division.[22]

On the morning of 14 August, all German tanks came under the command of Kampfgruppe Wunsche. The 1st Company Jagdpanzers were in an ambush position in the woods around Epancy and the Mont d'Eraines to repel any breakthrough in that direction. Given the deployment of the Panther company and transfer of artillery from the 85th Division on the night before the attack to Clair Tizon, the Germans may have expected the main effort to come from that direction, despite having the captured Canadian plans.[23]

Three other Tiger tanks of the 2nd Company 101st Battalion were ordered to move in the morning from Assy to Mazières along the northern bank of the River Laison to bolster the defences of the 85th Division. The leading Tiger suddenly met two Shermans coming the other way shortly after the start of the operation. The gunner in the leading Tiger, SS Rottenführer Lau, described the encounter:

After moving for about 20 minutes, Wendorff suddenly called out:
'Man … Two Shermans, Lau – fire!'
Then again:
'Fire! What are you waiting for, fire!'
A few things had to happen before that could be done – feet on the pedals, main gun released, turret traversed to 2 o'clock. And then I saw the Sherman in the optics

of the gunsight. It was only 30 metres away from us on a bend in the road. The first round got him. I had the impression the burst of fire was hitting us right in the fighting compartment. It was my 16th 'kill' with Wendorff since the middle of July 1944.

Wendorff was yelling again: 'Next to it … on the other side of the road … another one!'

I continued to traverse by hand and saw the next one. In the next moment it happened – a truly ear deafening hit, dead silence and the smell of burning. At some point I came back to my senses. It was as if I were paralysed. I was in shock and could scarcely breathe, hear or see. My first movement was upwards, where you could pull yourself up into the commander's cupola by grips above the gunner's seat. While doing that I had to catch my breath. Wendorff was sitting there but he did not move. I did not see any blood soaked clothes, I could not see his face. There must be something wrong with my eyes.

Then I hear the radio operator, Fred Zimmerman. He was screaming, I could barely understand him. No sound came from the driver, Franz Elmer. The loader lay dead in the fighting compartment. Zimmerman said that he was trapped and could not feel his feet. There were flames in the engine compartment and he wanted to put an end to it all with a pistol.

I also felt the burning smoke that took away your breath and biting pain – burns. I heard the shot of Fred Zimmerman's pistol – that also took my breath away. Probably because of the smoke, I started to feel quite calm and peaceful. I slumped forward with my head against the black rubber eyeguard of the optics. This was the end – or so I thought. I was unconscious until the 3rd September when I woke up in the 99th British field hospital. The driver, Franz Elmer, had bailed out and probably got help …[24]

The Tiger was hit by an armour-piercing shell from a Firefly of A Squadron of the 1st Hussars, which had already knocked out two Tigers that morning.[25] The shell did not penetrate the side armour of the hull but flakes of armour flew around the inside of the tank, wounding or killing some of the crew. As the main gun had traversed to the 2 o'clock position, the barrel was over the radio operator's hatch and so he could not get out.[26] The two remaining Tiger tanks and three others from the company then engaged the throng of tanks around Assy and Rouvres, taking a heavy toll. At some point the Tiger tanks crossed the River Laison at a usable crossing to avoid being cut off by the Canadian advance and to take up new defensive positions. After knocking out three Shermans advancing to Rouvres, the 2nd Company Jagdpanzers withdrew with the remnants of the 12th SS Panzer Regiment.[27]

Some Canadian tanks were fortunate in quickly finding a crossing point over the River Laison. In the east, No. 3 Squadron of the Grenadier Guards crossed an intact bridge at Ernes and swept into the village itself, knocking out an 88mm anti-tank gun and destroying artillery guns. The other two squadrons eventually crossed the bridge at Rouvres, which was made passable by three bundles of fascines dropped by the AVRE Churchills. The regiment then regrouped before pushing on a few more miles to near Olendon. However, valuable hours had been lost and again the momentum of the charge had been halted because of an elementary planning mistake.

The partially rebuilt British Columbia Regiment lost fifteen Shermans that day. One tank crossing the river toppled off a fascine at Rouvres and other tanks were lost while climbing the southern slope of the River Laison valley towards the waiting anti-tank guns.

After 2 miles of the advance to the river, the Foot Guards encountered a small wood that turned out to be a German strongpoint protected by mines and containing anti-tank guns and Mark IV tanks. The regiment divided to go around either side of the wood; No. 1 Squadron and RHQ went one way and the remainder of the regiment the other. Accurate armour-piercing fire hit some of their tanks in their thinner sides and six tanks were knocked out or damaged, including that of Colonel Scott, which hit a mine. No. 1 Squadron and RHQ arrived at Rouvres to join the tanks of the Grenadier Guards milling about looking for a crossing. A crossing was found south of Rouvres which No. 1 Squadron and RHQ used before waiting for the reminder of the regiment to arrive. Attempting to use a crossing that had been constructed by the engineers with fascines, No. 3 Squadron lost seven tanks, including one that overturned on the fascines and blocked the crossing. Before they reached the river, two tanks of No. 2 Squadron became bogged in a sunken lane and were destroyed by a pair of Mark IVs.[28] The Foot Guards eventually crossed the river at Mazières and regrouped before fighting their way to high ground near Olendon, advancing to a point just west of Sassy.

In the 2nd Canadian Armoured Brigade, C Squadron of the Fort Garry Horse found a crossing place over the River Laison 1,000yds west of Rouvres at about 1415 hours and attempted to improve it with logs and a bridgelaying AVRE. RHQ eventually found another bridge and by the time the other squadrons were notified and had crossed, it was 1630 hours. Several C Squadron tanks got bogged in this process. The 1st Hussars got one squadron across by means of the bridge in Rouvres itself by 1412 hours.[29] The tanks of the other two Hussars' squadrons had bogged or had strayed eastwards along the riverbanks until they met the units of the 4th Canadian Armoured Division. The subsequent delay whilst the regiments regrouped into forces large enough to continue the advance lasted another 3 hours and it was 1730 hours before the advance resumed.

However, more and more anti-tank guns of every calibre were encountered, often in lines behind hedges, and the advance was slow. Ignoring pockets of infantry the tanks pushed on, their route marked by flaming Shermans. The Fort Garrys got to Point 184 at Orme des Gresles just before dark with some of the infantry, whose advance had been similarly disrupted by the lack of crossing points. The infantry continued to arrive in dribs and drabs during the night.

The second bombing raid came in at 1400 hours and 3,723 tons of bombs were dropped by 417 Lancasters, 352 Halifaxes and forty-two Mosquitoes of RAF Bomber Command. They were used on six targets around Potigny, including

Quesnay Wood and Fontaine le Pin. Unbelievably, again there were misdirected or short bombs on Canadian troops. The bombs fell in the areas of St Aignan de Cramesnil and Hautmesnil and hit the rear echelons of the 4th Canadian Armoured Division, disrupting the artillery, fuel supplies and brigade communications. Unlike the previous two incidents which had been caused by planes of the USAAF, this time the planes were from RAF Bomber Command and forty-four of the seventy-seven planes that bombed short belonged to a Canadian bomber group, No. 6 (RCAF) Bomber Group.[30]

The Canadian First Army on 15 August reported sixty-five killed, 241 wounded and ninety-one men missing. The luckless Polish Armoured Division was again hit along with the rear echelons of the 2nd Canadian Armoured Brigade, causing many casualties. Two aircraft were shot down, one of them possibly by Canadian anti-aircraft gunners, unable to believe the aircraft were not manned by Germans. In another administrative error, Bomber Command, perhaps used to night-time operations, used yellow smoke for target markers which was the same colour as the yellow smoke used for identification by the Allied. It is likely that as the ground troops let off the smoke, this only attracted more bombers to target them.

Brigadier Booth was following the advance with his tactical HQ and protective troop. At about 1500 hours, fire from a German tank hit Booth's tank, killing another officer and mortally wounding Booth. The route taken by Booth had brought the troop too close to Quesnay Wood. Lieutenant-Colonel Scott of the Foot Guards was ordered to take over the brigade, despite having earlier broken his ankle when his tank ran over a mine. Other tactical HQ vehicles were destroyed and all radio contact between the brigade and the regiments was lost. Communications for the next few days remained either poor or non-existent as replacement command vehicles were sought.

After a rapid advance that saw the tanks break through the German lines and reach the river within 30 minutes, it then took another 4 or 5 hours for the river to be crossed and the regiments to regroup before the advance continued. When they eventually harboured for the evening, the harbour furthest south was 2 miles from the River Laison. The regiments of the 4th Canadian Armoured Brigade were in the vicinity of Olendon and the 2nd Canadian Armoured Brigade was on Hill 160 to the east of Soulangy.

In the 2nd Canadian Armoured Brigade, the 1st Hussars had only seven tanks left in A Squadron and four in C Squadron, and the two squadrons had to be amalgamated.[31] The Fort Garry Horse was also forced to do the same after its losses that day.

During the afternoon of 14 August, General Montgomery modified his original orders to General Crerar and gave the Canadian First Army the additional task of capturing Falaise itself, rather than the Second British Army. This was the fifth time that Montgomery had changed the responsibility for Falaise since the campaign began; no doubt Montgomery would see this as being 'flexible' and 'balanced'. Falaise was to be taken as soon as possible, but its capture was not to

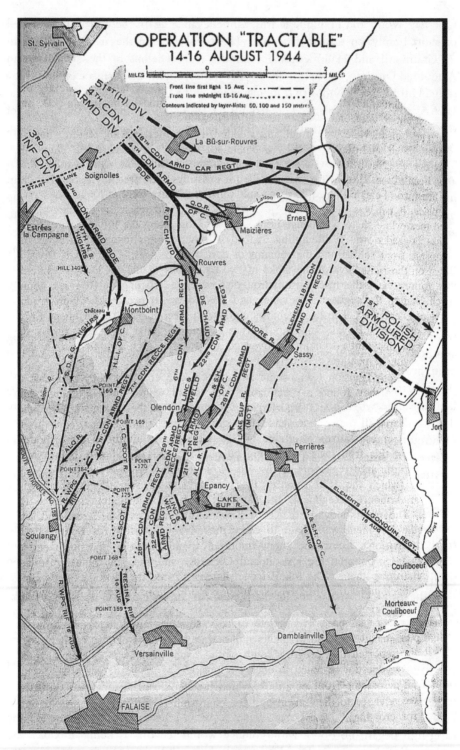

Operation Tractable: the limits of Canadian and Polish advances, 16 August 1944, adapted from the *Victory Campaign*.

interfere with the more important objective of driving south-east to capture Trun and link up with General Patton's forces coming up from the south.

At Clair Tizon, the 2nd Division and the Sherbrooke Fusiliers attacked, opposed by the few Tigers of the 2nd Company of the 102nd Schwere SS Battalion and the fifteen operational Panthers of the amalgamated 2nd and 3rd companies.[32] The Germans were overwhelmed and began to fall back under the weight of Canadian artillery, tanks and infantry. At 1400 hours, the Panther company was ordered to withdraw to Olendon but had to wait for the bombing to finish. The three remaining operational tanks arrived at Olendon at 1900 hours. The other tanks were destroyed by artillery or encircled by Canadian infantry and knocked out. Two tanks that were bogged had to be blown up.

The Tiger company, after losing two Tigers, was forced to retreat towards Soulangy. At 1800 hours the Tigers took part in the fighting on Hill 184 just off the Caen–Falaise road where they 'found our own infantry running from the front line, in battalion strength, chased by twelve Sherman tanks. At last daylight, we quickly set three of them on fire whereupon the infantry began to dig in on the hill.'[33]

15 August

After spending an anxious night in their harbours in forward positions, next morning the 4th Brigade regiments made plans for the continuation of the operation although 'no guidance was received from above' from the acting brigadier, Lieutenant-Colonel Scott.[34] An immediate problem for the regiments was that their supporting echelons had not arrived overnight. The Grenadier Guards A echelon was the first to come up in the morning and the fuel and ammunition was shared amongst the regiments. The three regiments attempted to reach Point 159 near Versainville above Falaise but the village of Epancy proved to be an obstacle all day.

The four remaining Jagdpanzers of the 2nd Company were positioned in the orchards south of Epancy whilst the 1st Company had been sent north-east to Hill 120 near Jort to cover the Jort–Falaise highway. A decision by the Luftwaffe to withdraw the remaining batteries of III Flak Korps to behind Falaise was not well received by the soldiers in the front line.[35] There were two companies (sixteen guns) of the 88mm Flak guns of the 12th SS Panzer Division defending the area around Point 159 and the third company was defending the line near Jort.

Epancy was defended by the grenadiers of the 3rd Company of 1,054th Regiment of the 85th Division, reinforced with a medium artillery battery and a few tanks of the 12th SS.[36] The remaining German armour had withdrawn during the night to the defensive positions previously reconnoitred by Wunsche. Kampfgruppe Kraus moved to defend Soulangy with two Tigers on the night of 14/15 August. Forming a thin defensive screen from Soulangy to Point 159 were the three Panther tanks, a dozen Tiger tanks of the two SS battalions and a few Jagdpanzers to secure a front line 2km long without supporting infantry.[37]

On 15 August, General Crerar instructed Simonds that as soon as Falaise had been taken and handed over to an infantry division, the advance on Trun by the two armoured divisions should get underway as soon as possible.

Not till 1030 hours did the Grenadier Guards begin the day's advance, the intention being to proceed to Point 159 (codenamed Idaho) by going around Epancy to the north and then moving west towards Points 168 and 184. Anti-tank gunfire was encountered from Epancy but with the aid of a smoke screen, the regiment continued to move on. Just west of Epancy, No. 1 Squadron lost a tank to anti-tank fire from the south.[38] The regiment halted in some dead ground to plan a combined attack with the South Albertas and the British Columbia Regiment whose tanks were in the vicinity. The high ground of the proposed route to the objective was very exposed, and a number of tanks were already burning in the area. A plan involving extensive artillery and infantry support was devised. However, there was little artillery support available as the field regiments had not yet crossed the River Laison and the required targets were out of range, so, unsurprisingly, the artillery support did not come down as ordered and the attack was cancelled.[39] An ominous report from 4th Armoured Brigade was received at 1406 hours of ninety German tanks assembling in the Monts d'Eraines just to the south, and this cannot have generated much enthusiasm amongst the Canadians for a further advance.

The British Columbia Regiment rejoined the attack on Epancy and towards Falaise at 1030 hours and experienced considerable German anti-tank fire from the orchards on the ridge to the east of Epancy. C Squadron attempted a left-flanking manoeuvre and after crossing a road and entering a field, lost two tanks brewed up and two damaged. A subsequent right-flanking attack around Epancy was also unsuccessful. The A echelon finally arrived in the afternoon and each tank got three cans of petrol at 1500 hours but any advances to Point 159 were continuously blocked by the German armour. German artillery and mortar fire from Falaise was also making life exceedingly uncomfortable for the Canadians.

The Foot Guards after an earlier start to the morning left their harbour to advance to Falaise. One squadron of tanks was sent to support the Lake Superior motorised battalion to secure Epancy.[40] Petrol and ammunition finally arrived at 1030 hours and was carried forward by ARVs and half-track to the individual squadrons. Several tanks were lost in armoured duels to the east of Epancy but, as with the other regiments, any advance southwards was strongly resisted by the concealed Tigers and Jagdpanzers. When ammunition and petrol ran low, the regiment was forced to leave the attack at 1417 hours and seek replenishment at the forward rally point. This irritated Lieutenant-Colonel Scott and the tanks were given only 20 minutes to refuel, rearm and get cracking towards Point 159.[41] Spurred on by this, the regiment advanced towards the objective, encountering the tanks of the South Alberta Regiment seemingly headed the same way. The Foot Guards then reported (incorrectly) that they had reached Point 159 (Idaho) and this was duly relayed by 4th Brigade HQ at 1713 hours to the other units which could see that the Foot Guards unfortunately were not on the objective but a mile short of it. In the face of heavy, accurate anti-tank fire, the regiment retired, losing another tank. General Kitching was elated at the news of the capture of Point 159 and promptly went off to see Simonds, believing that his division had at last achieved its objective. The subsequent report that this was a mistake was not well received by Simonds. According to Simonds' aide de camp, 'Simonds could not have been more disappointed or exasperated over this new example of faulty communication and misinformation.'[42]

A little earlier, Scott had reported that he could not continue with his broken ankle and another temporary brigade commander would have to be found; Kitching appointed Lieutenant-Colonel Halpenny of the Grenadier Guards as acting commander. Epancy was finally secured at 1850 hours.[43]

The 2nd Canadian Armoured Brigade was not idle this day, either. An attack on Point 168, the next hilltop south, was originally scheduled for 1130 hours with one squadron of Hussars to advance just over a mile with the Canadian Scottish Rifles supported by artillery and tanks of Fort Garry Horse from Point 175 but this did not get underway until 1300 hours. The advance by the infantry and composite squadron of tanks got within a few hundred yards of the objective before a mortar barrage descended on the infantry and heavy anti-tank fire came in from the left flank in the direction of Epancy, temporarily halting the advance. Epancy was supposed to have been cleared but some German tanks and anti-tank guns were still in the woods and orchards to the west and south-west of the village and had a clear line of sight up the hill to the crest.[44] The infantry struggled on alone and secured the hilltop at 1630 hours as the tanks of the Hussars could not expose themselves to the withering anti-tank gunfire. Six more tanks were lost that afternoon but when the squadron returned to the harbour, two Y casualties had been repaired, bringing its strength to seven.

The attack was opposed by two Tiger tanks from the 2nd Company 101st SS Battalion and a company of infantry which were eventually surrounded by the Canadians. The infantry and tanks broke out under heavy artillery fire, with one Tiger towing another. The Tigers claimed twelve Canadian tanks knocked out.

With the failure of the 4th Brigade to achieve its objective in the afternoon, the 2nd Canadian Armoured Brigade was ordered to make a further attack that evening on Point 159. As the last details for the attack were being worked out at about 1800 hours, a report was received that Point 159 was already in the hands of the 4th Brigade and that the mission would just be to clear the ground between the two points which was welcome news to the exhausted crews. The plan of attack was adjusted accordingly. As the tanks were moving to their start line, they met tanks from the two 4th Brigade regiments that were supposed to be on the objective. Then before the 2nd Armoured Brigade tanks even reached the start line, heavy anti-tank gunfire came in from directly ahead and on the left flank, the Fort Garry Horse on the left quickly losing four tanks. German artillery joined in, and the Canadian advance faltered and became confused in the smoke and fading light. Infantry lost touch with tanks and both found their visibility severely reduced by smoke shells fired by the Germans. The infantry were finally ordered to consolidate on the start line whilst the brigade's tanks withdrew for the night, losing other tanks in the process.[45]

Counterattacking from Soulangy, three Tigers of the 2nd Company claimed to have destroyed ten Shermans of the Fort Garry Horse at Point 184.[46] The Tigers, three Panthers and Jagdpanzers fought a successful delaying action all day, breaking back past the Canadian tanks to new positions when surrounded.

Furious at the false report of the capture of Point 159 and the failure of repeated attacks, Kitching ordered the British Columbia Regiment to attack that evening. The new plan was for the regiment to advance at 2100 hours to take Point 159 via Point 168 in the south-west but when the remaining tanks of the regiment (by then nearly all replacement tanks and crews) got to Point 168, the attack was cancelled. Here A and B squadrons were fired on by the same Tigers and anti-tank guns that had previously destroyed the Fort Garry Horse tanks. The recce troop used the superior speed of their Stuart tanks and advanced almost to the objective before they were forced to withdraw.[47]

Aftermath

For the 4th Canadian Armoured Division, 15 August was a day marked by confusion and lack of coordination, as reflected in the records. Nightfall on 15 August saw the division planning to resume operations next day to take the high ground above Falaise while its infantry attacked the town. However, at 1000 hours on 16 August, Simonds issued orders that the 2nd Division would instead clear Falaise and the two armoured divisions would be directed eastward on Trun. The armoured division now began to plan for the capture of a bridge over the River Ante at Damblainville and this marked the end of Operation Tractable, no doubt to the relief of the exhausted tank crews of the two brigades. The 4th Division war diary for 15 August observed:

> … it appeared that the enemy had once again established an anti-tank screen on the southern slopes of the high ground which the Armoured Brigade was unable to penetrate.[48]

During Operation Tractable, the division had advanced about 6 miles but Falaise had not been captured. Simonds later claimed that the failure to take Falaise earlier was due to the Germans finding the Canadian plans before the operation and this was an example of the carelessness of individuals.[49] Simonds could not accept that the operation had failed because of his planning and therefore it had to be the fault of the units involved. 'What looked good to Guy's precise engineering mind looked good on paper but seldom worked out in practice once the human element was added.[50]

A 2nd Canadian Corps report on Operation Tractable did not even mention the difficulties crossing the river and expressed disappointment in the progress of the 4th Canadian Armoured Division.[51] The division was still under interim command and had suffered heavy tank losses.[52]

The Foot Guards were reduced to twenty-three Shermans and three Stuarts.[53] The Grenadier Guards were down to only twenty-three tanks operational.[54] The brigade had made little progress again on 15 August and was beset by poor co-ordination and communication problems. Many of the problems were a result of the death of Brigadier Booth the previous day, the destruction of radio command vehicles and the temporary appointment of Scott before he had to relinquish command to Halpenny. Nevertheless, basic routine functions such as the resupply of the armoured regiments also did not work well. One reason for this is the late start of Operation Tractable designated by Simonds which did not give the armoured regiments the maximum number of daylight hours for operations. The reduced hours combined with the blunder concerning the passage of the River Laison cost the advance precious hours and this meant that the armoured regiments were fighting until darkness fell on 14 August; the supply echelons were then unable to get forward and find their regiments. Once again, the rear areas of the Canadians had been disrupted by the friendly fire of the air forces. This time the second wave of bombers had not been directed at targets along the axis of advance so the attack would not need to be temporarily halted as during Operation Totalize. The bombing, however, was not aimed at any defensive screens south of the River Laison and did not contribute positively to the operation in any way but rather hindered it with the bombing of the rear echelon areas and the disorganisation of the supply echelons of the armoured regiments. The bombing was primarily to eliminate opposition in Quesnay Wood and as such was more designed to finally achieve the objectives of Operation Totalize. Unfortunately, the Germans had already largely withdrawn from Quesnay Wood, so the effort was largely wasted. A report on Operation Tractable by the 2nd Canadian Armoured Brigade was critical of the lack of information available to it regarding terrain, the position of friendly units, i.e. the 4th Armoured Brigade, and the short space of time to plan operations.[55]

The advance of the three regiments of the 4th Brigade was poorly co-ordinated with the regiments trying to advance along the same route as two regiments of the 2nd Canadian Armoured Brigade. To some extent, this was caused by the dominating forested hills of Monts d'Eraines to the south that allowed the Germans to easily defend the line of advance with the few tanks they had available. Yet despite being funnelled into an attack in one direction, the Canadian tanks could not exploit their concentration and break through the German positions. Canadian artillery had also not come forward in any strength to support the armour and the infantry battalions were preoccupied all day with clearing Epancy. This left the Shermans and Stuarts very much on their own and vulnerable to the high-velocity armour-piercing shells of the few Tigers, Panther and Jagdpanzers lurking in the area.

Operation Tractable, in spite of its apparent shortcomings, did however finally cause the thinly stretched German lines to break. This was not appreciated by Simonds and the 4th Canadian Armoured Division remained stationary for 16 August; it took a phone call from Montgomery to Crerar to get the division moving again. Further German casualties were enough to reduce the already depleted fighting abilities of two divisions to almost nothing; the 85th Division was all but annihilated and the 12th SS Panzer Division was reduced to little more than a battle group. The tanks of Kampfgruppe Wunsche had been either destroyed or surrounded, having to fight their way south-eastwards to where the new German lines were supposed to be. The surviving Tigers of the 102nd Schwere SS Battalion reassembled near Vignats, south east of Falaise. This success of Tractable owed more to the material superiority of the Canadians than any tactical genius on the part of Simonds. The armoured tactic to breakthrough in phalanxes was successful, but the armoured regiments lost so many tanks crossing the river and on the other side that their effectiveness the next day was severely impaired, as most regiments were down to half strength or less. Losses in the armoured brigades of men killed or wounded were high.

	Officers		Other ranks	
	Killed	Wounded	Killed	Wounded
BCR	0	2	10	13
GGFG	1	4	13	27
CGG	2	5	17	28
FGH	0	3	11	32
1st Hussars	4	0	5	9
	7	**14**	**56**	**109**

Following the phone call from Montgomery to Crerar, Simonds in turn ordered the 4th Canadian Armoured Division to get moving.[56] However, the division did not advance at all that day and it was not until 0330 hours next morning that a squadron of the South Albertas moved off with the infantry of the Algonquin Regiment to Damblainville.

Meanwhile, a further attack on Point 159 was made at 1400 hours by the tanks of the 1st Hussars and the Regina Rifles in tandem with an earlier thrust by the Sherbrooke Fusiliers and 4th Infantry Brigade of the 2nd Division along the Route Nationale 158 to Falaise, and this made good progress. By 1130 hours, the Sherbrooke Fusiliers tanks and infantry had entered Falaise and by 1900 hours Point 159 had been secured. Two Tiger tanks and some 1st Company Jagdpanzers, which were hull down on the reverse slope of the Point 195 feature, made life very difficult for the Hussars' tanks: two tanks were knocked out and one damaged, and the Jagdpanzers claimed another eight Shermans.[57]

Detailed records for the 4th Canadian Armoured Division have not survived but before the operation, the division reported 259 tanks fit and on 16 August there were only 194 fit, sixty-five tanks having been knocked out or damaged.[58] In the Foot Guards, No. 2 Squadron was reduced to four tanks, and No. 3 Squadron had only one officer left and a similar number of tanks as No. 2 Squadron. The next day, the Foot Guards got five replacement tanks but were forced to operate on a two-squadron basis until the end of the month. The losses in the 2nd Canadian Armoured Brigade were even higher; on 13 August the brigade had a total of 134 Shermans and twenty-seven Fireflies fit in the three regiments, and on 16 August the regiments only had a total of seventy-three fit Shermans (plus fifteen damaged) and twelve Fireflies (plus one damaged).[59] Therefore the brigade had lost more than fifty Shermans and twelve Fireflies. A and C squadrons of the 1st Hussars each had only four tanks operational and the regiment could barely field a complete squadron. Total Canadian losses in Operation Tractable were more than 110 tanks.

Operation Tractable Losses

	Sherman	Vc	M5
GGFG	15	4	
CGG	11	1	
BCR	14	1	
SAR	2		1
1H	19	5	2
FGH	20	4	1
SFR	11	3	4
Total	**92**	**18**	**8**

Following Operation Totalize, the strength of the 12th SS Panzer Division had been severely reduced. At the start of Operation Tractable the division had no more than thirty-five tanks and self-propelled guns – ten Mark IVs, fifteen Panthers and ten Jagdpanzers.[60] At the end of 16 August, the division had lost a further twenty tanks and there were only fifteen tanks of all types operational.[61] At least twelve Panthers and three Jagdpanzers were destroyed.

The SS Tiger battalions also lost several of their tanks. The 101st Battalion lost three Tigers while the 102nd Battalion on 11 August had seven Tigers operational and seven in short term repair, having lost at least two Tigers.[62] In total the Germans had lost only thirty-five tanks compared with the more than 100 lost by the Canadians, but unlike the Allies, there were no replacements for the German tanks. Tiger tanks were harassed continuously from the air and supplies of ammunition and fuel were increasingly difficult to find, resulting in several tanks having to be abandoned or blown up by their own crews. The 12th SS Panzer Division had virtually ceased to exist, and there were no forces to speak of to oppose the advance of the Canadian First Army to Trun. The only problem was that the replacement Allied tanks were back in the ordnance parks at the beachhead and the delivery squadrons had very few tanks in their holdings. The 4th Canadian Armoured Division would have to enter the next phase of operations at less than half strength.

Notes

1 Hastings, M., *Overlord: D-Day and the Battle for Normandy 1944* (London, Michael Joseph, 1984), p.290

2 CAB 44/248 Liberation Campaign NW Europe – the Breakout 16 June–29 Aug 1944, TNA

3 RG319 FMS B-725 von Gersdorff, Seventh Army at Avranches, p.50, NARA

4 WO 229/72/21 Montgomery M518, 11 August 1944, TNA

5 CAB 44/248 opcit

6 Jarymowycz, R., *Tank Tactics from Normandy to Lorraine* (Mechnicsburg, PA, Stackpole, 2009), p.190

7 Meyer, H., *The 12th SS – The History of the Hitler Youth Panzer Division Volume 2* (Stackpole, Mechnicsburg, PA, 2005), p.58

8 Zetterling, N., *Normandy 1944 – German Military Organisation, Combat Power and Effectiveness* (Manitoba, JJ Fedorowicz, 2000), p.361

9 Szamveber, N., *Waffen SS in Normandy – The Combat History of the SS Panzer Regiment 12* (Solihull, Helion, 2012), p.138

10 WO 179/2806 War diary 4th Canadian Armoured Division workshop, August 1944, TNA

11 RG24 vol 13792 War diary 4th Canadian Armoured Division AA and QMG Adrep, 13 August 1944, LAC

12 RG24 vol 13788 War diary 4th Canadian Armoured Division HQ, G branch, August 1944, LAC

13 Graves, D.E., *The South Albertas – A Canadian Regiment at War* (Toronto, Robin Brass Studio, 1998), p.120

14 Bradley, O., *A Soldier's Story* (New York, NY, Holt, 1951), p.373

15 Weigley, R., *Eisenhower's Lieutenants* (London, Sidgwick and Jackson, 1981), p.209

16 Bradley, *opcit*, p.373

17 Duguid, A.F., *History Canadian Grenadier Guards 1760–1964* (Montreal, Gazette, 1965), p.271

18 CMHQ report #65 Canadian participation in Operations in NW Europe, vol.III, August 1944, DHH, Ottawa, p.67

19 Szamveber, *opcit*, p.133

20 Szamveber, *opcit*, p.174

21 Schneider, W., *Tigers In Normandy* (Mechanicsburg, PA, Stackpole, 2011), p.276

22 Anon, Special Interrogation report Kurt Meyer, Canadian Military History, vol.11, No. 4, 2002, pp.59–70

23 RG319 FMS B-846 Schuster, The 85th Infantry Division Feb–Nov 1944, p.19, NARA

24 Schneider, *opcit*, p.255

25 Stark, F.M., *History of the 1st Hussars Regiment 1856–1945* (Ontario, London, 1951), p.92

26 Agte, P., *Michal Wittmann, Volume 2* (Mechanicsburg, PA, Stackpole, 2006), p.204

27 *Ibid*, p.176

28 Jessup, Maj. A.R., *Regimental History of Governor General Foot Guards* (Ottawa, private, 1948), pp.111–14

29 RG24 vol 10992 War diary 2nd Canadian Armoured Brigade signal log, August 1944

30 Stacey, *opcit*, p.243

31 Stark, *opcit*, p.96

32 Szamveber, *opcit*, p.140

33 Fey, W., *Armour Battles of the Waffen SS* (Mechanicsburg, PA, Stackpole, 2003), p.160

34 RG24 vol 14260 War diary Canadian Grenadier Guards, August 1944, LAC

35 Meyer, *opcit*, p.62

36 RG319 FMS B-846, *opcit*

37 Szamveber, *opcit*, p.141

38 RG24 vol 14260 War diary Canadian Grenadier Guards, August 1944, LAC

39 Duguid, *opcit*, p.274

40 CMHQ Report #65, *opcit*

41 RG24 vol 14052 War diary 4th Canadian Armoured Brigade Signal log, 15 August 1944, LAC

42 Roy, R.,*1944: The Canadians in Normandy* (Ottawa, Macmillan, 1984), p.279

43 RG24 vol 14255 War diary Governor General Foot Guards, August 1944

44 RG24 vol 10992 War diary 2nd CAB August 1944, Report operation Tractable, LAC

45 *Ibid*

46 Schneider, *ibid*, p.269

47 RG24 vol 14292 War diary British Columbia Regiment, August 1944

48 RG 24 vol 14052 War diary 4th CAD HQ G Branch, August 1944, LAC

49 Roy, *opcit*, p.279

50 Foster, T., *Meeting of Generals* (Lincoln, Authors Choice Press, 2000), p.368

51 RG24 vol 10673, 2nd Canadian Corps Immediate Report on Tractable, 22 August 1944, LAC

52 Stacey, *opcit*, p.249

53 RG24 vol 14255 War diary Governor General Foot Guards, August 1944, LAC

54 Duguid, *opcit*, p.275

55 *Ibid*

56 Stacey, *opcit*, p.250

57 Szamveber, *opcit*, p.176

58 RG24 vol 13792 AA and QM 4th Canadian Armoured Division reports adreps 13 and 16 August 1944, LAC

59 RG 24 vol 10992 War diary 2nd CAB August 1944, Events log, August 1944, LAC

60 Szamveber, *opcit*, pp.131–8

61 Zetterling, *opcit*, p.361

62 Zetterling, *opcit*, p.181

13

Falaise Gap

Well aware of the developing encirclement, von Kluge and Hausser conferred on 14 August and decided that whatever happened, the shoulders of the remaining gap in the Allied lines must be reinforced to keep the lines of communication open for supplies and for the troops in Normandy to withdraw through when Hitler finally gave the order. However, Hitler remained firmly in control and still retained the idea of a new offensive against the Americans at Alençon. Begrudgingly recognising the strategic situation after a protracted debate, Hitler gave permission for the front line to be shortened but only to free up troops for a future attack. On this basis, von Kluge authorised the 2nd SS Panzer Korps to move to the Argentan area and other non-essential units to start withdrawing out of pocket.[1]

On 15 August von Kluge was on his way to the front in his tactical headquarters convoy when the vehicles were shot up by Allied fighter-bombers which destroyed all the communications equipment. After von Kluge apparently spent a torrid day harassed by aircraft and out of communication with Army Group B, Hitler, suspecting that von Kluge may have been trying to contact Allied leaders, directed von Kluge to report to the Fifth Panzer Army HQ outside the pocket.[2] Later, von Kluge discussed the urgent need for a general withdrawal with Jodl. The next day, Hitler finally sanctioned a general withdrawal to east of the River Orne but had already appointed Field Marshal Model to replace von Kluge. Summoned to see Hitler, the despairing von Kluge wrote a last letter affirming his loyalty to Hitler and committed suicide on the journey back to Germany.

At 1530 hours the same day, Montgomery had telephoned Crerar and told him that a German force containing elements of five panzer divisions was reported to be planning to counter-attack the American pincer of XV Corps stretching north to Argentan. The German divisions identified included the remnants of the 1st SS, 2nd SS, 12th SS, the 2nd and 21st Panzer divisions whilst the 116th was occupying Trun.[3] Montgomery believed that when the Germans discovered that the American advance to the line between Argentan and Carrouges blocked their potential escape route, they would try to force a way out through the gap between Argentan and Falaise. The capture of Trun, in the middle of the gap, was thus vital to the Allies and an hour later Crerar ordered Simonds to start out immediately for Trun.

Montgomery also ordered Bradley to start pushing his forces northwards from Argentan but owing to changes in the command structure of the First and Third US armies, it would be another 36 hours before the Americans could get moving.[4]

The 4th Armored Division had been ordered to accelerate its move and meanwhile, the 3rd Division had pushed south from Point 168 and the 7th Brigade with the tanks of the 1st Hussars had occupied the high ground about Point 159.

Polish Advance

As the reserve division for Operation Tractable, the 1st Polish Armoured Division had been given the task of clearing up the Quesnay Wood, Potigny and Fontaine le Pin on 14 August immediately after the second wave of aircraft. In the short RAF bombings of this wave, one officer and forty-seven men were killed, 103 men wounded and a further fifty-three men missing. Despite this episode, the objectives were all secured by 0900 the next day as the Germans had largely withdrawn, leaving behind only a few stragglers. The initial objectives of Operation Totalize had finally been taken. The Polish 24th Uhlan Regiment reportedly captured two Panthers and a Mark IV in these mopping-up operations.[5]

Next morning, the 1st Polish Armoured Division began its advance towards Falaise, which was to start from the open territory on the left flank of the Canadians in the sector of the German 85th Division, largely destroyed by the previous day's attack. In a well-organised march beginning at 1100 hours, the division moved in two columns across the rear echelons of three Canadian divisions to its start line in the east. From there, the division with the 10th Mounted Rifles in the vanguard advanced rapidly to seize the river crossing at Jort which was defended by a battery of 88mm Flak guns, the 1st Company Jagdpanzers from the 12th SS Panzer Division and a company of Pioneers of the 85th Division supported by artillery. The Cromwells of the 2nd and 3rd Squadrons cleared the woods of German infantry to the north-west of Jort and occupied the high ground on Hills 74 and 76 overlooking the river and town. The 2nd Squadron moved northwards towards Vendeuvres but when the tanks entered the village, the Germans blew up the bridges over the River Dives in front of them. The 1st and 3rd Squadrons then moved south and entered Jort where the bridge was found to be damaged. Two tanks from the 1st Squadron found a way down the marshy banks and managed to cross the river using a ford but the following six tanks got bogged and had to be dragged across using their towing cables.[6] By this time, 1st Squadron had lost three Cromwells to anti-tank fire and two had become immobilised.[7] Once across, the 1st Squadron tanks set about shelling the German positions with high explosive but advanced no further. The infantry of the Dragoons, supported by Canadian artillery, then crossed the river and helped establish the bridgehead over the River

Dives. That evening, Jort itself was cleared and the tanks of the 1st Tank Regiment arrived to relieve the 10th Mounted Rifles which harboured back across the river in Jort. That night, sappers improved the ford by laying steel mesh and prepared to build a Bailey bridge over the river.

During the night, the remnants of the German defenders established a new line from Courcy to Louvagny and were reinforced by 300 men from an artillery regiment but contact was lost with the 12th SS Panzer Division. A kampfgruppe from 21st Panzer Division arrived from Estry to help fight the breakthrough in this area.

Next day, 16 August, the Polish advanced in two battle groups, each led by a tank regiment, southwards along the eastern bank of the River Dives to L'Homme Couleboeuf and Barou to the east. The remaining Panthers that had been attached to the 102nd SS battalion were moved across at 1800 hours to defend Jort.[8]

The 4th Canadian Armoured Division spent the day reorganising, replacing tanks and crews and planning the next phase of the advance, codenamed Operation Smash, despite the orders from Montgomery and Simonds to move to Trun as soon as possible. Welders at the armoured regiments worked frantically at fixing track links and armour plating to their replacement vehicles for extra protection. Meanwhile, the 2nd Division fought its way into Falaise against strong German resistance and the town was finally secured about midnight after having been largely reduced to sandstone rubble by the fighting. The acting 4th Brigade commander, Lieutenant-Colonel Halpenny, held his own Orders Group at 2315 hours that evening, again not leaving much time for any preparations for an advance next day by the time the regiment commanders had briefed their squadron leaders.

17 August

The Polish units advanced steadily for most of the day cross-country, eschewing the road network and meeting little opposition. The 10th Mounted Rifles moved in advance of the other battle groups towards Trun, Hill 159 and Hill 259. The 3rd Squadron captured Hill 159, finding an abandoned fuel dump and a battery of artillery before trying to take Hill 259 above Hordesseau. The regiment reconnoitred towards Trun and saw many German columns moving eastwards along the Falaise-Trun road which they engaged and called down artillery fire on. A patrol further to the east was fired at by two anti-tank guns which were eventually destroyed, losing one Stuart tank being lost and another damaged.

The left-flank battle group of the 2nd Tank Regiment and the 8th Rifle Battalion advanced via Norry en Auge to Hill 259 above Hordesseau. On the right flank the 24th Lancers and 10th Dragoons battle group advanced to Hill 159 west of Moutiers en Auge.

At the same time, the South Albertas Regiment with a company of infantry had moved ahead of the main advance by the division to the outskirts of Damblainville before dawn. The recce troops reported the village clear, and A and

C squadrons moved in, capturing the stone bridge over the River Ante; one tank was knocked out.

The 4th Canadian Armoured Division's main advance began at 0900 hours on 17 August, with B Squadron of the British Columbia Regiment leading from Epancy towards Damblainville with a company of the Lake Superior Regiment. German tanks were reported at 1037 hours by the South Albertas.[9] On the ridge overlooking the River Ante just south of Damblainville, a Tiger tank knocked out one of B Squadron's Shermans that were shelling Angloischeville.[10] Three Tiger tanks and several Jagdpanzers were in position to block any advance south.[11] Heavy artillery and mortar fire then hit the Canadian columns moving into Damblainville and the decision was taken by Simonds to shift the axis of the advance 2 miles further east to the crossing over the River Dives at Morteaux-Couliboeuf which had been 'seized' by a patrol earlier in the day after the 1st Armoured Polish Division had passed through. The Polish advance had opened the way for the Canadian 4th Armoured Division to advance to Trun. The British Columbia Regiment was left in position to pin down the German troops south of Damblainville whilst the Foot Guards took over the advance at 1600 hours, followed by the Grenadier Guards. Morteaux-Couliboeuf and the river were reached without incident but while proceeding south, the CO's tank was hit by an anti-tank gun and burst into flames. The regiment then harboured 1,000yds north-east of Crocy, an advance of just 3 miles from the river crossing. Shortly before dark, another tank, this time a Sherman Vc, was hit by three 75mm armour-piercing shells, probably from one of the Panther tanks that had redeployed the previous day.

In the meantime, the British Columbia Regiment, less B Squadron, was ordered to advance through the Grenadier Guards to Hill 118 just north of Trun but only got as far south as the Foot Guards, harbouring at Moutiers en Auge through which the Polish had passed earlier in the day. The Grenadier Guards were last in line but advanced the furthest south to Louvieres en Auge just over a mile from Trun and without loss, shooting up some soft vehicles of the 1st SS Panzer Division on the way and taking a few prisoners. It was only 12 miles from Falaise to Trun, but the advance was slow and hesitant, as evidenced by the 4th Armoured Brigade's radio signals log.

At 1445 hours, Montgomery issued new orders to Crerar that it was essential that the gap between the Canadian First Army and US Third Army be closed as soon as possible. At 1750 hours, Simonds arrived fresh from a meeting with Montgomery and with new orders to take Chambois that same night. In view of the numbers of German forces assembling around the developing bottleneck, Montgomery realised that an encirclement needed to be completed further to the east at Chambois rather than Trun which was now to be captured by the Canadians and not the Polish. The 2nd Canadian Corps was also to create blocking positions at the heights above Chambois at Coudehard and Mont Ormel.

General Maczek in turn issued his new orders at 1900 hours for the 1st Polish Armoured Division but it was not until 0200 hours that the division, divided into two battle groups, had been refuelled and rearmed. The 2nd Tank Regiment battle group was to move directly to Chambois with the 10th Mounted Rifles and link up with the Americans whilst the 1st Tank Regiment battle group was to occupy the imposing heights at Coudehard and Mont Ormel which commanded the Chambois–Vimoutiers road that ran through the valley below. On 17 August, the US Third Army's V Corps was ordered to advance to Trun to complete the southern pincer of the encirclement.

18 August

The 2nd Tank Regiment battle group started off at 0200 hours for Chambois but took a wrong turn in the darkness, even though they had a French guide, and headed east towards Les Champeaux. Herman Mietek was a tank commander:

After a short, but fierce battle, we captured our objective just as darkness fell and the night sky was illuminated by the fires of the battle. We rounded up the prisoners and had just started to heat canned rations in billy-cans over primus stoves when the order was received to check fuel and ammunition – supplies had failed to arrive and we were low on both. Despite this, we were ordered to move out immediately, without food or rest from the day's battles. Our plan was to get as close as possible to Chambois under cover of darkness. Carrying the 8th Light Infantry on our tanks and vehicles, our orders were 'complete radio silence, no lights; tank column must not be broken and no firing except on order from the CO himself'. Behind enemy lines, in total darkness and with no sleep, this was a nerve-racking journey. The Germans also had a similar plan — to escape under cover of darkness and as we moved down a narrow lane towards a crossroads, our scouts reported a German column approaching from the right. To turn 60 tanks and 20 other vehicles in such a narrow lane would have been courting disaster, we just had to press on. Then, a stroke of the greatest good fortune, the German traffic controller at the crossroads halted the German column and waved us forward. We will never know if he mistook us for a fellow German division or had recognised us and wanted to avoid a disastrous close range encounter. That was not the only luck we had that night! Later we were fired on and took some casualties, but we held our fire and the enemy firing ceased. Again, the Germans must have concluded we were part of a retreating German Division.

As dawn broke on August 18th, we suddenly found ourselves looking upon an unexpected cluster of vehicles of the 2nd SS Panzer Division. All hell broke out; our tanks went into position and the infantrymen spread out and we opened fire with tanks and machine guns. German cars and trucks were on fire, people were running everywhere and the Germans seemed to be in a panic. They started to drop their guns and equipment and surrender. We took about 80 prisoners. Suddenly there was a roar of aircraft and we thought we were being attacked by Messerschmitts, perhaps 20 in all. Then we recognised they were Thunderbolts and we quickly lit flares to alert the pilots, but too late to avert the first attack. As the lead plane came in for the second attack, the pilot saw the signal and with a waggle of his wings quickly climbed, followed by the others. They circled for a while, probably making sure we really were Allied forces, wondering how we could be so far behind enemy lines. The narrow lanes and the dust from the dry roads had protected us and we took only a few casualties from the planes.[12]

The Polish had stumbled into the command post of the 2nd SS Panzer Division preparing to attack back towards the gap (or pocket) to keep it open. Other German tanks were then heard close by. The German infantry regrouped and assaulted the column but this time a platoon of tanks from the 2nd Squadron were able to deploy and met the attack with a 'hurricane of fire' that turned it back. German attacks came in all along the length of the Polish column with the rear being attacked by panzergrenadiers with Panzerfäuste and grenades. The leading elements of the column then managed to break through the roadblocks at Les Champeaux and reached the village of Besson Rousseaux. Here they were forced to halt due to a shortage of fuel as Allied Thunderbolts had destroyed the fuel trucks in the column.

The 3rd Squadron of the 10th Mounted Rifles was directed towards Chambois, hoping to link up with the Americans advancing from the south. The squadron reached Hill 124, a mile north of Chambois, at 1650 hours. Here it proceeded to shell the road through St Lambert and Chambois, causing tremendous destruction and confusion amongst the retreating Germans. A vigorous counterattack was made by German tanks and as Chambois was obviously still held by the Germans, the squadron withdrew to Hill 259, having to fight its way through German columns to get there.

The 2nd Tank Regiment battle group remained in the vicinity of Hill 240, a kilometre to the east of Ecorches, as it was unable to move for a lack of supplies while confusion over their exact position made it impossible for supply trucks to link up with them. As the day progressed, General Maczek became increasingly concerned at the inability to resupply or even locate the battle group and dispatched the 1st Mountain Rifle Battalion to Les Champeaux to try and find the missing regiment, without success.

Like the Polish 10th Mounted Rifles, the South Albertas were also operating well ahead of their division. B Squadron cleared the hamlet of Le Marais la Chapelle, and A Squadron with a company of Lincs and Welland infantry occupied Trun after RAF Typhoons had a field day shooting up German vehicles in and around the town. German trucks and cars continued to stream into Trun where they were promptly taken prisoner, the Germans being under the mistaken impression that Trun was still in their hands.

C Squadron reached the heights to the north of Chambois and spent most of the day in observation:

Could see rising clouds of dust, and on closer examination by field glasses, found that we were witnessing, what we later found out to be the remnants of the German forces in France trying to escape the pocket. The columns were about three or four miles from our location and seemed to consist of every type and kind of vehicle, gun, tank and horse drawn equipment that the German army possessed. The column stretched as far as the eye could see. It was an awe inspiring sight and from a distance appeared to be a crushing force.[13]

At 1800 hours, the fifteen Shermans of C Squadron and a depleted company of fifty-five men of a company of Argylls advanced the 2 miles to St Lambert sur Dives where one tank was promptly knocked out by an anti-tank gun in the village. The squadron was then strafed by two Spitfires and, unable to locate the hidden anti-tank gun, withdrew to a harbour just to the north of St Lambert.

There were many Allied Thunderbolts and Typhoons in the area that day and friendly fire incidents became increasingly common in the fluid battle where both German and Canadian ground forces were on the move. After the episodes during Tractable and Totalize, Canadian troops were very wary at the approach of any aircraft. The South Albertas regimental HQ had just arrived in Louvieres en Auge when it was attacked. The commanding officer, Colonel Wotherspoon, made an angry report afterwards:

> One squadron of Spitfires of the RAF started to engage my headquarters shortly after and two flights had bombed and strafed the headquarters and set fire to a vehicle from another formation a few yards away. Yellow recognition smoke was thrown and vehicles with Allied recognition markings were in the open but with no effect even with the planes diving as low as 200 feet.[14]

As bullets and cannon shells hit the tank and vehicles, the CO ordered his own Crusader AA tanks to open fire on the Spitfires but was forced to countermand this when the regiment padre, realising that something had to be done to stop the attack, grabbed a Union Jack flag normally used for burials from his vehicle and held it down on the ground in the village square as the planes lined up for another pass. The padre displayed the flag during the attack by the first plane but fortunately was not injured and the rest of the flight passed low overhead without firing. Afterwards, the padre was apparently shaking like a leaf but was recommended for the Military Cross.[15]

The Polish were also frequently attacked by Allied aircraft and that night they reported, 'Units and brigade headquarters have been continually bombed by own forces. Half the petrol being sent to 2nd Armoured Regiment was destroyed through bombing just after 1700 hours.' The Polish casualties from such friendly air attacks during the three days of 16–18 August were seventy-two men killed and 191 wounded; the friendly fire casualties of the 2nd Canadian Corps in the same period totalled seventy-seven killed and 209 wounded.[16]

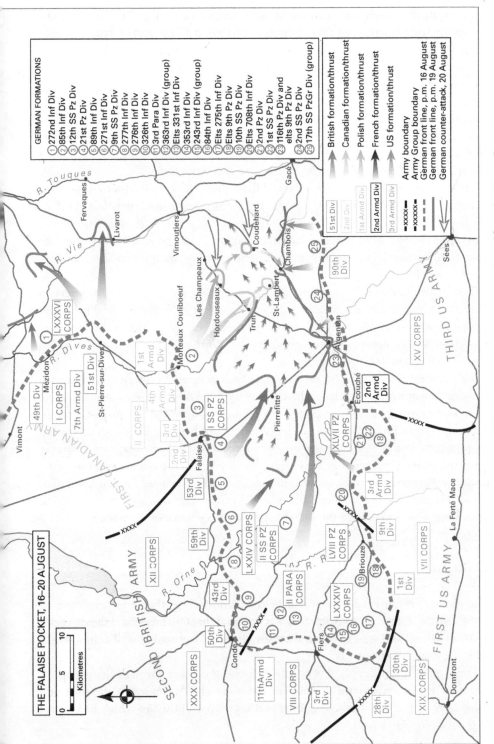

GERMAN FORMATIONS

1. 272nd Inf Div
2. 85th Inf Div
3. 12th SS Pz Div
4. 21st Pz Div
5. 89th Inf Div
6. 271st Inf Div
7. 9th SS Pz Div
8. 277th Inf Div
9. 276th Inf Div
10. 326th Inf Div
11. 3rd Para Div
12. 363rd Inf Div (group)
13. Elts 331st Inf Div
14. 353rd Inf Div
15. 243rd Inf Div (group)
16. 84th Inf Div
17. Elts 275th Inf Div
18. Elts 9th Pz Div
19. 10th SS Pz Div
20. Elts 708th Inf Div
21. 2nd Pz Div
22. 1st SS Pz Div
23. 116th Pz Div and elts 9th Pz Div
24. 2nd SS Pz Div
25. 17th SS PzGr Div (group)

British formation/thrust
Canadian formation/thrust
Polish formation/thrust
French formation/thrust
US formation/thrust

51st Div
2nd Div
1st Armd Div
2nd Armd Div
3rd Armd Div

Army boundary
Army Group boundary
German front line, p.m. 16 August
German front line, p.m. 19 August
German counter-attack, 20 August

THE FALAISE POCKET, 16–20 AUGUST

Kilometres
0   5   10

The closing of the Falaise Gap: movements of Allied units 16–20 August 1944, adapted from the *Victory Campaign*.

The Canadian regiments continued their cautious advance. At first light, the Grenadier Guards advanced a short distance to a point 1 mile east of Trun and proceeded to shell the town and targets to the south while waiting for the infantry to arrive and the USAAF to bomb the town. Eventually, at about noon, the infantry came up and a plan was devised to support them into Trun with seven tanks from B Squadron. The advance did not start until 1423 hours and veered too far south, running into opposition from anti-tank guns that forced the attackers to return to their starting point.[17] A message was then received from the Argyll and Sutherland Highlanders to say that they had already secured Trun.[18] The regiment harboured that night near Point 259 with the Polish 10th Mounted Rifles.

Meanwhile, the Foot Guards advanced from their harbour in Moutiers en Auge to Point 118, just north of Trun, only to find a Polish motorised battalion of infantry already there. The regiment shelled the road below for most of the day before moving in the late afternoon to a harbour in an orchard 2,000yds further east. The operational strength of the regiment that night was only twenty-two Shermans and three Stuarts.[19]

The British Columbia Regiment, after its late night journey to Les Moutiers en Auge, resumed its advance at 0600 hours to Trun but suffered two fatal casualties at about 0900 hours when a Thunderbolt strafed their tanks. One of the casualties was Major Worthington, the brother of Colonel Worthington who had been killed during Operation Totalize.

The general withdrawal by the Germans was now well underway and the retreating Seventh Army was being hammered by the Allied airforces. Any assembly of vehicles during daylight was quickly pounced on by the swarms of aircraft. Although the ordinary German soldier often did not have the luxury of motorised transport, he could at least move cross-country and take advantage of whatever cover the countryside offered. This meant, however, that the withdrawal was being made by thousands of men at walking pace; the problem was not if the Allies could complete the encirclement but when. As time was running out, this created a growing sense of panic in the infantrymen still to get out of the pocket.

19 August

The closure of the Falaise Gap as it became known was the single objective of 2nd Canadian Corps on 19 August. It was essential that Chambois and the exits east to Mont Ormel and west to St Lambert sur Dives be captured as well as linking up with the Americans that day.

During the night, supply trucks finally found their way through the groups of Germans intent on leaving the pocket and were able to replenish the men and equipment of the 2nd Tank Regiment battle group on Hill 240 which had orders to proceed to Coudehard.

All three squadrons of the 10th Mounted Rifles advanced to the south-east towards Chambois, retracing their steps of the previous day. A German column was bumped 1,000yds from Bourdon and the regiment was constantly engaging German forces from then on. In the morning, the tanks occupied Hill 124 to the north of Chambois and opened fire on the traffic on the road below, halting it completely before moving closer to Chambois at Hill 113 in the afternoon. At 1700 hours, the regiment was ordered to support the 10th Dragoons directly into Chambois and a tank was lost while engaging a pair of anti-tank guns on the outskirts of the town. The attack was successful and finally, at 1920 hours, the Canadian First Army was able to report that Chambois was secured and that Polish troops had met soldiers of the US 90th Division in Chambois.[20]

The tanks and infantry of the 1st Tank Regiment battle group climbed a winding, narrow road to Coudehard on the top of the northern Hill 262 and, after a brief firefight against the defenders, which were supported by a few Panther tanks, took up positions where they could shell and call down artillery fire on German convoys moving along the Chambois–Vimoutiers road below between the two hills of Coudehard and Mont Ormel. This caused great destruction amongst the vehicles, tanks and soldiers on foot and the Germans reacted quickly to the sudden appearance of the Polish troops on the hill overlooking them by directing heavy artillery and mortar fire at the hilltop. The Polish Sherman tanks from a ledge near Point 262 had a clear view of the valley below and were able to shoot at German targets with relative impunity as their tanks were difficult for the Germans to hit with armour-piercing fire.

During the afternoon, the 1st Tank Regiment received orders to occupy the southern hill at Mont Ormel with the 9th Rifle Battalion from the 2nd Tank Regiment battle group when it had moved up. Units from this battle group began to arrive in the positions at Coudehard from 1700 hours, but the 9th Rifle Battalion was amongst the last troops to arrive in the evening and so the attack had to be postponed until next day.[21] However, there were now eighty Polish tanks and 1,500 men on the Coudehard position which was effectively cut-off from Allied lines by the groups of Germans trying to leave the pocket to the west. Fuel and ammunition were running low for the tanks, as were medical supplies and food. Finding any shelter or protection for the Polish and German wounded from German artillery was proving difficult. At 1700 hours, a message was received that the Canadians had been stopped 5 miles away and later that evening further bad news arrived to the effect that the Americans had been unable to progress from Chambois. The Coudehard position was organised so that the infantry held the lower positions while the tanks were kept in a wood near the Boisjois manor house in a counterattack role as they were low on fuel. Artillery was the only form of support as Allied air support had been called off because of the increasing number of friendly fire incidents.

German troops manoeuvred all around the Polish positions day and night, either seeking to leave the pocket or attack from the north-east to keep the pocket open. Maintaining supply to the Polish regiments became a major problem due to the numbers of German soldiers moving along the roads and countryside which prevented any supplies from getting through and wounded men from being evacuated. The Polish 10th Dragoons took Hill 137 to the west of Coudehard and then reinforced Chambois itself against the increasingly desperate Germans looking for a way out of the encirclement.

At first light, the South Albertas began moving to reoccupy St Lambert. A Squadron held a line east of St Lambert while RHQ was established on Hill 11, where the regiment had haboured overnight. At 0630 hours C Squadron and the infantry moved cautiously into St Lambert from the north and again a Sherman was immediately knocked out by a German tank. A Mark IV was spotted and a Sherman quickly hit it with an HE round followed by six armour-piercing rounds that caused the tank to catch fire. A second Sherman was then destroyed but the Argyll infantry surprised the crew of a Panther tank in the town centre and after a short fight at close range, a grenade was dropped into the one of the tank's hatches which ended all movement; a PIAT was brought up to finish off the tank. By mid-morning, the village was secure and the twelve remaining tanks deployed to the west to face the expected German attacks.[22]

With the occupation of St Lambert, the Polish at Coudehard and a link-up having been made with the Americans at Chambois, the Falaise Gap was closed in accordance with Montgomery's orders and the German Seventh Army now encircled. Whether there were sufficient forces to ensure the Gap remained closed was another matter.

With the British Second Army advancing from Aunay sur Odon to the west of the River Orne, acting as beaters to drive the remnants of the Seventh Army back on its lines of communication through Argentan and Trun, the Germans retreated in a north-easterly direction over the Falaise ridge to the south of Chambois and Trun towards Vimoutiers. Thousands of soldiers could be seen emerging from the forest covering the ridge, heading straight for St Lambert. Whilst the Canadians held the towns and controlled the roads, the fleeing Germans were able to cross the roads and flee cross-country. The hedgerows and woodlands permitted their movement between the Canadian and Polish positions which were like islands in a human sea. Darkness also offered the Germans protection from observation and subsequent attacks either from the air or by artillery. Word quickly spread of the locations of gaps in the Allied line and that as they neared St Lambert and Chambois, Allied air attacks were no longer taking place.

The South Albertas' A Squadron and a troop of M10s on Hill 117 with RHQ fired at a German convoy moving on the far side of the river valley at long range before another German armoured unit emerged from its camouflaged positions only 2,000yds away. A furious firefight broke out before the German vehicles disappeared from view. The countryside was full of German soldiers trying to infiltrate past the Canadian positions and it was necessary to constantly machine gun nearby hedges and the edges of woods to ensure that no Germans armed with Panzerfäuste got too close to the tanks. St Lambert itself began to be overrun with

German soldiers trying to pass through while others preferred to surrender to the Canadians; the South Albertas took 2,000 prisoners that day alone and this became a logistical problem of its own. Fortunately, the prisoners had no fight left in them and could be loosely guarded by the tanks of RHQ on Hill 117. The AA Crusader tanks, with their 20mm cannon, were also used with devastating effect to try and stem the human tide of field grey.

Despite the battle reaching a climax with the closure of the Gap, the other tank regiments of the 4th Canadian Armoured Division had a curiously quiet day and saw little action, having been ordered to stand down for the next few days.[23] The regiments were ordered to occupy positions along the Trun to Vimoutiers road from Hordessau to Les Champeaux which denied the road to the Germans but left a 2-mile gap between them and the Polish at Coudehard. The British Columbias moved to just north of the highway at Neauphe sur Dives, being shot at by anti-tank guns on the way but arriving without any tank casualties.

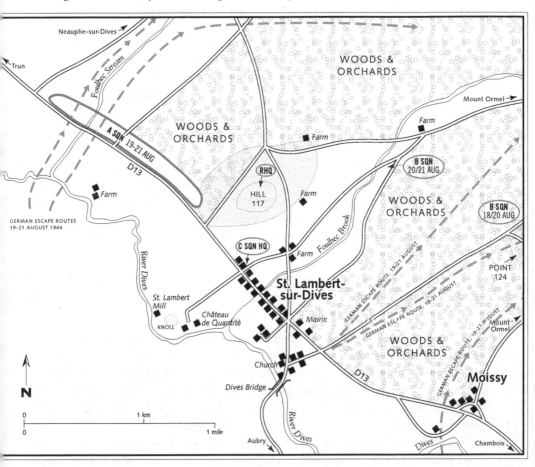

The South Albertas in St Lambert. *(Map by Molly Brass, from Donald E. Graves,* South Albertas: A Canadian Regiment at War)

The Foot Guards were ordered to move to the high ground at Point 258 just north of Ecorches and two patrols were sent out to deal with a German convoy in the area, only to find that Polish troops were already attacking the Germans. The regiment lost two Stuarts to anti-tank guns during the day and claimed to have been attacked by Tiger tanks and infantry.[24] The Grenadier Guard tanks stayed at Point 259 near Hordesseau and as this position was a Polish responsibility, spent the day in reserve, performing necessary maintenance on their operational tanks.[25]

Booth's replacement, Brigadier Moncel, had arrived the previous evening to take command of the 4th Brigade. The brigade's war diary for 19 August reported some uncertainty about the position of the 1st Polish Armoured Division which is curious as the Polish had occupied Coudehard that morning as ordered. That evening at 2130 hours, Moncel held his first Orders Group and immediately cancelled the stand-down; an advance to Vimoutiers was planned in detail, with Moncel declaring that he wanted progress reports by radio from the regiments every 30 minutes. The Foot Guards and one company of motorised infantry were to move to Vimoutiers after first establishing a firm base on Point 261 at Les Champeaux. At the very time when the last elements of the German Seventh Army were planning their breakout, the 4th Canadian Armoured Brigade was preparing to move away from the blocking positions held at Chambois and St Lambert. Only the South Albertas (the reconnaissance regiment) stood between the desperate Germans and their passage out of the encirclement.

Between von Kluge officially ordering the withdrawal on 16 August and 19 August, five panzer divisions and two infantry divisions plus hordes of rear echelon personnel and non-combatants had left the pocket. Whereas the withdrawal had started in an orderly fashion, the constant Allied artillery and aerial attacks had delayed the progress of many units and panic had begun to set in. That day, Hausser and Model realised that the coming night was their only chance to get the rest of the Seventh Army out of the encirclement and a last-ditch breakout operation was planned.

20 August

All the Allied units on the front line spent another restless night: German vehicles could be heard moving along the valley roads below and there were large groups of German infantry moving cross-country that could stumble into the Canadian positions at any time. The remaining German units in the pocket planned their final breakout, which would be assisted by attacks from outside the pocket on the shoulders of the gap to try and keep escape routes open.

There were still seven infantry divisions, one parachute division, the remnants of six panzer divisions plus countless stragglers and rear echelon staff in the Falaise pocket, an estimated maximum of 70,000 men and 150 tanks. The attack from outside the pocket would employ the divisions of the 2nd SS Panzer Korps; the

9th SS Panzer Division would attack on the right and the 2nd SS Das Reich on the left. Some of the Germans trapped were veterans who only moved at night and were content to lie up during the day and let the Canadians target other units on the move. The 2,000 survivors of the 3rd Parachute Division would lead the way via Coudehard whilst the 353rd Division would attack the southern Hill 262 to keep the road between the two hills open. The panzer divisions would follow behind with the remaining infantry further back. The artillery had fired off all its remaining ammunition the previous day and destroyed its guns. The fleeing tanks and armoured vehicles needed bridges over the River Dives capable of carrying their weight and these were located at Trun, Chambois and St Lambert. With the first two towns firmly in Canadian hands, St Lambert provided the only escape route. At Moissy, just to the east of St Lambert, was a ford that the infantry on foot could use.

Early in the morning, the 3rd Squadron of the 1st Tank Regiment with a company of infantry had occupied the wooded hills to the north-west of Coudehard near Hill 239 to keep open the line along which any relief was expected to come. This line was directly in the path of the attacking 2nd SS Panzer Korps and the intended route of the German breakout. The squadron reached the woods at Hill 239 and could see lines of German troops marching towards them from the west and other tanks and troops advancing from the north-east. The targets below to the west were engaged for more than 1 hour which broke up some of the columns, scattering the infantry and setting fire to four self-propelled guns.[26]

From the 2nd SS Panzer Division, the 3rd Battalion of the Der Führer Regiment with infantry in half-tracks supported by two Mark IVs and a Panther tank attacked at 0545 hours either side of the minor road Champosoult to Vigan. One company advanced towards St Leger while a second attacked Boisjois. The Polish commander recognised the importance of the Hill 239 feature and ordered the 2nd Squadron of the 2nd Tank Regiment which was responsible for the defences to the north, to support the 3rd Squadron of the 1st Tank Regiment there. However, the 2nd Squadron was heavily engaged and could not carry out the orders. The Germans also recognised the importance of Hill 239: whoever occupied it effectively controlled Coudehard. The German advance reached the high ground at St Leger and ten Shermans from the 3rd Squadron were spotted on a ledge, lined up side on and firing HE westwards into the valley below:[27]

Our own panzers are still in Champosoult near 3rd Battalion HQ. I jogged back about 2 kilometres to TAC HQ outside which stands a Panther which has just been repaired. I order the platoon commander to bring his vehicle forward where it is urgently needed. This he refuses to do as he is awaiting orders from the Panzer regiment. I insist that he comply with my order but he still refuses and at last I draw my pistol and tell him that I am the one issuing orders here. He agrees. I clamber on the back of the turret and guide him to the point I had left earlier from which we can observe heavy shell fire falling upon nos. 9 and 11 companies. The Obersturmfuhrer and I go forward on foot and I show him the Shermans still standing on Point 262 and firing into the pocket. The young commander issues orders and within a minute three enemy tanks have been knocked out. He continues firing until he has knocked out five Shermans and inflicted damage upon several others.[28]

The other Sherman tanks withdrew from sight and the shelling on troops making their escape below was eased. Two tanks from the 3rd Squadron (2nd Tank Regiment) were knocked out by Mark IV tanks supporting the 3rd Battalion Der Führer.[29] During the fighting in the morning, a convoy of trucks carrying supplies for the Polish was wrecked by German artillery as it approached Coudehard from the north.

Despite the German pressure from the north, at 1000 hours the Poles attacked across the valley as ordered the previous day with two squadrons of the 1st Tank Regiment and two companies of infantry to take Mont Ormel on the southern Hill 262. The progress was slow through the wreckage littering the Chambois-Vimoutiers road and the fierce German defence. With the losses to the 3rd Squadron (1st Tank Regiment) seriously weakening the defenders to the north, the decision was made to abandon the attack southwards and recall the battle group as all forces were needed to defeat the German attacks from the north.

While German troops continued their attack on Coudehard, others fled eastwards as fast as they could under a continuous bombardment from Canadian and Polish artillery. The roads were choked with destroyed vehicles, wrecked guns and the bodies of men and horses. The lack of mobility of German infantry divisions was now coming back to haunt the Germans: what was left of the panzer divisions had been able to move out of pocket during the night, leaving the walking infantry. The 2nd SS Das Reich panzergrenadiers were able to create a thin semi-circular line north of Coudehard to contain any offensive actions from the Polish that could interfere with the withdrawal. The simultaneous attack by a few tanks of the 9th SS Panzer Division on the right flank down the Champeaux to Trun road with the objective of Louvieres only reached the high ground at St Gervais where it was stopped by the tanks of the British Columbia Regiment. The panzergrenadier regiments were too weak to make a decisive attack and could only fight defensively to keep the northern shoulder of the corridor open.

Attempts were made to drop supplies by parachute to the Polish during the day, but these supplies fell behind German lines. Infuriated by the Polish resistance, Hausser ordered the Coudehard position be eliminated and from noon onwards the entire position was subjected to concentrated artillery and mortar fire. A second attack from the north-east by a battalion of infantry supported by some Mark IV tanks was beaten off in the afternoon. At 1700 hours, the perimeter defences to the north were broken by three Mark IVs that penetrated the Polish lines and were able to set free a number of German prisoners before being knocked out by a counterattack from tanks of the 1st Tank Regiment. Another Sherman tank was lost, but 800 more prisoners were taken. The Germans continued their attacks until about 1900 hours when they withdrew to resume their retreat under the cover of darkness. The Poles, exhausted and virtually out of food, fuel, medical supplies and ammunition, were desperately awaiting the arrival of the Canadians.

The harbour of the 10th Mounted Rifles on Hill 113, north of Chambois, had been attacked during the night by a large German reconnaissance force. At dawn, infantry supported by fifteen Panthers and four Mark IVs mounted a strong German attack. The brunt of the fighting fell on the 3rd Squadron which was able to hold its ground with the support of the rest of the regiment. The German infantry pushed so close to the Polish position that when their armour was knocked out and the Polish tanks' machine guns began to take a heavy toll, many of the Germans surrendered rather than risk being killed by continuing to seek a way out of the trap. Entire companies gave themselves up, including commanders of units of the LXXXIV Korps and a panzergrenadier battalion from the 2nd Panzer Division. For the Polish, the ammunition shortage was becoming a major problem, as were the numbers of wounded and prisoners. In the afternoon, when the 10th Mounted Rifles made contact with the 385th Infantry battalion from the US 90th Division at Chambois, the Americans were able to assist with the wounded and took responsibility for the prisoners of war. The regiment then decided to move closer to the relative safety of the American positions on the eastern outskirts of Chambois. In a savage day of combat, the 10th Mounted Rifles had four men killed and four wounded and lost two Cromwell tanks, but they destroyed four Panthers and four Mark IVs as well as several armoured cars and took more than 1,200 prisoners.[30]

The 4th Canadian Armoured Division's plans for an advance to Vimoutiers were cancelled at 0637 hours that morning on the orders of Kitching. Intelligence had been received overnight that a massive German breakout was to be attempted that day, spearheaded by an armoured column. The division was to be used to block the German forces escaping through the high ground to the north-east of Chambois. However, these new orders were not received by the Foot Guards, which set off at 0530 hours from Point 258 towards Vimoutiers with A Squadron and two companies of motorised infantry as previously ordered, getting as far as Camembert with little opposition. The rest of the regiment had moved up to join them before the operation was cancelled and the regiment had to hastily turn around and return to its previous position, Point 258, which was directly in the path of the retreating Germans.

During the night, many Germans had worked their way past the South Alberta tanks which were unable to stem the human tide or do much more than speculative shooting in the darkness. Waves of men led by the 3rd Parachute Division broke on the positions of the South Albertas. As there were only a few infantry with C Squadron to interfere with the German retreat, the bulk of the remaining Germans began to bypass the Canadians, aided by the morning drizzle from low clouds which had also grounded most aircraft. There was no organised attack, just a mass of moving men, which despite heavy losses, began to overwhelm the positions in St Lambert and at RHQ on Hill 117. A Tiger tank entered the main street and began to fire at the infantry positions; a Sherman tried to engage it but was knocked out.[31] A second Sherman was also lost to the Tiger tank which continued on its way northwards. Sherman tank machine guns fired until the barrels grew red hot and had to be changed. A Squadron was ordered to move back and support the RHQ tanks that were being attacked by waves of infantry and as the Germans had no anti-tank weapons with them, a slaughter ensued.

Eventually the Canadians in St Lambert were pushed back from the bridge at the southern end of the village and the Germans madly rushed forward to use it. The ford at Moissy was also captured by the Germans, who now had two clear escape routes at St Lambert and Moissy towards the waiting lines being held by the 2nd SS Panzer Korps north of Coudehard that meant safety.

At 1100 hours, the Polish forces reported that the Germans had broken through at St Lambert and were heading towards Ecorches and Hill 240; the Foot Guards were asked to take action along with the Grenadier Guards.[32] As they were still returning from the aborted mission to Vimoutiers, the Foot Guards were unable to immediately comply with this instruction. The Grenadier Guards had received the orders cancelling the early morning advance to Vimoutiers in view of the impending German breakout and the regiment had been stood down for the day until orders were suddenly received at 1115 hours to go to Point 240 and reopen the Polish lines of communication. No. 3 Squadron moved immediately and was followed later by the other tanks. The Shermans destroyed many soft vehicles as they advanced and thousands of rounds of machine-gun fire were sprayed into every hedgerow which more often than not contained hiding German soldiers. No. 2 Squadron moved to Point 147, closer to Coudehard and ended up spending an anxious night with eight tanks and seventy prisoners and surrounded by fleeing Germans. Heavy rain then began to fall, reducing visibility and providing a welcoming cloak for the German soldiers on their eastward migration.

That evening, Maczek met with Simonds to explain the plight of his forces. Simonds contacted Kitching and requested that the 4th Canadian Armoured Division mount a relief mission. Kitching's response was completely inexcusable:

> To hell with them. They have run out of food and ammunition because of the inefficiency of their organisation; our people have been fighting just as hard but we have managed to keep up our supply system.[33]

Simonds refused to listen and ordered Kitching to act at once. At 1931 hours, the Grenadier Guards were ordered to set out immediately for Point 262 and Coudehard to render all assistance to the cut-off Polish force. The intention was to advance via Point 239 and meet the Poles in the vicinity of Point 147 north-west of Coudehard. Encountering Germans hiding behind nearly every bush and hedge, which they duly shot up with machine guns as they advanced, No. 2 Squadron moved to Point 147.

By this time, it was getting dark early because of the heavy rain and low clouds, and it was hard to identify friend or foe in the conditions. At 2154 hours, after numerous misidentifications, claims of being fired on by friendly troops, messages asking to confirm positions and the sending up of green flares, the Grenadier Guards reported that it was unwise to proceed as it was getting too dark.[34]

After a quiet morning, the British Columbia Regiment had moved to Les Champeaux in anticipation of a rumoured German attack which did not eventuate. The regiment was directly in the path of the attack by the battle group of the 9th SS Panzer Division which only got as far as Les Cosniers, a mile from Les Champeaux. One troop of C Squadron cleared a 'pocket' of Germans just to the east of Les Champeaux, which may have been enough to halt the German advance. That night, at 2200 hours, the regiment moved back to Hill 240, east of Ecorches.

Despite occupying positions directly in the path of the German counterattack by the 2nd and 9th SS Panzer divisions, the Canadian regiments were remarkably inactive. The British Columbia Regiment was directly in the path of the 9th SS at Les Champeaux but saw no major action. The Grenadier Guards were actually stood down for the day whilst the Foot Guards had been sent off to Vimoutiers. Either the German attack did not advance as far as the Canadians positions or the Germans were able to easily infiltrate past them by making skilful use of the terrain to avoid contact with the Canadians. The brunt of the effort of keeping the cork in the bottle fell on the South Alberta Regiment and the besieged Polish units at Coudehard which were more preoccupied with their own survival than attacking to prevent any breakout. Chambois remained a focus of strong fighting that day that involved the 10th Dragoons, the 24th Uhlans and Americans from the 90th Division trying to halt the thousands of Germans flowing past.

21/22 August

Early on 21 August, 1st Squadron of the 10th Mounted Rifles attempted without success to link up with the forces at Coudehard losing two tanks in the process. The close terrain and fog meant that the German units were difficult to intercept and many continued to slip through the loose cordon. The hillside harbour of the Foot Guards at Point 258 was disturbed by a German mobile column proceeding eastwards:

> At 0815 hours, just as the first crews were dismounting to cook breakfast under their tanks, the hill suddenly became alive with machine gun and anti-tank fire. An escaping German column of tanks was attempting to pass the regiment's position. The only route open to the enemy was the narrow road at the bottom of the hill held by the regiment, and for once the crews and their friends the Lake Superior regiment and the anti-tank gunners were able to enjoy the most frequently encountered German

method of doing battle – that of sitting back on a good defensive position and picking off the attackers as they advanced.

The firepower of the defensive formation was very high and a brisk fight developed as all guns opened up. Sgt Mclean's tank destroyed a Mark IV and No. 2 troop of No. 2 Squadron caught a solid company formation of German infantry before it could disperse. The situation was a hopeless one for the enemy and the fighting ceased as suddenly as it had begun.

Casualties were light. The regiment lost one tank and one man L/Cpl Mullins was seriously wounded … the enemy column was completely smashed. Three SP 75mm guns, one Mark IV and more than a dozen transport vehicles of various types were destroyed. Fifty dead littered the fields and hedges as well as many wounded, and many prisoners including several officers were taken. Although SS troops predominated, the prisoners were a motley crowd from several formations. Dirty, bearded and servile, they seemed almost pathetic as they stumbled up the slope to surrender …[35]

The Foot Guards spent the reminder of the day in the same position.

The morning saw renewed German assaults on Coudehard from both along the Chambois–Vimoutiers road and up the western slopes of Hill 262 towards the church. Both attacks were accompanied by heavy artillery and mortar fire and determined German infantry got into several Polish positions where hand-to-hand fighting broke out; some Poles were even taken prisoner.

A second rescue mission was planned for the isolated Polish at Coudehard and a supply column was assembled to follow the leading units tasked with breaking through to the Polish line. The mission was to be led by the British Columbia Regiment but the 4th Armoured Brigade HQ was unable to contact their commander, so at 0633 hours it was delegated to the Grenadier Guards.[36] At 0800 hours, the leading squadron of Grenadier Guards moved off in the pouring rain to Point 239 which was occupied by the tanks of the Foot Guards; the squadron lost three tanks to two concealed German Stug IIIs before even arriving at Point 239. Using a smoke screen, the battle group charged across the valley towards the Polish positions, breaking through a line of German infantry. Captain Ghewy in No. 1 Squadron knocked out a Panther, two Stug IIIs and a Mark IV tank. One more Sherman was lost on the way to Coudehard. Periodically halted by artillery fire and the confused fighting around Point 239, No. 1 Squadron slowly moved towards the Polish positions where fighting could be seen in progress on the northern perimeter. A final halt was made to establish an identification procedure and then at about 1200 hours, firing green flares, the Canadian Shermans met two Polish Stuart tanks which guided the convoy into Coudehard. The Grenadier Guards war diary describes the advance:

Number 1 Squadron led off at 0800 hours in the pouring rain. The road, as were all the roads in the area, was lined and in places practically blocked by destroyed German vehicles of every description. Horses and men lay rotting in every ditch and hedge and the air was rank with the odour of putrification. Most of the destruction must have been caused by the airforce but the Poles had done their share ... No.1 Squadron's co-axes fired almost continuously from leaving Hill 239 until arriving at Point 262 and the results were devastating. All the Germans in the area were either killed or ran away and the line of communication was opened up. The picture at Point 262 was the grimmest the regiment had so far come up against. The Poles had had no supplies for three days; they had several hundred wounded who had not been evacuated, about 700 prisoners of war loosely guarded in a field, the road was blocked with burned out vehicles both our own and the enemy. Unburied dead and parts of them were strewn about by the score. Before the last of the squadrons had arrived Captain Sherwood was on the scene with his A1 echelon, bringing in supplies and for the Poles and evacuating the wounded. To do this job he was equipped with Priests; Captain McDonald the MO pitched in with all his resources to assist in the evacuation of the casualties. The Poles cried with joy when we arrived and from what they said I doubt if they will ever forget this day and the help we gave them.[37]

Five Priests were used to bring in supplies and carry the wounded to the field hospitals, each one making ten trips. Polish losses in the battle at Coudehard were eleven tanks, and 351 men killed, wounded or missing.[38] The German attacks lessened with the Canadian arrival but by then most of the German forces had infiltrated through the bottleneck and were in retreat to the River Seine. The British Columbia Regiment arrived in Coudehard at about 2100 hours and immediately put in an attack on Mont Ormel across the valley which was quickly captured by the tanks driving through the carnage caused by the Poles, Allied artillery and fighter-bombers.

The battle of Normandy was over. The valley floor and road were scenes of terrible destruction with much of the German Seventh Army lying broken on the ground below the Polish Coudehard positions.

As the pursuit of the Germans to the River Seine got underway, there was no celebration by the 4th Canadian Armoured Division. On 21 August, Simonds removed Kitching from the command of the division. The advances of the division had been slow and hesitant compared with those of 1st Polish Armoured Division. The division had played only a minor part in the closing of the gap and seemed disconnected from the reality of what was transpiring in the pocket. As the battle reached a climax, the Grenadier Guards were inactive or in reserve for two days, the Foot Guards had gone on an excursion to Vimoutiers and the British Columbia Regiment saw little action. It could be argued that the mere presence of the armoured regiments forced the retreating Germans to detour around them but this only put more pressure on the Polish at Coudehard. By not linking up sooner with the Polish at Coudehard, gaps were left in the territory held by the Canadians through which the Germans were able to make their escape. Kitching was understandably upset at his dismissal but with the death of Brigadier Booth, Kitching was responsible for the poor performance of the division. However, Simonds and

Montgomery also have to share some of the blame: Montgomery's constantly changing orders put Simonds under pressure and he in turn had to make frequent changes to his own orders for the 2nd Canadian Corps. In his defence, Kitching had requested Brigadier Moncel as Booth's replacement but Simonds inexplicably delayed this appointment for several days, requiring successive commanders of the armoured regiments to temporarily act as brigadier with subsequent reductions in the performance of their own regiments. Scott, from the Foot Guards, took over after Booth's death but as he had a broken ankle he had to be replaced by Halpenny of the Grenadier Guards after 24 hours. Scott was then hospitalised, so both regiments then had temporary commanders for the closure of the Falaise Gap. Major Smith took over the Foot Guards on 15 August but was relieved next day by Major Baker who was then wounded by a sniper on 17 August when he had to bail out of his tank after being hit by an anti-tank gun. Therefore, all three regiments had inexperienced commanding officers, the British Columbia Regiment having lost Colonel Worthington during Operation Totalize. As Operations Totalize and Tractable were the first time in battle for the armoured division, this lack of experience seriously affected its performance with devastating consequences such as befell the British Columbia Regiment during Totalize. Simonds should have recognised this and ensured a rapid replacement for Booth.

Although the armoured regiments controlled the roads and hilltops, the regiments were not very active, largely remaining stationary in their positions without aggressive patrolling. This was a result of the inexperience of the acting regimental commanders and the heavy tank losses already sustained by the regiments, each being reduced to half strength by this time. It is also possible the Canadians were not too keen to tangle with the desperate Germans scurrying through the fields and woodlands, ideal terrain for infantry wanting to hide or ambush tanks.

The CO of the South Albertas had requested several times that more infantry be sent forward to support his tanks and the 9th Brigade from the 3rd Division was ordered forward at noon on 19 August but did not arrive until the evening of 20 August when the crisis had passed. The 3rd Division was waiting to be relieved by the 2nd Division and Simonds seemed to have shown no urgency in organising reinforcements for the South Albertas. It was left to C Squadron and fifty men to hold St Lambert. Had Simonds been more aggressive, then many more German troops would have been cut off. With the standing down of the 4th Brigade regiments on 19 August, Simonds may have believed that most of the Germans had left the pocket already.

It could also be argued that the advances of the Polish Armoured Division were foolhardy and reckless following the division's relegation to the reserves after its inauspicious first day of fighting in Totalize; Kitching certainly thought so and refused to go their aid when isolated. Despite the 2nd Tank Regiment being lost to the battle for a day after taking a wrong turn and so delaying the capture of Chambois by a day, permitting thousands of Germans to escape, it is the Polish forces and the South Albertas that have been deservedly recognised for the part they played in the closure of the Falaise Gap.

But Montgomery and Bradley made other mistakes as the Falaise Gap could have been closed much earlier. When Bradley halted Patton's divisions on 12 August, Argentan was defended by only a few German security detachments and it was the opinion of Hausser that it and Chambois could have been taken on 13 August with little effort.[39]

The Gap was sealed in the end by the efforts of just three divisions: the Polish Armoured Division, the US 90th Division and the South Alberta Regiment from the Canadian 4th Armoured Division. The French 2nd Armoured Division blocked the easternmost part of the Gap south of Mont Ormel but seems to have seen little action, perhaps distracted by the plans being hatched for the liberation of Paris. While Bradley was concerned about any blocking unit being destroyed by the Germans desperate to escape, Simonds was apparently content for a reconnaissance regiment, the South Albertas, to occupy St Lambert as the only blocking unit.

Having missed the opportunity to close the Gap on 13 August, this mistake was then compounded by the reorganisation of US commands. A reinforced Argentan was not captured until 20 August by the 317th Regiment after stiff resistance from the 116th Panzer Division. The distance from Argentan to Chambois was only 10 miles, yet the Americans effectively took a week to get there.

When Montgomery ordered the capture of Trun on 16 August after the fall of Falaise, the inter-army boundary was never changed, so it is difficult to see why it was such an issue on 13 August. On 16 August, Patton created a new provisional corps containing the three divisions that had been holding the line south of Argentan, the 80th and 90th divisions and the French 2nd Armoured Division. Patton put General Gaffey in command and ordered him to attack Trun next day. Bradley chose this moment to restructure the US inter-army boundaries and made Argentan the responsibility of FUSA rather than Patton's Third Army. Bradley also appointed General Gerow, previously of V Corps, to command the new corps, much to Gaffey's disappointment. It is almost as though Bradley was determined to delay any operation to close the Gap in the light of his views that this should have been done by the British, so the opportunity was lost. Gerow promptly discarded Gaffey's plans to make his own and the attack northwards was postponed until 18 August. This meant the American advance northwards was delayed for more than four days, during which time the Germans had ample time to bolster their defences of the southern shoulder and for many units to safely withdraw from the threatened encirclement.[40] After two days' fierce fighting, the Americans and Polish were able to finally link up at Chambois on 20 August. But the Allies held the towns only, the countryside between them continued to be an avenue of escape for the Germans.

Neither did the British advance very quickly: after reaching Necy, which is 4 miles from St Lambert, on 18 August, the British took 48 hours to make contact with the Canadians at Trun.[41] The consequences of the Allied tardiness in closing the Gap was that the more mobile panzer divisions got out of the encircle-ment, as did many infantrymen on foot. However, as many as 40,000 soldiers did not get through, as this statement from an SS officer captured on 21 August at St Lambert, reveals:

> At 2 o'clock, we received a report that the Gap had been forced. We were to move accordingly and drove off in three cars. We drove two or three kilometres and then came onto roads which were completely blocked. There were four or five columns which had run into each other with dead and wounded in between. We put our vehicles into one column and got stuck in it. Then we were on foot from 3 o'clock in the morning until six o'clock. Eventually we arrived forward at the place where the Gap was supposed to be and met about two or three hundred men. They were composed of a parachute battalion to which SS and army and GAF and Navy person-nel had attached themselves. The tanks joined us, a Mark IV and a Panther; they were put in the vanguard with scouts aboard and a platoon behind then the troops. Suddenly there was heavy firing into the sunken road. At first it sounded like fire from anti-tank guns and mortars and machine guns interspersed with rifle fire. The tanks immediately reversed and ran over some of our men whereupon all the infantry streamed back. I took up a position at the rear to hold up the retreat and shot the first one who came along. An RSM stood beside me and brought them to a halt. Then the tank drove up and I ordered it to drive forward again. Soon the tank was hit and set on fire. We lay down flat and then some heavy firing came along the sunken road from ahead. We had a great many dead and wounded. We lay for ten minutes and then the fire eased off a bit. I heard the sound of tanks so I made two men came forward with Faustpatrone which we still had with us. It slowly became light and then we saw Americans in the opposite hedge. We fired at them with machine guns and automatic weapons. Then the enemy started firing again. There was suddenly heavy cannon and machine gun fire out of the whole hedge. Then someone at the rear started to wave a white flag. We shot him at a distance of 100 metres. After a second attempt with a white flag had also proved unsuccessful, we heard the noise of an enemy tank ahead again. In the meantime we had brought up our second tank, the Panther. This was given orders to take up a position behind the shot-up Mark IV and shoot up the advancing tanks with its gun. The Panther made a mistake in not taking up a position directly behind the Mark IV and drove past it. It was hit and burst into flames. Later another white flag appeared and we fired at the troops surrendering. We were in the process of trying to approach the enemy tank with the Faustpatrone when American troops captured us.[42]

Tank Losses

Polish tank losses, despite the intensity of the fighting at Coudehard, were not as heavy as in Operation Totalize. Eleven tanks were lost on Hill 262 and nine

Shermans and five Fireflies had been destroyed over the preceding week.[43] Since 15 August, the 10th Mounted Rifles had lost eleven Cromwells and two M5 tanks, and seven others had been damaged.

The Canadian losses are difficult to determine exactly as no records exist for the period. A comparison of regiment strengths at the conclusion of Operation Tractable with the estimated strengths on 22 August gives the following losses:

- BCR one Sherman and one M5
- GGFG two Shermans and two M5
- CGG three Shermans
- SAR six Shermans and one M5 knocked out

Four Vcs in the armoured regiments were damaged, as were another twelve Shermans, mostly from South Albertas. There is anecdoctal evidence that the South Albertas lost at least twenty tanks. On 21 August, the engineers of the Canadian First Army had 157 tanks awaiting recovery or repair after two weeks of fighting, ninety-two of them from the three armoured brigades in the 2nd Canadian Corps. Other tanks knocked out on the battlefield had not yet been discovered by reconnaissance or reported.[44]

Notes

1 RG319 FMS B-727 von Gersdorff, Battle in Northern France ch VI, Falaise, p.25, NARA

2 Cave Brown, A., *A Bodyguard of Lies* (London, W.H. Allen, 1976), p.792

3 CAB 44/248 Crerar notes 16 August – Liberation Campaign NW Europe – the Breakout 16 June–29 Aug 1944, TNA

4 Stacey, Col. C.P., *The Victory Campaign* (Ottawa, Dept of National Defence, 1960), pp.249–51

5 Maczek, Gen. Report of Operations 1st Polish Armoured Division, Canadian Military History, vol.15, No.2, Spring 2006, pp.51–70.

6 McGilvray, E., *The Black Devils March. A Doomed Odyssey – the 1st Polish Armoured Division 1939–1945* (Solihull, Helion, 2005), p.30

7 McGilvray, *opcit*, p.29

8 Szamveber, N., *Waffen SS in Normandy – The Combat History of the SS Panzer Regiment 12* (Solihull, Helion, 2012), p.142

9 RG24 vol 14052 War diary 4th Canadian Armoured Brigade signal log, August 1944, LAC

10 RG24 vol 14292 War diary British Columbia Regiment, August 1944, LAC

11 Graves, D.E., *South Albertas – A Canadian Regiment at War* (Toronto, Robin Brass Studio, 1998), p.134

12 Mietek, H., BBC History website http://www.bbc.co.uk/history/ww2peopleswar/stories/46/a2879346.shtml accessed 13 October 2011

13 Graves, *opcit*, p.136

14 Graves, *opcit*, p.136

15 *Ibid*

16 Stacey, *opcit*, p.257

17 RG24 vol 14052 War diary 4th Canadian Armoured Brigade, signals log, August 1944, LAC

18 RG24 vol 14260 War diary Canadian Grenadier Guards, August 1944, LAC

19 RG24 vol 14255 War diary Governor General Foot Guards, August 1944, LAC

20 CAB 44/248 *opcit*, TNA

21 McGilvray, *opcit*, p.47

22 Graves, *opcit*, p.142

23 RG 24 vol 14260 War diary CGG, August 1944 Appendix 23, LAC

24 RG24 vol 14052 War diary 4th CAB HQ, August 1944, LAC

25 RG24 vol 14260 War diary CGG August 1944, LAC

26 McGilvray, *opcit*, p.50

27 Lucas, J., *The Military Role of the 2nd SS Division* (London, Arms and Armour, 1994), p.147

28 *Ibid*, p.147

29 *Ibid*, p.150

30 *Ibid*, p.144

31 *Ibid*, p.155

32 RG24 vol 14052 War diary 4th CAB signals log, 20 August 1944, LAC

33 Kitching, G., *Mud and Green Fields* (Langley, BC, Battleline, 1986), p.204

34 RG24 vol 14052 War diary 4th CAB signals log, August 21 1944, LAC

35 Jessup, Major A.R., *Regimental History of Governor General Foot Guards* (Ottawa, Mortimer, 1948), p.125

36 RG24 14052 War diary 4th CAB signals log, 21 August 1944, LAC

37 RG24 14260 War diary CGG, August 1944

38 *Ibid*, p.54

39 RG319 FMS B-726, von Gersdorff, Fifth Panzer Army, 25 July to 25 August 1944, p.21, NARA

40 Stacey, *opcit*, p.251

41 Graves, *opcit*, p.175

42 WO 205/1164, Report 15, *opcit*

43 RG24 vol 10736, Canadian First Army Tank States, 26 August 1944, LAC

44 WO 179/2636 War diary DDME branch, Canadian First Army, August 1944, Appendix 2, TNA

14

Summary

After ten weeks of hard fighting in Normandy and the closure of the Falaise Gap by the Americans, French and Canadians, the Germans were in full retreat and the Normandy campaign was over.

Von Kluge had ordered a general withdrawal over the River Orne on 16 August, and following his dismissal and replacement by Field Marshal Model on 18 August, Hitler sanctioned a further withdrawal to behind the River Dives and then the River Tocques on 21 August. However, the retreat to the River Seine by the German Fifth Panzer and Seventh armies was orderly, although beset by severe fuel and ammunition shortages and harassed by Allied ground attack aircraft during the day. Plans were hastily drawn up for defending a line at the River Seine. The Seventh Army was placed under the command of Dietrich and the SS were then commanding all the German forces in Normandy. That day, Dietrich was also given permission to withdraw across the Seine if necessary.[1]

The Allied armies did not pursue the Germans aggressively, much to the surprise of the Germans, who were concerned that a concerted attack northwards by the Americans to seize all the River Seine crossings south-east of Rouen would have cut-off the escape of the entire army group.[2] Most of the crossings were in the zone of the Second Army and there were again concerns about American troops entering the British zone. An attack in this direction did not begin until 21 August with the US XV and XIX Corps driving towards Conches. On 22 August, the 2nd Canadian Corps was also instructed by Montgomery to advance to the Seine. Four days later, the American advance had reached Elboeuf and any plans for an organised German withdrawal were abandoned; all units still west of the river were ordered to retreat as quickly as possible. The Germans urgently required time to reorganise their forces and the line of the River Somme further east was the only realistic future defensive position that Model could hope to use to stop the Allied advance, provided it was not too rapid:

Despite some disorder and panic, the Germans managed to get a surprisingly large number of troops to the east bank of the Seine, mostly on 26 and 27 August. To the Germans, it seemed that the British and Canadians did not push as hard as they might have. Neither did the Allied air forces seem as active as usual during the critical days of the withdrawal. The Seine ferries that remained in service operated even during daylight hours.[3]

An opportunity to roll up the Seventh Army was missed. What was left of each German division that got over the river was reinforced and re-equipped where possible to form a single regiment but a lack of communications equipment made command and control difficult.[4]

The Germans had suffered a major defeat. Losses in vehicles, artillery and equipment were particularly severe and German industry could not replace this valuable material easily because of the effects of Allied strategic bombing. The German forces lost more than 458 tanks after the fall of Falaise in the last two weeks of August 1944.

Whilst the numbers of men and tanks that escaped from the pocket or were lost in fighting is matter of some post-war debate, a German Army Group D count of the survivors on 22 August was as follows:

- 12th SS Panzer – ten tanks, 300 men, no artillery
- 1st SS – no tanks, few men, no artillery
- 10th SS – no tanks, four weak bns, no artillery
- 9th SS – twenty to twenty-five tanks, 460 men, twenty guns
- 21st Panzer – ten tanks, four weak battalions, unknown artillery
- 2nd SS Panzer – fifteen tanks, 450 men, six guns
- 9th Panzer – not reported
- 2nd Panzer – no tanks, one battalion, no artillery
- 116th Panzer – twelve tanks, one battalion, two batteries[5]

Only about seventy German tanks or assault guns were operational after the fighting in the Falaise Gap and many had to be abandoned because of shortages of fuel.

As the mobile panzer divisions were able to escape the pocket and several had attacked back in to it to keep it open, it is likely the figures above represent combat troops rather than total divisions. It is claimed, for example, that the 12th SS Panzer Division still had 12,500 men after the Falaise Gap.[6] The administrative and support troops of many divisions certainly moved out of the pocket ahead of the combat troops once von Kluge approved the general withdrawal on 16 August. More than 50,000 prisoners of war were taken by the Allies and an estimated 200,000 men killed, bringing total estimated German losses to 400,000 men in Normandy.[7]

With the Normandy campaign won, Montgomery expected the war to be over by Christmas.

German Losses

The British No. 2 Operational Research unit travelled extensively around the pocket and the Falaise Gap after the battle and counted the destroyed vehicles as well as examining selected samples in detail.

A total of 1,223 German tanks and self-propelled guns were found abandoned, destroyed or knocked out in three areas called the 'Pocket', the 'Shambles' and the 'Chase' (to the River Seine). In the 'Pocket' from Falaise and Argentan to Barenton (excluding the Mortain battlefield) through which the Seventh Army retreated, eighty-one of a sample of 121 tanks and assault guns had been abandoned or destroyed by their crews. In the area known as the 'Shambles', which was the mouth of the pocket from Argentan to Trun and Chambois, a further 187 tanks were found. A detailed examination of eighty-two of these vehicles found that seventy-one of the eighty-two were destroyed or abandoned by their crews. In the 'Chase' area to the Seine, another 150 tanks and assault guns were found of which eighty-one of a sample of ninety-eight had been abandoned or destroyed by their crews.[8]

The Germans committed to Normandy a total of 2,248 tanks and assault guns, and the total of 1,233 armoured fighting vehicles found in the retreat represents more than half of the German tank forces that were deployed in Normandy.[9] This underlines the outstanding success of Operation Cobra, the encirclement to close the Falaise Gap and Allied air superiority which constricted German supply lines and caused shortages of fuel and ammunition. From the detailed samples studied in the OR surveys, more than 75 per cent of the German tanks and assault guns in the pocket were abandoned or destroyed by their own crews which is approximately 925 tanks.

If the number of tanks and assault guns abandoned or destroyed by their own crews is taken into account with those that escaped the pocket (a minimum of sixty-seven) then 1,256 tanks and assault guns were lost by the Germans in actual combat from all causes in the Normandy campaign.

British Losses

The 21st Army Group losses for the first three months of the Normandy campaign were reported by the RAC in its six monthly progress report as follows:

	Sherman	Cromwell	Churchill	
June	86	42	18	
July	186	28	17	
August	547	145	142	
	819	**215**	**177**	**1,211**

Clearly, this report contains some errors for June and July, as 179 tanks were lost on D-Day alone and more than 200 in Operation Goodwood in July. The August figure has apparently been corrected to arrive at the total for the first three months of the campaign.

A report prepared by RAC for its Liaison Letter to 21st Army group shows losses to 5 August which when combined with First Canadian and British Second Army tanks knocked out in the period 6–26 August gives the total of Allied tanks knocked out as follows:

	2nd Brit Army SOS to 5 Aug 1944*	Recovered to 5 Aug	nett	1st Cdn Army to 26 Aug**	2nd Brit Army 6–26 Aug***	Total 21 Army Gp	US 12th Army Gp to 26 Aug	Gross losses
Sherman/M4	631	94	537	257	133	1,021	824	1,845
Vc	86	7	79	40	14	140		140
Cromwell	193	8	185	40	2	235		235
Stuart	79	4	75	26	5	110	175	285
Churchill	92	9	83	10	48	150		150
Churchill 95	9	1	8	0	2	11		11
	1,090		**967**	**373**	**204**	**1,667**	**999**	**2,666**

* RAC Liaison Letter No. 2[10]
** Sum Operation Totalize, Tractable and Falaise Gap losses inc. I Corps (Weekly AFV losses, vol. 10736)
*** Second Army DME figures not inc. Bluecoat plus Operation Grouse plus XXX Corps losses[11]

Therefore almost 2,700 Allied tanks were knocked out or written off in the Normandy campaign, of which nearly 1,700 were British. The British total is approximately 25 per cent higher than the previously accepted total as per the RAC Progress Report for tanks lost by 21st Army Group. The difference in the two totals is because the RAC Progress Report gave tanks written off and did not include those knocked out and repaired, which are included in the RAC Liaison Letter.

Another example of this type of dual reporting was an earlier report prepared by the RAC for the Wastage Rates committee, which gave tank losses after six weeks of fighting to 20 July as:

- Shermans – 931 knocked out of which 493 were write offs with 297 of the remainder having been repaired
- Churchills – 140 knocked out with eighty-one written off and thirty-nine of the remainder having been repaired
- Cromwells – 205 knocked out with eighty-one being written off and forty-three of the remainder having been repaired[12]

This report gives a total of 1,276 British tanks knocked out to the 20 July before the heavy losses of August 1944 which is again higher than the Progress Report.

In reality, by the end of July the effective wastage rate for the month for Sherman equipped units was 35 per cent of the unit entitlement and much higher than the planned 25 per cent rate. A shortage of Sherman tanks developed as only 246 had been shipped to Normandy to replace the 493 written off. One of the factors influencing the planning of Operation Goodwood was the ready availability of reserve tanks, yet by the end of the month the British had a shortage of tanks because of the Goodwood losses.

Another way of examining total British tank losses is to look at the numbers of replacement tanks supplied. Total issues from Corps and Army delivery squadrons in the 2nd Armoured Replacement Group of the 21st Army Group from June to August were as follows:

	Sherman	Churchill	Cromwell	M5	
FDS initial	137	34	37	14	
June	115		42		
July	355	92	113	29	
August	264	50	198	87	
	871	**176**	**390**	**130**	**1,567**

A total of 1,567 replacement tanks were issued to the Field Delivery Squadrons during the campaign, which is again higher than the RAC Progress Report.[13] A small proportion of the tanks issued would have been for mechanical break-downs, so the total of tanks issued corresponds well with the total 1,667 knocked out or destroyed in the campaign; most armoured units were still understrength at the end of August 1944 owing to the shortage of replacement Shermans.

American tank losses were also considerably higher than forecast and by mid-August there were no reserves of M4 tanks left at all. A replacement factor of 7 per cent of unit strengths had been used by the War Department for planning before the invasion and the actual losses from combat were 25 per cent which caused reserves to be rapidly used up. This depletion was accelerated in July by the emergency transfer to the British of 388 M4 tanks to help meet their losses. Attempts by the AFV section at FUSA to have the transfer to the British cancelled and to procure more tanks were refused by the War Department which only agreed to raise the replacement factor to 9 per cent on 15 August. As a consequence, most US tank units were only at 75–87 per cent of full strength for most of September and October.[14] The greater than expected American losses culminated in the borrowing back of 350 tanks from the British in December after the Ardennes Offensive and all Sherman shipments to the British being suspended from January 1945 to channel all tank production to US units.

If the number of German tanks destroyed or abandoned by their own crews is excluded then the Germans lost in combat 1,256 tanks to the Allies' 2,693 tanks written off, a ratio of more than 2:1. Given the immense resources committed to tank production in the United States and numbers of tanks in the field, this was a ratio the Allies apparently could afford. The 2:1 average ratio of Allied to German tank losses supports the claims of journalists and regimental war diaries that two or three Shermans were lost for every German tank knocked out.

Flesh and Blood

Tanks are machines crewed by flesh and blood; each time a tank was knocked out in the Normandy campaign, there were usually men killed or wounded. The more thinly armoured the tank, the higher the number of casualties that could be expected.

A late-war survey in 1945 of 333 British tank casualties showed that:

- 41 per cent of tanks were knocked out by AP (tanks and anti-tank guns)
- 35 per cent of tanks were knocked out by Hollow Charge weapons (Panzerfaust)
- 20 per cent of tanks were knocked out by mines[15]

The figure of 35 per cent for Panzerfaust is due to this weapon being available in large quantities in the last few months of the war during fighting in Germany and is believed to be unrepresentative of fighting in Normandy. A more accepted figure for tank casualties in Normandy due to Panzerfaust was 6 per cent.[16] While 333 tanks were damaged or destroyed, 769 men became casualties (2.3 for every tank) of which 278 officers and ORs were killed.

During the Normandy campaign to 28 August, in the RAC in 21st Army Group (including the Canadian and Polish forces) 2,038 men were killed or died of wounds.[17] This represents an average of 1.2 men killed per tank knocked out. In the same period, the RAC suffered a total of 7,889 battle casualties, including those killed, which is a ratio of 4.65 casualties for every tank.

According to the same survey, 50 per cent of casualties to tank crews occurred inside the tank and 40 per cent outside when hit by mortar or shell fire, a further third of the 40 per cent outside being due to bailing out.[18] Therefore, 62 per cent of RAC casualties, which is 4,891 casualties, were statistically due to tanks being hit and knocked out by German tank and anti-tank weapons.

In a detailed survey sample of 214 tanks knocked out by AP or HC in 1945, there were 325 battle casualties, of which 123 men were killed and 202 men wounded, an average of 1.5 casualties per tank.[19] Of these casualties, 84 per cent were caused by a single penetration of the fighting compartment. On average, 0.58 men were killed for every tank lost.[20] Applying this factor to the number of tanks lost by 21st Army Group to the end of August, a total of 982 men would be expected to have been killed in action by AP or Panzerfäuste. In the late-war study, the expected numbers killed inside the tank were 17.8 per cent of casualties (1,405 men) with a further 1,025 men killed outside the tank, so the total fatal casualties in Normandy were actually fewer than expected for the number of tanks lost.

As the total RAC casualties in Normandy per tanks lost (4.6) was double that of the 1945 survey (2.3) but the fatalities less than expected, many more casualties were therefore due to other causes, such as artillery, rockets and snipers, and this is consistent with the repeated Allied attempts to break through the German lines and the intensity of the fighting in this period.

Of particular note is that the percentage of men killed did not vary much with the type of Allied tank, i.e. Sherman, Churchill or Cromwell.[21] The study also highlighted the importance of thick frontal armour, as 40 per cent of tanks that were hit on the hull were hit in a sector 22.5 degrees either side of the forward axis as were 50 per cent of those hit on the turret.[22]

American casualties for the campaign were similar, with 1,627 men killed in the 2nd and 3rd Armored Divisions in the same period but fewer tanks being lost: total battle casualties were 7,922 men.[23] These casualty figures also include those which occurred in the armoured infantry regiments of the divisions, so are higher than expected. The 66th Armored Regiment lost 111 M4s and twenty-eight M5s in the campaign with 120 officers and men killed and 601 wounded or missing. These casualties equate to one man killed per tank lost, a slightly less average rate than that of the RAC. In a US study of FUSA tank casualties, 174 men were killed in a sample of 274 tanks, which was 0.64 men killed per tank, a ratio very similar to the British study.[24]

So great were the British losses in men and tanks that the British replacement system was unable to keep up. A severe shortage of trained men and tanks immediately following Operation Goodwood meant that the 2nd Armoured Replacement Group had to be 'combed-out' for crew members, and the Field Delivery Squadrons were similarly scrutinised for every available man.[25]

As the planned replacement system could not cope with demand, five tank regiments had to be disbanded to make replacements for other armoured regiments. Generally, the most junior regiment in a brigade was disbanded but the reorganisation saw the entire 27th Armoured Brigade broken up with the Staffordshire Yeomanry going back to England for amphibious training, the East Riding Yeomanry going to the 33rd Armoured Brigade in place of the 148th RAC and 13th/18th Royal Hussars to the 8th Armoured Brigade to replace the 24th Lancers. The 24th Lancers were disbanded and the two County of London Yeomanry regiments were merged. The 2nd Northants Yeomanry was disbanded on 15 September and replaced by the 15th/19th Hussars in the 11th Armoured Division.

One reason for the shortage of British tanks at the end of July was that the 2nd Armoured Replacement Group at that time was only delivering sixteen battleworthy tanks a day to front-line units. Tanks were accumulating in the Ordnance parks at the beachhead Rear Maintenance Area but not getting through to the regiments in the front line. This was because of a bottleneck in the servicing and kitting of AFVs, which had an initial output of only ten tanks a day in June. With the arrival of the First Canadian Army this rose to sixteen tanks a day, then twenty tanks with extra REME assistance. With the attachment of the workshop from the disbanded 27th Armoured Brigade, the daily output was able to rise to thirty tanks by the end of August.[26] LADs from the disbanded 148th RAC, 153rd RAC and 2nd Northants Yeomanry regiments were required to boost this further as output still did not keep pace with losses in the front line.

Tank Performance

Following the defeat at Villers Bocage, the first mutterings of discontent regarding British tanks were heard in Normandy. Brigadier Hinde of the 22nd Armoured Brigade wrote a critical report immediately after the action. To the weight of this report was added a report by an XXX Corps General Staff Officer, Brigadier Pyman, who wrote on 16 June:

> The result is that while the 75mm shot has been failing to penetrate the front face of the Tigers and Panthers at ranges down to 30 yards, they can knock out Shermans and Cromwells at ranges of up to 1500 yards with ease.[27]

General Erskine seized on the comments made in the reports to excuse the turn of events at Villers Bocage and added his own comments in his report to XXX Corps to the effect that the Allies were now fighting at a disadvantage similar to that of 1942 when the Crusader tank with a 2-pounder gun was outclassed by the Panzer Mark IV. [28]

The reports made by Pyman and Erskine were further elaborated on by another report from an XXX Corps liaison officer (Lieutenant-Colonel J. Bowring) which found its way to Montgomery and somehow, the War Office in London. These were reports from some of Britain's most experienced tank officers and were the opening shots in a debate about the merits of Allied tanks that would come to haunt the north-west Europe campaign. The 21st Army Group Chief of Staff, Francis de Guingand, received copies of these reports and wrote to Montgomery:

> I feel that any further broadcasting of the sentiments expressed in Bowring's and Pyman's letters needs to be jumped on. If we are not careful, there will be a danger of the troops developing a Tiger and Panther complex – when every tank becomes one of these types; compared to the old days when every gun was an 88mm.[29]

Montgomery's reaction was swift; the writing of further liaison reports was prohibited and on 25 June he wrote a public letter, copied to James Grigg, Secretary of State for War, claiming that there was no problem:

We have had no difficulty dealing with German armour, once we had grasped the problem. In this connection British armour has played a notable part.

We have nothing to fear from the Panther or Tiger tanks; they are unreliable mechanically, and the Panther is very vulnerable from the flank. Our 17-pounder gun will go right through them. Provided our tactics are good, we can defeat them without difficulty.[30]

Grigg, for his part, was under pressure to respond to the critical Parliamentary Select Committee report on British tank development and was alarmed at the reports emanating from Normandy, according to Lieutenant-General Weeks, the DCIGS:

... He is nervous of two things

(i) Ill-informed criticism arising from first impressions
(ii) Deliberate criticism almost amounting to defeatism as regards or armour (in this respect watch the Guards Armoured Divn which I think the S of S has spoken to you.)[31]

This letter was followed by a directive on 6 July from Montgomery (M506) to the War Office reiterating the above comments and his views on the future requirements of British tanks. This document, with its demands for more 17-pounder equipped tanks, demonstrated that Montgomery was well aware of the situation on the battlefield.

All was quiet for a few weeks until, following the failure of Operation Goodwood, further criticism broke out, this time concerning the Sherman tank. According to Grigg at the War Office, the MP Major William Anstruther-Gray, serving in the Coldstream Guards in Normandy, was suspected of passing information to another MP, Richard Stokes, about the poor performance of British tanks.

Churchill, having delayed making a proper response to Parliamentary questions for three months, was forced on 21 July to state that a full report would be made to the House in the future. Visiting Montgomery in Normandy after Operation Goodwood, Churchill requested a copy of the letter Montgomery had written to Grigg on 25 June and then used sections of it in his speech to the House of Commons on 2 August. Meanwhile, another question was asked by Stokes in Parliament:

HC Deb 25 July 1944 vol 402 c567 567

Mr. Stokes asked the Secretary of State for War whether he will assure this House that our troops in Normandy are equipped with tanks at least the equal of both the German Tiger and Panther in armour and armament.

Simultaneously, reports began appearing in the British and foreign press about the problems of British tanks:

> Our Shermans, with special 17-pounder guns, are fine tanks. They can match the Germans' best in fire power but not in thickness of armour. But our ordinary Shermans are inferior to Tigers and Panthers. Roughly, out of every 20 German tanks we destroy, nine are Mark IVs, eight are Panthers and three are Tigers.[32]

Churchill delayed making a reply to the Select Committee until after Operation Cobra when there was better news from Normandy. On 2 August Churchill finally made a statement to the House of Commons before sending a reply to the Select Committee the same day:

> <u>The Prime Minister</u>: General Montgomery has written as follows about the recent battle: 'In the fighting to date we have defeated the Germans in battle, and we have had no difficulty in dealing with the German army once we had grasped the problem. In this connection British armour has played a notable part. The Panther and Tiger tanks are unreliable mechanically and the Panther is very vulnerable from the flanks. Our 17-pounder guns will go right through them. Provided our tactics are good we can defeat them without difficulty.' Well, they say the customer is always right.
>
> The Cromwell, of course, possesses superior speed, which will be especially effective when, and if we come, as we may, into more open country. As to the Sherman, I saw with my own eyes last week an example of the work of the 17-pounder. It was on the approaches to Caen. There was an expanse of large fields of waving corn out of which a grey stone village rose. Generals Montgomery and Dempsey brought me to this spot and invited me to count the broken-down Panther tanks which were littered about. I counted nine in the space of about 1,000 yards square. The generals then told me that all these nine had been shot with a 17-pounder from one single British Sherman tank from the side of the village wall. One cannot help being impressed by these things when one sees them with one's own eyes. Of course, you will never get the same armour in a 30-ton tank as you will in one of 60 tons. But mobility, speed and manoeuvrability also count high, and when the 17-pounder gun is added to all these qualities, no one has the right to say that these lighter tanks are not fitted in every way for their task and are not a wise and far-seeing employment of our war power …
>
> … But when I last saw General Montgomery in the field he used these words which he authorised me to repeat if I chose. He said: 'I doubt if the British War Office has ever sent an Army overseas so well equipped as the one fighting now in Normandy.' That is what he said, and I must say I think it is a well-justified statement.
>
> <u>Mr. Stokes</u>: My experience as a soldier has been that I know how good and how bad my weapons are, and my grouse is that the House of Commons does not do more about it. I find that to be the point of view of almost every soldier I talk to. I spoke

to a friend of mine, who is the commander of a squadron of a very famous regiment, about the relative merits of the Sherman tank, of which we have heard so much to-day, and the Tiger. He told me: 'I know what happens, because it has happened to me twice. My squadron goes over and bumps into one of these Tigers. There are four bangs and there are four of my tanks gone.' So far as I know, we have nothing in production which is a complete answer to the Panther or the Tiger.

The criticisms made by the Select Committee were largely justified and questions raised by Stokes in Parliament deserved a better response than the evasion and obfuscation that they were met with. However, despite the problems of tank design and production, the armoured units had to go into battle with the equipment they had and emerge victorious. Montgomery in particular did not want there to be a slump in morale as a result of what he perceived as alarmist reports being generated, no matter how true they were. Morale was an important component of Montgomery's strategic thinking and he was determined to suppress any such thoughts or reports. Even the RAC attracted Montgomery's ire when it published its first Liaison Letter which commented on tank policy and some aspects of the performance of 21st Army Group armour in the first few weeks of the campaign. As well as stifling all further liaison reports from Normandy, Montgomery ordered the RAC not to include any reports in its six-monthly Progress Report to the end of June 1944 until the 21st Army Group itself had reported.[33]

Whilst Churchill was attempting to quell the negative reports on the Home Front, those in the front line were not deceived. The war diary of the 2nd Irish Guards the following day recorded:

The advantage, of course, lay with the Germans as, no matter what is said in Parliament, their guns penetrate our armour, and the 75mm does not penetrate theirs.[34]

The Irish Guards were not alone in their opinion: most of the men in the other Sherman-equipped regiments had similar views.

In mid-August, Montgomery and Grigg, on a goodwill tour to Normandy, visited the Guards Armoured Division which was resting after Operation Bluecoat. On 16 August they saw the Irish Guards and two days later attended divisional HQ for medal presentations at which Montgomery made a speech about the fighting in Normandy. The regimental historian of the Irish Guards was unimpressed with this visit and made the Guards' views on the deficiencies in their tanks known:

... the problem was that only one Sherman in every four was equipped with a 17 pounder gun and that Allies defeated the Germans in Normandy only because they could afford to lose 6 tanks to every German tank.[35]

Within three more weeks the campaign in Normandy was over and the Allies were victorious, making the Select Committee reports largely redundant. The shortcomings of the British tank industry remained a passion of Stokes, who went on to publish a small booklet after the war entitled 'Some Amazing Tank Facts'.

Just how vulnerable was the Sherman tank to German weapons? Given the developing furore over the number of Sherman tank casualties, a battlefield survey was conducted by the No. 2 Operational Research Unit that examined Sherman tanks knocked out and/or destroyed in the fighting between 6 June and 10 July 1944. The hulks of forty-five Shermans were examined and forty were found to have been penetrated by 75mm or 88mm German armour-piercing shells, of which thirty-three tanks had subsequently caught fire and brewed up.[36] This was believed to be due to fragments of metal hitting the ammunition stored in the tank which then caused the tank to catch fire. Out of sixty-five hits by armour-piercing shells on these tanks, sixty-three penetrated the tank completely. This was evidence, if not proof, that the armoured protection of the Sherman was completely inadequate. Twenty-five tanks were knocked out by just one hit.

As in most cases the Shermans were attacking, they were often victims of concealed German anti-tank weapons which had the benefit of first fire; this was often all that was required, as the high-velocity German tank and anti-tank guns were able to penetrate the Sherman's frontal armour with ease.

British and Canadian Performance

The British and Canadian armour in the Normandy campaign did not perform well, but this was more often due to the poor way in which it was employed by the corps commanders. Once badly deployed, the numbers of tanks lost were exaggerated by losses due to the thin armour and ineffective gun of the Sherman/M4.

Operation Overlord required the seizure of Caen, Evrecy and Bayeux by armoured columns advancing inland on D-Day, and none of these objectives were achieved. These objectives proved to be too ambitious and unrealistic; Caen and Evrecy were not taken for another six weeks. Despite overwhelming naval firepower and complete air superiority on 6 June, the Allies were not able to capitalise on the success of their initial landings. There is not one particular cause of this but rather a series of compounding factors.

The late afternoon attack by the 21st Panzer Division was enough to prevent the capture of Caen on D-Day. The bad weather on D-Day (and the preceding days) caused higher tides than predicted with subsequent traffic congestion and delays for the follow-up units in getting off the beaches and moving inland. In addition to this, the D-Day forces had been cooped up in their assault craft since 3 June, most without proper facilities for sleeping or eating which meant that many men were simply exhausted by the afternoon of 6 June after the tumultuous events of the day. The Overlord plan was so detailed and intricate with landings and operations scheduled to the nearest minute and no time allowed for unexpected delays that the timetable was always in danger of being considerably delayed by a single event or obstacle.

The DD tanks, while coming as a surprise to the Germans, were largely inef-fective, failing to arrive on time to support the engineers and the first wave of infantry which achieved their tasks quickly and largely without support from the DD tanks. In the Gold and Omaha sectors where the naval and air bombardments were not as effective as in other sectors and the enemy bunkers were largely intact, the reduced numbers of DD tanks were even less effective in the absence of any AVRE firepower and the fighting continued all morning on these beaches.

The British tank brigades arrived in Normandy after two changes to the doctrine for working with infantry in the previous six months. With the emergence of the threat of the Panzerfaust, yet another recommendation was made by the War Office on 10 June that tanks and infantry should advance together. Tank and infantry co-operation often came down to individual squadron and battalion commanders or tank troop leaders and company commanders working out hastily, often just a few hours before they went into action, how they would work together. First attempts in Normandy were not always successful, as the 4th/7th Royal Dragoon Guards found out at Cristot in June and the 31st Tank Brigade during Operation Epsom. The lack of a proper doctrine for tanks and infantry to work with Sherman tanks has been cited as the 'greatest failure of the war in the field of doctrinal dissemination'.[37] Another historian has suggested that the British failure to enforce any doctrine at all was a major factor in the way tanks and infantry co-operated in the campaign.[38] Certainly, had the British been forced to follow a faulty doctrine, the results would have been more catastrophic for the tanks which were required to lead, according to de Guingand's notes of February 1944. This tactic had been found to be faulty after two years of fighting in North Africa and yet Montgomery and the 21st Army Group tried to insist it be followed in Normandy.[39]

In 1943, the War Office had actively come out against infantry being carried on tanks because of the discomfort caused by the hot engine exhausts and the vulnerability of the riders to small-arms fire. However, during the Normandy campaign, time and time again, the only way for the armoured brigades to get infantry forward to work alongside the tanks was for the tanks to carry the infantry into battle. Only the armoured divisions, with their motorised battalions, were equipped with enough suitable vehicles to keep pace with the tanks cross-country.

Ultimately it was the bocage hedgerows that determined how tanks and infantry co-operated. Current doctrine and training went out the window when the Allies entered the first small field surrounded by thick, high hedges. As the 21st Army Group did not deliberately or otherwise enforce any doctrine at all, the tanks and infantry were given the flexibility to develop new tactics for the hedgerow environment as neither arm could work alone. Though this happened the hard way, the best methods for tanks and infantry to work together eventually evolved during the campaign.

British and American armoured divisions were not handled well during the first half of the campaign by army and corps commanders. In many instances the armoured divisions were expected to operate against established doctrine and instead of being used as a force to exploit gaps in the German lines, were used as blunt instruments to make the gaps in conjunction with the support from heavy Air Force bombers.

The 7th Armoured Division had struggled in the bocage during the advance to Villers Bocage and only made slow progress against small numbers of tanks and anti-tank guns supported by a few infantry. The division's own infantry brigade was unavailable and the tanks had to work with infantry they had never trained with before which resulted in a predictably slow advance. Having been created as a weapon of exploitation, the 7th Armoured Division was forced by the bocage to act as an infantry tank brigade.

Once Villers Bocage was reached, the leading regiment pushed on without a reconnaissance, even though enemy units were around. At the objective, the regiment stopped in a column as if it was on a peace-time training exercise, allowing a few German Tiger tanks to fully exploit the opportunity and the desert veterans of Britain's most experienced armoured division were forced into an ignominious retreat halfway back to Bayeux.

The next action of the 7th Armoured Division was during the breakout attempt of Operation Goodwood. However, the 7th Armoured Division was missing in action for virtually the whole day and did not enter the fighting until about 1700 hours.

The 7th Armoured Division's unfortunate experiences in Normandy continued in Operation Bluecoat. The division was held in reserve ready for exploitation by XXX Corps southwards to Vire or Le Bény Bocage as the opportunity arose. With the rapid advance of the 11th Armoured Division, the division was again committed to the attack in a battering role, not one of exploitation. Progress was slow against German mines and anti-tank guns in the bocage and the division was unable to capture Aunay on schedule. The XXX Corps plans were changed on 5 August with the division being redirected towards Thury Harcourt.

With a new commander, General Verney, a period or rest and reorganisation followed while 100 new personnel were absorbed. A slow advance to Seine began on 17 August in an operation which lasted ten days. Free of the bocage, the division advanced in series of more familiar textbook operations and, with the changes in personnel, the morale of the division gradually improved. Buoyed by the enthusiastic reception from the French population liberated in Livarot and Lisieux, the spirit and confidence of the men improved further. For the Desert Rats further challenges lay ahead in northern France, Holland and Germany. General Verney could not find solutions to all the division's problems and he himself was replaced in November 1944.

However, by this time Montgomery's plan to reinforce the unexperienced units of the British Second Army with combat seasoned troops he had previously commanded had badly misfired. Doubts were being openly expressed within 21st Army Group about the performance of the 7th Armoured, 50th and 51st (H) Divisions. There were high numbers of desertion and subsequent court-martials in the 50th Division and the commander of the 51st (H) Division was replaced with the division regarded as unfit for battle.[40] The 7th Armoured Division were not alone in believing they had done their share of fighting.

The 11th Armoured Division began the Normandy campaign as an inexperienced green division, although its 29th Armoured Brigade had been leavened with the experienced 3rd RTR which had seen action in North Africa and Italy. Its combat debut during Operation Epsom was characterised by the splitting up of the divisional troops by the VIII Corps commander, General O'Connor, and their subsequent independent actions, which was disappointing for General Roberts as the division had trained extensively before D-Day in infantry/tank co-operation.

O'Connor and Dempsey repeated this separation of the infantry and tanks in Operation Goodwood. Because of the limited room for deployment at the start of the attack, instead of the advance being made by two divisions side by side, the Guards Armoured Division could not come up alongside the 11th Armoured Division which was forced to advance alone into the intact German gun lines.

It was in Operation Bluecoat that the 11th Armoured Division really came into its own. This time General Roberts was able to plan his own battle and the division was at last able to operate as one unit. The armoured regiments and infantry battalions of the 159th Brigade formed two battle groups which rapidly penetrated deep behind German lines to Chenedolle and Burcy. The division also demonstrated flexibility and aggression in advancing at night with the capture of St Martin des Besaces. Roberts was then able to boldly exploit the situation further through the rapid reinforcement of the Household Cavalry patrol which had penetrated the Forêt l'Evêque and seized the bridge over the River Soulevre. But Roberts's aggression was not matched by O'Connor and the division's advance was halted. The Guards Armoured Division, designated to safeguard the left flank, had again not kept pace with the progress of the 11th Armoured Division and had left its flanks exposed.

During the furious counterattacks by the 2nd SS Panzer Korps to eliminate the 11th Armoured Division battle groups, which were already behind the new front line the Germans were trying to establish, the battle groups were able to defeat the German attacks with the considerable assistance of divisional and corps artillery plus air support. The 11th Armoured Division showed that it could operate with infantry successfully, like the infantry tank brigades. The appointment of Roberts in December 1943 as an experienced commander of a green division proved to be a particularly good decision.

The Guards Armoured Division made its combat debut in Operation Goodwood in the role of a battering ram. The division experienced its first casualties around Cagny, faltered, and on seeing the burning 11th Armoured Division tanks on the rising slopes the other side of the railway line, advanced no further. By the Guards not eliminating German flanking fire from villages like Frenouville, Le Poirier and Four, the 11th Armoured Division was left exposed. The division hastily reorganised during Operation Bluecoat to achieve a better combined arms structure when it found itself in the bocage. Strangely, the division did not allow the same infantry and armoured regiments to work together, apart from the Irish Guards. Although directly in the path of the later German counterattack, the Guards initially made only slow progress and were halted for long periods such as at Le Tourneur and Corteil. A divisional history blamed the bocage countryside and the Germans for not forming proper defensive lines and for fighting in ad-hoc battle groups.[41] Progress was firstly slowed by the 21st Panzer Division and then halted altogether by the counterattack of the 9th SS Panzer Division.

Though perhaps more favoured by the fortunes of war, the 11th Armoured Division was better trained in infantry/tank co-operation, had an experienced commander and was ready to exploit any advantages on the battlefield. Arguably, the assignment of an inexperienced divisional commander to the new Guards Armoured Division was not such a sound decision by Home Forces in 1942 and Montgomery did try to have General Adair removed in February 1944, without success.[42] The Guards would be given one more opportunity in north-west Europe to lead an attack during Operation Market Garden in September 1944. Debate continues to this day as to the division's performance in this operation, although once again British planning was rife with basic errors.

The Canadian 4th Armoured Division also went through a process of development in response to its first battle experiences but its commander, General Kitching, was replaced. Simonds, to his credit, tried new armoured tactics and virtually threw away the training manual in order to find solutions to the superior firepower of the German tanks and anti-tank guns. His plan initially worked well and gaps were created in the German lines for subsequent exploitation. Simonds's own planning then derailed the operation: the exploitation attack by the armoured divisions could not get underway until after the second bombing as a German counterattack was regarded as inevitable by Simonds. The subsequent delay afforded the Germans nearly 8 hours to reorganise their forces and construct a new front line. The 4th Canadian Armoured Division's regiments subsequently attacked straight into this new line which buckled but again held.

A few days later, the same tactic was tried again, this time in daylight with the Canadian tanks lined up in armoured phalanxes in parade ground fashion. The initial advance went well until it reached the River Laison which was supposedly easily crossed. The opposite proved true and chaos ensued with valuable time being lost; those tanks that got across continued their advance but by then were separated from their infantry. With tank casualties mounting and the loss of daylight, the attack that had not started until noon was stopped. This allowed the Germans to again regroup and progress next day was negligible.

Both of these operations are notable for the planning function being taken over entirely by Simonds and his corps staff; Kitching was completely bypassed so cannot be held solely responsible for the outcome of Operations Totalize and Tractable. The operation to close the Falaise Gap saw the division curiously unengaged, except for the South Alberta Regiment. The division was certainly handicapped by the death of Brigadier Booth who was killed on 14 August, his place being taken at different times by two commanders of the divisional regiments. Lieutenant-Colonel Scott of the Foot Guards took over first, followed by Lieutenant-Colonel Halpenny of the Grenadier Guards, so at a critical stage of the campaign an inexperienced armoured brigade was twice led by temporary commanders with acting commanders in all three armoured regiments. Kitching struggled to retain control in the circumstances just when it was most needed. Simonds was also at fault for not arranging the requested replacement for Booth more quickly, despite the officer being in the area. Nevertheless, the strain finally got to Kitching: his refusal to send troops to the aid of the 1st Polish Armoured Division alone warranted his dismissal.

The 1st Polish Armoured Division also went through a steep learning curve. From the rash tactics in Operation Totalize which resulted in the loss of many tanks, the division executed a successful exploitation deep behind German lines in Operation Tractable, opening up the way for the Canadians. When ordered to close the Falaise gap at Mont Ormel, the division fought heroically in appalling conditions during the German retreat, despite outrunning its own supply lines and one battle group losing its way.

American Performance

The initial operations of the Americans in the capture of Cherbourg saw the independent tank battalions operate successfully with their infantry divisions against very sparse German armoured resistance. However, in June, including D-Day losses, FUSA reported 209 M4 and thirty-five M5 tanks lost despite FUSA having been opposed by only one and a half panzer divisions.[43]

The US tank battalions generally remained assigned to the same infantry division during the Normandy campaign and this allowed good working relationships to be developed. An exception was the 747th Tank Battalion which complained of friendly fire and a lack of artillery support from the 29th Division; the battalion was even forbidden on occasions to use their own 105mm assault guns for support.[44]

As in the British sector, the main problem faced by the armoured force of FUSA was the effectiveness of German tanks and anti-tank guns. The Americans found out the hard way what the British had already known: the armour of the Sherman was little protection against the high velocity German tank and anti-tank guns. There was also a growing realisation that a better tank gun similar to the British 17-pounder was needed by the Americans to combat the German armour. In late June, some testing was done by firing all available Allied anti-tank guns against some Panther tank hulks. The poor results provoked an angry response from Eisenhower:

> You mean our 76 won't knock these Panthers out? Why, I thought it was going to be the wonder gun of the war. Why is it that I am the last to hear about this stuff? Ordnance told me this would take care of anything the Germans had. Now I find out you can't knock out a damn thing with it.[45]

On 2 July, Eisenhower wrote a memo to his Chief of Staff, Lieutenant-General Bedell-Smith, demanding that the special ammunition similar to the British 6-pounder SABOT be developed for the newly arrived M4A1 with the 76mm gun as tests had shown that existing guns could not penetrate the frontal armour of the Panther tank. Eisenhower also queried the effectiveness of the proposed 90mm gun for the M4, demanding that a gun equivalent to the British 17-pounder be developed as quickly as possible.[46] Eisenhower followed this up by dispatching Brigadier Holly to the USA with a personal letter for General Marshall:

> None of our present ammunition for the 57mm, 75mm and 76mm guns and 105mm howitzer can penetrate the front armour of the Panther or Tiger tanks and due to the restrictive terrain and narrow roads in which we are fighting, we are unable to consistently attack these tanks from a favourable angle. Moreover, even from the flanks, our present weapons and ammunition are not adequately effective.[47]

For a more powerful anti-tank gun, Eisenhower was forced to wait for the arrival of M36 tank destroyers with a 90mm gun from late August onwards; the future supply of all M10s was cancelled altogether as these were regarded as ineffective. However, the M36s and an improved Sherman, the Jumbo M4A3E2 with better sloped frontal armour of 47 degrees that was half in inch thicker than the standard, arrived too late to take part in the Normandy fighting.

While the chorus of British complaints about their tanks was loudest in the Normandy campaign, it was not until later in the war that American complaints reached a crescendo, negative reports from Italy having been previously suppressed by the War Department. This was precipitated by tank losses during the Battle of the Bulge and was fuelled by adverse press articles in March 1945. Eisenhower had commissioned the commanders of the 2nd and 3rd Armored divisions in March 1945 to write a report comparing German and American equipment and the reports they produced were both very critical of the M4 Sherman. One tanker remarked that the best American tank weapon was the P-47 Thunderbolt aircraft.[48] The newspaper articles echoed these sentiments and reported that the German Tiger and Panther tanks were far superior, with three Shermans needed to knock out every Tiger tank.[49]

The difficulties of fighting in the hedgerows forced the infantry and armour to work together, although early experiences were unsuccessful. When an advance was going well, the average infantryman disliked having tanks nearby as they often attracted German artillery and mortar fire. Conversely, when the advance was held up or being threatened by German tanks, the infantryman was naturally very keen to have the support of tanks.

The Allies quickly discovered they could not use the roads because of well-sited, powerful anti-tank guns, so they went cross-country. This worked for a while until the Germans dug in assault guns and tanks as strongpoints and covered any open ground with anti-tank guns. American ingenuity and improvisation then devised ways to improve the communications between tanks and infantry. There was no question of whether the infantry or tanks should lead; undisputedly, the two arms needed to advance side by side. The infantry could not get through the hedges and trees without the tanks and vice versa. In the bocage, both the Allies and the Germans found defence much easier than attack.

The American armoured divisions, like their British counterparts, had trained for an exploitative role and found themselves unexpectedly having to work very closely with their armoured infantry. In the advance to St Lô, the 3rd Armored Division was employed in late June by XIX Corps to eliminate a small salient in the front line by a direct frontal assault, which was an inappropriate use of an armoured division. It was the first time in combat for Combat Command A, which found itself fighting in hedgerows unlike any terrain they had trained in. The results were high casualties in men and tanks, and these became typical of later operations as the advance on St Lô continued. Around St Jean de Daye the operations of the division's CCB were hampered by congested lines of advance, friendly-fire incidents and tanks advancing across the front of infantry regiments. Relations with XIX Corps degenerated to such an extent that CCB's reports of having reached the objective at Les Hauts Vents were not believed and next day its commander was replaced.

The veteran 2nd Armored Division, after its initial action at Carentan, remained in reserve until Operation Cobra in expectation of a German attack that never came. Despite its inexperience, the 3rd Armored Division was then given the most important objective in Operation Cobra of charging across the Cotentin peninsula from St Lô to Coutances and cutting the retreat of the left wing of the Seventh Army. If ever there was to be a battle of exploitation through a gap blasted in the German front lines, this was it. Unfortunately, the gap proved to be too narrow with only a single road to carry the vehicles of two armoured divisions. Traffic congestion, increasing German resistance and rigid VII Corps orders that prescribed an advance by steps, all served to impede the advance of the 3rd Division's CCB and the 1st Division. Consequently, on 28 July the mission of capturing Coutances was given to another corps and the division's commander, Major-General Watson, was relieved as a consequence of his division's poor performance.

The 2nd Armored Division, having previously been allocated the role of protecting the eastern flank from German counterattacks, was ordered to take over the mission of the 3rd Armored Division. The 'heavy' structure of the division had sufficient strength in tanks to allow its CCA to continue the flank guard by pushing east to Tessy while CCB eventually formed the blocking force at St Denis and Lengronne.

The stage was now set for the launching of Patton's Third Army into the gap at Avranches created by Operation Cobra. Patton's rapid advance eastwards was with three armoured divisions in a classical armoured division exploitation role through the weakly defended rear areas of Seventh Army with the Germans unsure of his intentions. It was only when the armoured divisions turned northwards on 10 August towards Alençon that the American plan of encircle-ment became obvious.

By the end of August, the 3rd Armored Division had overcome its baptism of fire and became a formation that befitted its nickname of 'Spearhead'. It had suc-cessfully fought through the hedgerows by adopting combined arms tactics learnt the hard way. Free of the hedgerows after Operation Cobra, both the 2nd and 3rd Armored Divisions rapidly advanced great distances, ably assisted by the cab rank of fighter-bombers overhead.

German Strategy

The Germans in Normandy knew how their panzer forces should be used but were unable to employ them. This was for two reasons: firstly, the lack of mobility of their infantry divisions and secondly Montgomery's most successful strategy of keeping the Germans off-balance by repeated blows in different places. This 'keep hitting' strategy allowed the Allies to nearly always retain the initiative in Normandy and forced the Germans to continually commit any available reserves. The panzer divi-sions were the only forces capable of rapid movement to meet such blows and this inevitably resulted in them becoming caught up in the fighting, unable to disengage to move back into reserve or assemble for their own attack. In the entire campaign, the Germans did not mount a single offensive that ever threatened the beaches and after June, they were continually on the defensive until Mortain. However, the reputation of the panzer divisions was such that the threat of an attack by them was enough for Montgomery to halt any British offensive in progress.

The German strategy in the first half of the campaign was considerably influenced by Operation Fortitude which succeeded beyond the wildest dreams of the British. Nine German infantry divisions remained along the coast at Calais during the entire campaign, although these were largely static coastal defence divisions. The 1st SS Panzer Division remained in Belgium in anticipation of a landing near Calais until mid-June by which time the Allied build-up had all but assured success in Normandy.

The German forces in Normandy had a complicated command structure that was almost designed to fail. The three panzer divisions ordered to throw the Allies back into the sea received orders from five different formations in the first few days after D-Day, to which a sixth was added with the creation of Panzer Gruppe West. The first attempts at counterattacks by the panzer divisions commanded by Dietrich and the 1st SS Panzer Korps were poorly coordinated and hastily con-ducted. With the destruction of the Panzer Gruppe West HQ on 11 June, five days had passed since D-Day during which time not a single coordinated mass panzer counterattack was made, allowing the Allies to quickly build up their forces and expand the beachhead.

The initiative then remained firmly with Montgomery. Although the Germans prevented the capture of Caen and Carpiquet airfield, the strategy of constant blows prevented the Germans from regrouping their forces and moving the panzer divisions back out of the front line to form a mobile reserve for a counterattack. The Germans were hampered by a lack of aerial support from the Luftwaffe, particularly reconnaissance information on Allied units and their concentrations. The subjugation and absence of the Luftwaffe allowed Allied fighter bombers, reconnaissance flights and low-flying artillery spotter planes to roam at will over the Normandy countryside during the day, reporting on the movements of all German units and attacking them whenever they could be found in any concentration.

The Seventh Army then became preoccupied with the American attempt to capture Cherbourg and cut the Cotentin peninsula while the British Second Army continued to exert pressure all along the front from Caen to Tilly, ensuring that the three panzer divisions were continuously involved in fighting, which served to both keep them in the line and continue their attrition. Other panzer divisions as reinforcements were on their way to Normandy, including the 2nd, 2nd SS and the two divisions of the 2nd SS Panzer Korps from Russia. According to von Schweppenburg after the war, there had been an opportunity for an attack on 13 June by the panzer divisions and the wheeled elements of the newly arrived 2nd Panzer Division towards Bayeux but this was not ordered by Seventh Army.[50] Only the reconnaissance and wheeled elements of the division had arrived by this time and immediately became embroiled in the fighting around Caumont and Villers Bocage.

The gales and storms of 19–23 June perhaps represented the German's best opportunity for a successful counterattack. The bad weather kept Allied aircraft grounded and therefore naval and air support were not available. However, the three main panzer divisions were still holding the front line at that time. On 17 June, Hitler met von Rundstedt and Rommel to discuss future operations. Rommel drew up several scenarios for a counterattack but all of these depended on the arrival of the 2nd SS Panzer Korps and a massed panzer attack would not be possible until the end of the month. This was forestalled by Montgomery's Operation Epsom, which completely disrupted the German plans and saw the newly arrived SS panzer divisions roughly handled.

Paradoxically, the only massed panzer counterattack of the Normandy campaign was Operation Luttich at Mortain and then only at the express orders of Hitler himself which is an indictment of the poor performance of the German commanders in Normandy. Despite Operation Luttich being conceived in fantasy by Hitler, the offensive was duly carried out by the army commanders. The fact that none of them would voice their objections illustrates how moribund Army Group B and von Kluge had become, although the numerous arrests and deaths of many senior officers after the attempted assassination of Hitler on 20 July no doubt helped bind them to his will.

Despite the importance of the panzer divisions to any future attack plans, the German commands regularly detached parts of the panzer divisions so that they rarely fought as a cohesive unit. Ad-hoc kampfgruppen were used to restore the front line and support other units but this process left the parent unit considerably weakened. For example, parts of 2nd SS Panzer Division were continually detached to support other divisions so that in the entire Normandy campaign, the division did not once fight as a single entity. Panzer Lehr, when it initially moved to the American sector near St Lô, was forced to leave a tank and artillery battalion behind to support the infantry division that had relieved it with the result that the division was at half strength when it launched its attack on 11 July at St Jean. The division escort company of the hard-pressed 12th SS Panzer Division was even sent to reinforce Panzer Lehr for the period of 16–20 June.[51]

What of the Rommel versus Rundstedt invasion strategy? The course of the Normandy campaign closely followed the intended strategy of von Rundstedt and others in that the Allies were allowed to land and establish a beachhead. However, because of the Allied air superiority, their immense resources and Montgomery's 'keep hitting' strategy, the Germans were never able to mount a decisive counterattack. Therefore von Rundstedt's strategy was proven wrong but the question remains as to whether Rommel's strategy of having the panzer divisions near the coast would have worked either. The location of the billets and assembly areas of any panzer divisions would have been well known to the Allies prior to D-Day and would have been subjected to heavy naval and air bombardments. The survivors of such attacks would have been forced to make an advance towards the beaches late in the evening or at night, as any observed concentration of tanks during the day would have again been subjected to naval gunfire. Even this would be no guarantee of success, but Rommel's strategy and appreciation of Allied capabilities was the more correct of the two strategies.

As history has shown, once Eisenhower made the decision to go ahead with D-Day, given the overwhelming superiority of the Allied war machine, aerial dominance, the success of Operation Fortitude and the ineptitude of the German command, there was only one possible outcome for the Allies: victory. The German command structure rather sidelined Rommel who was a firm believer that the Normandy landings were a feint for further landings in the Pas de Calais. Rommel had been a strong advocate of Calais as the likely location of any landings and he continued to tour Fifteenth Army defences right up until being wounded on 17 July. Within four days of D-Day, Rommel was pessimistic about the outcome of the fighting in Normandy.[52] Perhaps disappointed at not being made commander-in-chief after von Rundstedt or overwhelmed by the forces apparently arrayed against him as projected by Operation Fortitude, Rommel did not play a major part in the Normandy campaign, declaring that because of Hitler's interference a sergeant major could have carried out his role.[53] Rommel's strong opinions regarding Calais certainly helped perpetuate the Allied deception and prevent the early movement of troops to Normandy. No doubt the machinations of the plot against Hitler distracted him further.

The Allies succeeded despite their own shortcomings in infantry/tank doctrine, the existence of the tank development gap and stresses in command at a senior level.

Montgomery's bold plan of armoured thrusts moving rapidly inland to stake out large tracts of Normandy failed in the first few days of landing in the face of German opposition. The two armies of 21st Army Group were unable to deepen and broaden the initial lodgement as planned with the result that the intended pivot by the armies was delayed and there was a fear of a stalemate developing. With the failure to capture Caen, this movement was not possible until after the relative success of Operation Cobra in July. The US Third Army's original mission was to capture the Brittany ports further west and a line would be held by the Allies while this was achieved. Patton was then tasked with defending the supply corridor through Avranches and did not commence a general eastward movement until 4 August. Only when Hitler committed the bulk of the remaining panzer forces to a desperate counterattack westwards did Bradley, not Montgomery, recognise the strategic opportunity for encirclement that had arisen and the German Seventh Army was eventually destroyed in the Falaise Gap. Montgomery was intent on carrying out his Overlord plan and did not see this opportunity. Had Hitler not committed the panzer forces at Mortain, the Allies would have faced considerably more opposition in their advance to Germany. Nevertheless, the Allies and Montgomery had in less than 90 days advanced to the River Seine, liberated Paris and destroyed two German armies, achieving far more than was ever envisaged in Operation Overlord.

On 1 September, Eisenhower assumed control of all the Allied land forces in France as previously decided owing to the greater contribution being made by the United States, and by then Bradley and his staff were thoroughly disenchanted with Montgomery's leadership. Montgomery was very disappointed and felt that he had carried out his mission in Normandy well enough to deserve to remain commander.

Victory in Normandy came to the Allies in the end through their dominance of the air and their superiority in firepower, numbers, logistics and code breaking skills. For the first six weeks of the campaign until Operation Cobra, the Allied battle plans were unsuccessful until the Allied overall superiority had severely weakened the Germans. Final success was in no small part due to the bravery and sacrifice of the men of all arms, including the tank crews in their thinly armoured Shermans and Cromwells that continually went out to do battle every day with more powerful enemy tanks and anti-tank guns. The Shermans and Cromwells were not the match of German tanks but they got the job done and the Allies won the campaign in Normandy, despite the many casualties amongst the tank crews. General Bradley commented after the war:

> The Sherman with its powerful engine could always be counted on to run without a breakdown. This advantage, together with our US superiority in numbers, enabled us to surround the enemy in battle and knock out his tanks from the flanks. But this willingness to expend Shermans offered little comfort to the crews who were forced to expend themselves.[54]

Notes

1 Blumenson, M., *Break Out and Pursuit* (Washington, DC, US Army CMH, 1961), p.576

2 FMS B-727 von Gersdorff, Campaign In Northern France Chapter VI, p.62, NARA

3 Blumenson, *opcit*, p.583

4 FMS B-841 Hausser 7th Army 22nd to 31st August 1944, NARA

5 CMHQ Report no. 50 Campaign in NW Europe – Information from German sources – Sitrep 22 August, p.138

6 Meyer, H., *The 12th SS – The History of the Hitler Youth Panzer Division Volume 2* (Stackpole, Mechnicsburg, PA, 2005), p.117

7 WO 205/972A Notes on Operations of 21st Army Group, 1946, TNA

8 WO 291/1331 ORS, Report 15 Enemy Casualties in Vehicles and equipment during the retreat from Normandy to the Seine. TNA

9 Zetterling, N., *Normandy 1944 – German Military Organisation, Combat Power and Effectiveness* (Manitoba, JJ Fedorowicz, 2000), p.418

10 WO 32/11035 RAC Liaison letter no. 2 1944, TNA

11 WO 171/248 War diary DDME Second Army August 1944, TNA

12 WO 205/112 21st Army group equipment wastage rates, letter 21 July 1944, Appendix A, TNA

13 WO 171/902 War diary 2nd Armoured Replacement Group, September 1944, TNA

14 AFV section ETOUSA Preliminary Historical report, 9 December 1944, p.50, NARA

15 WO 205/1165 Wright, Capt. H., and Harkness, Capt. R., A Survey of Casualties amongst Armoured Units in NW Europe, January 1946, p.15, TNA

16 WO 205/1164 Operation Research in NW Europe, Report no. 33 Use of Panzerfaust in NW Europe, p.240, TNA

17 WO 219/1550 21st Army Group casualties by arm and branch of service, reports to 28 August 1944, TNA

18 WO 205/1165 Wright and Harkness, *opcit*, p.6

19 WO 205/1165 Wright and Harkness, *opcit*, p.26

20 WO 205/1165 Wright and Harkness, *opcit*, p.26

21 WO 205/1165 Wright and Harkness, *opcit*, p.26

22 WO 205/1165 Wright and Harkness, *opcit*, p.23

23 US Adjutant General, Army battle Casualties and Non-battle deaths in World War II, Archives, Fort Leavenworth, Kansas

24 ORO-T-117 Coox, A., and van Loan Naiswald, L., Survey of Allied Tank Casualties in World War II, Operational Research office, John Hopkins University, Washington, 1951, p.38

25 WO 205/631 letter RAC to G(SD) 28 July 1944, 2nd ARG Part IV June to Nov 1944, TNA

26 WO 32/11305 RAC liaison letter number 2 Sept 1944, TNA

27 WO 205/422 21st Army Group Combat reports – Brigadier Pyman to Gen Erskine, 16 June, TNA

28 WO205/422 21st Army Group Combat reports GOC 7AD to XXX Corps Immediate report 6:Impression of fighting in Normandy, 17 June 1944, TNA

29 WO 205/5b, Letter de Guingand to Montgomery, 24 June 1944, TNA

30 Buckley, J., *British Armour in the Normandy Campaign 1944* (Oxford, Cass, 2004), p.109

31 WO 205/5c Chief of Staff demi-official correspondence, letter DCIGS R. Weeks to C of S F. de Guingand, 26 June 1944, TNA

32 Clifford, A., German Tanks are Superior (*The Mercury* newspaper, Hobart Press, 28 July 1944)

33 WO 165/135 *opcit*, p.4

34 WO 171/1256 War diary 2nd Irish Guards, 3 August 1944, TNA

35 Fitzgerald, D., *History of the Irish Guards in World War II* (Aldershot, Gale & Polden, 1949), p.427

36 WO 291/1331 WO 205/1164, No. 2 Operational Research Section Final report, Report No. 12 Analysis of 75mm Sherman casualties suffered between 6 June and 10 July, TNA

37 Harrison Place, T., *Military Training in the British Army 1940–1944* (Oxford, Routledge, 2000), p.126

38 Buckley, *opcit*, p.81

39 Harrison-Place, *opcit*, p.149

40 Hart, S., *Colossal Cracks – Montgomery's 21st Army Group in NW Europe* (Mechanicsburg, PA, Stackpole, 2007), p.29

41 Howard, M., and Sparrow, J., *The Coldstream Guards 1920–1946* (London, Oxford University, 1951), p.274

42 Harrison Place, T., *opcit*, p.126

43 FUSA Operations report 19431944, Armoured Section Appendix 2 Annex 9, NARA

44 Wilkes, H., *History of 747th Tank Battalion* (Illinois, University of Illinois, private, 1976), p.21

45 Zaloga, S., M4 76 mm Sherman Tank 1943–1965 Osprey, Oxford, 2003, p.17

46 WO 229/83/8 Memo Eisenhower to Bedell Smith, 2 July 1944, TNA

47 WO 229/83/8 Letter Eisenhower to Marshall, 5 July 1944, TNA

48 White, Gen I.D., *United States v German Equipment* (US Armour Museum, Fort Knox, Kentucky, March 1945)

49 *New York Herald Tribune*, 5 April 1945

50 *Ibid*, Appendix 3

51 Meyer, *opcit*, p.291

52 Irving, D., *The Trail of the Fox* (London, Futura, 1977), p.539

53 Cave Brown, A., *A Bodyguard of Lies* (London, Sidgwick and Jackson, 1976), p.704

54 Bradley, *opcit*, p.53

Bibliography

Unpublished Primary Sources

DHH Canada

CMHQ Report #50 Campaign in NW Europe – Information from German Sources, DHH, Ottawa

CMHQ Report #54 Canadian Participation in the Operations in NW Europe, part 1, June 1944, DHH, Ottawa

CMHQ Report #58 Campaign in NW Europe, part II, July 1944, DHH, Ottawa

CMHQ report #65 Canadian Participation in Operations in NW Europe, vol III, August 1944, DHH, Ottawa

CMHQ Report #107, The Operation at Dieppe 19 August 1942, Further personal stories, 2 November 1943, DHH, Ottawa

CMHQ report #169 Canadian Participation in the Operations in NW Europe, August 1944, DHH, Ottawa

TNA National Archives, Kew, London

ADM 199/1660 Operation Neptune (Naval Aspects of operation Overlord) – Final report Force S commander, July 1944

AIR 37/763 Operation Totalize air support notes, 5 August 1944, TNA

CAB 44/248 Liberation Campaign NW Europe – the Breakout, 16 June–29 August 1944, TNA

CAB 44/249 The Liberation Campaign, Book 2, Chapter V, Operation Goodwood

CAB 66/51/15 Cabinet paper Draft Instrument of Surrender, 10 June 1944, TNA

CAB 106/959 Operation Goodwood, TNA

CAB 106/998 79th Armoured Division Final report, July 1945

CAB 106/1061 Liddell Hart Dempsey notes, TNA

PREM 3/427/1 Tank Policy discussion paper, March 1943, TNA

WO 32/11035 RAC Liaison letter no. 2, September 1944

WO 106/4469 79th Armoured Division Final report, 1945

WO 165/133 RAC Half yearly progress report no. 7, January–June 1943

WO 165/135 Memorandum Montgomery M506 on British Armour, 6 July 1944

WO 165/135 RAC Progress Report no.9, Montgomery letter to War Office VCIGS, 28 August 1943

WO 171/139 War diary 21st Army Group A branch, 1944, TNA

WO 171/248 War diary DDME Second Army August 1944, TNA

WO 171/386 War diary CREME Guards Armoured Division, 1944, TNA

WO 171/439 Intelligence summary no 57, part II, 7th Armoured Division G branch, August 1944

WO 171/456 War diary G section 11th Armoured Division, 1944, TNA

WO 171/583 79th Armoured Division Operational Bulletin no.1, June 1944

WO 171/613 War diary 8th Armed Brigade, 1944

WO 171/619 War diary 22nd Armoured Brigade, June 1994, TNA

WO 171/620 War diary of 22nd Armoured Brigade, July 1944, TNA

WO 171/627 War diary 29th Armoured Brigade, 1944, TNA

WO 171/628 War diary of 29th Brigade, 1944, TNA

WO 171/838 War diary 4th/7th Royal Dragoon Guards, 1944

WO 171/845 War diary 13th/18th Hussars, 1944

WO 171/848 War diary 23rd Hussars, 1944, TNA

WO 171/853 War diary 2nd Fife and Forfar, 1944, TNA

WO 171/856 War diary 4th County of London Yeomanry, 1944, TNA

WO 171/859 War diary 1 Northants Yeomanry, 1944, TNA

WO 171/860 War diary 2nd Northants Yeomanry, 1944, TNA

WO 171/861 War diary Nottinghamshire Sherwood Yeomanry, 1944

WO 171/863 War diary Staffordshire Yeomanry, 1944, TNA

WO 171/866 War diary 3rd RTR, 1944, TNA

WO 171/867 War diary 5th RTR, 1944, TNA

WO 171/868 War diary 7th RTR, 1944, TNA

WO 171/873 War diary 44th RTR, 1944, TNA

WO 171/878 War diary 144th Regiment RAC, 1944, TNA

WO 171/892 War diary 263rd Field Delivery Squadron, 1944, TNA

WO 171/902 War diary 2nd Armoured Replacement Group, 1944, TNA

WO 171/1256 War diary of 2nd Irish Guards, 1944, TNA

WO 171/1258 War diary 3rd Scots Guards, 1944, TNA

WO 171/1325 War diary 2nd KSLI, 1944, TNA

WO 179/2622 War diary BRAC First Canadian Army, 1944, TNA

WO 179/2636 War diary DDME branch, Canadian First Army, 1944, TNA

WO 179/2806 War diary 4th Canadian Armoured Division workshop, 1944, TNA

WO 205/2 COSSAC Operation Overlord; Appreciation and outline plan

WO 205/5C Chief of Staff demi-official correspondence

WO 205/5D Commander In Chief demi-official correspondence letter

WO 205/5E Commander In Chief personal signals, COS copies

WO 205/112 21st Army group equipment wastage rates, letter 21 July 1944, Appendix A, TNA

WO 205/422 Combat reports 21st Army Group G (Operations)

WO 205/631 2nd Armoured Replacement Group, 1944, TNA

WO 205/631 G(RAC) Armoured Replacement Group part IV, June to Nov 1944, TNA

WO 205/748 79th Armoured Division DD tanks training, vol II

WO 205/972A Notes on Operations of 21st Army Group, 1946, TNA

WO 205/1164 Operation Research in NW Europe, Report no.33 – Use of Panzerfaust in NW Europe, p.240, TNA

WO 205/1165 Wright, Capt H., and Harkness, Capt R., A Survey of Casualties amongst Armoured Units in NW Europe, Jan 1946, p.15, TNA

WO 219/1550 21st Army Group casualties by arm and branch of service, reports to 28 August, 1944, TNA

WO 229/72 C in C and HQ 21 Army group directives 1944, TNA

WO 229/83 SHAEF Secretariat General Staff – Supplies, 1944, TNA

WO 291/246 Opposition on British Beaches Operational Research Report, 1944

WO 291/1331 ORS Report no. 4 Air Attacks on Enemy Tanks and Motor Transport in the Mortain Area, August 1944, TNA

WO 291/1331 ORS Report 15 – Enemy Casualties in Vehicles and equipment during the retreat from Normandy to the Seine, TNA

WO 291/1331 No.2 Operational Research Section Final report, Report No. 12 Analysis of 75mm Sherman casualties suffered between 6 June and 10 July, TNA

NARA, Marylands Washington

RG38 Action report of DD in the Assault, 11th Amphibious Fleet, letter dated 22 Sept 1944, NARA

RG38 J. L. Hall Jnr, Report Force O Commander, 14 July 1944, NARA

RG313 12th LCT Flotilla report, Launching DD tanks on D-Day, 14 July 1944, NARA

RG313 LCT(A)2307 AAR, June 1944, NARA

RG319 EHINT 66 Bayerlein, Lt Gen F., interview Panzer Lehr division, January–28 July 1944, NARA

RG319 ETHINT 17, von Schwerin, 116th Panzer Division in Normandy, NARA

RG319 FMS A-973 275th Infantry division Combat Operations in Northern France, NARA

RG319 FMS A-984 353rd Infantry division, 14 July–15 September 1944, NARA

RG319 FMS B-234 Pemsel, M., The Seventh Army Pre-Invasion, NARA

RG319 FMS B-258 von Schweppenburg History of Panzer Gruppe West, NARA

RG319 FMS B-284 Blumentritt OB West 6 June–24 July, NARA

RG319 FMS B-388, 352nd Infantry division 6 June, 1944, NARA

RG319 FMS B-425 89th Infantry Division – Part 1 Invasion to 15 August, NARA

RG319 FMS B-441 Feuchtinger, 21st Panzer Division on 6 June, 1944, NARA

RG319 FMS B-455 LVIII Panzer Korps, NARA

RG319 FMS B-466 von Schweppenburg Panzer Gruppe West, June–July 1944, NARA

RG319 FMS B-725 von Gersdorff, Seventh Army at Avranches, NARA

RG319 FMS B-726 von Gersdorff, Fifth Panzer Army 25, July to 25 August 1944, NARA

RG319 FMS B-727 von Gersdorff, Battle in Northern France ch VI, Falaise, NARA

RG319 FMS B-763 Pemsel, M., The Seventh Army, June and July 1944, NARA

RG319 FMS B-841 Hausser 7th Army, 22–31 August 1944, NARA

RG319 FMS B-846 Schuster, 85th Infantry Division, February–November 1944, NARA

RG319 FMS C-024 Kraemer, 1st SS Panzer Korps in the west

RG319 EHINT 49 Jodl and Keital, NARA

RG338 70th Tank Battalion After Action Report, June 1944 dated 20 August 1944

RG338 741st Tank Battalion, Field order #1, 21 May 1944, NARA

RG338 741st Tank Battalion Journal, June 1944, NARA

RG338 741st Tank Battalion After Action Report, 6 June 1944, NARA

RG338 743rd Tank Battalion, AAR B Company, 6 June 1944, NARA

RG338 AAR 743rd Tank Battalion July 1944, NARA

RG338 AAR 82nd Reconnaissance Battalion, July 1944, NARA

RG338 FUSA Operation Neptune Plan, 1944, NARA

RG338 FUSA Report of Operations 20 October 1943 to 1 August 1944, NARA

RG338 V Corps Operations Plan Neptune 26 March 1944, NARA

RG407 3rd Armored Division G-4 journal, July 1944, NARA

RG407 30th Division G-2 Periodic report, 12 August 1944, NARA

RG407 603 AAR CCB 3rd Armored Division, July 1944, NARA

RG407 603 AAR 3AD CCB July 1944, NARA

RG407 603 AAR CCA 3rd Armored Division, July 1944

RG407 603 Call Me Spearhead, NARA

RG407 AAR 3rd Battalion 120th Infantry Regiment, 11 July 1944, NARA

RG407 AAR 30th Infantry Division, July 1944, NARA

RG407 AAR 67th Armored Regiment, Operation Cobra, 1944, NARA

RG407 After Action Report 66th Armored Regiment, June 1944, NARA

RG407 Box 1788 Adjutant General, 12th Army AFV section reports, June 1944, NARA

RG407 FM17-10 Armored Force Field manual US Army, March 1942, NARA

RG407 TM E9-369A German 88mm Anti-aircraft gun manual, US War Dept, June 1943, NARA

RG498 FUSA Army Intelligence bulletin, January 1944, NARA

RG498 Miller, Capt E., Interview by Capt Hechler for Operation Cobra, 6 September 1944, NARA

RG498 Korrison, Lt D., Interview by Capt Hechler for Operation Cobra, 6 September 1944, NARA

RG498 AFV section ETOUSA Preliminary Historical report, 9 December 1944, NARA

US Adjutant General, Army Battle Casualties and Non-Battle Deaths in World War II, Archives, Fort Leavenworth, Kansas

US Army CMH, The General Board, US forces ETO Report no 52 Armored Special Equipment.

LAC Ottawa

RG24 vol 10455 Report 2nd Canadian Armed Brigade, Operation Overlord Sequence of events June 6–11, report 5, July 1944, LAC

RG24 vol 10649 First Canadian Army HQ, Enemy appreciation, 7 August 1944, LAC

RG24 vol 10673 2nd Canadian Corps Immediate Report on Tractable, 22 August 1944, LAC

RG24 vol 10736 Canadian First Army Tank States, 26 August 1944, LAC

RG24 vol 10798 2nd Cdn Corps HQ log 9 August 1944, LAC

RG24 vol 10942 Report 1st Polish Armoured Division in Operation Totalize, LAC

RG24 vol 10992 War Diary 2nd Canadian Armoured Brigade, May 1944 Appendix 6, Operational Order, Operation Overlord

RG24 vol 10992 War diary 2nd CAB August 1944, Events log, August 1944, LAC

RG24 vol 13645 First Canadian Army Intelligence Summary no. 33 of 1 August 1944, LAC

RG24 vol 13788 War diary 4th Canadian Armoured Division HQ G branch, August 1944, LAC

RG24 vol 13792 War diary 4th Canadian Armoured Division AA and QMG Adrep, 13 August 1944

RG24 vol 14052 War diary 4th CAB, Signals Log 8 August 1944, LAC

RG24 vol 14213 War diary 1st Hussars (6 CAR), June 1944 Appendix 5, LAC

RG24 vol 14234 War diary Fort Garry Horse (10 CAR), June 1944, LAC

RG24 vol 14255 War diary Governor General Foot Guards, August 1944, LAC

RG24 vol 14260 War diary 2nd Canadian Grenadier Guards, August 1944, LAC

RG24 vol 14287 War diary Sherbrooke Fusiliers, June 1944 Appendix A, C sqdn account, LAC

RG24 vol 14292 War diary British Columbia Regiment, August 1944, LAC

RG24 vol 14295 War diary South Alberta Regiment, August 1944, LAC

RG24 vol 15000 War diary Algonquin Regiment, August 1944, LAC

RG24 vol 15122 War diary North Nova Scotia Highlanders, 7 June 1944, LAC

RG24 vol 15233 War diary Royal Winnipeg Rifles Regiment, June 1944, LAC

RG24 vol 13792 AA and QM 4th Canadian Armoured Division adreps, 13 and 16 August 1944, LAC

Liddell Hart Centre Military Archives, KCL, London

de Guingand, F., Notes on the Employment of Tanks in support of Infantry in the Battle, 21st Army Group February 1944, LHCMA de Guingand 4/1/7

Dempsey, M., Letter and notes to Liddell Hart, 28 March 1952, LHCMA, LH1/230/22

Imperial War Museum

Baker, A.E. Memoirs in Private papers, 1945, IWM document #569

Brownlie, Lt-Col W.S., And Came Safe Home, Private papers, 1944, IWM document #2204

Dewar, D., Memoirs in Private papers, IWM document #3987

US 3rd Armored Division Archives, University of Illinois

2nd Battalion 33rd Armored Regiment log and journal July 1944, University of Illinois

32nd Armored Regiment S–2 report 30 June 1944, University of Illinois

32nd Armored Regiment journal and log, July 1944, University of Illinois

AAR 33rd Armored Regiment, July 1944, 3rd Armored Division Archives, University of Illinois

Dugan, H., First Combat – essay dated 17 July 1986, University of Illinois

Dugan, H., The 3rd Armored Division Saga in World War II, University of Illinois, 1986

Corbin, C., Letter to Dugan Haynes, 3rd Armored Division Archives, University of Illinois, Urbana

Haynes, D., The 3rd Armored Division Saga in World War II, 1988, University of Illinois, Urbana

Wilkes, H., History of 747th Tank Battalion, University of Illinois, Illinois

Others

4th/7th RDG Association newsletter, September 2011

Barnum, Maj J., et al – Committee 6 The Armoured Division in a Double Envelopment – The 2nd Armoured Division in the Mortain Counterattack, Appendix V, MCOE paper, Fort Knox, Kentucky, 1948

Baumgarten, Private Harold, eyewitness, American D-Day.org website http://www.american-dday.org/Veterans/Baumgarten_Harold.html (accessed 21 Jan 2012)

Breakthrough, 26–30 July 1944, MCOE Monograph, 1946–47

Bryan, Maj. J., The Operations of Task Force Y, CCA at Villiers Fossard, MCOE Fort Benning paper, 1948–49

Bullock, R., *D-Day Remembered – Personal Recollections of the Westminster Dragoon Guards* (unpublished, Westminster Dragoons Regimental Association)

Clifford, A., *German Tanks are Superior* (The Mercury, Hobart Press, 28 July 1944)

Collins, J.L., Letter to Eisenhower, 1 August 1944. J. Lawton Collins Papers, Box 3, 201 Personal Letter File, 1944, Dwight D. Eisenhower Presidential Library

Committee 3, Pilsbury, G., et al, Employment of the 2nd Armoured Division in Operation Cobra, MCOE paper, 1950, p.56

Committee 10, Armour in Operation Neptune, US Army, Fort Leavenworth, Kansas, Armour School report, May 1949

Creamer, Maj F. W., The Operations of XIX US Army Corps in Normandy, MCOE Fort Benning, 1946

D-Day – the untold story, BBC History website http://www.bbc.co.uk/history/ancient/archaeology/marine_dday_underwater (accessed 3 December 2011)

D-Day to VE Day – History of 741st Tank Battalion (unpublished history)

Doubler, Capt M., Busting the Bocage – American Combined Arms Operations in France 6 June to 31 July 1944 (Combat Studies Institute, Fort Leavenworth, 1988)

Eisenhower, Gen I., letter to Montgomery S-55476, 13 Jul 44 (Eisenhower Centre, Abilene)

Hansard HC Debate, 16 March 1944, vol.398, cc.393–4

Hopper, Corporal, quoted in Vitamin Baker (unpublished history 741st Tank Battalion)

Johnson, Lt-Col B., P., The Operations of the Second Armoured Division in the Saint Lo 'Move Out, Verify: The Combat Story of the 743rd Tank Battalion' (unpublished history)

Mietek, H., BBC History website http://www.bbc.co.uk/history/ww2peopleswar/stories/46/a2879346.shtml (accessed 13 October 2011)

Neave, J.A.S., War diary of Julius Neave (Tyne and Wear Museums)

New York Herald Tribune, 5 April 1945

RAF Air Historical Branch letter to the author, October 2013

Slarks, E., 'On the Perrier Ridge, August 1944', BBC History website http://www.bbc.co.uk/history/ww2peopleswar/stories/36/a6115736.shtml (accessed 2 December 2012)

Smith, E.E., Lt, The Assault 6–23 June – The Story of C Squadron (Tyne and Wear museums)

Special Interrogation Report Kurt Meyer (*Canadian Military History*, vol.11, no.4, Autumn 2002, pp.59–70)

War diary 2nd bn Grenadier Guards narrative July 1944 (Guards Museum, London)

War diary narrative 2nd Grenadier Guards, August 1944 (Guards Museum, London)

War diary narrative 4th Grenadier Guards, August 1944 (Guards Museum, London)

White, Gen. I.D., United States v German Equipment, US Armour Museum, Fort Knox, Kentucky, March 1945

Wormald, Maj. A., D-Day Recollections (Tyne and Wear Museums)

Zien, Col H., Operations of the 3rd Battalion 66th Armoured regiment in the St Lo breakthrough, MCOE paper, 1946–47

Published Secondary Sources

Agte, P., *Michal Wittmannn Vol. 2* (Mechanicsburg, PA, Stackpole, 2006)

Allen W., and Cawston, R., *Carpiquet Bound – A pictorial tribute to 4th County of London Yeomanry (Sharpshooters), 1939 to 1944* (Epsom, Chiavari, 1997)

Ambrose, S.E., *D-Day June 6, 1944 The Battle for the Normandy Beaches* (New York, NY, Simon & Schuster, 1994)

Anderson, R., *Cracking Hitler's Atlantic Wall* (Mechanicsburg, PA, Stackpole, 2010)

Anon, *Vanguard – The Fort Garry Horse in the Second World War* (Holland, private, 1945)

Anon, *History of the 7th Armoured Division* (BAOR, private, 1945)

Anon, *Move Out Verify – The Combat History of the 743rd Tank Battalion* (Frankfurt, private, 1945)

Anon, *Club Route History of XXX Corps* (Germany, private, 1946)

Anon, Special Interrogation Report Kurt Meyer (*Canadian Military History*, vol.11, no.4, 2002)

'Army Group B weekly report 27 June – 2 July 1944' in Wood, J.A. (ed.), *The Army of the West* (Mechanicsburg, PA, Stackpole, 2007)

Bando, M., *101st Airborne – The Screaming Eagles at Normandy* (Minneapolis, MN, Zenith, 2011)

Bando, M., *Breakout in Normandy – The 2nd Amoured Division in the Land of the Dead* (France, Editions Heimdal, 2013)

BAOR, Operation Bluecoat Battlefield study tour, Appendix 6, BAOR, 1946

BAOR, 50th Northumbrian Infantry Division Battlefield Tour, 1947

BAOR, Study Tour Operation Totalize, June, 1947

BAOR Battlefield Study Tour Operation Goodwood Spectator edition, BAOR, Aug 1947

Barnard, Lt-Col W.T., *The Queen's Own Rifles Of Canada: 1860–1960* (Ontario, Ontario Publishing, 1960)

Beale, P., *Tank Tracks* (Stroud, Sutton, 1997)

Bechthold, M., Lost in Normandy – The Odyssey of Worthington Force August 9 1944 (*Canadian Military History*, vol.19, no.2, Spring 2010)

Belfield, E., and Essame, H., *The Battle for Normandy* (London, Parnell, 1965)

Blacker, C.H., *The Story of the 23rd Hussars 1940–1946* (Germany, private, 1946)

Blumenson, M., *Breakout and Pursuit* (Washington, DC, US Army CMH, 1991)

Blumenson, M., *The Battle of the Generals* (New York, NY, Morrow, 1993)

Boscawen, R., *Armoured Guardsmen* (Barnsley, Pen and Sword, 2010)

Bradley, O., *A Soldier's Story* (New York, NY, Holt, 1951)

Bradley, O., *A General's Life* (New York, NY, Simon and Schuster, 1983)

Bramwell, Sgt, quoted in Neillands, R., *The Desert Rats – the 7th Armoured Division 1940–1945* (London, Weidenfeld and Nicholson, 1991)

Bryant, A., *Triumph in the West* (London, Collins, 1959)

Buckley, J., *British Armour in the Normandy Campaign 1944* (Oxford, Cass, 2004)

Carafano, J.J., *After D-Day – Operation Cobra and the Normandy Breakout* (Mechanicsburg, PA, Stackpole, 2008)

Caravaggio, A., A Re-Evaluation of Generalship: Lt-General Guy Simonds and Major-General George Kitching in Normandy 1944 (*Canadian Military History*, vol.11, no.4, 2002)

Carver, M., *Out of Step – Memoirs of a field Marshal* (London, Hutchinson, 1989)

Carver, M., *El Alamein* (Ware, Wordsworth, 2000)

Cave Brown, A., *A Bodyguard of Lies* (London, W. Allen, 1976)

Chamberlain, P. and Doyle, H., *Encyclopaedia of German Tanks* (London, Arms and Armour Press, 1993)

Churchill, W., *The Hinge of Fate: The Second World War – Volume 4* (London, Cassell, 1951)

Churchill, W.S., *Triumph and Tragedy: The Second World War – Volume 6* (London, Cassell, 1953)

Clark, L., *Operation Epsom* (Stroud, Sutton Publishing, 2004)

Close, Maj, W., *View from the Turret* (Tewkesbury, Dell and Bredon, 1998)

Coox, A., and Naisawald, L., ORO T117 – A Survey of Allied tank casualties in World War II (US Army Operations Research Office, March 1951)

Copp, T., 'Reassessing Operation Totalize' (*Legion Magazine*, Part 27, 1 September 1999)

Dalglish, I., *Over the Battlefield – Operation Epsom* (Barnsley, Pen and Sword, 2007)

Dalglish, I., *Goodwood* (Mechanicsburg, PA, Stackpole, 2009)

Dalglish, I., *Over the Battlefield – Operation Bluecoat* (Barnsley, Pen and Sword, 2009)

Danchev, A. and Todman, D. (eds), *War Diaries 1939–1945 Field Marshal Lord Alanbrooke, 20 July 1944* (London, Weidenfeld and Nicholson, 2002)

Daugherty, L., *Battle of Hedgerows,* MBI Publishing, St Paul, 2001

Delaforce, P., *The Black Bull – From Normandy to the Baltic with the 11th Armoured Division* (Stroud, Sutton, 1994)

Delaforce, P., *Battles with Panzers – The Story of 1st RTR* (Stroud, Sutton, 2003)

Delaforce, P., *Churchill's Desert Rats* (Stroud, Sutton, 2003)

Dempsey, quoted in D'Este, C., *Decision In Normandy* (London, Collins, 1983)

D'Este, C., *Decision in Normandy* (London, Penguin, 2000)

Dugan, H., *Spearhead in the West – The Third Armoured Division* (Paducah, KY, Turner, 1991)

Duguid, A.F., *History Canadian Grenadier Guards 1760–1964* (Montreal, Gazette, 1965)

Eisenhower, D., *Crusade in Europe* (New York, NY, Doubleday, 1948)

Ellis, Maj L.F., *Victory in the West Volume 1: The Battle of Normandy* (London, HMSO, 1962)

Exton, Col H.M., The 2nd Armoured Division in Operation Cobra (*Military Review*, August 1947)

Fey, W., *Amour Battles of the Waffen SS* (Mechanicsburg, PA, Stackpole, 2003)

Fitzgerald, D., *History of the Irish Guards in World War II* (Aldershot, Gale & Polden, 1949)

Folkestad, W., *The View from the Turret – the 743rd Tank Battalion During World War II* (Shippenburg, White Mane, 1996)

Foster, T., *Meeting of Generals* (Lincoln, Authors Choice Press, 2000)

Graves, D.E., *The South Albertas – A Canadian Regiment at War* (Toronto, Robin Brass Studio, 1998)

Hall, C., *History of the 70th Tank Battalion* (Louisville, KY, Southern, 1950)

Harrison, G., Cross-Channel Attack (Washington, US Army CMH, 1993)

Harrison Place, T., *Military Training in the British Army 1940–1944* (Oxford, Routledge, 2000)

Hart, S., *Colossal Cracks – Montgomery's 21st Army Group in NW Europe* (Mechanicsburg, PA, Stackpole, 2007)

Hastings, M., *Overlord D-Day and the Battle for Normandy 1944* (London, Michael Joseph, 1984)

Hewitt, R.L., *Workhorse of the Western Front – The Story of the 30th Infantry Division* (Washington, DC, Infantry Journal Press, 1946)

Hill, Col E.R., and Parsons, Capt L.M.H, *The Story of the Guards Armoured Division* (London, Geoffrey Bles, 1956)

Hills, S., *By Tank into Normandy* (London, Orion, 2002)

Horne, A., *The Lonely Leader, Monty 1944–1945* (London, Macmillan, 1994)

Houston, D., *Hell on Wheels – the 2nd Armoured Division* (Novato, CA, Presidio, 1995)

How, Maj. J.J., *Normandy – The British Breakout* (London, Kimber, 1981)

How, J.J., *Hill 112 – The Cornerstone of the Normandy Campaign* (London, Kimber, 1984)

Howard, M., and Sparrow, J., *The Coldstream Guards 1920–1946* (London, Oxford University, 1951)

Hunnicutt, R.P., *Sherman: A History of the American Medium Tank* (Novato, CA, Presidio, 1978)

Invasion of Normandy: Operation Neptune. Administrative History of US Naval forces in Europe 1940–1946, vol.V, London, 1946

Irving, D., *The Trail of the Fox – The Life of Field Marshal Erwin Rommel* (London, Futura, 1977)

Irving, D., *Hitler's War* (London, Focal Point, 2002)

Jackson, Lt-Col G.S., *Operations of Eighth Corps* (London, St Clements, 1948)

Jackson, Lance Corporal R., quoted in Fowler, W., *D-Day the First 24 Hours* (Leicester, Silverdale, 2004)

Jackson, H.M., *The Sherbrooke Regiment* (Montreal, Christian Bros, 1958)

Jarymowycz, R., *Tank Tactics from Normandy to Lorraine* (Mechnicsburg, PA, Stackpole, 2009)

Jensen, J., *Strike Swiftly: the 70th Tank Battalion* (Novato, CA, Presidio, 1997)

Jentz, T., *Panzertruppen Vol 2* (Atglen, PA, Schiffer Military History, 1996)

Jessup, Maj A.R., *The Regimental History of the Governor General Foot Guards* (Ottawa, private, 1948)

Kennett, B., and Tatman, J., *Craftsmen of the Army* (Barnsley, Cooper/REME, 1970)

Kitching, G., *Mud and Green Fields* (Langley, BC, Battleline, 1986)

Kortenhaus, W., *The Combat History of the 21st Panzer Division* (Solihull, Helion, 2014)

Lehmann, R., and Tiemann, R., *The Liebstandarte, Vol IV* (Manitoba, JJ Fedorowicz, 1993)

Liddell Hart, Capt B.H., *The Tanks – The History of the Royal Tank Regiment, Vol 2, 1939–1945* (London, Cassell, 1959)

Lindsay, T.M., *The Sherwood Rangers* (London, Burrup, Mathieson, 1952)

Lindsey, O., *A Guards' General: The Memoirs of Major General Sir Allan Adair* (London, Hamilton, 1986)

Lucas, J., *The Military Role of the 2nd SS Division* (London, Arms and Armour, 1994)

Maczek, Gen, Report of Operations 1st Polish Armoured Division (*Canadian Military History*, vol.15, no.2, Spring 2006)

McGilvray, E., *The Black Devils March. A Doomed Odyssey – the 1st Polish Armoured Division 1939–1945* (Solihull, Helion, 2005)

McKee, A., *Caen – Anvil of Victory* (London, Souvenir Press, 1984)

Meyer, H., *The 12th SS – the History of the Hitler Youth Panzer Division, Vol 1* (Mechanicsburg, PA, Stackpole, 2009)

Meyer, K., *Grenadiers* (Mechanicsburg, PA, Stackpole, 2005)

Milano, V. and Conner, B., *Normandiefront: D-Day to St Lô through German Eyes* (Stroud, Spellmount, 2012)

Miller, Maj-Gen C.H., *History of 13th/18th Royal Hussars (QMO) 1922–1947* (London, Chisman, Bradshaw, 1949)

Mitcham, S., *Retreat to the Reich – The German Defeat in France 1944* (Mechanicsburg, PA, Stackpole, 2007)

Montgomery, B., *Normandy to the Baltic, Vol. II* (London, Hutchinson, 1947)

Neville, R.F. and Scott, G.S., *History of the 1st and 2nd Northamptonshire Yeomanry* (Uckfield, Naval and Military, 1946 reprint)

Newton, C., *A Trooper's Tale* (Self-published, 2000)

Owen-Smith, Lt Col M.S., Armoured Fighting Vehicle Casualties (Journal Royal Army Medical Corps, vol.123, 1977)

Palamountain, E.W.I., Taurus Pursuant, The History of the 11th Armoured Division, 1946

Perrun, J., Best-Laid Plans: Guy Simonds and Operation Totalize, 7–10 August 1944 (*The Journal of Military History*, vol.67, no.1, 2003)

Pogue, F.C., *The Supreme Command* (Washington, DC, US Army CMH, 1989)

Reardon, M., *Victory at Mortain* (Lawrence, KS, University of Kansas Press, 2002)

Reay, Sgt, quoted in Moore, W., *Panzerbait – With the Third Royal Tank Regiment 1939–1945* (London, Leo Cooper, 1991)

Reid, B., *No Holding Back – Operation Totalize, August 1944* (Mechanicsburg, PA, Stackpole, 2009)

Ritgen, H., *The Western Front, 1944: Memoirs of a Panzer Lehr Officer* (Manitoba, JJ Fedorowicz, 1995)

Roberts, G.P.B., *From the Desert to the Baltic* (London, Kimber, 1987)

Rockwell, D., in Drez, R., *Voices of D-Day – the Story of the Allied Invasion Told by Those who were there* (Eisenhower Centre, 1994)

Roy, R., *1944: The Canadians in Normandy* (Ottawa, Macmillan, 1984)

Ruppenthal, Maj R., *Utah Beach to Cherbourg – US Army Forces in Action* (Washington, DC, US Army CMH, 1948)

Ruppenthal, Maj R., *Logistical Support of the Armies – 2 vols*, (Washington, US Army CMH, 1995)

Schneider, W., *Tigers in Normandy* (Mechanicsburg, PA, Stackpole, 2011)

Sellars, R.G.B., *The History of the Fife and Forfars* (Edinburgh, Blackwood, 1960)

Shulman, M., *Defeat in the West* (London, Secker and Warburg, 1947)

Stacey, C.P., *The Victory Campaign, Operations in North West Europe 1944–1945* (Ottawa, DHH, 1960)

Stark, F.M., *History of the 1st Hussars Regiment 1856–1945* (London, Ontario, 1951)

Stirling, Maj J.D.P., *The First and Last – The Story of the 4th/7th Royal Dragoon Guards 1939–1945* (London, Art and Educational, 1949)

Szamveber, N., *Waffen SS Armour in Normandy – the Combat History of the SS Panzer Regiment 12* (Solihull, Helion, 2012)

Taylor, C., *St Lo 7 July–19 July 1944* (Washington, DC, US Army CMH, 1946)

Taylor, C., *Omaha Beachhead, US Army Forces in Action* (War Dept Historical Division, 1984)

Taylor, V., *The Armoured Micks 1941–1945* (Irish Guards HQ, 1997)

Tieke, W., *In the Firestorm of the Last Years of the War* (Manitoba, Fedorowicz, 1999)

Tout, K. A., *Tank – 40 hours of Battle – August 1944* (London, Robert Hale, 1985)

Tout, K.A., *A Fine Night for Tanks – The Road to Falaise* (Stroud, Sutton, 1998)

Trahan E.A., ed., *A History of the Second Armoured Division 1940–1946* (Atlanta, GA, Love, 1947)

Urban, M., *The Tank War* (London, Little Brown, 2013)

US Army Office of Adjutant General, Army Battle Casualties and Nonbattle Deaths in World War II, Final Report: 7 December 1941–31 December 1946 (1953)

Verney, Maj-Gen G.L., *The Guards Armoured Division – A Short History* (London, Hutchinson, 1955)

Von Luck, H., *Panzer Commander* (Westport, CT, Praeger, 1993)

War Office Military training pamphlet no.41, The Tactical Handling of the Armoured Division and its Components, July 1943, Bovington Museum

Weidinger, O., *Das Reich 1943–1945* (Manitoba, JJ Fedorowicz, 2012)

Weigley, R., *Eisenhower's Lieutenants* (London, Sidgwick and Jackson, 1981)

Whitehead, A., quoted in Yeide, H., *The Infantry's Armour, The US Army's Separate Tank battalions in World War II* (Mechanicsburg, PA, Stackpole, 2010)

Wilkes, H., *History of 747th Tank Battalion* (Illinois, University of Illinois, private, 1976)

Wilmot, C., *The Second World War – the Struggle for Europe* (London, Collins, 1952)

Winter, G.J. (Sr), *World War II* magazine (November 2003)

Zaloga, S., *M4 (76mm) Sherman Medium Tank 1943–65* (Oxford, Osprey, 2003)

Zaloga, S., *Armored Thunderbolt – The US Army Sherman in World War II* (Mechanicsburg, PA, Stackpole, 2008)

Zaloga, S., *Sherman Medium Tank 1942–45* (Oxford, Osprey, 1993)

Zaloga, S. and Ford, K., *Overlord – The Illustrated History of the D-Day Landings* (Oxford, Osprey Publishing, 2009)

Zetterling, N., *Normandy 1944 – German Military Organisation, Combat Power and Effectiveness* (Manitoba, JJ Fedorowicz, 2000)

Zuehlke, M., *Juno Beach: Canada's D-Day Victory* (Vancouver, Douglas and McIntyre, 2004)

Zuehlke, M., *Breakout from Juno* (Vancouver, Douglas and McIntyre, 2011)

Index